LOS ANGELES
place of possibilities
the people and resources that created Los Angeles
by Lynn C. Kronzek

FOREWORD

At the Los Angeles Conservancy, our citywide historic preservation organization, we often get puzzled inquiries from local residents and friends in other cities. "Historic preservation in Los Angeles?", "What history do you have that's worth saving?"

While Los Angeles has certainly seen more than its share of bulldozers and wrecking balls, our city retains great monuments from a rich architectural history dating back to its founding in 1781. From grandiose movie palaces to modest bungalow courts, from ornamented Victorian gems to minimalist Modernist icons, from civic gathering places to private estates, and from grand cathedrals to playful hamburger stands, Los Angeles architecture has always been worth noticing, and visual markers of our city's past are remarkably evident.

The Los Angeles Conservancy's mission is to preserve and stimulate public awareness of Los Angeles' built heritage. The Conservancy has created a dozen Downtown Walking Tours and hosted over 100 educational programs on Los Angeles' architectural history. We have also introduced more than 90,000 people to the historic Broadway movie palaces through our "Last Remaining Seats" film series. Yet, all too often, Los Angeles is still thought of as a city without history.

That is why the Conservancy is proud to sponsor this outstanding book on Los Angeles, part of Heritage Media's national series of city histories. Lynn Kronzek, best known locally for her acclaimed chronicle of Los Angeles' Fairfax district, was the ideal author because she is acutely aware that Los Angeles history is about more than our great monuments; it is also about the people, neighborhoods and cultures that shaped our history. Many thanks are also due to the entire staff at Heritage Media.

This look back on Los Angeles' history comes at a fitting time. The Conservancy has just finished looking back on its own first two decades. The Conservancy's creation in 1978 heralded the launch of an organized historic preservation movement in Los Angeles. From a handful of volunteers meeting to discuss how to save the Los Angeles Central Library, the Conservancy has grown to become the largest local historic preservation organization in the nation, representing more than 6,000 members — (another surprise for the "L.A. has no history" crowd.)

Over our first 20 years, the Conservancy has helped save many of Los Angeles' most important landmarks, including the Central Library, the Wiltern Theater, the Sheraton Town House Hotel, St. Vibiana's Cathedral, Downey McDonald's, Los Angeles Memorial Coliseum, and the Wilshire May Co. Building.

Because Los Angeles is a city of neighborhoods, preservation can only succeed neighborhood by neighborhood, block by block. The Conservancy therefore helped create Los Angeles' Historic Preservation Overlay Zones, protecting and enhancing the city's most historic residential neighborhoods.

As we move into the 21st century, the Conservancy recognizes that historic preservation can no longer only be about saving individual buildings, as important as that may be. Preservation must also include saving and revitalizing entire historic districts in our city.

At the Conservancy, we are dedicated to using our past to build Los Angeles' future. We truly love L.A. Now, read on to see why.

Linda Dishman,
Executive Director, Los Angeles Conservancy
October 1998

To Robert,

Child of the Nineties,
Angeleno of the Future.

With love forever

First Edition

Copyright ©1998 by

Heritage Media Corporation

All rights reserved. No part of this book may be reproduced in any form or

by any means, electronic or mechanical, including photocopying,

without permission in writing from the publisher.

All inquiries should be addressed to Heritage Media Corp.

ISBN Number: 1-886483-13-2

Library of Congress
Card Catalog Number: 97-077580

Author/Photo Editor: Lynn C. Kronzek

Publisher: C.E. Parks

Editor-in-Chief: Lori M. Parks

VP/National Sales Manager: Ray Spagnuolo

VP/Corporate Development: Bart Barica

Regional Sales Manager: Kathee Finn

Production Manager: Deborah Sherwood

Project Art Directors: Darlene Kocher and Gina Mancini

Editorial Manager: Betsy Blondin

Sales Coordinators: Linda Camerino, Victoria Coles,

                       Merrilyn Fleming, Alan Lindquist, Al McPherson,

                       Rex Oppenheimer, Marcus Quintana, Karen Ritter

Editorial Coordinators: Lesley Abrams, Susan Ikeda, Renee Kim, Betsy Lelja

Production Staff: Sean Gates, Brooks Gregg,

                     Brad Hartman, David Hermstead,

                     Steve Trainor, Ray Williams

Operations Manager: Marla Eckhoff

Administration: Michael Bayon, Regina Read, Scott Reid

                   Cory Graham, Ellen Ruby, Erin Davis

Profile Writers: Barbara DeMarco Barrett, Jeb Callan,

                    Connie DerTorossian, Donna Englander,

                    Libbe HaLevy, Jenifer Hanarahan, Nora Horn,

                    Howell Hurst, Christine James, Scott Okamoto,

                    Debra Rahal, Michael Sonnenschein,

                    Christopher Trela, Laurie Wiegler,

                    Jody Marquez Wood, Sherrie Woodbury

Sponsored by:

Los Angeles Conservancy

919 South Grand Avenue, Suite 102A

Los Angeles, CA 90015

Published By

Heritage Media Corporation

6354 Corte del Abeto, Suite B

Carlsbad, CA 92009

www.heritagemedia.com

Printed in the United States of America.

CONTENTS

216

234

196

438

356

262

410

540

292

484

PARTNERS

INDEX

If a passion for history is inherited, my genes are certainly owed to my father. But it was my mother who, when I was eight or nine, lovingly began hauling home from the library those weighty illustrated history books. The pictures seduced me, and lured my eyes to the text in search of more substantive information. Knowledge of the local environment was first derived from "before and after" pictures; works about U.S. Presidents introduced me to American history and public policy. (To write a book such as *Place of Possibilities*, I'm sure, then was a dream far beyond even my vivacious childhood imagination.)

I later learned to study the vast, impact-filled distance between the "before and after" shots. By the time I was commissioned to write this volume, I had totally abandoned the approach that for so long dominated "coffee table" histories: pure chronology, punctuated by laundry lists of local celebrities and sites. The title *Place of Possibilities: The People and Resources that Created Los Angeles* (through 1945) is cumbersome, but the appellation reflected, and still reflects, my intent.

Place of Possibilities may be the first coffee table book locally to have benefitted from the discipline of public history. The emphasis here tends to be on the broad terrain — and populace — rather than on Hall of Famers. In short, Amy Semple McPherson will not be found in these pages. Another characteristic of public history is a "multimedia" orientation that engages readers at several levels — and invites their active involvement. Appropriately, *Place of Possibilities* offers three access channels: the illustrations; chapter opening "vignettes;" and the text itself. Although strong connections exist between them, each can be read (or viewed) independently.

Illustrations remain the most outgoing — and least demanding — of the three elements. Educational values notwithstanding, the old adage is true: pictures can evoke feelings or moods better than words. Abundant black-and-white photos grace this book, as they do in most popular histories, but readers will be treated to a much more diverse display here. Whether classically-trained painters of the last century or today's exuberant muralists, artists have long drawn inspiration from Los Angeles. In encouraging broader participation, *Place of Possibilities* beams with creative interpretations of L.A.'s social and physical environment. The range of periods, styles, subjects and media is truly vast.

As for the vignettes, they evolved from my own style and for organizational reasons: I was commissioned to write this book with the understanding that the narrative would end in 1945. The cut-off point is sensible. L.A. changed so drastically during World War II and the years immediately following it that a temporal leap to the 1950s probably demanded an entirely new framework. Still, as the manuscript developed, both the publisher and I felt there should be a way of bringing the reader from 1945 to the present.

The answer was found in the chapter introductions. Consisting of several pages and preceding the actual text, these vignettes entail visits to — and observations of — sites that reflect each chapter's theme. The style is first-person journalism, with each composition appearing as a sort of travel article. My interviewees/tour guides are professionals and volunteer activists alike who, in multidisciplinary ways, apply history to contemporary situations. Most of the sites featured here are or will be publicly accessible. Again, the goal is to promote a tangible Los Angeles heritage.

Please note that the mood and style swings dramatically between the vignettes and the text. To avoid confusion, the transition is formally marked, in each chapter, by a snapshot of Boris Deutsch's massive Terminal Annex mural (see the endpapers for an example.) The vignette ceases — and the text begins — at this graphic interlude.

Overall, *Place of Possibilities* has been organized topically. I opted for a narrative approach: serious content that often reads like a story and, in its telling, encourages readers to ask questions, to observe the omissions or inconsistencies. Academicians "specialize." My endnotes attest to the fact that this book rests on a variety of authoritative sources. In assuming the role of writer, photo researcher, travel agent, and longtime Angeleno, however, I was left to bridge the gaps. It may have been safer for me to have hidden behind chronology; bald spots do occasionally emerge from under this topical approach.

I hope, more than anything else, that this book is intellectually honest. At times, I express outrage over past injustices or puzzlement over phenomena which I believe still lack concrete explanations. My directness serves as an invitation for you to further explore and interpret the City of Angels.

Ƀ

My own explorations have been facilitated by many people. I believe it was Barbara Hoff Delvac, then of the Los Angeles Conservancy, who originally connected me with this book project 18 months ago. Charles E. Parks, publisher at Heritage Media, made it all seem so easy and pleasurable. My editor, Lori M. Parks, deserves a lifetime supply of champagne, most of all for her patience, and for encouraging a creative approach to popular history. I also owe thanks to the editorial and design staff at Heritage who worked diligently — and overtime — in bringing this book to press. Kathee Finn and her field representatives kept me informed of their findings: privately held photo collections and other gems.

As I mentioned earlier, the subtitle of the book is "The People and Resources that Created Los Angeles." At several critical and very different junctures, I called upon William D. Estrada of El Pueblo de Los Angeles Historic Monument. I can think of few who so capably and enthusiastically link people and resources. I am very grateful to Roberta S. Greenwood, Greenwood & Associates, for allowing me to raid her personal library collection and for knowledgeably responding to my many queries, great and small. Having just concluded her own research into the city government, Anne V. Howell of the Los Angeles Department of City Planning reviewed Chapter 3. Her comments were comprehensive and extremely helpful. Hynda Rudd of the Los Angeles City Archives offered her time for a special part of this project, and her energy is always appreciated.

In the photo category, two individuals deserve particular recognition. Jeanne Taylor Baird, of the L.A. Conservancy, told me about her postcard collection and granted repeated access. *Place of Possibilities* surely would not have been as richly illustrated without this fine resource. Several years ago, I read about a cache of California Plein-Air paintings that had recently opened to the public; I couldn't get it out of my mind. Jean Stern, Executive Director of the Irvine Museum, has been most gracious in availing this treasure trove — and that of Joan Irvine Smith Fine Arts — to *Place of Possibilities*. Thank you.

In addition to those whose names appear in the text, I owe gratitude to the following people and institutions for easing my editorial and photo research: Academy of Motion Picture Arts and Sciences, Linda R. Mehr and the staff of the Margaret Herrick Library; Arcadia Public Library, Mary Beth Hayes; Bob Baker (puppeteer, longtime local resident); California Historical Society, Patricia L.

Keats; Centinela Adobe, Margaret Bates and Evelyne McEntire; Chinese Historical Society of Southern California, Gene Moy; City of Los Angeles, Department of Water and Power, Robert Dalton and Valerie Roberts-Gray; County-USC Medical Center, Toby Horn; Drum Barracks Museum, Marge O'Brien; Robin J. Dunitz Enterprises, Robin J. Dunitz (mural historian, publisher); El Pueblo de Los Angeles Historical Monument, Suellen Cheng; Goethe Institut/German Cultural Center, Stephan Kloo; Getty Research Institute, Karen L. Stokes; Immigrant Genealogical Society Library, Gwen Christensen and Lura Perkins; Jewish Federation Council of Greater Los Angeles (Planning), Pini Herman; Jewish Historical Society of Southern California, Stephen J. Sass; Los Angeles City Historical Society, Don Esacove; Los Angeles Conservancy, Mary Sullivan; Los Angeles Public Library, Carolyn Cole, Jane Nowak, and Cindy McNaughton; Metropolitan Transportation Authority, Laurie Garris; National Archives and Records Administration, Sharon Culley; Playa Vista, Ken Agid and Jennifer Fidelman; Social and Public Art Resource Center, Reina Prado; Southwest Museum, Kim Walters; Swedish Consulate, Elisabeth Kiehlsberg; UCLA External Affairs Division, University Communications Department, Marketing and Communication Strategies Office, Michael Stone; UCLA University Archives, Dennis Bitterlich; UCLA Young Research Library, Department of Special Collections staff; USC Regional History Center, Dace Taube; Randy Young (independent historian, publisher); and, any others who I may have missed.

Most importantly, my family nurtured this book with great love and understanding. My son, Robert, demanded that I take a "time out" every day from 5:30 to 9:30 p.m., to remind myself what life is really about. And I am unfailingly grateful to my husband, soon-to-be Rabbi Richard Flom, for the love and emotional security that allows me to journey through the past and elsewhere. I cherish our personal history and anticipate our future together.

✍

They say that L.A. — and its people — are always reinventing themselves. To me, this claim perpetuates the stereotype we so vigorously protest: a city weak in traditions, where self-proclaimed gurus (or crazies) continuously concoct fads *du jour* void of meaningful effect.

I prefer to think of Los Angeles as a place where people can find reconciliation and liberate aspects of themselves that may have been latent elsewhere. I am a first- generation American, with all of the hopes and confusion that the title bears. In Los Angeles, I perceive a city that provides multiple opportunities to highlight — or bury — social, economic, moral, political or creative standards that are in internal conflict, or in conflict with each other. Yet, the process of finding personal harmony on a grand, urban scale sometimes erupts: we do battle when reminded of who we were — or are — rather than what we might become. Critics claim Angelenos forget their past; perhaps it's easier that way.

I realize that I cannot please all of the readers all of the time. Any sociological or political grouping encompasses many subsectors. While it might have been simpler to portray L.A. as home to 3.5 million utterly variegated individuals, such a tactic would deflect from intelligent dialogue. I can only hope that *Place of Possibilities* will be truer to the city's complexity.

Lynn C. Kronzek
Los Angeles, California
September, 1998

CHAP

TER 1

chapter

Introduction

Multicultural Los Angeles of the late 1990s is an assertion of individual group identities. Addressing the National Society of Fundraising Executives (NSFRE) in L.A., a foundation director told the audience that they should start paying attention to new constituencies at around the same time that politicians do. Does the "Other" on the application form refer to yet-to-be-recognized groups demanding separate space, or is it a place for those who have mingled to proclaim their point of view?

Cy Wong is a longtime board member of the Chinese Historical Society of Southern California. I chose to start this book with him because his culturally mixed background recalls the pobladores, settlers of the pueblo we now call Los Angeles. Wong's name tells only part of his story. He is both African- and Chinese-American, with some Native ancestry, too: the same highly literate tribes who were forced to march on the Trail of Tears from their Southeastern homes to Oklahoma reservations.

More unusual than Wong's background, however, is the fact that he's cared to preserve it. In the wake of the Civil War and Reconstruction which freed African-American slaves, the South needed additional field hands. Some Louisiana and Mississippi planters turned to Chinese contract laborers. While employers sought to create a workforce rivalry between the Asian newcomers and the African-Americans, a few intermarried. Most of their progeny blended into one culture or the other.

Wong has kept his genealogical records and his multicultural heritage. It is this combination of awareness and sensitivity that leads me to ask for

(Right and bottom photo) The plaza in transition, circa 1880. The historic, rectangular nucleus has given way to a newly-landscaped, park-like round. With a population of over 11,000, Los Angeles now has a water system, run by the private L.A. City Water Company. The main storage tank appears recessed from the center of the picture, but clearly visible through signage. *Courtesy The Southwest Museum, Los Angeles, photo N.42523 and N.42520.*

his help. I want to find a place where those from different backgrounds truly mingle. In complex, 1990s Los Angeles, the goal seems to be co-existence. My quest is more ambitious: a multicultural environment that even extends beyond civility — to conviviality. What I hope to discover, no matter how small or idiosyncratic the space, is a late 20th-century version of the pueblo.

Wong is unable to help. He knew of a Chinese-Cuban restaurant that came close to my description, but it has closed. Drawing a parallel to that spot where the states of Arizona, Colorado, New Mexico and Utah meet, I ask if there is a "Four Corners of L.A." that marks the convergence of three or four communities. Wong talks of tiny ethnic enclaves within differently-composed neighborhoods; he knows his demography — but no four corners.

With limited time, I try a different approach. When the present does not translate to the past, I invariably go to the historic source. And in Los Angeles that means El Pueblo de Los Angeles Historical Monument. My guide here is William Estrada. Gracious and thoughtful, he cites among recommended readings W.W. Robinson's classic, *Los Angeles from the Days of the Pueblo.* Yet, Robinson is gone now, and I seek Estrada because he probably knows more about this area than almost anyone else today. An historian by training, he works as a curator at El Pueblo and has been been finishing his doctoral dissertation on the plaza, a subject which has led him to study Southwestern historic sites, railroads, preservation movements and everything in between.

Our tour starts by circling around the old plaza twice, a spontaneous ritual acknowledging the dizzying array of historical topics that cannot be reduced to 90 or so minutes. Estrada offers "a dialectic between the plaza and Olvera Street, as sacred and contested spaces." More generally, he discusses "what it means to be a Mexican in late 20th-century North America."

The plaza refers to the communal center of the Spanish land grant specifically designated for the creation of a city. Housing lots of equal size (roughly 55 x 110 feet) surrounded the rectangular "town square" on three sides. The remaining side was reserved for public buildings and a church. Although the land uses changed, the plaza remained center-city until the second half of the 19th century. Estrada makes the connection between the coming of the railroads and the plaza's decline, during the 1870s. In his words, the event signified a "point of departure." Spanish subsequently was spoken to the

north of the plaza, and English, to the south. St. Vibiana's rose as the Cathedral of the Roman Catholic Archdiocese, challenging the primacy of the Church of Our Lady Queen of the Angels, the old Placita Church. The area around Temple and Main constituted the new government center.

As civic leaders abandoned the plaza, it became home to poor, immigrant communities, the socially and politically disenfranchised. In 1907 the City Council banned free speech everywhere — but here. A concrete rostrum accommodated speakers, including the exiled Mexican revolutionary Ricardo Flores Magon, socialist mayoral candidate Job Harriman and anarchist Emma Goldman.

Estrada points to the "bum proof" wall around the plaza, a gift to the unemployed of the 1930s. The top row of bricks have been laid vertically at an angle, rendering a crown of spikes. We perch there anyway, with — at least, in my case— some natural padding to cushion the effects; still, it is no place to sleep.

Everything looks different this 9:30, Wednesday morning than when I've visited in the past. I have taken classes here, always on Sunday afternoons, because I love the plaza's authenticity — the natural wedding of people to place. And for one who has never gone beyond 100 miles of the Canadian or Mexican borders, the scene is interestingly foreign: we simply do not use urban space in the same way. Sunday afternoon will find packed masses leaving the old Plaza church every few hours. A folk shrine immediately outside offers departing Spanish-speaking worshippers a more personal perspective, recalling spiritual celebrations and icons from back home. Street vendors grill meats, sell fresh juices and churros. Burial and life insurance policies also are available here, a reminder of the issues which always have been most important to immigrants with time for little else than labor.

Across the street, the plaza itself draws both worshippers and casual strollers for live performances. Dozens of Mexican and Central American immigrants circle around the dance troupes, singers or musicians. Spectators hovering toward the center are entranced by the rhythms, while people around the rim socialize, rest

or chase kids. Even on this Wednesday morning there are musicians, gliding the sound of clear, windy Andean elevations through their reed instruments. Yet, these performers seem out of place because there are no crowds to interact with them.

Museums often pay tribute to a past void of heirs; the plaza is living history. Although its constituents have come here during different times than the pobladores, they use this place in much the same way as it was intended over 200 years ago.

Estrada and I make a turn on Olvera Street. Just as the plaza has been bum-proofed, Olvera Street has been emptiness-proofed. It always looks crowded, by design. Two contiguous rows of small booths (or *puestos*), with only cloth walls to separate them, run down the center of the typically narrow, 19th-century thoroughfare. Most stalls are staffed, immediately populating the area. Historic structures on each side of Olvera Street contain shops, too, selling similar clothing, crafts and affordable items bearing a Mexican or Mexican-American imprint. Merchants find additional display space by hanging their wares from the sides of these buildings. Encouraged by gentle breezes, the goods flutter outward, banners for Olvera Street.

I linger on and near the plaza when I'm with my students; conversely, I usually hustle them through this commercial sector, pointing only to the brickwork that marks the historic *zanja madre*, (mother ditch.) Today's tour provides a different view. Estrada slices through the equivalent of a multi-layered archaeological dig, emphasizing the history which, if not coherent or

The 1818 Alvia Adobe, Olvera Street, belonged to one of Los Angeles' pioneering families. Its patriarch, Don Francisco Alvia, hailed from Sinaloa, Mexico and moved here during the 1790s. He became alcade, or mayor, in 1810. The building might not be here today were it not for the leadership of Christine Sterling. As this 1950s postcard illustrates, however, historic preservation through much of the 20th century was almost exclusively connected with tourism. *Courtesy The Postcard Collection of Jeanne Taylor Baird.*

immediately visible, is always present. The Pelanconi House (1855-1857), Los Angeles' oldest remaining brick structure, recalls a once-vibrant Italian presence. Olvera Street was known as Vine Street when Antonio Pelanconi arrived here from Lombardy during 1853. He soon joined with fellow Italian immigrant, Giuseppe Gazzo, in the winemaking business and married Isabel Ramirez, whose father owned several grape-covered acres to the east of Alameda Street. The couple's oldest son Lorenzo developed his own winery complex, including business and warehousing functions — on Olvera and Alameda streets.

By the time that Los Angeles developed what may be considered the nation's first zoning ordinance (1908), Olvera Street had declined in its residential value and was reserved for light industry. Henry Huntington built his Plaza Substation there (1903, expanded 1918,) generating electricity for the street cars serving his Los Angeles Railway Company.

We move to the Avila Adobe. It's akin to San Antonio's Alamo or Boston's Fanneuil Hall. With the

namesake Olvera adobe torn down in 1917, this structure became a rallying symbol for early preservationists and a landmark subsequently familiar to local history buffs. If you know nothing about any of the neighboring buildings, you might know about the Avila Adobe. It is Los Angeles' oldest surviving residence and the home of an early mayor, the structure tourists visit because they want to learn about local history.

"Christine Sterling died in this house," Estrada informed me. I was taken aback.

Sterling had been responsible for bringing Olvera Street to its present state. And when old Chinatown fell to Union Station, she developed China City, which was as thematic and tourist-friendly as Olvera Street.

It is easy — but wrong — for the late 20th century Angeleno to dismiss Sterling. When citizens of L.A. in 1926 passed a referendum to construct a new railroad station, they were simultaneously given a choice of five locations. They opted for the plaza, which would have meant certain destruction of this historic district. Christine Sterling's passion may have kindled a local preservation movement but, according to Estrada, the *Times'* Harry Chandler and real estate-railroad politics were responsible for reversing the public decision. In terms of developing Union Station, it proved easier, less expensive and more strategic to acquire land in Chinatown. And a renovated plaza could only add to the commercial gains stimulated by improved transportation and trade networks. (Old Olvera Street even complimented the Spanish style of Union Station!)

Sterling summarized her motivations: "Olvera Street holds for me all of the charm, and beauty which I dreamed for it, because out of the hearts of Mexican people is spun the gold of Romance and Contentment. No sweeter, finer people live on this earth, than the men and women of Mexico, and what ever evil anyone believe about them have been bred in the darkness of ignorance and prejudice. Olvera Street claims no architectural distinction. It is just simple and plain with every day usefulness, but beneath the surface it is sincere. It is not enough that we just remember the pioneer Mothers and Fathers. We must carry forward some part of their work, some definite, tangible thing to pass on to future generations; and in giving this respect to those who came before us, we earn the remembrance of those who follow us."

Some of these words are timeless, others sound dated and condescending. Yet, as Estrada reminds me, Mexican restaurants in those days were called "Spanish kitchens." The movement to save the pueblo began the long battle to correct historic perceptions, proclaiming a Mexican past and, ultimately, a well-mixed cultural heritage.

California B.C.

Many Angelenos now know of the multicultural backgrounds of the pobladores, settlers who in 1781 bestowed on Los Angeles its urban identity. Their origins are celebrated because many of us — whether tracing our own lineage to Africa, Asia, the Americas, or Europe — can claim kinship. If we were to begin in the late 18th century, however, we would be ignoring prehistory and a society that boasted immense cultural complexity. Yet, there are few left who can speak with family pride to the ancestry of the very first settlers.

Today's City of Los Angeles extends from the San Fernando Valley to the border of the San Gabriel Valley. Circumventing the independent City of Santa Monica, it greets the coast from Pacific Palisades to Playa del Rey, engulfs a huge basin, and narrows through a 20-mile "neck" to San Pedro. Before the pobladores, this expansive territory was primarily the domain of two peoples, the Chumash and the Tongva. Their boundary has been staked somewhere in or near

Chumash rock art still can be seen at Burro Flats in Chatsworth. *Courtesy The Southwest Museum, Los Angeles, photo CT.86.*

(Left) Boris Deutsch's "Cultural Contributions of North, South, and Central America" begins by focusing on Native populations and comes to include the European and Asian immigrants who subsequently settled in the western hemisphere. In fact, Deutsch's own profile pops up occasionally among those of his subjects. The Terminal Annex Post Office downtown, which contains Deutsch's masterpiece, currently is undergoing restoration. *Courtesy, The National Archives and Records Administration, Washington, D.C.*

Topanga Canyon, with the Chumash occupying the Western San Fernando Valley and its southerly shoreline, into Ventura County and up the Central Coast. The Tongva roughly claimed the coast from Chumash territory south to Orange County, and all of the present city's interior basin. (In time, the Tongva became known by other names. The Spaniards applied the term "Gabrielino" to those who lived near the San Gabriel Mission and "Fernandeno" to those who resided close to the San Fernando Mission.)

Native Americans often are identified by language group. A Hokan-speaking people, likely related to the Chumash, may have arrived in Greater Los Angeles tens of thousands of years ago. During 1936 at Ballona Creek, the discovery of a human skull and mammoth bones hinted that residency could be dated 25,000 years ago. Contemporary archaeologists appear more comfortable referring to the existence of well-established settlements between 7000-8000 B.C.

The Tongva, by contrast, were relative newcomers. Arriving in waves from the Great Basin of Utah, Nevada, and California between 2500 B.C and 700 A.D., this Uto-Aztecan (formerly called Shoshonean) language group probably sought more bountiful food and water sources. They eventually integrated with or displaced older residents of the area.

The Chumash may have been involved in the merger; beside their possible kinship to the original Hokan people, they continued to maintain a language

The signs of coastal living — reed huts and tomol (plank canoe)— dominate in this sketch of a Chumash village. The Pacific provided skilled Chumash fishermen a variety of products for personal consumption and trade. *Courtesy The Southwest Museum, Los Angeles, photo N.37072.*

distinct from the Tongva. If the two cultures bonded by means of invasion, however, it was commerce and advancing civilization that brought them closer together.

From Los Angeles to Central California — the Chumash population totaled 15,000-20,000; merely 1,300 dwelled in the vicinity of the Santa Monica Mountains. These people built a reputation on maritime industries. They crafted sturdy plank canoes (*tomol*) which, when fully shaped, were polished with sharkskin sandpaper. Up to 20 men propelled the boats and, under the right conditions, the vessels might sail at six to eight knots. With their canoes, the Chumash routinely traded with kindred peoples on the Channel Islands.

Chumash fishing methods were precise, offering sustenance and fodder for trade. A late 18th-century observer described prosperous harvests of bonita and yellowtail tuna:

> They (the Chumash) were always seen out by the dawn of day either examining their fish pots in the bay or fishing in the middle of the Channel where they never fail to catch a plentiful supply of Boneto and a kind of Herring with a yellow tail.

Although known for their nautical ways, L.A.-area Chumash also took trade excursions inland. They enticed the Tongva with arrows and, possibly, mortars and yucca cord.

The Tongva, like the Chumash, possessed maritime skills and interests. In a society where the environment molded culture, however, the more diverse Tongva landscape likely created greater internal variances. Archaeologists often characterize Southern California as a region of four biomes: interior mountains and adjacent foothills; vast prairie extending from the mountains; exposed coast; and, sheltered coast. Each boasted its own natural resources — and subsequently, ecosystems — confronting human inhabitants with different adaptational challenges. Simply stated, the Chumash spread over two of these micro-environments, the Tongva covered all four.

The 5,000 or so Tongva also found themselves at the physical, cultural and commercial crossroads of five peoples: the Chumash, Tataviam, Serrano, Cahuilla and Luiseno. It is hardly surprising, then, that the Tongva language included three Los Angeles-area dialects, which could be generally understood. Sibangna was spoken by those who lived near the San Gabriel Mission and Fernandeno, by peoples residing in the proximity of the San Fernando. Santa Catalina Islanders and their cousins from Redondo to San Pedro spoke "pure" Tongva or possibly, Playasano.

Artistry and trade mingled in the Tongva world. Quartz, soapstone and clay yielded eating and cutting utensils, effigies and implements of all sorts. Craftspeople fabricated rope from plants, colored it with natural dyes, and wove it into baskets. Today's athlete-on-the-run owes the Tongva thanks for an important innovation, the water bottle. Composed of rushes or tules and made impermeable with asphalt, these vessels stood up to three feet tall; the larger receptacles were used to store a family's water supply. An observer, Captain George Nidever, described the enterprise of one Tongva:

"She had built a fire and had several stones about the size of a walnut heating in it. Taking one of the vessels, which was in shape and size very like a demijohn, excepting that the neck and mouth were much longer, she dropped a few pieces of asphaltum within it, and as soon as the stones were well heated they were dropped in on top of the asphaltum. They soon melted it, when, resting the bottom of the vessel on the ground, she gave it a rotary motion with both hands until its interior was completely covered with the asphaltum. These vessels hold water well, and if kept full may be placed with safety in a hot sun."

So sophisticated were Tongva craftspeople and professionals (particularly, the shamans, ritual leaders/healers,) that they organized guilds — which sometimes paralleled and intersected with like organizations among the Chumash. The Tongva also sent what we might call "trade emissaries" to their northern neighbors' communities. Many instances of cultural blending subsequently occurred. For example, storytelling was an important art form, an engaging, entertaining method of conveying tradition and history to future generations. Chiefs sometimes ordained youthful bards to cultivate the skill of repeating, word-for-word, revered legends, tales, and orations. Yet, narrative also evolved: the Tongva occasionally inserted Chumash or other details for their effect.

It is important to emphasize that cultural contributions diffused in all directions. Whereas American settlers often carried with them a malodorous scent of horses, food, whiskey, and biophysical activity, the largely unclothed Tongva purged themselves of these smells daily; as a rule, they bathed each dawn. Hygiene indeed had been commanded by Chengiichngech, the supergod who presided over a hierarchy of other deities and advanced a strong code of behavior. This religion spread to southerly peoples — the Luiseno, Cupeno, and Diegueno — and remained important long after Christianity took hold regionally.

In addition to imparting new cultural and religious practices, Los Angeles-area chiefs enforced their power through marriage. Various communities were beginning to consolidate and, thereby, develop larger, more unified networks as early as the first century. The Chumash lived close together, physically, their small villages often no more than five miles apart. One political-economic confederacy, based in Humaliwo or Malibu, extended all the way to the Tongva western-central San Fernando Valley.

Similarly, marriages between the southern Chumash and north-

As identifiable native (Chumash and Tongva) populations diminished by the late 19th century, ethnographers began to document their lifestyles. Fernando Librado was photographed here in 1912 or 1913, unearthing edible roots with his digging stick. The Chumash villager had been legendary: church authorities claimed he was 125 years old. *Courtesy The Southwest Museum, Los Angeles, photo N.42522.*

This elderly Tongva woman resided at San Gabriel long after the priests left. The crucifix dangling from her wrist affirms an ongoing religious commitment. *Courtesy The Southwest Museum, Los Angeles, photo N.20056.*

western Tongva proliferated. Mission records indicate several of the Santa Monica Mountain-area villages were bilingual. Some sociocultural compromise probably was necessary, as the Chumash tended to live with their wives' families, while the Tongva adhered to more strictly defined patrilineal communities.

What mingling did not occur of its own accord took place during the Spanish era: the San Gabriel and San Fernando missions recruited from both peoples. Although the padres sometimes enlisted the chiefs to forge better cooperation, the larger effort was not primarily directed at cultural preservation.

Early Multiculturalism, and the Becoming of Californios

One of the reasons often cited for Spanish settlement of Alta California is the perceived encroachment of the English and Russians from the north. The native peoples — each with their own distinctions but intertwined by trade, kinship and religion — must have presented a large, befuddling obstacle. The three-pronged Spanish strategy of presidio (fort), pueblo (city) and mission was a way of tapping existing human resources, while building a machine that could halt, if not eventually conquer, more traditional (and easily understood) opponents.

But what was the incentive for the native Californians? Excluding debate about instances of forced relocation, why did so many voluntarily confine themselves to the mission system? Recent scholarship about the local populations renders the answer increasingly elusive. Some argue that the missions offered physical protection from warring factions, yet this runs counter to the interest of societies which had in many ways transcended a military orientation. True, skirmishes were not unknown to the Tongva. There had been, for example, ongoing battles between the landbound people of the Whittier Narrows and certain western villages, who halted their fishing expeditions to the ocean. Yet, the overall view is one of peace. The Chumash possessed no standing army; they could muster forces, when the need arose, through their other social and trade connections.

Economic arguments fall short, too. Native peoples had long developed a regimen of seasonal hunting, fishing and gathering activities. Food processing techniques, plus formal storage and distribution methods (often, the chief's responsibility), generally yielded provender year-round; trade could make up for some deficits. The Spanish added novelties, among them colorful clothing and corn, tortillas and other culinary adaptations to New World ingredients. Was a more stationary agricultural society (and the resulting products) a lure? Did the Chumash and Tongva ponder and reconcile the differences between newly-introduced food production technologies and their own?

The draw of Catholicism — already blended with some of the native, and possibly related, religions of Mexico — also is a topic for discussion. Indeed, the Spanish had used the mission system to settle parts of Mexico, and boasted well-honed recruitment techniques. Furthermore, classical California archaeologists and anthropologists (Hugo Reid, Alfred L. Kroeber, Bernice E. Johnston and others) indicate that the Uto-Aztecan language of the Los Angeles basin was similar to that spoken by the Comanche, Aztec and Pueblo peoples; the Tongva's original travel route may have commenced in Northern Mexico. Perhaps certain religio-cultural characteristics endured through this evolution, and the Spaniards' earlier conversion successes, if not directly applicable, at least might have been helpful.

In truth, we cannot settle the initial appeal of the mission here, but the ramifications are important

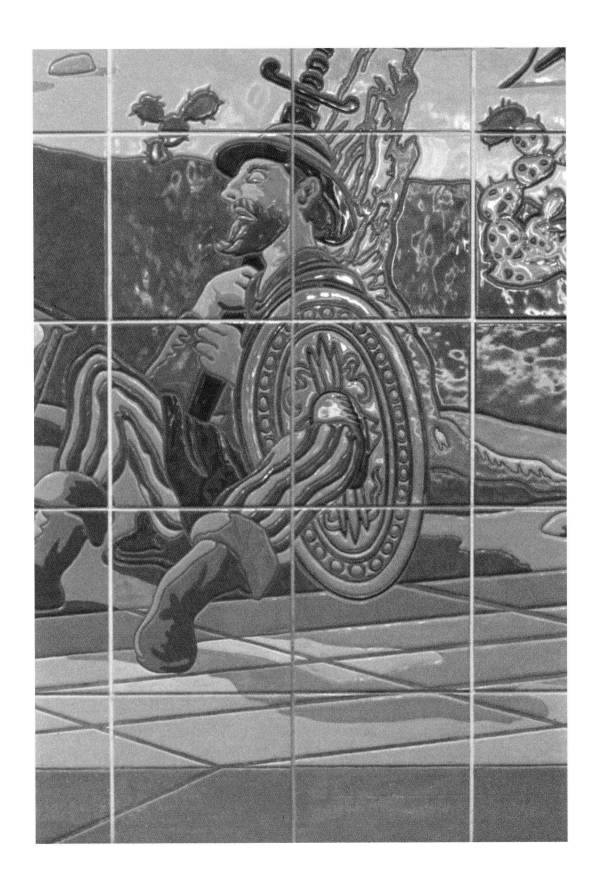

because of sheer numbers: San Gabriel and San Fernando each counted about 1,000 neophytes (Native converts) between 1817-1819, whereas the City's population probably did not even reach four digits until 1840. Had they not been recruited for mission service, the native groups may have directed themselves more toward the El Pueblo de la Reina de los Angeles.

The relationship between the indigenous populations and the pobladores differed, too, from that framed by the padres. If Spain launched a complex strategy for control of Alta California, its executioners came with divergent backgrounds, purposes and approaches. Advancement to the highest military ranks, for example, likely depended on pedigree as well as on service. And before being anointed for religious duty in this totally alien New World, the padres' spiritual growth had been carefully cultivated in Spain. (Note: the issue of church-state separation predated the U.S. Constitution by years. The prominent roles — and shared leadership — of military and clerical men in various California expeditions indicate that the rationale for settlement was debated on both macro and micro levels.)

But the original 44-foot soldiers who committed themselves to building a pueblo here in 1781 boasted no heraldry, little education, few direct ties to Spain. In fact, the term "Spanish" has been used more thus far to describe the geopolitics of the 18th century than the demographics. Of the 22 adult pobladores, eight were listed as Indio/India; eight, Mulato/Mulata (mixed African and European descent); two, Negro; two, Espanol; and one, Mestizo (mixed Native American and European descent).

This classification system is reminiscent of that employed for the Cherokee census, conducted during 1835 over a substantial swath of the Southeastern United States. Categories such as White, Full-blooded and Half-breed (Native American), Mixed Catawbys, Mixed Spanish, and Quadroon (partially of African ancestry) linger on the historic rolls. France and Spain dominated the Southeast early on, and the census clearly acknowledges racial/cultural blending. Conversely, the view of the English Northeast is more homogeneous.

Perhaps Franco-Spanish Catholicism — as opposed to Anglicanism or Protestantism — was an element in early multiculturalism. But the underlying issue really may have been how religious freedom (or more accurately, oppression) manifested itself. The Spanish Inquisition imposed Catholicism on the population through individual means, conversion or death. By contrast, the British sought more institutional answers to religious dissension, effectively outlawing certain denominations. The latter approach actually might have encouraged minorities to organize. Some groups of Northeastern American colonists chose to exercise religious freedom by living alone, among themselves, in isolation from the oppression they had known in England. For the pioneering Spanish (and French) masses here, these factors appear to have been less unifying — and intimate association with other populations, greater.

The term Espanol, used to describe several of the pobladores, is instructive, too. Its synonyms include *criollo* and *Espanol americano*, American-born Spaniard (or more appropriately, Mexican). Additionally, the designation was bestowed upon individuals — no matter what their race — who possessed talents vital to the community or who became prosperous on account of their personal integrity and efforts. A multiracial person of light skin also could don the title. Parallels with the southeastern U.S. surface again. One especially thinks of the French creole , and a subsector of the Louisiana population that *passe blanc* (literally, "pass as white") for a better chance at social and economic mobility.

The pobladores of African heritage, however, were not connected with the then-thriving Southern plantation system. As the global power of the 16th century, Spain drew — and captured — many foreigners: both slaves and individuals who freely sought to enter its kingdom. In turn, Spanish (and Portuguese) explorations included black crew members, artisans, laborers and servants. Some disembarked, and helped the Iberian influence to spread over the Americas. By 1810, New Granada (a territory encompassing present-day Ecuador, Colombia, Venezuela and Panama) boasted a population of 1.4 million; 210,000, or roughly 15 percent, were of African descent. And, like other voyagers from Spain and Portugal, they intermingled socially and culturally with the indigenous populations. The mulato/mestizo composition of the pobladores indeed reflects what also had been happening in parts of their homeland, Mexico, for several centuries.

More generally, the pobladores came from the Northwestern Mexican provinces of Sinaloa and Sonora. Their physical movement originated with Spanish colonial designs, which typically settled Mexican regions from the south to the north — using missions, presidios, pueblos and mining districts, where applicable. Immigration to the United States basically followed the same geographic pattern throughout the first half of the 19th century. Drawing increasing numbers of people, the movement frequently began in Sinaloa, then pressed northward into the Sonora, Baja California, and over the border to Southern California. Other Mexican cities and provinces also contributed to the flow.

When talking about migration, we often refer to "push-pull" factors: social, economic and political conditions that simultaneously cause massive relocation. The most southerly of the three provinces, Sinaloa, served as the starting point for many Spanish — and later Mexican — families who entered Alta California. It was the first of the three provinces settled, during the early part of the 1500s. By the time of the pobladores, agricultural Sinaloa long since had been carved up, creating class distinctions between landowners and those who more directly tended the soil, supported the

agrarian infrastructure, and crafted the earth's many bounties into usable products.

Some members of the working class saw new opportunities in Sonora's silver mines. They pushed northward to explore the challenges. The impending frontier existence was marked by horrendous labor, a speculative income and ongoing, unpredictable confrontations with the Apaches. Again, North seemed a plausible direction. Military duty carried particular cachet. For a person of little means, it offered a regular stipend and possible promotion to lower officers' ranks. Exemplary service also might be rewarded with a land grant upon retirement.

Actually, the pobladores had been part of an expedition that included both soldiers and settlers. Recruited simultaneously, the former were to fill vacancies at presidios, while the latter would settle at what later became Los Angeles and Santa Barbara. (Another Spanish expedition, under the leadership of Lieutenant Colonel Gaspar de Portola, Governor of Baja California, already had "discovered" Los Angeles during 1769, camping in the general vicinity of the soon-to-be pueblo).

The requirements and rewards for pobladores proved different than those for soldiers. In outlining their credentials, Teodoro de la Croix, Commandant General of the Interior Provinces, desired that each settlers be the "head or father of each family, must be a man of the field, a hard-working farmer, healthy, robust, and without known vices or defect..." Skilled artisans of similar constitutions and ethics also were enlisted. For their hardships, the pobladores would receive three-years' sustenance: a monthly stipend; rations and clothing for themselves and their families; a pair each of cows, oxen, ewes, goats and horses; one mule; three mares. Arrival in Los Angeles then would guarantee a housing lot and small plots for farming, along with communal pastorage. Taxation and tithing were waived for five years, allowing the pobladores to repay Spain's initial investment.

Recruitment of settlers proved difficult. The sole land route equated to a parched march, first across the Sonoran, then the Mojave, deserts — with a trek over the Colorado River — while orchestrating children,

The mission buildings, themselves, impart a romantic aura which has ensured their preservation long after other historic structures were razed. San Fernando Rey de Espana (1797) is captured here by professional and amateur artists, respectively. Henry Ford Chapman created the black-and-white etching in 1883; major restoration had occurred four years earlier, reversing to some extent earthquake damage and decades of neglect. *Courtesy of Joan Irvine Smith Fine Arts, Laguna Beach, California.*

the recruits, pobladores and families which he brought, under his charge, should camp at a distance from of one league [from the mission] because of the fact that some of the children among the party had but recently recovered from the smallpox. From [their camp] they went to establish themselves on the ground where they are founding the pueblo of Los Angeles, and now having finished the Zanja madre they are continuing with building their houses and also corrals for the stock. The latter has not as yet been distributed because they are concentrating their efforts on finishing the pueblo and when its is completed, they begin to plow the fields for the sowing of the wheat.

That to the pueblo there arrived but 11 pobladores, and that of these eight alone are of any use.

(Left and bottom photo) Eva Scott Feynes started as a Sunday painter. When afflicted by arthritis, she took the advice of her physician and, for therapeutic purposes, devoted herself increasingly to art. Fenyes' renderings of the missions and historic Los Angeles residences are scattered throughout this book. The illustration at the top is her view of the San Fernando belfry (1905). Drawn 15 years later, the second work captures the door to the priest's house. *Courtesy The Southwest Museum, Los Angeles, photo FEN.19 and 20.*

livestock and equipment for various climatological and military contingencies. The pobladores were spared somewhat. Leaving on February 2, 1781 from Alamos, they initially went by sea to Baja California. The expeditions subsequently proceeded to the established presidio of San Diego before heading to the Mission San Gabriel. From there, they would enter Los Angeles and begin building their community.

The trip was not so simple, however. An epidemic of smallpox waylaid the settlers. Small groups, several families at a time, trickled into L.A. rather than moving jubilantly in unison. The first party may have come during late June, 1781. Governor Felipe de Neve reported on October 21, 1781 that though still somewhat debilitated, the pobladores nevertheless commenced the hard work for which they were recruited:

That having arrived at this Mission on August 18, the Lieutenant Jose Zuniga provided that

Unlike the retired soldiers and government administrators whose names became associated with the large ranchos, the pobladores essentially exchanged their labor for self-sufficiency and community property. El Pueblo de la Reina de los Angeles — the village — itself was considered a land grant. The settlers' plots were small, and their commission came with demands: collective responsibility for creating and maintaining the city's social/commercial nucleus, the pueblo, and an urban infrastructure.

Together, the pobladores developed the zanja system, a network of open, wooden irrigation ditches that — through gravity — tapped the Porciuncula (L.A. River) and mountain runoff for farming. The zanja madre , the mother of these channels, ran near to the pueblo and crossed what is now Olvera Street. From the voluntary, communal irrigation system evolved today's Department of Water and Power.

In choosing an actual site, the pobladores opted for a place near the Tongva village of Yaangna. Similar rationales guided many Spanish-financed expeditions: native populations were familiar with the land and knew where natural resources converged. Furthermore, settlers may have considered their future progeny; in sparsely settled territory, they were not totally opposed to intermarriage — or less formal relationships.

The situation was mutual from the Tongva-Chumash perspective. As discussed earlier, L.A's first inhabitants accepted cultural and social intermingling.

Their societies also imparted moral values that appear complex and, in some ways, contemporary. Hugo Reid, a 19th-century Scotch-Angeleno who, himself, married a Tongva chief's daughter (see the sidebar), alluded to their need for intermarriage: "Incest was... punished with death: being held in such abhorrence that marriages between kinsfolk were not allowed." And while rape was cause for war, the Tongva likely tolerated premarital relations among consenting parties.

If mutual accord about intermarriage existed, the pobladores' racial views were mixed and their behavior reflected this confusion. An acculturation dynamic began immediately in the pueblo. Of the original adult pobladores, eight changed their racial/cultural identification by the 1790 census, within 10 years. Four mulattos and three Indians either became mestizos or coyotes, and one of the mestizos was now listed as espanol. Though the sample is small, such realignments possibly indicated weakening ties to African or Native backgrounds, or movement toward what was becoming a dominant, new culture.

However motivated, this process did not stop intermarriage and other cultural integration. Perhaps most telling was that orphaned or abandoned children of Native American/mixed heritage parents were adopted with relative frequency. Similarly, early settlers of African lineage merged into what came to be called the Californio culture. Los Angeles by 1850 contained 1,610 residents, only 12 of whom were termed "colored." Eleven of them lived and worked in other households, an extension of the system transported from the American South. Although the last Mexican Governor, Pio Pico, and others claimed African heritage, it was of the old order. An identifiable black presence — by today's parlance, African-American — did not really emerge until the late 1800s.

From the new millennium through 1850, Los Angeles remained a small agricultural village. Natural reproduction yielded population increases, but the pueblo appeared isolated to new residents. California was first part of Spain — then of Mexico — until mid-century and, therefore, at least conceptually, not as inviting to Easterners as official U.S. territories or states.

Like a mountain road pelted with avalanches, overland routes from Mexico often proved hopelessly impassable. The government closed large portions due to recurring battles with Native peoples; more generally, northern passages were untrammeled and difficult to traverse. Spain and Mexico nevertheless continued to encourage settlement of Alta California, including the southern sector.

Their methods were different. Spain had taken an institutional approach, with its three-pronged pueblo, presidio and mission. There was considerable regulation: to control the distribution of wealth, the Spanish government confined the pobladores to no more than

50 heads each of sheep, cattle and horses. And while Spain awarded land grants, they tended to be few — and large. Mexico won independence in 1821. Land grants became the primary method of settlement here, as the new government gifted nearly 40 ranchos through 1845. (Secularization of the missions, during 1833, added extra acreage, plus coveted administrative posts that were necessary to replace the mission priests' oversight.)

Descended from poor farmers, laborers and peasants, the newly-landed held positions as soldiers and government agents — a rise in their inherited status. Their grants were typically smaller than what had been awarded under Spain, though they represented a huge improvement over the situation back home, where miniscule family plots allowed no room for subdivisions among future generations. The combination of land and status bestowed by military/civil service produced an elite Californio culture. Though often of mixed parentage, these early Angelenos saw themselves as socially and intellectually superior to Native Americans and subsequent Mexican immigrants. Physical distance and communications gaps further severed them from the realities of their homeland.

A trip to the old ranchos is instructive. The refurbished and rehabilitated estates differ in size and decor, and one might sense the extent to which operations depended on outside labor. Places like the Rancho Los Alamitos must have been palatial by the standards of the day, with 28,027 acres surrounding it.

Aguaje de la Centinela remains closest to where I live and work. It is difficult to really see the "Centinela Adobe" at first, because from the street, visitors are pleasantly overwhelmed by the mature trees and a dense, vast, calming shade. Ignacio Machado, recipient of the original 2,200-acre land grant, built Aguaje de la Centinela in 1834. While calculations of worth and absolute size may confound contemporary homeowners, this holding actually was one of many smaller parcels apportioned by the Mexican government. The Aguaje de la Centinela estate today has been reduced to a large, if beautiful, lot on the Westchester/Inglewood border. Its back overlooks (and probably was nipped by) the San Diego/405 Freeway.

The adobe contains three rooms — a living room, dining room and bedroom — of good size, aligned, with no space other than the walls between them. The original floor was earthen, and all cooking was done outdoors. A separate bunkhouse arose (after Machado's time) as sleeping quarters for children. There is no evidence of ballrooms or workers' quarters here. By reason of the economy and climate, the rancheros surely traded indoor for outdoor space. Fiestas took place al fresco and laborers could sleep in the fields. Adobes were never intended as Newport (Rhode Island)-style mansions. Rather, they must be viewed in perspective: variable, gracious, but generally not ostentatious. Land use mattered far more.

Courtesy The Irvine Museum, Irvine, California.

Bartholomea/Victoria Reid (1808-1868)

Of the four dozen-plus Spanish and Mexican land grants awarded locally, only a few went directly to women: Victoria Reid came to own 128 acres in the San Gabriel Valley, near present-day San Marino. I investigated Dona Victoria's life. Her title alone indicates public esteem, and I was hoping to find a long-forgotten feminist exemplar. Instead, I uncovered a less idealized tale, but an honest nexus between Native American, Californio and, finally, Californian cultures. This life scetch also shows how one dignified woman could rise in a limited society and, simultaneously, suffer for her position. And Victoria might have disappeared from our view altogether were it not for public interest in her Scotch-born husband, Hugo, a respected local citizen and writer whose works about her people — derived partially from her testimony — are now legendary.

Born in 1808, the infant started her life in the village of Komikranga, in or around Santa Monica. The family soon moved to San Gabriel Mission; there, the eight-month-old baby was christened Bartholomea. It is interesting to note that the village was a mixed community. Mission records indicated that of the 13 personal names identified with it, eight spoke the language of the Chumash and five, of the Tongva.

Bartholomea was descended from a patrilineal chain of chieftains, in the Tongva way. Her lineage, if nothing else, probably bestowed a modicum of respect: some mission administrators viewed chiefs as conduits to their followers and, therefore, treated them better than average neophytes. Yet, none other than Hugo Reid reports that Indians who were baptized "lost 'caste'"among their people. Bartholomea pursued intimate relations among those of disparate cultures, however.

A friend from the mission days and fellow land grant holder, Eulalia Perez de Guillen Marine initially taught the younger woman the arts of cooking and embroidering. The two remained very close. In subsequent years, Eulalia provided Victoria with sanctuary during times of loss and depression. Similarly, Victoria later was to lavish her affections — and jewelry— on a Caucasian girl, Laura Evertson. The two met through the San Gabriel Mission, at roughly the same time that most of Victoria's own children died of smallpox.

Victoria (still Bartholomea) married at the age of 13, to another neophyte, Pablo Maria, 28 years her senior. The couple had four children. For some reason now lost, after mission secularization, Pablo was granted the large Rancho Santa Anita. Victoria came to secure the Huerta de Cuati, also called La Huerta de Peras, for its fecund pear orchard. With the exception of one even smaller parcel, the other 52 land grants in the county exceeded 1,000 acres. La Huerta de Cuati's miniscule proportions may fuel the argument that the property was given to Victoria, though a woman, out of respect.

Victoria probably met Hugo Reid at Eulalia's home. They initially may have been attracted physically and by mutual interests in the sociology of mission life. Victoria possessed lavish raven hair and a royal demeanor, either because of a tall, slender frame or maybe just because she carried herself erectly, with dignity. (Most Gabrielinas were referred to as "squat.") Hugo, too, is portrayed as tall, handsome and educated.

Upon Pablo's death during the mid- to late-1830s, Hugo left a teaching job in Mexico to woo the attractive, landed widow. They soon wed. Visitors commented on a happy, well-managed home. Hugo's friend, William Heath Davis, wrote: "A Castillian lady of standing could not have bestowed on us any greater attention or graciousness..." The couple cooked together. Commented Davis, "both Reid and his wife are epicures who have everything to entertain sumptuously."

Hugo held public office and was elected a delegate to the first California Constitutional Convention, where he proved a strong advocate of Native rights. But perhaps the idealism that served him so well from a human relations perspective set him back as a frontier capitalist. The Reids invariably depleted their (probably, her) finances. Hugo once tried to recoup them through a trading expedition; unfortunately, the customs duties he paid exceeded the worth of his cargo.

Financial duress forced the Reids to unload their property. During Hugo's final illness in 1852, Victoria sold the La Huerta de Cuati to B.D. Wilson. She later lost some smaller lots at the hands of the U.S. Land Commission, which revoked many Mexican grants.

Like her four children and first husband, Victoria Reid, nee Bartholomea, died of smallpox. She was 60 years old. Victoria was buried on the grounds of the San Gabriel Mission on Christmas eve, 1868. Her legacy survives, albeit fairly removed from reality. A long-departed daughter, Maria Ygnancia, was said to have been the model for Helen Hunt Jackson's *Ramona*. And Victoria herself is the central figure in a fictional work, *The Listening One* (1962).

Native populations are said to have bolstered the success of the ranchos, but they made contributions across economic sectors since the earliest days. Most were engaged in the mission system. San Gabriel nevertheless viewed the pueblo as a serious competitor for their labor: Los Angeles enticed the Gabrielino, they believed, deflecting them from more important work. (The pobladores and the fathers also clashed over water resources which, as mentioned earlier, were being channeled via zanjas.) Observing the rivalry from Mission San Buenaventura in 1795, Franciscan Father Vicente de Santa Maria wrote:

> The whole pagandom between this Mission and that of San Gabriel, along the beach, along the camino real, and along the border of the north, is fond of the Pueblo of Los Angeles and the rancho of Mariano Verdugo, of the rancho de Reyes, and of the [Rancho La] Zanja. Here we see nothing but pagans passing, clad in shoes, with sombreros and blankets, and serving as muleteers to the settlers and rancheros, so that if it were not for the gentiles, there would be neither Mission nor rancho. Finally these pagan Indians care neither for the Mission nor for the missionaries.

Indeed, the relaxed frontier/family orientation of the pueblo may have been a draw. The San Gabriel

Symbols of the rancho era, historic adobes often are associated with wealth. In their heyday, they were for the most part functional, not uniformly palatial, family dwellings. (Many of their owners, however, also kept townhomes near the plaza.) Located on Western Avenue near West 36th, this house probably belonged to Vicente Sanchez, of the Rancho Cienega o Paso de la Tijera, an 1843 Mexican land grant. Eva Scott Fenyes painted the property 74 years later. *Courtesy The Southwest Museum, Los Angeles, photo N.FEN.121.*

Mission suffered repeated revolts. One of the first, in 1773, stemmed from numerous rapes of Tongva by Spanish soldiers stationed at the mission. Such violations against Native women recurred, contributing to the syphilis epidemics that killed thousands. While secularization freed some Tongva for jobs at the ranchos or in the pueblo, their numbers had dwindled over the years. Nevertheless, Native Americans from the County and other outlying areas were migrating to Los Angeles — often, seasonally — to fill gaps in the workforce. Attitudes toward them probably differed from those which had guided earlier relationships between cohabitants of the L.A. basin.

Extending the Definition

The situation was to change in mid-century, by a series of monumental, inter-related events. Two stand out: the Gold Rush in 1849 and Statehood, the following year. The Northern-based Gold Rush distinguished California as more than just another endless outpost; it accelerated settlement statewide and spawned a variety of supporting, regionally-centered indus-tries. (In Los Angeles, cattle reigned.) American prospectors of all types were inspired by the momentum, and came with legal/economic assumptions than what had prevailed under Spanish-Mexican rule. (Chapter III for details.)

Furthermore, the fledgling United States sought to gain better control over a huge area that already had grown on its own; bad roads and poor communications permitted only delayed, generally muted responses to mandates from earlier governments. The legacy remains: 150 years later, the rest of the nation tends to view California as intransigent, a state that will have its own way (whatever it is), regardless. Demographics and popular will ultimately prevailed over circumscribed government mandate.

As for Southern California, efforts to impose a monochromatic order failed for two reasons. First, there was little homogeneity among Americans, even during the mid-19th century. Second, the Native populations and pobladores bestowed a heritage, unin-tended and whisperingly subtle. The sophisticated land use practiced by Tongva and Chumash set the pattern for later settlers, as immigrants availed their well-honed skills to Los Angeles' diverse natural resources: Japanese newcomers could advance their horticultural talents; maritime Portuguese found the harbor area a welcoming home; and, multiethnic Jewish merchants again felt comfortable, as they had in Europe, at com-mercial and cultural crossroads.

One other point needs to be emphasized. Immigrants often flock to areas where geographic/

climatic conditions are familiar or where their kin have established community. The mixed and variegated backgrounds of the early settlers — though at times suppressed — encouraged the multicultural melange that today is so much a part of Los Angeles.

Statehood and its incumbent changes brought pain, along with growth, to the city. Perceptual differences soon surfaced between the Spaniards of legend and real Californios. Before Statehood (and later, as part of early-20th-century boosterism) Americans glorified the exotic, yet urbane "Spanish dons." Indeed, there were few pure-blooded Spaniards and just a handful of Euroamericans prior to 1850. Anglos who came here were greeted: conversion to Catholicism allowed Euroamerican men to become citizens, marry Californio women and inherit their land. These new residents also accepted titles of status, a process which transformed Benjamin D. to "Don Benito" Wilson.

The notions of property changed quickly after Statehood, undermining the Californios' rights and position. Anglo-American squatters pressed for legislation to create a commission challenging Mexican land grant claims. Named after its sponsor, the Gwin Bill also left the burden of proof on existing property holders. Californios soon were enmeshed in lawsuits, set within an system foreign to them. (In all fairness, though, some of the land grant boundaries had been very informally determined, with such transitory objects as animals' silhouettes or trees dividing properties.) Friction heightened; incidents of violence between the two factions erupted, too.

Census data from 1850 showed 61 percent of Mexican-American heads of families holding parcels worth more than $100; the figure dropped to 29 percent a decade later. A depressed cattle market during the 1860s — combined with several natural disasters and a different form of taxation— put an end to the Californio land grant tradition. Gender also figured into the equation. Abel Stearns and John Temple held distinct as two of the largest individual taxpayers locally; both had wed Californios. The early

Euroamerican male settlers often came to their acreage through marriage, an 1861 law passed by the California legislature skewed inheritance in their favor.

Other human rights literally were being bought on the auction block. Ostensibly to defray the costs of "holding" public inebriates, an 1850 ordinance permitted parties to "bid" on Native Americans who had been arrested for drunkenness. Nearby vineyard and ranch owners utilized the system heavily. They typically paid the city a requisite fine — and reimbursed the workers with brandy. This city-sanctioned measure did little more than to introduce forced labor based on alcohol dependency.

The local Native population dwindled, due to both assimilation and an exploitative environment. One Dr. Oscar Loew visited the San Gabriel Mission (still a functioning rancho) in 1875, and discovered only two

Pio Pico and his wife, Ignacia Alverado de Pico, flanked by two nieces. Pico's long life (1801-1894) in many ways told the story of 19th-century Californios. Of mixed European, African and Native ancestry, he served as governor several times, though his tenures were abbreviated by political change. Land holdings yielded Pico considerable wealth. His fortune tumbled during the great cattle bust of the 1860s. He rebuilt, but died impoverished. *Courtesy The Southwest Museum, Los Angeles, photo N.42519.*

Tongva speakers; Spanish had prevailed among the rest. By the end of the 18th century, other observers noted that within the city's boundaries, Tongva only resided in the Eagle Rock-Highland Park vicinity and on the Palos Verdes peninsula.

Although the economic and political bases were shifting, the feeling of old Los Angeles lingered. Bilingualism existed in most spheres of life at least through the 1850s. And according to 1860 census figures for the County, there were a total of seven

remains at the pueblo to this day, was dedicated in 1823. The first priest arrived during the 1830s. As the century progressed, French and Italian fathers soon began to replace those of Spanish background. The 20th century saw Irish clerics, as was typical throughout much of the United States.

Jewish immigrants arrived in Los Angeles at mid-century. During the waning days of the Californio era, the 1850 census shows eight men. Uniformly foreign-born, they had landed in the East and explored other outposts on the way to this frontier town. All but one of the eight pioneers were single, in their late teens or twenties; the married man, tailor Jacob Frankfort, had just turned 40. Frankfort excepting, groups of two or three shared quarters and lived next door to each other, near the pueblo.

Jews had been in the United States since the 1600s. The oldest surviving Jewish residence, the 1714 Gomez Mill House, is on the banks of the New York's Hudson River. But by California Statehood, American Jews of Spanish or Portuguese descent were comfortable, or at least acculturated, Easterners. In the same way that Californio scions took a long, long time (if ever) to discover New York, first-wave Jewish immigrants with names like Cardozo had easier options than to speculate on the wild frontier.

Indeed, six of the pioneer Jewish Angelenos were born in Germany, two in Poland. These demographics reflect, respectively, the second and third phases of Jewish immigration to America. (The first was the Spanish-Portuguese.) Western-Central European Jews came at around mid-century, while those from Poland, Russia and Eastern Europe generally were part of the "great wave," 1880-1920.

All added to Los Angeles' multicultural heritage. Jews cut across ethnic classifications. As a people, they

churches: four Roman Catholic, with a collective property value of $16,000; two Methodist (totaling $3,000); and one Congregational, $1,000. In addition to being the wealthiest, the Catholic parishes drew the largest number of congregants: about 2,450 people between them, or on the average of 600-plus each. The lone Congregational Church attracted 200 and the two Methodist institutions, 300 in total.

But Los Angeles hardly could claim to be the spiritual nucleus of the Western world, or even the Western United States. These seven churches together welcomed 2,950 souls, of a population hovering at 11,333. Basic calculations reveal that as many as 74 percent of the County's residents shunned regular or formal religious participation.

The city lagged in observance, too. Residents of the pueblo typically traveled nine miles to San Gabriel Mission for religious ritual. Though hardly optimal, this arrangement sufficed almost 30 years, until 1810. Agitated by ongoing disputes over water and the Tongva labor force, the settlers finally broke away when duties at the mission prevented the two resident priests from coming to Los Angeles to administer last rites; they soon petitioned the Father President of the Alta California Missions for permission to construct their own church. La Placita (535 N. Main Street), which

had no homeland until the creation of the State of Israel in 1948, and the speed with which they flowed into the mainstream typically depended on where they had been immediately before. Periods of liberalization in Europe and elsewhere often hastened assimilation, for Jews might briefly acquire the legal means to advance economically and socially. Then, just as easily, outbreaks of virulent anti-Semitism, including pogroms, enforced Jewish isolation. Even after their arrival in the United States, a memory stretching 2,000 years would not let most forget their collective minority status: Jews were historically (or racially) related but ethnically diverse — with their own religion.

They also had been forbidden to own land at various points throughout history; in fact, during oppressive regimes, their connection to a given municipality or country might be abruptly — and altogether — severed. All factors considered, they could best adapt to new surroundings by relying on their own abilities. The first Jewish Angelenos therefore were not the squatters who coveted Californio parcels. (Although some later became major real estate developers, they did not amass land as a personal possession; rather, it was generally viewed as a resource to be tapped.) As they came in increasing numbers, the Jewish pioneers initially established themselves as merchants and skilled tradespeople.

And they arrived in Los Angeles at an opportune time. Quickly becoming bilingual or trilingual, they conducted trade and enjoyed communal relations with both the Californios and emerging Anglos. Their general lack of familiarity with or interest in land titles helped them to escape the intense friction that embroiled the other two groups.

Several of the original Jewish settlers ascended to public offices.

Morris Goodman was elected to the first City Council in 1850, and Arnold Jacobi secured a similar post three years after. A slightly later L.A. arrival, French-born Maurice Kremer moved around local government like an energized knight on the chessboard. He was County Treasurer, a City Councilmember, County Supervisor, City Clerk and Board of Education commissioner.

By 1860 there were 200 Jews in the area, including French and Bavarian contingents. The immigrants often encouraged their relatives to join them here, and while ensuing business partnerships formed and dissolved rapidly in those days, Bells (or Mellus') Row, continued to be the hub of the growing Jewish community. The central structure, itself, was a two-story adobe at the southeast corner of Angeles and Aliso streets, across from the current Federal Building. Bell's Row (a mixed-used rowhouse, really) might be called one of our earliest mini-malls: individual doors, at both street levels, beckoned customers to small shops carrying dry goods, clothes, groceries, general merchandise. Single, young men often saved their limited financial resources by sleeping in back rooms.

A growing population also brought more of a family orientation to the community, and Jewish life on the frontier initially survived with the assistance of committed volunteers and lay leaders. As anyone who has ever visited historic burial sites knows, babies and very young children claim a shockingly high percentage of the graves. And Judaism, like most religions or cultures, has unique rituals for handling death and grief. The Hebrew Benevolent Society was founded during 1854, with the community's first cemetery located in Chavez Ravine. (From its inception until 1874, only three of the 28

Joseph Newmark (1799-1881), patriarch of the Los Angeles Jewish community, helped to organize several Eastern U.S. synagogues before settling here in 1854. Trained as a ritual slaughter (shochet) of kosher meat, an occupation demanding considerable observance, he guided the spiritual life of Congregation B'nai B'rith until 1862, when a rabbi was hired. The synagogue became the Wilshire Boulevard Temple, which continues to thrive today. *Courtesy The Security Pacific Collection, Los Angeles Public Library.*

interments were for individuals 21 years of age or older, an indication of the youth mortality rate.)

The Jewish community had always gathered to worship, but its first spiritual center, Congregation B'nai B'rith, was officially founded in 1862, when the ordained Rabbi Abraham Edelman ascended to the pulpit. Members subsequently commenced fundraising for a permanent structure. Hailed by the *Los Angeles Star* as "the most superior church edifice in Southern California," it opened in 1873 on what is today Broadway, between Second and Third, downtown. The historic synagogue later became the Wilshire Boulevard Temple; its present site, a regal Byzantine-inspired building on Harvard Street, itself, has attained landmark status.

But Congregation B'nai B'rith also was a microcosm of American Jewry at the time. The Polish-born Edelman might have been hired to please his landsmen (Jews from the same hometown or in this case, country) who were numerically smaller but religiously more observant than their German brethren. Still, certain conditions provoked change. The Reform Movement began in Germany during the early 1800s, and together with the exigencies of rough, demanding frontier life, it held practical appeal for the community of coreligionists here. Rabbi Emanuel Schreiber, Edelman's successor, openly flew the Reform banner in 1885; it was the culmination of a 20-year evolution for the synagogue. During that same year, the Pittsburgh Platform (named for what turned out to be a historic conference in the Mid-Atlantic city) carved a permanent demarcation between radically reformed and traditional orthodox American Judaism. The Conservative movement, which through its own maturation, strikes an often complex middle-ground, was about 15 years away.

Today's Jews who grieve over the image of internal — and projected external — divisiveness might be comforted by the lessons of history. Congregation B'nai B'rith went through yet another schism: Rabbi Moses G. Solomon rebelled against Reform Judaism, and in 1899 left the synagogue to found People's Congregation Beth-El. This new shul attached itself to the fledgling Conservative movement, soon merging with a like-spirited synagogue, Kehal Israel. The result: Beth Israel, Los Angeles' oldest surviving Orthodox congregation.

To some extent, this incident represented a pattern of the community's diversification process. Disagreement about anything from deeply-held spiritual or philosophical views to operational details could cause synagogues, social/cultural clubs and Jewish political organizations to split. Often, both factions remained to build (or rebuild) their constituencies. And as Jews dispersed around the city, they opened neighborhood "chapters" of philanthropic and social/cultural societies. Jewish L.A. grew to be a broadly-accommodating home.

Though involvement in organizational and political life surely was a strong trait, caution borne out of a long history of persecution — plus religious strictures against intermarriage — have at times made the Jewish community appear insular. Dangerous stereotypes mask a complex dichotomy. Pioneering Jews, like pre-1850 Anglos, sought to become part of Los Angeles, yet they grappled more with issues of cultural/religious preservation versus assimilation. Unfortunately, emotional distance from one's background occasionally was an outcome of worldly success. Isaac Lankershim, an influential Angeleno whose name lives on in the San Fernando Valley, converted to Christianity. A different approach was employed by John Jones. Originally from England, the wealthy wholesale grocer intermarried, but both he and his Christian wife, the former Doria Deighton, remained active in Jewish communal affairs. Overall, Jewish families married within their religious faith, while merging into Angeleno culture — given the acceptable boundaries of the time.

A government surveyor sketched Los Angeles in 1853, a few years after California entered the union. The city had not grown much since its founding over 70 decades earlier. *Courtesy The Southwest Museum, Los Angeles, photo N.30579.*

The hurdles could be difficult. As was seen repeatedly, groups just beginning to gain power felt the need to keep newer arrivals from ascending. Spontaneous arousal of xenophobic instincts led to some ugly incidents in Los Angeles history, but economic actions were more regular and, sometimes, officially sanctioned. Boycotts and special excise taxes, for example, struck at the precise trades that engaged certain minority groups.

Economically-driven, anti-immigrant legislation might come from any level of government, often representing a perceived regional, state, or local threats to the status quo. In 1855, for example, Speaker of the California State Assembly William D. Stow tried to pass blue laws for Santa Cruz and Santa Clara Counties that sought to close businesses on Sunday. (Jewish merchants thus would be forced to work on their Sabbath, if they wished to remain viable.) Although such restrictions did not always carry anti-Semitic overtones, in Stow's case his motivation was clear. The *Sacramento Union*, reported that the Speaker also advocated a special tax on Jews "as would act as a prohibition to their residence among us." On a less formal, local basis, Prudent Beaudry, the largest merchandiser south of San Francisco and future mayor, proclaimed during the mid-1860s that he would drive every Los Angeles Jew out of business if only he could.

Such ill-will often was rebuffed because Jews — and subsequent immigrant groups — were too firmly rooted and proved too valuable to L.A.'s economy (see chapter 4). Despite occasional barriers, the Jewish community flourished here, rising to 330 people — or 5.76 percent of L.A.'s population — according to the 1870 census. In New York, considered then as now to be the premiere American Jewish city, it stood at just a smidgen over five percent.

While drawn to the United States as a result of push-pull factors, Jews were not officially recruited here. The situation was different for various Asian ethnic groups. In cultivating, exploiting and/or otherwise taming its huge Western acreage, Washington often derived its immigration policy from business interests. And corporate California specifically scoped economic problems overseas and lured workers who wanted to escape those privations.

What a difference 20 years makes! Looking north toward the mountains is the older, more populated section of the city. The southern outskirts appear devoted to farming and orchards, as seen in the bottom center and lower right-hand corner of this postcard. Spring Street and Main Street were among Los Angeles' first thoroughfares to be named, in 1849. *Courtesy The Postcard Collection of Jeanne Taylor Baird.*

Largely viewed for their potential as cheap contract labor, many Asians nevertheless came here with entrepreneurial intent: they saw unmet gaps — for service providers (cooks, gardeners) and merchandisers — as opportunities, and sought to fill them. Others did work on the railroads or in the mines, trading old privations for uniquely American ones. They paid with sweat equity, giving "their all" until harsh conditions expended most of it. When they protested, the robber barons responded by replacing them with other ethnic groups of laborers. (These newcomers might be Asian, too.)"Unassimilable" often was the word used to dismiss entire populations who proved less compliant — and complacent — than anticipated.

It is important to remember, too, that Los Angeles was not the first destination for most trans-Pacific immigrants. Many sojourned in Northern California and, during a slightly later period, Hawaii. Angel Island served as a less-than-hospitable port of entry from 1910-1940. The West Coast equivalent of Ellis Island — with an even dreamier appellation but just as vile a reputation — its location ensured that Asian immigrants would be required to pass through San Francisco on their way to other California locales.

The Chinese were the first to settle in Los Angeles. Two immigrants, both house servants, appeared on the 1850 census, but soon left. Ten years later, Los Angeles could claim only 14 Chinese. An herbalist established his shop here in 1861, laying the groundwork for a culturally-centered commercial quarter.

Alexander Harmer was a Santa Barbara-based artist who visited Chinatown, returned to his studio, and painted this picture during 1886. The small poster on the building in the lower right-hand corner recalls an ugly moment in L.A. history. The Los Angeles Trades and Labor Council picked May Day — May 1, 1886 — a holiday celebrating workers — to call for a boycott of Chinese labor and businesses. *Courtesy of The Irvine Museum, Irvine, California.*

The Burlingame Treaty (1868), a national act of diplomacy supported by California interests, altered the equation. By awarding "most favored nation" status to China, it opened both doors across the expansive Pacific. Chinese immigration to the Golden State peaked during 1873, with 23,000 individuals arriving that year alone. Restrictive laws soon would counter the early population increases. The highest portion of Chinese immigrants in Los Angeles, vis-a-vis the general population (5.4 percent, or 605 individuals), occurred at around the time of the 1880 census. As for sheer numbers, the 2,111 Chinese-Americans living in L.A. in 1900 was unmatched until 1930.

Early demographics can be explained by "trickle down" immigration from Northern to Southern California. San Francisco was the Golden State's jewel in the 1800s, and the Gold Rush had spurred vast regional growth. But urban existence, even then, could be taxing, particularly for immigrants when the economy cooled. Leaders in San Francisco's overcrowded Chinatown recommended that some of their citizens relocate to Los Angeles; a small delegation arrived during 1866.

Railroad construction also generally began in the North, with Chinese immigrants contributing mightily to the efforts. As transportation connections moved southward, the workforce followed. About 1,000 of the 1,500 workers on the San Fernando Tunnel, which brought the Southern Pacific to Los Angeles, were Chinese. L.A. was transformed into a boomtown with the completion of the span in 1876. Immigrants from everywhere — the eastward-lying United States and overseas alike — flocked here, many aboard trains.

Today's Los Angeles is graced by an enormously cosmopolitan Chinese-American population. Large contingents descend from Hong Kong or Taiwanese families, while Vietnamese nationals of Chinese ancestry make their homes in historic Chinatown. And judging from the culinary diversity, many mainland provinces are represented, too. No matter how they initially arrived, however, the pioneer Chinese of the mid- and late-19th century traced their origins to Guangdong (or, Kwangtung) Province.

But provincial life needs to be set against a larger background: China's Qing Dynasty (1644-1912), had been responsible for phenomenal population and economic growth. The 1800s, however, saw a regime falling to corruption. Officials embezzled millions, as the infrastructure crumbled and made farming and other pursuits increasingly difficult. Treaties resulting from the Opium Wars further pinched China with harsh economic sanctions: payments in silver and the forced opening of ports. Lucrative Hong Kong was ceded to the British. Restrictions on tariffs destroyed China's import-export balance. Foreign goods — and opium — entered en masse.

To comprehend China's geography, it is helpful to think of a family tree. Under the nation itself, there are provinces and, beneath them, individual counties or areas. Guangdong (or Kwangtung) Province of the mid-nineteenth century tallied 680,000 citizens and had as its capital Canton, or Quangzhou. (Hong Kong was another major asset before being turned over to the British.) However, it was a Guangdong county called Taishan that yielded 60 percent of those who later would opt for the transoceanic adventure.

The Taishanese farmed whatever they could, but poor soil could not sustain them. Always resourceful, they engaged in commerce or day work, depending on their skills. Taishanese drive and versatility — the ability to challenge a perverse, diverse environment — later suited them for the many roles they would assume in California.

Beside a tough economy, relocation and resettlement policies instituted by the Qing dynasty purposely pitted two ethnic groups, the Hakka and the Punti, against each other. A civil war escalated from 1854 to 1868, leaving villages gutted and thousands wounded and homeless.

With the China Sea ports of Canton and Hong Kong in close proximity, the Taishanese had long been exposed to urban life and far-flung travel. Foreign capitalists used these cities as bases from which to lure a prodigious labor-force in need of a more fertile work climate. The most unscrupulous "pig traders" almost literally kidnapped workers with various alibis, placing them in pens during the long voyage across the Pacific. More generally, the immigrants paid their own way or had their fare advanced through labor contractors. In the latter case, wages subsequently would be deducted. This recruitment method was commonly employed by the railroads.

Although conditions in Guangdong Province pushed the Chinese to seek refuge in Los Angeles and other Western shores, most of these pioneers did not consider the United States a permanent residence. Burial practices included shipment of bones to the true homeland, China, where decedents often wished to return.

Like their compatriots, too, Chinese Angelenos were confronted by personal and systemic discrimination. The most hideous incident was the massacre of October 24, 1871. The bloody details are clear and often retold, but the actual cause remains clouded. According to the oldest, most popularized account, two Chinese men bitterly disputing their "rights" to a woman, engaged friends in a pitched battle. Scholars have set forth two other possible explanations: tong rivalry fueled by some police corruption; and, interracial reverberations stemming from a Chinese merchant's self-defense during a robbery attempt by a Caucasian.

Cause notwithstanding, the police chief at the time, Emil Harris, tried to quell what started as a neighborhood episode. (The Chinese community later recognized this Prussian-born Jewish immigrant for being, in today's parlance, a peace officer.) Violence peaked when a Euroamerican was mortally wounded. The massacre ensued and Angeleno mobs became involved. The ultimate price was 19 Chinese lives and a looted, singed community.

There also were formally organized efforts to uproot the Chinese from Los Angeles. Independent Labor Union No. 1, founded in 1885, soon became known as the Anti-Chinese Union. Collecting 1,271 signatures during a Fourth of July parade, the group petitioned the Los Angeles City Council to expel all Chinese residents. This initiative failed and the group technically dissolved; yet, perpetrators continued to pursue their goal under other guises, using different techniques.

Local incidents pale, however, with the long-term, systematic effects invoked by the Chinese Exclusion Act (1882). The Burlingame Treaty had facilitated immigration, and the Chinese were becoming a larger presence in California. The economy changed almost simultaneously. The Panic of 1873 shook the entire nation, while here in California, the initial railroad-building spree — which employed first the Irish, then the Chinese — ended, causing displacement. Various interests confronted each other during the economic pinch: workers who viewed the Chinese as competitors for jobs, different types of employers with either pro- or anti-immigrant interests, nativists clinging to their sometimes unexplainable distrust of the foreign-born.

The Chinese Exclusion Act abruptly halted the flow of Chinese workers for 10 years. (Its provisions were re-enacted in 1892, with changes under the Geary Act, before being made permanent a decade later.) Although merchants and educated classes were still welcomed, broad definitions effectively kept Chinese from entering the U.S. Resident aliens could not become citizens, but their American-born children were entitled naturalization. From 1902 until the 1920s, when more universal immigration restrictions were imposed, the Chinese needed to register and maintain papers. Failure to do so might lead to deportation.

Beside the demographic ramifications, exclusion had very painful personal effects on the Chinese living here. Certain families were separated forever. Those who sought reunification sometimes concocted fictionalized lives, using "paper sons" and friends or relatives with double identities. Even the excepted classes were put to severe scrutiny: the INS could interrogate both American residents and their foreign family members on hundreds of minute details; any discrepancy might invalidate one's application and, in the worst case, send the other back to China. And this dual existence brought such shame to Chinese Americans that the topic was literally excluded from their conversation until recently. As one contemporary who never got to know his brother wrote: "...if my father were alive today, these revelations would not be forthcoming because he would not wish our family tragedy to be the subject of public discourse."

Los Angeles' Chinese community nevertheless continued to grow, albeit slowly, because of inmigration. People from other parts of the U.S. gravitated to a small, poorly served, but hospitable Chinatown in a ever-promising city. The exclusion laws were repealed altogether during 1943. The 1960s brought more open immigration policies generally, and today Los Angeles claims a larger Chinese-American population than anywhere else in this country, save New York.

L.A.'s African-American community similarly remained small until the 20th century, but its foundation had been built earlier. One of the pillars was Biddy Mason. Born in Georgia, Mason had moved as a slave with her three children to Utah, then San Bernardino County. A court case ensued when her master attempted to take the family out of state. Because they had resided in California for three years, the judge ruled that Mason and her children were no longer property — nor fugitive slaves. The family moved to L.A in 1856, their freedom secured. A single mother, Mason initial-

ly earned $2.50 per day as a confinement nurse and midwife. She saved her money, gaining distinction within 10 years as the first African-American in Los Angeles to own property. A decade later, she decided to work on independent terms: Mason parlayed her midwifery skills into a self-employment option.

Personal accomplishments notwithstanding, Mason is best known for her philanthropy. She founded a child care service and orphanage, and those in-need knew that they could obtain personal assistance at her 331 South Spring Street residence. "Grandma Mason," as she became known by her many friends and beneficiaries, died in 1891, at 73, but not before bequeathing a permanent legacy: her home was site of the initial meeting of L.A.'s first black church. The African Methodist Episcopal (AME) exemplifies a local trend: a once-small assemblage — that served a once-small population— and subsequently accepted the role of community-builder, preparing growing numbers of constituents for broader civic involvement. Out of its membership, for example, came the Los Angeles Forum, an organization directed toward political discussion and debate. The First AME Church today remains a powerful voice in African-American L.A., and one that is willing to engage other ethnic, racial and religious groups in dialogue. But at the turn of the century, the term "community relations" held an internal focus, for all Angelenos.

The 2,435-foot "Great Wall of Los Angeles" beautifies the Tujunga wash, a San Fernando Valley flood control channel, with scenes of California history. A collaborative project involving artists, historians and 300 youth, the gigantic mural was painted during the summers of 1976-1983. This segment is titled "1868 Sojourners." African-Americans in the Gold Rush, Asian immigrant railroad workers, Sojourner Truth, and Joaquin Murrieta all appear here. *Mural sponsorship and copyright by The Social and Public Art Resource Center (SPARC), Venice.*

(Opposite page) This panel of the "Chicano Time Trip" by the Eastlos Streetscapers, focuses on el hacendado, the wealthy Mexican landowner. Los Angeles' pioneers probably moved here with dreams of attaining similar status. The scenes surrounding the central figure allude to his economic evolution, and Mexican history. While the remote pueblo did not relate to Mexican events as intensely, relationships with the Native population were equally complex. *Mural sponsorship and 1977 copyright by The Social and Public Art Resource Center (SPARC), Venice.*

CHAP

TER 2

chapter

Introduction

No matter how compelling the societal factors, cultural identity is a weighty personal choice all along the preservation-assimilation continuum. Current history books don't talk much about Oscar Hudson, owner of one of Los Angeles' earliest African-American papers, *The New Age*. Hudson also was a linguist, real estate investor and lawyer, perhaps the first black man or woman to hold a state bar membership. During World War I, he mustered African-American Angelenos for military service. His efforts were rewarded by appointment as U.S. consul to Liberia — at about the same time that local followers of black nationalist Marcus Garvey pondered massive emigration to that country.

Although decisions of cultural preservation and assimilation raise important questions for the individual, heritage only begins here: it is longitudinal, conveyed from one generation to the next. The process demands balance. Too great an emphasis on ethnic struggle and hardship cause the second generation to rebel, forsaking their past for a more upbeat "American way"— if available to them. Yet, festivity without historic substance reduces culture to a few days of ritual gorging, with the chopped liver, haggis and menudo tossed out because they are no longer courante.

When tabulating census figures from early in this century, I was surprised to discover that Los Angeles once boasted large German, Irish, Italian and Swedish communities. (I challenge readers to find a comprehensive article about any of them!) Popular history books have very tight deadlines, not much time for footwork. Yet, these missing

elements of Angeleno cultural drove me to the streets. The results of my initial treasure hunt were fragmentary. En route to a meeting in the Mid-Wilshire towers, I saw a sign directing visitors to the Goethe Institut/German Cultural Center. Inquiries to friends made me aware of a local Italian Hall in San Pedro.

They say that the so-called Generation X is truly — and almost naturally — multicultural. The rest of us mingle rather easily in the workplace and share public spaces, but our social lives largely remain apart. You cannot grasp a culture different from your own unless you actually enter another's home and, even better, party with his or her high school friends.

In a case of the personal-becomes-editorial, I chose to trace the evolution of L.A.'s Swedish community as a tribute to Rose-Marie Swid. Ms. Swid operates a family child care center that actively, lovingly engaged my son for the first three years of his life. Many in this country choose infant and toddler care as an occupation out of a love of children, certainly, but also out of default: an absence from the conventional workforce. They think that their own parental experiences — or perhaps elevation to "favorite mom on the block"— automatically qualifies them. Although a mother herself, Ms. Swid's pursuit rests on a stronger commitment: in her native Sweden, infant and toddler care requires education well beyond high school. Rose-Marie Swid opted for the intensive curriculum, including a six-month residential internship with a severely handicapped child. She continues her education here, meeting formally with other child care providers, reading, and

attending classes. It is the immigrant legacy of new approaches and attitudes — sometimes more refined than our own — that can enrich the United States, if we let it.

Swedish Americans can be divided into two groups. The first wave typically arrived before World War I. They either stayed in Midwestern farm country — Illinois, Minnesota, the Dakotas — or tarried there for awhile before moving on. The 1900 census showed that of all American immigrant groups, only the Danes and Norwegians surpassed the Swedes in agricultural occupations. The first generation purchased (or homesteaded) their own farms, while their children strayed. Los Angeles was a perfect beacon; positioned between an agricultural past and an industrial present, it offered choices. The second wave of Swedish immigrants, post-World War II, came directly to L.A. Better educated and traveled, they specifically sought the city and the coast.

If anything portrays the Northern European heritage for me, it is a small, overlooked corner of the Angelica Lutheran Church. A corridor leads visitors from the circa 1950s education wing, once home to the California Lutheran Bible College, to the 73-year-old sanctuary. Along this hall, close to a stairwell, I happen upon my landmark: a narrow stained-glass window, with simple diamond segments emitting soft light in shades of amber and muted ligonberry. A small shaker-style table, probably maple judging from its cheery burnishment, stands nearby. This piece of furniture epitomizes space economy: if opened, its two leaves might easily quadruple the surface, accommodating homework, bookkeeping, an informal meeting or culinary tasks.

More people are likely to remember the main sanctuary. Although average in size, the edifice is dramatized by the seemingly vast distance between its floors and the ceilings. A simple flower pattern, folk art, repeats itself midway up the walls and at strategic points it turns and curves. During services, however, all eyes peer toward the podium and the full-length, sapphire-stained glass window that glorifies it. The central figure, luminous in white, is an energetic young woman whose massive curly locks seem to tangle (or tango) with the wind — not the usual image of Mary. Might she be Saint Lucia, lending warmth to long, Swedish winter nights? In a later conversation, Assistant Pastor Sue Devol corrects this notion. The female figure indeed is the Virgin Mary, but Angelica's early members demanded that her halo be "removed" before the impressive stained glass window was installed.

Abundant personality, exemplified by many hand-crafted touches, speaks of a church literally built by its congregants. One member, G.S. Larson, was its architect and C.G. Hokanson left his imprint on its interior decor. But the congregation's history actually dates to February 12, 1888 when a small group gathered to charter the Svenska Evangelisk-Lutherska Angelika forsamlingen I Los Angeles, California. Two structures preceded the current Burlington Avenue edifice. The last, on Seventeenth and Hope, sold for $70,000 in 1924. The present building was erected a year later — and cost twice that amount.

Other reminders of pre-Depression L.A. linger, in different formats. Though well maintained, the palatial, single-family homes on nearby Alvarado Terrace generally have been subdivided; one shelters the homeless, according to Reverend Carlos Paiva, senior pastor of Angelica Lutheran. The Peruvian-born spiritual leader says that his Pico-Union neighborhood is the second poorest in Los Angeles. The average family of five earns about $9,000 annually, he adds. Local residents are approximately 85 percent Latino, 5 percent African-American, 10 percent Korean-American.

Paiva and Devol are the first non-Swedes (and Devol, the first woman) to guide the church. Preservation of the cultural heritage has been important to them. When the 1987 earthquake caused $275,000 in damage, repairs were made. But the old plaster, embellished at points with flowers and stars, is cracking. A preservationist might need to be called from Sweden. Cost: $75,000. The congregation cannot easily under-write such projects, though standard operating funds

have been secured in very contemporary ways. A Korean church rents space in what previously was the Bible College, and filming of the television show, "Nothing Sacred," netted about $51,000 during 1997.

While the structure would be recognizable to a founder, Angelica's composition has changed. Paiva estimates almost 425 members: 375-400 Latino and about 25 Caucasian. As the minister greets congregants engaged in weekday activities — seniors gathering informally to chat and play games, women attending Bible studies — he emphasizes their diversity. "Nicaraguan, Guatemalan, Salvadorean, Finnish," he says as looks back at me, with an arm simultaneously scanning the recreation room. Angelica is now a mission church, representing Protestant outreach to a large population historically imbued with a mixture of indigenous and Catholic religious traditions. As any spiritual leader, Paiva is proud of those who pursue the faith devoutly. Two of his young congregants have entered California Lutheran University, an educational institution also known for its annual Scandinavian festival.

But among the Caucasian members of Angelica, Swedes are a minority. Julotta — literally, Yule morning — is an important Christmas ritual that commenced at 5 a.m. in the old days. (Mercifully, starting time has been moved up two hours.) Services drew as many as 300 a decade or so ago, according to Thyra Anderson, 92, a committed 58-year member who has

Los Angeles

WHEN I came up town on the bus
The porter called "Loss Anjy-lus!"
But others—when I talked with
these—
Pronounced it thus: "Loss Anjy-lese!"
A few days since a bright young miss
Surprised me with "Las Anjy-lis!"
But, 'mongst the cultured, one soon sees
The real thing is "Lows Ankylese!"

F. W. W.

Probably due to the incredible range of accents — both domestic and foreign — pronunciation of "Los Angeles" was a topic for discussion. Staff at the history department of the L.A. Public Library have cited nine formal sources on the subject. *Courtesy The Postcard Collection of Jeanne Taylor Baird.*

baked her share of Swedish coffee cakes for the event. "Now we're lucky to get 75," she laments. Nor are the services rendered in the mother tongue. "All of our ministers have gone." Indeed, things cannot be the same as they were when Angelica claimed 3,000 mostly Swedish members. Yet, the language and customs have not been totally lost. Second and third generation Swedish-Americans, disbursed throughout Los Angeles, return to the church to sing holiday songs and contribute Julotta spirit.

Who had insight into the historical and communal expanse between Angelica's founders and their 1990s descendants? I was referred several times to a woman

now living in Las Vegas. Could I — or should I — assume there were no closer connections to the past? Reverend Paiva had given me a copy of the *California Veckoblad*, the newspaper of the Southland's Swedish community since 1910. The name Jane Hendricks appeared repeatedly. Hendricks is the publisher, a position she inherited in 1980 from her father who had purchased the journal 22 years earlier. She also serves as president of the Swedish American National League and the Swedish American Woman's Club of Los Angeles, founded here in 1913 and 1919, respectively. For someone of just 51 years, Jane Hendricks has amassed a lot of responsibility for the community's history.

When asked whether the new multiculturalism has inspired the children, grandchildren and great-grand-

children of immigrants, Hendricks affirms. "During the late 1960s, readers thought the paper should be in English. That changed." (Some parts are in English, others in Swedish.) "People who know that they had Scandinavian blood way back are reconnecting (with cultural organizations)," she noted a few minutes later. "They're even enrolling in language classes at UCLA and Cal Lutheran."

The *California Veckoblad* lists 19 Southern California lodges of the VASA order, a fraternal organization. Pacific Southwest District No. 15 owns a park in Agoura which is leased out during the year, except for three Swedish festivals. There also are nine other organizations engaging the community. Each appoints three representatives to the Swedish American Central Association of Southern California, a coordinating council that meets monthly at Angelica Lutheran.

The relationship between human need and enduring cultural commitment is interesting. One organization, the Swenska Hollywood Klubben, started during the pre-war years as a group of young Swedish immigrants who wanted to gain a sense of belonging: "a single's club, more or less" summarizes Hendricks. The older, married membership now speaks English, but the organization still provides its contact information in Swedish.

Hendricks believes that despite an aging population, most of these groups "are holding their own." Immigrant communities of the early 20th century remained insular — until they assimilated. The Swedes were no exception; they didn't even interact much with other Scandinavians. Yet, in these days of inclusivity, the publisher jokes, it would be unfair to keep a Norwegian spouse from joining a Swedish cultural society. Beside multicultural kin, the organizations to some extent are being maintained by new generations reconnecting with a centuries-old heritage. Still, Hendricks admits that the only group to witness real growth has been the Swedish Women's Educational Association. SWEA attracts the under-55 crowd; a large portion of its members are around 40.

The founder of this worldwide organization, is a near-Angeleno (actually, a resident of the South Bay),

Agneta Nilsson. Comparing her members to previous generations, she comments: "Few of them wanted to speak Swedish again. It is very important to us that our children speak Swedish and have Swedish culture." As a result, these "affluent, highly educated" women raise money for: Scandanavian language and literature departments at universities; scholarships; and, Swedish churches, retirement homes and social services. The organization counts 7,000 members in 56 chapters throughout the world. Asian groups are flourishing, according to Nilsson. Branches recently have started in Chile and Buenos Aires, and Mexico is the next country targeted. SWEA is making inroads into Eastern Europe, too — as Nilsson says, "anywhere that Swedes live."

In addition to "networking," a concept popularized during the 1980s, L.A.'s Swedish-American community is experimenting with two distinctly 1990s forms of organization: "partnership" and "collaboration." Sensing renewed cultural interest, the Swedish American Historical Association of California (SAHAC), decided to investigate the possibility of developing a heritage center. The organizing committee discovered that Norwegian Angelenos were doing the same thing — at a perfect location. SAHAC member Wayne Pierson soon found himself involved in a Scandanavian-American collaborative.

Nansen Field covers eight acres of prime property in the Palos Verdes Peninsula. Named for a Norwegian native son, the Nobel Prize-winning explorer and zoologist Fridtjof Nansen (1861-1930,) the land was once owned by the Government of Norway. The Norwegians tired of paying taxes and ceded the property to a nonprofit group. Complications arising from the tax code yielded a $280,000 debt. The plan became to clear the title and use the property for heritage preservation. About two years ago, said Pierson, an organization formed under the name Scandinavian Center At Nansenfield.

"Nansen" and "field" were combined so that the resulting acronym might embrace all of the Northern nationality groups. According to Pierson, SCAN will celebrate Danish, Finnish, Icelandic, Norwegian and Swedish cultures, with each visible in the larger environ-ment. A Norwegian stave church, distinguished in its design and wooden structure, shall be used for a wedding chapel and to host small events. Special places may be highlighted or otherwise demarcated by a Swedish long fence. This decorative border features vertical poles rendered into a herringbone pattern by cross-bars ascending — with uniform space between them — at a 30-degree angle. In addition to these individual ethnic contributions, SCAN will include common display and meeting areas, and a memory garden, part way up a canyon bluff. Could the Swedes have proceeded independently on a heritage center? Certainly VASA Park could provide an adequate, though less scenic, venue. The strongest devotees to cultural preservation are older, says Pierson, and the Scandinavian communities can do far more — and elicit broader interest — collectively than alone. Pierson also admits that Nansen's Field is a valued site because of its L.A. location.

Many others attest to the draw of Los Angeles. Swedish-Americans in California today number 570,000, according to Andreas Ekman, the Consul General here. Minnesota, for so long the beacon, contains about 525,000. Ekman arrived in L.A. just three weeks earlier, changing the Consulate from an "honorary" status — with unpaid staff— to a "career" operation. Like so many other organizations, this diplomatic office had been downsized in 1994. Ekman confesses that the decision was "widely critized," but understandable. The Consulate's purpose appears much clearer today. "It is right to reopen," he asserts.

(Left) Boris Deutsch's "Cultural Contributions of North, South, and Central America" begins by focusing on Native populations and comes to include the European and Asian immigrants who subsequently settled in the western hemisphere. In fact, Deutsch's own profile pops up occasionally among those of his subjects. The Terminal Annex Post Office downtown, which contains Deutsch's masterpiece, currently is undergoing restoration. *Courtesy, The National Archives and Records Administration, Washington, D.C.*

While Los Angeles spawned various ethnic and religious communities, late 19th- and early 20th-century primacy generally has been ceded to the "Midwesterners," an ostensibly homogeneous group of hyper-Americans hailing from the central part of the United States. The simplification is troubling. Given that improved railroad transportation and increased booster-ism inspired cross-country migration beginning in the late 1870s, the 1880 census may provide useful insights.

Los Angeles County totaled 33,381 residents at the time: 14,798 (44 percent) were born in California, 11,313 (34 percent) throughout the United States, and 7,270 (22 percent) in other nations. As noted elsewhere, it is reasonable to assume that a good number of the natives boasted Hispanic — or mixed — backgrounds. The Mexican-American population within the city,

itself, has been cited as 19 percent. Although the numbers clearly revealed declining representation since 1850, they remained significant. And of the 7,270 foreign-born, 1,721 (five percent of County residents in 1880) came from Mexico and another 1,144 (three percent) from China. Germany had been the birth place of 1,075 (also three percent.)

Even the Midwesterners were deceptively complex. The 1880 census lists the native lands and U.S. territories that contributed most heavily to each state's population, subsequently showing how these demographics manifested themselves in the counties. Only 6,495 (57 percent) of the 11,313 Los Angeles residents born within the U.S., but outside of California, came from the nine Northeastern and Midwestern states cited by census statisticians.

The elk of the Great North Woods meets Southern California citrus. Even as late as 1909, when this postcard was sent to Neosho, Missouri, the myth of pumpkin-sized oranges pervaded. Courtesy The Postcard Collection of Jeanne Taylor Baird.

One might speculate on other regional origins. For example, during the Civil War — and out of fear that Confederate sympathizers might rally political support here — the federal government went so far as to build a fort in Wilmington, a half continent away from the military action. Might a head-count through unaggregated, handwritten census rolls locate a sizable delegation of Southern-born Angelenos? (Or were these politically-charged citizens vocal far beyond their numbers?) More to the point, however, when the nine "contributing" states are divided by region, we discover that 43 percent of the L.A. County's inmigrants came from the East and 57 percent, from the Midwest. The Midwestern overstatement deflates further when the 4,818 newcomers of unspecified U.S. origins enter the equation. These heartlanders constitute only 33 percent of the Americans born outside of California — and just 11 percent of all L.A. County residents in 1880.

There is one comical footnote to our statistical dabbling. The L.A.-New York rivalry — a media creation which, considering the incomparability of the cities, probably owes more to population growth than to anything else — apparently has a historic basis: according to the 1880 census, the largest contingent born outside of California, but within this nation, hailed from the Empire State. A documented 1,413 people, four percent of County residents or a whopping 12 percent of those who inmigrated here, boasted New York credentials.

Still the legendary Midwestern association cannot be discounted. At a time when New Yorkers and other Easterners were undergoing a mighty urbanization, the large (if not majority) group from the heartland shared with Angelenos agricultural interests. And it was this green, bounteous image that real estate promoters used in their Midwestern recruitment campaigns.

There also is a tendency to equate certain civilized values with the new population influx. In contrast to the 1860 census figures quoted earlier, as many as 40 percent of L.A. residents now were church affiliated. A centennial edition of the Los Angeles Times (1888)

proclaimed the former gunslingers' paradise "developing into a highly moral town." Education became more important. Throop College (now Cal Tech), Immaculate Heart, Occidental, Whittier, the University of Southern California and the two-year State Normal School (with later connections to UCLA) all emerged during the 1880s.

The new, mixed-ethnic, primarily Protestant culture may have lent some inspiration, but it should not be given credit for singlehandedly transforming the city. L.A.'s first college, St. Vincent's (which merged into what later became Loyola Marymount,) was a Catholic school dating to the 1860s. Obviously, a growing metropolis now could fill more and different types of classrooms. USC was conceived by the regional Methodist Episcopal Conference, but it drew sustenance from representatives of diverse religious, philanthropic and professional spheres: Ozro W. Childs, a Protestant horticulturalist; John G. Downey, a Catholic businessman and former California governor; and, Isaias W. Hellman, a Jewish banker, not only donated the land for the campus, but also provided residential lots, the sale of which would be channeled into an endowment fund.

Under whatever name, a more organized society may have appealed to a town which was growing wildly and yearned for order. Each census showed a population doubling, tripling, quadrupling: from 11,183 (1880) to 50,395 (1890) to 102, 479 (1900) to 310,198 (1910). Indeed, L.A. was no longer a provincial murder-a-day town.

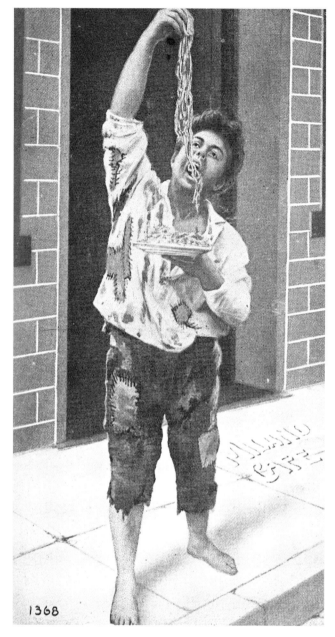

Most Angelenos preferred to quiet their past, though discrimination isolated — and thus, forcibly preserved — some cultures. (Even in the 1791 census, when those of truly variegated backgrounds highlighted the Hispanic elements of their lineage, there had been a desire to blend into what was seen as the emerging majority.) The chart on the following page shows the most prominent foreign stock of the early 20th century.

How many readers have heard of L.A.'s German, Canadian, Italian or Swedish heritage, or considered the discrimination that these groups faced when they first arrived?

The California Commission of Immigration and Housing published a community survey of Los Angeles during the late teens. A cooperative effort, the study had involved the state government, local elementary schools and libraries, public and non-profit social service agencies, police bureaus, churches. Its purpose was to understand living conditions of the foreign-born and, subsequently, to provide informed outreach. The letter of transmittal (a short introduction) to Governor William D. Stevens, states:

This report is valuable not as a piece of individual research, but as a splendid beginning toward united effort in the solution of community problems… Such frank discussion should be of service locally and in other cities, in producing greater and renewed support for those who are directly in the field carrying out the wishes of all members of the community.

The stated intent was progressive for the times. Yet, the survey — like census data from the same era — reveals inconsistencies of thought, as shown in the following passages:

In the second district, there are principally Mexicans and Italians. The Palo Verde neighborhood is entirely isolated by hills from the rest of the city. Here, after a summer of primitive freedom, the children's minds have to be reclaimed from the desert waste to at least a sluggish interest in education.

In the Ann Street district, situated among the tracks, there is poverty and the resulting disease to be expected among Mexicans and Italians…

Indeed, by contemporary standards sensitivity was a largely unknown concept. Mexicans and Italians were often linked via their neighborhoods and to some extent, physical appearance — despite differing cultures. Census officials also considered both as "white," a classification that many Latinos today would question.

FOREIGN STOCK IN THE CITY OF LOS ANGELES, 1910 and 1920*

	1910	1920
Total Population	310,198	576,673
Foreign Stock, Number	135,340	252,406
Foreign Stock, Percentage	44 %	44 %

Country	Germany	Germany	Country	Mexico	Canada
Number	28,591	38,522	Number	8,917	20,585
Percentage of Foreign Stock	21	15	Percentage of Foreign Stock	7	8

Country	England	Mexico	Country	Russia	Russia
Number	16,920	31,173	Number	7,478	20,209
Percentage of Foreign Stock	13	12	Percentage of Foreign Stock	6	8

Country	Canada	England	Country	Italy	Italy
Number	14,574	28,324	Number	6,461	15,415
Percentage of Foreign Stock	11	11	Percentage of Foreign Stock	5	6

Country	Ireland	Ireland	Country	Sweden	Sweden
Number	12,804	20,948	Number	6,150	10,462
Percentage of Foreign Stock	9	8	Percentage of Foreign Stock	5	4

* In the terminology of the 1920s, these figures pertain solely to "white foreign stock"; it is interesting to note, however, that Mexicans are included. The only Asians counted were immigrants from part of Turkey (the second part of the country was considered European) and a group simply referred to as "all other."

Leading Countries of Origin

Identity seems to have been closely aligned to politics, at least for Caucasians immigrants. The Leonis Adobe — where the San Fernando Valley meets Calabassas and, from there, the Conejo Valley — reflects the Basque presence. A separate nationality and language group hailing from the Pyrenees Mountain region of the Spanish-French border, these people frequently were shepherds who brought their occupational skills to the hills and outlying valleys of the West. Basques were counted as Spaniards when they came to California in the early 19th century; later, passports identified them as being French. (One subsequently wonders if the number of Koreans listed here during the first half of the 20th century was low because they were counted as Japanese, again due to political factors.)

In analyzing the white foreign stock, the 1920 census cites only two Asian birthplaces: "Turkey in Asia" and "All other." Similarly, a chart in the Commission study bears a footnote: "Turks include Syrians and Armenians." The Armenians, who had just suffered a genocide of as many as one million people under Turkish rule, would have been outraged at such an association. Furthermore, some of the Turks were Jews, a different population group altogether, who nevertheless migrated here at the same time — with the dissolution of the Ottoman Empire. So much for cultural sensitivity at the turn of the century!

as a vehicle for assimilation. Various denominations established missions in Los Angeles to reach out, as individually appropriate, to the disparate non-Caucasian and/or non-Protestant populations: Filipinos, Koreans, Mexicans, others.

On Sundays in turn-of-the century Chinatown, a busy street corner would find several missionaries joining together for a cooperative service of singing, prayer and preaching. One Reverend A. Michelson even attempted, during the desperate Depression, to convert members of the Boyle Heights' Jewish working class. His Hebrew Christian Synagogue

(Above) In addition to their hopes for a better future, immigrants came to Los Angeles with diverse skills — and occasionally, plant cuttings. This Italian family owned an olive farm. *Courtesy Shades of L.A. Archives, The Los Angeles Public Library.*

When confronted with obstacles, immigrant groups of the early 20th century sometimes created their own institutions. The German-American Savings Bank, "The Bank with the Efficient Service," stood at Spring and Fourth. *Courtesy The Postcard Collection of Jeanne Taylor Baird.*

Indeed, the Commission report was written on behalf of the immigrants, not for them. No matter how public-spirited, civic leaders equated ethnic/cultural identity with the need for social improvement; heritage simply was not an independent issue.

While Caucasians were lumped into super-categories based on geopolitical factors, the Commission report tried to maintain the distinctiveness of non-Christians. The most comprehensive ethnic breakdown in the study, a chart of arrests, enumerates 58 different population groups. Included are Jews and "Hindoos," ostensibly immigrants from the Indian subcontinent. (Jews, at least in part, accounted for the heavy influx of Russians on the 1910 and 1920 census rolls. So did approximately 7,000 Molokans, a break-off religious group which defied Russian Orthodox ritual and had strong pacifist inclinations.)

If the will to "become American"— to blend in — was a strong one, civic leaders frequently saw religion

flashed a neon sign, proclaiming in Yiddish and English, "Jesus the Messiah Is the Light of the World." With regard to Mexican-Americans, George Sanchez relates what was a more universal approach: Protestant parishioners contributed financially to conversion efforts, but the missions were quite a distance — phy-sically and emotionally — from their own churches.

If assimilation was the goal, it was fashioned to produce prospective employees and contractors, not peers. And this philosophy manifested itself outside of religion. While Californio (Mexican-American) and immigrant Jewish Angelenos figured prominently in Los Angeles' early municipal government, they and other ethnic groups were effectively disenfranchised by the late 19th century. It was only Edward Roybal's run for City Council in 1947 that re-opened political culture to a broader base.

The dawn of a new century seemed to bring a settling influence to Los Angeles. Small groups of immigrants arrived to build communities that endured prejudice and adverse public policy. Unless enraged by some particular injustice, they generally tried to be as inconspicuous as possible, fearing that too public a presence might evoke hostility. Subsequent events— the Great Depression and World War II— brought different cultural groups together, and empowered them individually. New Americans

38th annual

bazaar

June 29, 1986   program

St. Bridget's Catholic Chinese Center
510 Cottage Home Street, Los Angeles, California 90012

Christian missions traditionally have offered social services. An early goal was assimilation; today the emphasis is on increasing affiliation. *Courtesy Shades of L.A. Archives, The Los Angeles Public Library.*

enlarged the quiet ethnic enclaves, and by the 1980s, truly diverse Angelenos grew confident enough to openly celebrate their longstanding, if veiled, heritages.

Recruited for Work

The story of the Japanese in Los Angeles bursts with unique ironies and tragedies, but settlement patterns parallel those of other immigrant groups. Coincidentally, like the earliest Chinese, the first two

Japanese were young house servants. This pair of teenagers surfaced during the 1870 census and disappeared within the decade. (In all fairness, though, they had been employed by Judge E.J.C. Kewen of San Marino — not by definition an Angeleno.) No Japanese resided here as of 1880. The 1890s brought the first real "rush" of immigration, and about 150 were counted at the turn of the century.

Both commerce and labors of the field and sea subsequently engaged Japanese Angelenos. This duality of occupational interests hearkens to a land-short heritage. In Japan, oldest sons inherited their family farms, plots seldom amounted to more than two and one-half acres — too small for practical subdivision. Younger children were forced to find a livelihood in the cities, or elsewhere. But excessive internal taxation spawned the emigration fever, or *netsu*. Fearing a Western-style colonization that they perceived was destroying China, Japan's leaders sought to strengthen the country from within. The reinstated Meiji emperor enacted high levies for a three-pronged initiative of centralized government, industrialization and militarization. Tales of American-colonial wages — manifold their own taxed-stressed earnings — tantalized Japanese citizens. Approximately 380,000 migrated between 1885 and 1924.

Western settlement originally translated to two centers: the Hawaiian sugar plantations and the booming metropolis of San Francisco. Although virtually all of L.A.'s Japanese population came from Northern California, their presence on the island territory had ramifications for other groups. Many Korean and Filipino Angelenos originally had been lured to Hawaii by commercial growers seeking to replace Japanese farm laborers, who actively protested poor conditions and compensation. But worker solidarity was unlikely, at least between two of the groups: Japan ruled Korea against popular will, and the distrust and resentments extended to foreign shores.

The first tangible Japanese community in L.A. consisted of about 25 men, arrived from San Francisco in 1884. A handful established their own businesses on East First Street. This was the very beginning of what later became known as Little Tokyo. Although Japanese pioneers also opted for other downtown locations — and working class Angelenos of all types shared the turf — Sho Tokyo may be considered the oldest neighborhood continually identified with one ethnic group. But these settlers were community-builders in other ways. As early as 1897 and with few residents here, they formed the Japanese Association of Los Angeles, both to resolve internal problems and to act as a civil rights arbiter.

The turn of the century brought population growth. A mimeographed sheet, *Rafu Shimpo*, first appeared in 1903; it was a daily community newspaper by the following year. With the exception of a period during World War II, *Rafu Shimpo* has been published regularly since. An estimated 3,387 persons of Japanese birth resided in Los Angeles as 1905. The great San Francisco earthquake — combined with episodes of outright racial hostility — caused between 2,000 and 3,000 to move here, soon bringing the population total to 6,300. Unlike many other people of color, the Japanese also showed a willingness to disperse around Los Angeles, often to fulfill their agricultural and fishing interests. Tiny communities soon were reported in Hollywood, along Jefferson and Washington boulevards, on the coast from Santa Monica to San Pedro.

The Japanese may have been able to move beyond town because their reconstituted neighborhoods were small enough to escape much attention. Numbers were long important in community relations and, subsequently, public policy. As Japanese immigration climbed and the newcomers proved economically versatile (and vital,) resistance mounted. The method of curtailing their enterprise was a familiar one, previously waged against the Chinese: exclusion. Most of the Japanese immigrants had been laborers, and the federal government in 1908 prohibited the entry of this nationality and class into the United States. This became known as the "Gentleman's Agreement" because the emperor, usually protective of his citizens abroad, tacitly caved into U.S. pressure. California's Alien Land law (1913) prohibited Japanese nationals from acquiring land, either through purchase or lease. When Congress passed generally restrictive immigration laws in 1924, specific provisions for the Japanese were included. And a court case, brought by a Japanese-American, had confirmed a federal statute of 1790: non-Caucasians from overseas were to be denied naturalization.

The native-born second generation, known as *Nisei*, experienced other forms of discrimination despite their U.S. citizenship. Similar to Chinese-Americans, sizable numbers pursued college degrees, only to graduate and work in one of Little Tokyo's retail shops. Angeleno Togo Tanaka made 119 inquiries in his efforts to buy a home. In 114 instances, he was informed: "You cannot live here. Your money is not good enough. The deed has a racially restrictive covenant, and only members of the Caucasian race may reside here." (Such tactics were applied to many other groups: African and Jewish-Americans, to name a few. A common acronym of the time was NINA. Hardly a woman's name, it was a warning that "No Irish Need Apply.")

Just as the United States government regulated its workforce composition through immigration policies, Japan sought to protect the economic interests of its citizens — at home or abroad. Koreans were most effected by these practices. Excepting a few students who came to study here in the 1870s, Koreans were inclined by longstanding religious and cultural traditions to remain on their peninsular home. A severe drought (1901-1903), combined with displeasure about a corrupt and largely ineffective government, forced many to reconsider their position.

At the same time, Hawaiian labor recruiters successfully solicited Korean crews to counter what they saw as the unduly recalcitrant Japanese. The Koreans tended to be more educated and urbanized than other Asian field hands: fully one-third were white collar or professional. Brutalized by the unfamiliar conditions of colonial agricultural labor and, lacking the ability to communicate in English, they became particularly vulnerable to harsh physical treatment. Fear of losing their jobs and a distaste for an alliance with the Japanese workers caused them to seek their own alternatives to the oppression. A delegation returned home; its leaders tried to persuade their king to intervene either by establishing a consulate in Hawaii or limiting the activities of labor recruiters.

The effort proved futile. The Meiji dynasty gained a protectorate over Korea in 1905 and five years later, annexed the country. All U.S. restrictions on Japanese immigration subsequently applied to Koreans, and priority for the few available visas went to citizens of the ruling empire. Limited Korean entry became the norm when the immigration laws of 1924 (effective for more than 40 years) based quotas on the existing population figures. Ironically, too, as the early 20th century sociologist Bogardus pointed out, the same prejudice directed to the Japanese — and, indeed, other Asian groups — also afflicted Koreans; hardly any substantive distinctions between populations were made.

The recent immigrants to Hawaii were

Before moving to the United States in 1933, three generations enjoy a visit to grandmother's house, Sun Chun, Korea. *Courtesy Shades of L.A. Archives, The Los Angeles Public Library.*

These two women stand outside of the Korean National Association, 1734 Jefferson Blvd. Founded in the early 1900s, the organization developed chapters all over the west and, in lieu of a consulate, became a political voice for Koreans here. *Courtesy Shades of L.A. Archives, The Los Angeles Public Library.*

and vegetable stands, and the largest in size, an "Oriental foods" wholesaler, engaged 18 employees. Limited in their career ambitions by prejudice, Korean youth nevertheless craved education. Thirty Korean students were counted among Los Angeles City College, UCLA and USC in 1939.

The community's premiere institution, the Korean Presbyterian Church, was founded in 1905, when there were only 60 Koreans countywide. It subsequently established a permanent home at 1374 Jefferson Boulevard. Several doors away, the Korean Center was comparable to a YM/WCA, a multipurpose facility sponsoring a variety of age-specific clubs and varied social and recreational activities. This building also held distinction as headquarters of the Korean National Association (1910), a wellspring for the expatriate independence movement.

The old neighborhood — between Vermont and Western, and spanning from Adams to Slauson — is not far from the present Koreatown. The difference is one of identification. The few Korean Angelenos of yesteryear got lost in the multiethnic community of which they were a part. Today's residents define their district. But it was the fact that a vibrant neighborhood existed, regardless of its size, that drew others here. After the pioneering generation, there were the Korean War refugees of the 1950s. Much larger numbers arrived later, subsequent to the change in immigration laws (1965). Los Angeles circa 2000 holds the second largest Korean population, somewhere between 150,000 and 200,000 people, outside of Seoul.

The Filipinos who settled here during the earlier part of the century were recruited to fill labor shortages of American invention. Their 7,038-island homeland had been turned over to the United States following the Spanish-American War, creating a unique immigration status. Filipinos could legally escape the restrictions that befell most of the other Asian populations

stuck: unhappy about their current existence and now without an independent home, the more urbane and urbanized left for the mainland. After arriving in San Francisco, the small, emigre Korean population began to spread. Other destinations included Oakland, Dinuba, Reedley, Sacramento, Delano, Riverside and Los Angeles. By 1940, there were an estimated 650 in L.A., probably an understatement. Albeit small, L.A.'s population was the largest nationally and served as a political and cultural center for the Korean-American community. It exuded internal energy, too, with 73 small businesses. The largest in number (33) were fruit because they were under a U.S. "guardianship." Like Koreans, they were initially recruited for field work in Hawaii. Unlike Koreans, many had been accustomed to a tropical plantation economy. They were as much "pulled" to this country as "pushed" out of their own.

A polyglot people, Filipinos spoke a total of 87 dialects. Over three centuries of Spanish influence also had spread the language of the Iberian peninsula. (Many of the islanders embraced Catholicism, too.) With Americans present from 1893 through 1946, large numbers became trilingual, adding English to their linguistic repertoire. They welcomed new cultures more than other nationalities of the time, while managing to retain their own identity. And a substantial number greeted the personal opportunities possible through Western civilization.

A long history of trade and travel simplified the Hawaiian journey for Filipinos. (Their most well-known adventures had occurred during the early Spanish colonial era when the Manila Galleons, originating in the Phillipines but carrying riches from all over Asia, brought cargoes to the New World.) Single, young men especially accepted the challenges of overseas employment. Once exposed to outrageous conditions on the islands, they also willingly entered into multiethnic labor coalitions. Similarly, those who later came to Los Angeles (and agricultural plains throughout the West) made common cause with Mexican, as well as Japanese and other farmworkers.

From 1922 to 1929, a period that overlaps with the changing immigration laws, some 5,513 Filipinos — over 95 percent of them men — entered via the Port of Los Angeles. They included workers seeking an alternative to the labor-glutted fields of Hawaii and, to a lesser extent, students. Though they soon were to be found in various parts of the city,

the first arrivals often roomed and boarded downtown. One national described the inherent loneliness of being single and foreign:

In Los Angeles, the people of all nations drift almost every hour of the day up and down Main Street and thereabouts. It is generally conceded that these places are not wholesome places. There is a reason: the cheaper amusements in the city are found there. Pool halls, public dance halls, sideshows which are calculated to appeal to the feelings and imagination, and other "whoopee" attractions make Main Street a magnet to the homeless and friendless, among whom are the Filipinos…

In spite of whatever good qualities he may possess, he grows tired and lonesome and restless. He is young; he craves for freedom, sunshine, expression, and recreation. If he works in a kitchen, he is harassed by cooks and waitresses and excited by the din of pots and dishes. In his spare hours he seeks consequently the places and companionship that make him forget, even for a moment, that he has become a slave…

Restaurants engaged many Asian immigrants, but their styles and purposes varied. Although the population

First Street downtown, circa 1900, bustles with retail and service activity, as evident by the dentist's office and bookstore on the far left, and the street traffic. *Courtesy The Postcard Collection of Jeanne Taylor Baird.*

was minute at the time, 16 Japanese-operated establishments existed in 1896. They cooked to satisfy general tastes: chicken dinners and beef stew, 10 to 15 cents a meal, with apple pie and ice cream for dessert. (L.A.'s first sushi-ya opened only after the San Francisco earthquake; a sufficiently large clientele then could appreciate the authentic tastes and textures of raw fish rolls.) Somewhat differently, the Chinese became known for finding a middle ground between their own culinary delights and what would please American palates. Of the 55 businesses owned by Filipinos in 1938, 16 (29 percent) were restaurants and cafes. They served their diners the multiculturally-seasoned food of the homeland; virtually none of the customers were outsiders. These eateries nurtured the Filipino immigrant soul and provided an expatriate meeting place.

While L.A.'s Asian communities typically began with single men, such a demographic pattern obviously could not sustain them. Chinese and Japanese friends or family members abroad often facilitated "picture" marriages; after being assigned a match, the couple-to-be would exchange letters and photographs. Filipino Angelenos, particularly the early settlers, handled the situation differently. Of 200 men studied in 1952, almost exactly half (49.5 percent) had intermarried, 33 percent to Euroamerican women. Discounting survey

validity and reliability, this rate still is high. (A study of 1,200+ Mexican immigrants and Mexican Americans, for example, indicates that only 17 percent of the marriages were exogenous.) During the 1950s, however, when Filipino women emigrated in greater numbers, the trend toward intermarriage receded somewhat.

L.A.'s Mexican-American community was complex. On an individual basis, assimilation into or distance from mainstream culture depended on when a family arrived here, whether or not they had status to defend, and their sensitivity to what by most accounts was an increasingly inhospitable social/political environment. Physical appearance — light or dark skin color — and name (a factor for the scions of intermarried Californio women) mattered, too.

As mentioned earlier, the first chasm between Californios and Anglo settlers had occurred in the wake of Statehood. The ensuing power play created skewed government and legal systems. Three respected Californios had served as judges at various times from 1853-1873, but from 1887 to 1900, only three of 194 attorneys admitted to the California bar possessed Spanish surnames. Lack of representation may have bolstered the conviction rate: 30 percent of those found guilty of criminal offenses in L.A. courts during 1887 were Mexican-American.

There were issues of group solidarity. As with many people, the comfortably situated, long-time residents (in this case, Californios) often distanced themselves from fresher immigrants. The term *La Raza*, the race, was first used in the 1850s, addressing Mexican-Americans by ethnicity rather than class. It may not have been a common concept then, but by the end of the century, the phrase had worked its way into the pages of community newspapers espousing radically divergent political perspectives. Mexican-Americans now were isolated,

and depended on each other for everything from mutual aid to the loftier goal of cultural enrichment. Still, differences continued to exist. The founding during the 1880s of two local organizations, the Sociedad Progresista Mexicana and the Spanish-American Republican Club, exemplify the phenomenon of diversity.

Immigration to L.A. from the Southern border had steadied toward the end of the century. (In fact, increasingly hostile conditions throughout the Southwest even evoked a small repatriation movement.) Yet, the open Mexican border remained a safeguard against the laborforce vicissitudes caused by U.S. immigration policies; the growing legion of commercial growers and industrialists assumed that when other sources diminished, an abundant supply of hands from the South would appear.

This arrangement held appeal for Mexican laborers, too. They could cross the border to take advantage of seasonal harvest work, and return home with relative ease, more or less at their own choosing. Of the 35,886 aliens who entered the U.S. via El Paso in 1910, almost all indicated stays of under one year. American wages went far in the Mexican economy, and workers would not be forced to relocate their families.

Trains proved to be both the vehicle and economic motivation for some immigrants. The building of a Mexican national railroad system under the regime of Porfirio Diaz (1876-1910), radically increased mobility. With operations booming and the traditional supply of Chinese workers dwindling (thanks to exclusion), the railroad industry became a large employer of Mexican-Americans in Los Angeles and elsewhere.

Outlined by train tracks, the border also boasted a commercial economy of its own. The Mexican government had initiated free trade privilege along its Northern boundary in 1885. Without having to pay customs, merchants could sell imports at drastically reduced rates. The combination of location and transportation spurred the rapid growth of border towns on both sides of the divide. El Paso and its sister city, Juarez, together merged into a metropolis of about 24,000 in 1900. Ten years later, the population had more than doubled and by 1940, it rose to over

145,000. Lacking as tight a rail connection, Tijuana — the gateway to Southern California — counted only 242 souls in 1900 and approximately 16,500 within 40 years. (San Ysidro had not yet been developed.) Indeed, El Paso became the main port of entry from Mexico, accepting immigrants en route to a variety of destinations. Many Angelenos now in or approaching retirement age recall their sojourns through the Texas border city.

But if rail and other signals pointed North at the turn of the century, the Mexican revolution (1910) caused some immigrants to choose one-way streets rather than revolving doors. Diaz's 35-year reign rapidly pushed the country toward capital development, shifting the rural masses into urban and/or wage-earning existences. With the economy squeezing them, heads of households often sought supplemental income in the U.S. The stability of home and family life, however, dictated against more permanent moves.

The revolution changed attitudes. It created and destroyed national leaders in quick succession, particularly from 1910 to 1920. Although these heads of government typically did not propose radical reforms, the political volley caused speculation about many raw issues, including land distribution. In the meantime, Emilio Zapata and Pancho Villa led popular regional rebellions, and U.S. troops entered Mexico, elevating the chaos. Factionalization — both real and perceived — manifested itself in politically-motivated executions, street anarchy, the destruction of communities. All told, 1.5 million Mexicans left their birthplace from 1900-1930. Most chose to settle in the Southwestern U.S., and Los Angeles was a beneficiary.

With domestic calm no longer assured, movement across the divide became more of a family affair. The U.S. Immigration Act of 1917 furthered that motion. Extending its jurisdiction well beyond Mexico, the law sought to limit the influx of war-ravaged people generally. A fortified Southern border patrol soon administered head taxes, medical examinations, interrogations. Crossing the boundary wasn't hopscotch anymore. The term "public charge" had entered into Immigration Service's operational vocabulary, too. Foreign women, children, and aging relatives, ostensibly economic drains, were scrutinized. Yet, all of this heightened anxiety — combined with conditions in Mexico — deepened a commitment to permanent resettlement. If families were to endure expense and indignities from the border patrol, they should do so infrequently.

These demographic changes affected Los Angeles. The Aztecs had a special word for the communal space inhabited by extended families; Spanish conquistadores translated it into *barrio*. L.A.'s Mexican-Americans population historically resided north of the Pueblo in a section called Sonora Town, bounded by Short, Main, Yale, and College streets. A growing population stretched the barrio eastward; transient Mexican workers also shared large sections of downtown with immigrant Asians, African-Americans and Caucasians, often single men.

A central location eventually would make the land valuable from a commercial perspective, but for the time being, cheap rentals dominated the old and neglected housing stock. With the arrival of more immigrant families in the early 1900s, Mexican-American Angelenos continued a flow that had just begun during the end of the previous century: they traversed the Los Angeles River. The modest homes of East Los Angeles, Boyle Heights, Belvedere would draw couples with kids, while singles occupied less-wholesome quarters downtown.

Independently Exploring the Terrain

Indeed, the notion of becoming "propertied" has been a powerful force in Los Angeles' growth. Expansive land under perennially sunny skies attracted more than just the monied classes sought by real estate

Like this couple, many Russian Jewish immigrants of the 1920s chose to live in Boyle Heights; the Venice beachscape was reserved for weekend relaxation. Ocean Park subsequently became a favorite retirement spot. *Courtesy Shades of L.A. Archives, The Los Angeles Public Library.*

promoters — or the immigrant laborers needed to build the rails and houses. L.A.'s multicultural infrastructure, subdued though it was at times, beckoned a variety of ethnic, racial and religious minorities who were not specifically recruited.

The public relations and promotional campaigns, for example, filtered down to Eastern European immigrant Jews who disparately wanted to flee the tubercular ghettos of the industrialized U.S. for a place where air blew freely and tenements did not obstruct an often-shy sun. These were not the Newmarks or Hellmans, the merchants of the previous century. "There are great numbers of the poorer class of Jews" reported the Commission of Immigration and Housing. And L.A. offered them mobility. The turn of the century saw roughly two-thirds of the Eastern European Jews living downtown, though 87 percent moved at least once from 1900-1910. Subsequently, the younger couples joined Mexican and other immigrants in the more residential communities across the Los Angeles River.

Although they shared the same beliefs as their coreligionists, the Jews of Turkey and Greece claimed their own ritual customs and practices. Many infused Ladino — a language with Hispanic roots — into their worship, rather than English. To this day, confusion may result the first time one hears Sephardic strains of "Ayn K'Elohenu," a Sabbath morning song of praise to God. The Ladino translations (with verses such as "Nuestro Senor" and "Nuestro Salvador") almost could be mistaken for Church Latin.

Often from the Island of Rhodes, the Mediterranean Jews also established different demographic patterns. They tended to live in what is now considered South Central L.A., and remained there much longer than most Euroamericans. Their first synagogue, called the Sephardic Hebrew Center, only closed its doors during

the mid-1990s, having moved from its original building on Hoover and 55th (now an AME church) to its final location on West 59th Street, bordering Baldwin Hills and Inglewood.

Of all the congregations currently serving Near and Far Eastern Jews, however, Sephardic Temple Tifereth Israel remains the largest; its Westwood structure is starkly imposing from the outside and strikingly true to Middle Eastern Jewish culture on the inside. This synagogue also has a historic background, dating to 1919 when it called itself La Communidad. The term "Sephardic" envelopes not only the original Turks and Greeks, but Jewish people who can trace their birthplaces to anywhere *but* Western, Central and Eastern Europe. La Communidad proved to be more a mission than a simple moniker: in the years that followed, a Sephardic infrastructure evolved from this small nucleus of mostly Turkish and Rhodesli Jews. The community now consists of Israeli, Moroccan, Persian, Yemenite, Syrian, Iraqi, Mexican and South American; some even have come from as far away as China, India and Burma. More generally, L.A.'s Jewish population — Ashkenazim and Sephardic alike — is thought to exceed 519,000 people.

St. James Armenian Church is within a five-minute walk (so rare in L.A.) from the building that until recently housed the Sephardic Hebrew Center. Jews and Armenians have shared the status of people without a country, and neither were specifically recruited to Los Angeles. During the first third of the century, the Armenians' immigration route stretched from their former homeland — occupied by the Turks and later, the Soviet Union — to other parts of Eurasia. Those who came to the U.S. arrived on Eastern shores. If they subsequently chose the West, it usually was Fresno.

Armenians had settled in this Central Valley farming community since the 1880s. Accustomed from their birthplace to subsistence agriculture, they thrived as California growers, developing the fig and raisin industries. Their success yielded prejudice, however. In Fresno they were called "Fresno Indians;" housing was segregated by way of restrictive covenants. The Depression proved to be a turning point: many Westward-heading Armenian-Americans now opted for L.A. over Fresno. As in so many other instances, they were welcomed by a small, viable community.

Their occupational pursuits revolved around food-related interests and trades learned while in exile. A study of first-generation Armenians who came of age during the Depression indicates a propensity to own or manage small businesses, most often farms, grocery stores/markets, dry cleaning operatives, tailor shops. They also were largely responsible for introducing Oriental carpets to Angelenos.

Disbursed among so many lands prior to arriving in the United States, they were masters of adaptability: Armenians-Angelenos thus tended to live alongside immigrants from their host countries. For example, Boyle Heights was home to many Russians — and Armenians who had once taken exile there. Some evidence suggests that those with a recent Middle Eastern past lived south of downtown, as did the Sephardic Jews. But the Armenian community became more prominent — and geographically concentrated — in the 1970s. The Soviet Union had for decades limited emigration; with changing diplomatic relations, these restrictions were eased. The local population rose from 100,000 in 1980 to 250,000 a decade later. L.A. thus boasted a greater Armenian population than any other country or

jurisdiction — save the Republic of Armenia. Immigrants now gravitate toward the "East Hollywood" section of Melrose Avenue, as well as the independent city of Glendale.

For those groups not specifically recruited here, one of the most important factors was the existence of a community. The pobladores represented a unique African/Hispanic/Indian melange, but African-Americans per se — individuals whose lives had been touched by the nation's subservience to the vile institution of slavery — did not appear in great numbers until after 1900. Philanthropist Biddy Mason (see Chapter 1) and Robert Owens (1805-1865), another former slave who earned a fortune through real estate investment,

Born a slave, Biddy Mason used the financial success she achieved in L.A. to build a community and offer aid to those less fortunate. Part of the "Witness to History Project " of the UCLA/Cesar Chavez Center Mural Digital Lab, this work draws on the Angel's Flight theme to emphasize Mason's transcendent qualities and to give them a permanent, local context. Images of other African-Americans, from Rosa Parks to Angela Davis, surround her. *Copyright, 1996, The Social and Public Art Resource Center (SPARC), Venice.*

were examples of mid- to late-19th century pioneers: the few African-Americans who either came here with slaveholding families and/or who had defied incredible obstacles to amass the resources necessary to establish themselves independently.

For blacks, the post-Civil War South was a seesaw of optimism, then despair. Reconstructionism brought the promise of landownership and political enfranchisement. Yet, the continuum of small-scale agriculture/sharecropping/farm labor was confining in itself. Nor did constitutional rights guarantee enfranchisement, let alone political power. The blacks who came to California during the post-Civil War period typically chose the North for its mining and transportation opportunities; nascent interest in Los Angeles was generated during the 1880s via Southern-sweeping railroad ties and "trickle down" promotional campaigns, intended for monied people but inadvertently capturing working class dreams.

The San Francisco earthquake contributed to the demographic slide. As with everyone else, Bay-area blacks lost their property and jobs. Yet, egregious discrimination — combined with obvious shortages — prevented them from regaining their previous status. Los Angeles contained 19 percent of the state's African-American population in 1900; by 1910, it was 35 percent, or 7,599 people. Caution must be exercised in implying direct cause and effect, however. During the same time period (1910-1920), California's African-American population doubled, from 11,045 to 21,645. We cannot say with certainty that black San Franciscans moved south, or that newcomers to the Golden State saw L.A. as a better option.

But a vibrant community spirit nevertheless proved an asset. The National Association for the Advancement of Colored People was formed in 1909, and soon boasted an L.A. chapter. Members vigorously protested the racist film, "Birth of a Nation." Visiting

Los Angeles in the early teens, the African-American scholar and activist W.E.B. DuBois wrote, "Los Angeles is wonderful. Nowhere in the United States is the Negro so well and beautifully housed, nor the average efficiency and intelligence in the colored population so high...Out here in this matchless Southern California there would seem to be no limit to your opportunities, your possibilities."

DuBois and others soon noticed a color line forming, however. Due to housing discrimination beginning in the 1920s, a growing population consolidated around Central Avenue, which evolved into the community's commercial and spiritual nucleus. African Methodist, Baptist, Presbyterian and Episcopal churches thrived. Like the barrio and other enclaves created by segregation, the neighborhood produced mixed feelings of resentment and solidarity. The situation was perhaps more blatant on Central Avenue than elsewhere, as 70 percent of black Angelenos resided in its vicinity by 1930. Yet, the concentration may have allowed the district to vote one of its own, Frederick M. Roberts, to the California Assembly in 1918. When other groups were totally disenfranchised, Roberts held distinction as the first African-American elected official. Central Avenue also motivated people to community service, although discrimination limited their ability to gain wider recognition. At the same time that Roberts gained his Assembly seat, USC granted a dental degree to an African-American woman, Dr. Vada Jetmore Somerville.

The Great Migration, a population phenomenon unique to African-Americans, expanded the community farther. Ninety percent of the nation's blacks lived in the South as of 1910, but more than 2,000 lynchings during the two preceding decades — plus segregation laws newly imposed at the state level — forced action. When World War I slowed the pace of immigration and the industrialized states called for workers, the rural black population responded. Most flocked to the job-rich Northeast, where the rapid influx

was sometimes met with violence. During the teens and 1920s, race riots and ghettoization urged other options.

The Great Migration lasted from 1915 to 1929. Los Angeles benefited in part by default. The climatic conditions attracted African-Americans just as it did other newcomers. There was now a larger population here than anywhere else in California, so the presence of community alone proved to be a draw. And although racial incidents certainly happened here, Los Angeles was not infamous for anti-black violence. (Californios had suffered a rash of lynchings at Statehood, however. Extreme and repeated incidents of physical violence seem to be directed toward numerically large population groups, perceived as threats during periods of rapid demographic, economic and political change.)

A history of civic activism and determination had elevated a few exceptional people above the walls of prejudice; the same spirit continued to enrich the community generally. Yet, the average African-American endured privation in the pursuit of urban jobs and wages. Few sought agricultural labor, nor were they (as a rule) recruited. Concerned about the shortage of decent jobs available to African-Americans, their leaders occasionally tried to sway residents, particularly newcomers, toward rural alternatives.

Allensworth State Historic Park is an inviting landmark along the otherwise dead zone of SR 43, just off California Highway 99. The now-defunct farming

(Left photo and top of following page) Deportation of Mexican workers was a smokescreen response to the Depression. A rare shot from the August 18, 1931 issue of *La Opinion*, shows 1,300 leaving Los Angeles for Mexico. Earlier that year, 11 Mexicans had been arrested in a raid at the Plaza. Perhaps one-third of the officially listed Mexican population of the United States were forced to depart this country by 1940. *Courtesy La Opinion and El Pueblo de Los Angeles Historic Monument.*

LA OPINION

1 MEXICANOS PRESOS EN U
PARATOSO RAID A LA PLACIT

community began in 1908 with a national advertising campaign, promising African-Americans that they could "live on an equity with whites…" By 1914, the town elected its own officials and utilized 800 acres for the cultivation of alfalfa, grain, sugar beets, chicken, turkeys, dairy cattle and Belgian hares. The farming village was the brainchild of its namesake, a career military officer and Angeleno, Colonel Allen Allensworth. Although the community attracted resident-buyers from Ohio, New York and Kansas, it evolved from the founder's L.A.-based California Colony and Home Promoting Association, a group which consisted entirely of African-Americans.

Not many Angelenos followed Allensworth's lead, though, and their roots were somewhat removed from the rural South. The African-American population here rose from 38,894 to 63,774 in the decade between 1930 and 1940 — the Depression. Over half came from various parts of the nation, but the largest single block arrived from the West South Central States, particularly Texas and Oklahoma. To a greater extent than the white Dust Bowl migrants, the African-Americans had been urban dwellers prior to their move.

Los Angeles could offer them jobs at comparable wages — once they found suitable employment. Yet, only 20 percent had attained union memberships in 1930, and approximately 50 percent were domestic workers. Maid service was common employment for immigrant women of various ethnic groups, including many Caucasians; they needed to contribute to their family income (or to support themselves), but their gender, combined with often limited formal education, relegated them to unskilled labor. What may have distinguished African-Americans were issues of wage and working conditions. A writer for the *California Eagle*, the black community newspaper, described their situation :

> There is a great horde of jobless domestics who are forced to work at whatever wages they can get. Employers have taken advantage of this condition and Negro women and school girls are being hired at wages ranging from five to ten dollars a month in many cases. For these wages, they are forced to remain on the premises seven days a week with a half day off on Thursday. In other cases there are women working for mere room and board.

At least African-Americans had a community to welcome them on their arrival. Not so for nearly 100,000 white refugees from the Dust Bowl states of Texas, Oklahoma, Arkansas and Missouri. Confounded by a regional drought, a failed bank system that could offer no credit, and the multiple effects of an depressed national economy, these families abandoned their homes and farms during the 1930s. They loaded their cars and drove to California hoping to work the fields — and find a more abundant food supply. Without an established community or kinship network here, they met derision and hostility: Los Angeles Police Chief James E. Davis dispatched 136 of his officers in 1936 to stave off their entry at the eastern border.

If the Depression compelled communities to take better care of their own and forged some solidarity between grounded working class Angelenos of diverse nationalities, Mexican-Americans were given a colossal exit visa: approximately 50,000 retraced earlier passages, this time crossing the border — from the north. The exodus owed to several factors. First, in reaction to a choked job market, the U.S. Immigration Service conducted public or workplace raids (the same type conducted here by the Reagan Administration during the 1980s); undocumented workers were deported. But Mexican nationalism colluded, both directly and unintentionally, with U.S. Depression-era immigration

Terminal Island was the first place in the U.S. to force the evacuation of its Japanese population. This picture, however, captures the scene on Vermont Avenue, February, 1942. *Courtesy Security Pacific Collection, The Los Angeles Public Library.*

Different emotions, all vividly expressed, appear as these four men pass time before being sent from Santa Anita to the intern- ment camps. *Courtesy Security Pacific Collection, The Los Angeles Public Library.*

"policy." In the years that followed the civil war, the Mexican government created a formal constituency in L.A., with various "Honorary Commissions" established through the consul's office. The goal was repatriation: experienced workers from an advanced industrial environment could rebuild the ravaged Mexican economy. Equally important, such a movement would add to the spirit of nationalism. During the early 1930s, Consul Rafael de la Colina and community leaders encouraged poorer residents to emigrate, and sometimes helped to organize or otherwise finance their train transport.

Many nativist policies were created in the name of national interests, however defined. Perhaps the most egregious occurred at the onset of World War II, when President Franklin Roosevelt's Executive Order 9066 removed 120,000 people of Japanese ori- gin, two-thirds of them U.S. citizens, from their

homes and isolated them in remote, inland relocation centers; there were over 23,000 Japanese Angelenos at the time. But whereas other racist incidents had taken place throughout the nation's — and indeed L.A.'s — history, this one differed in the responses it evoked. A *Los Angeles Times* poll of late 1943 indicated that about 90 percent of the almost 10,000 readers surveyed would in- deed exclude Japanese from the coast. On a personal level, howev- er, there was an outcry among certain seg- ments of the pop-

ulation. Mixed ethnic communities existed, and a fledgling sense of solidarity united Angelenos who worked and lived together, recently through the Depression.

The Lopez Farm Ranch is a large produce market with a Halloween pumpkin patch, a Christmas tree grove and country charm — in Los Angeles. Its Jefferson Boulevard location remains difficult to describe geographically: the long, wide, high-speed street straddles Culver City, the Marina, and the Mar

following the revolution. According to Cressy's son, Chris (who with his sister now runs the successful second-generation enterprise), the family chose Little Tijuana, "Tijuanito"— an unplumbed, dirt shack, community near the Overland-Venice intersection of Culver City — as their home. The senior Lopez became a farm hand, while at the age of 12, Cressy obtained a job as a dishwasher at the landmark Culver City restaurant, Joe Petrelli's. The boy

The withdrawal of Exclusion during the 1940s and new immigration laws two decades later at last gave Asian-Pacific Americans their full rights of U.S. citizenship. *Courtesy the Social and Public Art Resource Center (SPARC), Venice, and taken from the Great Wall of Los Angeles (copyright, 1976-1983).*

Vista and Playa del Rey sections of L.A. An agricultural remnant of a former era, the land was originally owned by the Frias family. When young Cressy Lopez first laid eyes upon it circa 1940, however, Japanese tenant growers were harvesting celery there.

Cressy had been born in Tijuana, where his parents stayed for exactly three days before continuing their journey from Michoacan to L.A. They were part of the massive Mexican migration in the years immediately

worked six days a week. On Sundays he went to Playa del Rey beach via Jefferson Boulevard, walking three or four miles to save bus fare. The celery fields were in view.

Cressy soon decided that a second income was more important than a day off. He petitioned the tenant farmer, a Mr. Mayurama, for a Sunday farm labor job. Beside English and Spanish, the youth quickly learned basic Japanese. He worked at Mayurama's farm full-time; his industriousness and trilingual capabilities won him a foreman's post.

Executive Order 9066 pulled Mayurama away from his crops during the middle of a 1942 harvest. In his hasty departure, he signed over the lease "to ride out the rest of the year," as Chris Lopez explains the situation, to his young foreman. This was not a gift, nor did it involve any monetary transactions other than a purchase of equipment. Yet, Cressy visited Mayurama frequently at the Manzanar relocation center, bringing him food, candy and sundries unavailable at the naked, windswept outpost.

The young Mexican immigrant signed two more leases. Ample harvests yielded him $160,000 him in profits over the two-year period. By the time the war was over, Cressy owned the 18-acre Lopez Ranch. And the Mayurama family lived on it for more than six months, until they could heal and rebuild from Manzanar. Cressy's respect for his former boss, developed without financial patronage, may strike us as odd in an era when we can scarcely exchange authentic compliments, let alone give of ourselves in any "inconvenient" way. But appreciation for color-blind opportunity — a shared value from one immigrant to another — spoke to the best aspects of a changing social environment.

World War II converted Los Angeles from a large city with

Feeling trade pressure first and, ultimately, political change, the Soviet Union after a long hiatus allowed its citizens to emigrate more freely from the 1970s until its dissolution. A participant at the 1977 West Coast Song Latvian Song Festival is pictured. *Courtesy Shades of L.A. Archives, The Los Angeles Public Library.*

A Los Angeles-area family reunites with relatives in Ghana, possibly for a wedding. The term "African-American" has a much more diverse connotation now with a small community of recent African immigrants now calling L.A. home. *Courtesy Shades of L.A. Archives, The Los Angeles Public Library.*

strong agricultural undertones into a metropolitan manufacturingcenter. And people of all colors, genders and backgrounds were desperately needed to fuel military industries which later came to hold civilian applications. Certainly racism and nativism have emerged many times since. Yet, after the McCarthyite ravages of the 1950s, the multicultural melange now associated with Los Angeles assumed a new posture and pride.

Today's African-American community includes some members whose life experience is rooted more in Africa than America. Once small Armenian, Filipino, and Korean communities have increased manifold. Joining sizable contingents of coreligionists from Persia and Israel, Russian Jews arrived here en masse for the first time since 1920, and Chinese immigrants come from a far wider sphere than Canton Province.

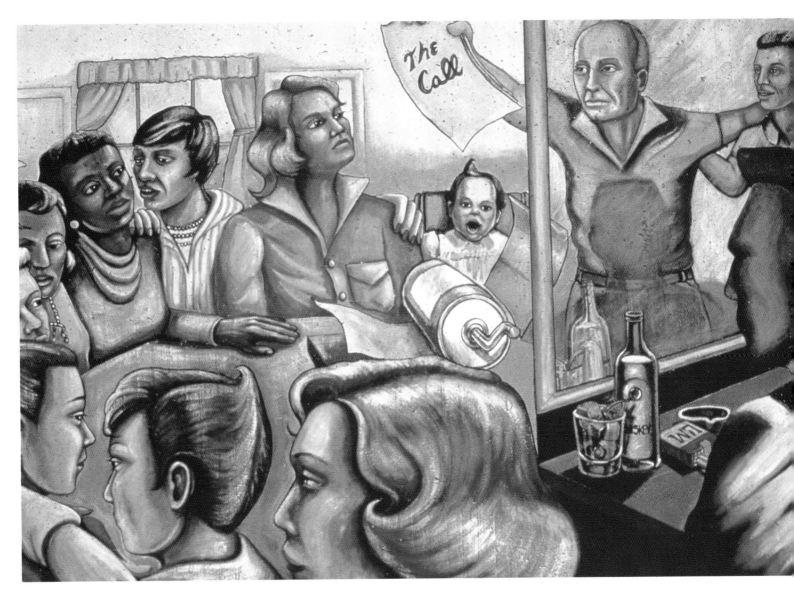

A latter-day British invasion, not necessarily musical, has swept the Westside coastal communities, as Little Tokyo welcomes globally-vested Japanese business people. "Latino" entered common parlance because "Mexican-American" and "Chicano" proved too limited to embrace the influx of Central American refugees.

The multicultural melange envelops groups who had never been here before, or only in small numbers. Samoans arrived slowly, steadily since World War II wracked the Pacific. Domestic and foreign policy, invariably beyond the control of individuals, urged Greeks, Thais, Vietnamese to relocate to these shores.

As for the erstwhile "Midwesterners," they had reason to celebrate when, in 1960, Los Angeles overtook Chicago as America's second largest metropolis. The incredible number of Wind City refugees here leads one to believe that their exodus alone caused our ascendancy, but I know this is not true. And while there are only four million people to go, the local media constantly remind us that the Big Apple should be vigilant.

Dare the Easterners threaten our status? Hardly! History teaches us that New Yorkers arrived here in droves, at least since the 1880 census. We seduced them: they're Angelenos now.

A relatively early sense of community fostered strong gay and lesbian identity in Los Angeles. The right-hand corner of this picture introduces Harry Hay, who helped to organize the Mattachine Society, the city's first gay rights-culture organization, in 1950. The Daughters of Bilitis, the premiere lesbian group, coalesced shortly afterward. often meeting around kitchen tables. The bar scene depicts masked identities. *Courtesy The Social and Public Art Resource Center (SPARC), and taken from th Great Wall of Los Angeles (copyright, 1976-1983).*

GOVERNANCE:
AUTHORITY, INVOLVEMENT

CHAP

D MUNICIPAL SERVICES

TER 3

chapter

Introduction

The city of Los Angeles is currently designing its Information Technology infrastructure (or I.T.) I.T., as it is affectionately known to practitioners, should be to new millennium what freeway construction was to the 1950s and 1960s. L.A. wants the long boulevards and surface streets to converge into an extra-wide, customized ramp to the Information Superhighway, merging needs for service delivery, data-gathering and purposeful dissemination, economic growth, municipal entrepreneurism.

In bringing issues of governance from the past to the present, therefore, it seems appropriate to click on L.A.'s website: http//www.ci.la.us. One can easily take a link from the homepage to a section describing the Los Angeles Charter Reform Commission. Simply stated, the charter is a municipal constitution. In its almost 150 years as a formally governing city, L.A. has gone through the act of incorporation, three charter overhauls, dozens of amendments, and several major reorganizations. The current charter was enacted in 1925, and though revised hundreds of times, it remains more or less true to nearly 75-year-old dictates.

According to the website, the current movement for reform embraces 11 issues. These topics can be distilled to embrace: the nature of the charter, itself, whether it should be detailed, or broad enough to readily accommodate future input; the roles and power of the mayor and city council; charter specification about the Los Angeles Unified School District (LAUSD), city personnel management, and municipal service delivery; neighborhood services and participation; the election (or appointment) of the city attorney and city controller; possible reorganization of financial management operations; changes in city and LAUSD electoral systems; and, management and governance of the proprietary departments.

Of all the issues, neighborhood governance has perhaps elicited the most media attention. How would communities be defined, geographically and politically? And who would be the arbiters? While it is too premature to set physical boundaries, the political considerations stir debate among members of the Charter Reform Commissions. Alternatives have ranged from neighborhood advisory councils (which would serve as conduits for input and consultation), to staffed, locally based, decision-making authorities. The irony is that the issue and choices have been primarily raised by the commissioners. When focus group tests were conducted in nine communities, none of the 113 likely voters — not even those aware of charter reform — suggested neighborhood councils.

Grassroots government is ideal, philosophically, but it defies L.A. history. As the website informs us, the 1909 Charter included an option for the creation of boroughs, which can determine such issues as zoning, street maintenance and repair, tax rates and other related issues. The provision languished, was virtually ignored, until its repeal in 1973. Advisory commissions during the second half of this century recommended decentralized service delivery and increasing responsiveness to local needs.

The issue of neighborhood government surfaces now, according to the charter reform commission staff, "as the solution to the alienation of many city residents, and as the best way to keep the city together." The most recently discussed secession of the San Fernando Valley — with its huge population and tax base — has a discomforting effect on elected officials, city personnel, other Angelenos. However, if any neighborhood were likely to walk, it probably would be San Pedro, stated Raphael Sonenshein, political science professor and now the commission's executive director, at a recent public policy forum.

Secession has been voiced in the past by San Pedro, Valley, and Westchester residents, and there are similarities between those communities. Distance

proves to be the most obvious factor. Virtually all travelers from the basin to the Valley must traverse a hill or canyon, before descending into a microclimate often 10-20 degrees different. San Pedro is even more remote. One can access the Valley through combinations of surface streets and freeways, many within L.A.'s borders.

But the trip to "Pee-dro," as the locals call it, forces travelers to leave city limits for about half an hour, before re-entering the port. Indeed, geophysical factors have separated San Pedro and the Valley since pre-colonial times, when the local Tongva spoke dialects distinct from their kin in the basin.

The unifying characteristics of San Pedro and Westchester are of a more modern vintage, with each community developing an economic culture around its primary municipal industry. Westchester, of course, is home to Los Angeles International Airport (LAX), while San Pedro, with neighboring Long Beach, boasts the busiest port in the nation. Both trade/transportation hubs are overseen by commissions that control their long purse strings, and need not consult with the mayor or the council when conducting business.

And this is the line dance of charter reform: 11 issues whirling, interlocking momentarily before moving on to find another and, hopefully, more fitting connection. Appointments — along with veto power, override strictures, and budgetary authority — have been weapons in the historic struggle between mayor and city council. Past charters detail which senior management and commission positions are chosen by the chief executive, and which ones by the legislators.

Parker Center, home of the L.A. Police Department, and City Hall are cast against a classic, 1950s-noire sky. The postcard caption reads: This is the city...Los Angeles, California," referring to the opening lines of *Dragnet. Courtesy The Postcard Collection of Jeanne Taylor Baird.*

The commissions themselves diverge wildly. The new Information Technology Agency crosses bureaucratic boundaries and provides services to virtually all city government departments; it has no policymaking functions, however, and therefore, no commissioners. On the opposite end are the independent "proprietary" agencies. As the name suggests, these departments — Airports, Harbor, Water and Power — have real assets. They consume grand budgets and generate multimillion dollar revenues.

Due to the "propertied" status enjoyed by these agencies, their commissions are empowered to act as business agents, negotiating powerfully and independently of elected officials.

Beneath the commissions (of varying potencies) are citizen advisory groups. The charter reform website lists 17 of them, engaging at very minimum 1,187 Angelenos. Selection methods mimic those of the commissions: 10 of the 17 boards appoint their members (754+ citizens, at least 64 percent, collectively), rather than opening involvement to all interested parties, or establishing an election process — a missed opportunity to promote a more active political culture.)

The website asserts that the "primary mechanism of ensuring citizen representation is the ballot box." Initiatives and referenda were pioneered in Los Angeles, via a 1903 charter revision. They offer grassroots movements with potentially immense influence. Yet, these mechanisms demand an informed, inspired electorate. Furthermore, initiatives and referenda often seem isolated in context; placement of individual issues on a ballot box eschews a systems approach to municipal governance and isolates voters larger from larger federal and state policy agendas. Controversial topics attract (or buy) media attention, but the choice of operational alternatives — sometimes overlapping, sometimes contradictory — only adds to the confusion. In short, what's lacking is identity, affiliation as a way to strengthen mental associations.

The same problem exists in municipal politics. Justifiably responding to the corruption and bossism of the late 19th century, L.A. Progressives did away with formal party identification through a 1909 charter amendment. Yet, who doubted that Tom Bradley was a Democrat, or Richard Riordan, a Republican — albeit L.A. versions? In fact, these tangential party affiliations always lend a bit of excitement to elections, when national pundits speculate on the mayor's plans for higher office. Ultimately, however, neither controversy nor candidate move the voter. Turnout in general elections over the past 12 years has only once exceeded 40 percent.

Neighborhood governance is likely to be an expensive proposition. The website offers examples of four other cities that have implemented it: New York, Portland, St. Paul and Washington, D.C. Tax dollars are the primary funding source for all. St. Paul, alone among the cities, also secures foundation and corporate support. Powers and purposes vary, too. With a strong tradition of grassroots involvement, self-organized groups in Portland direct their energies to eight community development advisory boards. Washington, D.C. claims 37 neighborhood commissions; one for each 2,000 residents. The scope envelops "city issues" generally, but a primary function may be community veto of local liquor licenses.

As charter reform crystallizes, will Angelenos continue to shuffle from one ballot issue to another, or slowly create community approaches that work within a municipal system. Which way, L.A.?

Supreme Authority, Occasional Chaos

Spain's zeal to colonize the New World was years ahead of its ability to develop a true and uniform management system. But noone thought of "government" at

(Left) Boris Deutsch's "Cultural Contributions of North, South, and Central America" begins by focusing on Native populations and comes to include the European and Asian immigrants who subsequently settled in the western hemisphere. In fact, Deutsch's own profile pops up occasionally among those of his subjects. The Terminal Annex Post Office downtown, which contains Deutsch's masterpiece, currently is undergoing restoration. *Courtesy, The National Archives and Records Administration, Washington, D.C.*

the time; "rule" was the operating word. A viceroy, directly accountable to the monarchy, presided over the Spain's territory from South to North America. As if the area wasn't large enough, the Mexican-based governor at one time also had been responsible for the Phillipine Islands.

There were very real reasons for this consolidation of global authority. Lucrative Manila trade galleons helped to underwrite royal expeditions and convey a wealth of supplies and materials to (and soon, from) new colonies. Religion threaded itself into this fine weave of trade and settlement, but goals often conflicted. Spain invaded Holland to preserve Catholicism, with devastating political consequences.

The monarchy's commercial and religious interests nevertheless manifested themselves in four New World settlements patterns: mining districts, presidios, missions and pueblos. But for most of the Spanish rule in North America, relatively little structure existed under the viceroy's office. A commandant usually oversaw both military and civilian affairs, although a separate governor sometimes dealt with the latter. (Disputes between the two sectors might go before a supreme court, or *audencia*, in Guadalajara). Depending on the nature of the settlement, the commandant or governor would

appoint a mayor, military officer, or priest to execute official decrees and handle daily matters. The problem was that when close together, these differently-oriented communities developed fractious relationships. As noted in Chapter II, resource allocations — specifically, the use of water and Native American labor — created rifts between the pobladores of Los Angeles and the priests of San Gabriel.

Forced dependence and cross-purposes caused political havoc, too. Since there was no presidio near Los Angeles, a small band of guards accompanied the priests to San Gabriel and remained there. One of the first misunderstandings with the Native Americans occurred because the soldiers had been given different instructions than the priests about gatekeeping — literally, how many of the then-friendly Tongva might enter the walls of San Gabriel at a given time. Confusion resulted, and the locals stampeded.

(Opposite page, above, and bottom left) Spain's systematic approach to colonial rule and the realities of frontier life occasionally clashed at San Gabriel Mission, depicted in an 1890 water color by Eva Scott Feynes. Feynes returned 12 years later to paint distinguishing features, notably the belfry and orange grove. The mission priests proudly cultivated fruit trees, but the mayordomo, chief caretaker, is thought to have lived their midst. *Courtesy, The Southwest Museum, Los Angeles.*

The rape of a chief's wife by a soldier later that first year (1771) provoked an outright battle; the chief subsequently was killed and his body, mutilated. This incident foretold future violations: at least twice during the 1770s groups of mission guards ravaged Tongva women. The soldiers also frequently viewed Native American females as commodities to be "purchased." Venereal disease spread among the local population, to the extent that 300-400 cases were reported at a mission hospital in 1810. Certainly much criticism has been hurled at the priests for San Gabriel's cramped, unsanitary, often harsh conditions — and the way that the environment eroded Tongva culture. But the stationary guards, who seldom numbered more than 10, added to the chaos by leading mission life into their own unsavory direction.

Government Structure and Political Organization in Colonial Los Angeles

The distance between supreme monarchy and grassroots anarchy settled somewhat toward the end of Spanish rule. Los Angeles' first titular mayor (alcade), Jose Vanegas, came to his position in 1788. A prosperous farmer of Mexican/Indian descent, he was the only poblador to so serve; he accepted the alcade's position again eight years later. In an era well before term limits, Angelenos held the position for one or two years.

The viceroy's office had become more regionalized, too. Jose Joaquin de Arrilaga, Governor of Alta California, strengthened rudimentary local democracy in 1812. Cities would choose their own mayor-judge (alcade) to preside over the council (ayuntamiento); the number of seats depended on the size of the community. Matters that elicited local interest were put to public discussion, debate and vote. The process was rather akin to a New England town meeting, with one notable exception: those who did not attend were fined. And while the alcade and councilmembers (regidores) served without remuneration, the syndico received commissions for the revenues he brought in as combined treasurer, tax collector, and city attorney. The only salaried staff was a secretary, who recorded both civil and court proceedings.

The Plan of Iguala (February 24, 1821) decreed Mexican independence from Spain. There may have been an effort to suppress the news from supposed Spanish loyalists, particularly the priests and military commanders. Word arrived approximately one year later. By 1823, Mexico created a republican form of government. Gone was the position of comisionado, which during the late years of Spanish rule could — and did — seize authority from the ayuntamiento. Mexican leaders also inaugurated a representative process: the population voted electors, who in turn would choose a territorial legislature, or diputacion. This body then selected a deputy (diputado), to the Congress in Mexico City. Jose Palomares was the first to speak for L.A.

The pueblo's growth soon elevated its position in Alta California. Los Angeles officially became a city during 1835. During the following year, General Antonio Lopez de Santa Ana took charge of the Mexican government and moved toward increasing political centralization. The "Department" of Alta California subsequently would contain two prefects, the southern one headquartered in Los Angeles. Furthermore, the new system carved out a territory running from Santa Barbara to San Diego, with both cities

Hostilities between local Californios and U.S. troops officially came to an end at the Treaty of Cahuenga (1847), named for Tomas Feliz's ranch, where Universal City stands today. However, the terms of California's departure from Mexico and entry into the United States would be officially stated in the Treaty of Guadalupe Hidalgo (1848). *Courtesy The Southwest Museum, Los Angeles.*

being partidos of Los Angeles. A prefect or subprefect, respectively, presided over each of these divisions.

With Los Angeles having gained supremacy in the South, the stakes became higher. As early as 1828, a young, first-term deputado to the Congress, Pio Pico, proposed that L.A., rather than Monterey, be the capital of Alta California. He and fellow Angeleno Jose Antonio Carillo led three revolts for the cause of Southern California primacy; Pico briefly won the governorship in 1832, exhorting his position — from Monterey. Nicolas Guiterrez, a successor, transferred the capital to Los Angeles four years later. This move incited Juan Bautista Alvarado to invade Southern California, place Los Angeles under martial law, and subsequently establish his claim as governor. Pico's ultimate gubernatorial victory, in 1845, assured that Alta California's legislative and administrative center would be moved to Los Angeles. (A compromise with then-rival, the northern-based General Jose Castro, allowed military and customs functions to remain in Monterey.) Los Angeles now boasted both political clout, with administrative authority extending to present-day Orange County, as well as parts of Riverside and San Bernardino.

But Pico had little time to enjoy the realization of his career-long vision. A year later, he and Castro together fled for Mexico, on a less well-rehearsed mission. The Bear Flag Revolt invited another changing of the guard. Monterey was captured by U.S. naval command on July 7, 1846, and a crew under Commodore Robert F. Stockton sailed for San Pedro. Pico and Castro did not stay to greet the navy; they may have sought reinforcements from Mexico or more simply, refuge. Four hundred armed American troops landed, marched into and occupied Los Angeles on August 11. Stockton secured the city and left Captain Archibald Gillespie to maintain order. Virtually all historical accounts agree that the latter's actions provoked rebellion — quickly. Frustrated by oppressive conditions and a lack of responsiveness from the Mexican government, Servulia Verila and Leonardo Cota organized grassroots resistance. La Pronunciamiento Contra Los Norte Americanos , signed on September 24 by over 300 of a total of 675 male Angelenos, was their manifesto:

Early Los Angeles relied heavily on volunteer leadership. Following the first municipal elections, in 1850, Antonio F. Coronel was instated as chief fiscal/tax officer for the city — and the county. He is seen here reviewing church records. Coronel later became mayor and a county supervisor. *Courtesy The Security Pacific Collection, Los Angeles Public Library.*

For a month and a half, by a lamentable fatality resulting from the cowardice and incompetence of the departments's chief authorities, we see ourselves subjugated and oppressed by an insignificant force of adventurers of the U.S. of N. America, who, putting us in a condition worse than that of a slave, are dictating to us despotic and arbitrary laws by which, loading us with contributions and onerous taxes, they wish to destroy our industries and agriculture, and to compel us to abandon our property, to be taken and divided among ourselves. And shall be capable of permitting ourselves to be subjected and to accept in silence the heavy chain of slavery?... Therefore, the majority of the inhabitants of this district, justly indignant at our tyrant, we raise the cry of war...

Typically outnumbered, the Californios nevertheless prevailed at several major battles. One of their most memorable weapons was an antique cannon, left over from the Spanish era, that became known as the "old woman's gun." When Stockton's troops first entered L.A., the instrument had been rescued from its site at the plaza by nearby resident Francisca Reyes — and buried in her backyard for safety. The cannon resurfaced during battle, fueled only by the rocks and shrapnel that the Angelenos could afford.

Los Angeles proved the last and most durable bulwark of Mexican California. The U.S. responded by more zealously concentrating its resources. Freemont invaded the city from the north and Stockton from the south, each with about 600 soldiers. Personal fire power, swords, and the "old woman's gun" were no match for a larger, well-equipped army. The local resistance simply could not endure. Officially representing the Mexican government — but perhaps more closely identifying as Californios — Andres Pico and Jose Antonio Carillo signed the Treaty of Cahuenga (named for the ranch where Universal City now stands) on January 13, 1847. Hostilities thus ended. A year later, Mexico ceded California in the Treaty of Guadalupe Hidalgo, granting residents all the freedoms of the U.S. Constitution — or the right to return, with equal liberty, to Mexico.

But mid-century L.A. was a baffling place, socially and politically. From 1847-1850 martial law prevailed over California. The military governor for the southern portion of the state, Colonel J.D. Stevenson, clashed with local officials and, in the ensuing 1848 confrontation, appointed Stephen C. Fosters as mayor. Foster was a man who represented the changing times. Arriving here only the year before as a soldier of the U.S. Mormon Battalion, he spoke fluent Spanish and married into a leading Californio family, the Lugos. While Angelenos protested his appointment and at first refused to follow his lead, he became mayor (no longer called alcade) again, twice during the 1850s.

Becoming A California City

Foster joined Jose Antonio Carrillo, Manuel Dominguez, Abel Stearns, and Hugo Reid (see Chapter 2) as popularly-elected delegates to the California Constitutional Convention of 1849. This bicultural contingent consisted of Californios, plus Euroamericans who had married either California or Native American women. The assembly, gathered at Monterey that fall, passed a constitution with a bilingual clause. Article XI, Section 21 asserts: "All laws, degrees, regulations, and provisions, from which their nature require publication, shall be published in English and Spanish." This early push for inclusivity was dropped by amendment in 1879. (The first Constitution also prohibited lotteries, but...)

Upon entering the union, California's vast interior yielded 27 counties (today, there are 58). Article XI, Section 5 called for the formation of governments overseen by boards of supervisors. Subsequently: "Each county, town, city and incorporated village shall make provision for the support of its own officers, subject to such restrictions and regulations as the Legislature may prescribe." (XI, 9.) The newly formed legislature then was responsible for transforming vague clauses into operational detail. Vast boundaries bore 27 counties (today there are 58). "An Act to Provide for the Incorporation of Cities," passed on March 11, 1850, mandated that municipalities contain: no fewer than 2,000 residents; a ward system determined by the number of white male inhabitants (of both Mexican and Euroamerican origin, per the Constitution;) and, certain identifiable municipal offices.

The Mexican pueblo spanned 112 square miles and housed the requisite number of residents. July 1 marked the first municipal election. However, U.S. cities were to be no more than 28 square miles. L.A. shrunk to roughly the same size as the original Spanish land grant, thus losing its 2,000-person population requirement. Debate over its municipal status ensued. After a survey and arguments about census methodology, however, L.A. was allowed to maintain its authority as a city.

Possibly out of the confusion regarding geographic and governing turfs, local city and county positions overlapped. County Coroner A.P. Hodges simultaneously served as mayor of L.A., while A.F. Coronel and Samuel Whiting, respectively, assumed fiduciary and law enforcement duties for both entities. Governing powers evolved. Voters during a 1916 election rejected

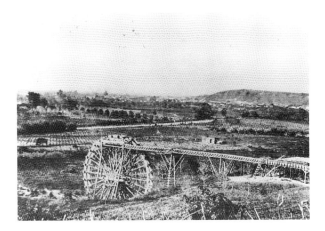

consolidation of the city and the part of the county (from the Pacific Ocean the San Gabriel Mountains) that surrounded it. A 1935 motion for the city to secede from the county and form a consolidated city-county government also failed.

In its early years, Los Angeles looked like nothing so much as a volunteer organization. The Common Council's very first resolution, drafted during its inaugural meeting of July 3, 1850, read: "It having been observed in other places the council members were drawing a salary it was unanimously resolved that the members of this council shall receive neither salaries nor fees of whatsoever nature for discharging their duties as such."

If grassroots government had been introduced hesitatingly in the Spanish era and eradically during the Mexican years, it was now a part of local life. Little distinction existed between legislating and physically carrying out municipal duties. An 1852 state law, for example, required mayors to cosign every check that came from city treasuries. With plenty of hands-on duties at work and home, some of these nonpaid officials grew tired: only two of the seven original council members remained at their posts by the end of the first year, 1850. Still, the same local faces appeared repeatedly, extending themselves over a small — but growing — government infrastructure. The newly created school board (1854) extracted the energies of then-mayor Stephen C. Foster, as superintendent, and three commissioners, who also were council members.

Local ordinances demanded that citizens draw on their own resources in lieu of municipal services.

Saturday in L.A. was street-sweeping day, and every individual or family took care of the unpaved dirt passageway in front of their houses. Homeowners whose properties faced the street were made to hang lamps on the doors during the first two hours of darkness. Care of the zanja (water/irrigation) system had forever been problematic. Looking back in his memoirs on an 1821 trip to Los Angeles, Pio Pico recalled: "I was ordered by Alcade Avila, an ignorant fellow who ruled 'a la fuerza de machete' to go to work with the citizens on the new aqueduct, but being on horseback and armed with a musket, I escaped the task." (Translated very roughly from the Spanish, Avila used the threat of the machete knife.) Water diversion was not uncommon, either. Enrique Sepulveda in 1846 thus received permission to develop a system that would process and distribute this precious resource more justly.

A Municipal Workforce, Contractors, and Franchisees

What eventually transpired is that the city awarded salaries for positions that consumed too much time, assumed substantial expertise, or entailed work that no one really wanted. For the year ending early in 1870, the zanjero and his deputies earned $1,800, as opposed to the mayor's $1,000. An interesting position was overseer of the chain gang. Convict labor (including Native Americans arrested under charges of public inebriation) proved to be valuable resource. It was worthwhile for the city to pay such a "supervisor" $80 per month, not far from the mayoral salary.

Zanjeros entered the law enforcement system, too. A June 13, 1879 order of city council outlined the duties of the position:

ALL DEPUTY ZANJEROS shall be under the control and subject to the order of the Zanjero, and it shall be their duty to patrol and keep close watch over any and all Zanjas, Reservoirs, Ditches, etc. placed under their

The zanjas — crude, wooden irrigation ditches — were almost as old as the pueblo, itself. This large wheel hoisted ground sources to a zanja, at which point gravity took over. The water tank below was constructed during the 1850s. *Courtesy The Southwest Museum, Los Angeles.*

supervision; to see that the water is properly divided to those who have claims, and the only proof of such claims shall be the production of Water Permits, and they shall acknowledge no exchange of water by irrigators inside the city with those outside city limits; they shall wear a police badge, and arrest all persons using the water without a Water Permit, and report their names to the Zanjero and also to the Committee on Zanjas of the Council in writing, and the Zanjero shall also report the same to the Council in his weekly reports…

From the start it appeared that in its delivery of municipal functions, Los Angeles distinguished between human services and natural resources/infrastructual development. Service providers were salaried, not exceptionally well, with circumscribed responsibilities. The pueblo had engaged a school master intermittently since 1817. Monthly wages of $10 to $15 were supposed to be supplemented by the parents, depending on income, but this did not always work. Just before statehood — and perhaps sensing an impending public education requirement — the ayuntamiento contracted with teacher Francisco Bustamente at $60 per month. He also was required to be something of a facilities manager, for he was given an additional $20 to defray the cost of renting a school.

An outbreak of small pox pushed the city to contract ad hoc with Dr. H.S. Orme. His $10/day seemed generous by contrast to other salaries, but this emergency commission probably took him away from his regular practice — at greater health risk. As the epidemic lingered, the common council created a board of health commissioners, whose main duty was to hustle sick people to the "city hospital" or elsewhere for treatment, and to enforce vaccination.

Mercifully, religious and cultural societies lent continuity to human services. The Daughters of Charity, a Catholic order originating in Belgium and more commonly known as the Sisters of Charity, came to Los Angeles during the early-mid 1850s, establishing a educational and health care complex to the immediate north of where Union Station stands today. The Sisters maintained their infirmary at least partially though a contract with the city, and it is to this facility that the health commissioners brought smallpox-stricken Angelenos. The nuns also operated both boarding and day schools offering culturally enriched learning: French, Spanish and German; tapestry and embroidery; art and music; piano and guitar. Jewish Angelenos were apparently so glad to finally have a school of caliber, that some of them even enrolled their children there.

The Sisters hold distinction as the first to provide health care in Los Angeles. But while they moved to the East Side and created St. Vincent's Medical Center, the French Benevolent Society remains at its original site, 531 W. College Street in Chinatown. Thirty-three members of the French community — apparently displeased with the inadequacy of services locally — decided to create their own model of health care in 1860. The fledgling organization secured $2 contributions from

each member and subsequent monthly assessments of $1. A cornerstone was laid in 1869. "French Hospital" opened one year later to "care for the sick, regardless of background." Hospital management and Society functions split in 1969, with the latter continuing as landlord. Membership is still available for $4 monthly, allowing for medical reimbursement up to $25,000 at what has become known as the Pacific Alliance Medical Center.

By contrast to sparse and tightly circumscribed social/educational services, the municipal government displayed a fluid management style with regard to natural resource and infrastructural development. In 1857, a lease was granted to John Dryden to supply the city with water from his property. Contractual responsibilities for pipe-laying went to Jean Louis Sansevaine. A third party, David W. Alexander assumed liability and agreed to process and stock a 30-day supply of potable water. Sansevaine eventually took over Alexander's lease, but within several years transferred it to the partnership of John S. Griffin, Prudent Beaudry and Solomon Lazard. The trio obtained a 30-year franchise (1868-1898). Beaudry became mayor in 1874. Among other contributions, his legacy included expanding the city's water system. Apparently, "interest" was not a conflict in the civic leadership of Old Los Angeles (or, for that matter, in many cities of the era).

In the same year as Griffin, Beaudry and Lazard obtained their contract, the city purchased $75,000 of capital stock in Phineas Banning's Los Angeles and San Pedro Railroad Company — which had been built with a state subsidy. Banning knew the value of contracts and contacts. His wagons had supplied government posts at Tejon, California and Yuma and Tucson, Arizona; Camp Drum, Los Angeles' only Civil War fortress was constructed on land that Banning either sold or donated to the federal government. The Los Angeles and San Pedro Railroad became part of the mammoth Southern Pacific network. With Benjamin D. Wilson as a leading advocate, the city relinquished land, $600,000 and Banning's former line so that the SPRR would not circumvent L.A.

Local governing mechanisms advanced at the same time as the infrastructure. California Senate Bill 581, known as the Charter of 1878, changed the 1850 Act of Incorporation. The legislation spoke directly to the phenomenon of L.A., with increasingly complex municipal needs mandated by growth. (Population here rose 4,385 in 1860 to 5,728 in 1870 to 11,183 in 1880.) The mayor had previously been a member of city council — the one with the public voice and "ribbon-cutting" duties. S.B. 581 created distinctions and checks and balances between two separate governing powers. Council grew to 15 members, three from each of five wards, with staggered two-year terms. The mayor gained membership on standing committees, and citizens' boards and commissions were formally written into the charter. Council now needed a four-fifths vote to override a mayoral veto.

Unheralded economic growth and an ever-burgeoning population compounded the city's sense of importance. Council in 1888 raised the number and salaries of municipal employees. Payroll now included about 50 full-time staff members; 20 more fulfilled seasonal duties. That same year, an amendment to the state constitution carved two distinctive modes of governance: general law, a uniform structure for new or small municipalities, and home rule, an option for cities with over 10,000 residents. The latter encouraged locally-determined government expansion and reorganization, but required public approval before such measures were initiated.

In order to fully grasp these capabilities, Angelenos chose a Board of Freeholders charged with developing a

(Opposite page and left) Government involvement in public health really did not occur locally until the founding of County Hospital in 1933. The Sisters of Charity founded L.A.'s first hospital, situated to the east of the plaza, and later moved their facilities to Boyle Heights (pictured opposite); they also founded St. Vincent's pictured on this page. *Courtesy The Postcard Collection of Jeanne Taylor Baird.*

home rule charter. The ensuing document identified elective positions (Board of Education, Tax Collector, etc.) and citizen commissions. It also gave Council fiscal power over the budget, tax rate and salary schedules. The voters approved home rule on October 20, 1888, and it went into effect the following year.

Charles Dwight Willard was a newspaper editor, chamber of commerce member, L.A. booster. Looking back on the increasingly large government apparatus and the process that created it, he commented:

> But the document was faulty in providing too many elective offices and in failing to definitely locate responsibility. There is no such percentage of foreign element as is to be found in most American cities, neither is there an illiterate or impoverished element. On the other hand, the exceptionally large portion of people of comfortable means who have the time that they might devote to the duties of citizenship, gives an opportunity such as few cities enjoy for a high quality of government.

Willard's assessment holds some truth (and much ignorance). Government and grassroots organizations have become as separate as two branches of a tree that was split almost to the trunk. Indeed, Los Angeles could have preserved its spirit of civic involvement. Fire fighting was purely a voluntary pursuit until the formation of a formal department in 1885. L.A.'s few steam engine companies benefited from the leadership skills of officers (president, treasurer, etc.) and the knowledge of technicians (hook-and-ladder operator) — all unpaid. Even after bureaucratization, Hose Companies 2 and 3 remained voluntary.

It is interesting to speculate on the career of George Bright, who in 1897 became L.A.'s first black firefighter. He arrived at his position having passed the necessary civil service exams, but extra letters of endorsement from his minister and church are said to have furthered his candidacy. Bright later commanded the city's first segregated fire crew. By 1909, the long-standing volunteer company (No. 2) also was black. Although segregation is objectionable, this historic volunteer/community connection probably enabled

African-Americans to enter firefighting in large numbers during the 1920s — and to reap the advantages of civil service — when other fields were beginning to shut them out.

Public employees notwithstanding, development and management of utilities tended to be awarded via franchise. A private company was engaged in 1865 to design L.A.'s first sewage system. (The firm unceremoniously tossed the muck into an uninhabited arroyo.) The city also awarded gas franchises during 1865 and 1866. Similarly, when the municipal fathers realized the necessity of an urban transportation system toward the end of the decade, they knighted an entrepreneur, Judge Robert M. Widney. (Many others subsequently speculated in transportation.)

Some of the more misguided contracts (water works and sewage, for example) forced the city to assume greater responsibilities. In other instances, greedy vendors brought their own obscurity. The Gas Company tampered with its prices to the point where a a boycott was threatened (1876). L.A. soon became one of the first U.S. cities to abandon gas lamps for electric lights. Outgoing Mayor James K. Toberman pulled the switch on New Year's Eve, 1882. This time, user fees underwrote the growing utility system.

Indeed, as Willard wrote, L.A.'s civic spirit was fading in the wake of growing government and demanding business interests. But while the writer's perspectives on community involvement remain insightful almost 100 years later, the rest of his statement is vintage 1900. The myth of a homogeneous, affluent population belongs to a Midwestern transplant (Willard came from Illinois,) blindly in love with his adopted city. Disparities between Angelenos grew.

The city government ordained senior civil servants — building, plumbing, engineering overseers — during the late 19th century, but they enforced codes differentially. A 1914 report to California Governor Hiram Johnson by the state's Commission on Immigration and Housing studied living conditions. The Macy Street district, among the "most cosmopolitan" in Los Angeles, contained large numbers of Chinese, Mexican and other newcomers. The boundaries stretched north

of First, from Main Street to the L.A River. Researchers examined 252 apartments within the Macy Street District; in 133 of them (53 percent), toilets were located in the kitchens. This layout undoubtedly was cost-effective, with plumbing being directed to only one part of the house. Furthermore:

> Cellars were found full of standing water and rubbish. In the rear of one restaurant there was a large, deep hole near the cellar door, filled with several feet of water, and, at the time of the investigation, a dead chicken and rotting garbage floating in the water polluted the air throughout the neighborhood...
>
> Little attention seems to be paid by the city officials to the insanitary plumbing conditions that were found. Five instances were noted where the sink was not connected with the

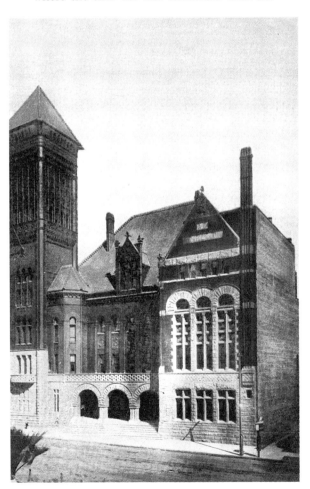

Prudent Beaudry (1818-1893) served as mayor during the mid-1870s and was a partner in the water works franchise that lasted through the turn of the century. *Courtesy The Security Pacific Collection, Los Angeles Public Library.*

Circa 1900 downtown features what Angelenos later called the "old" County Court House. The Portland tourist who originally bought this postcard seemed smitten by the city's outward charms. He playfully wrote to his wife: "This is where we go for divorces in Los Angeles. Your affectionate old man." *Courtesy The Postcard Collection of Jeanne Taylor Baird.*

sewer at all, and other cases where it was improperly connected. In one case the water from the sink drained into a tin bucket; in another, it drained into a Chinese basket, and the floor underneath was a slimy mass of wet, rotten refuse and vermin; a third sink emptied into a deep hole worn under the flooring. Leaking drain pipes were numerous in both sinks and toilets, making the floors wet and causing them to rot.

Shoddy, hasty construction caused additional problems: Of the 1,572 rooms investigated, kitchens included, 878 were found totally dark and windowless, lighted only by a dim candle…or gas jet which seemed to enhance the blackness. These rooms, partitioned off from the store in front, are often hidden away behind heavy bolted invisible doors.

The built-in mezzanine-like floors found in almost every house are also dark and even more stuffy than the rooms below. They are reached by steep, narrow, ladder-like stairs, or by ladders which hang on the wall when not in use. The ceilings are sometimes less than four feet high and usually only six feet. Dust, dirt, and filth accumulate here in the darkness and provide breeding places for diseases…As shown by the health records, the deaths from tuberculosis…

Enter, the Independent Sector

Citizen activists — originally from outside of the government sphere — sought fully-functioning municipal operations, better oversight and human services that would fill an obvious void. During the 1890s and early 1900s, the city's response to disease, poverty and other social maladies was reactive rather than proactive. The national nonprofit Associated Charities established a presence in Southern California by 1893. A precursor to the United Way, this organization's membership consisted of various local philanthropic institutions. Associated Charities also obtained funding from time to time from the city government, possibly in response to crises or to special projects. (A more contemporary feature of this organization, however, was its independent fundraising. Early and longtime President Herman W. Frank circulated 20,000 direct mail letters at Christmas time; he enjoyed a five percent response, often quoted as standard by professional fundraisers today. Associated Charities also ran a "tag day" for five years, with the inaugural event gleaning $15,000.)

Commenting on the group's philanthropic mission, Frank said: "It cannot be denied that the poor have the

COURT HOUSE - LOS ANGELES, CAL.

A number of Los Angeles communities had their own women's clubs — and club houses. While each organization determined its agenda, the broader movement fostered leadership skills and public involvement. Women and children's welfare issues frequently provided the motivation, however. *Courtesy Shades of L.A. Archives, The Los Angeles Public Library.*

same right to seek the sunshine of California as have the wealthy. Many emaciated men were to be seen on our streets, coming here often too late to obtain the results." But Frank's work was confounded by residency requirements: recipients of municipally-funded services had to have lived here for at least one year before obtaining benefits. One of Associated Charities' responses was a small-scale "repatri-ation" of erstwhile Midwesterners, or Easterners. Foreshadowing the treatment of Mexican immigrants during the Depression (see Chapter 2), the organization arranged discounted fares with the railroad companies, and sent indigents on return trips to the heartland. A more proactive approach guided the organization's work program. Here, local merchants donated materials for repair, recycling or repackaging by unemployed men,

who often lived at the Associated Charities' bunkhouses while engaged in these short-term stints.

The late 19th century saw the rise, too, of another important institution: women's clubs. They met the disenfranchised population to hone organizational and communication skills, enter public forums and articulate new (or understated) philanthropic visions. Second, because members' primary point of reference was the home, they tended to focus on women and children, whose special needs were largely ignored by government and other agencies. Activists made important such issues as child labor laws, working and living conditions (particularly for single women,) and suffrage. Another women's club emerged in response to the San Francisco quake of 1906 by efficiently collecting and distributing emergency aid it became the Assistance League of Los Angeles. Today's San Pedro chapter holds distinction: it raises funds by running the only volunteer-staffed U.S. post office in the country!

The two goals of political organizing and philanthropy merged in Caroline Severance (1820-1916). An activist who had worked with abolitionist William Lloyd Garrison and pioneering feminists Susan B. Anthony and Lucretia Mott, she founded the nation's first women's club in Boston. Severance came to L.A. at the age of 55, seeking the climate for her husband's health. She was the motivating force behind the Friday Morning Club, which called civic leaders on a variety of issues from health care to conditions for women in prison. Severance also had oratorical and leadership abilities that stirred her peers. Addressing club women on the Alameda Street crib district — the hub of local prostitution — she affirmed it "would disgrace any city... A scoundrel place where the horrid mills grind on."

Severance went on to organize the International Federation of Women's Clubs. The biennial convention met locally, in Venice, but drew delegates from as far away as China, Iceland and New Zealand. The nationally respected activist then became the honorary president of the state Suffrage Convention and the L.A. Political Equality League. When Californians gave women the right to vote in 1911, county officials honored Severance by allowing her to be the first to register. The ever-articulate 91 year old commented: "We have come to the dawn of a glorious tomorrow! A landmark in the most sacred crusade of the ages, when woman is heroically released from the bondage and superstition of the past and liberated from the political black list in our free country."

Women began to serve on government advisory boards at all levels — but mainly in the fields of health, education and welfare. Los Angeles voted its first city councilwoman, Estelle Lawton Lindsey (1915-17), and Friday Morning Club member Mary Gibson was appointed to the State Commission of Immigration and Housing. During her stay, Gibson effectively lobbied for home visits to immigrant women, furthering their English language instruction.

But if there is a pattern to the philanthropic movements described above, they dealt to a considerable extent with poor "singles:" those widowed, divorced, unmarried. A structurally-rigid, middle or working class family model was almost universally upheld at the turn of the century; those who lifestyles didn't quite conform — no matter what the cause — sometimes faced isolation. Broad-based, religiously-inspired groups like the Women's Christian Temperance Union and Young Men's/Women's Christian Association often provided housing for singles or female-headed families. Historian Gloria Ricci Lothrop aptly describes the atmosphere of the YWCA residences: "The facilities, run on a not-for-profit basis, catered to women under thirty in need of

temporary housing. Characteristic of these hostels was a unique blend of religious probity and general decorum…"

By contrast, missionary churches usually sought the participation of families, with programs appropriate for members of different ages (youth were a "target group). As mentioned in Chapter II, they also tended to be associated with established Protestant denominations (Nazarene, Methodist, etc.) and did outreach to individual nationality groups. Settlement houses (and, later, some of the Y's) followed similar patterns, though the Jane Addams/Hull House prototype — a Chicago import — was multicultural. Virtually all of these organizations strived for the eventual assimilation of their clients.

Newcomers here built organizations on the principle of self-help, within a cultural context. The issues of day-to-day subsistence (particularly during periods of unemployment), health coverage, burial costs and survivor benefits loomed large for working class families. Some approaches were very intimate. Both Mexican and Italian immigrants widely practiced godparenting to create deeper bonds between family members — for the well-being of children. Philanthropy appeared on an ad hoc basis, too. When the L.A. River flooded during the 1880s, leaving many community members without resources, Biddy Mason (see Chapter 1) opened an account at a local grocery for all to use. In a larger sense, the church had been the only African-American institution allowed to grow during the long period of slavery, and its religious, charitable and communal functions remained closely connected.

More typically, however, aide was divvied out by ethno-cultural — rather than purely religious — organizations. Associated Catholic Charities, which has grown into a large social service provider here, only started in 1918. Mexican-Americans, a major constituency, had long since operated their own mutualistas. The Spanish American Benevolent Society (1875) was the earliest of these, but many subsequently flourished.

The Hebrew Benevolent Society (1854) actually held distinction as the first nonprofit agency in L.A. Under the direction of Rosa Newmark, the Ladies Hebrew Benevolent Society joined the philanthropic

Chinese benevolent associations extended aid to members united by ties of kinship and/or birthplace. This one stood on Marchessault Street, the hub of Old Chinatown before Union Station was built. *Courtesy The Regional History Center, University of Southern California.*

community in 1870. Ten years later, the two organizations together were collecting and distributing $20,000. Different types of institutions existed simultaneously among Jewish Angelenos — synagogues, charities, political and cultural clubs, and later, landsmanschaften (societies of people from the same European town or region). In many cases, however, these diverse groups maintained parallel structures. The standard model consisted of: a male-dominated decisionmaking and fundraising arm (similar to the Hebrew Benevolent Society;) a women's auxiliary (The Ladies Hebrew Benevolent Society;) and, as they grew more sophisticated, an operational or direct benefits unit headed by paid professionals, often social workers (Jewish Family Services). Youth clubs or divisions were frequently attached to the network, too.

Chinese aid also was elaborately organized, along traditional family and community lines. At the top of the structure were the district societies, consisting of

Los Angeles High School, Southern California's first, was constructed at a cost of $25,000 in 1873. It is pictured at its original Temple and Fort Street site. The school subsequently relocated to Olympic Boulevard and Rimpau. *Courtesy The Postcard Collection of Jeanne Taylor Baird.*

individuals from the same region of China. Family associations engaged the local emigre community to a great extent, with the Wong and Louie societies being among the largest and most influential. Multifamily groupings also sprung up, arising from the need of the smaller clans to unite and influence local community affairs. These societies proved versatile, as Kit Fong Tom wrote: "In times of emergency and distress, the members can go to their family association for help. They may get a loan directly or indirectly from it. In case of unemployment, the Kung Saw can give a recommendation to its members and sometimes provide them with room and board." Bachelors even received permission to sleep in some of the local headquarters.

Whereas mutual aid societies dealt with a variety of basic needs, other organizations focused on particular problems — or promoted new philosophies and approaches. Many services at the time were crisis-oriented. By contrast, the German community took a proactive stance; instead of supporting hospitals, they advocated physical fitness and built gymnasiums. The

local fellowship of "Turners" resulted from an 1871 merger of the Teutonia-Concordia (founded here during the late 1850s) and the Turnverein Germania. Other organizations grew well beyond their ethnic confines. What started in 1912 as the Jewish Consumptive Relief Association became City of Hope, which claims thousands of donors nationwide and has long since added research to its health care functions.

It can be said that a dearth of municipal services begged for nonprofit involvement. The state government, however, was more responsive than the city and even enabled grassroots organizations to pursue their missions. By the turn of the century, California had developed a dependent children's subsidy. Every institution which cared for an abandoned or orphaned youth under the age of 14 received $100 from the state. Few bureaucratic strings were attached; the state neither required official investigations nor established standard admissions policies. Institutions only had to be in existence for one year and serve 20 children. Subsidies from the California treasury totaled $410,000 in 1901.

Higher learning in Los Angeles also gained greatly from state intervention. The ultimate goal was to cultivate a talented workforce, first nurturing the capabilities of school children and, later, providing a college education to young people who otherwise might not afford it. UCLA's history reflects a rapidly-evolving commitment to this mission. Its earliest incarnation, dating to 1882, was as the State Normal School in Los Angeles. Like most institutions of this type, it offered a two-year curriculum designed to enrich California's supply of professionally-trained teachers. The Normal School entered into the University of California system becoming its "Southern Branch" on May 23, 1919. Students defied local college loyalty, instead reveling in their new affiliation with Berkeley, singing its songs and flaunting its traditions. Southern Branch President Ernest Carroll Moore warned them, "You must do twenty-five percent better than Berkeley to be recognized at all."

In 1923, the state authorized teachers' colleges to award four-year education degrees. The Southern Branch granted B.A.'s to 100 women and 24 men in June, 1925. But a true mark of recognition came when the school moved from Vermont Avenue to the barley-covered fields of Westwood during the late 1920s. Today, UCLA boasts 81 academic departments, 30 interdepartmental programs, and almost 300,000 living alumni. Distinguished faculty and advanced research have earned the university a national reputation, indeed quite separate from Berkeley's.

An interesting footnote to the story of higher education in Los Angeles: junior or community colleges are often thought to be a post-World War II invention, satisfying the immediate learning needs (plus limited time and budgets) of returning veterans under the federal G.I. bill. L.A. City College emerged during 1929, however, occupying the campus vacated by UCLA. The school remains at this Hollywood-area site.

What is now the California State University at Los Angeles was created in the late 1940s to fill the burgeoning demand for educators, as a result of the Baby Boom. During the next decade, and following the organizational path orginally taken by UCLA, the "San Fernando Valley Campus of the Los Angeles State College of Applied Arts and Sciences" came to occupy a Northridge site. The new campus separated from its parent in 1958, becoming San Fernando Valley State College, and later, the California State University at Northridge. Both Cal State institutions subsequently have assumed a variety of functions.

Visions of an Activist Local Government
In addition to fostering new social and educational services, philanthropic leaders strived for a more proactive, professionally-run local government. The Progressive spirit of the late 1890s and early 1900s slowly managed to secure a foothold in L.A.'s influence-trodden City Hall. For one thing, "corporate responsibility" was

(Above and bottom left) In its slightly less than 50 years (1881-1929), UCLA evolved from a two-year "normal school" for teacher training, to a four-year institution of higher learning. Courtesy The Postcard Collection of Jeanne Taylor Baird.

anathema. When the franchise for municipal water management expanded in 1898, officials discovered that not all infrastructural improvements (mandated by contract) had been implemented. The city regained control over its most precious natural resource only after four years of haggling — and a reacquisition cost of $2 million. Most other utility and transportation systems likewise were being installed and overseen by private contractors. Walter Francis Xavier Parker, the Southern Pacific Railroad's agent, allegedly controlled both political parties, and every major government within the state.

Much can be said about the Progressive movement. Its leaders could move the public as readily as industrial titans could influence elected officials. They also typically possessed education, boundless personal energy, and forceful, passionate natures that had been sensitized to some form of injustice — whether social, economic or environmental. Furthermore, the Progressives represented a political compromise position: a middle road between unregulated corporate socialism and all of the radical working class "isms" then being imported from Europe and fueled by substandard urban conditions.

The Progressives' national standard bearer was the frenetic patrician President Theodore Roosevelt who used the White House as his "bully pulpit." John Randolph Haynes (1853-1937) released the Progressive spirit locally. The Ivy League-trained physician accrued sufficient wealth so that he could retire from medicine early to work— and underwrite— some of his most dearly-held political causes. His legacy is the John and Dora Haynes Foundation, which still distributes grants today. (Dora Haynes was a suffragette; she helped to

organize the Los Angeles chapter of the League of Women Voters in 1920.)

Haynes' earliest endeavors revolved around direct legislation, the movement to implement and safeguard a publicly-inspired, proactive government. After several tries, he and his allies successfully rallied in 1903 for three charter amendments: the initiative, encouraging grassroots legislation through the balloting process; the referendum, allowing City Council to place issues to the public vote; and the recall, granting citizens the right to remove elected public officials from office. (Recall was tested initially, and in 1904 led to the downfall of one councilmember. Mayor Arthur C. Harper, known for both corruption and carousing, resigned in 1909, just before he could be publicly booted.)

Haynes' tactics were as invigorating as his ideas. Though crusading early in the century, his organizing techniques could be applied without modification today. Haynes would petition government commissions, often secure appointment himself, and work with a variety of related grassroots groups (some of which he founded) to implement or advance progressive goals. He also understood that, if unguarded, his direct legislative measures could easily be reversed. When the initiative came under scrutiny before the California Supreme Court in the Phaler case, Haynes paid two lawyers from his own pocket to successfully defend the concept. He also acted as a lobbyist — and engaged professionals, too — so that direct legislation might be enacted statewide. His Los Angeles-based innovations were approved by both the California legislature and the electorate in 1911.

Haynes deemed political education, research and information dissemination essential for public involvement. He once brought the nationally respected reformer Lincoln Steffans to Los Angeles, and would periodically wine and dine potential supporters who attended what now might be called "issues forums." In a move that presaged Ralph Nader by about 60 years, Haynes began to suspect that local motor cars were unsafe. He sent a survey about accident and

mortality rates to 70 mayors around the country and, indeed, discovered that L.A.'s soared above the rest. The problem could be stopped through the installation of front fenders that scooped and protectively cradled would-be victims. Haynes advanced his campaign by mobilizing a variety of resources. A corporation publicly tested the fender, to some fanfare. Haynes obtained support from the Voters League for a massive petition drive and, himself, hosted a dinner to "educate" City Councilmembers. An ordinance passed about a year later, in 1906, requiring fenders on all L.A. streetcars.

Another cause dear to Haynes was public ownership of utilities. As mentioned earlier, private mismanagement of water made this an increasingly popular cause. Yet, the outcomes — a far greater public domain than anyone ever imagined — rested on some traditional political machinations that ran counter to community spirit.

Everyone thinks of William Mulholland (1855-1835) as the visionary behind L.A.'s water conquest. Indeed, the Irish immigrant may have had more hands-on knowledge than any contemporary. He chose L.A. as his permanent home in 1878, settling into a job as deputy zanjero for the privately-owned Los Angeles City Water Company. Mulholland's early approach to resource management was organic, locally-tailored, and derived from his intimate relationship with the environment. Years later, he wrote:

"The country had the same attraction for me that it had for the Indians who originally chose this spot as their place to live. The Los Angeles River was a beautiful, limpid stream with willows on its banks...It was so attractive to me that it at once became something about which my whole of live was woven, I loved it so much."

In response to a decreasing water supply tapped by a spiraling population, Mulholland advocated groundwater conservation and forestry. His environmental ethic would soon change; primary influences included a period of severe drought, and Fred Eaton.

Eaton was Superintendent of the privately-operated L.A. City Water Works. In 1888, he drafted the municipality's first sewage system master plan, expanding the infrastructure from 20 to 160 miles of pipelines. Eaton and Mulholland became colleagues. When the former resigned from the utility company to enter politics (he served as L.A.'s mayor from 1898-1900), Mulholland inherited his position. The friendship grew. Eaton suggested that his protege follow a different water course — the Owens River, 250 miles away. Los Angeles could not survive on its own, according to Eaton. Some sources were closer, he argued, but given the difference of elevation between the mountainous region and low-lying L.A., the Owens River could be tapped relatively easily through gravity.

Mulholland ascended to superintendent of the newly-created city Water Department; his first act, in 1904, was to publicly push for an enlarged supply. Mulholland already knew where to look, but a potentially major intergovernmental conflict existed. The federal Reclamation Service, recently charged by Theodore Roosevelt with its own conservation mandate, had been developing plans for effective utilization of Northern California resources. A native Angeleno and professional engineer, Joseph Lippincott, had been chosen to head the effort. As part of the hiring agreement, however, the previously well-paid consultant was allowed to maintain his private practice.

Lippincott served as tour guide for Eaton and Mulholland on their early water-prospecting trips through the Owens Valley. When the federal agent needed to make a decision between two competing power-license applications, he sought the advice of a paid consultant: an old friend from L.A. and fellow engineer, Fred Eaton. Three days later, the City of Los Angeles entered into a what is now called a "sole-source contract" to assess its water options. No bidding process was necessary, though, as the project had Lippincott's

name on it. Soon, Eaton purchased a large tract of land from the same rancher in whose favor he had decided as the Reclamation Service's consultant. The property contained a site ideally suited for a reservoir. Eaton wired to Mulholland, "the deal is made."

But L.A.'s water chief wanted insurance against future competing projects. Since all of this maneuvering had transpired outside of public processes, Mulholland guarded the secrecy. He organized a delegation of potential investors to the Owens Valley, with Mayor Owen McAleer and two water commissions accompanying them. William Mulholland secured his insurance policy.

The irony about all of these actions is that they were exacerbated by hasty decisions. Unaware of the Reclamation Service's double-dealing and on the advice of his friend and chief forester Gifford Pinchot, Theodore Roosevelt quickly approved the project. Mulholland later abandoned Eaton's property for another reservoir site, ostensibly because he felt the former was overpriced. The project ultimately cost the city a lot more. Possibly Roosevelt, and almost certainly Mulholland, realized their mistakes. Both were powerful enough that had they relented, different courses — water and otherwise — might have evolved.

City residents in 1907 voted a $23 million bond to finance the Owens Valley project. The *Los Angeles Times*, under the ever-vocal Harrison Gray Otis, led the campaign. (It was discovered that Otis and other leading citizens benefited from land deals associated with the project's terminus, in the San Fernando Valley.) A 1909 charter amendment formally authorized the board of public works to oversee the design and construction of 233-mile aqueduct. Promoting the dual rewards of such a massive undertaking, Ezra Frederick Scattergood became to hydroelectricity what Mulholland was to water. A charter amendment in

1911 united them by creating a Department of Public Service, with two bureaus: Water Works and Supplies and Power and Light. William Mulholland commandeered a crew of 5,000 men, and in 1913, completed the first phase of what was to be a permanent quest for water resources. During the inaugural ceremony on November 5, he proclaimed his famous words, "There it is. Take it."

Meanwhile, Scattergood was charged with building hydroelectric facilities along the aqueduct. San Francisquito Power Plant No. 1 emerged from construction in 1917. (Another irony: this historic hydroelectric facility was located below the site of Mulholland's Waterloo. The engineer's newly enlarged Saint Francis Dam burst in 1928, hours after he inspected it. The flood initially released 200-foot waves and took over 400 lives before receding into the Pacific near Ventura.)

Subsequent land grabs in the Eastern Sierra — all for the sake of water — led to incidents of sabotage and violence that need not be recounted here. At one point, Owens Valley residents reactivated an old water pump, forcing the fluid to revert its rightful locale. But what started as a stream has been transformed into a virtual water and power empire. Even discounting the massive Colorado River Aqueduct and Hoover Dam, the local traveler who enjoys long, weekend car rides can pass facilities without connecting them to the City of Los Angeles. The physical and environmental distances simply seem too great. Just over the Orange County border, the road to the Leisure World retirement community displays L.A. utility towers. This complex is called the Haynes Generating Station, giving John Randolph tribute in a scheme probably light years beyond his imagination. The Castaic Hydroelectric

Power Project — so close to the woodland splendor of Mt. Pinos — similarly surprises the road-happy Angeleno. All told, the City of Los Angeles claims 108 reservoirs and tanks; 7,030 miles of distribution main; 85 pump stations. Water storage capacity spans 365,000 acre feet. The old Owens Valley pipeline now extends an additional 100 miles to Mono Lake, making it the longest municipal aqueduct in the world.

The advanced engineering of the teens and twenties in a sense heightened contrasts between the old and the new. Plague struck Los Angeles in 1924. Otherwise known as the Black Death, this reviled rodent- and flea-borne disease killed an estimated quarter of the population during the 14th century. (Fortunately, here it was confined to approximately 40.) The latter-day epidemic arrived in the San Francisco port when infected rats descended from Asian trade ships, spreading the disease to their American cousins and to ground squirrels. San Francisco sustained the plague for four years in the early 1900s and Oakland, briefly, in 1919. Robert G. Cleland wrote of the epidemic's L.A. origins, in the Macy Street district, which he described as "a populous Mexican-American community…Clara Street bustled with activity. Its greatest boast, and the center of its social life, was the boarding house at 742, run by Guadalupe and Lucena Samarano."

The plague captured this close-knit community chain-fashion, first killing a man thought to be ridden by venereal disease. His daughter became ill, and was nursed by Lucena Samarano, then six months pregnant. Within about a month, both Samaranos had fallen. Guadalupe was already smitten at Lucena's funeral, exposing the couple's many friends to the epidemic. The Mexican-American community on both sides of the border, the Macy Street district (city) and Belvedere (county) suffered disparate and unpredictable symptoms. Dr. Emil Bogen, resident physician of the Los Angeles General Hospital, conducted a site visit, but scientific diagnosis ultimately came from a Dr. Hammock, who recognized the plague from his work in the Philippines. Analyzing a sputum-stained slide, he exclaimed: "Beautiful, but damned."

The city and county maintained a tight quarantine; each unit of government also contributed $25,000 for pest control and extermination. Of the almost 125,000 animals examined, 157 rats and five squirrels contained the bacterial infection. Plague-bearing rodents were found as far away as Beverly Hills; one even carried the strain to the Harbor area — in the days before freeways facilitated travel.

Disease more frequently attacked those with limited access to care. During the mid-1920s, the health department reported that one-sixth of all tuberculosis-related cases and one-fourth of the resulting deaths occurred in L.A.'s Mexican-American community. Children proved most vulnerable. Infant mortality statistics revealed that two to eight times more Mexican and Mexican-American babies died than Euroamerican newborns. Although it took a disportionate toll on some communities, disease ultimately knew no boundaries. In 1919, the state permitted county governments to take charge of health care — and required such responsibility by 1935. Somewhere between those dates, the transference of services occurred here.

Other municipal bureaus were assuming their current forms, too. The City's Charter amendment of 1925 stated virtually the same government we have today. Boards of commissioners varied radically before 1925, ranging in size from three to 51 members. The five-person standard entered under the Charter of 1925, and it has fairly much persisted. Bidding (and bonding) procedures for city contracts were formally outlined, as well.

Departments have been added, consolidated or split since 1925, but the structural nucleus remains. Some government bureaus were created by ordinance, and City Council had (and has) the authority to modify those with relative ease; conversely, departments established via charter are subject to public vote before they can undergo change. In 1936, the City counted some 77,000 ordinances. A cleaning process began that year: laws were sorted, organized by subject matter, rewritten for clarity and brevity, and compiled into the Los Angeles Municipal Code (a.k.a. Ordinance 77,000). Duplicative or invalid statutes, as well as those which

(Opposite page) Thousands celebrate the opening of the 233-mile aqueduct at its San Fernando Valley terminus, November 5, 1913. Los Angeles then had a population well over 310,000, but the water system could satisfy a much larger metropolis. *Courtesy The City of Los Angeles, Department of Water and Power.*

conflicted with other local and state laws, were tossed. Mayor Fletcher Bowron in 1941 implemented a numbering system for city ordinances and commission actions. The Los Angeles Administrative Code (Ordinance 138,000) of 1969 consolidated administrative and regulatory statutes.

Otherwise, Los Angeles during the immediate pre- and post-World War II years was moved by larger, external forces. The Depression galvanized left-leaning political sectors — socialists, communists, self-help activists and veterans of Upton Sinclair's End Poverty in California (EPIC) campaign — seeking a public or collective response to a dysfunctional economy. Together, their organizers inspired "homeguards" to fight evictions; Hoovervilles sprung up on the dry bed of the L.A. River. The New Deal of President Franklin D. Roosevelt, a more activist government than had been known before, subsequently replaced Herbert Hoover's pleas for private philanthropic aid. Public works projects, including housing complexes, were brought onto the national agenda. Fortified with support from Washington, the City Housing Authority

began the Ramona Gardens project in 1939. The Maravilla and Hacienda Heights followed.

Another product of the New Deal, the federal Wagner Act (1937) boosted labor unionism here and throughout the country. One-half million Americans had been involved in strikes between September, 1936 and May, 1937; the largest number of arrests, well over 300, occurred locally at the Douglas aircraft plant. Yet, the Wagner Act's effects were soon apparent. As World War II engaged young men, the whirring industrial machine embraced a previously-untapped workforce: African-Americans and women availed themselves of new opportunities and realized higher standards of living through union wages.

Personnel shifts took different forms, depending on the economic sector. Japanese-Americans had been leaders in local agriculture, both supervising cultivation and literally tending many parcels of Los Angeles farmland. When they were forced into internment, the bracero program, a cross-border system of contracting for labor, replaced them with Mexican workers.

The war indeed became a storm front where old prejudices and new insights collided. Children of immigrants and small town, fifth-generation Americans often for the first-time shared makeshift living quarters, friendship, ignorance — all in the atmosphere of combat. An Aryan bookstore had opened sometime during the 1930s, vending anti-Semitic venom from a downtown storefront.

Prejudice was put on trial, too. Following the death of a local Mexican-American boy, police literally descended upon his community, took 300 suspects and arrested 20-some. These "Sleepy Lagoon" murder defendants were not informed of their rights, nor was there time to change their clothes and present themselves well for court. Lawyer, historian, and later *Nation* editor Carey McWilliams headed the successful defense team, which gathered allies well beyond the Mexican-American community.

The Sleepy Lagoon case led to another incident, however. Responding to the trial with xenophobia, servicemen stationed here attacked "zoot suiters," primarily Mexican-American teens who wore the garb

While great strides occurred in labor during the late 1930s, many locals barred African-Americans. The police officer beating the worker in the background represents the "red squads" formed to squelch various union and left-leaning organizations. *Courtesy The Social and Public Art Resource Center (SPARC), and taken from the Great Wall of Los Angeles (copright, 1976-1983).*

of a 1940s youth culture: oversized jackets, pleated, ballooning pants tapered at the cuffs; hair slicked back and crowned with flat brimmed-hats. Individual incidents peaked in a rampage during June, 1943; sailors stationed near Chavez Ravine positioned themselves as vigilantes, joyriding around the the city and randomly beating and stripping the youth. Police either stood by — or harassed the teens.

Angelenos of all races and ethnicities nevertheless embraced patriotic duty during World War II. Some experienced segregation in the armed forces; still, American soldiers, sailors and pilots generally received the "hero's welcome" by the embattled peoples they freed. Reminded of their potential sacrifice on a daily basis, uniformed Angelenos contrasted overseas triumphs with the racism they suffered in the U.S. The most highly decorated unit during World War II was the segregated 442nd Regimental Combat Team. Called upon for a rescue mission, 800 of these Japanese-Americans died saving 211 of their countrymen. Members of the 442nd, also were among the first to liberate Dachau death camp in Germany.

World War II left L.A. a radically changed metropolis. Many veterans from across the country gained exposure to Los Angeles through their military service; they liked what they saw and relocated here. Although the city's boundaries had been more or less set since the early 1930s, the empty spaces now filled rapidly. An ensuing demand for municipal services — articulated by burgeoning, young, relatively homogeneous populations throughout Southern California — led to the Lakewood Plan (1954). Under its tenets, newly incorporated towns did not need to invent full-blown bureaucracies or merge with existing cities; instead, the upstarts could contract with the county for police, fire and other services. Communities used the

Lakewood Plan to meet needs while maintaining autonomy.

At about the same time, Angelenos moved farther and farther away from the central city, taking advantage of new infrastructures, modern facilities and better services. The urban core was left to those who could not access such options. Starting with President Lyndon B. Johnson's "Great Society" in the mid-1960s, federal programs addressed disparities caused by: urban decay; racial prejudice that limited opportunities for personal advancement; and, differential state and municipal expenditures in the areas of health, education and welfare. Intergovernmental revenues subsequently helped Los Angeles to deal with these issues.

Federal and state dollars also allowed the region to build its trademark freeway network during the 1950s and 1960s, and L.A. officials learned the value of regional systems — and cooperation. The latter part of the century has seen the growth of such entities as the Southern California Association of Governments, the South Coast Air Quality Management District, and the Metropolitan Transportation Authority. Yet, perhaps residents interpreted regionalization as an urban/suburban existence way beyond their personal control.

In the wake of the civil unrest, talk of neighborhoods has resumed. Geographic identity — as expressed through homeowners' associations, block clubs, and ad hoc committees formed to oppose development — reflects self-interest just as much as community pride. Thus, we are left to ponder the same question raised at the beginning of the chapter: can this latest bout with charter reform inspire (or reinstate after a very long hiatus) a broader, more sustainable civic activism? Or is our collective attention span now captured by single-issue politics and single-event responses?

CHAP

OMES ENTERPRISING

TER 4

chapter

Introduction

Light, the artist's ingredient, dances in many directions at the Sante Fe Arts Colony. Communal windows outside of the individual units and facing the street appear to have been scrubbed for Open Studio on this April day. Still, there are idiosyncrasies within the fenestration, as befits an artist's abode. Years of exposure to the sun and to the dust emanating from the truck route below have etched and stained the glass slightly, but permanently; it can never be truly clean. Gray, transparent sunshield adheres stubbornly to one of the multipane windows, a reminder of the building's industrial days.

Such features are external; inside, the mood brightens mightily. A central skylight probably was the circa 1988 contribution of Community Redevelopment Agency when it converted the factory to its present use. Sloped and, therefore, self-cleaning (rain permitting), this overhead window transmits an uninterrupted golden stream from above.

2401 S. Santa Fe Street is largely unnoticed in a heavily industrial district along the past and future Alameda transportation corridor. The symmetrical, two-story rectangular edifice— made of clay-brown bricks and sealed tightly with a flat roof — looks solid enough to have withstood the three major earthquakes that struck since its 1916 construction as the C.B. Van Vorst Furniture Company. To the north (2349 S. Santa Fe) and south (2415-2421 S. Santa Fe), respectively, the manufacturer operated a display/storage room and a mill; 2401 anchored this small complex. Technically within L.A. borders, today's colony skirts the city of Vernon, where the population fluctuates from 55,000 during the working hours to 150 at night.

Los Angeles has never shown a tolerance for old buildings. Survivors like this one on the fringes of downtown are rather like the artists who inhabit them: they don't always produce, for that would stunt their creative potential. Rather, they evolve. Artists and enduring industrial structures adapt to — and indeed flourish under — conditions of change. And as partners, they interact, borrowing from and displaying each other's assets, and contributing to a unique urban environment.

Some of the artists at Santa Fe show work that is grand in scale, and, therefore, cumbersome to move. A vintage freight elevator — the size of a small bedroom — now draws on its industrial capacity for creative purposes. The lift bears antique diamond gates that so fascinated me as a child, and continue to delight me today. Even the mechanics are visual: cable rolls round and round on a huge bobbin, propelling the elevator's movement. The old ventilation system attracts attention, too. Small grates open from the some of the individual units to the sky. Around them whirl corrugated steel knobs, shaped like the ridged, buttercream rosettes on top of birthday cakes.

A courtyard in the back provides the central thoroughfare for Open Studio. Reaching this area from the main building, visitors notice two other structures: artists' quarters both. These elongated edificies may have been furniture finishing plants; one probably

served as a 20-car garage, during a 1950s incarnation. Its redwood siding and narrow, one-story construction, though, recall a mews.

The courtyard is "urban rustique" in style. A vendor, appropriately t-shirted for this event, dispenses links, lemonade, and potato salad — American country fare, scratch the diet. Resin chairs around tables and lined alongside the main building allow guests to enjoy the food and the bustling, makeshift "street." Bougainvillaea cling to a trellis at the front of what we believe to have been the garage, adding considerable charm. Other permanent features include tall, wooden crocks brimming with succulents, geraniums. Salvia are resident, too, and the concrete pavement occasionally breaks for small, square dirt plots. Trees were planted here some time back; ever resourceful, the artists have filled the space between the trees and the concrete with cacti. Birds of paradise nod their heads in the gentle breeze, thankful for their home and approving the scene.

I follow the silver threads from the courtyard to the back of the property. These are tracks, remnants of a transportation system that saw hundreds of trains and street cars passing daily. The historic volume of traffic makes it difficult to pinpoint the exact usage and route; most likely the tracks were spurs, conveying freight — in this case, furniture — for shipment aboard the trains. Today, the silver threads provide another interesting element to the Santa Fe Arts Colony.

If the artists enliven this old, manufacturing plant, the structure and its location strengthen their urbanist commitment to seeing the beauty in industrial products and processes. About five years ago, my close friend and conduit to 2401 S. South Santa Fe, Laurel Paley, rescued somewhat less-than-sprightly lime and grapefruit shells from near our garbage disposal, where they were headed as drain fresheners. "These are beautiful," she exclaimed, "may I have them?"

A late 20th-century successor to Chaim Soutine, Paley digitized them and miraculously infused color into each differently eroding nook of pulp and rind. The results were splendid, especially considering that most of us at that time were using computers for word processing. Technology notwithstanding, Paley's primary medium is paint. Today, she exhibits a floral burst in browns and roses — executed on ticking, the fabric that covers pillows. The thin, uniform, navy and white stripes discreetly segment her painting, adding character without detering from the carefully laid colors and brush strokes.

Next, I enter the studio of Terri Lenahan, one of the few original tenants remaining from the colony's beginnings in 1988 or 1989. Lenahan has imparted three-dimensional life to dress patterns — without relying on mannequins. Cut-out clothing designs are laquered so that they stand firm and full, and do not

collapse into their tissue paper textures; minimalist skeletons derive from wire. Although connected to a block on the floor, these clothed figures, sans body parts, truly seem suspended in air. Lenahan has framed some Barbie-sized versions, too. Pins and threads extend their forms, and visitors are free to inspect the lacing with a magnifying glass. Invited guests also can have unique views of Lenahan's dinner parties: a row of wooden theatre benches lines the eating area. Lenahan initially salvaged these from an old auditorium for use in her master's show; she estimates that they to date to the 1920s or 1930s.

Paley and her peels, Lenahan and her theatre seats, exemplify the artist's talent for urban recycling. Creative souls have moved to abandoned neighborhoods where no one else would settle, brought their patrons and design sensibilities, and made generally glum industrial quarters inviting. At the opposite end of downtown, 650 S. Avenue 21, is the Brewery Arts Complex. A group of 14 buildings constructed from 1904-1928 (including the old Pabst plant) offers a different flavor than Sante Fe, but performs the same community service. And there is Downtown Arts Development Association (DADA), an organization "founded to support and promote artists and businesses" here.

Benefits run two ways. Arts associations have succeeded in applying the concept of cooperative marketing, gaining an audience/clientele by uniting practitioners for the common good. Indeed, downtown more and more frequently is called the "loft district," referring to an economical arrangement where combined studio and living quarters are situated above factory floors.

It also helps that artists fit into the late 20th-century individual-entrepreneur mold. Fifteen years ago, few understood why anyone would voluntarily remain outside the corporate sphere. "What is another word for consultant?" the joke went. Answer: "Unemployed." Imagine my shock, several months ago, to hear an ad on

(Above) Noted sculptress Anna Mahler completed the 15-foot "Tower of Masks" in 1961 as a commissioned work for UCLA. The daughter of Austrian composer Gustav Mahler, she represented the emigre community of renowned artists, musicians, and writers who during the 1930s chose Los Angeles as a refuge from Nazi-occupied countries. Lion Feuchtwanger, Thomas Mann, Arnold Schoenberg, Bruno Walter, and many others came to call this city home. *Courtesy UCLA University Archives.*

the radio for a culturally-oriented singles groups. Among other professionals, one could meet doctors, lawyers, consultants and artists!

According to a 1992 report commissioned by the California Arts Council, some 59,528 artists call the L.A. metropolitan area home. Generalizations about their death from hunger are greatly exaggerated. Individual artists earned an average of $38,400 here during 1992, exceeding the $36,869 median household income in Los Angeles County at the time. The figures varied across disciplines, however; those engaged by Hollywood or otherwise unionized sectors showed the greatest incomes. Musician/composers averaged $47,200; actors/directors, $36,700; authors/writers, $33,900; visual artists, $31,700; and, dancers, $24,200. (There also is a direct correlation between income and gender: only about 25 percent of the musicians/composers — but 85 percent of the dancers — were women.)

In an era when social contributions are measured in monetary rather than creative terms, collective earnings of between $3 and $4 billion add to the local tax base. Artists were employers, too. The 1992 figures show that some 35 percent had hired or contracted with other individuals to assist them in their art-related activities. Each artist who entered into such a relationship spent an average of $8,211 for these services. Finally, two separate surveys tallied anywhere from 536-1,000 arts organizations in the metropolitan area. It can be assumed that their workforces reached beyond purely creative occupations, to include a variety of administrative and support staff.

But artists probably have earned respect because from a 1990s business viewpoint, they seem to be doing all of the right things. They direct their own careers, and do not rely on interpreters to issue economic prognoses, or pink slips. Artists also have built a diversified economic base for themselves: only 53 percent of their income owes to creative endeavors; they have honed additional skills, ventured into new markets. Finally, as a professional group, they address quality of life. Twenty-four percent may be considered home-based business owners, narrowing the lamentable (and down-right inconvenient) space between residence and work.

In sum, artists shine as sole proprietors in this post-industrial age, nevertheless paying homage to — and keeping alive — an older industrial heritage.

While the daily lives of Chumash and Tongva were closely governed by the authority of their leaders and of spiritual practices, relationships with the outside world proved dynamic. Connections between villages could be cemented and severed with relative ease. The centrality of commerce to Native American life here — and its fluidity — demanded common tender; strings of olivella shell beads served as the medium. Value was derived from the length of each strand, as well as the quality of the individual beads. Knotted cords marked trade transactions. One of the oldest shell-bead exchange networks at one time linked all the Cahuilla, Serrano, Luiseno and Gabrielino lineages from San Gorgonio Pass to the Pacific Ocean.

The Spanish way was much different. As illustrated in Chapter III, daily life could be anarchical, yet the economy was planned. Each sector — mines, missions and pueblos — contributed to the whole. Land grants were not permanent, but rather loans to be repaid from the yields of newly-cultivated fields. Otherwise, barter reigned and internal currency was scarce. Spain issued three large grants outside of the pueblo in 1784, with a purpose: cattle raising. Little changed, at least from a commercial perspective, under Mexican government. It is no wonder, then, that when liberated to explore its trade potential for the first time in the 1850s, Los Angeles' "company" was kept with cattle.

Actually, opportunity had beckoned earlier. Trade with outsiders was forbidden, yet some commerce began during the early 19th century. Eastern ships arrived in search of relatively durable, nonperishable cattle products, specifically hides and tallow. The former became known throughout the hemisphere as the "California bank note." Hides substituted for currency and were used to purchase even the smallest commodities: a few yards of cloth, a pound of sugar, a box of raisins.

Still, it was the Gold Rush that catapulted Los Angeles' first commercial industry. Northern California's population surged. Precious metal lured prospectors, but a whole regional economy spun off the discovery at Sutter's Mill. And Statehood brought more Easterners to California. These settlers needed sustenance — and craved beef. Combined with the recent political changes, the Gold Rush called Los Angeles to a new trade realm.

is all owing to the cold weather that the stock is reduced in flesh — two partidos ahead of us Forsters and Lugos both lost cattle between here and San Buenaventura cattle.

Grass destroyed above San Luis Obispo by frost and cold — 3,500 head 'have gone up'....

Raids by Native Americans, problems with the vaqueros, cattle diseases and roadway rustling all made this a risky undertaking. Some of the wealthier Angelenos leased Northern grazing rights so that their herds might be fattened immediately before sale and, therefore, fetch a premium. While the boom lasted, these efforts provided immense compensation. The cost of a drive alone might run up to $4 per head, insignificant compared to the low-end ticket of $50.

Gracing the Compton Post Office, this 1936 mural romantically captures the old ranch lifestyle. Artist James Redmond died during World War II combat. *Photo copyright* ©*Robin J. Dunitz.*

The movement of cattle from south to north began during late winter; herds averaged 700 to 1,000. Range grass, freshly cultivated by the seasonal rains, would provide the animals nourishment along the month-long trip. Yet, the cattle drives were fraught with obstacles. A vaquero wrote from Santa Barbara:

We arrived here last evening with our number of cattle and horses complete but can't say much for their good condition....While encamped on the beach at Buenaventura it rained verry hard and the wind blew as hard as ever I saw it, the cattle consequently on the stir all night but we have not had a Stampeed since we left Los Angeles. It

The cattle boom coincided with — and introduced — changes in the local economy. As mentioned earlier, the newly-inaugurated Land Commission reviewed property holdings awarded during the Spanish and Mexican periods. The ensuing transfers mainly affected Californio families. Furthermore, the assessed value of grazing lands had been cut in half (from 50 cents to 25 cents an acre) during the early 1850s. At around the same time, the state handed down the Trespass Act, which imposed expensive fencing requirements on farmers. All of the factors noted above — plus certain economies of scale — had the effect of consolidating wealth. By 1858 half of the county's valuation, as measured by taxes, was concentrated in the hands of fewer than a dozen men. The Eastern journalist Charles Nordhoff looked back on the lifestyle that emerged:

The Yankee demand for beef made the cattle owners suddenly rich, and they made haste to spend what they so easily got. Saddles trimmed with solid silver, spurs of gold, bridles with silver chains, were among the fancies of the men; and a lady in Santa Barbara amused me by describing the old adobe houses, with earthen floors covered with costly rugs; four-post bedsteads with the costliest lace curtains; and these looped up with lace again; and the senoras and senoritas dragging trains of massive silk and satin over the earthen floor. It must have been an odd mixture of squalor and splendor.

The cattle boom was short-lived. The market became glutted by the mid-late 1850s, with fierce competition from Midwestern and Southwestern states. A parochial economic outlook, evoked by the long years in isolation, had been apparent: many of local cattle owners clung to the lean, long-horned stock introduced

Between duties, vaqueros rest at the then-crumbling San Fernando Mission. *Courtesy, Department of Special Collections Young Research Library, UCLA (C.C. Pierce Box 1).*

by the Spaniards rather than experimenting with beefier breeds. (Angelenos made the same mistake in subsequent sheepraising ventures.)

What remained of the industry, after market forces intervened, was lost to a severe, three-year drought (1862-1865). Even at the beginning of this natural disaster, ranchers found that they could get more for hides and tallow, and started to slaughter their herds; toward the end, the animals literally died of thirst. Cattle never again were as important to the economy here, and over the years, the industry could not begin to satisfy local tastes for meat. One Chamber of Commerce official, writing in 1924, lamented:

> Our present shortage in animal industry products is made evident when we realize that the amount of our annual out-of-state purchase comprises millions of pounds of cheese and butter, practically all of our meat and poultry, 85 percent of our pork products, 60 percent of our beef products, and a considerable amount of our mutton.

Industrious Agriculture

Viticulture, another historic L.A. enterprise, shared one key quality with the cattle industry: it was a part of everyday life just as much as an economic opportunity — at least in the beginning. The mission priests were the first to cultivate the grape. As early as 1831, landowners Ballesteros, Jean Luis Vignes, Maximo Alanis and Juan Ramirez boasted vine-covered acres to the east of Alameda. (The names Ramirez and Vignes survive in local street names.) L.A.'s first corporate seal (1850) featured a cluster of grapes. And Olivera Street then was known as Vine Street.

Young Los Angeles depended on viticulture for both revenues and, in a processed form, recreation. The early 20th century historian Guinn wrote:

> The municipal funds for the pueblos were obtained from revenues on wine and brandy; from the licenses of saloons and other businesses; from the tariff on imports; from permits to give balls or dances, from the fines of transgressors, and from the tax on bull rings and cockpits... Then men's pleasures and vices paid the cost of governing.

Grapes even could be found at the center of property transfers, as was the case in an 1848 transaction between Rosalia Dalton and a newly arrived Chilean immigrant, Juan Apablasa:

> She delivers the place to Juan Apablasa at the rent of half the products and expenses, and when she dies, if it happens after the year 1849, Apablasa will give as the value of the vineyard and appurtenances, $250, and it will remain his property; but if she wishes payment before to conclude the sale, Apablasa will give to the said Senora one barrel of grape brandy each year during her life.

Apart from the fruit, itself, Los Angeles achieved a reputation for varietal and fortified wines. Improved shipping during the 1850s nourished the market, and the city boasted 15 of the nation's 36 distilleries by 1867. Northern California ultimately conquered the industry and Union Station took many of the remaining local acres devoted to viticulture, however, a 1939 picture shows the Padre Vineyard Company enduring in the old neighborhood.

A prime mover behind this enterprise was an Irish immigrant, Matthew Keller, who

So pervasive was viticulture, that Los Angeles' first seal featured grapes. This design represented the city from its 1850 incorporation through 1905, but no one is sure of the exact colors. Starting with an old black-and-white line drawing, members of the Los Angeles City Historical Society added green, purple and gold for a commemorative t-shirt. *Permission and copyright, LACHS.*

Vintner-enologist and civic leader Matthew Keller (left) posed with Phineas Banning, "Father of the L.A. Harbor" (standing), and a local cattle rancher, sometime during the 1870s. *Courtesy Department of Special Collections, Young Research Library, UCLA.*

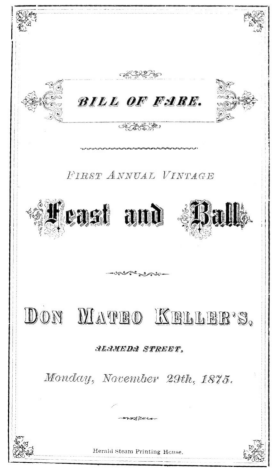

Winemakers traditionally have celebrated the crush, and the quickly-acculturated Irish immigrant "Don Mateo" welcomed the custom. The Bill of Fare for his First Annual Vintage Feast and Ball listed multiple courses, richer and more meat-laden than anything imaginable in the last 70 years. Keller also noted (at the bottom of the menu) a handful of his wines, followed by the word "etc." *Courtesy, Department of Special Collections, Young Research Library, UCLA (Ephemera file 200, box 159).*

BILL OF FARE.

FIRST ANNUAL VINTAGE

Feast and Ball,

DON MATEO KELLER'S,

ALAMEDA STREET,

Monday, November 29th, 1875.

Herald Steam Printing House.

arrived here at mid-century. Keller began as a grocer, packing and shipping grapes. Within a decade he built a home at 726 Alameda Street, and planted approximately 100,000 vines on the surrounding acres. He strived for an empire, sending his nine-year-old son, Henry William Workman Keller, to New York to study German. The boy subsequently toured Europe, speaking the languages of — and learning enology from — French and German masters.

When Austrian Archduke Ludwig Louis Salvator traveled through the United States during the 1870s, he noted that Keller "largely controlled" the vineyards in and around Los Angeles. The "garden... on Alameda...merits mention," wrote the Archduke. Here, Keller's vines yielded "claret, port, white wine, madeira, sherry, and angelica." His sherry earned special distinction, capturing the silver medal at the Centennial in Philadelphia. According to the *Los Angeles Express*, Keller's estate was state-of-the-art:

> The wine and brandy manufactory and cellars are located on the home place, Alameda Street. The machinery has a capacity for crushing fifty tons of grapes in a day, and turns out during the season, 200 gallons of brandy and 1,000 of wine daily. The wine cellars, of which there are two — one 60x60 and the other 50x300 — are located on the home place adjoining the works. With all the old stock sold and only the vinegar of 1879 on hand, he still had one hundred thousand gallons of wine in the store.

Keller succeeded because he pushed himself hard and far, in every direction. The Irish native served as an L.A. City Councilman and County Supervisor, joined the boards of the Pioneer Oil Company and Farmers and Merchants Bank. His property holdings ultimately reached Malibu. He was said to have been the first in Los Angeles to use glass-embossed beverage bottles. And beside his reputation as a vintner and enologist, Keller creatively pursued agronomy, importing Central American and Hawaiian orange seeds for his Southern California orchards.

While Keller added to the local orange culture, it already had a rich history by the time he arrived. As the association with "Valencia" implies, the Spaniards grew citrus in their homeland before introducing it to the New World. (The fruit allegedly tasted more bitter than the varieties we know today.) Mission San Gabriel was the greatest agricultural producer among the Spanish colonies in California. Most of the yield could be attributed to neophyte labor, but the fathers may have taken a personal interest — and directed their own energies — toward the oranges. The process started in mission nurseries, as there was roughly a seven-year incubation period between seeding and the initial harvest.

A Kentucky-born trapper and Rocky Mountain rambler, William Wolfskill obtained his orange stock from San Gabriel. He planted about two acres at Central and East Fifth Street in 1841. When the crop thrived, he proceeded to fill some 70 acres with groves. Southern Californians quickly developed a taste for oranges. Wolfskill had more than enough to satisfy local hunger — and, indeed, thirst. He subsequently traded his fruit north, to the gold miners.

By the mid-1870s, the estate, now overseen by Wolfskill's son, counted thousands of trees. The orange hier was poised for a national market, and Los Angeles had just been firmly linked with the rest of the country via railroad. Wolfskill loaded a train car full of oranges to St. Louis, the first time such commerce had been undertaken. The trip took one month, but the fruit proved durable, and delicious, to those largely unaccustomed to it. Wolfskill's enterprise soared.

At around the same time, a couple recently transplanted from Maine to Riverside, read in a U.S. Department of Agriculture bulletin about a variety of exceptionally sweet, high-yield, seedless oranges. Luther and Eliza Tibbetts sought further information from a commissioner in Washington. Since "navels"

hadn't taken to Florida very well and the official was eager to test them, he sent the Riverside couple three trees; two of them survived to transform the Riverside citrus industry. The Tibbetts soon commanded $5 for each budstock from their original plants.

Orange cultivation also became one side of a huge marketing triangle — the Real Estate Boom — that additionally embraced land and transportation development. Easterners or Midwesterns with some savings could retire to several sunny acres and a small orange grove. The railroad companies vied vigorously for their business by offering reduced fares to encourage previously expensive cross-country relocation. (Since many railroad firms also were large landowners, they had a vested interest in real estate. The Southern Pacific, as one example, obtained 60 prime acres near downtown as part of the deal that brought its services to Los Angeles.) Unscrupulous marketing and sales practices occurred: the proverbial offering of the Brooklyn Bridge, with a western agricultural accent. Overselling and unreal expectations on the part of consumers contributed to the real estate bust of the mid-1880s.

The growth of the citrus depended on advanced transportation. California oranges became nationally prized after the Wolfskill family shipped a carload of fruit to St. Louis during the late 1870s, via railroad. Jim Doolin's "Los Angeles Circa 1910" (at the Metropolitan Transportation Authority headquarters downtown) emphasizes the primacy of citrus — and trains. *Courtesy The Metropolitan Transportation Authority, Los Angeles.*

(Below) Citrus-growing attracted Easterners and Midwesterns who wanted both a lifestyle and an investment. *Courtesy The Postcard Collection of Jeanne Taylor Baird, with permission of Flag Studios, Pasadena.*

Some of the blindly-optimistic new growers hadn't calculated the time and patience required of orange cultivation, nevertheless, orchards bloomed all over Southern California: Riverside, Claremont, Ventura, San Diego, Los Angeles, and the jurisdiction that recently broke away, Orange County. But profits depended on factors beyond the growers' control: the weather, certainly, but also unregulated markets and the demands of commercial brokers.

The answer was in cooperatives, an innovative concept that spread west from Riverside. Growers would form associations to: judge the "grades" of produce based on market value; package and broker the crop; and,

redistribute the proceeds according to each member's contribution. As an article in the *Riverside Press and Horticulturalist* explained: "The damage done by the shipping of inferior fruit at prices leaving profit only to the railroad, the packer, and the commission man, is far greater than could possibly result from pooling."

Small orange cooperatives emerged throughout Southern California. Determined that these efforts should be solidified on a regional basis, two early organizers/practitioners embarked on a crusade. They called a meeting for August 29, 1893 at the L.A. Chamber of Commerce, and the Southern California Fruit Exchange was born. (Ultimately, the cooperative became known as Sunkist.)

By 1925, California, (primarily the Southland), furnished the U.S. with more than 50 percent of its oranges and 89 percent of its lemons. The Exchange counted 11,000 grower-members, cooperatively sending their produce through a network that included: 1,000 established carlot markets; 3,500 jobbers; 400,000 retailers; and 118 million American and Canadian consumers. According to this same (trade) estimate,

members received a total of over $50 million for their production efforts.

In the course of its long development, the citrus industry brought new realizations to agriculture. First, growers learned to apply cooperation broadly. Second, they gained sensitivity to subclimates within Southern California. As early as the late 1860s, a world-wide wheat shortage motivated Isaac Lankershim, who was then cultivating grain in Northern California, to look for additional farm land; as he rode through the San Fernando Valley, he observed wild oats growing madly all around him. Wheat had failed elsewhere in the basin, apparently because of the coastal fog. But Lankershim knew his product; he bought half of the Valley from Pio and Andres Pico for $2/acre, or $115,000 in all. The Valley subsequently became known for grain production. Similarly, Angelenos harvested grapefruits, figs, nuts, grain, celery and other table vegetables, though in different locales.

The produce business — both directly and indirectly — also spurred mobility for immigrants who found it easier to carve their own economic niches than to rise through industry or union spheres. (Lankershim, himself, was a Bavarian-Jewish immigrant.) Certainly, they met with adversity. In 1878, for example, city officials tried to impose licensing fees and otherwise regulate vegetable peddling, an industry in which Chinese immigrants played a major role. Having gained the cooperation of Chinese truck farmers, the vendors went on strike. By the 1880, 50 out of 60 of L.A.'s vegetable peddlers were Chinese.

It is also interesting to note here the stages of mobility achieved through agriculture-related industries. From 1900 to 1910, Chinatown residents identified as "farm laborers" declined from 19 to 10 percent. Over the same 10-year period, vegetable peddlers increased from 21 to 41 percent among the identifiable working population. Easier, more lucrative pursuits followed. Approximately one percent of the people living in the vicinity of Apablasa Street had become grocers as of 1900. Within the decade, eight percent were so

Chinese immigrants tending the vines, probably during the 1880s or 1890s. Agricultural labor provided entry on a path that, for Chinese-Americans, led to vegetable peddling and, ultimately, retailing and wholesaling. *Courtesy University of Southern California, Regional History Center.*

engaged. Wholesaling became yet another pursuit, although its practitioners were semi-jobbers, who simultaneously conducted retail operations.

These recent immigrants also translated their experience into more universal terms. Produce merchant Louie Gwan organized the City Market at Ninth and San Pedro during 1909. He offered Japanese farmers substantial loans to join him there, although the latter community exhibited divided loyalties between Gwan's plan and one of their own. City Market nevertheless came to include many small, independent growers: Anglo, Chinese, Italian, Japanese, Russian.

Ultimately, however, the secret of Chinese — and later, Japanese success — in produce was the ability to trade both ethnic and general merchandise. (African-American businesses, as one example, could not benefit from the same type or level of bicultural commerce.) The vegetable peddlers' strike emphasizes the important place Chinese immigrants held in the larger economic-agricultural scheme; at the same time, these merchants needed to attract and maintain their neighborhood customer bases. Grocery stores therefore contained fresh and imported goods. A Euroamerican reporter visited old Chinatown's Yee Sing Chong market in 1933, and talked of the mix:

> A great brown and white striped awning keeps the direct rays of the sun from the sidewalk array of vegetables, terrapins, snails, Chinese cabbage, long stalks of sugar cane and stacks of rice. Inside, the numerous shelves are literally groaning under the weight of imported foodstuffs:

green jars of candied lichee nuts, preserved in their own syrup; containers of the delectable amber plum sauce, without which no good Chinaman will eat roast meat; tinned bamboo shoots, mushrooms, pottery jars of preserved ginger, bean sauce or soeuy sauce — and a thousand and one interesting delicacies....

Strings of flat, dried fish hang from the ceiling. Piles of shredded wood — in reality seaweed — a choice soup ingredient. Shark finds and dried birds' nests — two of the finest Chinese epicurean treats.

Japanese immigrants similarly engaged in agriculture and related commerce, often overseeing operations and cultivating the soil themselves. They also experienced discrimination on a statewide and national basis, including "Swat the Jap" trade campaigns. In response to discrimination — and for practical business reasons — Japanese Angelenos fully adopted the cooperative spirit. They founded the Nippon-California Farmers Association in 1909. Twenty years later, Japanese grower organizations from the central coast — Guadalupe, San Luis Obispo, Pismo Beach and Lompoc — teamed with the Japanese Produce Merchants' Association of Los Angeles to create the Japanese Cooperative Farm Industry (JCFI) of Southern California. The JCFI, in turn, distributed agricultural products through Japanese-owned outlets such as the Southern California Flower Market and the City Market.

The dual forces of self-reliance and isolation rendered the JCFI more sensitive than most agricultural associations to the welfare of its members. The Japanese-American cooperative established a fund to reimburse farmers whose produce had to be dumped in order to maintain competitive advantage. And of the JCFI's general income, 40 percent went to operating costs and 60 percent for welfare and relief functions.

Japanese-Americans also pooled their resources — financial and physical — in the purchase/lease and cultivation of small farms. The financial rewards ultimately repaid them for their labors. But economic and social situations can change quickly. Mexicans arrived en masse between 1910 and 1920, a decade or so after the Japanese influx. The large numbers of Mexican immigrants, seeming to appear at once, heightened prejudicial attitudes against them. Joining other newcomers to Los Angeles, they also experienced a scarcity of urban jobs. Farm labor was not necessarily the first choice of employment, but many resorted to it. The early 20th-century sociologist, Emory Bogardus, summarized their plight: "The Mexican has been a victim of the seasonal labor situation. In order to make a living, he has piled his family into 'the old Ford' and almost become a transient in seeking out the widely separated seasonal labor fields."

During the first decades of the 20th century, industry was changing — in the direction initially pioneered by Chinese-, then Japanese-Americans. Truck farming, the production of vegetables on relatively small plots, seemed to be aligned with future land use demands. One portend occurred in 1909. Possessing "insider" information about the aqueduct and its likely San Fernando Valley terminus, the well-heeled syndicate led by Moses Sherman and Harrison Gray Otis sought to multiply manifold their already hefty personal fortunes. The group offered Isaac N. Van Nuys (Lankershim's son-in-law and wheat heir) $2.5 million for the sale of his immense holdings; Van Nuys agreed.

In what was billed the "Sale of the Century," the developers also auctioned off some 2,000 horses and mules, the same number of harnesses, 250 plows, 200 farm wagons 25 tank wagons and 10 combines.

Large-scale farming gradually waned in 20th-century Los Angeles. The new water supply permitted population growth; housing boomed during the pre-Depression years, competing mightily with agriculture for land. Family dwellings and apartment houses under constuction amounted to 34.5 percent of the building permits issued in February, 1925 alone. More telling, their value was estimated at over $5 million, about 46 percent of that month's total. Home builders adopted mass-production techniques. Pacific Ready-Cut Homes, the largest of its type, boasted its ability to "produce a house every twenty minutes." The cost to buyers was

(Opposite page)An impoverished Mexican immigrant family is huddled in front of their well-traveled car. Agricultural workers pursued seasonal labor, following the harvests from one crop to the next. The situation proved particularly acute during the Depression-wracked 1930s, when this picture was taken. *Courtesy The Bill Mason Collection.*

$3,750, complete with built-in breakfast nooks and cabinets, fold-down ironing boards, and the latest electrical appliances.

In light of these developments, ranchers became justifiably sensitive to resource allocations. George P. Clements, M.D., manager of the Agriculture Department for the L.A. Chamber of Commerce, wrote: "Every fourteen people coming into the City of Los Angeles deprive agriculture of water sufficient to handle an acre of land." Clements talked big business. Afterall, the 1920 agricultural census "announced to the world that Los Angeles county led all other counties in the United States in agricultural production."

Ranch-style specialization meant only a few types of fruit, vegetables or grain per harvest. There was "down time" between plantings. Conversely, truck farms were organized so that multiple crops could grow simultaneously on small plots. New seedlings pushed up immediately behind the produce that had just been harvested. "Intensive farming" was constant, almost year-round use. No matter how efficient, though, agriculture within the city's borders soon lost to real estate. Wartime industries — and an unheralded urban influx — finalized changing land use patterns.

Urban Developments

From an 1850s perspective, it would have been difficult to envision Los Angeles at the nucleus of a thriving metropolitan economy. The city had little financial infrastructure — neither credible lending

Although real estate development was rapidly encroaching, vast acreage remained devoted to farming. Artist Phil Dike conveyed the San Fernando Valley's agricultural lifestyle and topography in "Well of Gold" (1928). *Courtesy The Irvine Museum, Irvine, California.*

institutions nor much hard currency. During the bloated 1850s, interest rates of three to five percent per month were common. (Simple promissory notes documented these costly transactions.) The debts and inflated lifestyles of the cattle boom proved difficult to finance as fortunes eroded. Banking in those days simply meant stashing gold in a safe, often kept by local merchants as a type of customer service.

One of the first bankers here, Isaias W. Hellman, had no experience in the financial field when he entered it. According to a long-time associate, the dry goods merchant simply tired of free "safekeeping" and the sometimes abusive customers who demanded such services:

> He got hold of a good friend who was running a paper, and between them they fixed up some passbooks and some deposit slips marked "I.W. Hellman, Banker." He had a carpenter fence off a corner of his store, in which he put the safe, and hung up the sign, "I.W. Hellman, Banker." The next miner who came along with gold dust was told he could not leave it there, "but," said Mr. Hellman, "I will buy your gold dust, at current rates, and I am running a bank. Here, see this book. After I buy your gold you can deposit the money with me, take this book and check it out as you please. All checks drawn on me, while your money lasts, will be paid!"

The narrator indicates that under these terms, the miners spent less — and saved more — than they had previously. And Hellman managed to watch his money, too. Within several years, he and another banking industry pioneer (and, later, Governor) John Downey, each contributed $100,000 for a merger of their interests. The result was the Farmers and Merchants Bank of Los Angeles. Hellman, Downey and Ozro Childs — the three who endowed USC — all served on the first board. Others who joined in subsequent years represented a multicultural swath of the city's business and civic community: Charles Ducommon, Jose Mascarel, Matthew Keller, Frank Lecouvreur, Domingo Amestoy, Phillipe Garnier, Tomas L. Duque, Henry E. Huntington, Henry W. O'Melveny, Moses H. Sherman, Victor H. Rossetti, Maurice H. Newmark, Lloyd W.

Dinkelspiel, and many more. Los Angeles was not to rival San Francisco as a banking capital until late in the 20th century, but this modest start gave the city a financial infrastructure from which to build its enterprises. And Farmers and Merchants lasted until its 1956 merger with Security-First National Bank.

In addition to a fledgling financial sector, small businesses and professional services grew with the population. A summary of the Los Angeles Directory for 1875 revealed: 107 carpenters, 72 fruit dealers, 50 attorneys, 43 blacksmiths, 33 printers, 32 physicians and surgeons, 30 boot and shoe dealers and makers, 30 butchers, 28 teachers, 28 wagon and carriage makers, 234 upholsterers, 22 clergymen, 22 livery, feed and sale stables, 2 real estate brokers, 19 clothing/dry goods dealers, 18 hotels and lodging houses, 18 general merchandisers, 14 jewelers, 13 editors and publishers, 11 restaurants, 10 drug stores, and two real estate agents.

The abundance of carpenters surely underscores the power and scope of the real estate boom: the need to keep promises to those who had often purchased land based on little more than an advertisement. To an even larger extent, the directory provides insights into the labor situation here. Los Angeles was never known for trade unionism. The California Labor Commissioner's report of 1902 noted 125 union organizations in San Francisco. Even after a recent and successful flurry of organizing, Los Angeles could claim only 68. (The cities of Sacramento and Oakland counted 45 and 36, respectively.)

Still, labor activity reflected local economic needs and strongholds. Typographical Union No. 174, chartered on October 1, 1875, was the first labor organization of record in L.A. Printers subsequently became strong advocates for the eight-hour day, a national rallying cry; they won reduced hours in 1887. Two years later, Arthur Vinette, a carpenter and secretary of the Los Angeles Council, was instrumental in organizing the Eight Hour League here. In general, if unions gained ground, it was primarily through the skilled trades. New residents flocked to Los Angeles and flooded the job market; it was particularly difficult for those with no specific — or applicable — trade to find employment during these periods.

Transportation workers, however, constituted another early, vigorous union sector. Here, the influence may be explained partially by the nature of their industry. In building a tangible, visible network, the rail and shipping magnates also inadvertently, but necessarily, linked their employees. Transportation workers came into contact with each other — and even in this union-adverse city — with the world outside. Protesting discharges by ship owners, for example, sailors and longshoremen together struck at San Pedro. Local members of the American Railway Union cooperated with a national action against the Pullman Company in 1894; not a single train left L.A. on June 27. A federal injunction, acts of violence, and intervention by U.S. infantrymen ensued. Although both the shipping and Pullman strikes ultimately failed, local transportation workers gained potency from their interactions with other unionists across the United States.

During the last decade of the 19th century, the Los Angeles business community also adopted a more expansive view of itself. Trade leaders sought increased

Merchant Isaias W. Hellman teamed with former California Governor and real estate investor John W. Downey in 1871 to create the Farmers and Merchants Bank of Los Angeles. This institution lasted until the late 1950s; it merged into Security Pacific, which later was absorbed by Bank of America. *Courtesy Department of Special Collections, Young Research Library, UCLA.*

political and economic influence, and realized that these objectives depended on organizing. Chambers of commerce historically had two functions. First, they sought municipal trade advantages: prime locations, reduced taxes, economic incentives, and various forms of political support. Second, they collectively marketed the city or region's products. The first chamber of commerce appeared in Marseilles, France sometime around 1600; New York's dated to 1768. Whenever it emerged in a city's history, the chamber usually signified a new economic awareness.

Business organizing here accomplished many of the same purposes, but took a slightly different form. The Los Angeles Chamber of Commerce, officially organized in 1888, set forth its mission "to foster and encourage commerce; to stimulate home manufactures; to induce immigration and the subdivision, settlement and cultivation of our lands; to assist in the development of the material resources of the region; and generally to promote the business interests of Los Angeles city and county..."

A more insular approach guided the Merchants and Manufacturers' Association. The "M & M" (as it is commonly abbreviated) evolved through an 1896 merger of two separate, recently-organized groups, respectively representing the interests of merchants and manufacturers. The consolidated association initially pursued a multiple-issue agenda. Soon, however, the M&M became steadfastly, at times brutally, committed to one goal: keeping unions out of Los Angeles.

The employment situation had already gone beyond local boundaries in 1896. L.A. companies developed branch offices in other parts of California, and enterprises founded elsewhere opened here. Labor actions to some extent could not be effective unless they gained regional or statewide support. When San Francisco brewery workers rallied during 1897, their cause looked hopeful. The large Maier & Zobelein Brewery of Los Angeles was open to organized labor. Yet, the workers, many of whom owned company stock, claimed that their wages and hours were at very least comparable to the union's. The San Francisco local called for a boycott of Maier & Zobelein, and Los Angeles labor supported it. Yet, the M&M asserted itself for the first time in its short history, and brought down the action.

The new association was to build an arsenal of tactics. Commanding loyalty — and large contributions — from its affiliates, the M&M hired strike breakers; imposed blacklists against those who were uncooperative; and, much later, through its political influence with City Hall, initiated the LAPD "red squads" which physically threatened and disrupted organizing activities.

The AFL-CIO realized the obstacles to be overcome and at the turn of the century dispatched an experienced organizer, John C. Ince, to Los Angeles. His leadership largely was responsible for bringing the number of unions from 26 to 68 between 1900 and 1902. Pasadena locals formed their own federation in 1904, and San Pedro, Santa Monica, Long Beach and Glendale groups soon followed.

After a period of relative calm from about 1905 to 1910, business-labor confrontation heightened. Actions were brought by Mexican-American employees of the electrical railway companies, leather workers and the brewers' union. Also during 1910, organized labor in San Francisco was warned by employers that unless they unionized Los Angeles and equalized wages and conditions between the two cities, they should be prepared for open shop. L.A. metal workers simultaneously were struggling over wages and hours. Employers' intransigence — an unwillingness to even communicate with workers — and agitation from Northern unions propelled a series of actions and reactions: strikes and lockouts that essentially shut down local metal plants in June, 1910. Scattered incidents of violence occurred. The L.A. City Council passed an anti-picketing ordinance on July 16, and 470 strikers were arrested.

Labor-management acrimony literally exploded with the October 1 dynamiting of the new *Los Angeles Times* building. Immediate losses tallied 21 deaths and $500,000 in property damage. Although no suspects could be found, the symbolism was powerful. *Times* publisher Harrison Gray Otis had been an M&M leader who railed against labor in his newspaper and, on a personal-business level, dealt heavy-handedly with his typographers and pressmen.

A subsequent dynamiting, this time of the Llewelyn Iron Works, allowed investigators and prosecuters to cobble together a case against several prominent labor officials. Although represented by Clarence Darrow, perhaps the most well-known trial attorney of his time, the unionists were undermined when one of their own turned state's evidence and implicated others. Ultimately, a federal grand jury convicted 39 labor officials of illegal transport of dynamite and nitroglycerin. Some were the most prominent labor leaders in California; their removal from public life had considerable effects on union activism. And within three and a half years of the *Times* bombing, San Francisco boasted its own Merchants and Manufacturer's Association.

As Chapters II and III of this book demonstrate, multiculturalism survives because it has been a more or less constant factor in L.A. history, beginning with the pobladores. The reverse holds for organized labor. It only

The Chamber of Commerce markets L.A. bounties, circa 1900. The display on the left spotlights local wines, while the elephant to the right is composed of — and serves as an advertisement for — walnuts. *Courtesy The Southwest Museum, Los Angeles, photo N.42525.*

The *Los Angeles Times* at the turn of the century was a symbol of the strong anti-labor stance here. Its publisher, General Harrison Gray Otis, helped to organize the Merchants and Manufacturer's Association and, on a personal level, brought in strike breakers against his printers and typographers. The *Times* building was bombed in 1910, during a peak period of labor-management acrimony. *Courtesy, The Postcard Collection of Jeanne Taylor Baird.*

started to take hold here during the 1930s. While San Francisco unionists lent organizing assistance, their support could not match the power of the M&M. Furthermore, the American Federation of Labor favored skilled craft unions (already existing here) over industry-wide organizations which would have added growing numbers of non-European immigrants groups to the ranks. Finally, corporate interests, at least through the 19th century, kept government at all levels in sway.

Mexican-American workers were an exception for several reasons. First, the physical closeness between Mexico and the United States encouraged political and economic interplay. Union leaders in the United States, ranging from the AFL to the radical International Workers of the World (IWW) established relations with their counterparts vying for position in revolutionary Mexico. Similarly, Mexican immigrants could keep track of and relate to the changes transpiring in their native land.

The politics and economics of the Mexican revolution may have evoked labor issues. The pro-development dictator Porfirio Diaz created a Mexican national railroad system, building 19,000 kilometers of track from 1876 to 1910, when the revolution ousted him. American investment by 1911 had comprised almost 62 percent of the capital supporting this massive project, and the same financial magnates who controlled the Southern Pacific, Santa Fe, and other Southwestern transportation enterprises were major shareholders in the Mexican rail system.

Mexican-American labor involvement in transportation industries was especially strong. Southern Pacific employees struck during 1903, and interurban workers seven years later. Members of the Huntington family held major interests in both systems, and also had invested in the Mexican rails. With the SPRR reviled in many populist and progressive quarters for its excessive influence, recent immigrants from the southern border may have been moved by a double entendre.

African-Americans did not benefit from the international implications that bolstered Mexican-American unionism. Yet, because they performed important service functions, the SPRR and others eventually acknowledged their labor: "We generally started work at 5:30 in the morning, and probably worked until 9 at night. They paid us overtime, but not time and a half. We were on our feet all day. If there were still people in the dining room, the waiters could sit down at the table, but we (cooks) had to stay in the kitchen because we were dressed in cooks' clothes."

African-Americans railroad workers united in the AFL, craft-specific mode, joining the Brotherhood of Sleeping Car Porters, the Dining Car Cooks and Waiters Union, the Bartenders Union. The irony was that the primary vehicle for labor credibility, AFL affiliation, had been denied them. Some African-American organizations, like the Dining Car Cooks and Waiters, independently gained recognition from the SPRR. Black bartenders declared themselves as an auxiliary of the white union; they paid dues and engaged in limited bargaining, but had none of the voter rights.

Although African-Americans were divided on unionism, the activism it fostered was transferable to other settings. The local director of the Cooks and Waiters Union in Los Angeles was Clarence Johnson. His nephew, Byron Rumford, would become a state legislator and author of the Rumford Act, outlawing housing discrimination.

Mining — and Minding — Natural Resources

While labor history is fascinating, its importance within L.A. industrial spheres should not be overstated. Union tradition was strong in Europe, but for other non-European immigrants there were few such entryways. More to the point, the lack of a vibrant labor sector here explains why Angelenos were otherwise-directed. Entrepreneurism, a longstanding local trademark, has long presented an alternative. What in other towns was a working class in L.A. became venturers and salespeople! (So much of this phenomenon is evident in our discussion of agriculture.) Prospectors of all types were willing to pour some sweat into their endeavors, but independence and financial rewards were the goals.

The process began in the 1850s. Through the cattle industry, Angelenos had been indirect beneficiaries of the Gold Rush. But northern journeys inspired them to unearth their own local riches. The *Los Angeles Star*, December 3, 1959, gave credence to the fledlgling efforts:

> Another field of labor is opening up to us and that is the development of our mineral resources. In this branch, it has been heretofore considered that we were efficient... that the deposits of the precious metals, ores, and minerals were confined to the northern portion of the State; but such is very far from being the case. Lately investigation has directed itself to the mountain ranges of our county and district, and we are glad to say that discoveries have been made which prove them to be rich indeed in all the metals which attract emigrtants to the north. Gold, silver, copper, tin, lead, are found, and not in one locality either, but spreading throughout the whole range of mountains which bounds our valley.

The *Treasure of Sierra Madre*, a classic film starring Humphrey Bogart, refers to a Mexican adventure, though the San Gabriel Valley town of the same name saw its share of prospectors, too. Roughly 300 men descended into the canyon area immediately following an 1859 gold discovery. Stagecoaches left and returned to Los Angeles three times each week, with stops to the San Gabriel Mission (for a $1 fare), Santa Anita mines ($2.50), the mouth of the canyon ($3), or through to Prospect Bar ($6). Towns rose instantly and were just as quickly deserted, leaving behind their remnants of saloons, shacks and gambling houses.

But events across the country translated to a more enduring and profitable local industry. Oil fever commenced immediately following Drake's 1859 extraction in Titusville, Pennsylvania. Tar (*brea* in Spanish), a form of the substance, had long been used by Native Americans to mend leaky boats and to waterproof fiber or reid vessels. Pioneers paid relatively attention to it, except for roofing and axle grease. Because of their advanced manufacturing processes, however, Easterners prized oil. An interesting footnote: those on the Atlantic coast used whale oil as a lubricant, and to light their homes, before Titusville. In fact, a whale merchant clandestinely prospected Henry Hancock's Los Angeles property, until Hancock forced him off. Whale oil soon went the way of the "California bank note," in large measure due to petroleum.

Indeed, external factors — and a profit motive — were needed to spark interest here. Yet, despite a credible number of starts beginning in the 1860s, most efforts came to naught. Of the close to 3,000 wells drilled, less than 1,000 produced oil by the end of the century. Fields were detected purely through seepage (oil's obvious presence), and many sites primarily yielded water or a mixture of the two fluids. In general, location and extraction methods remained unsophisticated until geological science began emerge, circa 1903.

Edward Doheny is recognized as the father of the Los Angeles oil industry mainly because in 1892, he happened upon a colossal, oozingly fertile field at the corner of Second and Glendale Boulevard downtown. Within five years, the 20-block site contained 2,500 wells owned by 200 companies, and was the major producer of California's oil. The uses for the new product, as a lubricant and heating fuel, were apparent. But Doheny earned his reputation (and commensurate wealth) because he sought broader, institutional markets. He convinced railroad companies to switch from coal to oil. Within a few years, the automobile

made its debut and relied on petroleum through the present time, when electric cars are being discussed, if not widely deployed.

Even in its colorful infancy, the industry went beyond Doheny. The so-called wildcatters who owned small drilling companies scanned the fields themselves, assisted by mini-crews of English, Canadian, Irish and Scottish workers. This mobile laborforce established a shanty town near the corner of Santa Monica Boulevard and Vermont Avenue. Emma Summers shared the ethnic background, if not the temperament, of the crews. A New England Conservatory of Music graduate with Scotch-Irish lineage, she drilled during the day and taught piano by night. Summers finally struck — at the right location — between Temple and Court Street. Her wells bore so much oil that she quickly graduated into the wholesaling and refining businesses. By

1900, Summers controlled half the production of the original oil field.

The discovery of abundant oil in L.A. County during the 1920s created a glut. As anyone who remembers the gasoline lines of the late 1970s can attest, the cycle of market factors, internal agreements among industry leaders, and price realignments have long typified the oil industry. Still, the bobbing mechanical dinosaurs that slurp buckets of crude from wells throughout the city and county are proof that this historic enterprise has not only defied extinction, but developed an enduring presence in Los Angeles.

The Technology-Dependent 20th Century

Oil also provides a useful bridge in understanding the differences between 19th- and 20th-century business environments. What once had been not much more than a "gathering" activity flourished through science: detection of oil advanced from seepage to geology to, in the late 1930s, applied geophysics — complete with instrumentation. More broadly, an industry originally inspired by natural resources turned into a technological process. Refinement meant refineries. Similar economies of scale reduced an assembly of dream-driven, mom and pop enterprises (the wildcatters) to a relatively small pool of large corporations.

Technology transfer is a related issue, and its power can be seen through the canning industry. Agricultural plenitude gave rise to fruit and vegetable preservation, one of California's oldest manufacturing enterprises. In 1900, it ranked fifth among Golden State industries as far as the value of its products; within 25 years, it climbed to second, right behind petroleum refining. California also was the nation's top fruit and vegetable canning state by that time, with 309 establishments, employing 23,384 people. The value of the product hovered at the $181,272,830.

More noteworthy is that by the first quarter of the century, fruit and vegetable canning could claim a commercial offspring. Fish preservation — though not nearly as large an industry — derived from the same technology. California also had risen to number one fish canner in the U.S., quite an accomplishment considering the industry's recent vintage. The three major locations for this activity were Los Angeles, San Diego and Monterey. L.A. held a monopoly on world tuna production by the late 1920s. If the average U.S. citizen were asked to name the capital of fish canning, however, he or she would probably respond with "Monterey." Similarly, advanced drilling techniques allowed other fields throughout the county and state to contribute to California's reputation as a petroleum producer. Texas tapped its own huge supply, ultimately grabbing the national title.

One fledgling industry — motion pictures — would become and remain synonymous with Los Angeles. Yet, the multi-layered technical, commercial, and artistic elements that comprised film were hardly indigenous. Motion pictures evolved from late 18th-century developments in photography and sound. Thomas Edison of Menlo Park, New Jersey was just as much a businessman as an inventor. Beside his role in the phonograph, he developed the Kinetoscope, which produced individually-operated "peep shows." Edison also purchased the patent on the Vitascope, an early projection technology. The idea of celluloid "film" belonged George Eastman's. And Hollywood's legendary lavishment on costumes and sets, of course, were inherited from theatre, with New York as its hub.

Entertainment simultaneously was drifting toward cost-efficiency and centralized or regional talent. Live stage had added culture to many small cities and towns through the late 19th century. "Combination companies" (itinerant acting troupes paired with centralized production staff and facilities) soon replaced community theatre. Stage mechanics responded to their collective loss of jobs, forming New York Local 1 during 1886. This early organizing effort grew into the International Alliance of Theatrical and Stage Employees.

Photographed in 1959, these oil wells probably had weathered years of service. *Courtesy Department of Special Collections, Young Research Library, UCLA.*

With the introduction of moving pictures, theatre owners transitioned toward even smaller production and payroll costs — at least for a few years. Furthermore, low-ticket "movies" appealed to the rising immigrant populations, for economic and other reasons to be discussed later. In short, it is hardly surprising that Los Angeles had its first theatre well before any such "industry" was known locally. T.A. Tally opened a "Phonograph and Vitascope Parlor" at 311 S. Spring Street in 1896. With a nine-person capacity, this pioneering theatre featured both peep and screen shows, with accompanying music rendered by phonograph.

How did L.A. become the "motion picture capital?" Historians offer two explanations: the natural environment and an anti-union, open-shop stance. The first is undoubtedly true. There was no need for false advertisement (oranges the size of beachballs) here: with extremely heavy, fussy equipment, and payroll expenses, early producers could ill afford false starts. Los Angeles offered them a year-round climate to shoot pictures. Furthermore, the terrains that lift late 20th-century pleasure seekers from the sea to ski slopes within two hours held a practical, techno-artistic appeal got film pioneers. One *Los Angeles Times* writer

continued on page 135

Los Angeles' agricultural plenitude gave rise to the canning industry. Seen here during the late 1920s, women and children are removing the pits from apricots for processing. *Courtesy The Bill Mason Collection.*

A report titled "Growth Industries and The New Economy," published by the Mayor's Office of Economic Development (1996) highlights the apparel, or women's fashion wear, industry. Consisting of almost 2,000 firms and one of the largest employers in the local manufacturing sector, it interacts with "a burgeoning textile industry and extensive networks of wholesale distribution and retail companies."

Apparel has historic roots in Los Angeles — and diverse inputs. With women's clothes largely handmade through the teens, manufacturers concentrated on men's pants, shirts, undergarments. Some enterpreneurs, however, utilized existing technologies to create new markets. Engaged in a family business, West Coast Knitting Mills, Fred Cole realized that women's swimsuits were not that far removed from men's underwear. Cole of California thus entered the fashion world in 1925.

(Upper left) Gwen Wakeling's elaborate, yet sleek, costume design for Rita Hayworth in "Cover Girl" (1944), demonstrates just how enticing fashion sketches could be, even to the average buyer glancing through department store advertisements. (Photographs have largely replaced this genre, however.) *Courtesy The Gwen Wakeling Collection, Margaret Herrick Library, Academy of Motion Picture Arts and Sciences, Beverly Hills.*

(Above) With its extravagant budgets and specialized staff, Hollywood may have perfected certain textile and design crafts. The two women pictured at the top, MGM employees of the late 1930s, are hand-painting bunches of flowers on a fine silk or satin background. *Courtesy The Margaret Herrick Library, Academy of Motion Picture Arts and Sciences, Beverly Hills, with permission from Warner Brothers.*

charted locations. Palmdale could double as the African desert and Newport, as an Atlantic coastal resort town. A producer might choose Portugese Bend when simulating the Israelites' arrival at the Red Sea. With it climate and mission architecture, Santa Barbara could provide a reasonable facsimile of Spain. Moreover, all of these places were within 90 miles of Hollywood.

Returning to the labor issues, it can be stated that L.A.'s unquestionning corporate openness (and distance from self-regulating business associations) drew refugees from the East Coast and, more specficially, from the Motion Picture Patents Company. The MMPC owned rights on production processes and zealously guarded its territory against independent producers in 1911. Two English brothers, David and William Horsley opened the first permanent motion picture studio, transferring their operations from New Jersey to Hollywood. Erstwhile underdogs became moguls. Cecil B. DeMille, Jesse Lasky, Samuel Goldwyn and William Fox all found Los Angeles a welcoming escape from the MMPC.

In terms of staffing, the situation is complex and variegated. The first department heads and performers likely came with New York-honed technical skills. Mack Sennett, as one example, hired former vaudevillians like himself. Jesse Lasky's 1914 quote lends insight into hiring practices, while illustrating the rapid transformation of freewheeling independent producers into studio bosses: "It occurred to us that we could use Bill (Bowers) at the studio to take charge of obtaining all the odds and ends needed to dress the sets. I think Bill established the principle upon which the props departments function today, namely that a director gets whatever he asks for without argument, no matter how crazy or impossible the task."

In discussing blue collar trades earlier in this chapter, it is apparent that national unions viewed L.A. locals as infirm, isolated orphans needing plenty of outside sustenance to survive. The motion picture industry changed this perception to some extent: Los Angeles became a place of possibilities. IATSE entered Hollywood advocating an industrial approach — regional jurisdiction over all production fields. Threatened by this challenge and suffering from a period of high unemployment, the International Brotherhood of Electrical Workers (IBEW) and Carpenters' locals sought assistance to defend craft unionism. Both IATSE and the AFL-CIO dispatched professional staff to L.A. by the mid-teens. The 17 largest production companies responded by forming the Motion Picture Producers (and later) Directors Association. While the open shop remained, a 1926 Studio Basic Agreement centralized labor negotiations.

Motion pictures — and Franklin Roosevelt's New Deal — generally strengthened unionism in Los Angeles. The industry also instituted the concept of "talent." Through various labor-related organizations, screenwriters, actors, musicians and others ultimately

Angelenos are queuing up near a small "moving picture" theatre, in the days before a film "industry" existed (probably the first decade of this century). *Courtesy The Hollywood Museum Collection, Margaret Herrick Library, Academy of Motion Picture Arts and Sciences, Beverly Hills.*

An example of early color, this shot comes from The *Devil and Tom Walker*, a 1913 production by William Selig. *Courtesy The Margaret Herrick Library, Academy of Motion Picture Arts and Sciences, Beverly Hills.*

were guaranteed standard wages and conditions, though work typically was divvied out on a project-by-project basis. "Star" status indeed elevated one to the upper firmaments, high above the union level; with a corps of agents, lawyers and other handlers, celebrities could finance and script their own elaborate lifestyles.

More generally, however, Hollywood had global impacts, springing from very humble beginnings. A number of the motion picture pioneers were Jewish immigrants: Carl Laemmele, Adolph Zukor, William Fox, Samuel Goldwyn, Louis B. Mayer. Many entered production through the retail side of things, the

theatres and nickolodeans. Even if they did not admit it, their immigrant experiences may have led to an appreciation of pure entertainment. New arrivals to the U.S. had little time or money for amusement. Consider the Yiddish theatre, a Jewish cultural manifestation borne during the late 1800s: the sparse, unadorned venues found immigrant neighborhoods were more than compensated by amplified, vividly expressed emotions ranging from intense euphoria to deep depression. The same can be said for klezmer music, its instuments alternatively blasting laughter — or wailing; little was neutral. With their subtitles, the first "movies" presented

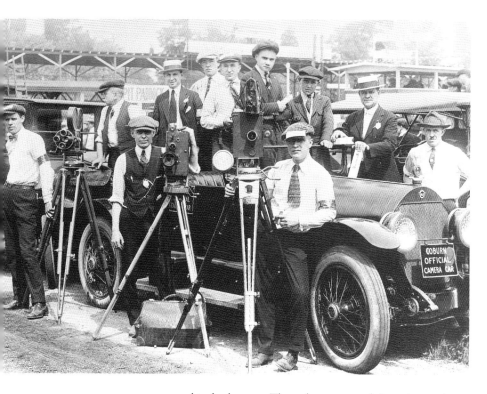

The Horsley Brothers were first to establish a permanent presence in Hollywood during 1911. A production crew from the David Horsely Studio is pictured above. *Courtesy The Hollywood Museum Collection, Margaret Herrick Library, Academy of Motion Picture Arts and Sciences, Beverly Hills.*

a kindred genre. They also conveyed American culture (as well as universal conditions) sans the mockery and derision immigrants usually faced.

The genius of the early, largely uneducated moguls is that they would remember, but not be confined to, the past. They elevated their fledgling medium with increasingly sophisticated technology (probably beyond their own comprehension) and craft, while never forgetting the importance of "audience." Therefore, it is not surprising that by 1920s, motion picture production, distribution and exhibition were tightly aligned. Here in Los Angeles, Sid Grauman managed to maintain his independence, choosing films for their individual qualities rather than their "brand names." He erected several noteworthy movie palaces: the Million Dollar Theatre downtown (1918); Hollywood's Egyptian Theatre (1922); and, the Metropolitan (1923) in Pershing Square, the largest ever built in the city. Grauman sold his interests to Paramount shortly thereafter. The RKO, Fox, and Warner theatre chains, as their names implied, reflected more directly on the studios' investments.

The exemplar for innovation in regional marketing was the Balaban & Katz organization out of Chicago.

B&K provided its audiences total escape, opening the first air-cooled theatre in the U.S. (1917) and generally equipping facilities with plush, spacious lobbies that offered a respite from Chicago's bipolar climate. Auxiliary services extended to supervised child care. The B&K organization also was sensitive to diverging markets wrought of socieconomic changes. By launching what might be called the first three suburban theatres in the metropolitan area, the chain was able to underwrite the costs of building a 4,000-seater downtown.

An entertainment-clamoring market created dynasties. Even during 1934 (and partially as an escape from the Depression), Loew's reported profits of 130 percent. Some 85 million people in the U.S. and 150 million abroad viewed motion pictures on a weekly basis, according to 1938 figures. And many people were indirectly tied to Hollywood: of each dollar taken in at some 16,251 movie theatres across the country, 65 cents stayed at home for payroll and other exhibition expenses and 10 cents went toward distribution-related costs. Hollywood producers claimed only 25 cents. Indeed, an international industry had been established.

Possibly because its benefits were so far flung, the industry demanded an economic and artistic nucleus. Film became uniquely wedded to Los Angeles, while grabbing for the city a chunk of the larger enterprise — call it arts, entertainment and electronic media, or just plain communications. By 1938, when radio was the home entertainment magnet for most American families, Hollywood and environs boasted studios of the Columbia Broadcasting System, National Broadcasting Company, three smaller networks, and 10 stations.

The forties would see war, the dissolution by anti-trust litigation of the studio-distribution-exhibition linkage, and the emergence of television, then deemed a competitive industry. Yet, film bisected and continues to bisect other media. Talent glides easily between them, corporate megastructures engulf both motion pictures and television, the same productions ultimately appear on big screen and small. It is hard to believe that M-TV is over 15 years old. As happened a generation earlier, some viewed the arrival of videos as a threat to older, more established media.

passage below traces the origins of a modern, commercial port, assessing the then-sleepy coastal trade and appraising its potential.

> The number of coasting vessels which arrived during the year (1891) at Wilmington was 546 and at Redondo 255, and 41 vessels entered from foreign ports, making a total of 842 vessels. The principal export was wheat, the value of which was about $40,000. The principal imports from foreign countries were coal, cement, and glass, the value of which was about $370,000. The coal, most of which comes from Australia, was about $340,000....
>
> It will appear from the above that the maritime exports of this region are at present insignificant, and that the imports from foreign ports, with the exception of coal, are of little consequence. The coast-wise traffic, consisting principally of the importation of lumber, forms by far the most important part of the seaport business....The present demands for commerce, either for safety or convenience, do not appear to be such as would

Nevertheless, if balance of trade has become a 1990s issue, entertainment remains one of the United States' largest exports. No matter what their packaging, performances are still captured on film, to be viewed later by global audiences. And many begin in the City of Angels.

World War II: Investments Pay Off

Just as motion pictures spread way beyond the boundaries of Hollywood, the local economy grew too diverse for L.A. to be labeled a "company town." World War II welded port-related enterprises and aviation into a formidable defense sector, which would share the economic spotlight with motion pictures. Yet, while film quickly united many artistic and technical fields, the varied origins of transportation — hobbyist, commercial and military — resurfaced for many years.

The federal government showed an interest in L.A. harbors as early as 1890. Far more than curiousity, this interest was backed with a pledge to build a $4 million breakwater. Although subsequent politics are keenly remembered, the initial reason has been lost. The

justify the construction of a deep-water harbor at great expense by the General Government.

By far the most important aspect of this subject, however, is its relation to the probable future development of the deep-sea commerce of this country. Heretofore the Asiatic trade has naturally gone to San Francisco....Two through lines, the Southern Pacific and the Santa Fe systems, cross the continent from Los Angeles at much lower elevations than the northern lines, and also connect the Pacific with the Gulf of Mexico, and their operation is never obstructed by snow or ice....

Should the Nicaragua Canal be completed the importance of the proposed harbor will become greater still. At the present time the most convenient course for sailing vessels coming around the Horn is to go out into the mid-Pacific and strike the trade winds to make the port of San Francisco...

A deep water harbor on the southern Coast would...receive the Asiatic and Australian freights for shipment over the most favorable transcontinental lines, accommodate a large part of the commerce passing through the Nicaragua Canal...and finally furnish a port...not only for the productive territory in its immediate vicinty, but also for the great interior plateau...beyond the mountain ranges....

The present interests of...coastwise and foreign transportation of southern California do not justify the construction of such a harbor... but the propsective requirements of foreign commerce amply warrant...its establishment, even at large expense. *Source: Report of Board of Engineer Officers on Deep-Water Harbor at San Pedro or Santa Monica (Washington: U.S. Department of War, 1898), pp. 3-4.*

Thus, the federal government, not always known for its foresight, emphasized the Pacific Rim trade concept, if not the name. Note, too, the mention of the Nicaragua (Panama) canal. In their report, the engineers had the right to be tentative: the canal pro-

ject dated to 1879, but the waterway would not actually open until 1914.

Cogent arguments notwithstanding, the main obstacle to the breakwater was in selecting an exact location. The choices were: San Pedro-Wilmington, the oldest local port; Redondo; and upstart Santa Monica. The engineers visited Southern California several times to evaluate options. The storm-protected San Pedro site was their first choice, although its shallow mud flats would require considerable dredging to accommodate large, oceangoing vessels.

But politics stood in the way. All three sites were connected to downtown by railroads. The oldest link dated to the 1850s, when Phineas Banning purchased coastal land from the Dominguez family and began port operations at Wilmington, named after his Delaware hometown. To consolidate transportation networks, the "Father of the L.A. Harbor" also developed the Los Angeles and San Pedro Railway Company. Banning's line subsequently was purchased by the city for $75,000, and transferred to the Southern Pacific as part of the deal that brought the "octopus" to Los Angeles.

SPRR still controlled this route when the harbor initiative began. Redondo and Los Angeles were connected via the Santa Fe Railroad, which, though a giant in its own right, held less sway locally. The SPRR was the dominant political mover.

Here, the interpretations differ. According to one account, SPRR co-founder and political lynchpin Collis Huntington took seriously the opposition to San Pedro voiced by Senator William B. Frye of Maine, powerful Chair of the U.S. Senate Commerce Committee. On a visit to San Pedro, Frye was quoted as having declared: "You say this harbor will cost close to five million dollars?....If the Los Angeles people want a good harbor why don't they move their city down to San Diego?" Most

other accounts, however, indicate that Huntington dominated the politics. When a group of St. Louis speculators commenced rail service to nearby Terminal Island in 1891, the SPRR showed its might and abandoned its initial inclination toward a San Pedro breakwater.

Fifteen years earlier, the SPRR had bought out a line to Santa Monica. Now Huntington purchased additional land there and proceeded to construct a rival harbor. Pre-empting the impending congressional decision, Huntington opened his "Port Los Angeles" in 1893. SPRR subsequently pressured local firms into shifting their business from San Pedro to Santa Monica, and had it designated as a sub-port of entry for the U.S. Customs District. This was unprecedented recognition for a private, partly completed port with no federal approval, but a good example of Huntington's influence. Angelenos proceeded to rally against the SPRR in what was known as the Free Harbor Fight, led by Senator Stephen M. White and the *Times'* General Harrison Gray Otis.

The opposition prevailed on two different fronts. First, as pro-Santa Monica legislation was put to the Senate in 1896, White added an amendment that ensured any railroad's right to use the harbor for a reasonable fee. This measure mitigated the obvious and predatory trade advantages sought by the SPRR. Second, local activists on both sides lobbied Washington. President Grover Cleveland appointed one more committee — deemed neutral by its composition: half civilian engineers, half ranking military personnel — to render an authoritative decision. San Pedro again proved victorious. In April, 1899, the first load of rock for the Harbor breakwater was dropped into the San Pedro bay. The project concluded 13 years later.

The harbor grew as a magnet for workingclass entrepreneurs. Portugese, Italian, Norwegian, Greek and other immigrants groups with seafaring traditions gravitated to the San Pedro-Wilmington area to ply their skills. (Some of the fish processed here came from as far away as Mexico.) When Japanese-Americans discovered abalone at White's Point in San Pedro circa 1901, they created for themselves an export market: the fish could be easily dried and shipped to Japan. Hostility by other residents ultimately forced these entrepreneurs to relocate on nearby Terminal Island, but they diversified their catch and prospered commercially. Mexican-Americans also were important to the local economy; they figured heavily not only in fish canning, but in canning generally; food processing employed more Mexican women than any other local industry.

While the U.S. Congress originally expanded the harbor for commercial rather than military purposes, strategic advantages immediately became apparent. Fort McArthur, named for General Douglas MacArthur's father, was dedicated in 1914. It housed Battery Osgood, with guns that could fire projectiles 17 miles — farther than any battleship at the time.

The shipbuilding industry increased mightily following World War I, soon employing 20,000 people. The California Shipbuilding Corporation, or Calship, one of the nation's largest shipyards was launched on Terminal Island in 1940. Within several years, World War II brought an impressive new neighbor: the Long Beach Naval Shipyard was being commissioned for military service during 1943. All told, the local industry engaged 90,000 at its World War II peak. Giant Todd Shipyards and the Long Beach Naval complex continued as major local employers, but both were casualties of the defense cutbacks of the late 1980s and 1990s. By that time, however, the Port of Los Angeles had become containerized, allowing for automated loading and unloading of commercial cargo. Long Beach and Los Angeles, together, now hold distinction as the busiest harbor district in the United States.

By contrast to the port's carefully deliberated beginnings and political maneuvering, Southern California aviation commenced, almost literally, as a flight of fancy. Glenn Martin built his first airplane in a Santa Ana garage during 1909; when he moved his business to L.A. three years, he listed it in the phone directory under "amusements." Indeed, early aviation used entertainment for its public relations value. The first major air show in the nation, held at Dominguez Hills during January, 1910, is said to have been responsible for fueling Angelenos' interest in flying. The weather suited this particular occasion, as well as the ensuing promotional, research and development functions that boosted local aviation more generally.

Privately-manufactured airplanes, however primitive, were ordered by the government for duty in World War I. Afterward,

the industry survived primarily through airmail contracts and some passenger service, though control of the skies came under federal purview. Career diplomats usually have a reassuring way, particularly when they're 85 years old, but George F. Kennan's experience aboard a vintage World War I craft is as jolting as Russian frost:

"At two o'clock my plane finally arrived from Rostov. It was an ancient affair; an open bi-plane with all the paint worn off the struts. They gave me a helmet and glasses which effectively blinded me for the duration of the journey, and in addition, a shaggy old shuba such as night watchmen might wear in Moscow, but with all the buttons missing, and with a gaping rent in the back. For more than two hours on the way to Rostov, I being partly out in the wind, fought blindly with the wind for the shreds of that shuba. The odds were against me. I had only two arms; the wind had a hundred. In the end, the wind had most of the shuba. I had a magnificent cold."

Admittedly, there were multiple degrees of difference between the Soviet Union and Southern California, long-distance travel and joy rides. During the 1920s, an open air field stood at the corner of La Brea and Wilshire, with a World War I Jenny beckoning courageous pleasure-seekers.

Excitement about the industry was shared by civic leaders, too, albeit for different reasons. The Chamber of Commerce formed an aviation committee to woo companies here. According to one account, the *Times'* Harry Chandler helped raise $15,000 to put Donald Douglas in business.

Immigrants from a variety of seafaring traditions found opportunities to utilize their skills in the harbor area. This veteran fisherman cast his net during 1939. *Courtesy Los Angeles Times Collection (number 15696,) Department of Special Collections, Young Research Library, UCLA.*

The young, Massachusetts Institute of Technology graduate originally had been hired during 1914 by aviation pioneer Glenn Martin; whether at the chamber's urging or through his own inclination, he established his own shop in Santa Monica and built the DC series that for many years propelled the commercial airforce.

The twenties and thirties saw fledgling companies locating to Southern California, and considerable improvements altering mainframes, Still, aviation was a small commercial sphere, and firms traded prime employees and technologies. John Northrup traveled Donald Douglas' career path, working for the Lockheed brothers before starting the company that bears his name. As preparation for his record-breaking flights, Howard Hughes took an active role in modifying Northrup, Lockheed and other planes to increase their fuel-storage capacity, safety features and navigational aids, such as radio. Lockheed later adopted some of these changes in their World War II Hudson Bomber.

The 1928 National Air Races brought construction of three 7,000-foot runways in the middle of a Westchester bean field, with the medium-range goal of developing a municipal airport. The city leased the property and built an oiled landing strip and two 100-foot hangars, with capacities of 20 planes each. The dedication of Mines Field, later Los Angeles International Airport (LAX), occurred on June 7, 1930. Originally more manufacturers flocked to the airport than did carriers. Improvements soon were necessary, however, and they began during 1935, courtesy of the federal government.

The government also purchased some military aircraft prior to World War II, though its system of fixed-priced contracts did not make it a particularly valued customer. A loose infrastructure for military procurement nevertheless was established. By the time Hitler invaded Poland, 60 percent of the nation's airframe manufacturers were in Los Angeles. And of course, the war radically elevated the industry. Aviation was catapulted to aerospace, and subsequently embraced commercial and military applications, as well as exploration of the solar system. The city-proper was home to relatively few headquarters, which generally preferred the South Bay of the County. Still, aerospace manufacturing divisions blanketed L.A., and employed many Angelenos.

The Cold War officially ended during the early 1990s with the formal dissolution of the Soviet Union. Even before the closing act, however, the megafirms that had been the backbone of the local economy began downsizing. Robotics — and far less sophisticated processes — seemed to be replacing human labor.

More accurately, however, a massive workforce transformation was taking place. Studies repeatedly indicate that the fastest growing sector is in small business. The U.S. Small Business Administration for years has characterized its constituency as having fewer than 500 employees, yet "gazelles" of the 1990s often claim far scantier payrolls. Perhaps the greatest irony is that as the 20th century closes, technology appears to favor latter-day wildcatters, efficient, persistent enterprisers tempered with a just enough vision to help them endure the drilling.

The *Spruce Goose* holds the record as the world's largest airplane ever to fly. Howard Hughes built it in a hangar which still can be seen on Jefferson Boulevard near Westlawn. So huge was the craft that its major components (like this wing) were constructed piece-by-piece and later joined together. *Courtesy Playa Vista.*

CHAP

EIGHBORHOODS

TER 5

chapter

Introduction

If books have lives of their own, this one is positively feline. Its pulse has dropped and accelerated to the point of emotional fever many times, with each resuscitation bringing new purpose. One early and often repeated pledge was to tour the L.A. River, from start to finish. The bigger issue, of course, became how would such an excursion would fit into the book. This chapter introduction seemed to be the best place, but a variety of logistical problems arose. I needed a tour guide who knew both the geography and the history of the river; finding any volunteer in August, let alone an interdisciplinary expert, was virtually impossible. I then convinced myself that the tour could be self-guided — an idea that exploded almost immediately. Riding on the freeway to some now-forgotten destination, I spotted the river. My glance quickly diverted from roadway to waterway, where it remained until I realized I could well be the cause of collision. I did not want *Place of Possibilities* to end with quite as much of a bang; a walking tour, therefore, seemed to be a safer alternative.

Indeed, the dissolution of my L.A. River fantasy gave me the excuse to embark on a more personal odyssey: a return to Fairfax Avenue. Fairfax was the focus of my first history book, a project made intensely meaningful by the fact that I lived in the neighborhood for four years. I have since moved away. Now, when my Jewish reserves dwindle, I head to Pico-Robertson. It is closer to my home and more convenient. Metaphorically speaking, one does not need to eat fast food to realize that the art of dining has been lost. Pico-Robertson is straightforward. You know what it offers, get what you want, and can begin the trip home within an hour. Fairfax, however, demands exploration. Because it cannot be neatly packaged, it is sometimes neglected. A 323 (formerly 213) area code and urban identity shut once-suburban Fairfax out of "Westside" — Jewish and otherwise. Different voices ignore the community's current problems, clinging instead to a false label of "affluence."

I would argue that the Angeleno who appreciates an urban vacation can spend a phenomenal weekend here. Within perhaps two and a half miles, one finds Ethiopian culture, variegated Jewish culture, and culture-culture — the latter around the corner from Fairfax on Wilshire Boulevard. Here, stand the massive Los Angeles County Museum of Art complex, the Museum of Miniatures, and the Peterson Automotive Museum. Tourist tendencies may be satisfied by participation as a "live" audience member at CBS studios, on Fairfax just to the south of Beverly Boulevard. Next door, the

Farmer's Market beckons. Created as an outlet for local growers, this almost 65 year-old landmark offers produce stalls and food booths of all types. (Generally, Fairfax boasts more culinary options than could be explored within a month's dining out).

Today, however, I skip the attractions and concentrate on neighborhoods. Fairfax makes an interesting study by anyone's standards. It was perhaps Los Angeles' first modern suburb, and in this capacity, its growth cannot be attributed to any single factor. The community was annexed in parcels; the earliest, an northeastern section known as the Melrose Addition (1922) owed to residential sprawl from Hollywood. Pacific Electric street car lines ran down Santa Monica Boulevard, too, further encouraging this westward movement.

Contrary to its image, Fairfax did not start as a Jewish community. Two of its oldest synagogues both were founded within several blocks of Western

Avenue. The shuls moved with their congregants, and/or to tap a growing pool of prospective members.

On the South, Wilshire Boulevard was being built as a commercial/shopping magnet that would attract a middle- and upper-middle income clientele, autobound from a four-mile radius. This suburban planning concept, which we now take for granted, proved novel — and it worked. Angelenos then, as today, were enamored with the new; for the children of immigrants (many departing from aging, crowded Boyle Heights), an address near the "Miracle Mile" brought

L.A.'s first Jewish settlers, often dry goods and clothing merchants, established themselves near the pueblo. Anti-semitism was less pervasive here during the mid-1800s than it was 50 years or so years later, and those who prospered generally blended into the larger society. French-born Jews Maurice Kremer and Solomon Lazard, whose stores are viewed in the picture, were brothers-in-law and one-time business partners. Lazard became a chamber of commerce president and an owner of the L.A. City Water Company; Kremer served as city clerk. *Courtesy Department of Special Collections, Young Research Library, UCLA.*

cache. They could be Jewish, but were not forced into such an identity. Fairfax residency primarily signified the arrival of modern, upscale Angelenos.

The scions of these suburban pioneers themselves have moved, and return mainly to visit family. Simon Rutberg, owner of Hatikvah, a Jewish music store known for its wide klezmer selection, laments their desertion. He says that many complain about the relatively short driving distance from the Valley or Westside. "Fairfax gets smaller and smaller," Rutberg asserts. "It is a begrudging journey a lot of people make... (Jewish) Fairfax will eventually disappear."

Rutberg's arguments hold some validity. When the Los Angeles Jewish Community Council conducted a population study during the early 1950s, slightly more constituent households resided in Wilshire-Fairfax (the area bounded on the south by Venice Boulevard) than in Beverly-Fairfax. The Jewish community's geographic borders surely have shrunk over time.

Despite changing demographics, neighborhoods maintain natural boundaries shaped by topography and similar architecture styles. Fairfax Avenue extends all the way to Hyde Park, but its Mid-Wilshire division is

a long runway that begins at the Santa Monica Freeway and ascends to the Hollywood Hills. And, as a Fairfax resident, I knew I was almost home when I reached Venice Boulevard. The section between Venice and Airdrome for most of the 1980s and 1990s contained lovely, single-family homes (the oldest probably dating from the 1920s) — that appeared to be deteriorating rapidly. Today, I see gardeners tending local yards; the houses glow with fresh paint and clean windows reflect a variety of positive changes. Indeed, this largely African-American neighborhood seems to be rebounding mightily.

Not so for the section of Fairfax immediately north, from Airdrome to Pico. Though fundamentally sound, the low-density apartment houses cry for a facelift. Their darkening paint and occasionally chipped plaster are further demeaned by broad signs stating the obvious: that vacancies exist.

In 1989, I noted four businesses at the northwest corner of Pico and Fairfax, catering to Indian-, Bengali-, and Pakistani-Americans (and/or those, like myself, who admire their cooking). All but one of these establishments have disappeared, victims of the 1992 civil unrest. The district from Pico to Wilshire nevertheless remains commercial. Anchored by Hansen's Bakery, a family business now celebrating its 50th anniversary, the most obvious presence here is Ethiopian: five restaurants; one merkato; a women's clothing and jewelry shop; and, two travel agencies specializing in trips to the African homeland.

When I lived in Fairfax, I enjoyed meals at perhaps the premiere Ethiopian establishment, Messob restaurant. Owner Rahel Woldmedhin arrived on the Avenue in 1985. Her decision to go into business was inspired by the abundance of successful Ethiopian eateries in another international city, Washington, D.C. Why Fairfax? "It was a growing place; I saw a future for the area," Woldmedhin explains. "(Fairfax also) was a big street, with lots of local traffic." Proper signage, she believed, would surely entice ethnic food-loving Angelenos. Other Ethiopian-American restaurateurs joined her in short order. Some of these immigrants have committed themselves to Fairfax as a home. Woldmedhin and her manager, for example, both live in the giant Parklabrea complex (my former residence), to the north of Sixth Street.

This neighborhood appears to be undergoing gentrification. Sixth and the smaller streets that cut across it once boasted vintage apartment buildings, containing perhaps no more than eight units each and displaying Tudor or other charming designs. The old structures have succumbed to 1990s complexes, likely inhabited by a mixture of well-heeled singles, young couples, and retirees. The four- or five-story Barnaby's building at the corner of Colgate and Fairfax apparently has been purchased after a long vacancy. Now fashionably washed in gray, its first floor is dedicated to a trattoria and bakery; the natural wood panes and window boxes brimming with white roses echo an upscale, 1990s American aesthetic. Yet, generalizations are never easy on Fairfax. Right across the street, Hancock Park Elementary School invites enrollment, with banners in English, Spanish and Korean.

I drive to the historic Jewish section, north of CBS and Beverly Boulevard. Parking dictates my itinerary; I start on Oakwood, momentarily passing the previous block. Rutberg's warning rings true here; I'm somewhat confused about where I am. After visiting his store with the Yiddish classic, "By Meir Bis Du Shayn " ("To Me, You Are Beautiful,") blaring, I spot the Nova Express Cafe. Its upper facade bubbles a molten orange styrofoam, and though not yet open, the place ordinarily serves "cosmic pizza." Next door is the Blitzstein Museum of Art, a gallery.

The under-35 crowd, undefined ethnically or religiously, has situated itself here. As Rutberg points out, a tattoo parlor stands along side Solomon's bookstore, which during the 1940s relocated its Judaica collection from Boyle Heights. The Bang Improv Studio — hardly an early-morning haunt — offers classes and shows, most for an affordable $5 admission. Even Canter's Deli, another venerable Eastside transplant, plays to a new audience, announcing through signage that customers may purchase cappuccino and espresso inside. Fairfax is "totally different at night," informs Haim Kario, who owns Musicall, a store selling Israeli music, videos and books.

Youth-oriented businesses can be found all over this block, but they hardly constitute a majority. In response to the Avenue's jumbled array, however, shops serving distinctly Jewish constituencies seem to have banded together, asserting identities for themselves and their customers. Three glatt 2 kosher establishments — Hadar Glatt, Western Kosher and La Glatt Delicatessen — can be found on the northeastern quadrant of Fairfax between Oakwood and Rosewood. The Israeli merchants have chosen the western side of the street, to the immediate north of Rosewood.

At the hub of these six or so shops is the Fairfax Grocery, now just as readily known by its informal Hebrew name, Sami (or, Sammy) Makolet. This store awaited me when I moved to Fairfax 15 years ago, and it immediately became my favorite. Back then, it was unique among the local businesses, and tiny. The owner, Sammy, and his wife carried Middle-Eastern specialties — the freshest nuts, dried fruit, four or five types of feta cheeses. Spices were not entirely visible; if I wanted something that wasn't displayed, I asked for it. No matter how obscure my request, the hard-working proprietor would respond with Yaish! ("I have it!"), retrieving the fragrant substance from what must have been a miniscule storage space piled to the ceiling.

Sammy later won money in the lottery and expanded his store. Customers filled the space; the enlarged makolet frequently is as packed as that old storage room must have been. Bilingual (Hebrew and English) signs — their red letters professionally-rendered — now direct shoppers to several cashier booths and other noteworthy corners. And Sammy has become dean of the local Israeli merchants. Perhaps unintentionally, all their street signs contain red letters on a white background. Returning south, I notice that Sami Makolet and El-Ad Nuts have dangled slender plaques, of uniform size, from the awning posts at high eye-level, alerting passersby to their presence. No urban planner could have done it better!

My last stop is the section that I missed, between Beverly and Oakwood. With the notion of various constituencies in my mind, I perceive an impending social service center. A massive old kosher butcher-produce mart has been replaced by Out of the Closet Thrift Store, one of seven such enterprises that raise funds for the AIDS Health Care Foundation. HIV oral testing is offered here every Saturday, and the sign outside lists the organization's four clinics and three hospices. Another new addition to the Avenue, the Hirsch Family Kosher Kitchen provides elderly community members with hot lunches. The Freida Mohr Multiservice Center follows to the south, attracting senior clients at its longtime location.

Chatting with two of the diners at the kosher kitchen, I look out the window for a broad view. A surprise awaits me. Many of the neighborhood's old businesses remain: Diamond Bakery, Freddy's Deli, Famous Bakery, Dave's Cut Rate Deli Rite and the Bargain Fair. Some changes have occurred, of course. When my father visited me in L.A., he invariably made pilgrimages to Dave's; generous portions of schmaltz herring, well-packed, returned with him and my mother to Pittsburgh. Dave no longer runs the Deli Rite, and a new generation, in the persona of family member Steve Friedman, has taken over. The 1994 earthquake offered an excuse for the business to move into bigger,

refreshed quarters a few doors away. As for the Bargain Fair, it has dropped the prefix "Honest Max's" from its name.

Indeed, this section of Fairfax exudes American Jewish sensibilities of the 1950s and 1960s, when I was a girl. Few were culturally enlightened then, seldom acknowledging the existence, let alone the politican plights, of Syrian or Ethiopian coreligionists. But here, too, one recalls a community that in some way seemed more accepting, less ritually hierarchical. "Jewish" food did not always need to be kosher, and keeping kosher alone was commendable prior to the imposition of glatt standards.

It is hard to write off Fairfax; people have tried before. Newspapers 25 years ago disparaged the district, referring to it as "A Grey Area" and the "Lower East Side of the West." Baby boomers of all backgrounds, rebels then, established local headquarters with an underground press, free clinic and coffee houses. Nothing — and everything — is different today. According to a 1997 survey conducted by the Jewish Federation, Fairfax still holds a larger number of Jewish Angelenos than any neighborhood in the city, though the figure has declined from 75,000 in 1979 to 55,000 currently. But more importantly, the substantial aging population is being replaced by young Jewish singles and married households, including immigrants.

This is not to say that the majority of folks who transform Fairfax at night are Jewish. People under 30 relate more to their generation than to religion or culture. If they stay long enough, however, they will be free to promote their growing identities — no matter how defined — somewhere on this Avenue.

Born in Eastern Europe of Jewish parents, artist Boris Deutsch (1895-1978) demonstrated an awareness of— and interest in — diverse cultures. He probably would have felt comfortable on Fairfax Avenue. *Courtesy The National Archives and Records Administration, Washington, D.C.*

Today's City of Los Angeles is the product of some 10 consolidations and 151 annexations. Already incorporated, the consolidated communities came from positions of greater civic or commercial strength. These neighborhoods had thrived in an early era because they often were founded for a specific purpose — an identity beyond sheer housing development. Wilmington (consolidated, 1909) and San Pedro (1909) grew through their harbor tradition. Contrary to its later image, Hollywood (1910) had been intended as a religious bastion and Tujunga (1932), a utopian, socialist colony guided by environmental principles. Watts was known for farming and had an African-American presence by the time it entered L.A. in 1926. The remaining consolidations were: Sawtelle, now West L.A. (1922); Hyde Park (1923); Eagle Rock (1923); Venice (1925); and, Barnes City, today part of Mar Vista (1927). Twenty parcels, all under one-half square-mile, separated from the city in the years immediately following World War II. These "detachments" merged into Burbank, Beverly Hills, Culver City, El Segundo, Inglewood, San Fernando and Torrance.

From its 1850 incorporation until 1895, however, Los Angeles had only one addition, the annexation of a small "southern extension." The future leviathan developed internally, populating its original 28-square- mile Spanish land grant. The acreage is not insignificant. Arlington County, Virginia, a comfortable Washington, DC suburb with plenty of parks, backyard space and other amenities today squeezes 170,000 people into approximately five square miles. Of course, land uses are different now, but Los Angeles of 1890 contained only 50,000 people.

Within the original borders lie communities as varied as Little Tokyo, parts of East L.A., and Angelino Heights. The integration of housing and work space defined Los Angeles' earliest neighborhoods, its core communities.

The Core

The plaza area served as the original "center city." Each of L.A.'s first families, the pobladores, were assigned residential lots with two nearby fields for agriculture. Community property included grazing grounds and facilities such as La Placita, to be shared by all. Everything then could be accomplished within a short distance. Spanish land grants for purposes other than the urban settlement were relatively few but expansive, consisting of thousands of acres outside the city limits and reaching from Ventura to San Diego County.

The political changing of the guard altered population patterns. Mexican grants typically were more numerous but not as generous in acreage; they also hewed closer to the pueblo. Greater numbers of rancheros created their own lifestyle — yet the city clearly was part of it. Grantees often built "second homes" around the plaza to be near a growing commercial and social hub.

Though not a direct recipient of a Mexican land, Abel Stearns became a ranchero in all but the legalities — and someone whose daily existence combined these urban and rural spheres. The New Englander erected a spacious house near the plaza in 1842, and emerged as the county's largest property owner, eventually boasting 200,000 acres. He was heavily vested in the most prosperous enterprises of the era — cattle and viti-culture — but his enduring historic legacy has been forgotten: Stearns constructed what is now Capitol Milling (1831), the oldest manufacturing concern within the borders of Los Angeles. The building remains at its original site, 1231 N. Spring Street. Milling operations, however, are more closely associated with two Jewish families, the Loews and the Levis, who bought the business from Stearns; Capital Milling remained in their hands from 1883 until the late 1990s, when the Levis left.

The story of Capitol Milling reflects on certain the geographic and demographic changes that took place during the mid- and late-1800s. The rancho period declined with the cattle bust and the reallocations of property judged by the U.S. Land Commission. Holdings diminished, but those could afford it chose space over highly urbanized settings.

Moreover, a pattern of movement already was indicated. The Hancock survey of Los Angeles (1856) divided southern-lying land into 35-acre tracts. Washington, Adams and Jefferson streets — east-west thoroughfares all — separated the parcels. The railroads

came to town within the next three decades, creating
north-south transportation corridors first along Alameda,
then Santa Fe and Central avenues. Manufacturers
hovered closeby, and the resulting industrial grime literally yielded right and wrong "sides of the tracks." Given
the natural terrain and these newly-drawn boundaries,
monied settlement generally thrust southward and westward from its original downtown locus.

Immigrants inherited homes near the plaza, which
declined in value as newer residential addresses were
sought. Vintage properties were subdivided, rendering
more profitable — but less commodious — rental space.
Landlords demonstrated fewer concerns about maintenance and upkeep than when they, themselves, had
lived in the properties.

Quantitative methods recently have been extended to history, once strictly a "humanities" discipline. If
late-19th century social and economic segregation
could be calculated mathematically, in degrees of sever-
ity, "points" would be assigned in four categories to
immigrants who: displayed signs of poverty; spoke a language other English; held a religious affiliation outside of
Protestantism, and were not Caucasian. Individuals
who scored in every category would suffer the most
discrimination; those with none of the above-traits, the
least. When the general population diffused in about
the 1870s, the plaza became the domain primarily of
Chinese and Mexican immigrants.

Sonoratown, so named because most of its residents
hailed from that Mexican province, existed on the
north end. A growing population and a lack of affordable housing presented problems, even then. One- and
two- room shacks, jacales, were interspersed between
older buildings. The Los Angeles Housing Commission,
formed shortly after the turn of the century, viewed
conditions in the historic barrio: "Here we found filth
and squalor on every hand. Miserably constructed
homes, made of scrap sheet iron, old bagging and
section of dry goods boxes, were huddled together without any attempt at proper construction or order. The
more Mexicans to the lot, the more money for the
owner." The shacks, which housed four and five family

members, ultimately were condemned, and the property sought for more valuable commercial uses. Many of the residents moved eastward, over the river.

L.A.'s first Chinese neighborhood emerged on a narrow passageway directly southeast of the plaza, Calle de los Negroes, or Negro Alley. (This appellation probably recalled the mixed-African heritage of earlier settlers.) Maps through the mid-1880s indicate a heavy Chinese concentration, but by 1887, the population had crossed Alameda Street en masse. Some laborers were there before, working the vineyards; still, such a major relocation — achieved over the course of a few months — probably owed to arson, as described in this *Los Angeles Times* article:

> The removal of Chinatown from its present quarters on "Nigger" alley and on the east side of the Plaza to a section more remote and less obtrusive, is a good fortune which has literally been forced upon Los Angeles....Undoubtedly the late incendiary fires and the withdrawal of insur-

ance from the Chinese quarters...have been the most potent influences in securing this quick result. THE TIMES denounced the lawlessness which sought to burn the Chinamen out, but the good results which unwittingly sprung from an evil cause cannot be gainsayed or deprecated. Now Los Angeles Street, which has so long been held in suspense, can be put through to a junction with Alameda Street, and an unsightly and noisesome quarter or town can be revolutionized.

The fire also may have spawned another, smaller Chinese community to the south, on San Pedro Street; a produce market subsequently grew at this locale. Nevertheless, a crowded, new Chinatown rose east of Alameda, on the property of the Apablasas, a Chilean family tracing its ancestry to Portugal. The central thoroughfares were Apablasa and Marchessault streets; narrower, intersecting passageways derived their names from the Apablasa children — Cayetano, Juan, Maria, Conchita, Lara, Candelaria and Benjamin.

The original buildings were wooden shacks, probably inhabited at an earlier date by Mexican and Native American laborers. Fifteen of these fell to a blaze in 1899, and were replaced with brick edifices, utilizing the most common building material of the day. Chinatown subsequently acquired a distinctive look:

One of the most striking points in viewing Chinatown is its bright color. The houses are for the most part of red brick, built flush with the street, two stories in height and offering a surface unbroken by any apparent division between properties. The windows are small and are usually barred or covered with solid wooden shutters. Here and there are wooden balconies ornamented profusely in brilliant hues, yellow, red, and green. Occasionally are window boxes filled with bright flowers. On holidays variegated lanterns are hung on all porches and doorways and gay pennants flutter thick in the air.

The community lasted for almost 50 years, until the finalization of the Union Station project. Formal demolition notices were sent to Chinatown residents during the latter part of 1933, and the first wrecking crews arrived on December 22. Older residents clung to their homes, ignoring the inevitable. Relocation had yet to be decided and the Chinese Chamber of Commerce, under Peter Soo Hoo, successfully stalled the demolition several times pending a viable strategy. Ultimately, two competing plans emerged; both materialized. The brainchild of Christine Sterling, China City was the Asian twin to Olvera Street, thematic with rickshaws and a vintage Hollywood "Great Wall" donated by Cecil B. DeMille. The development contained rental lots and attracted 50 small shops. Located between Ord, North Spring, Macy and North Main, China City burned down in the early 1940s.

Apablasa and Marchessault Streets constituted the nucleus of Chinatown. Just before the community was razed to accommodate Union Station, Charles C. Apablasa, a descendant of the original property owner, took his wife, Panchita, and their young children, Carlos and Ernestine, to visit the homestead for the last time. The sign on the corner of the building echoes their heritage. *Courtesy The Collection of Carlos B. Abaplasa.*

New Chinatown owed to Peter Soo Hoo in two respects: he negotiated with the Santa Fe railroad for the vacant property west of Broadway and North of College, and he had the vision and perserverence to bring to fruition a multiuse, Chinese-owned and developed-community. Initial investments amounted to $500/share, and New Chinatown opened during 1935 with 18 stores and a bean cake factory. It welcomed tourists, but its primary mission was to serve the social and economic needs of its constituents. Buildings assumed a contemporary Chinese-American appearance, representing the community's leadership. By 1942, $1 million had been invested in the complex.

Neither New Chinatown nor China City could be defined solely by business activities, however. Residential units surrounded both commercial districts and, despite their different histories, the two developments merged into what is now commonly Chinatown. Enduring as a walking community, the area also remains true to the spirit of its predecessors — and, in a sense, to the old Los Angeles that could be navigated without third-party intervention.

The Japanese began to arrive here at around the same time as Chinese Angelenos moved across Alameda Street. The plaza area then was tightly occupied, and newcomers from around the world settled to the south, in newer, brick parts of downtown that where they, too, could live and work in close proximity.

Earlier, we explored the people who turned grapes into wine. But in the vicinity of today's Little Tokyo, one Kiln Messer parlayed his native craft, utilizing the vineyards for the German beverage of choice. L.A. chronicler Harris Newmark describes Messer's enterprise and changing land use: "After brewing beer for a while at the corner of Third and Main streets, Messer brought a twenty-acre vineyard which, in 1857, he increased by another to forty-five or fifty acres; and it was his good fortune that this property was so located to be needed by the Santa Fe Railroad, in 1888, as a terminal."

By 1909, no trace of Messer or the other neighboring vineyards existed; an industrial sector had burgeoned in their place. Warehousers flanked the railroad tracks, storing anything from furniture to crockery to dried fruits. Large grocers and food purveyors of all types established themselves locally: a division of the Spreckels Company, H.J. Mercer Honey and Bee Supplies, Globe Mills A-1 Flour, Newberry's Groceries.

Laborers lived in the adjoining area, as did small retailers and service workers. The community surrounding East First and Second streets, between Los Angeles and Central Avenues was known as "Little Berlin" just before the turn of the century; Germans (brewery workers and those otherwise engaged) constituted the largest nationality group. The Japanese presence was small, with a few restaurants scattered in the midst of Jewish, Irish, German, African-American and Chinese businesses. All catered to the community's vast working class, foreign-born and ill-paid.

Arriving around 1900, the Russian-speaking Molokans settled slightly to the north. They could be distinguished by their commitment to their church, and by their national dress: men sported long beards and shirts left outside of their cloth-belted trousers; women opted for bright, multi-colored garb, draped with black shawls. Family people who worked as laborers and domestics or laundry workers, respectively, they saved rigorously to purchase neighborhood homes. Freestanding brick ovens and banyas (saunas) came to occupy their backyards.

Japanese moved in increasing numbers to Los Angeles from 1901-1906. A sizable group had been recruited from San Francisco in 1903 to replace the Mexican workers then striking the Pacific Electric Railway; other job hunters in pursuit of better employment opportunities followed. As mentioned previously, however, the dislocation caused by the San Francisco earthquake was perhaps the largest factor in sending many south.

While the Japanese-American population in Los Angeles had been diffused, by 1905 the area around First Street acquired the nickname "Little Tokyo." A rival district existed at approximately Sixth and Olive; its trademark was the "employment agency," a unique Japanese-American enterprise that fed, clothed and housed workers, and dispatched them to temporary window-washing or housekeeping assignments — likely the predecessor of today's clean-up crews.

Little Tokyo ultimately gained primacy. It was central to the other small, Japanese enclaves. Furthermore, at the same time as the local Japanese population grew, downtown residents began searching for newer, more family-friendly quarters away from the singles-oriented bars and pool halls; some moved across the river to the multicultural Boyle Heights community. Japanese-Americans maintained a strong presence in Little Tokyo until forced out during World War II. To some extent, African-Americans temporarily filled the emptiness. Many had flocked to L.A. for defense industry jobs, and their crowded, segregated neighborhoods were bursting. Vacated by Executive Order, Little Tokyo provided local African-Americans more living space.

Japanese Angelenos returned after the war. Again, rival communities emerged, with places like Gardena (an independent city) and West Los Angeles greatly nurtured by the *Nisei*, or second generation. Little Tokyo nevertheless remains the spiritual center of Japanese Los Angeles, paying reverence to the turn-of-the-century commercial district that brought sustenance to its earliest residents, while enticing Angelenos and world travelers alike with a culturally-proud, almost futuristic urban setting.

Suburbs Within City Limits

Robert M. Widney incorporated the city's first public transportation line, the Spring and Sixth Street Horse Railroad Company, on February 7, 1874. He was not speculating in mass transit but in real estate. Widney recently had moved from his home on Spring Street below Second to Hill near Fourth, where he owned building lots. Transportation was needed to lure future residents there. Laying tracks proved the costliest part of the venture, though funds also were needed to buy the passenger cars and horses. Widney opened his enterprise to stockholders; 42 bought into it, with banker Francis P.F. Temple owning the largest share at $500. Nevertheless, property owners along the route provided two-thirds of the capitalization. Widney inaugurated his one-horse line with hourly service from 6:30 a.m. to 10:00 p.m weekdays, and a reduced schedule on Sundays to accommodate

(Left and bottom) Hardly a Merry Christmas if you were stuck in downtown traffic! The street rails had been built by many proprietors, each maintaining distinct lines, facilities and equipment. While ownership consolidated, the system's anarchical origins rendered downtown a tight weave of congestion. The pace of the electric cars accelerated, however, upon leaving the city. *Courtesy The Postcard Collection of Jeanne Taylor Baird.*

churchgoers. Fare ran 10 cents per trip, but four were available for the special price of a quarter.

By 1890, L.A. counted some 20 independent street railcar companies. Histories varied, but underlying themes repeated themselves: new housing developments often waited at the end of the lines. The name of Moses Sherman, a entrepreneur heavily vested in both street rails and real estate, lived on in Sherman, California, (later West Hollywood,) as well as Sherman Oaks.

Horse-drawn cars, cables and electric trolleys ran simultaneously through the late 1890s, sometimes under the auspices of a single operator. Street cars mimicked the railroads: very little was shared, and most had their own stops, repair facilities and equipment. A tight weave of routes soon crisscrossed downtown, their names indicating destinations: Main Street & Agricultural (Exposition Park), Los Angeles & Aliso Avenue, East First Street & Boyle Heights, Main & Fifth Street, Los Angeles & Vernon, Pico Street & Maple Avenue, East Los Angeles & San Pedro, Second Street Cable Railroad, Temple Street Cable Railway, Mateo Street & Sante Fe Avenue, Los Angeles & Vernon, Cummings Street.

Even before fierce competition from the automobile, ownership in the street rail system changed rapidly. Companies went into bankruptcy; they were quickly bought, sold, consolidated with others. What resulted from this chain of mergers, in 1910, was the Los Angeles Railway Corporation (LARY), known more popularly by its "yellow cars." The Pacific Electric Company owned the "red car" line. LARY endured as a local street system; PE was "interurban", transporting passengers to the ends of Los Angeles County, and beyond.

But names — or even routes — did not tell the complete story. With extensions, street cars drove suburban development in several ways. Obviously, they provided conveyance to new communities. Furthermore, the lack of centralized transportation planning caused unbelievable congestion downtown. The resulting crowdedness, noise, dirt, and sometimes dangerous traffic conditions helped to push outward movement.

The first suburbs actually were within the limits of the old Spanish land grant, though they were separated by natural features, such as hillside locations or sites across the L.A. River. A physical division between work and home remained the most distinguishing suburban feature, at least until about 1920. Residents depended on town for livelihood, shopping and entertainment, and the street railways allowed them to lead a dual existence.

Bunker Hill, probably the first neighborhood to meet the definition of an urban suburb, was developed during the late 1860s, appealing to newly-arrived, well-heeled Angelenos — not quite the landed gentry, but the professional and business classes. Its Queen Anne and Eastlake homes, then fashionable throughout the United States, clearly defied the earlier L.A. vernacular. Bunker Hill's trademark link to downtown, Angel's Flight, only opened in 1901, a good 30 years after the community itself developed. The neighborhood later confronted a situation which was to become familiar in L.A. Vacated by upper-middle class owners for bigger yards and clearer air, its spacious Victorians were subdivided to accommodate older people and families who could not afford to move from center-city. The Community Redevelopment Agency, founded in 1948 to reverse urban blight, chose Bunker Hill as its

first project. During the 1950s and 1960s, the neighborhood was leveled. The Music Center, office towers, and a large apartment complex rose in its place; a restored Angel's Flight is the sole reminder of the formerly gracious neighborhood.

The ending is happier for Angelino Heights. Spurred by the opening of the Temple Street Cable Car, which cut over the hilly terrain to what is now East Edgeware Road, William Stilson and Everett Hall began their development project in 1887. They erected 13 Queen Anne and Eastlake homes before the 1880s land boom fizzled. Nearby oil discoveries rekindled local housing construction in about 1905, but this time Angelino Heights added California and craftsmen-style bungalows. Spanish, Dutch, and other colonial homes joined the streetscape, too. The neighborhood later went through some of the same deterioration and subdivision that plagued Bunker

the river became impassible, or flooded, during rainy seasons. Therefore, the "bluffs" overlooking it were considered more desirable for settlement.

Boyle Heights actually had been part of the pueblo's original land grant. Henry Hancock conducted a second survey in 1858 to clearly identify city borders for the U.S. Land Commission. Indiana Avenue was confirmed as the line of demarcation between Los Angeles and unincorporated parts of the county. When city lands east of the river subsequently were sold during the late 1860s to raise revenues, some of the most influential Angelenos — Isais W. Hellman, Prudent Beaudry, Ozro W. Childs, John W. Downey, Andrew Boyle and William Henry Workman — speculated on them. At the same time, Hansen's survey noted 12 structures. Almost all were associated with Mexican-Americans. While Victorians rose on Bunker Hill, these early residents of Boyle Heights likely preferred adobe.

Boyle and Workman were the only two major investors who actually chose to make their homes in the community. True to his times, Boyle was a vintner. He grew grapes on the flatlands near the river, and built a wine cellar into the bluffs. This structure is believed to remain. Workman married Boyle's daughter, Maria Elizabeth. And it was he who decided to develop Boyle Heights in earnest, subdividing the Brooklyn, Crescent View and Mount Pleasant tracts. According to a 1880 report: "In 1876 he laid out the village of Boyle Heights, which now contains fifty or sixty families. A horse railway connects the settlement with the city. Mr. Workman has expended some ten thousand dollars in procuring water for this upper land, and now has it in sufficient quantities. He has laid out a park of fifteen acres, beautifully planted with citrus fruits."

Like all other land in Los Angeles, Boyle Heights went through the ups and downs of the real estate market. Workman wielded considerable influence. This president of the Boyle Heights Board of Trade carried downtown credentials, too: he subscribed to the first public library and high school, helped organize the Chamber of Commerce, and served as mayor from 1886-1888. As a result of Workman's advocacy, the Los

Hill, but the 20-year age difference coincided with a changing attitude. Angelino Heights became the city's first Historic Preservation Overlay Zone, a factor that has brought a new generation of homeowners here and united them into a community.

Another historic suburb is more confusing: first, because it actually consists of several neighborhoods; second, because everyone has their own definition of it; and, third, because today it seems to be decidedly urban. One current Los Angeles City Councilmember, Richard Alatorre, represents the "Eastside"; yet, his district also embraces Highland Park, Eagle Rock and other Arroyo Seco communities that have their own geo-cultural characteristics. Most parts of what is generally considered "East Los Angeles" — Belvedere, City Terrace, the area around the Maravilla housing development — are out of city limits. Definitions converge, however, in Boyle Heights.

The neighborhood begins immediately to the east of the L.A. River. Whatever its other early amenities,

Angeles Cable Railway came to Boyle Heights, at a cost of over $1 million.

Although some wealthy families initially resided in the area, its frame houses were inhabited mostly by the middle class. Workman was not the only community-builder in the Heights. Two Jewish developers, Louis Lewin and Charles Jacoby, added affordability to the equation by allowing prospective homeowners to buy "on time," a practice then not common. Perhaps this new ethnic presence — and more importantly, a stretched payment schedule — lured a variety of other working class Angelenos to the area. Additionally, by the turn of the century, the original housing stock was not so new and, therefore, more affordable.

The average circa 1906 home was a wood frame, single-family dwelling, constructed on a large lot but without stables. Some apartment buildings existed, too. Horse and buggy was still the vehicle of choice then, but probably for financial reasons, most Boyle Heights residents relied on public transportation. With the exception of a mixed commercial-residential zone on First Street, the area contained few businesses. People in the Heights continued to go downtown for work, shopping and entertainment.

Within the next 20 years, the community changed rapidly. At the same time as small, local business districts grew, automobile garages slowly emerged on some of the residential properties. The area was truly multicultural, a draw for working-class Angelenos of Mexican, Jewish, Japanese, Molokan, Italian and African descent. There were indeed ethnic concentrations. The greater East Los Angeles area counted 30,000 Mexican-American families by the late 1920s. Brooklyn and Soto is lovingly remembered as the major center of Jewish life then, home to as many as 90,000 residents and 27 synagogues. Yet, the Jewish population was diffused throughout Boyle Heights. Groups not generally associated with the area even had a presence there: for example, St. Johannes Evangelical Lutheran Church, located near the southwest corner of Evergreen Cemetery, attracted Scandinavian worshipers.

While relations may not have been uniformly harmonious, a cross-cultural, community spirit often existed. Norma Alvarado, a friend who was a Boyle Heights child during the late 1950s, said that since many mothers worked, those who were home at a given time tended to look after other kids on the block — regardless of ethnic background.

Yet, there also was an exodus from Boyle Heights. The 1920s saw the birth of a neighborhood, City Terrace, so physically close that the casual observer might have failed to notice a border. The new community "had larger, convenient, better-plumbed and heated homes — with more elbow room," observed former area

The pueblo's land grant originally extended to Indiana Avenue in Boyle Heights, but the community truly emerged during the late 19th century as a middle and working-class suburb, along a growing industrial corridor. The bridges that span the Los Angeles River were not mass-produced, however. Different classical and contemporary styles are displayed, and features such as old streetlights have been preserved. *Courtesy The Postcard Collection of Jeanne Taylor Baird.*

resident Hy Solomon. "It was situated on a hill and sought for its wonderful climate." Although its growth was hindered somewhat by the Depression and World War II, City Terrace became a stopping off point for young, mobile Boyle Heights families or the American-born children of immigrants who sought a more modern, upscale lifescale. Many subsequently headed to L.A.'s Westside or to newer parts of the San Gabriel Valley.

From the 1930s onward, but particularly after 1950, Boyle Heights and unincorporated East Los Angeles attracted greater numbers of Mexican-Americans. The demographic change owes to a burgeoning population and housing simultaneously vacated by previous residents (including Mexican-Americans). In addition to a large wave of immigrants who came north during the Mexican Revolution, longtime Angelenos were searching for homes. The city period-ically leveled deteriorating Mexican-American or ethnically-mixed communities — first parts of the plaza and, much later, Bunker Hill — necessitating relocation. Other neighborhoods fell to freeway construction and commercial development; Chavez Ravine, where Dodger Stadium now stands, once was Mexican-American.

More generally, Boyle Heights' initial suburban trappings have been lost at least since the 1920s. Still, those who lived there then bear a fondness for the multicultural neighborhood that was community.

Extending City Limits, North and South

The Highland Park and University annexations, repre-sented by USC and Occidental College, respectively, took place in 1895 and 1899. Both institu-tions had existed since the 1880s, but their formal admission to the city mirrored both population and perceptual growth. Angelenos craved as communities verdant "campuses;" they also sought a more sophisticated cultural identity.

Yet, the parks — Exposition and Highland — differed mightily. USC soon teamed with West Adams to form a respected, fashionable district. The newly-riche Dohenys chose a domicile in the vicinity. The area may not have had much history at the time, but it handcrafted its own destiny: many classic structures — residential and institutional alike — have endured, in the heart of what is now the inner-city.

By contrast, the Arroyo Seco communities of Eagle Rock, Highland Park, Mount Washington and Glassell Park claim a long, if radically understated, history. Their vivid prehistoric and colonial past largely escaped the written word. Furthermore, a location between Los Angeles and Pasadena spurred modern growth, but simultaneously concealed the unique identities of these communities. The Arroyo nevertheless retains natural beauty and echoes regional history, all the while staying elusive — difficult to define. In that sense, it is very much like Los Angeles.

Eagle Rock is a gigantic bolder still visible from the 134 Freeway. The impression of a bird embedded in the rock was explained by the Tongva who lived nearby. Many years ago, an eagle absconded with a human infant. Villagers threw stones at the bird until his flight was halted. As the wounded eagle fell, he dropped the baby safely into his mother's arms before crashing into the rock and casting his permanent contour.

Later, passersby included priests and settlers. The Austrian traveler, Archduke Ludwig Louis Savaltor, commented on his 1876 journey through the arroyo:

A valley was reached where directly ahead rose the mysterious Piedra Gorda (fat rock)...At the right is Cienega del Garvanza, a small green swamp with clumps of bunch-grass, and the bottom, Sacate de Matiago, which never dries out. From here we emerge on a plain where enormous herds of sheep, guarded by strong, fat, shaggy dogs, pastured. The Piedra Gorda, towering above....also was used at one time by the Indians as a natural bulwark, a rock fortress, since this spot was an excellent location from which to observe the movements of the first settlers.

A 1923 publication produced by a local bank indicated a "Greater Highland Park" composed of "five friendly valleys." Beside Highland Park proper, other historic names included Garvanza, York Valley (likely Eagle Rock), Hermon, and Sycamore Grove. Andrew Glassell and A.C. Chapman purchased over 114,000 acres from the Verdugos, Spanish land grant holders whose indebtedness forced them to sell at a low price. A Basque couple, the Goldaracenas, leased land and established a sheep herders camp.

Often-mentioned Garvanza (now part of Highland Park) was the first community settled; fed by the real estate boom and accessible through the Santa Fe Railroad line, it boasted 500 residents by 1887. Its first community newspaper, the *Garvanzan* — an exchange sheet, really — was the inspiration of a local realtor. Moses Sherman and Eli P. Clark soon built an electric railway from Los Angeles along the arroyo. Service reached Sycamore Grove and Garvanza during 1894, and the line to Pasadena, completed the following year. Highland Park (1895) and Garvanza (1899) soon became annexed to L.A. In general terms, local residents wanted to maintain civility: some sources say that the move was designed to help the communities stay "dry," others talk about the difficulty in dealing with bandits who regularly traipsed through the area.

Eagle Rock developed on its own, first as an agricultural community:

Its area was broken up into truck gardens and orchards, and the reputation of the famous Gates (Eagle Rock) strawberries and Eagle Rock winter vegetables was about the only medium by which the district was brought to the attention of those living outside its hilly boundaries. A country wagon road leading from Glendale and the San Fernando Valley into Pasadena roughly bisected the valley from west to east; another road, running southwest, connected with the main San Fernando Road, along which the truck gardeners drove their produce to the markets of L.A.

Eagle Rock incorporated as an independent city in 1911; Occidental College moved there three years later. Community planners interwove natural elements with the transportation features of an advanced, early 20th-century suburb. The following excerpt describes Eagle Rock in 1909:

With the comparatively small area lying west of Townsend Avenue there are now completed or under construction for immediation completion over twenty-two miles of heavy concrete street curbings and wide cement sidewalks. Eagle Rock's main boulevard, Colorado Street, is dedicated to the county at a uniform width of 120 feet and is to be paved with macadam. One of the most beautiful streets is the famous Hill Avenue, which follows closely the contours of the foothills, bounding Eagle Rock on the north. The portion of Hill Avenue now completed gives a smooth hard surface for autos and carriages, winding in and out close to the hills and flanked by wide parkways planted with cork oaks and the beautiful double-blooming scarlet hibiscus.

Los Angeles annexed or consolidated almost 70 communities between 1910 and 1930. The primary reason was the opening of the aqueduct — and, more basically, water. After 12 years on its own, Eagle Rock likewise entered the union. There were exceptions to the water- and transportation-driven rationales for annexation, however. Watts was developed by a man whose family also built parts of the arroyo. The southern community's early history resounds transportation themes, but the consolidation occurred for unique reasons.

Shortly after the turn of the century, Charles Watts donated 10 acres of land so that the Pacific Electric could connect some of its lines in his development. Watts Junction, incorporated during 1907, soon found itself in the middle of routes that reached from downtown to Redondo, San Pedro and Long Beach-Santa Ana. The

"South Central Suite" (1995), one of a series of panels at the Metro Blue Line/Slauson Station, depicts community history and the aspirations of local residents. This commissioned work was completed by a team of artists, the East Los Streetscapers. *Courtesy The Metropolitan Transportation Authority, Los Angeles.*

community attracted working class residents and farmers of various backgrounds: German, Scotch, Mexican, Italian, Greek, Jewish, Japanese and African-American.

African-Americans during the first decade of this century were encouraged to buy land in Los Angeles. The 1910 census shows that 36.1 percent of African-American Angelenos owned their own homes, quite a high figure for the times. Among other advertisements, black newspapers throughout the country carried announcements like the following: "Buy Lots now in Watts: where values are sure to double — where a five cent car line is started — where the price is within reach of all....Terms $10.00 cash and $5.00 per month."

Watts counted a large African-American population by the 1920s; encroaching segregation was apparent, too, as they lived in a quarter called "Mudville." When it seemed that the African-American community might be strong enough to elect a black mayor, other residents successfully appealed to Los Angeles, in 1926, for consolidation.

Actually, the area commonly referred to as "South Central" represents a less official consolidation. Six African-American neighborhoods existed throughout the city circa 1910: West Temple Street-Occidental Boulevard; First to Third Street, San Pedro Street to Santa Fe Avenue; Seventh to Ninth streets, Mateo to Santa Fe; Boyle Heights (First to Broadway, Evergreen to Savannah); 35th Street and Normandie Avenue; Pico Heights.

Prejudice grew with increasing population and visibility. From the late teens and accelerating after the Depression, African-Americans faced discrimination in consumer services and housing. As a result, they concentrated along Central Avenue — and in all directions from it. This north-south thoroughfare, itself, had long been a transportation hub, with the Southern Pacific's Arcade Depot located at Fifth and Central. The railroads brought newcomers to Los Angeles and employed perhaps more African-Americans than any other single local industry until that time.

Indeed, Central Avenue confined African-Americans, but allowed for unique cultural expression and solidarity. The neighborhood brimmed with personality, as those of every class, education and experience level lived in close proximity. The noted African-American architect Paul Williams, who designed a number of homes in posh Windsor Square and Hancock Park, also was the creative force behind South Central's most distinguished community and commercial structures: the Mediterranean Revival 28th Street Y; the Angelus Funeral Home and the second office of the Golden State Mutual Life Insurance Companies, one of the largest African-American owned businesses of this type in the country.

Under artist Eva Cockcroft's direction, high school students painted "Compton: Past, Present and Future" (1995), for the Metro Rail Blue Line. The ceramic mural could just as easily portray cultural fusion in neighboring South Central Los Angeles. Here, the rhythms of traditional Mexican-American sounds, classical jazz, and folk-inspired music from the Pacific and Caribbean islands meet in new forms — and forums. *Courtesy Metropolitan Transportation Agency, Los Angeles.*

Central Avenue became synonymous with jazz, and all the greats who played Harlem toured here as well: Duke Ellington, Lionel Hampton, Bill "Bojangles" Robinson, the Jimmy Lunceford Band, Charlie Parker, the Inkspots and many others. The Lincoln Theatre hosted full-fledged concerts and a Saturday afternoon talent search matinee, where young, rising stars were brought to the attention of major performers. Smaller venues, with crowded dance space also lined the Avenue, and even brought Euroamerican patrons. Habitues will remember Club Alabam, Last Word, Apex Night Club, Chicken Shack, Parisian Room, Kentucky Club, among many other establishments that flourished through the 1950s.

African-American visitors to Los Angeles — whether musicians, NAACP activists attending conventions, or sleeping car porters on break — welcomed the opportunity to stay at the Dunbar Hotel. With first-rate accommodations, it originally had been named the Somerville after its owner and builder, dentist Dr. John A. Somerville who met his future wife, Dr. Vada Jetmore while they both were receiving their professional training at USC.

An interesting footnote: The Dunbar Hotel of the 1990s has served as a catalyst for local revitalization efforts, most directly through the Dunbar Economic Development Corporation. And, ironically, as I write this section, a jazz concert is taking place at the historic venue. Gospel and big band appear on the program. An addition of fairly recent vintage is Latin jazz, reflecting the demographic changes that have come to the community — and a laudatory move toward inclusivity.

After World War II, when new housing developments emerged to meet a growing population and legalized discrimination diminished, middle-class and affluent African-Americans moved west. Neighborhoods like Baldwin Hills, Hyde Park and nearby Ladera Heights (in the County) became their homes from the 1960s onward. Crenshaw drew a broader sphere, and within that large district, Leimert Park is the possibly the African-American community's cultural hub.

Walter H. Leimert, creator of City Terrace and other developments, purchased 231 acres west of Arlington Avenue from Clara Baldwin Stocker for $2 million during the mid-1920s. (Mrs. Stocker was the daughter and heiress of E.J. "Lucky" Baldwin, once owner of a vast expanse near Santa Anita; her name is evident in Baldwin Hills and Stocker Street.)

Leimert engaged the firm of Olmstead and Olmstead, scions of park advocate Frederick Law Olmstead, to design what emerged as one of L.A.'s first planned communities. Leimert Park was featured, several times, at the Los Angeles Small Homes Exposition. Intended for upwardly-mobile, middle income families and not then open to African-Americans, the development retains many of its original characteristics: a layout that insulates it somewhat from city ongoings; pedestrian walkways; ample and now-mature shade trees; courtyard configurations; artful tile work.

African-American identity has broadened. Of culturally-related enterprises, cafes and bookstores now share the spotlight with jazz clubs. Comparisons are impossible. Still, Leimert Park may be the late 20th-century rendition of Central Avenue — smaller and more physically attractive, but a center for expressiveness nevertheless.

Moving south, we would be remiss in omitting San Pedro and Wilmington. Since the neighborhoods already have been discussed extensively, however, this section is somewhat abbreviated. The two communities are often mentioned in unison, but the differences remain important. San Pedro probably was more densely settled from the start. The activities of the Tongva, as detected by their fires, caused Juan Rodriguez Cabrillo to name its natural harbor "the Bay of Smokes." Sebastian Vizcaino contributed the lasting appellation, San Pedro.

Wilmington grew less from obvious natural advantage than from the visions of Phineas Banning. Initially a teamster, he applied transportation technologies zealously and early. When Wilmington became incorporated as an independent city in 1872, 16 years before its older sister, Banning nearly deferred to history, calling the town New San Pedro. He changed his mind, however, and decided to leave his own imprint: the name Wilmington was derived from his Delaware hometown. Wilmington's most distinguished landmarks reflect on its historic economic development. Most prominent are Camp Drum, the civil war outpost that did its share to build Wilmington, and Banning's spacious and well-maintained estate.

Separated physically from downtown L.A., Wilmington and San Pedro shared doubts about their 1909 consolidations; Wilmington kept its school

Thos.L.Hunt.

"board of trustees" until the following year. Even now, the formerly independent cities maintain identity partially through history. Old housing stock that might have been torn down in other sections of L.A. stands resolutely in Wilmington and San Pedro. Both communities also have large branch libraries.

San Pedro exudes public history, the past of ordinary people: captain's houses; revered churches; a small, but richly detailed 1901 shopping arcade; the Art Deco Warner Theatre; a monument to longshoreman who suffered a bloody strike during 1934. Ethnic culture has survived over decades. Whereas the Italian Hall on Olvera Street is long vacant, Pee-dro still has such a gathering place. Similar establishments draw Slavic and Norwegian residents, among others. And though barely visible throughout most of the metropolis, unionism carries its own voice and contributes to the port culture.

Outward Bound

Considered competitors from the start, the interurban rail system and automobile-oriented boulevards unintentionally conspired to give urbanites a taste of healthier environments. The turn of the century, for example, inaugurated a "Great Age of Hiking." Pacific Electric red cars carried health-conscious passengers to such distant posts as Sierra Madre. Visitors would trek several rigorous miles into the San Gabriels, with changes of clothing, destined for "mountain resorts" — often nothing more than large lodges surrounded by canvas tent cabins. Both male and female guests enjoyed lengthy day hikes and evening socializing. Outdoor attire consisted of an old "business suit," according to a contemporary *Los Angeles Times* article.

For those less physically inclined, the Mt. Lowe funicular and the Poppy Car to Monrovia nevertheless provided mountain attractions, and a change of air. Or families might spend the day on a "balloon route" excursion. Advertised as a "101 miles for 100 cents," the circular itinerary showcased eight cities and 10 beaches. Fare would include admission to the Venice aquarium and other sites. Of course, some might spend the day at a chosen spot. Even with the inevitable

downtown bottlenecks, roving red cars (circa 1911) travelled from L.A. to Playa del Rey in 43 minutes; Manhattan Beach, 53 minutes; and, Redondo, 63 minutes.

While playing a unique role in Southern California culture, the electric car system did not exclusively bring about settlement of the L.A.'s farthest-flung areas, the Westside and Valley. Its main contribution might have been in giving Angelenos that first exposure to formerly remote areas — and the promise of different lifestyles.

A rival transportation mode presented itself as early as the teens: jitneys were autos which ran alongside the congested downtown rail tracks and offered groups of passengers a lift for five cents apiece. Figures from 1915 showed 1,800 jitneys carrying 150,000 riders daily. Patronage on the Los Angeles and Pacific Electric cars, respectively, dropped by 17.7 million and 8.6 million between 1914 and 1916; operating revenues tumbled by 900,000 and 800,000. Both rail companies requested City Council intervention; impending regulations reduced the jitneys' profits, effectively eliminating their

(Opposite page) The independent cities of San Pedro and Wilmington consolidated with Los Angeles in 1909. Thomas L. Hunt's (1882-1938) undated painting evokes the ambiance of a fishing village. Even today, the port area maintains an historic, small-town character distinct from the rest of the city. *Courtesy The Irvine Museum, Irvine, California.*

A 1923 picture shows the transformation of a blacksmith shop (with horseshoeing capability) to a Ford motor specialist, offering "expert auto repairing", supplies, and Red Crown gas. Los Angeles already exhibited a propensity toward the automobile. *Courtesy The Mack Sennett Collection, Margaret Herrick Library, Academy of Motion Picture Arts and Sciences, Beverly Hills.*

PLACE OF POSSIBILITIES

service. (The electric cars continued to sustain losses, decreasing service but nevertheless functioning, until the 1960s.) In the meantime, Angelenos who could afford it — and many could — purchased their own vehicles. L.A. averaged one automobile for every 2.9 residents by 1928. With the growth during the 1920s of suburban residential districts and aligned economic bases, the public transportation system and automobiles together facilitated new (and less downtown-oriented) population movements.

Westward Expansion

For quite some time, Westlake (now MacArthur) Park stood at L.A's western edge. The parcel gained its status inadvertently during the 1860s, when the city attempted to raise revenues by selling municipal property. Unable to auction it off even at 25 cents per acre, Mayor William Workman reserved Westlake for parkland. Its large ravine later was filled with water and converted to a lake. (Central or Pershing Square, Lafayette and Elysian parks shared similar beginnings on the muncipal auction block.)

Westlake and Lafayette converged to form a stylish residential district by the 1890s. Another creation of the 1860s was situated immediately to the north. Initially a reservoir, Echo Park benefited from the

philosophies of Frederick Law Olmstead: the city dredged and richly landscaped it in 1895, ensuring its character for years to come. Hilly Silverlake crowned these contiguous, early "western" neighborhoods.

Though not considered a part of today's Westside, Hollywood nevertheless played a leading role in its development. The formerly independent city, founded as a religious community, consolidated with Los Angeles in 1910. Neighboring Colegrove had been annexed the year before, and water resources similarly beckoned Hollywood. Still, the community flourished around its homegrown economy — motion pictures. Its early "flatland" houses are said to be more densely packed than elsewhere in the city; work and residence became intertwined, bypassing older downtown-centered neighborhoods. Expanding beyond its initial borders, the industry, itself, quickly crossed the Cahuenga Pass to Studio City and Universal City. The names North Hollywood and West Hollywood (nee Sherman), also indicate a relationship — and Red Car connections.

The development of the Wilshire corridor owed to Hollywood, too. Even as early as the teens, celebrities led by Douglas Fairbanks and Mary Pickford sought more spacious, secluded surroundings. Beverly Hills grew with their arrival. (Some of the motion picture elite also paved the way for canyon living, from the Hollywood

(Opposite page) The PE Red Cars sustained financial losses since the teens, but ownership by the massive and diversified Southern Pacific Railroad allowed the system to endure. Here, two employees at a PE freight station account for their cargo. *Courtesy Department of Special Collections, Young Research Library, UCLA.*

Unused portions of the pueblo's original land grant were auctioned off during the late 1860s to raise municipal revenues. When some parcels failed to attract bidders, the city set them aside as green space. Elysian, Westlake (now MacArthur), and several other municipal parks resulted. A portion of Elysian Park appears at left. *Courtesy The Postcard Collection of Jeanne Taylor Baird.*

Griffith J. Griffith (1850-1919) likewise could not sell part of his Rancho Los Feliz property. He donated over 4,000 acres to the city in 1896, thereby creating the nation's largest municipal park. The Griffith House, captured in 1914 by Sunday painter Eva Scott Fenyes, was not the happiest of homes. Mercurial and a drinker, Griffith shot his wife in 1903. She survived and he went to San Quentin for several years. The Griffith Park Observatory was built with a portion of his $700,000 bequest to the city. *Courtesy, The Southwest Museum, Los Angeles, photo FEN.112.*

Hills westward.) Additionally, more modest residential quarters were needed to accommodate the legions of technicians, support staff, and aspiring talent who came from out-of-state to join the dynamic industry. As motion pictures boomed during the 1920s and 1930s, an influx of singles and newlyweds created a demand for apartment housing to the north of Wilshire Boulevard and to the south of Hollywood's commercial hub.

Indeed, Wilshire — as well as Sunset Boulevard — nourished the Westside. At their downtown geneses, both were old roads. The pobladores' cattle had grazed on latter-day Sunset, and livestock paths and feeding patterns created a 25-foot-wide passage. What became Wilshire Boulevard once was an Indian trail. Shortly after the city dedicated the road for use in 1885, Socialist millionaire Gaylord Wilshire subdivided it just to the west of today's MacArthur Park. The avenue that bore his name reached 16 miles to the ocean by about 1920, a breezy Sunday drive for motorists — with very

sparse development. A structure containing four storerooms stood at the intersection of Wilshire and Vermont, emptiness proceeded until a market appeared at Western, and the stretch to La Brea held only a few houses and vacant lots. A fruit store and two small commercial buildings distinguished the next lap, to Cochran Street.

Small communities were sprouting along the corridor, but there was nothing to unify or anchor them. With the automobile age now inaugurated, A.W. Ross understood the concept of a 20th-century suburb way before other Angelenos. The downtown realtor reckoned that residents would drive about four miles for their shopping needs. Ross purchased 18 acres of land between La Brea and Fairfax at a price of $54,000 during the mid-1920s. He asked buyers for $100 a front foot. Using his four-mile radius theory, Ross estimated that the soon to be named "Miracle Mile" would draw people from the Westlake, West Adams, Hollywood,

Beverly Hills and — just a short distance down the road — the emerging communities of Hancock Park and Windsor Square. All were at least middle-income; most, affluent.

Ross met with resistance. Downtown and Hollywood commercial interests thwarted his master zoning request, so that he had to pursue variances on an individual basis. Different voices spoke to the public benefits of Wilshire Boulevard as a wide, green, well-landscaped parkway; for some, this was a sincere crusade; for others, merely a smokescreen. Ross ultimately persuaded retailers of the area's potential. The Miracle Mile of the late 1930s came to encompass Desmond's, Silverwood's, and the oldest department store in L.A., Coulter's.

Companies flourished with the community. Railway Federal Savings and Loan, which established itself during the 1920s by catering to those who worked the trains, made a bold move in 1936. First, the company decided to open a branch office, something of an innovation given contemporary banking practices. It also opted for a site on "suburban" Wilshire Boulevard. The small savings and loan soon changed its name to California Federal and assets jumped to $1 million

within a year. Wilshire Boulevard subsequently welcomed a larger branch office and, later, corporate headquarters. The May Company came in 1939, locating its first Westside store in the Miracle Mile rather than in Hollywood, as originally intended. Ross' development spread rapidly. The shopping district extended westward from the original Miracle Mile, but Carnation moved its corporate headquarters east on Wilshire.

Sunset Boulevard ran a more winding path, resulting in a 27-mile journey to the Pacific. But the portion almost exactly to the north of Ross' Miracle Mile bore some similarities. The Sunset Strip was developed at around the same time, with a like display of Art Deco and other architecture styles. Both thoroughfares beckoned motor-happy Angelenos, and provided parking in the back or on the side — a new configuration. (Some rear entrances consequently proved more inviting than those fronting the boulevards.)

But the patrons varied. The Sunset Strip was a mecca for Hollywood celebrities and their admirers. A local landmark opened in 1927, the Garden of Allah housed Garbo, Bogart, Olivier, Deitrich and many more. During the early 1980s, comedian John

Western Avenue, pictured here in 1895, was a wide dirt road extending from Los Angeles to San Pedro. With Hollywood as their destination, members of the *Los Angeles Times* bicycle club are peddling just to the north of Pico Boulevard. *Courtesy Department of Special Collections, Young Research Library, UCLA.*

The Chapman Park

Hotel and Bungalows

3401 WILSHIRE BOULEVARD
LOS ANGELES 5, CALIFORNIA

Where the
BRIDE and GROOM
BROADCAST
IS HELD

Your Home in
A California Garden

Private Swimming Pool

Belushi died in the Chateau Montmart, a building of that same gilded vintage.

Moving west from Hollywood's commercial sector and the Sunset Strip, the noise and liveliness diminished. Wilshire and Sunset sandwich Beverly Hills, Westwood and Brentwood, yet these southern and northern boundaries, respectively, were (and are) different. Wilshire is the more active and commercial of the two; traffic aside, Sunset offers quiet and often palatial residential options. The boulevards part directions in Brentwood. Wilshire enters the heart of Santa Monica. A gateway to secluded canyons, Sunset climbs to Pacific Palisades and ends, almost literally, at the ocean.

The earliest Westwood settlements might now be considered West L.A., or Sawtelle. In 1884, Maximo

Alanis sold the Mexican land grant that had been his possession for over 40 years. The property stretched all the way from Pico to Sunset, from Sawtelle to the Beverly Hills border. Buyer John Wolfskill situated his residence near the site of the current Mormon Temple on Santa Monica Boulevard. He attempted to subdivide it, but that did not work. Other parties failed equally in their efforts to promote a new town, Sunset. At Sawtelle and Wilshire, also during the 1880s, two influential Santa Monica developers donated land for the construction of what Angelenos were to call the "Soldiers Home." (One of these builders, John P. Jones, owned the railway that the Southern Pacific soon bought and later used to fortify its Port Angeles harbor campaign.) The donated site turned into a huge institutional complex, with structures and landscaping so impressive that balloon excursionists stopped to visit. Today's Veteran's Administration Hospital is reduced in capacity, and though its grounds preserve a century-old feeling, many of the original, historic buildings (and plantings) are no longer there.

Wolfskill died in 1913. His vast holdings were bought at the end of the decade by Arthur Letts, founder of the Broadway department store. While Letts began to convert the Northern section into an estate community, Holmby Hills, his son-in-law, Harold Janss, focused on the area to the south of Wilshire, which he called Westwood Hills, with the intent of creating solidly middle-class residences. Janss already was vice president of the Janss Investment Company, known for having developed parts of Monterey Park, Boyle Heights and the San Fernando Valley. The corporation was a full-service firm, engaging its own staff of architects and engineers, completing such tasks as road grading, and even planning parks and school sites.

During the mid-1920s, what is now UCLA began looking for a larger campus. A search committee narrowed the selection to

Burbank, Fullerton, Pasadena, Palos Verdes and Westwood. The final decision was predicated on Westwood's pleasant physical environment, abundance of space, and the fact that over three-quarters of the student body came from Los Angeles. (Indeed, the "Southern branch" of Berkeley hewed to its local roots.) Janss set a price for the land, and Beverly Hills, L.A. and Santa Monica bond issues facilitated the

appreciation. Angelenos summered at Pacific Palisades as far back as the 1860s. Instrumental in its larger development, however, was Robert C. Gillis. The Canadian-born entrepreneur constructed San Vicente Boulevard as an automobile gateway to his Westside holdings. Because he was owed a favor, he convinced Moses Sherman and Eli Clark to build interurban tracks that would link the huge Westgate

On their 101-mile itinerary, balloon excursionists left tour the Soldier's Home (following page), a complex of stunning residential buildings, health and recreational facilities, and complementary landscapes. Today, the Westwood site is better known as the Veterans Administration Hospital. *Courtesy Department of Special Collections, Young Research Library, UCLA.*

financial transaction. Alphonso Bell, developer of neighboring Brentwood and Bel-Air contributed an additional eight acres. From the onset, Janss intertwined community and university. The Westwood Hills sales campaign resounded this goal. A 1929 *Los Angeles Times* advertisement shows a suited man, with one arm around a young boy and the other extending in the direction of the new campus. "Son! I am buying this lot in Westwood Hills to send you thru College."

By contrast to the corridor neighborhoods, ocean-adjacent parcels drew early recognition and

tract (annexed in 1916) to the city and to Santa Monica. Gillis developed the Huntington Palisades area during the 1920s at about $1 million ($2,000/lot), costly back then. In addition to following the land's natural contours and generally exercising taste, most of Gillis' expenses lie in infrastructure — sanitary sewers, gutters and paving needed for this still-remote district. The 1920s also saw a Methodist Chautauqua colony move to the Palisades; its members purchased house lots above Potrero Canyon for $1,000 each.

The beach communities from Venice to Playa del Rey share an early history. Native Americans harvested these coastlines for seafood, water fowl and edible plants. The area later became the Rancho la Ballona, a Mexican grant to two sets of brothers Augustin and Ignacio Machado, and Felipe and Tomas Talamantes. As partners, they raised the Spanish-variety of long-horned cattle and grapes, from which they produced a fine, sauterne-like white wine.

Only Agustin lived on the ranch, however. As was typical during early Statehood, the U.S. Land Commission called ownership into question. The deaths of two grantees, bequests to multiple heirs, and the ongoing dispute over title ensued. Squatters built shantys close to the oceanfront, filling a perceived population void. One was named Will Tell, and although his exact residence is unknown, he probably lived near Playa del Rey. (Venetians have claimed him, too.) The beachcomber was remembered, nevertheless, for luring friends to his own brand of hostelry, "Will Tell's Seaside Resort." Tell was either evicted by Machado's heirs or forced to leave when a rain storm destroyed the "inn." A successor, Michael Duffy appeared, opening "Hunter's Cottage." Ducks seemed to be a favorite target for lodgers under both proprietorships, and food, drink and ammunition were provided.

Duffy's establishment closed, perhaps like Tell's, with a pounding from the heavens and seas.

Serious speculation came during 1885, close to where Playa del Rey and the Marina meet today. Moye L. Wicks purchased part of the Machado estate and enticed the Santa Fe Railroad, an L.A. upstart, to build tracks to the ocean — with a purpose: Wickes was planning a harbor suitable for ocean-going vessels. Under the Ballona Harbor and Improvement Company, he engaged an engineer and commenced construction. Wickes also laid out lots for a town. Potential homeowners had just started to explore this prospect, when the real estate bust brought an end to "Port Ballona."

The rail connection was utilized anyway — by Abbott Kinney. A wealthy, cosmopolitan cigarette manufacturing heir who simultaneously maintained involvement in the Chamber of Commerce and the Angeles National Forest, Kinney is best known as the founder of Venice. He and his real estate partner convinced the Sante Fe in 1892 to extend tracks northward from a junction with the deserted Ballona line. Kinney began building from the Santa Monica neighborhood of Ocean Park, and by 1901, his unique development contained 200 cottages, a separate post office, pier, bath house, race track, experimental garden and stores. Three years later, Kinney started construction on the canals that would become the trademark of "Venice of America." He hired two dozen Italian gondoliers, including songsters, to give the waterways flourish. When subsequent plans for the expansion of amusement facilities were thwarted, Kinney mobilized the community to break off from Ocean Park and form an independent city.

Venice was culturally diverse from its early days and, indeed, has remained so. Kinney engaged African-Americans to staff his amusement parks and one, Arthur Reese, for many years served as an interior designer. (Reese's lasting contribution was said to be the revolving balls, surfaced with bits of mirrors, that reflect dance-hall/disco lights.) The African-American population grew large enough to organize its own First Baptist Church of Venice. Jewish Angelenos congregated in the area, too. As families, they came from the Eastside on day trips. Some later retired to Venice. Still, there is evidence that a tangible community already existed: Mishkon Tephilo, a Conservative Jewish synagogue celebrates its 80th year to date.

The Santa Fe tracks and Kinney's vision notwithstanding, the Pacific Electric was the vehicle for those seeking Venice's waterfront amusements. Some 33,000 visitors stepped off the rails on July 4, 1910 alone. Public transportation (albeit privately-owned) also spurred the development of Playa del Rey, otherwise only accessible via the old Santa Monica-to-Compton Road, now Lincoln Boulevard.

After the brief hunting lodge era of Tell and Duffy, Henry P. Barbour purchased 1,000 acres near the Playa del Rey lagoon. His Beach Land Company constructed a pavilion that featured dining, bowling and a double-duty dance floor and roller rink. A 1,200-foot pier attracted water sports enthusiasts, and an 18-mile automobile speedway raced through the community, bringing additional recreationists. The Los Angeles Pacific Railway Company, predecessor to the PE, extended its track to Playa del Rey in 1902. The firm promptly invested $200,000 in the 50-room Hotel del Rey, which boasted luxury accommodations and beach views. The exact demise of these early landmarks are debated; a combination of a massive fire and oil exploration activities probably consumed them. Residential properties rose during mid-1920s when a national developer, the Dickinson & Gillespie Company, moved to the corner of Vista del Mar and Speedway (today's Culver Boulevard). Approximately four decades later, airport expansion claimed these early

homes, and under the flight path of LAX, one can see still vacant, paved streets.

More generally, though, oil discovery in the 1920s affected the city's entire coastline. For Venice, drilling created blight. A Committee of One Hundred business and civic leaders sought consolidation with L.A. Their campaign purported to advance: "more and cheaper water, raise the real estate value of their property, give their childen better and finer schools, give the city wider, worthier streets, provide a police force...give them a real Board of Health, membership in the largest Chamber of Commerce in the world, and generally drag

(Left and below) Busses eventually assumed the urban transportation role once played by the street rails. The Pacific Motor Coach Company similarly embarked on Balloon Route-type excursions. No matter how one arrived, Venice nevertheless proved a popular stop. Its aquarium claimed to be the largest on the Pacific Coast. *Courtesy The Postcard Collection of Jeanne Taylor Baird.*

dear, blessed Venice out of the gutter." Opponents put up road signs, "To Los Angeles, Annexation, and Ruin."

Playa del Rey responded to oil with arrested development. Exploration kept the small community in abeyance and enabled some of the beach front to return to a more natural state. From the teens through the late 1980s, a horseriding stable stood at Culver Boulevard. PDR of 1998 is a quiet enclave of water, coastal fog, afternoon sun and residences of all sizes. Homeowners stay here for a long time, and the wetlands presently are being restored, helping the community to maintain a greenbelt like few others in L.A.

Playa del Rey marks the boundary between the City's Westside and the County's South Bay. Since World War II, the Westside has expanded greatly. Early 20th-century communities — Fairfax, Palms, Mar Vista — extended their borders through small annexations. It was the San Fernando Valley, however, which displayed lightning development.

The Big Valley

The Valley's earliest roads were trodden by Native Americans. Dating back several thousand years, Topanga provided a passageway for those journeying over the Santa Monica Mountains. The San Diego/405 Freeway and adjacent Sepulveda Boulevard constituted another important trail, and it was this path that guided Father Juan Crespi to Encino:

> We saw a very pleasant and spacious valley. We descended to it and stopped close to the watering place which is a very large pool. Near it we found a large village of heathen....We gave to this plain the name of Valley of Santa Catalina de Bononia de los Encinos. It is nearly three leagues wide and more than eight long. It has on its hills and in its valleys many live oaks and walnuts, though small.

The San Fernando Mission and several Spanish land grants notwithstanding, adventurers crossed the Valley long before they made a commitment to residing there. A gold deposit brought hundreds of miners through its plains to Placerita Canyon in 1842, seven years prior to the Northern California discovery. And before turning his energy on railroads and harbor facilities, Phineas Banning (or his crews) likely drove their stagecoaches along Fort Tejon Road to fulfill their government contract and deliver supplies to the military outpost of the same name. Lopez Station, a stage stop near the Mission, gave rise to the area's first post office (1869) and shortly thereafter, its premiere English-speaking school.

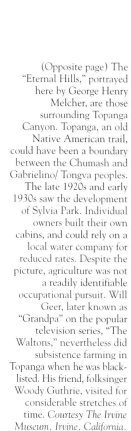

As discussed in the previous chapter, Isaac Lankershim and I.N. Van Nuys held vast acreage in the southern half of the Valley, spreading over Van Nuys, Reseda, North Hollywood, Canoga Park and other adjacent communities. The wheat growers formed a new company which added flour-milling to their existing agricultural pursuits. This empire developed into a network of seven ranches, with the main one located in Van Nuys. Each had a superintendent's house, several large barns, blacksmith shop, equipment shed, bunkhouses and a mess hall.

The northern half of the Valley, near the Mission, became more conventionally settled. Three men, two of them state senators, purchased land there. With the Southern Pacific right of way granted nearby, Senator Charles Maclay founded the town of San Fernando in 1874. He divided the future city into blocks, and allocated lots for farming and for purely residential purposes. Prospective buyers were rewarded with a half-fare train trip and a free lunch at the Mission. The biggest prize, however, came after the Southern Pacific established full service; lots subsequently realized a value far greater than Maclay's original asking price. It

is important to note, too, San Fernando continued to grow independently and did not seek annexation to Los Angeles.

Inspired by real estate but diverging in strategy, Maclay and his two partners split. San Fernando's creator went on to develop the area near Pacoima. With the toss of a coin, Benjamin F. Porter selected the northwestern portion of the Valley, including Chatsworth. He began to subdivide this community in 1888; later it was found to be oil-rich. His cousin, Senator George K. Porter took possession of the northcentral area. The senator apportioned some of the property into irrigated lots, and covered about 177 acres with navel orange trees. Visitor accommodations were facilitated through a street railway extending from the South Pacific depot — and leading directly to a new hotel. Today's large Porter, Ranch Development represents only a part of the original holdings.

Although not associated with either of the Porter or Maclay, North Hollywood also was a product of the late 1880s. First named Toluca, it became Lankershim (after its original owner) in 1911, and finally assumed its current name.

The real growth of the Valley, however, owes to the water. Earlier, we mentioned the speculators who invested in land near the proposed terminus of the aqueduct. All told, the Los Angeles Suburban Homes Company drew 30 investors. In addition to the *Times'* Harrison Gray Otis and his son-in-law Harry Chandler, its five-person board boasted considerable expertise in real estate and infrastructure development. Other members were: Moses Sherman, of street rail fame; H.J. Whitley, a master builder who had facilitated the

consolidation of Hollywood with Los Angeles; and, Otto F. Brant, vice president and general manager of the Title Insurance and Trust Company.

As a singular entity, the Los Angeles Suburban Homes Company purchased Van Nuys' wheat fields in 1909. This expanse, soon known as "Tract 1000," was bounded by the Santa Monica Mountains on the south and Roscoe Boulevard on the north, the San Fernando Mission on the west and present-day North Hollywood on the east. Subdivision had been completed in 1911. The resulting townsites — Marian, Owensmouth and Van Nuys — bore the legacies and motivations of the major investors. Marian (later Reseda) had been named for Otis' daughter, while Owensmouth (Canoga Park) paid tribute to the massive water project.

As new suburban developments evolved from the1930s onward, retailers and consumer services left the center-city to expand their markets. Downtown endured as a magnet for corporate offices. *Courtesy The Postcard Collection of Jeanne Taylor Baird.*

Sales proceeded apace. William Paul Whitsett, who had bought a half-interest in Van Nuys, personally directed that town's promotion. Owensmouth properties were sold by the Janss Company, which later assumed even larger commercial responsibilities in Westwood. Transportation knit these small townsites into the San Fernando Valley, and linked it with the City of Los Angeles. Enlarged crews toiled to complete one side of 16-mile Sherman Way in time for the official opening of the town of Owensmouth on November 30, 1912. The Pacific Electric extended its line to the fledgling city the following year. Lankershim/North Hollywood joined the Van Nuys-Owensmouth-Marian axis via automobile roads.

The infrastructure often outpaced community amenities, however. Owensmouth's first public library opened during the early teens — with a collection of 25 books. The facility initially utilized a school room, then a store room, before annexation yielded the resources of a large, urban library system.

Almost 170,000 square miles of the San Fernando Valley were added to the City of Los Angeles in 1915, more than doubling its territory. This huge parcel, including Tract 1000 but encompassing vastly more acreage, was to be L.A.'s largest annexation. The early towns grew. Burbank, a city which even today retains its independence, boasted a diverse manufacturing base by the 1920s, bringing people and urbanization to the subregion. Extensions of the burgeoning Hollywood film industry, Universal City and Studio City, also contributed. Approximately 80,000 new residents moved to the Valley in the 1930s.

As a distinctly 20th-century subregion, the Valley displayed contemporary theories about government and urban planning. The city established a municipal services center in Van Nuys during 1933, with the purpose of decentralization; this government complex still functions today.

Seeing immense growth but worried a post-war slump, city officials devised a plan for the Valley during the mid-1940s. The subregion's southeastern quadrant already was more urban than rural, and the plan acknowledged 10 nuclei closely linked by highways. The goal was to preserve the leading economic bases, industry and agriculture, while simultaneously utilizing farm lands as buffers against unbridled urban sprawl. The concept of "planning" demanded public input and elicited interest; comprehensive zoning changes facilitated implementation of the plan.

Yet, the whole scheme was being undermined from the start. A quarter of a million people moved to the Valley during the forties, with twice that many arriving in the next decade. Massive industrial plants — automotive and aerospace had just become local landmarks. Developers purchased ranches and farmlands, sought zoning changes, initiated subdivisions. A primary impetus was the county's reassessment of agricultural lands for

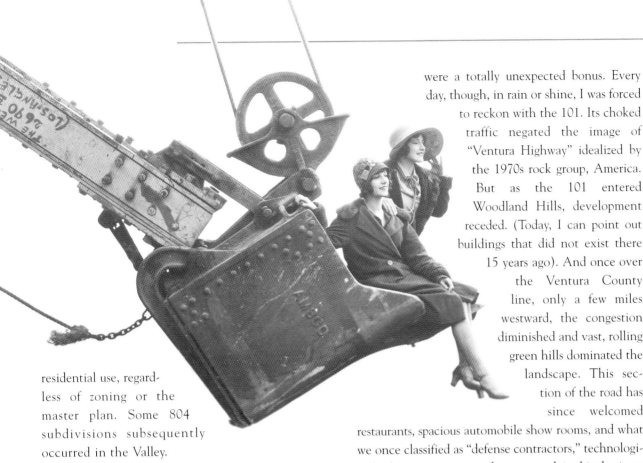

Circa early 1920s. *Courtesy The Mack Sennett Collection, Margaret Herrick Library, Academy of Motion Picture Arts and Sciences.*

were a totally unexpected bonus. Every day, though, in rain or shine, I was forced to reckon with the 101. Its choked traffic negated the image of "Ventura Highway" idealized by the 1970s rock group, America. But as the 101 entered Woodland Hills, development receded. (Today, I can point out buildings that did not exist there 15 years ago). And once over the Ventura County line, only a few miles westward, the congestion diminished and vast, rolling green hills dominated the landscape. This section of the road has since welcomed restaurants, spacious automobile show rooms, and what we once classified as "defense contractors," technologically-driven companies that engaged in big business with the government.

Statistics do not always match the scenery. Chatsworth has witnessed hundreds of years of history: as Native American village, stagecoach pass-through, Benjamin F. Porter's real estate turf. One might think that such a place would be long-settled. Yet, Los Angeles invariably offers room for growth. Chatsworth's population increased 361 percent in the 1950s alone, and I can remember during the mid-1980s when friends moved to a brand new townhouse complex on uncrowded and recently-developed Lemarsh Street. But just slightly to the north — at L.A.'s northwestern corner, near the 118/Simi Valley Freeway — huge boulders distinguish a natural wonderland that remains undisturbed, as it might have been for centuries. Though continuing to interact in other spheres, the people and well-tapped resources are missing from this picture, allowing the land to rightfully claim its legacy and limitations.

THE END

residential use, regardless of zoning or the master plan. Some 804 subdivisions subsequently occurred in the Valley.

New lifestyles echoed the burgeoning industrial patterns. Close to Van Nuys, Panorama City (1948) grew as a planned community of small homes and regional shopping. One of its chief builders was Fritz Burns, noted for his development, at around the same time, of Westchester.

Almost anyone can be an old timer in Los Angeles. My first job here, circa 1984, demanded a commute from Mid-Wilshire to Woodland Hills. Unfamiliar with the Valley, I was directed to Warner Center, a collection of refined, low-capacity industrial parks and a refreshingly understated, shaded, suburban shopping mall. The multistory Kaiser facility — soon a beacon to all the other nearby office towers — was literally a hole in the ground. A colleague referred to neighboring Pierce College as "Moo U;" livestock roamed on part of the campus, and the curriculum included animal husbandry. (These activities continue.)

I remember my frustration with the 101/Ventura Freeway. In order to avoid both the 10 and the 405, I approached the Valley via Laurel Canyon; its herbal essences, dramatically intensified during rain showers,

Courtesy The Irvine Museum, Irvine, California

TABLE OF CONTENTS

PARTNERS

MANUFACTURING & DISTRIBUTING

MARKETPLACE

NETWORKS

PROFESSIONS

QUALITY OF LIFE

TECHNOLOGY

PARTNERS IN LOS ANGELES
BUILDING A GREATER L.A.

Real estate and construction industries shape tomorrow's skyline, providing working and living space for the people of Los Angeles.

PLAYA VISTA
Rethinking Urban Living

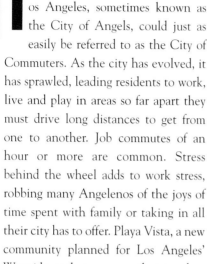

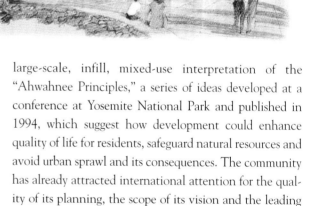

Los Angeles, sometimes known as the City of Angels, could just as easily be referred to as the City of Commuters. As the city has evolved, it has sprawled, leading residents to work, live and play in areas so far apart they must drive long distances to get from one to another. Job commutes of an hour or more are common. Stress behind the wheel adds to work stress, robbing many Angelenos of the joys of time spent with family or taking in all their city has to offer. Playa Vista, a new community planned for Los Angeles' Westside, seeks to reverse that trend.

Homes, apartments and shops will compliment each other in neighborhoods that recall the best architectural traditions in Los Angeles.

Located in an area with 400,000 fewer homes than jobs, Playa Vista is the last major piece of developable property in Los Angeles, the last real chance to build homes where jobs and community services are, and give people an opportunity to spend less time on the road and more time enjoying the outdoors.

The vision for Playa Vista is both simple and ambitious — build a community that balances the needs of people and the environment. Every design element, every construction choice is under scrutiny to maximize livability, minimize the ecological impact of the community and restore acres of wetlands that have been degraded by prior land use. It is believed to be the first

Playa Vista's one thousand acres stretch toward the ocean, straddling Jefferson and Lincoln Boulevards west of I-405.

large-scale, infill, mixed-use interpretation of the "Ahwahnee Principles," a series of ideas developed at a conference at Yosemite National Park and published in 1994, which suggest how development could enhance quality of life for residents, safeguard natural resources and avoid urban sprawl and its consequences. The community has already attracted international attention for the quality of its planning, the scope of its vision and the leading minds contributing to and guiding its development.

Playa Vista spans 1,087 acres, bordered by Marina del Rey to the north, Westchester and Playa del Rey to the south, the San Diego Freeway (I-405) to the east and the Pacific Ocean to the west. It is 3.3 miles long from east to west, and one mile from north to south at its widest point. Over the next 15 years, the community's developers envision completing approximately 13,000 homes on the property, plus 3.2 million square feet Campus at Playa Vista, an entertainment, media and technology district; an additional 1.9 million square feet of professional office space; 600,000 square feet of shops and services; 750 hotel rooms; 560,000 square feet for community serving public facilities; and about 500 acres of parks and open space, including a fully-restored Ballona Wetlands ecosystem. Initial construction is underway.

Cattle, Derricks, Planes and Movies

The community will take shape on land that has mirrored Los Angeles' evolution. The first record of its use appears in the history of Spanish land grants. Playa Vista was part of the Rancho La Ballona grant. The property was used first for cattle ranching, then dairy farming and other agricultural purposes.

Its next gift was oil and gas. Once these deposits were discovered, wells began to dot the area. But it was during the 1930s that features of the landscape began to change dramatically. First, the U.S. Army Corps of Engineers channelized the Ballona Creek, the stream running through the property. The fill from the project was piled onto a section of Playa Vista.

More changes came with the land's purchase by Howard Hughes around 1940. His Hughes Aircraft Company built hangars, support buildings and a 9,300-foot runway. During World War II, Hughes received a government contract to design and build a fleet of "Flying Boats" to ferry troops across the Atlantic out of reach of German submarines. His solution was a 200-ton, eight-engine craft nicknamed the "Spruce Goose." The wooden marvel, first and last of its kind, was finished too late to see action, and was put into storage on the site.

After the war, Hughes Aircraft adapted to fill new aerospace needs including design and manufacture of radar and missile systems, satellites, helicopters and aircraft. While this work was underway, fill from the 1960s excavation to create Marina del Rey was deposited on Playa Vista.

The Hughes facilities were in continuous use until 1994 when both McDonnell Douglas, a later arrival, and Hughes Aircraft relocated, leaving behind giant hangars, empty buildings that had once housed assembly lines and research labs, and one of the longest private airstrips in the world.

Their departure was timely. That same year the Northridge earthquake damaged or destroyed movie production spaces scattered across the Los Angeles area. The cavernous structures Hughes had built were reborn as soundstages. It's for this reason, and the fact that entertainment, media and technology companies are concentrated in Los Angeles' Westside, that the

Part of the Spanish land grant of Rancho La Ballona, Playa Vista was first cattle ranch, then oil and natural gas field.

design for Playa Vista includes a special district catering to entertainment industry needs, incorporating many former Hughes facilities.

Playa Vista's next incarnation is transforming the property, more than 80 percent of which has seen prior use, into a community that integrates jobs, homes and everyday services, balances those uses with major open space and restores hundreds of acres of degraded wetlands.

Playa Vista's history is linked to Howard Hughes' famous "Flying Boat." The giant wooden troop transport plane was built at Playa Vista during World War II and later stored there.

Rethinking Urban Living

Los Angeles once led the nation in a new growth pattern based on America's love affair with cars. Rather than the eastern city model of housing surrounding city centers that included government, industry, and commerce, with bus and subway routes connecting everything, Los Angeles evolved into a series of separate, but interdependent communities, linked across vast distances by a system of freeways. The quip "47 suburbs in search of a city" paints the picture.

But times are changing. The new Getty Center, new subway routes, plans for the Walt Disney Concert Hall and a new cathedral are symbols of Los Angeles' new direction. With the renewed energy of contemporary business, particularly in the fields of media and technology, and the nation's increasing interaction with the Pacific Rim, Los Angeles is coming into its own as a world center for art, commerce, culture and entertainment.

Playa Vista is also poised to signal a new direction in urban living — infill development, a reduced dependence on cars, an increased value placed on time, a sense of place, homes and neighborhood services side by side, and acres of open space to sustain residents and nurture native plants and animals.

A Sense of Place

Playa Vista is being designed as a collection of neighborhoods, or districts, each with homes, shops, restaurants, offices and recreational facilities. Each

district will have a different mix of architectural styles reminiscent of the best architecture in Los Angeles — Art Deco, Spanish, Mediterranean, Italianate, Postmodern, the bright white of Beverly Hills.

A great deal of freedom in the design process is being encouraged. In fact, designers are going to great lengths to create exterior designs and interior spaces that are not only exciting, but function in surprisingly creative ways to accommodate contemporary lifestyles with a fondness for high-tech devices and private, personal space.

The villas of early 1900s Los Anegles with open-air courtyards and towers provided the inspiration for mansion condominium designs, some with circular master bedroom suites, overlooking garden courts. A row of townhomes was not acceptable until it was redesigned into Brownstones with parking, and a living or storage space half a flight down from street level. Initial plans, calling for alleyways, have been redone to create street-level pedestrian "walk streets" through garden spaces instead, with parking below ground. Some two-level condominiums are stacked one on top of another, with the bedroom level of the top unit sitting atop the bedroom level of the lower unit, isolating the main living areas so one homeowner can sleep while the other winds down with music. There are private spaces for reading and study. There are formal dining rooms and outdoor decks with fireplaces for entertaining. Every design shows attention to views, maximizing living space and privacy.

Homes in each district will vary in size and price to appeal to a wide variety of residents and lifestyles. The housing mix will range from studio

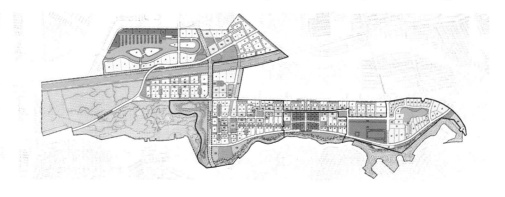

apartments to penthouses and from townhomes to million dollar manor homes.

Streets will interconnect rather than "keyhole" in cul-de-sacs, so districts throughout the community will open to one another. The streets will be well lit but more like village lanes than city thoroughfares, inviting residents to walk and to meet neighbors in the community's shops, restaurants and parks. Even the office districts will share their open spaces with residents, instead of walling them off for the enjoyment of employees only.

A Place to Grow

Some residents may work down the street from their homes. More than 20,000 jobs are projected for the completed community, many in The Campus at Playa Vista, the entertainment, media and technology district. Playa Vista designers seek to help the companies who take up residence in the community find the talent they need. An entertainment industry-oriented education center is being explored. And, continuing education programs are planned to provide ongoing education and training in many professional fields for Playa Vista residents and prospective employees.

Other public services included in the plans are police and fire stations, a school, theaters, libraries, museums, health and fitness centers and child care centers. In all, 560,000 square feet has been set aside

Titanic, Independence Day, Godzilla and *Virtuosity* are just a few of the movies produced in Playa Vista's aircraft hangars and related buildings since 1994. Playa Vista will incorporate 100 acres of space customized for the entertainment industry.

for community service uses, including public safety, cultural and support facilities.

Exploring the Possibilities

Community design, residential districts, housing mix, job potential, safety, sense of place, drive time and walking distances are still just the beginning of the way contemporary urban planning principles are being interpreted at Playa Vista. And that is what has garnered international attention. Playa Vista is exploring environmentally friendly techniques, until now applied primarily to demonstration homes in rural areas, with the intent to incorporate proven technology into residential and commercial structures in this infill community.

Like the best streets in any city, Playa Vista's residential districts will each possess a style of their own yet blend with the style of their neighbors to form a cohesive whole.

The importance of wetlands to ground water purification, erosion and flood prevention as well as fish and wildlife was not known for many years. At the time of initial construction, prior land use and adjacent development were slowly killing the Ballona Wetlands on Playa Vista.

Playa Vista, with ongoing input from respected environmental groups, will restore and enhance 340 acres of wetlands and uplands to renewed variety and vitality.

Street orientation, building locations, window placement and composition, natural ventilation and building shade are all under review as techniques to conserve energy. For example, reflective glass will be avoided, because it heats up buildings across the street. The impact of building height and angles may be adjusted if it severely compromises the availability of natural light indoors for adjacent structures. Long hallways will be avoided.

Landscaping will feature primarily native plants and de-emphasize both vast and "postage stamp" individual lawns. Efforts to control stormwater runoff and erosion may include paving that allows rainwater infiltration.

In addition, existing buildings that will not be incorporated into the final design are being dismantled, with close to 90 percent of their components recycled.

Construction materials are being evaluated with consideration given to whether they are produced locally, from a renewable or recycled resource, free of post-installation emissions, and lifetime cost and durability as compared to conventional materials. New technologies for core systems, like transportation within the community and perhaps heating and cooling of interiors, are also being explored.

Erasing Years of Neglect

Yet what may be most striking to visitors and residents alike is the open space. Half of Playa Vista will be open space at completion.

The Ballona Wetlands, Santa Monica Bay's largest coastal marsh, has long suffered from activities on and around it. Wetlands, one of nature's most productive and valuable ecosystems, perform critical functions such as erosion and flood prevention, purification and recharging of ground water, and serve as a haven for many varieties of fish and wildlife. Sadly, the importance of wetlands wasn't recognized for many years.

Like many wetlands, the Ballona Wetlands had been dying a slow death for decades. The 1930s channelization of the Ballona Creek also included a series of tide gates to keep adjacent marshes dry. As a result, native wildlife and vegetation dwindled almost to nonexistence.

With input from such respected groups as Friends of the Ballona Wetlands, Heal the Bay and the Audubon Society, Playa Vista's plans include restoring the existing, though severely degraded, saltwater wetlands; creating a freshwater marsh; and re-establishing a riparian corridor at the base of the Westchester Bluffs.

Once restored, the wetlands will include 190 acres of saltwater marsh, a 26-acre freshwater marsh system, a 25-acre riparian corridor and nearly 100 acres of dunes and upland habitat, creating one of the largest native habitats in any major United States city.

Additional open space at Playa Vista will include acres of more urban parkland and recreation fields. One of the first parks will be a "bark park," room to run for

Playa Vista's canine residents. Others include Concert Park, which will feature an outdoor amphitheater for concerts and other community events; Crescent Park, which will lend itself to outdoor art fairs; and Fountain Park, where the focus will be alfresco dining.

An Inclusive Process, an Inclusive Community

Plans for Playa Vista have been years in the making. The process embodies yet another of the Ahwahnee principles — involvement of local government and environmental advocates in plan development. This involvement will continue through project implementation and was a critical factor in obtaining permits for initial construction.

Grand opening for the first homes is projected for summer 2000. Eight hundred homes are expected to be finished that year. Initial construction includes a total of 3,000 homes over four years, creation of The Campus at Playa Vista and a portion of the wetlands restoration. Plans for future community areas will depend on the performance of the first buildings and initial freshwater marsh reclamation.

There will be more than 60 different house plans to choose from when the first homes are available. Floorplans will include townhomes, condominiums and individual homes priced from less than $200,000. Rental apartments will be available beginning at $1,000 per month.

Storefront retail space will be interspersed throughout the neighborhoods. Completed districts will offer coffee and juice bars, specialty dining, newsstands and upscale shops designed to appeal to residents and visitors. And in true Main Street fashion, there will be residences above the shops.

The Campus at Playa Vista will spread across approximately 100 acres just south of Jefferson Boulevard. This easternmost portion of Playa Vista will include soundstages and production and supporting office space for film, video, media and technology companies. The hangar for the Flying Boat, known as the "Spruce Goose," will witness movie marvels as production facilities occupy 11 former Hughes Aircraft buildings.

A Place of Possibilities

Playa Vista is the collective vision of many minds. Leaders in fields ranging from architecture to urban planning are contributing ideas to site and land use, street layout, architectural direction, housing mix, job creation, transportation, energy efficiency, materials, deconstruction and recycling, indoor ecology and waste reduction. They don't have all the answers. Solutions may still be coming as the community nears completion a decade into the new century. But what makes Playa Vista visionary is the questions it asks and its commitment to explore the possibilities, embrace the probabilities and produce a community that incorporates not only new thought, but also ideas that have proven their enduring value.

It is a vision thousands of residents will make their own as they live, work and play in Playa Vista. It is a vision others will enjoy when arriving for work or taking in the community's cultural and recreational opportunities. It is a vision thousands will appreciate as they see and learn about the rebirth of the Ballona Wetlands. It is a vision that will continue to attract attention as an improved model for urban living, a new model in community design that responds to the values of individuals and the larger society.

Playa Vista may not end Angelenos' love affair with cars, but as they explore life in this "Place of Possibilities" on foot, their cars parked home alone, they may well fall in love with the city all over again.

Playa Vista: Rethinking Urban Living

FORT HILL CONSTRUCTION

Take a drive through the neighborhoods of Beverly Hills or Bel Air, or stroll past the beach houses in Malibu. Chances are some of those homes were built or remodeled by Fort Hill Construction, a Los Angeles-based company that provides high quality workmanship to homeowners from Santa Barbara to the South Bay.

For over 25 years, Fort Hill Construction — the largest custom builder in the L.A. area — has served Los Angeles, New York and Boston residents by offering the finest quality residential construction and remodeling services in the industry. Founded in 1971 by several East Coast residents who began by remodeling their own homes, Fort Hill Construction was created as a small business with a love of fine craftsmanship and a personal approach to each project. The company has grown considerably over a quarter of a century, but the personal attention given to clients has remained the same.

Fort Hill has expanded primarily through personal referrals. While the company has experienced tremendous growth, they retain the character of a family business.

The company's commitment to quality, integrity and personal service continues to be overseen by the original partners. Today, the company offers years of experience in residential building, expertise in all phases of construction from concept to completion and a diverse range of other services such as cost analysis during the development stage of a project, project management and serving as client representative.

Fort Hill services include custom new home construction, residential remodeling, historical renovation, cabinet work and fine finish carpentry, coastal seawalls, tennis courts, swimming pools and screening rooms.

Custom new homes and major residential remodels comprise the majority of Fort Hill's business. The company has the ability to take an older residence, dramatically renovate the facade and reconstruct the interiors without altering the original integrity of the home. The craftsmanship and personal attention that go into each project, along with the company's record of being on time and within budget, have become Fort Hill trademarks. An experienced, full-time, on-site

Fort Hill added a grand staircase and an additional wing to a restored Wallace Neff home built in the 1930s.

supervisor is assigned to each major job for its duration. The owner receives weekly reports detailing construction progress and any design questions that may have arisen. Longstanding relationships with many subcontractors and an experienced in-house estimating team enable the company to offer highly competitive prices while still guaranteeing a high-quality, custom-finished project.

A special department is devoted to smaller projects where it is more cost effective to have a working carpenter/foreman on site serving a dual purpose. These projects include partial remodels and small additions to existing residences. The foreman is assigned for the duration of the project and works in conjunction with an office supervisor.

The company's field staff includes carpenters, cabinetmakers, masons and electricians, most of whom have been with the company for many years. The main office has departments for estimating, drafting and expediting, while a clerical support staff helps keep things running smoothly through all phases of construction.

Fort Hill has additional capabilities that make it a complete service company. An in-house drafting department can prepare incidental architectural renderings, small addition designs, or offer field drafting services. Although Fort Hill is not primarily a design-build firm, they do have the experience and expertise to handle architectural responsibility for projects if requested. The company also has a large reference library that contains current information about environmentally sound alternative building materials, products and procedures.

Jobs run smoothly and clients continue to use and refer Fort Hill because the company works to establish and maintain clear communication with clients and their architects. Regular site meetings are held with the owner and/or the architect/designer to review job progress, and project documentation is detailed and consistent from the start of construction to its conclusion.

Fort Hill Construction considers a project the start of a continuing relationship with a client. The company's service

Open porch overlooking pool area in Bel Air Estates. Fort Hill reshaped columns, added arch detail, and matching stucco.

department provides personnel who are consistently available to attend to the service needs of clients. Skilled workers are ready to meet a need as small as replacing an electrical circuit breaker or as extensive as an addition. Service staff have trucks equipped to handle a wide range of maintenance and emergency situations.

While the majority of Fort Hill Construction's projects are in Southern California, the company handles three to four projects a year from its New York office. They continue to do historical renovation work in Boston, where they also have a cabinet shop for custom woodwork needs. There are currently seven partners who oversee the Los Angeles and East Coast operations of Fort Hill: George Peper, Joey Goldfarb, Mike McGrail, Randy Foote, Jim Kweskin, Mark Spector and Geoffrey DeWan.

MATT CONSTRUCTION

ecause the company not only incorporated but thrived during the recession of the early 1990s, Matt Construction's formation could be called an overnight success story. Indeed, since its founding in 1991 by Paul Matt, his son Steve and his brother Alan, commitment to the Company's philosophy of full client service has resulted in a constant growth of new and repeat business. To call Matt Construction an overnight success, however, misrepresents the depth of experience the three principals brought to the organization: Paul in all areas of construction, Steve in the area of preconstruction planning and project management and Alan in the area of finance. Similarly, many of Matt Construction's employees have a long association with Paul Matt. It's this pooled knowledge and shared experience that has contributed to Matt Construction's still-growing industry reputation. Peter H. Segel, president of the company's Nevada division,

Disney Ice, interior

Disney Ice, exterior
Courtesy Ronald Moore

has more than 25 years of experience, having overseen preconstruction and construction for projects for Bally's Hotel and Casino, ITT Sheraton Desert Inn and Caesar's Palace. Robert L. Welch, vice president and senior project manager, has over 30 years of high-end construction experience which includes such hotels as the Bonaventure, Century Plaza, Sheraton Plaza La Reina Hotel, Sheraton Cerritos and Sheraton LAX. Richard W. Miller, vice president and senior project

manager, has nearly 40 years experience in the construction industry and has also run his family's construction business.

Paul Matt's 40 plus years of construction experience includes operational responsibility for more than 450 West Coast projects including landmark buildings that dot Southern California's urban landscape. His experience includes stints as a field surveyor in Oregon, an estimator in Los Angeles, and supervisory positions in Washington State and Los Angeles. As superintendent on the Salk Institute project in San Diego, Paul was exposed to high-end architectural concrete construction. This assignment led to additional architectural concrete work, an area of expertise he eventually brought to C.L. Peck Contractor in 1968.

Paul Matt first worked for C.L. Peck on a Robinson's Department Store in Mission Valley. He then moved to Newport Beach to work on the first high rise in Newport Center. He soon assumed responsibility for all field operations for C.L. Peck, eventually working his way up to the position of Executive Vice President of Construction. He led the vanguard for the 1970s and 80s construction boom in Southern California. While working at C.L. Peck, he planned and organized numerous significant projects, including the Orange County Performing Arts Center, the Crystal Cathedral, the Bonaventure Hotel, Fluor Corporate Headquarters, Hughes E.D.S.G., the Skirball Cultural Center, major department stores and countless office buildings and parking structures.

In 1987, C.L. Peck merged with the Jones Bros. Construction Company, the two premier construction firms embedded in Southern California history. Shortly thereafter, the Southern California economy, particularly the construction industry, began to slow down. Taking the long-term view that there were opportunities to be gained out of the recession, Paul started his own company. Along with his brother Al and son Steve, as well as with a number of former colleagues with whom he had worked over the years, Paul formed Matt Construction. As their reputation rapidly grew, so did the company. Matt Construction began with three employees in 1991; by 1997, the company numbered over 120 employees.

During its relatively brief existence, Matt Construction has initiated or completed many projects throughout Southern California: the remodeling of Disneyland's Tomorrowland, Wind Dancer Production Village, Niketown, Disney Ice, Tiffany's South Coast Plaza, Disney Concert Hall subcontracting concrete work for underground parking, Aimcor Coke Storage, Ice House, numerous schools, and office buildings' earthquake repair.

Matt Construction offers a full range of preconstruction and construction services. The project teams maintain a strong foundation of trust and mutual respect generated through positive relationships with clients, architects, engineers, subcontractors and suppliers. A company-wide policy encouraging shared performance responsibility ensures the highest degree of professional services and results on all projects undertaken.

Because of the company's proven track record and dedication to excellence, clients know to whom they should turn for their building needs: Matt Construction.

Barney's New York-Piccolo Cucina, South Coast Plaza.
Courtesy Ronald Moore

Christie's, exterior

TILE EMPORIUM/TROPICAL MARBLE & GRANITE

Founded in 1980 by James and Gitty Zohoury, Tile Emporium International and Tropical Marble & Granite are two of the nation's largest importers of natural stones and ceramic tiles housed in over 100,000 square feet of warehouse space and generating several million dollars in annual sales.

The family started the business in France in 1970, James Zohoury brings decades of experience to the industry and evolved his company through an ability to forecast future trends. He realized the increasing demand for quality floor coverings in Europe and capitalized on the trend by acquiring only the most unusual and exceptional marble to custom craft designs reflecting the ancient floors of Europe.

His company quickly grew to become one of the largest European distributors of high quality and hard-to-find marble and stone.

In 1978, Zohoury relocated to Los Angeles with his wife, sons Charles and Robert and daughter Marjan. Through his continuing business investments and alliances with a select group of precious stone quarries in France, Spain, Brazil, India, Israel and Italy, Zohoury's introduced the U.S. market to a level of production, technology, packing and shipping previously unheard of in this country.

(Right)They have gathered an exclusive collection of ceramic tiles such as Gianni Versace and other exclusive designer tiles.

(Below, left to right) Robert Zohoury, Charles Zohoury, sister Marjan Zohoury and father James Zohoury.

Natural stones, granite and marble are relatively new products in the American marketplace and many consumers are not aware of the variations of color and shading inherent to these natural products. The expert staff at Tile Emporium and Tropical Marble & Granite are trained to educate architects and designers on the subtle differences and latest designs in the product line, from tumbled marble to water-jet cuts.

Zohoury's reputation and trademark of quality comes from his hands-on approach and constant travels to instruct quarry owners on the demands and expectations of the American market.

Today, a second generation of Zohourys have enthusiastically followed in their father's footsteps. Charles and Robert learned the art of stone trade at an early age and have devoted their lives to maintaining the tradition of importing only the highest quality marble and granite from around the world.

Their passion, vision, contemporary business practices and commitment to offering the most innovative patterns, colors and designs have further propelled the firm to achieve even greater success.

Tropical Marble & Granite and the Tile Emporium International have stood the test of time. Both businesses not only survived, but expanded in spite of a depressed Southern California marketplace. As such, the Zohourys credit the knowledge and professionalism of their employees and the quality and diversity of their product line to the continued success of the company.

Since its inception, the company has catered to worldwide clientele ranging from renowned architects and established interior designers to small contractors, homeowners and Hollywood celebrities.

The Tile Emporium's products are included in some of this nation's most prominent architectural designs, from the newly renovated Caesar's Palace Hotel and Casino in Las Vegas to recent renovations in the White House. Other collaborations include renovation and

remodeling projects for the Four Seasons Hotel and Sheraton Hotel and participation on recent remodeling projects for Warner Bros. Studios, Sacks Fifth Avenue stores, Twentieth Century Fox studios, Disney's Animal Kingdom and some of the finest area restaurants, such as Spago and Chasens in Los Angeles.

Tile Emporium and Tropical Marble & Granite import and export products to and from all five continents. Zohoury likens his business to "a marble supermarket where we handpick the most beautiful stones from around the world and gather them all under one roof in Southern California."

Zohoury further illustrates the importance of "one-stop shopping" by citing that it is "cheaper for a client from Japan to visit our facility here in California to find the perfect stones for a particular project and inspect and pack the product here than attempt to travel the globe in search of the right color, texture and quality."

Zohoury adds that there are an infinite number of applications for natural stones, ranging from the

granite used for office buildings and marble in residential settings to the slate and sandstone, utilized in sidewalks, pool decks and other exterior applications.

As the Tile Emporium approaches the millennium, plans turn toward further expansion, more distribution and aggressively seeking new markets to merchandise its diverse product line.

"We're one of the few marble and tile companies with such a large selection," says Robert. "Because of that fact, we are able to offer our clients the highest quality product and the convenience of one-stop shopping. Everything they need can be found under one roof."

VENT VUE WINDOW PRODUCTS CO., INC.

Ina business climate characterized by change, Vent Vue Window Products Co., Inc. has remained at the forefront of the Los Angeles window and door industry by focusing on quality and service while keeping abreast of market trends.

The company began life in 1950 as Coor-Pender and Long Co., resulting from a collaborative entrepreneurial effort between Howard Coor-Pender, a pioneer in shop manufactured door and window frames, and Ralph L. Long, the designer and patent holder of Sav-a-Space pocket door hardware which he manufactured in El Cajon. Joining Coor-Pender to assist him and manage the office was daughter, Marceil.

Shortly after the company's formation to produce sliding pocket frames, the company added other items to its product line, including "Windowmaster" louvered windows designed and manufactured by Ralph Long Co.

In 1955, Coor-Pender purchased Long's interest in the firm and changed the name to Coor-Pender Co. Soon after, son-in-law Donald J. (Mac) McNally came on board to oversee shop operations.

As the local demand for louvered windows increased Windowmaster proved too costly to be competitive. In order to continue in this market, Coor-

Pender purchased a line of louvered hardware, manufacturing rights and equipment from Vent Vue Co., a Florida based manufacturing company, and renamed and incorporated the compnay as Vent Vue Window Products Co., Inc. In 1963, the company moved into two small buildings on Glover Place. Since that time, these facilities have been more than tripled as additional buildings and adjoining land was acquired.

The third generation joined Vent Vue in the late 1970s when Mac's son, Mitchell H. McNally came aboard to help with sales and new product development. The company continued to diversify in response to the financial ebb and flow of the industry and added many different products as demand dictated.

In the mid 1980s, Vent Vue made a major change in response to the East Coast window companies who were infiltrating the local market, and started manufacturing pre-assembled window and door units. The trademark "REDI-FIT" was attached to the product line that duplicated the look of windows and doors of typical California manufacture, but included improvements in weatherstripping and hardware.

Soon added to the product line were custom radius door and window units, bay and bowed units and detailed panel doors. Because of the increased restoration and remodeling markets, Vent Vue began to match existing doors and windows and to make such specialized products as "curved glass" double hung windows and other unique millwork items.

The company's skilled craftsmen start with the finest quality raw materials and carefully

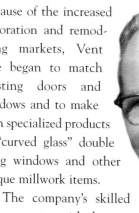

assemble each custom product. They take great pride in their workmanship and strive to achieve the exact look desired by the designer, dealer and end user.

As a local manufacturer with precision engineering standards, Vent Vue handles each order as a custom item. This enables them to make odd sizes as well as stock sizes and jamb widths to fit job conditions. There is no limit to the products the company can produce. Normal production includes a variety of specialty items — doors, windows, radius sash and doors as well as sliding and swinging patio doors. Vent Vue has a broad range of certified products, which comply with the current California Title 24 requirements and is moving forward into new product lines with emphasis on highly engineered European hardware.

Today, because of its reputation and expertise in the industry, Vent Vue is often specified in architectual plans and periodically, articles and pictures featuring its products appear in highly respected national magazines. The team of estimators and order takers are thoroughly qualified in the sash and door industry and their years of experience come to a high total. With the help of its employees and other family members, Diane McNally, Howard Coor-Pender's daughter, and Cheryl Aoyagi, his granddaughter, the company's goal continues to be quality and service.

The company has not been idle when it comes to community and industry participation. It has for many years supported local youth endeavors and has been a member of the "Friends of the Los Angeles River" organization whose goal is to clean up the river area and plant trees along its banks. It has been a member of the Southern California Lumber Association and BICA (Building Industry Credit Association). Marceil Coor-Pender is a past president and active board member of the latter. She was recently the recipient of the Donald M. Hollman Distinguished Service Award.

Vent Vue's 50th anniversary in the year 2000 is rapidly approaching. The outlook for the future is bright, as the company joins forces with others who are striving to preserve the historical integrity and improve the architectural panorama of Los Angeles.

STEINY AND COMPANY, INC.

In the early 1950s, Jack Steiny founded what is now one of California's premier electrical contracting companies, Steiny and Company, Inc. Postwar Los Angeles was truly the land of opportunity.

Steiny says, "Comparatively speaking, Los Angeles is a young city and we've been at this so long, we're part of the history of the place. We helped build L.A. We certainly did our share of the traffic signals in this famously traffic-heavy town."

In 1953, Steiny left San Francisco for what he felt was the more fertile ground of Los Angeles. He'd graduated in engineering from Stanford University, spent the war years in the Merchant Marines, and earned his contractor's license while working for a small contractor. The plan for the move was to start a company that would serve businesses throughout California. He chose electrical contracting because back then it was a business that required almost no start-up capital, which is what he had.

From an office in back of his home, he wired people's doorbells and porch lights, Loretta Young's house, and then advanced to larger buildings and a few traffic signals. He moved to a commercial office site, and in

Steiny and Company served as electrical contractor for the majestic Peninsula Hotel, located on Little Santa Monica Boulevard in Beverly Hills.

1958 he got his break with the United California Bank building. That job catapulted the company to state-level competitiveness, so it subsequently opened a second office in San Francisco and satellites elsewhere in the state.

Since then, Steiny and Company has done the electrical work on the J. Paul Getty Museum, the Bay Area Rapid Transit (BART) system in Northern California, the Lockheed Tristar Assembly Building in Palmdale, North American Aviation, Inc. in El Segundo, the Arco Center in Long Beach, the Forum in Inglewood and projects for Disney, Metro Rail and Bank of America — to name but a few of its projects.

The company's capabilities include industry-specific experience in airport terminals, armed services, co-generation facilities, life safety, security, prisons, refineries, mass transit, water treatment and telecommunication, but its bread and butter has always been traffic.

Such success does not occur without charismatic leadership. Jack Steiny has always been a savvy businessman and kind boss. He has served as president of The CORO Foundation, which trains college graduates with a hands-on course in civics and public policy. Earlier, he was a member of the Young President's Organization.

In April of 1949, Steiny married Nancy Thorp, a psychotherapist, with whom he has four children and eight grandchildren. The couple still live in the home that once housed the infant company. Steiny's daughter Susan is president and works out of the Northern California office, as she has since 1982.

Jack Steiny still has a soft spot for Northern California. When Steiny and Company installed the navigation lights on the Golden Gate Bridge, he couldn't help but take the little elevator and scale the steep orange ladder for a view from the top. But while he spends time gazing wistfully at the fog-shrouded San Francisco Bay, he always returns to Southern California. "I love the eclecticism of Los Angeles," he says. "It's a fascinating place."

MILFORD WAYNE DONALDSON, FAIA, INC.

Since its founding in 1978, Architect Milford Wayne Donaldson, FAIA, Inc. has established itself as one of the leading preservation architecture firms in the Western United States. Founder and President Wayne Donaldson, FAIA began working with historic buildings when the idea of preservation was still a new concept, opening his office in the Gaslamp Quarter, the historic center of San Diego. Wayne and his team of architects, conservators and historians have been instrumental in preserving, restoring and reconstructing hundreds of buildings throughout the Western states with an emphasis in Southern and Central California.

Architect Milford Wayne Donaldson, FAIA, Inc. has extensive experience in almost every variation of building scale, type and use. From small wood-framed agricultural buildings to adobe stagecoach stations, from Victorian hotels to mission style train stations, diversity is a hallmark of Architect MWD's work. The firm has over 20 years of technical know-how as well as a comprehensive knowledge of codes and how they relate to historic buildings — especially the Secretary of the Interior's Standards for Treatment of Historic Properties, the State Historical Building Code and the Americans with Disabilities Act.

Whether the project requires museum quality historic restoration, seismic stabilization, complete reconstruction, adaptive reuse or simply a report of existing conditions and space planning, Architect MWD can fill each client's needs in an expert and professional manner. Wayne Donaldson is also a licenced general contractor and President of Sixteen Penny Construction, giving him real world expertise for assisting clients during the construction phase, making sure that the project is completed on time and on budget.

Architect Milford Wayne Donaldson, FAIA, Inc. has been involved in many projects in the Los Angeles region, including: La Casa Primera adobe restoration, Laguna Beach High School restoration and expansion, Orange County Courthouse restoration, Ivy Substation and Media Park adaptive reuse and restoration, Smoke Tree Ranch House reconstruction, Catalina Island Casino conservation assessment program, Rancho Los Cerritos master plan, Riverside County Courthouse restoration, San Bernardino historic buildings survey, Padua Hills Theater planning, Calico Ghost Town repair and restoration, Navy Variable Angle Launcher documentation, San Bernardino Asistencia de Mission San Gabriel seismic retrofit, MCAS Tustin Blimp Hanger reuse study and Jensen-Alvarado Ranch restoration.

Architect Milford Wayne Donaldson, FAIA, Inc. has won numerous awards for preservation and design, including a Historic Preservation Award from the Los Angeles Conservancy and a Special Award for Excellence in Historic Preservation from the American Institute of Architects (AIA) California Council.

Smoke Tree Ranch House, Palm Springs.

(Top right) Ivy Substation & Media Park, Culver City.

(Far left) Calico Ghost Town, Mojave Desert.

THOMAS SAFRAN & ASSOCIATES

It takes a very special company to implement programs that will better its community.

Since 1974, real-estate developer Thomas Safran & Associates has married community involvement with its innovative, award-winning designs. Located in Los Angeles, the company is a small tightly knit organization that oversees the work of architects, contractors, social workers and administrative staff. The firm specializes in affordable family and senior rental apartment developments, and serves cities all over the Los Angeles basin — from Sun Valley to Hollywood, Inglewood, Camarillo, Carson and West Covina.

That many of TSA's buildings have won awards is important in combating "nimbyism" or "not-in-my-backyardism" to low income housing. Futhermore, Vice President David Ferguson says TSA has played an active role in revitalizing not only neighborhoods, but attitudes. Gang members have been transformed into responsible citizens, dilapidated rat-infested dwellings now boast lush landscaping and are a credit to the community. In fact, a quick glance at before and after shots of a TSA project demonstrates this point.

Among Safran's many recognized buildings are its Strathern Park Apartments in Sun Valley (see photo above), which received the 1992 Gold Nugget Award for Best Affordable Attached Housing Development from the Pacific Coast Builders, the Los Angeles Business Council's Beautification Award and the prestigious Urban Land Institute (ULI) Award for Excellence in 1993.

A variety of financing sources, including the HUD Section 8 and Block Grant programs, Federal Low Income Housing Tax Credits, local redevelopment agency loans and private sources are utilized to provide affordable rents.

TSA's employees include college and graduate student interns who are provided a small stipend to work on resident activities and social services. TSA also has an internship program for troubled youth, helping to rehabilitate them through their employment in the construction of its developments.

TSA provides complete property management services for all of its buildings, and its staff chooses to do the kind of work they do because they believe in it. They think it's important for a community to have affordable housing and are proud to support programs that make a difference in people's lives.

These are not different buildings — but before and after shots of Safran's celebrated El Centro Project in Los Angeles, completed in 1996.

PARTNERS IN LOS ANGELES
BUSINESS & FINANCE

Investment banking and securities brokerage, insurance and diversified holding companies provide a financial foundation for all of Los Angeles.

AON CORPORATION

Aon Corporation, one of the world's leading insurance services organizations with nearly $6 billion in revenue generated through 550 offices worldwide, began as the Ryan Insurance Group in 1964, specializing in the sale of insurance products and warranties through automobile dealerships.

Founder Patrick G. Ryan's entrepreneurial vision led to a series of mergers and acquisitions which propelled the company to its current position as one of the world's premier providers of insurance products and services.

In 1982, Ryan Insurance Group merged with Combined International Corporation and significantly expanded its brokerage and consulting business with the subsequent purchase of Rollins Burdick Hunter Co., a major U.S. broker.

Five years later, stockholders renamed the evolving insurance services provider Aon Corporation. The term "Aon," derived from the Gaelic for unity, captures the essence of the company's corporate philosophy.

As chairman and chief executive officer of Aon, Ryan's deal-making continued into the 90s with the purchase of several household names in the brokerage industry. Among them were: Hudig-Langeveldt Group B.V.; Frank B. Hall & Co. Inc.; Bain Hogg Group P.L.C and Alexander & Alexander Services Inc.

Since its inception, Aon's company culture has been defined by interdependence — sharing knowledge, skills and resources among all of its employees and clients. Driving Aon's vision and progress is a core commitment to create greater value for clients, policyholders and investors. As an industry leader with enhanced resources and expertise, Aon identifies and implements the most cost-efficient, innovative solutions for its clients.

Aon's numerous acquisitions over the years are part of the company's long-term strategic growth. Each acquisition is chosen for its individual strengths, and Aon only invests in specialized companies that enable it to bring greater value to its clients.

The corporation's services include the following areas of expertise: Aon Risk Services, a leading insurance brokerage and risk management services organization;

Located on Wilshire Boulevard, Aon Los Angeles acts as the primary hub for two other Orange County offices. With the third-largest office, Aon L.A. draws upon the skills of more than 800 people in Southern California.

(Left to right) Patrick G. Ryan, Chairman and CEO of Aon Corporation; Doug Judson, Chairman of Pacific Group, Aon Corporation; Doug Brown, President Aon Risk Services, Inc. of Southern California.

administration, premium financing, risk management and loss control consulting. Aon invests in professional talent and technology and develops the specialty products necessary to serve its clients in major industry groupings, including construction, energy, transportation, financial institutions, public entities, healthcare, utilities and others.

Aon draws on the intellectual capital of its global organization to provide creative risk financing and management solutions, with strategic risk planning, analytical and actuarial services, risk management information systems and risk control consulting services. Through its extensive distribution networks, Aon professionals offer value-added solutions to meet the local needs of its clients.

Aon maintains a leading position in providing specialty products that serve major industry groupings, including construction and land development.

Highly skilled professionals possess a thorough knowledge of the regulations and customs of the countries where they do business, benefiting marine and energy industries, as well as specialty nonmarine lines.

Aon Consulting Worldwide, a fully integrated human resource consulting organization; Aon Services Group, a provider of specialized insurance products and services for professional groups, service businesses, governments, healthcare providers and commercial organizations; and Aon Re Worldwide, which handles the firm's global reinsurance brokerage operations.

Brokerage & Consulting Companies
Aon Risk Services

Aon Risk Services offers a vast array of specialized services through locations worldwide to meet the complex needs of its diverse client base.

In addition to traditional risk transfer, Aon Risk Services applies a consultative and strategic approach to complex risks.

The company's spectrum of risk services includes insurance placement, program development and

Aon Consulting Worldwide

Aon specializes in linking human resource strategies with business initiatives for improved performance.

Aon Consulting offers services in employee benefits, human resources, compensation and change management. Specific services include organizational analysis and human resources strategic planning, job design and competency modeling, recruitment and selection, compensation and reward systems benefits design and management, training and development, human resources, compliance and risk management, and individual and organizational change management.

Aon Consulting's integrated consulting approach ensures that clients are effectively attracting, retaining and utilizing their people resources. The firm applies an objective, global perspective that provides customized solutions and consistent administration for client programs.

Aon specializes in linking human resource strategies with business initiatives, offering services in employee benefits, human resources, compensation and change management.

Pecos River Division

Pecos River is a world leader in helping organizations and individuals achieve specific, measurable business success through transformational change. By clarifying an organization's critical business objectives, and identifying the strategic and cultural changes required to achieve those objectives, the Pecos River Performance Breakthrough Process provides the necessary tools and skill sets vital to achieving change and improved business performance.

Aon Services Group

Aon Services Group, through its subsidiaries, designs and delivers specialized insurance products and services for professional groups, service businesses, governments, healthcare providers and commercial organizations.

For insurance companies, Aon Services Group provides outsourced underwriting management, claims and risk management expertise, and third-party administration services. Agents and brokers are served through a network of underwriting managers and wholesale brokerage operations. The unit also delivers specialized professional liability, life and personal lines insurance products to members of affinity groups and associations.

Aon Services Group's niche focus provides a deep knowledge of each client's profession or industry. Aon excels at cost-effective, multiple-channel distribution systems and state-of-the-art products for specific industries and professionals. Aon is a major provider of professional liability coverages, with emphasis on accounting, law and healthcare.

Aon Re Worldwide

Aon's global reinsurance brokerage operations are coordinated under the Aon Re Worldwide umbrella.

Aon provides reinsurance and specialty placement, alternative risk services, captive management services and catastrophe information forecasting. Expertise is organized around industries, including aviation, marine and energy, as well as in specialty nonmarine lines. Capital market products and techniques, including sophisticated security and risk portfolio analysis, allow Aon to address client exposures and alternative reinsurance options.

By developing new products and services, Aon addresses the dramatic changes in the telecommunications industry.

Aon's reinsurance and specialty brokerage expertise, market intelligence and analytical tools assist insurance underwriters and major corporate clients in making informed buying decisions. Through a combination of product line and geographical expertise, including significant presence in the United States and United Kingdom, Aon provides clients with efficient and cost-effective reinsurance and specialty coverage.

By bringing together the exceptional resources within Aon Re Worldwide, Alexander Howden, the Bain Hogg Group and Nicholson Jenner Leslie, Aon has created the world's premier reinsurance intermediary.

Aon Re Worldwide offers clients a global network of reinsurance expertise services and resources, coupled with access to virtually every reinsurance market around the globe. The breadth of the firm's organization and leadership in the industry enables it to negotiate extremely cost-effective placements for its clients.

Aon's talented, experienced professionals are dedicated to providing clients with innovative solutions to their reinsurance needs by employing both traditional reinsurance markets and alternative risk services.

Insurance Underwriting Companies

In today's unpredictable world, Aon's well-established insurance underwriting companies provide their policyholders with security and confidence about the future. These underwriting companies focus on markets

Utilizing sophisticated security and risk portfolio analysis provides reinsurance and specialty placements organized around the aviation industry.

Founded in 1927, Virginia Surety Company's major lines of businesses include new and used vehicles, consumer electronics and appliances, cellular phones, involuntary unemployment insurance, home warranty and credit card and financial institution enhancements.

As Aon's overseas specialty property and casualty company, London General Insurance Company's primary business is automobile, appliance and consumer electronics extended warranty as well as creditor disability, redundancy and critical illness insurance.

Aon Warranty Group

The Aon Warranty Group (AWG), part of Aon's insurance underwriting companies, is a recognized leader in specialty consumer warranty programs and serves as the largest service contract administrator in

in North America, Europe, Latin America and Asia/ Pacific by providing a variety of consumer insurance products, including accident and health coverage, traditional life insurance and extended warranties.

Combined Insurance Company of America

Since 1919, Combined Insurance Company of America (CICA) has maintained a leading position in the supplemental insurance market by providing accident, health and life coverages directly to individual consumers. Aon's specialty property/casualty underwriters, Virginia Surety Company and its U.K. affiliate, London General Insurance Company, serve consumers with a variety of extended warranty coverages.

CICA insures more than five million individual policyholders worldwide. Major product lines include disability income, supplemental accident and health and a basic portfolio of life insurance products.

America. AWG serves the world's premier manufacturers, distributors and retailers of almost every type of consumer goods including electronics, appliances, computers and telephone equipment.

In the rapidly changing, consolidating insurance industry, Aon pursues a sharply focused strategy, concentrating more of its resources in insurance brokerage and consulting.

Continued acquisitions provide Aon with enhanced resources, access to more insurance markets and a wider range of specialist capabilities, providing its clients with creative insurance and consulting solutions through local representation supported by a network of more than 500 offices in some 100 countries.

Size matters in today's marketplace because it allows Aon access to invaluable resources and geographic reach, which translates to efficiency and effectiveness for the company's clients.

"Size does matter," says company founder Patrick G. Ryan. "It gives you scale, which translates into efficiency. However, I believe the more important issue is quality. Size without quality does not serve our clients. It is not our goal to be number one in size; our goal is to be number one in quality."

The combination of a diverse product line and geographic reach, including a significant presence in all major insurance centers worldwide, allows Aon to provide customized solutions, seamless implementation and consistent, cost-effective administration.

CATHAY BANK

s the first Chinese-American bank in Southern California, Cathay Bank was founded to serve the financial needs of the Los Angeles Chinatown community. With just $550,000 in capital and seven employees, Cathay Bank opened its office in 1962.

With the establishment of Cathay Bank, the community had a bank to assist its Chinese-American constituents to own homes and start new businesses. Throughout the years, Cathay Bank has been fortunate to witness and participate in the tremendous growth of its community in California, and is proud to have contributed to its development and success. Many Cathay customers, having shared in that experience, started with a small store and grew into multinational companies. During those years, the Bank has learned to assist and work with customers to overcome both temporary and long term difficulty. In addition, Cathay Bank has continuously served its customers with consistency, strength and commitment.

In 1985, the Bank's first overseas representative office was opened in Hong Kong. In 1988, the Taiwan overseas office was added to facilitate the international banking needs of the Bank's expanding customer base. They have served as key links to the greater Pacific Rim business community and helped establish local business

Located in Monterey Park, our first branch's extraordinary design takes advantage of natural sunlight creating a greenhouse effect inside the bank.

contacts. Today, Cathay Bank has maintained an extensive correspondent bank network in Asia, Europe, South and North America, strongly reinforcing its business presence in the global market.

In 1990, Cathay Bancorp, a bank holding company, was formed to hold Cathay Bank and its shares began trading on the NASDAQ. Now, over three decades later, the Bank has grown to 19 branches throughout California. Today, the Bank's capital is nearly $140 million with assets over $1.6 billion.

In 1994, Cathay Bank received a "ten-year Continued Premier Performing Bank Award" by the Findley Reports, which placed it among the top six ranking California financial institutions for safety, strength and performance. According to the Findley Reports, Inc., a nationally recognized bank research and rating firm, Cathay Bank is the only Chinese-American commercial bank among over 300 California banks to reach this milestone since the founding of the award in 1976. This high level of excellence attests to the Bank's underlying financial stability, as well as its ability to respond promptly to changing market dynamics.

In 1996, Cathay Bank broke new ground in the Asian-American banking world by announcing a merger with First

Public Savings Bank, F.S.B. — the first merger between two Chinese-American banks. The acquisition made Cathay Bancorp the 15th largest publicly traded banking corporation in California and expanded the bank's locations, services and hours of operations.

One of the key components in Cathay Bank's success is building strength from within by providing employees with in-depth training programs. In view of this commitment, the bank implemented a sales and service training plan known as "CLASS" — Cathay Leads All in Service and Sales. This sales- and service-driven culture encourages relationship building and teamwork, resulting in greater customer retention, and sustainable increases in revenues and service quality.

Another equally important key component is technology advancement in Cathay Bank. The Bank has successfully used technology to improve operational efficiency and customer convenience. In 1996, the Bank took a leadership role among Chinese-American banks by introducing the PC Cash Management Service. This PC banking tool has helped business customers manage their company's finances more efficiently. The program allows customers to obtain transaction history and account information, make loan payments, initiate wire transfers and purchase investment securities to maximize their return. Recognizing the customer service potential of the Internet, Cathay Bank launched a site on the World Wide Web in 1997. The comprehensive Web site contains 60-plus pages providing updated information on the Bank's services and rates on foreign exchange, mortgage loans, auto loans and CD's, etc.

In keeping with increasing international trade on the West Coast and the needs of an expanding customer base, the bank introduced the first foreign currency exchange service among Chinese-American banks. Customers can buy and sell most major currencies at favorable rates over the counter at nine convenient Cathay Bank locations in Southern California. As a major Chinese-American bank in the foreign exchange market, their knowledgeable and experienced foreign exchange specialists have been assisting customers with prompt, personal and professional service.

Cathay Bank owes its history of growth to the individuals and communities it serves. Throughout the years, Cathay Bank has underscored its commitment to the communities through various speaking engagements, corporate contributions and thoughtfully designed financial products. Last year, the bank contributed over $100,000 to various charitable organizations in support of economic development, affordable housing and education, etc.

Looking ahead, Cathay Bank is confident about its future growth potential in the year 2000 and beyond. The Bank will continue to capitalize on its strong financial strength and solid organizational structure in achieving service expansion and maintaining superior customer service. Cathay Bank believes the future hold tremendous promise for both customers and employees.

The Lion Dance grand opening ceremony brought the Cathay Bank Monterey Park Office to Southern California in 1982.

FARMERS GROUP, INC.

The growth of Farmers Insurance Group of Companies, spanning nearly seven decades, is an outstanding example of America's free enterprise system working at its best. The steady rise of Farmers through the years to become one of the nation's leading insurance organizations is a classic American business success story. A number of factors combined to make possible the success of the nation's fifth largest property and casualty insurance organization. One of the most important was good timing. Farmers arrival on the insurance scene in 1928, coincided with America's growing love affair with the automobile. An increasing number of motor vehicles were rolling off the assembly lines onto an inadequate road system, resulting in an increasing number of accidents which generated the need for more and better insurance coverage. It was a good time to start an insurance company.

Using a common sense approach on how best to attract and keep customers, two successful California businessmen and experienced insurance professionals, Thomas Leavey and Jack Tyler, were attracted by the competitive advantage they would gain from insuring farmers and other rural residents at more favorable rates, reflecting the lower accident frequency in rural as compared to urban areas. This new competitive approach attracted many customers to Farmers

Sixteen thousand employees manage nearly 15 million policies-in-force.

Insurance and propelled the fledgling company into a growth rate that has continued steadily over the years since it opened for business in a small two-room office with just three employees.

Although the company has grown substantially from its humble beginnings, it still limits its operations to only 29 carefully selected states where it feels it can conduct a sound insurance business within the parameters of the state's legislative, regulatory and market environment. It is also constantly evaluating new markets and expects to be entering other states in the future.

Despite this measured expansion, Farmers today ranks fifth largest among the nation's property and casualty insurance companies based on direct written premiums and serves more than 8 million customers through some 14,000 agents and 16,000 employees. It has nearly 15 million policies-in-force and had total gross premiums written in 1996 of $9.8 billion.

The company's original philosophy of doing what is right for its customers has remained at the core of all Farmers' operations. Recently, to make it easier for customers to report and handle claims, Farmers set up a 24-hours-a-day, 7-days-a-week claims service and established a national catastrophe center in Kansas City staffed by specially trained Farmers claims adjusters who can be dispatched at a moment's notice to supply rapid aid to those in stricken areas. Such concern for its customers needs has never wavered over the decades. Today it is reflected in Farmers' advertising theme emphasizing Farmers' commitment to "Get You Back Where You Belong."

In the continuing evolution of its business, Farmers Group of Companies has been a leader in introducing state–of–the–art technology to assist its agents in providing their customers with the best in products and service. A Farmers agent is much like having a friend in the community who runs a local business and who also is an integral part of the community's civic and social programs,

often taking the lead in organizing needed charitable and fund raising programs like the March of Dimes "WalkAmerica" campaign.

Today, the Farmers agent offers personal, life and commercial insurance, centralized for maximum efficiency and to save time. Needed changes in policies can be handled online in the agent's office.

A recently established Asset Management Unit will allow Agents to offer products such as mutual funds, 401(K) plans, auto loans and leases, home and auto warranties and other financial products and services to their customers.

Part of the Farmers story is an on-going evolution that involves reorganization, restructuring and rethinking the way Farmers does business so as meet the new and increasing competitive forces now entering the insurance field.

Farmers believes in the value of personal contact with its clients, of having a local agent available to the insured whenever he or she has an insurance-related problem. Telephones and automatic machines can be helpful on a supplemental basis, but they will never replace the words of comfort, advice and assurance emanating from a community-based agent who knows what his or her customer needs and responds on an individual basis.

Martin D. Feinstein, chairman of the board, president and chief executive officer of Farmers provided an appropriate epilogue to the Farmers American Success Story recently during an interview when he summarized how he would like the company to be perceived as it enters the challenging 21st Century: "We want to be a company that is easy to do business with and to be our customer's resident expert for financial services. We want them to be comfortable in doing business with us. We want to be the company people can trust. We understand that trust is not something gained by saying or printing the word. It is something you have to earn and we believe Farmers has the capability of earning it."

Farmers began earning that trust by basing its original business philosophy on a simple idea that it made common sense always to do the right thing for its customers and by doing so earn their trust and loyalty. This, as the Farmers American Success Story has shown, is exactly what happened. That original pledge now is augmented with the company's reassuring promise "to get you back where you belong" whether you suffer a small or catastrophic loss.

And to think, all of this happened in just the first 70 years. Imagine what Farmers' growing legion of customers can expect from this unique American business institution in the years ahead.

HOULIHAN LOKEY HOWARD & ZUKIN

With nearly 30 years of experience and repeated rankings among the top-20 U.S. merger and acquisition advisors, Houlihan Lokey Howard & Zukin has established itself as one of the premier, middle-market investment banking firms in the nation.

Its more than 5,000 clients have come from virtually every industry and range from Fortune 100 corporations and Forbes 400 families to closely-held middle-market companies, state and federal agencies and foreign governments.

That's a significant achievement for an investment banking firm founded in 1970 in Century City in Los Angeles rather than the cobblestone streets of lower Manhattan more than 100 years ago.

Houlihan Lokey has carved out a rather remarkable place for itself in a very short time by recognizing specific market needs and being the very best in the business at meeting those needs. The fruits of that success are evidenced by the addition of offices in San Francisco, Chicago, New York, Minneapolis, Washington, D.C., Toronto, Dallas and Atlanta, and a staff of more than 280 employees.

This is the story of a private partnership which has grown through the vision and determination of its employees over the past 30 years. By creating an environment where professionals can develop and grow individual practices, the firm retains its most valuable asset, its employees. This entrepreneurial spirit has been the cornerstone of the firm and its leadership since the beginning.

O. Kit Lokey, founder and CEO, is a Los Angeles native who received his BS and MBA from UCLA. After graduation, he spent five years at Price Waterhouse. It was there that he met and developed a friendship with Richard Houlihan.

Houlihan left Price Waterhouse in 1970 to start his own financial management and consulting firm. Two years later, Lokey joined him and they incorporated as Houlihan & Lokey with individual investments of about $1,500. Initially, the company had no identified specialty and attracting business meant marketing a laundry list of 40 or 50 services to potential clients.

Then, a show business client in the midst of a divorce needed a number of jointly owned assets valued. Houlihan & Lokey recognized an underserved potential growth market and began to package their services as valuation experts. By 1974, business and securities valuation brought in 30 percent of company revenues. A year later, the figure was 75 percent.

In 1974, the Employee Retirement Income Security Act was passed and the firm decided to specialize in valuation services for Employee Stock Ownership Plan (ESOP) transactions. Today, the firm remains the nation's preeminent provider of ESOP financial advisory services, although they now account for a small percentage of the firm's revenues.

There were other significant changes during the 1970s as the company continued to grow and to mature. Robert F. Howard added his surname to the company in 1974 and James H. Zukin followed in 1976. Then in 1977, Houlihan left to pursue other

Founding partners (left to right) Kit Lokey, Robert Howard and James Zukin.

interests. Little did he realize that significant growth, success and excitement lay just ahead for the firm that still bears his name.

During the late 1970s and 1980s, hyperinflation ruled the U.S. economy and most of Wall Street's largest investment banking firms began calling upon Houlihan Lokey's independent valuation expertise in fairness, solvency and ESOP fairness opinions for the surge of merger, acquisition and leveraged buyout transactions. During this period, the firm advised in transactions totaling more than $200 billion.

In the mid 1980s, the firm recognized that some of the numerous leveraged transactions of the 1980s were potentially overleveraged and that a market for financial restructuring advisory services might be developing. Houlihan Lokey purchased Cheviot Capital Corporation and assembled what has become one of the most dominant financial restructuring groups in the country.

Today, forecasts are particularly promising for one of Houlihan Lokey's fastest growing practice areas. Houlihan Lokey's merchant banking experts have been extremely successful during the 1990s establishing private capital funds to assist companies with growth financing, recapitalizations and acquisition capital.

Strategic positioning and calculated assessment of potential market niches have been watchwords at Houlihan Lokey. But the real key to continued success has been expert analysis and an independent perspective. Whether it is a routine valuation, raising capital for a middle-market firm or helping a troubled company work its way out of financial distress, precise analysis is the core capability, which is combined with other experience acquired over the years.

Much of that experience focuses on the middle-market arena where companies traditionally have faced two options when selecting an investment banking firm. They could use one of the large, bulge-bracket investment banks and hope their engagement remained a priority or rely on a small regional investment banking boutique and hope for the needed breadth of services, industry specialization and professional and technical resources.

Houlihan Lokey Howard & Zukin corporate headquarters located in Century City.

Houlihan Lokey has positioned itself to offer an attractive third alternative. With nearly 200 financial professionals in nine offices across North America, Houlihan Lokey combines the resources and experience of national companies with the middle-market focus and senior-level attention of regional firms.

Timing also has been critical. It is a central factor in capital markets and in serving the needs of clients and broadening Houlihan Lokey's business. The firm has grown and diversified by staying ahead of shifting economic trends using the power of precise analysis and entrepreneurial philosophy to spur growth beyond expectation.

The list of Houlihan Lokey clients is impressive for its diversity as well as the prestige of the companies. A sampling of Southern California clients includes the Los Angeles Dodgers, Ralphs Supermarkets, SAIC, Merisel, QAD, Carter Hawley Hale Stores, Lockheed Martin, California Federal Bank, Koll Real Estate Group, Seven-Up/RC Bottling Co. of Southern California, The Restaurant Enterprises Group, Live Entertainment, Wolfgang Puck Food Company, Parson's Corporation and Calloway Golf.

Houlihan Lokey remains committed to providing only those specialized investment banking services where their research, development experience and professional personnel uniquely qualify the firm as a leader in the field. The firm will continue to excel by setting new standards of service in a highly competitive field. Professional competence and integrity will guide the firm into the 21st century, as Houlihan Lokey continues to meet the needs of its clients by providing value-added financial services from its core of market-leading specialties.

WILLIAM E. SIMON & SONS, LLC

William E. Simon & Sons, a private investment firm and merchant bank founded by former U.S. Secretary of the Treasury William E. Simon and his sons, William E. Simon Jr. and J. Peter Simon, is backed by years of experience and expertise in the fast-moving field of international finance and investment.

William Edward Simon, the company founder and chairman, served under two United States presidents as the Secretary of the Treasury before launching a series of successful global enterprises. He and his sons share responsibility for the firm's investment strategy and direction.

Founded in 1988, William E. Simon & Sons has over $4 billion of assets under management in a number of core businesses including private equity, capital markets, real estate investment and management.

An important core business for the firm is taking ownership positions in diverse businesses. William E. Simon & Sons researches and pursues those ventures the firm believes have strong growth prospects and excellent potential to appreciate in value from an opportune linkage of capital, management and market access.

Currently the Private Equity group has investments in companies with total revenues exceeding $4 billion, including aerospace, business services, transportation, specialty food, basic manufacturing and energy. The firm is a major force in the rapidly growing contract logistics industry, having acquired three companies with annual sales of nearly $1 billion, in partnership with Oaktree Capital Management.

"Intent on building for the future, William E. Simon & Sons has a clearly defined strategy for achieving superior returns while carefully balancing risk and reward."

Real estate traditionally has been an important component of the firm's portfolio of investments. William E. Simon & Sons actively invests in, develops or manages single and multifamily residential properties, industrial parks, office buildings, retail projects, hotels, mixed-use developments and land.

William E. Simon & Sons Realty group achieves superior returns by targeting smaller investments that are below the "radar screen" of opportunity funds and larger institutional investors and where there is not an oversupply of capital chasing deals. The firm's real estate portfolio includes such prime properties as the Phoenix Ritz Carlton and The Centrum in Los Angeles' vibrant media district.

Unrestrained by geographic or industrial boundaries, William E. Simon & Sons operates out of offices

William E. Simon & Sons is an international private investment firm and merchant bank founded by former U.S. Secretary of the Treasury William E. Simon (center) and his sons, William E. Simon, Jr. (left) and J. Peter Simon.

on both coasts: in Morristown, New Jersey near the heart of New York City and in Los Angeles, the United State gateway to the great emerging markets of Asia/Pacific and Latin America.

For many years, the senior Simon has been unshakable in his conviction that the 21st century will be the century of the Pacific. Determined to participate in, and benefit from, this economic and sociological miracle, he established a Hong Kong-based merchant bank, William E. Simon & Sons Asia, in 1991.

Drawing on the background of management, transactions pursued by Simon Asia tend to be corporate finance-driven with a variety of major investments in the areas of shipping, power, consumer electronics, eyewear, glass and steel throughout China, Indonesia, Taiwan and Hong Kong.

The Capital Markets group comprises William E. Simon & Sons Municipal Securities, Chadelaine Corporate Securities, Andrew M. Carter & Company and a convertible bond fund managed by J. Peter Simon. All of these enterprises serve the institutional market.

The firm's entry into municipal securities in 1990 was natural in light of William E. Simon's extensive experience and national reputation in the field. He began his career at Union Securities in the Municipal Bond Department and went on to head this department at both Weedon & Co. and Salomon Brothers.

William E. Simon & Sons Municipal Securities averages approximately $2 billion per month in secondary market transactions for institutional investors, and has managed or co-managed more than $5 billion in negotiated public finance transactions each year since it was founded.

Intent on building for the future, William E. Simon & Sons has a clearly defined strategy for achieving superior returns while carefully balancing risk and reward.

The success of this innovative firm is driven by its founders extensive experience in global financial markets, high-level personal relationships worldwide and their ability to make decisions to commit substantial capital in a short time frame.

William E. Simon & Sons operates on the premise that markets require timley decision-making and response. The firm's highly capable and qualified executives act quickly and effectively to assess and react to a wide variety of investment proposals. By addressing opportunities in a disciplined and prompt manner, William E. Simon & Sons has gained a well-deserved reputation in the investment world as an important and responsible player.

REAL ESTATE MORTGAGE ACCEPTANCE COMPANY

he success of Real Estate Mortgage Acceptance Company (RMAC) surpassed even the expectations of founders Ron LeClair and Harry Hedaya.

When the pair of young entrepreneurs opened their two-man Beverly Hills office at the start of 1995, the nation's residential mortgage business was just coming off the biggest refinance boom the industry had ever seen. The economy in early 1995 offered minimal opportunity for purchase and refinance loans, which forced many firms to close their doors.

Real Estate Mortgage Acceptance Company attributes its success to its outstanding employees.

LeClair and Hedaya found themselves in need of an income. But rather than work for someone else, the pair decided to sink or swim in their own start-up venture.

Despite seemingly insurmountable odds, the partners carved a niche in a previously untapped, and little known market: the Title I Home Improvement Loan. The beauty of these U.S. Department of Housing and Urban Development (HUD)-insured loans was that they were not "interest rate sensitive" and didn't require a formal appraisal.

LeClair and Hedaya started small with a single mission: to do as many of these loan transactions as possible. They sent out direct mailings to inform homeowners of the availability of these loans and encouraged them to utilize RMAC's services. Since there were virtually no competitors in the same market at that time, RMAC's phones literally rang off the hook.

Founders Ron LeClair and Harry Hedaya.

Less than six months later, the booming business expanded well beyond the walls of the Beverly Hills office. LeClair and Hedaya set up shop across town in their current 14,000-square-foot offices. Their employee base went from less than 10 to over 125 in the first two years at the Los Angeles corporate office, in addition to other locations including Orange County; Northern California; Boston, Massachusetts; Columbia, South Carolina; Tampa, Florida; Chicago, Illinois; Portland, Oregon; and Salt Lake City, Utah.

In the company's first ten and a half months in business, RMAC closed 414 loans. Today, LeClair and Hedaya's once-risky venture closes in excess of 4,500 loans annually.

The firm shows no signs of slowing down. Although LeClair and Hedaya had been offered millions for their bustling business, the pair decided to hold off on selling and "revisit the issue somewhere down the road." Future plans range from creating other spin-off ventures including a marketing and a computer company to a possible initial public offering.

PARTNERS IN LOS ANGELES

ENTERTAINMENT

As the world's largest entertainment center, Los Angeles is the hub for all artist-related businesses. Supporting industries that include management, production, marketing and distribution are an integral part of the city's economy and identity.

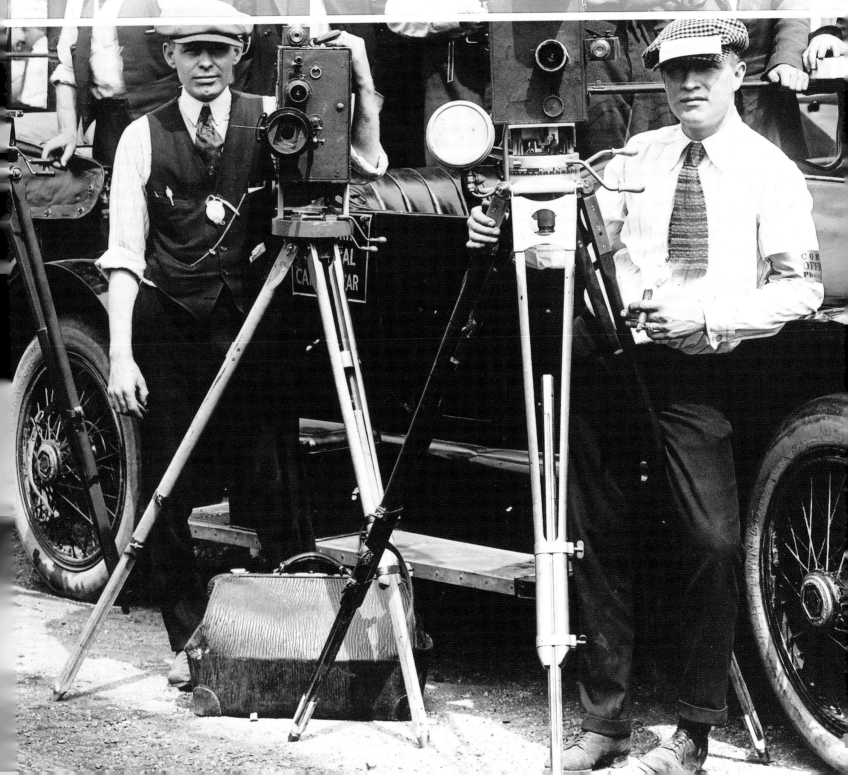

ACADEMY OF MOTION PICTURE ARTS AND SCIENCES

The Annual Academy Awards® Presentation is viewed by hundreds of millions of movie fans in more than 100 countries.

The Oscar® represents the best achievements of the year within the film industry and is easily one of the most recognizable awards in the world.

The Academy of Motion Picture Arts and Sciences is a professional honorary organization of over 6,000 motion picture professionals. Its primary missions are to advance the arts and sciences of motion pictures, to foster cooperation among creative leaders for cultural, educational, and technological progress and to recognize outstanding achievements.

The Academy was organized in May, 1927 with 36 original members under the presidency of Douglas Fairbanks. Membership is by invitation of the Board of Governors and is limited to those who have achieved distinction in the industry. Members represent 13 branches: Actors, Art Directors, Cinematographers, Directors, Executives, Film Editors, Music, Producers, Public Relations, Short Films and Feature Animation, Sound, Visual Effects and Writers.

The Academy recognizes outstanding achievements in motion picture arts and sciences during its Annual Academy Awards® Presentation to the best example in each of these 13 branches of the Academy. Because the Academy numbers among its members the ablest artist in the motion picture world, the Oscar® represents the best achievements of the year in the opinion of those who themselves reside at the top of their craft.

Awards have been presented every year since 1929. That year, the Academy Awards were presented at a private dinner with fewer than 250 persons attending. The event was broadcast on the radio from 1930 until 1952, when television enabled millions throughout North America to watch the ceremonies. Color television brought the full sparkle and glamour of the event to home viewers beginning in 1966. The program

now reaches movie fans in over 100 countries throughout the world.

While best known for its Academy Awards Presentation, the Academy of Motion Picture Arts and Sciences performs several other services of tremendous value to the industry.

The Academy Foundation, established in 1944, organizes and oversees the educational and cultural activities of the Academy. As such, the Foundation is dedicated to the preservation of early works to ensure their continued availability to students, filmmakers and scholars.

The Center for Motion Picture Study, in the restored historic structure that had formerly been the water processing plant for the City of Beverly Hills, is home to the Margaret Herrick Library and the Academy Film Archive. The library was founded in 1931 and maintains a world-renowned, non-circulating reference and research collection. It is regarded as one of the most complete collections of film-related materials ever assembled. The Photographic Stills Archive inventories and preserves its collection of more than six million prints or negatives. The Academy Film Archive contains approximately 25,000 films and videotapes made over the past 20 years.

The Academy has published the Academy Players Directory since 1937. The first directory was a single volume listing 1,800 performing artists; today, it is a four-volume set containing information on more than 27,000 artists and published on the internet. For nearly as long as it has awarded the Oscars, the Academy has published the Annual Index to Motion Picture Credits. This reference work contains film credit information for all feature films that qualify each year for Academy Awards consideration.

GOODYEAR AIRSHIP OPERATIONS

t is difficult to imagine a major outdoor spectator event without the familiar sight of a Goodyear blimp. Millions routinely expect the Goodyear blimp to be there transmitting magnificent aerial photography and flashing spectacular night-time messages from its elaborate network of colored lights.

The Eagle is one of the three-vessel fleet of airships that serve as goodwill ambassadors for the Goodyear Tire and Rubber Company of Akron, Ohio. Based just outside of Los Angeles during the winter, the Eagle travels throughout the continental United States and Canada during the other half of the year. Her sister airships, The Spirit of Akron, based in Akron, Ohio, and the Stars and Stripes in Pompano Beach, Florida maintain similar schedules.

The Eagle is a 192-foot long, 59.5-foot high and 50-foot wide, sausage-shaped craft that weighs 12,840 pounds and holds 202,700 cubic feet of helium inside of a rubber-coated, polyester fabric envelope. It is part of a proud tradition of the last U.S.-owned tire company and one that boasts seven decades of operating Goodyear airships without a single fatality.

A full-time staff of 21 people is required to keep the Eagle flying. There are four pilots, a public relations representative and 15 crew members.

With a carrying capacity of six passengers and a pilot, top speed for the Eagle is 50 mph. It cruises at 35 mph and is powered by twin, six-cylinder, 210 horsepower fuel-injected, air-cooled aircraft piston engines. It carries approximately 8,000 passengers a year at a normal altitude of between 1,000 and 3,000 feet with a maximum ceiling of 10,000 feet.

P.W. Litchfield, a former Goodyear chairman of the board, is credited with the company's involvement in airships. It was in 1910, after seeing an air balloon race in France, that Litchfield set Goodyear on the course to become a significant player in the fledging aviation industry. Goodyear built its first airship in 1911 and its first public relations blimp, the Pilgrim, in 1925.

Since then, Goodyear has built 312 airships, more than any other company in the world. That includes 65 commercial blimps and 250 airships under contact for the Army or Navy. Goodyear no longer manufactures airships, but continues its lighter-than-air heritage with the operation of the Eagle and its two sister ships.

Today, the Eagle serves Goodyear's public relations programs and is in constant demand by the news media, especially television networks, for use as an aerial camera platform for special events.

The Eagle also has "Super Syktacular," an intricate network of colored lights that flashes messages visible up to one mile away. More than 50 percent of the messages transmitted annually are devoted to public service.

Rides generally are limited to members of the press and a few corporate trade guests of Goodyear manufacturing and sales divisions by invitation only. No public flights are available. But the thrills and enjoyment provided by the unparalleled aerial photography shot from the Eagle will remain available to everyone as this gargantuan goodwill ambassador continues to be an indelible fixture of the American culture.

CAPITOL RECORDS

n a town filled with icons and legends, Capitol Records legendary Tower stands not only as a symbol for H-O-L-L-Y-W-O-O-D (whose letters are blinked in Morse Code from the beacon atop the building) but for innovation, excellence and quality in every aspect of the music business.

Newly renovated as part of the revitalization of Hollywood, Capitol Records Tower remains as vital today as it was upon its completion (as the world's first round office building and the first Los Angeles high-rise with air conditioning) in 1956. Multi-platinum albums from Capitol's established stars such as Bonnie Raitt, Paul McCartney, Bob Seger, Garth Brooks and The Beastie Boys line the lobby mingling with newly minted platinum albums from some of today's hottest new artists — Radiohead, Foo Fighters, Everclear, Meredith Brooks and Marcy Playground. Of the five albums nominated for Grammy's® 1997 Album Of The Year, two were on Capitol, which had an astonishing 18 nominations in all.

Johnny Mercer

Capitol's wide array of artists includes acclaimed singer/songwriters Roseanne Cash, Robbie Robertson, John Hiatt and Jeb Loy Nichols New artists like Sean Lennon (son of legendary Beatle John Lennon) and groups such as The Dandy Warhols, Supergrass and Bran Van 3000 are critics favorites poised for more mainstream breakthroughs. Capitol has also found gold and platinum for the silver screen with a recent foray into movie soundtracks for *Hope Floats*, *Clueless*, *Trainspotting*, *Good Will Hunting* (Academy Award nominated for Best Original Song

and Score) and the four times platinum *Romeo + Juliet*. With the just-formed Java Records (run by famed Grammy-winning producer and songwriter Glenn Ballard) housed on Capitol's twelfth floor and The Beastie Boys growing Grand Royal label, Capitol is assured of continuing its place as one of the most storied, successful and independent-minded of all music labels.

The extraordinary Capitol story began in 1942 when singer/songwriter Johnny Mercer, music store owner Glenn Wallichs and executive movie producer B.G. "Buddy" DeSylva joined forces to create a new label to compete with the "Big Three": Columbia, RCA-Victor and Decca. As Johnny Mercer put it in 1967, "we forged ahead with the undaunted enthusiasm of young men to whom nothing is impossible."

Nothing indeed. At first, with a war-time shortage of shellac and an industry-wide musician's strike, the new venture looked hopeless — so it was fortunate all three founders had "day jobs" to go back to. Mercer was one of the country's top composers, with four hits on

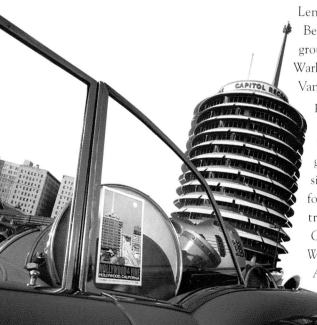

the 1942 Hit Parade. DeSylva, who put up the $10,000 seed money, was both a successful songwriter and an executive producer at Paramount Pictures. Wallichs was founder of the ahead-of-it's-time "super store" Wallichs music store — located at the corner of Sunset and Vine. With DeSylva's showbiz savvy and talent contacts, Mercer's uncanny musical instincts and top songs and Wallichs ingenious ways of getting hits manufactured and distributed (in a time when distribution was controlled by the Big Three), Capitol, as the new

label was named by Mercer's wife Ginger, was founded by a very fortunate melding of executive personalities who never did get back to those day jobs.

With a prevailing mood of optimism, Capitol swiftly developed a roster that included Mercer, Nat King Cole, Peggy Lee, Benny Goodman, Les Paul and Mary Ford and Kay Starr. In 1946, Capitol released the first Bozo the Clown album and promptly cornered the children's market for years to come. The "firsts" continued through the decade as Capitol, whose very survival

Frank Sinatra

depended on upsetting the status quo, became the first label to produce albums in all three speeds, the first to record on magnetic tape, the first to send DJs promotional copies of records, and the first to have world headquarters in Los Angeles, initiating the industry's growing emphasis on the West Coast. As a result, Capitol grew at an explosive rate. 1948's sales totalled nearly $18 million, compared to $195,000 just six years earlier. By the end of the 40s, upstart Capitol was already acknowledged as the industry trend-setter.

The 50s for Capitol can be summed with one word: golden. Between 1954 and 1958, annual sales more than tripled. In late 1955, Capitol had four out of five No. 1 hits. Les Paul and Mary Ford, Peggy Lee, Kay Starr and Margaret Whiting topped the charts along with new Capitol staples Tennessee Ernie Ford, Jackie Gleason and Ray Anthony. Innovators in album cover design and in servicing records to retailers, Capitol now had the ability to attract world-class talent. In 1953, the company signed Frank Sinatra who quickly became the label's signature artist, amassing 9 top ten singles and 17 top ten albums (four gold) throughout the fifties, including Come Dance With Me, Grammy's® 1959 Album Of The Year. Sinatra, whose re-ascendance coincided with the birth of the long-playing record, made music of such strength and expressive power that the world stopped viewing popular singers as mere entertainers and began seeing them as artists.

Another Capitol artist began the decade on a personal note, with the birth of his daughter Natalie in February 1950. Soon after, Nat King Cole recorded

"Unforgettable." Four decades later, Natalie Cole would overdub her part to turn this song into a unique Grammy®-winning father-daughter duet. In 1956, Nat landed his own TV series, the first major breakthrough for a black performer. In spite of 16 regional sponsors, the show never attracted a national sponsor and Nat gave it up after 60 weeks. Music fans love for Nat King Cole continued unabated. He compiled fourteen Top 10 singles (two No. 1's) and five Top 10 albums before the decade was through.

Capitol began the 60s with trademark success from Cole, Sinatra, The Kingston Trio, Nancy Wilson and Judy Garland's Live From Carnegie Hall album. Everything changed in late 1963 when Capitol released a single from four boys named John, Paul, George and Ringo who were known collectively as The Beatles. The single, "I Want To Hold Your Hand," quickly hit No. 1. By April 1964, The Beatles owned the entire top five. By

Paul McCartney, George Harrison, John Lennon, and Ringo Starr of The Beatles.

May, their singles had been No. 1 for 14 straight weeks. Long considered to be the most influential group in the history of rock and roll, The Beatles released 16 gold albums and 19 gold singles in the 60s. But more than sales figures, The Beatles become role models, recasting America's social fabric, their ever-changing music helping to define a decade of evolution, counter-revolution, assassination and disillusion from which we've never emerged.

Drawing on a creative well as deep as the nearby Pacific, Brian Wilson and The Beach Boys conceived musical innovations that would forever change the record-making process. The Beach Boys were the first group to decide what to record, to write the majority of their material, to own their publishing and to move out of the company's in-house recording studio. Fighting for these firsts took its toll on Wilson, who quit the music business in 1967, leaving behind what many of today's critics consider the most important pop music of our time, compiling an astounding 11 Top 10 albums and 13 Top 10 singles in a scant seven years on the label.

As the decade came to a close, Capitol saw success with artists as varied as Lou Rawls, The Letterman and Buck Owens, but it was five-time Grammy® winner Glenn Campbell (whose 35 pop/country cross-over hits are matched only by Eddy Arnold, Elvis Presley and Johnny Cash), who opened the door for singers like some-time partner Bobbie Gentry, a triple-Grammy® winner in 1968 for her "Ode To Billy Joe." As sales topped the $100 million mark for the first time, Capitol celebrated its 25th anniversary in 1967 with an astounding 16 Grammys®. "The best years are still ahead," the visionary Wallichs said at the anniversary party, his eye still firmly planted on the future.

One hundred days into the new decade, The Beatles, the biggest, most popular and prestigious act Capitol had ever had, called it quits. Luckily, Capitol's 1970 roster included several future top-sellers who would help off-set the loss of the fab four: Bob Seger, The Steve Miller Band, Helen Reddy, Anne

The Beach Boys

Murray, The Band, Linda Ronstadt, Merle Haggard, Natalie Cole, The Little River Band, Peabo Bryson, Grand Funk and Pink Floyd whose 1973 blockbuster The Dark Side Of The Moon is the best-selling album in Capitol Records history. By 1974, all four individual Beatles had become best-selling solo artists with their own No.1 hits (the first to do so, surprisingly, was George Harrison. The last, also surprisingly: John Lennon.)

The 80s began with a another tragic blow for the Capitol family, the loss of John Lennon, whose talent and impact are still deeply felt today. On a more positive note, the multi-platinum success stories continued with Bob Seger and The Silver Bullet Band, Anne Murray, Juice Newton, Billy Squier, Duran Duran and Tina Turner in the first half of the decade while Heart, Poison, Iron Maiden, Great White and M.C. Hammer were the big sellers in the second half.

It is possible to pinpoint the exact date a recharged Captiol Records went into overdrive — February 21, 1990 when the 32nd annual Grammy® Awards were presented. Bonnie Raitt's comeback hit, "Nick Of Time" won three Grammys® at the event including Album Of The Year. Within six weeks it was the best-selling album in the United States and Raitt became, after sixteen years in the business, an overnight multi-platinum star. "Nick Of Time" ushered in one of the most successful phases of Capitol's history with Hammer bringing rap to unimagined heights, Megadeth continuing their ongoing string of multi-platinum albums and Garth Brooks becoming the best-selling solo recording artist of all time. Hammer, Raitt and Brooks held the No. 1 spot on the pop album charts for a total of 32 weeks in 1990-1991. When Billboard published its "Year In Music" recap in December 1991, Capitol was the No. 2 label in pop album history, its highest year-end ranking since Billboard began keeping score in the early 70s.

More than sales figures and platinum albums, Capitol has never forgotten the independent spirit under which the company was formed. With artists like Bonnie Raitt (active in many worthy organizations, including the Rhythm & Blues Foundation) and The Beastie Boys (whose Milarepa Fund supports nonviolence and founded the wildly successful and meaningful Free Tibet Concert Series), Capitol is a label which has always had a social conscience.

Capitol's legendary Blue Note jazz label is now home to Cassandra Wilson, Joe Lovano, Jacky Terrasson and Charlie Hunter, some of the most critically lauded, musically adventurous and genre-blurring artists working today. EMI Classics is home to renowned talents like Itzhak Perlman and Vanessa-Mae while Angel Records has critical favorites like Bernadette Peters, Joan Baez and the hugely popular Chant Series featuring the Benedictine Monks. The recently formed New Media division has created Capitol's widely praised, eye-popping, Web site.

Capitol's famed recording studios, the first built for high-fidelity recordings, are still in high demand, boasting some of the most acclaimed recordings being made today including Chris Isaak, Missy Elliot, John Fogerty and several of Capitol's own artists.

(Left to right)
Bonnie Raitt
Photo by Dana Tynan, 1997

Bob Seger
Photo by Caroline Greyshock, 1995.

John Hiatt
Photo by Neal Preston, 1997

(Top row, left to right)
The Beatles

Beastie Boys
Courtesy Ari Marcopoulos, 1994

Meredith Brooks
Courtesy Neal Preston, 1997

(Second row, left to right)
Radiohead
Courtesy Tom Sheehan, 1997

Bran Van 3000
Courtesy James Smolka, 1997

Paul McCartney
Courtesy Linda McCartney, 1997

(Third row, left to right)
Foo Fighters
Courtesy Allison Dyer, 1997

Vic Chestnut
Courtesy Danny Clinch, 1996

Sean Lennon
Courtesy Tamra Davis, 1998

(Bottom row, left to right)
Cassandra Wilson
Courtesy David Mayenfisch

Robbie Robertson
Courtesy Andrew Macpherson, 1997

Megadeth
Courtesy Gene Kirkland.

Capitol has carved out an identity as an artist-friendly label, where newcomers Sean Lennon, Bran Van 3000 and Marcy Playground mingle with established alternative artists like Radiohead, Foo Fighters, Everclear, Luscious Jackson and The Beastie Boys, while veterans like Bonnie Raitt, Bob Seger and Robbie Robertson continue to make the most vital and acclaimed music of their careers. Thanks to new leadership which embodies the independent can-do spirit of its legendary founders, Capitol Records proudly enters a new millennium as a haven for artists and executives of vision.

STARLINE TOURS

ollywood is a state of mind much more than it is a geographic location. For millions and millions of fans across the country and around the world, Hollywood, in the heart of Los Angeles, is home to movie stars: home to all the glamour, all the glory and, of course, all the gossip. Never mind that, in reality, the stars moved a few neighborhoods west a long time ago. People still come to Hollywood to find them. And when the tourists arrive, Starline Tours is ready to take them where they want to go.

The sleek, comfortable Starline Tour bus passes L.A.'s signature palm trees.

First comes a visit to the kiosk in the forecourt of the Chinese Theatre. From that famous Hollywood landmark, Starline vans leave every half an hour for two hours of sightseeing through Beverly Hills and Bel Air. While star sightings are rare, the stars' homes are there to thrill the million visitors Starline escorts every year. Behind the gates and through the greenery, the mansions of the world's most glamorous people lure their eager fans, all hoping to catch a glimpse of the people who live in a style others only dream about.

Starline Tours has been in business since 1968, but the business of searching for stars' home began some 30 years before. Back in 1935, a young man named Bud came west in search of freedom and adventure. What he found was a job as chauffeur to Sid Graumann. Old-time Angelenos remember the Chinese Theatre when it was Graumann's Chinese, and it was through his high-profile movie palace that Sid Graumann became associated with some of Hollywood's principal players. Actors, producers, writers, Sid Graumann knew them all, and the young Bud knew where to find them because he drove his boss to visit them.

A hint from Graumann got Bud in business. Think of it, he was advised. All those tourists at Highland and Hollywood, they're just dying for a chance to find their favorite movie stars. Someone who knows where they live could make a pretty penny, even in the middle of the Depression. Bud took the hint, picked up his passengers, charged them a couple of dollars and showed them around. Eventually, Bud's Limo Service had four limousines and the license to drive the Beverly Hills route. (In those days, tourist routes were under the jurisdiction of the Public Utilities Commission, or PUC, which controlled who could drive where, but more on that later.) Bud had good ideas but limited vision. A great tour guide, he wasn't an ambitious businessman. Bud's Limo pretty much ended up driving around in circles.

Enter the Sapir brothers. In the late 60s Vahid managed the parking lot at the Chinese Theatre. He figured out pretty quickly that Bud was on to a good thing but wasn't doing much about it. Besides, Bud was getting on in years. So Vahid and his brother Fred, both electronic engineers by training, convinced Bud to sell them his business. Bud agreed, and Bud's Limo became Starline Tours. That was in 1968, and the Sapir brothers wasted no time making a good business bigger and better.

First they spiffed up the limousines. Soon they bought new ones. Then they bought vans and buses. Starline accommodated more tourists, but the company was still limited to Beverly Hills and Bel Air. That was fine, but not fine enough for two enterprising entrepreneurs. Southern California was filled with places to go and things to do, from Disneyland to San Diego, and the Sapirs were determined to take Starline Tours where everybody wanted to go. All it took was the license, and that was owned by the competition. To get a license of their own, they had to come up with something new and different.

That's where their engineering training came in. The Sapir brothers had the idea that non-English-speaking tourists would love to listen to recorded tours in their native language while they were Starline passengers. So, they invented foreign-language tour tapes which their clients could listen to with headphones. The Sapirs presented their invention to Southern California's major tourist attractions who understood immediately that tourists who were talked to in their own language would find it a lot easier to visit all the exciting destinations around the Southland. The Sapirs had little trouble convincing the theme park operators to testify on their behalf, and the PUC, acknowledging the unique appeal of their proposed service, granted Starline a license to conduct tours all over Southern California. Starline Tours was on the move.

So successful was the strategy that Starline's major competition approached the Sapir brothers who acquired The Grayline in the early 1980s. Then Tour Coach and American Pacific became part of the Starline fleet. The Starline vehicles combined the look and low cost of European touring vehicles with the power of American bus engines, guaranteeing sightseers a comfortable, dependable journey. Starline introduced its own exclusive and extremely popular tours of the Liberace Mansion and the Harold Lloyd Estate. Ever on the move, Starline's tours went further afield with excursions across the western United States, including Las Vegas and the Grand Canyon. Starline conducts its tours in partnership with major airlines and hotels. Starline tours of Hollywood has its own Charter Bus Services. They cover California, neveda, Arizona and Oregon.

But the heart and soul of Starline Tours is in Southern California. By far the most popular of Starline's many offerings is the tour of Movie Stars' Homes in Beverly Hills and Bel Air. Every day, visitors eager for a glimpse of the lifestyles of the rich and famous indulge their fantasies in air-conditioned comfort, searching for stars in the company's mini vans which go where big buses are prohibited. The two-hour trip includes approximately 60 homes, featuring the most glamorous stars of yesterday and today. Jimmy Stewart, Lucille Ball and Ronald Reagan get top billing, but many more enduring legends are included along with today's big names in the movies and television. In addition to visiting the homes of the stars, Starline drives by famous film location sites as well as the Sunset Strip.

Visitors get to know the other Los Angeles with Starline's Grand Tour of Greater Los Angeles. Quaint Olvera Street, home to LA's earliest history, starts the tour which escorts visitors through Chinatown, the

A Starline Tour Bus visits Magic Castle in Hollywood

Observatory in Griffith Park, Sunset Strip and the Farmer's Market. Rodeo Drive and Beverly Hills are included, as is lunch and shopping at the Farmers Market. For tourists who want to get to know Los Angeles as well as movieland, Starline offers a combination tour of the stars' homes and a grand tour of LA.

Big on the list of LA's must sees is Universal Studios Hollywood, and Starline obliges with two tour packages, one three-quarters day, the other for a full day. Starline allows visitors to avoid the hassle of navigating unfamiliar freeways, and the tour includes admission and all the shows. From the pyrotechnics of Backdraft-Live to the impressive shakeup of Earthquake — The Big One to Flying Home with ET, all the magic of Hollywood comes to life to thrill both locals and out-of-towners.

Once L.A.'s been discovered, visitors want to move farther afield, and Starline makes it easy to get to Disneyland and Knott's Berry Farm. Both Orange County theme parks are world famous destinations, and their many attractions are easily accessible when Starline makes the arrangements. During the summer, Starline makes it easy to stay late at Disneyland where fireworks and other evening treats add to the excitement of the Magic Kingdom.

Farther south, San Diego's Sea World and Mexico's Tijuana are served by Starline. The all-day trip to Sea World includes a ride along the beautiful Southern California coastline and an adventure with the ocean's mighty mammals Shamu and Baby Shamu, exotic bat rays and moray eels. Just across the border, colorful Tijuana offers a day's exploration of shops and restaurants, famous for leather goods, clothing and jewelry at bargain prices.

Back in Los Angeles, Starline makes it convenient to visit Catalina with a first-class voyage to Avalon and the romance and beauty of the island just "26 miles across the sea." The day's trip allows visitors to explore the island's beaches and back country. Returning to the mainland, Starline conducts tours of the insider's Westside, home to some of L.A.'s most interesting attractions. Starline takes visitors to the Getty, Marina del Rey, the movie studios at Culver City to relive the making of *Gone with the Wind*, and finally to Venice Beach, with its world-famous street scene. And for those who can't get enough of amusement parks, Starline escorts them to Six Flags Magic Mountain, an easy drive north of Los Angeles.

Los Angeles has much to offer visitors who flock there from all around the world, and they know about Starline through the company's vast marketing network. Many major tour wholesalers sell the Starline services to thousands of travel agencies all around the world, and Starline is a major exhibitor at a number of large conventions, both in the United States and in London and Berlin. The company advertises regularly in leading tourism magazines, promising the very best service for the most memorable vacation in glamorous and exciting Southern California. Starline maintains a high-profile presence in the Hollywood Chamber of Commerce and the Los Angeles Department of Tourism, and for immediate personal contact, Starline's brochures, offering more than a dozen tour packages, are available in hotels and tourist centers.

Just as Bud's Limo Service got its start at Hollywood and Highland, Starline Tours is poised for new growth with the rejuvenation of Hollywood from Highland to La Brea. Starline Tours, with its headquarters right across from the Chinese Theatre, is in the heart of a massive redevelopment project which

Downtown, will return to its own theater in the heart of Hollywood.

Home to the hopes and dreams of millions, downtown Hollywood will once again live up to its image of glamour and excitement. Fred and Vahid Sapir have been Hollywood players for much of Hollywood's storied history, and they have built a spectacularly visible and successful business that fulfills the expectations of all the star-struck fans who have flocked to Hollywood in search of the myth and the magic. Starline Kiosk has been located at forcourt of Mann's Chinese Theatre for many years where millions of tourists visit from all around the world.

promises to reinvigorate that strip of Hollywood Boulevard, long tarnished through years of neglect. Hotels, a shopping center, and an 13-screen movie theater are all on the drawing boards. And the Academy Awards ceremony, for years past presented at venues in

Starline looks foward to a very bright future because as long as there are movies, there would always be a "Hollywood". The tourist will come and Starline Van would be waiting for them.

Starline's tours begin at the world-famous Chinese Theatre.

DELUXE HOLLYWOOD

What if a person stepped into a theater and saw a blank screen? Were it not for the collaboration between the cinematographer and the film laboratory, the enjoyment of the latest Hollywood blockbuster would be limited, to say the least.

Deluxe Laboratories is the longest continuously operating film processing company in the history of motion pictures. The company processes, prints and distributes over two billion feet of film every year for customers worldwide, serving Hollywood's leading studios, independent film producers, directors and cinematographers.

Film take-off area of release print processors.

Its history began in 1915, when Deluxe opened its first processing plant in Fort Lee, New Jersey. In those days of black and white silent films, Deluxe's primary challenge was processing film. For the times, the facilities were relatively sophisticated, allowing Deluxe to process 50,000 feet of film each week. By the time the company moved to New York in 1921, the figure climbed to 50 times as much.

Main entrance way to Deluxe Hollywood laboratory.

In the 1950s, when Fox opened a small dailies lab — film talk for the film shot each day — in Southern California, Deluxe responded by opening its lab in Hollywood. The burgeoning film industry produced an increasing demand for Deluxe's services, and the company's facilities and capabilities grew in response. In 1996, Deluxe Labs was awarded the Technical Academy Award for developing a digital sound head for printing multiple sound formats on release prints.

In addition to its Hollywood labs, Deluxe operates a laboratory and rerecording studio in Toronto as well as a laboratory in London. The company is the sole processor for 20th Century Fox, Paramount, MGM, Universal, Miramax,

New Line Cinema and Artisan. Its impressive list of movie credits include The *X-Files, The Movie, Dr. Doolittle, Deep Impact,* all the James Bond movies, *Jurassic Park, Titanic, Braveheart* and *Forrest Gump.*

As a network of film processing and post-production facilities, each Deluxe lab features state-of-the-art technology that includes computerized process control and analysis, high-speed printing and processing equipment, and a highly advanced color timing system. When a couple is kissing on film, look at the background; Deluxe can turn a romantic sunset into an eery darkness with the turn of a dial.

Deluxe provided the look and feel of the restored Hitchcock classic, *Vertigo;* the spine-tingling darkness of outer space in *Star Wars,* and all the primary colors in *Primary Colors.* Deluxe also serves a variety of television shows, as it receives tens of thousands of feet of dailies every day, dailies that must be developed, selected, assembled and returned to clients in a matter of hours.

The front-end business involves the processing of the daily negative and making the daily work print so directors can see what they've shot that day. The same is true for both television shows and movies. Once the picture has been edited and spliced together, the completed director's cut is sent back to Deluxe, who will color time it scene by scene to make the necessary color corrections. Once the color's locked, Deluxe produces what is called an "interpositive," a master of the original negative. From that, Deluxe makes the "internegative," and from that they produce all the multiple release prints that go to theaters.

The process of developing a work print is slightly more complicated than developing a vacation photo. Processing passes through several departments — starting with Negative Developing before moving on to Negative Assembly, where print dailies are disassembled. This is followed by Color Timing to adjust and control the amount of red, magenta, blue, cyan, green and yellow in a picture; this is done by adjusting the opposite color of the one needed. For example, to control blue, the technician adjusts the amount of yellow. From this stage, the film advances to Printing, where the original negative is printed onto a color positive for the first time. Then comes Positive Developing, where the film goes through three stages: from the darkroom, to the chemical baths, to the "take-up" station. This is where the dailies are completed. At that point, the film is sent to the film editor.

The next stage is developing the answer print. This is done at the completion of film editing and sound mixing. Primarily, the film goes back for additional color timing for further adjustments: then it goes to the printing department, to Developing and finally to Screening. Once the film is carefully approved for quality, it goes into bulk release.

Many of the company's craftsmen and women are second-generation Deluxe technicians. President Cyril Drabinsky says that his technicians' experience in the workplace is more important than a college education. Deluxe Laboratories' is definitely a manufacturing environment, albeit one that marries art with technology.

The company is committed to excellence. For instance, if at any point the product does not measure up to Deluxe's high standards, procedures are repeated. Even in in the final phase of processing, where film is printed at 1,500 feet per minute and a feature print is produced in eight minutes, the role of the technician continues until the film is in the client's hands.

Deluxe is involved with the Hollywood Chamber of Commerce and the American Society of Cinematograhers, among its many community concerns. The company also plays a vital role in attracting new business to Los Angeles, and "color by deluxe" has become an industry staple.

Computerized printing area on high-speed loop printers.

Film feed-on elevator for a high-speed printer.

METRO-GOLDWYN-MAYER

Metro-Goldwyn-Mayer Studios has long held the tradition of the classic American icon, with a distinguished reputation, renowned moniker and roaring lion trademark. Since its founding in 1924, the company has prided itself on creating and shaping cinematic history, delighting audiences worldwide with entertainment of unparalleled distinction. Throughout its

MGM's Santa Monica Headquarters.

existence, MGM has endured memorable successes and overcome difficult obstacles, forging ahead with renewed vigor. Along the way, the Company has evolved and changed to meet the specific demands of modern audiences and maintained its foothold in rapidly emerging technologies, setting the stage for success in a new century of entertainment.

Theater magnate Marcus Loew formed MGM studios in 1924 by orchestrating the merger of Metro Pictures Corp., Goldwyn Pictures and Louis B. Mayer Productions. Headed by the pioneering visionary Louis

Pierce Brosnan as James Bond

B. Mayer and the equally renowned production genius Irving Thalberg, the studio rapidly attained fame as one of the foremost in Hollywood. The duo engendered a reputation for artistry and expertise in filmmaking that led to MGM's prominence as an indisputable force in the movie industry. Soon, the company had become the most profitable in the industry.

In 1928, in a move indicative of the studio's penchant for embracing and implementing new entertainment technologies, sound effects and a synchronized score were added to its esteemed trademark, Leo the Lion. Throughout the years, the lion and its accompanying roar came to represent MGM's illustrious history and preeminent status in the

entertainment world. This esteem led to some of the most celebrated talent of the day working under contract for the studio.

"More Stars Than There Are In Heaven," was the MGM slogan supported by legendary greats such as Clark Gable, Judy Garland, Spencer Tracy, Elizabeth Taylor and Joan Crawford, among others, who made their home at MGM. This unequaled pool of talent led to the studio's production of some of the most loved movies of all time in the succeeding years — films such as *Ben Hur*, *Gone with the Wind*, *The Wizard of Oz* and *Singing in the Rain*. The studio's course during the 1950s was no less pioneering. By licensing its film titles and contract players to the newly formed television networks, MGM began its foray into the rapidly advancing medium.

MGM achieved another milestone in 1981 when it purchased one of the industry's oldest and most revered film companies, United Artists, the company built for independent filmmakers by industry greats Charlie Chaplin, Mary Pickford, Douglas Fairbanks and D.W. Griffith. This union brought over 1,200 film titles into the studio's fold, including such acclaimed properties as *Rain Man*, *West Side Story*, *Midnight Cowboy*, the *Pink Panther* and *Rocky* series and the *James Bond* pictures, which represent the most valuable film franchise ever created.

In subsequent years, the company further broadened its presence in the entertainment community with the 1997 acquisition of Orion Pictures and Goldwyn Entertainment, which effectively doubled the size of

MGM's film library. These shared resources have led to what is unmistakably the largest post-1948 film library in the world, containing some 4,000 cherished titles. This unique collection is one of the most illustrious in Hollywood, with over 180 Academy Awards® to its credit. Furthermore, the library also includes more than 8,200 television episodes, including the current series "Stargate SG-1," "The Outer Limits" and the animated *All Dogs Go To Heaven*.

More recently, the company has moved aggressively to grow its additional businesses in the music, interactive and consumer products areas as well. MGM Music develops and acquires production music for all areas of the studio, as well as for the company's diverse marketing and advertising needs, and manages the company's substantial record and publishing catalogues from the film and television libraries. MGM Interactive was formed to create and produce products for a wide variety of multimedia platforms, creating interactive products based on both original ideas and the vast store of MGM-owned copyrights.

Another new division, MGM Consumer Products, was created in 1996 to take the concept of branding and consumer products to an exciting new level. Since its conception, the division has replaced conventional studio-type products with the introduction of a totally original brand portfolio, with distinctive collections specially created to offer licensees, retailers, and promotional partners the opportunity to ally themselves uniquely with Hollywood. Its first Hollywood-themed catalogue, in partnership with preeminent retailer Neiman Marcus, was introduced in 1998.

MGM also has placed itself in a prime position to be a key player in the burgeoning global market for its products. MGM Networks, including the first MGM branded movie channel launched in Brazil in 1997, has expanded into Latin America with plans for similar channels to follow in other International markets. The network includes a fall schedule of the studio's classic as well as contemporary movies.

Partnerships also have been formed to bring the studio's products to other parts of the world with licensing agreements to develop programming tailored to the overseas market and international output deals in major territories in Europe, Africa and Asia. These agreements have laid the groundwork for the studio as an essential player in the entertainment industry on an international scale.

Few companies have a presence in their industry as resounding as MGM has in the world of entertainment. Indeed, MGM is almost synonymous with Hollywood itself. Los Angeles is known the world over as a mecca for filmmaking, and the MGM lion personifies this mystique. As the pace of globalization has increased, the company has moved to take advantage of new opportunities, establishing a worldwide presence in distribution, marketing and production. As new technologies have emerged, MGM studios has broadened its scope to provide its trademark entertainment in new formats, whether it be in digital video discs, music soundtracks, computer games or uniquely branded merchandise.

This ubiquitous presence in a variety of markets ensures that the company is poised to continue its success into the next century. Yet even with these accomplishments in hand, MGM has never lost sight of the basic foundation of its achievements — motion pictures. Movies have always been nothing less than magical, captivating audiences since the first silent films debuted near the turn of the century. MGM's 15 Oscar®-winning Best Picture films are an indisputable testament to the fact that no other company has spun that magic quite like MGM. Nearly 75 years after its birth, MGM remains a major force in the entertainment industry, with a proud heritage, an enduring legacy, and a promising future.

MGM's esteemed trademark, Leo the Lion from 1924 to 1999.

PACIFIC TITLE ARCHIVES

ollywood is full of buried treasures and hidden secrets, and after nearly a century of movie making, every aspect of film production has its own fascinating history. In the very heart of Hollywood, Pacific Title Archives is a treasure trove of movie titles dating back to 1919. Young filmgoers today, accustomed to the miracles of computer-generated special effects, would probably be astonished to learn that in the early years, film titles and effects were generated by hand. By today's standards, the process was crude and time-consuming. But by any standards, it produced wonderful works of art, deserving to be preserved and shared with the world.

Film titles were originally hand-drawn by artists, who painstakingly inked them directly onto glass.

Formerly known as Pacific Title and Art Studio, the company began its work when film making was in its infancy, and over the decades and through three generations of family ownership, it grew up and kept pace with the ever-changing and fast-moving technologies of film and television. The company has been a leader in post-production work and film titling, and a recounting of its credits is like a march through movie history. From The *Jazz Singer* to *Schindler's List*, Pacific Title contributed to the artistry of thousands of landmark films.

The company traces its own history back to the Silent Era when Leon Schlesinger, who worked as an animator at Warner Brothers, established a film titling lab on Bronson Avenue off Santa Monica Boulevard in Hollywood. He was kept busy working on *Looney Tunes* when he was joined by a young Canadian artist named Larry Glickman. A decade later Glickman bought out Schlesinger and moved the business to a larger corner lot on Santa Monica Boulevard. It was a boom time for the movie title business, and Pacific Title flourished.

Love played a leading role, too. When Glickman's daughter Shirley married Gordon Hubbard, a family dynasty was founded. Gordon and Shirley continued in her father's work, and back in the early 1950s, it was Gordon Hubbard who predicted the immense potential of television and focused the company on future growth by expanding into the business of television titling. In 1962, following the death of Larry Glickman, Gordon Hubbard became Pacific Title's president and chief operating officer. Jerry Glickman, who was Larry Glickman's son, had come on board in August 1954, after serving in the United States Navy. He assumed the title of vice president until 1969. Gordon Hubbard retired in 1984, and, fulfilling a long-cherished ambition, his wife Shirley took over as president.

Peter Hubbard, son of Gordon and Shirley and the third generation family member of Pacific Title, came into the business in charge of sales. His successes included classic Fox series hits as "Trapper John," "The Fall Guy" and "M*A*S*H." In the mid-1980s he was appointed vice president of Pacific Title and worked closely with his mother as sales director until Shirley died in 1989. His astute insight into the rapidly changing needs of an ever-expanding industry guaranteed that Pacific Title kept pace through expansion and flexibility.

In 1979, Pacific Title Archives was founded as a division of the company. Its mission was to preserve the motion picture industry's vast library of film and videotape elements. In 1997, the technical side of the business, Pacific Title and Art Studio and Pacific Title Digital, was acquired by another company, and now Pacific Title Archives is focusing on its archival func-

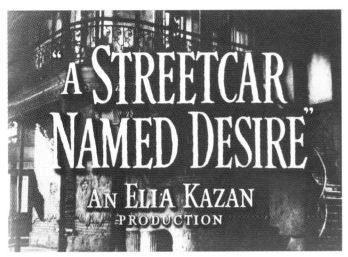

tion. Today, Peter Hubbard continues at the helm of his family firm and envisions an exciting new direction into education, exhibitions and licensing.

Throughout the history of films, the change in titling techniques has been dramatic. Titles for silent movies were created on just one black-and-white card, usually made of cardboard or slate. The next step was hand lettering on glass, which continued until the mid-1960s. Hand lettering was a true art form, and Pacific Title artists would occasionally paint backgrounds to accompany the titles. But hand lettering is time consuming and labor intensive, and the advance of automation technology rendered it obsolete while making the work faster and easier. Typositors allowed an artist to type out letters onto white-on-black strips that could be mounted on cards. In turn, Typositors were replaced by Linotronics machines which gave the artists the ability to type titles on a keyboard and print them onto a film strip for backlighting. Naturally, these "advances" themselves became obsolete with the arrival of Macintosh computers.

Protecting the work of all those decades is the mission of Pacific Title Archives. Four warehouses, located in close proximity to the major studios, are used as archival storage for them. Each piece in the vast collection is regarded as a precious and original work of art, and so the company stores its video and film elements in a controlled environment to ensure its future preservation. In addition to the storage of video and film elements, Pacific Title Archives has assembled images from decades of movie history: glass titles, photographs and original background paintings. These titles and backgrounds were used in the production of thousands of films, and most of those movies are indelibly etched in the memories of movie fans everywhere.

Pacific Title Archives believes that it's time to share these photo and glass-title treasures with the rest of the world. Mounting public exhibitions of its unique collection has already begun, with shows in Los Angeles, notably at The Hollywood Heritage Museum and the Academy of Motion Picture Arts and Sciences. Future plans include more exhibits in Los Angeles and other cities around the country such as New York and Chicago, while long-range goals include international exposure. In the future, Pacific Title Archives can rely on its successful history of predicting the next entertainment trend and perfecting the services it renders to the world of movie making.

Pacific Title has created movie titles for literally all of the great classics, including the majority of the Academy's Oscar winning films.

ROGERS & COWAN

"All the world's a stage," Shakespeare said, "and all its people, players." If so, America's foremost entertainment public relations firm, Rogers & Cowan, is essentially a worldwide stage director of our times. Relentlessly, the firms' guiding hand helps reflect life back upon itself in seemingly limitless media stories, news features and events. Tapping our insatiable appetite for entertainment, technology and new consumer products and services, Rogers & Cowan has precisely synthesized all three into a mirrored montage of life as it approaches the millennium.

Founded in Los Angeles in the early 1950s by Henry Rogers and Warren Cowan, the organization has broadened its base and honed its skills in the worldwide public communications arena to earn a venerable reputation in a growing and ever-changing industry. Rogers & Cowan has evolved formidably in its craft by capitalizing on the increasing interdependence of nearly 50 years, the organization has evolved from "pure play" press agentry to sophisticated communications strategies and executions, employing both traditional and new

media. If Marshall McLuhan was on the right track in his assertion that "the medium is the message," then Rogers & Cowan has had a direct role in helping to make this convergence of form and substance a reality.

From its original client base of actors, producers, directors and production companies, Rogers & Cowan quickly expanded its services in the technology-driven, talent-based business of entertainment. Rapidly, it encompassed television, motion pictures and music as it mastered the full range of the entertainment industry. Today, during an average week, the company introduces new media products and services, stirs up excitement that fills stadiums at world concert tours, rejuvenates brand images and showcases consumer products in blockbuster films for which it has generated massive viewer excitement and demand.

By 1987, the firm had opened offices in New York and London. Shandwick International, one of the largest independent public relations agencies in the world, acquired it. As a result, Rogers & Cowan boasts now a network of more than 90 affiliate offices in over 35 countries, offering its clients an unparalleled supply of resources. It is today co-chaired by Mr. Paul Bloch and Mr. Tom Tardio, who is also its managing director.

If you still think of public relations as amiably cajoling you into buying something, you should update your perception. Cordial enticements have become decidedly more complex. Rogers & Cowan, for instance, organizes its business into separate operating groups specializing in no less than

Rogers & Cowan Leadership. Paul Bloch, Co-Chairman (Left). Tom Tardio, Co-Chairman & Managing Director (Right).

12 areas of expertise: motion pictures, television, music, personalities, corporate and consumer marketing, interactive entertainment, youth marketing, fashion and beauty, special events, international entertainment, promotions and product placement.

Its stock in trade, of course, is publicity, but its success derives from a unique strategic understanding of the modern day intricacies of society. It knows that the key to mass communication today is based on a powerful triad and, accordingly, by meticulously and creatively blending elements of high technology, entertainment and consumer products and services, it defines modern PR practices. Producing a synergy for which it is rightly renowned, it has crafted endless innovations and implemented countless successful campaigns impacting on the lifestyle of the entire world.

Utilizing its excellent professional relationships with virtually every major newspaper, magazine and broadcast outlet, as well as its close association with major name world entertainment talent, and its sophis-

ticated sense of marketing, Rogers & Cowan has invented for itself a diversity of capabilities which set it distinctly apart from other practitioners of its craft.

If ever a company were to be described as having become, like our world, more than the sum of its parts, it is this firm. From Silicon Valley to Hollywood, from Sylvester Stallone to Daryl Hannah, from IBM to Nabisco, from NBC to Fox TV, from the Beatles to LeAnn Rimes, from Victoria's Secret to Mircrosoft, Rogers & Cowan reminds us who we are and who we intend to be. When the 21st century arrives, our presence will, in no small degree, have been orchestrated by this firm's imagination, organization and drive.

As actors in the world, our roles are substantially characterized for us by this unique firm's ability to sense our wants, anticipate our needs and — throughout dramatic communication — to help deliver them to us with unerring accuracy and timeliness via its clients' products and services.

Rogers & Cowan Senior Management (from left to right): Alan Nierob, Maureen O'Connor, Sandy Friedman, Cheryl Kagan, Steve Doctrow, Tom Tardio, Marci Williams, Julie Nathanson and Christine La Monte.

SMASHBOX

The space is ultra-minimal with soaring ceilings, poured concrete floors and industrial decor. Words like modern, edgy, hip, innovative and eclectic come to mind. But even those terms can't quite adequately define SmashBox Studios, L.A.'s five-star image factory.

Santa Monica SmashBox.

As architecturally impressive as it is, what goes on within these ultra-whitewashed walls are the stuff of legends and fairy tales. "Legends" in the sense that celebrities famous enough to be known by their first name alone (Demi, Uma, Jack and Tom) come here to be photographed by equally eminent shutterbugs, such as Herb Ritts and Annie Leibovitz.

And "fairytales" in terms of the phenomenal success of SmashBox, which evolved from a small photo studio at its inception in 1990 to its present status as one of the world's premier full service photography rental complexes. Its current Culver City location is home to five photo studios, a production company, beauty agency, equipment rental company, catering company and a newly designed sound stage.

(Left to right) SmashBox founders Dean and Davis Factor.

SmashBox was born when Davis Factor, a fashion photographer and graduate of the Pasadena Art Center, leased an old boat showroom in Santa Monica and renovated it into a photo studio. His initial motivation was to create a space to surround himself with hard-to-find equipment and amenities.

The vision of the company evolved into something altogether different when Davis' younger brother Dean came on board. Armed with an MBA from the University of Southern California, the younger Factor saw the enormous potential in the burgeoning business.

The great-grandsons of makeup master Max Factor focused on their respective strengths with Dean as CEO and president in charge of operations and Davis as creative director. By the end of the first year in operation, SmashBox was already well on its way to becoming what it is today...an innovation that is at once "high style and low-key."

SmashBox Studios comprises five state-of-the-art, private and self-contained photo studios, plus a sixth daylight studio in Santa Monica. "Softbox," "Skybox," "Stage 1," "Blackbox" and "Lightbox" each feature insulated walls to eliminate carry-over noise for video, commercial and film shoots and come equipped with their own production office complete with telephones and fax machines, wardrobe room, private lounge, hair and makeup room, coffee machine and refrigerator.

SmashBox Production offers full or "a la carte" services to assist clients with everything from production planning and coordination, casting, location scouting and permits, insurance, transportation and travel arrangements.

SmashBox Beauty is an agency representing stylists, hair and make-up artists, art directors and production designers working in print advertising, music video and film projects today.

Stage 1 is a 5,000-square-foot sound stage designed for commercial film and video clients as well as multi set still photographers. The studio features a full production office, private lounge, makeup room, darkroom, kitchenette as well as restroom and shower facilities.

The company has a complete line of carefully maintained rental equipment available for studio and location shoots as well as personnel who are experts in using the equipment to assist with any aspect of a client's shoot requirements.

Finally, GoodFood Catering, run as a separate division by company co-founder Phillip Weingarten, provides all meals, snacks and drinks for photo shoots and special events at SmashBox. GoodFood also caters location shoots and can make every-thing from a simple box lunch to an impressive sit-down dinner.

As children, Dean and Davis were always encouraged to pursue their own interests. But the great-grandsons of the man who put makeup on the map were destined to meddle in mascara and moisturizers. The Factor's family heritage has come full circle with their foray into a creative collection of cosmetics.

While the 215 plus product line, which includes a full range of moisturizers, foundations, lipstick, pressed powders and eye shadows, was originally targeted toward professional makeup artists, SmashBox has found its way onto retail shelves at such stores as Nordstrom, Lord & Taylor and Henri Bendels.

Given the Factor's corporate philosophy of pride in ownership, quality products, an unparalleled level of customer service and client satisfaction, SmashBox and all of its divisions will continue to set industry "firsts" that defy description.

Softbox Studio makeup and wardrobe area.

SPECIAL EFFECTS UNLIMITED

n the field of live action mechanical special effects, one company stands out — Special Effects Unlimited of Hollywood.

Since its founding in 1962, the need for its services has exploded. Special Effects Unlimited now designs the live action physical effects for innumerable motion pictures, television shows and commercials. *Live action* refers to the process of fabricating and rigging full-scale and model special effects. This may encompass recreating weather conditions, generating fires, explosions, break-away or collapsing sets, flying people or sets, flipping cars, robotics, mechanical animation and many other types of effects.

But back in the 1950s, when founder Joe Lombardi was working as a Paramount Studios construction work-er, special effects as an independent business didn't even exist. Lombardi got his big break designing a special spiral staircase for Lucille Ball, who ended up hiring him to work as the construction supervisor on *I Love Lucy*. The friendship provided a springboard for Lombardi's career, as he was able to gain the kind of clout necessary to make it in Hollywood.

Despite his experience in television, people thought Lombardi was crazy for leaving the studio

establishment to start Special Effects Unlimited. Yet he persisted, and his foresight would presage the coming decades in which films such as *The Godfather*, *Godfather II*, *Apocalypse Now* and *Clear and Present Danger* would require both his expertise and supervision. In fact, while on the set of *Clear and Present Danger*, Lombardi was profiled by "Entertainment Tonight."

In 1997, shortly before his death, the Academy of Motion Picture Arts and Sciences awarded Lombardi a special commendation for his 50 years of service to the industry as both a pioneer in pyrotechnics and special effects and for his commitment to safety on the set. The plaque sits on an illuminated shelf in his company's plush conference room.

Special Effects Unlimited president Gabe Videla says Lombardi was larger-than-life, an icon in the field of special effects. Lombardi's efforts and accomplish-ments paved the way for other top special effects pro-fessionals who would themselves go on to win Oscars, for films such as *Aliens*, *Jurassic Park*, *Forrest Gump*, *Titanic* and *Independence Day*.

Such Academy Award-winning work must be supervised by professionals who hold the highest grade of state and federal licenses. Such individuals and their

The explosion of a miniature replica of the White Hosue in *Independence Day* occurred in less than a second.

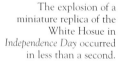

crews work a minimum 12-hour day, often under rigorous and dangerous conditions. Videla himself is up at 3:30 each morning, clocking into work by 6 o'clock. But all the effort pays off.

Special Effects boasts an impressive client roster that includes all major studios and networks. Since 1962, its crews have worked on hundreds of television series, and its movie roster is even more impressive. Films such as *Titanic*; *Air Force One*; *The Truman Show*; *The X-Files* movie; *Six Days, Seven Nights*; *Contact*; *Godzilla*; *The Mask of Zorro*; and *Tomorrow Never Dies* have all employed Special Effects Unlimited. The company is also able to provide its services on a global level, and its inventory of equipment is the largest of its kind.

As the cinematic process continues to become more sophisticated, more will be required of its special effects professionals. The company is up to the challenge, as it has a history of meeting Hollywood's needs with cutting edge technology. The people who work with and for Special Effects coordinate a multitude of tasks, all of which must be physically prepared and synchronized to work flawlessly when the cameras roll. Expertise and creativity are the hallmark of the company's special effects supervisors.

One such award-winner is Joe Viskocil, probably the film industry's leading pyrotechnics and small miniature effects supervisor. Viskocil, along with Clay Pinney, who supervised the full-scale special effects, won an Academy Award in 1997 for their work on *Independence Day*. The experience was rewarding, but Viskocil points out that it wasn't always glamorous: he had to wear a special Nomex racing suit and face mask, and several camera lights melted under the intense heat during filming. Due to careful precautions, no significant accidents were reported — an important feature in the special effects supervisor's planning. In fact, Viskocil stresses the importance of safety when handling high explosives and says a pyrotechnics supervisor must balance a variety of other considerations — the camera speed, the size of the model (if it's being exploded), how much explosive to use, what lenses to employ, how long the explosion will take and the speed between explosions.

The list of people associated with Special Effects Unlimited is a virtual who's who of the special effects field. From Joe Lombardi and the peers of his era to today's outstanding technicians, their combined talent continues to captivate audiences all over the world. And if there's any doubt, just listen to the audience next time the Mother Ship explodes or the *Titanic* sinks ... It's nothing less than magic.

Special Effects Unlimited has maintained an incomparable safety record — even when working with the types of high-grade explosives that can melt camera lenses.

Joe Viskocil won an Academy Award for his miniature effects and pyrotechnic wizardry on *Independence Day*.

UNIVERSAL STUDIOS

Universal Studios is one of America's largest and most diversified entertainment companies, and its history is an important element of the history of American show business.

The company's rich entertainment legacy dates back to 1912, when pioneer filmmaker Carl Laemmle, an immigrant from Bavaria, founded the Chicago-based Universal Film Manufacturing Co. Three years later, Laemmle moved his company to Los Angeles and on March 15, 1915 officially opened the gates of Universal City on a 230-acre ranch. While producing a steady stream of silent films — including Westerns, comedies and action-adventures — Laemmle invited visitors to the property to observe, thus establishing Universal's long-standing tradition of welcoming guests to enjoy the behind-the-scenes magic of movie-making. Over the years, Universal Pictures grew into a full-fledged movie studio and became a leader in motion picture production and distribution.

Meanwhile, the Music Corporation of America was founded by Jules Stein in 1924 as a Chicago-based agency that booked bands into clubs and dance halls. The legacy of MCA was expanded and enriched by Lew Wasserman, who joined the company in 1936 and, over the years, built MCA from a leading talent agency into a diversified global leader in the world of entertainment.

MCA and Universal officially merged in 1962. With activities in television and motion picture production well in place in the early 1960s, the succeeding years represented a period of growth and diversification for MCA/Universal, with the company expanding its interests in such areas as music and recreation, and later becoming a pioneer in location-based entertainment. In 1991, Matsushita Electrical Industrial Co., Ltd. acquired MCA. Four years later,

Universal Studios is nestled in the San Fernando Valley just north of metropolitan Los Angeles.

in June 1995, The Seagram Company Ltd. purchased a majority equity in MCA from Matsushita. On December 10, 1996, MCA INC. was renamed Universal Studios.

Today, Universal Studios spans 415 acres, including its famed theme park as well as offices and 32 sound stages, which together combine to form the largest motion picture and television production facility in the world.

Universal's theatrical motion picture division is perhaps its most visible element. Over the decades, Universal has amassed a library of such films as *To Kill A Mockingbird*, *The Deer Hunter* and *Field of Dreams*. These and countless others epitomize the distinctly American art of Hollywood movie-making. Now, Universal produces and distributes everything from special-effects event movies such as *Jurassic Park*, to family fare such as *Babe*, as well as specialty films such as October Films' *The Apostle*.

Universal is also active in the television arena. The company first began producing shows in the early 1950s under its original television production arm, Revue Studios, and quickly became a dominant force in the emerging industry, with such hits as "Alfred Hitchcock Presents" and "Leave it to Beaver." Universal's string of successful shows continued through the decades, including favorites such as "Dragnet" and "Law & Order." The present-day Universal Television & Networks Group was established following the strategic combination of Universal's television production operation with USA Networks Studios, Inc. The Group distributes Universal's more than 24,000-episode television library and feature film product to free and pay television outlets around the world, and is the exclusive international distributor for USA Networks, Inc.'s television production arm Studios USA. In addition to its current production and development slate, the Group has launched the Universal-branded channels 13th Street: The Action & Suspense Channel in France and Germany, and Studio Universal in Italy, with more channel launches planned.

Universal's music legacy continues into the present day via Universal Music Group, which encompasses: record labels; an international division; manufacturing, sales and distribution operations; music publishing; and a live event/concert promotion division. The Universal family of labels includes MCA Records, MCA Records Nashville, GRP Recording Company, Geffen/DGC Records, Universal Records, Interscope Records and Hip-0 Records — releasing a full range of music from cutting edge rock music to contemporary jazz to chart-topping country.

The Universal Studios lot itself is perhaps best known as the site of Universal Studios Hollywood, a recreational theme park. The park features movie themed rides and exhibits, giving visitors a behind-the-scenes look at a movie studio. It's one of the most popular tourist attractions in California. Adjacent to the park lies Universal CityWalk, a pedestrian promenade which has become a Southern California landmark in its own right. In partnership with The Rank Group, plc., Universal has a theme park in Orlando, Florida, Universal Studios Escape. Other parks include Port Aventura in Spain and the Universal Experience in Beijing, China. Plans are underway to open a park in Osaka, Japan.

Universal continues to expand its horizons in response to emerging technology, launching its New Media Group in 1996 in order to meet the challenges of the emerging global market for digital entertainment. The New Media Group includes Universal Studios Online, an interactive website, as well as Universal Interactive Studios, which is creating groundbreaking interactive games for CD-ROM and other media, such as the popular "Crash Bandicoot" game.

The entertainment business is legendary for its frenetic pace of change. New forms of media, as well as the ever changing tastes of the public, make for an

Universal Studios Hollywood attracts millions of visitors year-round.

industry marked by unpredictable evolution. However, no matter how the contours of the industry might shift, Universal will be at the forefront for many years to come.

The theme park offers behind-the-scenes views into the movie-making process.

PARTNERS IN LOS ANGELES
FASHION

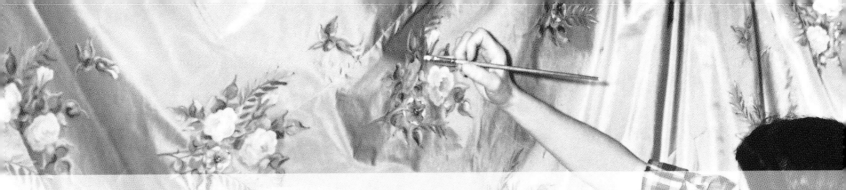

Los Angeles is the United States' largest fashion manufacturing center, with an annual retail amount of more than $43 billion. California apparel products reach consumers worldwide.

CALIFORNIA FASHION ASSOCIATION

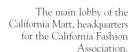

he California Fashion Association (CFA) is a statewide industry networking organization, providing information for international trade and labor law compliance. The CFA also serves to promote technological advancement and development of a positive image for the apparel and textile industries. Members include manufacturers, their suppliers, financial and professional services, allied industry associations, and applied educational institutions. The California Fashion Association, as a collective forum, focuses on the global recognition of the "Created in California" image.

Southern California's fashion industry combines elements of both casual and active lifestyles, and has created the largest apparel manufacturing opportunity in the nation. There are more than 7,500 registered garment manufacturers and contractors in the state. This number includes approximately 850 manufacturers of branded and private label merchandise, who generate over $60 billion of *retail* volume annually.

Fashion is the largest manufacturing sector in Los Angeles — it is a $35 billion wholesale business locally. That's $17 million more than the venerable New York garment trade, with employment in the California garment industry surpassing New York by 35,000 jobs. Nearly 4,400 firms are involved in fashion-related businesses in Los Angeles and surrounding counties, accounting for approximately 150,000 jobs.

Southern California has over 700 textile-related businesses including knitting, printing, finishing and dyeing plants. Fast response time, as an outgrowth of having local customers and suppliers, maintains the competitive advantage of Los Angeles' textile production against foreign imports. These Southern California textile companies employ approximately 15,000 workers and produce over $1 billion in sales annually.

Los Angeles has a growing labor pool of textile chemists and textile designers. Fashion and textile merchandisers, as well as corporate sales employees, are drawn to this creative profession. Jobs involving computer technology, such as computer-aided design and computerized cutters, also provide ongoing growth opportunities for domestic manufacturers, as well as importers and exporters of apparel. The combination of local design and production talent gives this thriving industry a unique advantage over other metropolises.

All eyes remain on Los Angeles, where all who wish to participate can benefit from the highly creative labor pool that is California.

Southern California has a very strong educational component which continues to deliver a steady flow of designers into the marketplace. Institutions such as the Fashion Institute of Design & Merchandising and the Fashion Center at Los Angeles Trade-Technical College train skilled artisans in apparel trades such as design, pattern-making and production management, using the latest in technological equipment. In addition, the California Polytechnic University Pomona offers programs to assist manufacturers and contractors to increase their productivity through the application of the new technology.

Los Angeles is also home to the California Mart, the nation's largest wholesale apparel center. This three million square-foot complex is where the world's manufacturers and retailers transact their business. More than 30,000 order-writing buyers travel to California each year, with an additional 10,000 to 50,000 visits registered by local one-day wholesale shoppers.

Serving as the networking source for information and representation, the California Fashion Association acts as the voice of today's California's fashion industry.

The main lobby of the California Mart, headquarters for the California Fashion Association.

ASSOCIATION OF TEXTILE DYERS, PRINTERS & FINISHERS OF SOUTHERN CALIFORNIA

hey are so easy to take for granted — the beautiful clothes we wear, the cottons and linens that brighten our homes, the denims and wools that keep us warm, the colors and textures that enhance our lives. They are all products of one of America's oldest and most prestigious vocations, an industry that contributes to every level of the country's rich history and economy, an industry that literally touches you every day.

The textile industry equates with fashion and to keep pace with the latest styles, production moves fast and is ever changing. The textile industry supplies fashion designers, fabric suppliers, garment and home furnishing manufacturers. This combination of local customers and suppliers, talent, technology and skill nurtured by Southern California's sunshine, celebrities, attitude and lifestyle creates fashion products that are recognized internationally as uniquely Californian.

The Association of Textile Dyers, Printers and Finishers of Southern California (ATDPF) was founded in 1991 as a nonprofilt organization by textile industry leaders from Anaheim Mills, L.A. Dye & Print Works, Matchmaster Dyeing & Finishing, Pacific Fabric Finishing and Tissurama Industries. Their mission: to continue the health and prosperity of the textile industry in Southern California. ATDPF's beginning was tentative and cautious. The founders were faced with detrimental issues that threatened the health and prosperity of their individual operations as well as that of the entire textile industry. Not used to associating with competitors butwith the foresight that there is power in knowledge and numbers, these industry leaders came together as a proactive united voice to play a definitive role in reforming Workers' Compensation, which had been rampant wit fraud and abuse.

With the strength that comes from a united voice, ATDPF educates government agencies and the general public about the textile industries' considerable impact on the local and national economy and it has become an integral part of the rules and regulations development process which ensures a cleaner environment and a viable textile industry.

ATDPF members are textile dyers, printers and finishers; associate members include utility providers as well as chemical and dyestuff suppliers. Technical production challenges — to keep the air and waters clean and pure while producing that vibrant red fabric the fashion designer needs by tomorrow, if not sooner — are surmounted daily. Vast quantities of water and energy are required; their input and output precisely monitored for regulatory agencies.

Like so many of Southern California's other industries, the textile industry is comprised of many diverse ethnic and cultural groups who brought their knowledge and skills with them from around the globe. They had to, because until recently local educational institutes had not begun to provide the highly specialized textile chemists or the technical training required. They created thousands of jobs that significantly enhance the local and national economy. They came, too, because of the sunshine, celebrities, attitude and lifestyle that is Southern California.

Southern California's textile manufacturing industries have grown steadfastly since the 1970s, requiring continuous new talent. Local educational institutes are responding to the remarkable growth by offering programs and degrees for tomorrow's textile professionals.

The founders remain active in the association today, and current membership has expanded to include textile industry leaders from other mills such as Beacon Laundry & Dry Cleaning, ColorAmerica Textile Processing, Paradise Textile, Texollini, U.S. Dyeing & Finishing and U.S. Namsung Textile. Associate members include Catawba-Charlab, DyStar, Hoechst-Celanese, Southern California Edison, Southern California Gas, Stev-Tex Laboratories, Tailheung U.S.A. and Trichromatic-West.

TEXOLLINI

From inception, Texollini was designed to be among the most technologically advanced knitting mills in America. Founded in 1989, the Company has quickly grown to become the largest knitting specialist for stretch fabrics west of the Mississippi. Texollini's size, capacity and flexibility enable it to serve large and small customers alike. It has the capacity for small customer orders as well as large program business.

Texollini is a vertically integrated knitting mill providing fabric development, knitting, dying, finishing, fabric print design and printing capabilities to their customers. Its 250,000-square-foot, state-of-the-art mill is located in Long Beach, California, minutes south of Los Angeles. In a relatively short time, the Company has become recognized within the textile industry as a leader in innovation and quality in textile fabrications containing Spandex and in creativity in print design and application. Product lines are focused on sportswear, body wear, active wear, performance wear, intimate apparel and swim wear.

Research & Development

New fabric begins in Texollini's Research & Development department. R & D responds to customer needs and market trends by creating and developing new fabric constructions and designs. Creating new fabrics is a comprehensive process that requires the involvement of highly skilled and innovative people who understand the intricacies of knitting, dying, finishing and printing. Once a fabric is developed it is then rigorously tested using Statistical Process Control (SPC) methods to ensure process capabilities and consistent product quality. Every fabric developed at Texollini must meet its exacting standards before being released for production.

The high quality of the Company's processes and products has won it official recognition by DuPont for innovation and quality fabrics containing LYCRA®.

Design

Here is where printed fabric takes on its particular look. The creative talent of Texollini designers and skill along with state-of-the-art computer-aided design (CAD) system have established the Company as one of the industry's leaders in creative design applications. In creating prints that are current in today's market, the design department takes into consideration many different variables such as fashion trends, merchandising and color.

Customers may either select from Texollini's large and ever-changing open line of print designs or the designers can customize prints for the customer.

Printing

Once the design is approved by the customer, the fabric is printed. Texollini is an expert at printing on the special fabrics it produces. The Company can accommodate both pigment printing and heat transfer printing which allows it to provide its customers with a very wide range of print designs. Its excellence in printing is a result of teamwork involving Texollini's creative design studio, top quality color matching laboratory, highly skilled printing professionals and its ability to apply the right finishing techniques for printed fabrics. The in-process quality control and inspection ensures that the result of this teamwork will produce the highest quality standards.

Quality Assurance

Before a new fabric moves on to knitting, it must meet quality assurance standards.

The goal of Texollini's Quality Assurance department is to ensure that it always end up with the desired product by using the highest quality raw materials and the most advanced process and process controls.

Raw Materials: By working in partnership with its vendors and certifying them, Texollini ensures the consistent high quality supply of yarns, chemicals and other raw materials.

* Honor our word
* Work in partnership with our customers
* Treat each other with dignity, respect and accountability
* Sustain growth through operational excellence
* Respond to the needs of our employees, environment and communities

"Start by doing what's necessary, then what's possible, and suddenly you are doing the impossible."

— St. Francis of Assisi

Process Control: As part of its Total Quality Management (TQM) program, Texollini starts the in-process quality control from the first step of production. Established manufacturing procedures and Statistical Process Control (SPC) methods support this control.

Testing and Inspection: Equipped with a state-of-the-art quality testing laboratory and highly trained technicians, Texollini ensures that its product is of consistent high quality before shipping.

Knitting

After a fabric is developed and tested, thus ensuring its quality, knitting can take place.

Knitting is performed on specialized, highly technical knitting machinery. The knitting of fabric that contains stretch yarns requires expert technology, special conditions, consistently clean machinery and constant maintenance over and above the standards of the textile industry.

Texollini has set new standards in knitting. Its continues to invest in new equipment customized to exact requirements in order to meet its own high expectations and to ensure its leadership place in innovation, quality and sophistication of knitted fabrics. Its investment in state-of-the-art knitting machines allows it to produce knitted fabrics in a wide variety of stitches and gauges.

The Company's knitting department operates 24 hours a day, seven days a week to fulfill its ongoing commitment to improving quality, response time and efficiency.

Dyeing

After the fabric is knitted, it moves on to Texollini dyeing department. Producing the most reliable color quality and steadfastness is a very sensitive and sophisticated process on any fabric. Stretch fabrics increase the level of sophistication required in the dyeing process. The quality of its dyeing equipment and the skill of its dyehouse technicians enable Texollini to excel in this very complex process.

Its dyeing capabilities include a modern color-matching laboratory equipped with the most advanced computerized color matching system and dyeing apparatus. Its laboratory sets new standards within the industry in response time and accuracy in matching colors.

Once colors are matched to its customers' approval, the fabric goes through Texollini's fully computer controlled, high performance pressure dye jets. Texollini customizes the dye jets to perform according to the exacting standards of quality and consistency it has developed and established.

Finally, Texollini's dyed fabrics go through various procedures designed by its technicians and chemists to ensure that every lot will have the same high level of color matching and consistency every time. They apply the same procedures to tests such as color fastness to washing, light and chlorine.

Finishing

Finishing is the last step the fabric goes through before it is printed.

Since finishing is one of the most important aspects in the final performance of fabrics, Texollini has developed a highly successful process based upon scientific methods and accumulated experience. Its modern computer-controlled finishing machines are modified to meet exacting requirements for quality, standardization and performance. Texollini technicians, working together with the machine manufacturer, design these modifications.

Customer Service & Support

Texollini would not be complete without its fine Customer Service staff. From the beginning, Texollini has made it a top priority to meet and exceed customers' needs. This commitment to customers goes well beyond providing the highest quality product. Texollini is also committed to providing its customers with the highest quality service available in the industry.

When customers place orders with Texollini, the Company enters into a working partnership. Texollini Customer Service department works closely with customers to ensure that they receive exactly what they expect, and when the customer expects to receive it. Texollini encourages customer feedback so that the Company can develop innovative solutions to serve current and future needs. It is Texollini's personal guarantee that its customers receive the very best service and product possible.

"The quality of a man's life is in direct proportion to his commitment to excellence, regardless of his chosen field of endeavor."

— Vince Lombardi

CALIFORNIA DESIGN COLLEGE

n today's highly competitive marketplace, even a long, costly education offers no assurance of landing a good job upon graduation. However, students in the growing field of fashion see a future filled with creative challenges, financial reward and personal self-fulfillment.

The apparel industry continues to thrive because it offers products everyone needs. Because the creative and manufacturing processes involve so many different steps to deliver a finished garment, students have a variety of specific career choices to select from and to grow into — including marketing and management.

For a truly cutting-edge education, however, the choices are much more limited. Many traditional colleges approach fashion design as "fine art," focusing heavily on theory and the evolution of apparel rather than offering its students the practical, hands-on experience they will need to find gainful employment upon graduation.

The founders of the California Design College (CDC) understand the importance of practical, state-of-the-art, hands-on training by experienced professionals for virtually every step in the creative fashion process; beginning with the basics and continuing all the way into professional careers.

While many colleges might frown on such a clever concept, CDC's instructors emphasize that "learning is doing," and teach their students how to make knock-offs and real garments, as opposed to merely original designs.

"There's nothing wrong with copying someone else's work when you are learning the basics of fashion design," says Sabrina Kay, Executive Director and founder of this innovative institution. "That's how you learn. At CDC, we try to offer a more realistic approach to our curriculum and teach our students the things they'll really need to know. We might not have many Christian Dior's walk out our doors right after graduation, but I can attest that our graduates will be highly skilled in the latest technology and be able to work in any of a variety of fields within the apparel industry."

Despite the glamorous image attached to the world of fashion, CDC's students are taught that the path to success is paved with long hours and hard work. Unlike many of their counterparts attending fashion courses at other institutions across the country, when CDC students enter the workforce, they will be armed with what is quite possibly the latest technological fashion education the field has to offer.

As the first specialized, computer-aided fashion design college on the West Coast, CDC's mission is simple: "To provide the most modern skills needed for a successful fashion career in the least possible amount of time, and at the lowest possible tuition cost."

The means to achieving this end meant investing in state-of-the-art technology. Located at the Central Plaza Complex on the corner of Wilshire and Normandie in Los Angeles, CDC serves as the authorized training col-

lege utilizing the LECTRA and PAD computer-aided design (CAD) systems in California. This CAD/CAM system eliminates the need for rushing handmade samples in alternate colors, fabrications and/or silhouettes to buyers and it also optimizes cutting patterns to save on labor and materials.

With on-screen high-resolution color imaging and hard copy of the same, those buyers who want to see designs in different color schemes or "in a looser knit," can view their changes in mere seconds. In the blink of an eye, a pattern is made. Within seconds, it is graded in six different sizes. The sample is stored, not on a hangar, but on a disk.

Because more and more manufacturers are turning to advancements in technology, CDC requires its students to spend long hours in front of the computer in industry-simulated fashion classrooms where they learn design, sketching, pattern-drafting, grading, marking and system management.

Kay knows that only a select few fashion students will join the ranks of the world's top designers. However, after graduating from CDC, most will be able to work in many aspects of the apparel industry as CAD illustrators, designers, graders, markers, CAD room managers and CAD operators.

CDC opened its doors in 1991 to teach professionals who were already working in the industry the elements of computer-aided design. The personalized attention and state-of-the-art equipment appealed to pattern-makers, designers and manufacturers who wanted a leg up on their competition. They, in turn, recommended the institution to their colleagues and enrollment has steadily increased over the years.

"We currently enroll 300 students a year at CDC," says Kay. "But we don't plan to ever grow to more than 500 students. We pride ourselves on being able to offer our students personalized attention and each of the faculty and staff members know all of the students by name.

CDC requires its students to spend long hours in front of the computer in industry-simulated fashion classrooms to learn design sketching, pattern-drafting, grading, marking and system management.

The four different degree programs, designed with an understanding that a "long career begins with a strong foundation," include:

- Advanced Fashion Design
- Visual Merchandising
- Apparel Manufacturing
- Fashion Merchandising

Advanced Fashion Design targets students whose long-term goals are to be successful in the fashion design and production field. The basic classes teach beginning students the fundamental techniques they need in order to enter the fashion industry. Even if they have never picked up a needle or drawn a single line, the advanced courses give students the opportunity to design and create a complete collection of garments and provide an overall understanding of the apparel production process. At the end of the program, students have an opportunity to display their collections to the public, including apparel manufacturers, retailers and community leaders in a professionally produced fashion show.

If we grew much larger, we would lose the personal approach that has made us as successful as we are."

Because the college aspires to keep its enrollment to a manageable level, the admission selection process is understandably selective. After a personal interview with an admissions representative, prospective students have a tour of the campus, see a computer demonstration and receive a career analysis prior to the application process.

CDC was granted approval from Bureau for Private Post Secondary and Vocational Education (BPPVE) to operate as a California degree granting institution and in 1995, CDC became a nationally accredited organization, which allows graduates to receive A.A.S. (Associate of Applied Science) degrees upon successful completion of the institution's degree programs, and be eligible for federal financial aid programs.

Apparel Manufacturing focuses on the production and business aspects of the fashion industry, giving graduates the tools they need to excel in the management or entrepreneurship of an apparel manufacturing operation. Students begin the program by taking fashion design classes in order to gain a solid understanding of the garment construction process. Advanced classes in apparel manufacturing give students the opportunity to study all facets of running an apparel manufacturing business and garment manufacturing process.

Visual Merchandising offers students an introduction to the basics of garment construction, graphic design and fashion forecasting by focusing on topics such as fashion displays, window displays, fashion graphic design, store planning and corporate images. In keeping with changes taking place in the fashion industry, CDC continually updates its computer equipment with the latest technology available for exploring the Internet and designing websites. Students learn how to design websites and market a line of clothing on the Internet. The knowledge and skills acquired in this program allow students to pursue careers as displayers, fashion graphic artists, trend analysts, fashion consultants or event coordinators.

Finally, **Fashion Merchandising**, an interdisciplinary program designed for those with some fashion or business background, allows students interested in a specific fashion program to achieve a proposed individual goal. This program addresses important topics and concepts, such as pattern making, trend forecasting and sales, and shows students how these concepts affect business decisions made by buyers, assistant buyers, retailers, fashion advertisers, trend analysts, personnel managers and a variety of other key positions in the industry today. Students completing the program will have created a professional fashion file featuring a clothing line based on their own fashion research and forecasting. This file is then placed on public display during the fashion show to be viewed by prospective employers and industry professionals.

In addition to the comprehensive degree programs, CDC also offers accelerated certificate programs in computer-aided fashion design for professionals in the field.

CDC is further distinguished from other institutions by its unique, individualized Job Placement Assistance Program. CDC staff members take student placement very seriously and provide extensive assistance to qualified graduates, including resume preparation and interview skills as well as providing qualified job leads, internships and interview appointments.

Perhaps the best testament to CDC's success lies in its alumni, many of whom have gone on to work for some of the nation's most renowned manufacturers, including Rampage, Chorus Line, Espirit, Carole Little and Steel Jeans.

"Talent is something you're born with, not something that can be taught," says Kay. "At CDC, we teach students the technical skills they'll need to work in the fashion field. They supply the commitment and pay their dues with hard work, and the rest is up to the faculty and staff at CDC to inspire, develop and cultivate their talents."

(Above) CDC students in the growing field of fashion see a future filled with creative challenges, financial reward and personal self-fulfillment.

(Left) Perhaps the best testament to CDC's success lies in its alumni, many of whom have gone on to work for some of the nation's most renowned manufacturers.

JONATHAN MARTIN

If change is the "life's blood" of the retail industry, Harkham Industries Inc. is the pulse that keeps the market moving.

ashion moves at a furious pace. The image is all glamour, but the reality is grittier. A fashion firm can be a shooting star one minute and burn out the next. Fashion is a business where yesterday is the only moment that counts and tomorrow is never guaranteed. To succeed in the fashion business, a company needs a talent for trendspotting coupled with prudent planning and a dedication to on-time delivery. Image is crucial, but style must be supported by integrity. A successful design line must build its reputation with both retailers and consumers, and to survive in the long run, establish brand awareness and customer loyalty. This is the strategy that keeps a fashion star shining brightly. And one of the brightest fashion stars is Jonathan Martin.

Jonathan Martin is the fashion label under the corporate umbrella of Harkham Industries, headquartered in Los Angeles. Harkham Industries is a fashion powerhouse with a worldwide reputation for its collections of sportswear, dresses and shoes for the junior/young contemporary, missy and girls markets. Four distinct divisions operate within Harkham Industries: Jonathan Martin, with junior/young contemporary sportswear, dresses and outerwear; Studio by Jonathan Martin, with missy career/casual sportswear and dresses; Jonathan Martin for Girls, with sportswear, dresses and outerwear; and Hype, with a contemporary collection of sportswear and dresses. The Jonathan Martin Shoe Group is the company's first licensed category and produces Jonathan Martin and Hype footwear.

The Jonathan Martin label was founded in 1975. In the generation since, it has expanded into a global design and manufacturing business catering to women of almost every age and attitude. The goal of the company is to develop a brand-loyal customer and dress her throughout her life. Each division has its niche, but all are recognizable for their creative styling, quality design and accessible pricing. Indeed, Jonathan Martin prides itself on having earned a strong reputation for fashion, quality, value and integrity. Every year, the company consistently outpaces the competition with its fresh fashion eye, innovative designs, unique signature prints and trend-setting styles.

The Jonathan Martin junior/young contemporary division is the largest in the company. It is targeted to young women ages 15 to 35 and appeals to these customers with consistently innovative and fast-moving styles, all defined by exclusive prints, fabrications and trend-setting silhouettes. The attitude of the clothing is defined as "understandable trend," meaning that the clothes are forward-thinking but not extreme. The collection includes sportswear and dresses with a look that is of-the-moment but a style that is not limited to a single, short fashion season. Jonathan Martin is known for its signature prints, many of which are produced by its in-house art department. By presenting ten collections a year, Jonathan Martin is always fresh and new, and its cus-

The Jonathan Martin label was founded in 1975. In the generation since, it has expanded into a global design and manufacturing business catering to women of almost every age and attitude.

tomers rely on the label for the right look for the moment as well as for pieces on which to build a wardrobe. Jonathan Martin's fashion message is always paired with great value: The price points are very affordable, and so the collection is accessible and not intimidating.

The young woman who relies on Jonathan Martin glides effortlessly into Studio by Jonathan Martin as she gets older. As with the younger Jonathan Martin line, Studio embodies the same fashion-with-an-edge sensibility while incorporating more luxurious fabrics and a more forgiving silhouette. Studio is designed with the understanding that fashion-sensitive young women will refuse to abdicate style just because they grow older, and the line offers a broad range of designs for every aspect of their lives, from casual to career. Comfort and ease with an emphasis on femininity are the hallmarks of Studio which, like Jonathan Martin, is famous for its signature prints. Each collection is comprised of dresses,

blouses, jackets, pants, skirts and sweaters, and to allow for maximum versatility, the designs are simple and clean.

With the introduction of the children's line, the loyal Jonathan Martin customer can introduce her daughter to the same fashion family. Jonathan Martin for Girls is a pared-down version of Jonathan Martin with similarly appealing prints and an emphasis on fashion and value. The line embraces every facet of a girl's lifestyle, from dressing up for special occasions to tearing up the playground. Sizing runs from 4-16, and the styling runs the gamut from demurely feminine to active and playful. Pretty dresses with beautiful prints happily coexist alongside rugged, functional outerwear. The clothes are spirited and playful and embody the Jonathan Martin philosophy of offering its customers great style at affordable prices.

Hype is the fourth Jonathan Martin division, with a sophistication and designer image all its own. It is the only division that is not labeled Jonathan Martin, and since its inception in 1996, it has met with resounding success. Hype is targeted to contemporary women, ages 25 to 50, who believe in their own personal style over commercially dictated trends and want unique and innovative designs. Hype is found in the most upscale and exclusive retail venues where it more than holds its own against the biggest names in fashion. With luxurious fabrications, exquisite embellishments and sleek styling, Hype is the epitome of modern style.

Jonathan Martin was founded by Uri P. Harkham who committed his business to its guiding principles of innovation and reliability. With his keen grasp of the marketplace, Harkham has guided his firm from its

early days as a simple blouse manufacturer. Harkham is the son of a schoolteacher, and his childhood included an odyssey from Israel to Australia where he spent most of his youth. In Australia he became enamored with fashion and began working in the garment industry. A vacation in California convinced him that Los Angeles was the land of opportunity, and with his background, L.A., home to the nation's second-largest apparel industry, was the logical place for him to found his own company. Harkham is quick to credit his talented team for having propelled Jonathan Martin to the forefront of the fashion business. That team includes the dedicated designers who are responsible for the signature style of the clothing and the large support staff which works both at the company's headquarters and around the world. Today, in addition to the Jonathan Martin fashion family, Harkham presides over an impressive and diversified investment portfolio, one that includes restaurants, hotels, real estate and contemporary art.

Harkham's ever-expanding Jonathan Martin business includes more than 400 employees. After years in a high-tech environment in L.A.'s garment district, Jonathan Martin outgrew its facility and moved to its new corporate headquarters in a landmark Art-Deco building a few miles south. The new site, with its surrounding seven-and-one-half acres, will allow the company to continue its growth and add more buildings to accommodate its future expansion. In addition to the corporate headquarters, Jonathan Martin maintains fashion showrooms in Los Angeles and New York.

While Jonathan Martin and Hype are prominently positioned in major department and specialty stores across the country, the company has taken the next important step in its development with the launch of its first retail store. The flagship Jonathan Martin shop opened in late 1998 on Santa Monica's Third Street Promenade, and plans are in place for more to follow. In the fashion business, the trend is for designers to join the ranks of retailers. Establishing a retail presence enables a clothing company such as Jonathan Martin, already successful and well-known, to showcase its line to its customers with no distracting competition. In turn, the loyal customer has a destination shop where she can go for both spur-of-the-moment finds and to build a consistent image with a wardrobe that works together season after season. For retailers, the freestanding designer store serves as a showroom where executives can go to experience the collections in their entirety. The retail strategy offers Jonathan Martin the opportunity to enhance its business by becoming more visible in the eye of both retailers and customers. In addition to its planned chain of retail stores, Jonathan Martin has designed an aggressive program to install individual boutiques in major department stores nationwide. The strategy capitalizes on the company's strong relationships with retailers who in turn welcome the firm's involvement and investment.

Having established Jonathan Martin and Hype as familiar and admired brands, the next move for the company is licensing. This is the arrangement whereby a successful fashion house loans its name to manufacturers of related businesses whose products are beyond the production capacity of a designer house. The result is increased profitability for both partners and an expansion of the presence of the company's name in the marketplace. The first licensing step was taken in 1997 with the introduction of the Jonathan Martin Shoe Group whose goal is to become the most desired shoe company in its category. Jonathan Martin and Hype footwear are available in specialty and department stores from coast to coast. Silhouettes range from casual to evening, combining unusual fabrics and designs. In keeping with the company's formula of always offering value, the price points are very affordable. Future licensing arrangements for both Jonathan Martin and Hype will include handbags, watches, small leather goods and fragrances. Expanding into the world of licensing, Jonathan Martin intends to move prudently, establishing each category on firm footing before moving on to the next.

Joining a growing trend, Jonathan Martin has entered the online world of e-commerce, beginning with its company Web site. Future cyber opportunities include virtual shopping, where customers can enter their body statistics and, with a quick click, layer on pants, skirts, sweaters, blouses, jackets and dresses to see exactly how they'll look. There is also an online catalog. With the world fast becoming a global marketplace, Jonathan Martin intends to be a part of the big picture.

Picturing Jonathan Martin and Hype is the job of the company's aggressive advertising program. The on-going, multimillion dollar national ad campaign includes placement in prominent fashion magazines, TV and on billboards and other outdoor media. The fashion images change with the seasons and feature

The fashion images change with the seasons and feature young women clearly in command of their world.

young women clearly in command of their world. Additionally, Jonathan Martin maintains close ties with magazine editors, a relationship which pays off tremendously, with positioning on the editorial pages of top fashion magazines giving the company enormous validation and name recognition. Fashion editors, always in need of what's-new-right-now, rely on Jonathan Martin to deliver the very latest exactly when they need it, which is usually immediately.

The impression that Jonathan Martin has made in the world of fashion is remarkable. Harkham Industries has succeeded so spectacularly by maintaining an excellent reputation for on-time delivery, superb quality and exceptional customer service, all accomplished while operating at a faster pace than most of its competition. Not content to rest on his laurels, Harkham is committed to his belief that there is unlimited potential to identify and develop new opportunities to complement his core business. With more than 20 years in the fashion business, Harkham has established Jonathan Martin on a solid infrastructure with a sound business philosophy, foundations on which Harkham and his motivated team stand securely as they face each new challenge with justifiable confidence.

THE FASHION DISTRICT

The Fashion District of Los Angeles is one of the most exciting and diverse wholesale and retail buying areas in the world.

California's reputation for fun, trend-setting fashion inspires designers on every continent. The district attracts millions of wholesale and retail buyers every year. Once a well-guarded secret of veteran shoppers, the district has become a must-shop experience for consumers attracted to the mix of fashionable merchandise at wholesale prices.

The Fashion District is also an important economic engine, producing over $7 billion in annual revenues. It is a major hub of the $16.5 billion Southern California apparel industry. The District houses the largest concentration of apparel related businesses in the Western United States. Nearly every type of apparel related product, including textiles, notions and accessories, is available in the district. More than 3,000 wholesale and manufacturing businesses occupy the upper floors and nearly 2,000 street level outlets sell merchandise to both business buyers and consumers. Fashion District businesses provide over 45,000 apparel-related jobs.

Although much of the district is devoted to wholesale and manufacturing activities, there is a large, well-defined retail corridor. Women's wear, men's wear, kid's wear, accessories, fabrics, beads

California's reputation for fun, trend-setting fashion inspires designers on every continent.

and trim — even flowers are available within this 56-block shopping paradise.

To protect their investment and to enhance this important commercial district, property owners voluntarily funded a pilot Clean and Safe program in 1993. The program was successful, and led to the establishment of a 56-block business improvement district (BID), a special service district funded by an assessment on commercial property within a designated geographic area. A private nonprofit organization, the Downtown Los Angeles Property Owners Association (DPOA), manages the Fashion District BID.

The BID generates $3 million annually, funding an array of services that directly benefit the district. The BID provides services beyond those provided by the City, such as maintenance, security, job training, homeless outreach and marketing. The BID has helped to create a stable business environment by protecting property values and encouraging private investment. This, in turn, has helped to preserve the employment base. The BID itself has created approximately 65 job opportunities. Many of these jobs have gone to formerly homeless and economically disadvantaged persons living in and around the district.

The BID has also inspired a renaissance of existing businesses as they improve their buildings to complement the enhanced surrounding environment.

Encouraged by the success of the BID, both the CaliforniaMart and the New Mart completed multimillion dollar renovations in 1996. The Los Angeles Fashion Building undertook a $500,000 renovation of its facility.

Most importantly, the BID has created a managed environment. The purple-and-gold-clad Clean and Safe Team are a welcome presence in the District as they work daily to maintain a clean, safe and friendly environment. These radio-equipped safety officers patrol the area on bikes and in cruisers. Clean Team members work daily to keep the District immaculately groomed. The Clean and Safe Team serve as important ambassadors in the district, assisting visitors with directions and information.

The BID places expectations on everyone's behavior. Together the community has demanded a certain level of cleanliness and personal behavior of those living, working and visiting the District. Consequently, the quality of life for everyone in the district and surrounding neighborhoods has improved dramatically.

A vital historic and economic landmark, the Fashion District has much to offer Los Angeles residents, visitors and the Apparel Industry. The DPOA provides a free orientation map and operates a free guided trolley tour (the best way to preview all the District has to offer). Call for information and reservations for the tour or visit the Fashion District web site.

The purple-and-gold clad Clean and Safe Team are a welcome presence in the District as they work daily to maintain a clean, safe and friendly environment.

WEARABLE INTEGRITY

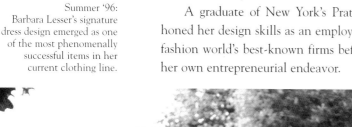

o matter how long a company has been in business, the name of the game for any garment manufacturer is giving customers what they want. Forecasting trends, researching ideas and adjusting product offerings are all strategies employed by companies on the cutting edge of fashion.

Barbara Lesser, designer of casual contemporary dresses, knows that today's busy woman wants clothing that is fashionable, yet practical. This innovative entrepreneur knows from experience that adapting to change and evolving a business to meet market demands is the way not only to survive, but to thrive in the fashion industry.

A graduate of New York's Pratt Institute, Lesser honed her design skills as an employee for some of the fashion world's best-known firms before embarking on her own entrepreneurial endeavor.

Summer '96: Barbara Lesser's signature dress design emerged as one of the most phenomenally successful items in her current clothing line.

In 1981, she and her husband, Mark, founded Felicity, a sportswear collection, and for nearly a decade, rode the financial highs and lows of a fickle fashion industry. By the late 80s, the couple began searching for ways to "find and give more meaning" to their chosen careers.

After taking a year off to travel and "regenerate" their souls, they returned to the City of Angels. Armed only with a creative concept and a shoestring budget, they launched Wearable Integrity as an "environmentally-friendly" clothing line created from organically grown cotton as a way of "creating a product we could be proud of that would also be a contribution to the environment and the community."

After three years of marketing their environmentally-friendly designs, the couple conceded that in the face of tough economic times, consumers were simply unwilling to spend money on what they considered "premium items."

"It was the whole mind-set that if a product was organic, it must therefore be more expensive," says Lesser. "If we wanted the company to succeed, we needed to adapt to survive."

The now-infamous Barbara Lesser signature dress survived the transition and emerged as one of the most phenomenally successful items in her current clothing line.

Building off of this signature dress — the thermal tank with crinkle rayon bottom in an expansive array of

colors — Lesser brings a wealth of new-
ness to each season's offerings, embracing
new fabrics and capitalizing on innovative
dye treatments.

One need look no further than the
ubiquitous Barbara Lesser signature dress
to understand why the Los Angeles-based
designer was named the "Dress Designer of
the Year" in 1997 by the International
Apparel Mart in Dallas, which recognizes
fashion industry leaders for outstanding
retail performance, design innovation and
quality workmanship.

Lesser lets lifestyle, rather than fashion
trends, dictate her designs, which are
currently sold through better specialty and
department stores and catalogs nationwide.
Though ever-evolving and introducing
new concepts, Lesser continues to offer
figure-flattering silhouettes in regular and
specialty sizes.

"It's a given that a garment has to
look good and be fashionable," says Lesser.
"But it needs to get her (the customer)
through the day in terms of versatility,
comfort and performance to be worth the
money she spent on it."

Lesser credits the company's success
to perseverance, hard work and "simply
not accepting defeat." Perhaps even more
telling to her success are the words by
which she runs her thriving business.

Fall '98:
Although ever-evolving and
introducing new concepts,
Barbara Lesser continues to
offer flattering silhouettes in
regular and specialty sizes.

Barbara Lesser's corporate mission statement is "to
produce a stylish garment that is affordable and
comfortable with easy care while adhering to our high
quality standards. In doing so, we strive to provide a
responsible, professional and positive work place with
growth potential for our employees."

This corporate philosophy helped propel Lesser to
the forefront of the fashion world. Wearable Integrity
and Barbara Lesser boast a reputation as an innovative
international company and an industry leader contributing to the growth of the garment industry.

BCBG MAX AZRIA

With award-winning collections, stellar advertising campaigns and a loyal following of Hollywood's top celebrities, BCBG Max Azria has earned its stature as a premier American design house. Marketing savvy and expansion in the realms of retail, wholesale, footwear, licensing and interactive media have branded BCBG Max Azria as a trendsetter and defined its niche in the marketplace.

BCBG Max Azria is the lifetime vision of one man: founder, designer and President Max Azria. In 1981, after spending 11 years designing contemporary women's wear in his native Paris, Azria moved to the U.S. and started the highly successful clothing company, Jess, as president and designer. In 1989, Max Azria set out to develop a collection that could "fulfill the needs of modern women" and thus BCBG Max Azria was born. Named for the French phrase Bon Chic, Bon Genre (Parisian slang meaning good style, good attitude,) the company is a true combination of European sophistication and American spirit.

BCBG Max Azria has effectively redefined the designer category by offering his collection at contemporary price points — a feat that none of his competitors can match. BCBG Max Azria first landed on the fashion map with the creation of the baby doll dress. Azria then developed a full ready-to-wear collection of designer clothing at reasonable price points that allow the modern woman to move easily from morning into evening, work to weekend.

Always looking ahead, Azria began to build a lifestyle

brand. Evening dresses, a jeans line, eyewear, footwear, swim, menswear and a variety of accessories are all now part of the BCBG Max Azria stable. Acquiring the Los Angeles based sportswear firm Francine Browner in 1996, Azria now addresses the needs of another tier of young women: the moderate to junior market. In addition to his collections under the BCBG Max Azria label, Azria now oversees three additional divisions from Francine Browner: To The Max, an edgy sportswear line; Maxime, a moderate misses' line; and Parallel, a contemporary line.

Dramatic successes on both the retail and wholesale fronts have defined BCBG Max Azria as a retail giant. There are currently over 60 freestanding BCBG Max Azria retail boutiques located throughout North America and Japan showcasing the diverse BCBG Max Azria collections. Further, BCBG Max Azria is sold at specialty stores across the country as well as major department stores including Neiman Marcus, Saks Fifth Avenue, Bloomingdale's, Macy's and Dillard's.

Status as a premier American designer was achieved when Max Azria decided to show his Fall/Winter 1996 collection on the runway at 7th on Sixth, New York City's fashion week. With a warm welcome and rave reviews, BCBG Max Azria returned the following season to show their Spring/Summer 1997 line. The New York Times hailed, "Mr. Azria imbued his collection with worldly elan." In April of 1997, with a packed house of nearly 1,100 guests, BCBG Max Azria previewed their Fall/Winter 1997 collection,

receiving praise from the ever-important *Women's Wear Daily* and *Los Angeles Times*, among others.

Recognizing his impact on the marketplace as both designer and marketer, Azria has been awarded a seat in the prestigious CFDA (Counsel of Fashion Designers of America). Azria has also won awards for 1995 California Designer of the Year, 1996 Atlanta Designer of the Year, as well as the 1997 Fashion Performance Award for outstanding performance and influence within the fashion industry. This past May, Azria was presented with the prestigious Spirit of Life award from the City of Hope; one of the country's leading research and treatment centers battling life-threatening diseases.

Outstanding editorial support coupled with the creation of a relentlessly hip advertising campaign each season continuously reinforces BCBG Max Azria's position in the market. The campaign, drawing upon the talents of top models, photographers and art directors, is featured in the pages of international fashion, lifestyle, and entertainment magazines as well as out-door venues in major U.S. cities. The collection can also be spotted regularly on top television shows including "Friends," "Melrose Place," Seinfeld," and "E! News Daily," while celebrities including Sharon Stone, Uma Thurman, Madonna, Ashley Judd, Minnie Driver, Neve Campbell, Julianne Moore and Sarah

Michelle Gellar have all claimed that BCBG Max Azria is a staple in their wardrobe.

BCBG Max Azria is one of the most sought after designer collections on the market. Ending 1997 with $141 million in sales, with projections to reach $180 million for 1998, Azria plans to continue to grow his fashion empire into an international lifestyle brand. With immediate goals to further expand the BCBG Max Azria product categories and retail store locations, Azria's long term goals involve opening stores in London, Milan, Paris, and eventually throughout the world — establishing BCBG Max Azria as a worldwide powerhouse of style.

CHORUS LINE

s one of the nation's largest apparel companies, Chorus Line Corporation's success stems from a simple philosophy to produce high quality merchandise utilizing cutting-edge technology.

The Vernon, California-based clothing manufacturer's roots can be traced back to 1975, when a pair of entrepreneurs launched a line of junior dresses from a 4,000-square-foot loft office in downtown Los Angeles.

By 1980, the once fledgling firm outgrew the small space and company founders Barry Sacks and Mark Steinman built their own 12,000-square-foot structure to house the expanding operation.

Throughout the turbulent business environment of the 80s and early 90s, Sacks, Steinman and partner Jay Balaban continually expanded the company's distribution and increased sales by following a simple corporate philosophy: to "react to hot, salable trends while maintaining high levels of quality."

This strategy led to Chorus Line's success in diversifying into new markets and becoming a key resource in the junior category. Chorus Line has five divisions: All That Jazz junior dresses; Jazz Sport junior sportswear; Molly Malloy women's dresses; More Jazz plus-size women's dresses; and Jazz Kids children's dresses.

President and CEO
Andrew Cohen

Since its inception, Chorus Line Corporation has maintained its focused approach to business. With showrooms in Los Angeles and New York, the company currently operates from a 450,000-square-foot complex of offices, design facilities, a piece goods warehouse and fully computerized cutting facility and distribution center in Los Angeles.

The company founders credit the firm's success to date to "having the right people in place to ensure the ability to make the right product at the right time and to distribute the merchandise to a wide variety of retailers."

"In this highly competitive industry, it's important to have excellent management," says Sacks, chairman of the board. "That means we need to encourage younger people to bring energy and enthusiasm into the company to help guide the firm's growth into the next century."

In response to the company's quest to remain on the cutting edge, the principals brought Andrew Cohen on board to serve as president and CEO in 1996.

With 27 years experience in the apparel business, Cohen knows how to manage a quality business, particularly within the challenging environment of a multi-division company.

"Finding and developing caring professionals that are able to continually focus their energies for the good of the company and its customers is a difficult task in the garment industry," says Cohen. "We have achieved that."

These resources allow Chorus Line to maintain its reputation for on-time delivery, value priced merchandise and unparalleled customer service. Fully equipped to accommodate future growth, Chorus Line boasts an expansive, state-of-the-art MIS department, which results in one of the industry's best records for quick response.

These tools have allowed Chorus Line to develop key relationships with the industry's most prominent national retailers, ranging from major department stores, such as May Co. stores, J.C.Penney, Federated Department Stores and Dillards to specialty chains, including the Dress Barn, Charlotte Russe and Wet Seal.

As part of its continued growth, Chorus Line opened the first of its outlet stores in Arizona in 1994. Subsequent sites, including multiple locations in Texas and California, are designed to heighten brand awareness and create a retail destination for its consumers.

Chorus Line's commitment to excellence and strategic focus ensures this premier apparel company's success into the millennium and beyond.

Sacks, Steinman and partner Jay Balaban continually expanded the company's distribution and increased sales by following a simple corporate philosophy: to "react to hot, salable trends while maintaining high levels of quality."

FASHION INSTITUTE OF DESIGN & MERCHANDISING

ounded in 1969 by Tonian Hohberg, the Fashion Institute of Design & Merchandising (FIDM) is an internationally recognized, WASC accredited, 2-year private college specializing in preparing students for careers in the fashion, interior design, and entertainment industries. Approximately 3,000 full-time students each year pursue Associate of Arts and Associate of Arts Professional Designation degrees in Merchandise Marketing, Apparel Manufacturing Management, Cosmetics & Fragrance Merchandising, Fashion Design, Theatre Costume, Textile Design, Interior Design, Garden Design, Visual Communications and Graphic Design. The specialized curriculum is taught by industry professionals and combines essential theoretical education with the practical application of skills and abilities.

Students at work in the Interior Design classroom. Courtesy Robert Cavalli

FIDM has four campuses in California: San Francisco, Costa Mesa, San Diego and the main campus on South Grand Avenue in downtown Los Angeles. The college began in 1969 by concentrating on the merchandising curriculum, adding fashion design and other areas of emphasis as the fashion industry dictated. The worldwide advisory board, comprised of industry leaders, helps shape the FIDM curriculum by providing input on industry trends and international innovations.

Over the years, FIDM has earned a reputation as a source of professional talent. More than 20,000 graduates are working internationally in the fashion, interior and entertainment industries. The talented faculty is comprised of working professionals who provide students with the most current information on industry trends and practices. The placement of alumni around the world has created a network of advisory board members, faculty and alumni that allows communication about the most up-to-date developments in these fields.

Students receive experience in the form of hands-on instruction from the beginning of their program. Depending on the area of interest, a student can learn everything from management skills to pattern drafting to computer assisted design techniques. This instruction enables students to actively enter their chosen professions upon graduation. Due to the campuses close proximity to Hollywood, many students opt for FIDM's advanced program in theater costume and graphic design. Practical courses in business, finance, promotions and related areas of study help students prepare for jobs in the working world.

One of the most exciting new programs, the International Manufacturing & Product Development Professional Designation, is designed to provide a quality professional education that will meet the needs of students entering the community of global manufacturing and product development. Students are involved in forecasting and analysis, production, sales and finance in the global marketplace. Students intern in Europe and Asia to experience, first hand, all phases of international apparel manufacturing from the development of the product, through costing, marketing, production cycle and purchase by the consumer.

The Cosmetics & Fragrance Merchandising curriculum prepares students for careers within the cosmetic retailing and/or manufacturing industries. Career preparation leads to selling, merchandising, training or management positions. Students learn practical principles of cosmetic product knowledge, merchandising, management and industry systems.

The Fashion Design major prepares students for careers in the fast paced world of fashion. The curricu-

lum stimulates talent and builds a framework for the translation of creative ideas into fashion. Courses in fashion sketching, draping, pattern drafting and creative design develop the skills necessary for a career in the apparel industry. There is also a separate program in Theatre Costume which encompasses many aspects of costuming for stage, television, film and video.

The FIDER accredited Interior Design curriculum is a comprehensive program combining theoretical elements of interior design with practical creative approaches to the solution of functional and aesthetic design problems in the living, working and recreational human environment. Students learn architectural drafting, illustration and presentation skills, design proficiency, and a working knowledge of the materials, resources and business procedures pertaining to the interior design profession. After mastering the basic course work, students may elect to study specialized programs of decorative arts, set design, kitchen and bath design, or garden design. This program enables students to qualify for the National Council for Interior Design Qualification (NCIDQ) examination.

The Apparel Manufacturing Management Program prepares students for eventual ownership and/or management of an apparel manufacturing facility. This "hands-on" program involves students in all phases of production, sales, financial and human resources management. Industry specialists act as special advisors to the department and the teaching faculty brings experience and specialized knowledge into the classroom.

The School of Merchandise Marketing is geared toward preparing students for careers in retail and wholesale organizations in buying, product development, merchandising, store operations, management, distribution and sales support.

The Textile Design Program prepares students for careers in the design and styling of textiles for the apparel and interior design industries. Courses emphasize the technical skills required to serve the textile industry in both surface and structural design.

The Visual Communications Program offers its students a diversified business background in visual presentation, exhibit/trade show design, retail and special event display, and store planning. Emphasis is placed on the knowledge of composition and design, the structure of form in a given space, the understanding of color, and the meticulous placement and presentation of merchandise.

The Graphic Design Program has been developed in response to rapidly expanding opportunities in the apparel and entertainment industries. Leading companies in these fields urged FIDM to create this comprehensive major to help fill their ongoing needs for well-trained graphic designers. Career possibilities are diverse and include print and apparel graphics, internet and corporate communications.

FIDM campuses, located adjacent to major retail and entertainment centers, include costume collections, specialized libraries, lecture halls, exhibits and a variety of student services including counseling, tutoring centers, and computer labs.

Students and staff participate in a variety of community service projects including the Jimmy Stewart Marathon, support for Para los Ninos, and fundraising for the Child Care Center at St. John's Hospital. FIDM founder Tonian Hohberg has been recognized by numerous organizations for her years of community service and civic contributions.

The FIDM campus in downtown Los Angeles. Courtesy Assassi

A student gets hands-on experience in the Graphic Design Computer Lab. Courtesy Brian Sanderson

GUESS?, INC.

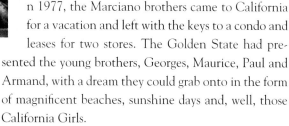

n 1977, the Marciano brothers came to California for a vacation and left with the keys to a condo and leases for two stores. The Golden State had presented the young brothers, Georges, Maurice, Paul and Armand, with a dream they could grab onto in the form of magnificent beaches, sunshine days and, well, those California Girls.

The Marciano brothers' first business venture, men's ties, was designed and manufactured by the foursome and sold in France out of the trunk of their car. Both the challenge and success of the business led the brothers to move onto bigger endeavors. In 1973 they opened their first retail store, MGA (which stood for Maurice, Georges and Armand), in the south of France. The overwhelming demand of MGA's original inventory, women's peasant blouses, was responsible for drawing a steady clientele into the store. By 1976, there were 20 stores in France and MGA's merchandise had expanded to include dresses, pants and, finally, stonewashed jeans — a concept that had not yet hit the American market...but it would.

The Marciano's brought the stonewashed jean to America in 1978 when Georges and Maurice returned to California to open the two stores leased during their first West Coast holiday. The pair ran the two new stores under the MGA name while Paul and Armand wrapped up the businesses in France. After two years the brothers were joined together again in Los Angeles, their new home.

Georges possessed a European sense of design, keen business savvy, creative inspiration and an instinctual knowledge of the women's cloth-

ing market. With these qualities and an unprecedented amount of determination, Georges and Maurice started GUESS?. Following the name, came the product — the Marilyn jean, the first American design under the GUESS? brand. Originally met with skepticism, two dozen pair of this sexy 3-zip jean were bought by Bloomingdale's and sold out within hours.

In addition to retail success, GUESS? is recognized for its signature provocative images which continue to break barriers within the world of advertising. The brand's history and cachet are illustrated by these captivating images. The campaigns, shot by world renowned photographers under the art direction of Paul Marciano, have made the GUESS? name synonymous with sensuality and creative innovation. The image of the GUESS? model has become an icon; past campaigns are responsible for launching the careers of some of the most beautiful faces in the world including Claudia Schiffer, Eva Herzigova, Carey Otis, Anna Nicole Smith and Laetitia Casta.

What began as a small California jeans company in 1981 has since developed into GUESS?, Inc., a global

(Top right and below)
Photos by Ellen Von
Unwerth, August 1988.

(Far right)
Photo by Daniela Federici,
September 1992.

lifestyle brand. While jeans remain the foundation of the company's history and success, GUESS? designs, markets and distributes its full collections of women's, men's and children's apparel, as well as accessories, shoes and home products. GUESS? became a public company in August 1996, and is still headed by three of the Marciano brothers. Maurice serves as the Chairman of the Board and Chief Executive Officer, Armand as Senior Executive Vice President and Secretary and Paul as President and Chief Operating Officer. GUESS?' corporate headquarters are located in Los Angeles, and has sales offices in New York City, Dallas, Atlanta, Chicago and Milan. GUESS? is distributed in fine department stores, retail, specialty and factory stores throughout the United States. The company has selectively granted licenses for the manufacture and distribution of many of its product categories. Additionally, GUESS? has licensees and distributors in Europe, South America, Asia, Canada, Africa and the Middle East.

Photo by Dewey Nicks, May 1995.

(Bottom right)
Photo by Neil Kirk,
March 1987.

(Bottom left)
Photo by Ellen Von
Unwerth, September 1991.

LUCKY BRAND DUNGAREES

More than 25 years ago in Miami, Florida, Gene Montesano and Barry Perlman worked as store clerks at the Red Hanger, a local jean store. From such humble beginnings legends sometimes arise, and dreams are made real. Such is the story of Lucky Brand Dungarees, a company that seems to have a future limited only by the imagination. Indeed, the company has captured the fancy of a skyrocketing number of customers, from movie stars to everyman, from grandfathers to teenagers, and all those in between. A combination of hard work, experience, a little luck, and above all, an unexcelled product, has pushed the company into that rarified air of unqualified success. The story of Lucky Brand Dungarees is above all the story of the American Dream, the idea that anyone with a hundred bucks and an idea can achieve their goals.

Lucky Brand jeans are a culmination of years of work that have left the founding duo with an all encompassing knowledge of their basic product and passion — denim. Their start as clerks at the Red Hanger was only preparation, a beginning to what would eventually become Lucky Brand. After their stint as clerks, the pair started their own store, Four

One of the growing number of Lucky Brand Stores.

Way Street, a jeanswear store based in Miami, Florida. Gene Montesano left to pursue other interests, and in the early 80s, he had his biggest success to that point, launching Bongo — a mass-market junior jeans label that would eventually grow to annual sales of more than $100 million dollars. During this time Perlman continued to work in Miami at Four Way Street. After several years of coaxing from Montesano, Perlman finally gave in and moved to Los Angeles to launch a new jeans line. Montesano wanted to start a new product, one that wasn't bound by the constraints of the mass market. Additionally, the pair had their own ideas of what made the perfect blue jean, ideas that were the fruition of decades of experience in the market and were typified by an irreverent outlook that was unique in an arena dominated by big players with conservative outlooks.

The first product of the new company, and still the most popular, was the 102, a relaxed fit jean that embodied the two men's dedication to making the best-fitting pair of blue jeans at a reasonable price. The phenomenal success of the 102 has led to the growth of the product line to several different styles of denims for men and an equal number for women, and a variety of different wash treatments, as well as a burgeoning line of sportswear and accessories to complement their primary product. Adding to the charm of Lucky Brand Dungarees is the tongue-in-cheek humor evident throughout the entire product line. Printed in bold red letters behind the fly are the words "Lucky You" and a four leaf clover is stamped into the zipper pull, thus spawning dozens of anecdotes and furthering the red-hot word-of-mouth advertising that remains one of the companies strongest selling points. Their blue jeans were such a success that as word spread major retailers soon approached the company about broadening their distribution. The two partners had distinctive ideas, however, about just how they wanted the company to approach the market and their newfound success. The company has refused to grow too rapidly, and thus avoided the pitfalls of opening up the distribution of their products to mass-market levels.

Lucky Brand has kept its focus on the specialty stores and upscale shops that first brought them success. Such stores as The Buckle, Nordstrom, Neiman Marcus, Fred Segal and JMR continue to be sources for the company's products. The limited outlets have further added to the mystique of Lucky Brand, along with their unique advertising campaigns. Savvy ads in carefully chosen markets such as George, GQ, Elle and InStyle magazines have contributed to the company's place as one of the hottest companies in denim. Additionally, the company has opened up Lucky Brand specialty stores in Santa Monica, Santa Barbara, Los Angeles and San Diego, two stores in Florida, one in Tempe, Arizona, and a store in the SOHO district of New York. The company's founders hope to eventually expand to 50 of the stores throughout the United States.

Adding to the pair's satisfaction with the company is the fact that they have managed to produce every single pair of Lucky Brand Jeans in the United States. The company now employs several hundred workers in the Los Angeles area at a time when many if not most clothing manufacturers have moved their production overseas to save on cost. The company has a deep commitment to sharing its success with local communities as well. Lucky Brand Dungarees and the charity formed by the company — the Lucky Brand Foundation, has been extremely active in several communities throughout California as well as New York City. Various benefits staged by the company have raised money for a variety of children's charities such as The Bridge School, the Chase Foundation, the Association for Children with Down Syndrome, and a benefit CD produced by the company attracted notables such as Rod Stewart and Suzanne Vega to contribute tunes. The Foundation raised over $350,000 at its first charity ball, the Black

Tie and Blue Jeans gala held at the Beverly Hills Hotel, and the company remains strongly committed to sharing in its success with those less fortunate.

Lucky Brand Dungarees is truly an American Success story, as American as hot dogs, apple pie and, well, blue jeans. From a start decades ago as clerks at a retail clothing store, Barry Perlman and Gene Montesano have risen to the pinnacle of the market with an unswerving commitment to making the best fitting pair of jeans at a reasonable price. Along the way they've managed to capture the fancy of the public, and in a big way, while at the same time sharing in their success with those less fortunate. With plans for more stores and a growing variety of products under the Lucky Brand label, the future seems bright indeed. The company's story is perhaps best summed up by the philosophy of its founders, that "anyone with a hundred bucks and an idea" can realize their dreams. Los Angeles is a city that has seen innumerable dreams realized, but surely few as compelling as that of Lucky Brand Dungarees.

An example of Lucky Brand's unique marketing campaign on the Sunset Strip in Los Angeles.

GREAT FABRICATIONS

eslie Deane's professional and personal life has been guided by a sense of "seeking the right balance."

The successful Los Angeles-based entrepreneur credits her success in the fast-paced world of fashion to "taking chances," by surrounding herself with calming influences and understanding the importance of polarity in her quest toward creative harmony.

Leslie Deane's flair for fashion began as an adolescent in Norfolk, Virginia where she roamed the local discount and thrift stores in search of the most unusual fabrics and unconventional clothing.

Even during the "hippie era" of the late 1960s, Deane was drawn to the clothing store racks which were rife with exotic fabrics and textiles from India and around the world.

But because in those days the field of fashion design wasn't considered a "true" profession, Deane opted instead to follow an altogether different path. Although she was well-paid as a lab technician, the Washington, D.C. native always felt that her true calling lay in a "more creative" field.

So the one-time aspiring designer spent her days off combing the CaliforniaMart, the hub of Los Angeles' fashion industry. In awe of the energy and excitement she encountered, Deane pounded the pavement in search of a new career.

Despite a significant decrease in salary and without

Company founder Leslie Deane with associate Ron Roessle, whom she credits with "creating harmony" in her work environment

any experience in the industry, Deane took on a position as a fabric broker to sell excess materials purchased by garment manufacturers. Six short months later, her tremendous success prompted Deane to take another leap of faith in her own abilities and Great Fabrications was born.

In 1980, the young single mother and her aptly-named son, Chance, relocated to Colorado where she launched a fabric business on the first floor of their loft apartment. This arrangement allowed Deane to be at home for her son and still create clothing and broker designer sample fabrics for clientele, who ranged from artists and costumers to homefurnishing designers.

Deane's reputation preceded her move back to Los Angeles. Through recommendations, she became a representative for one of the nation's oldest velvet mills just as various forms of the quality fabric were gaining popularity on the fashion scene.

In 1991, while she sought to strike a balance between her growing business and personal life, the answer arrived in the form of yoga instructor Ron Roessle.

"Ron is someone who is able to empower women, which is a gift since most designers are female," she says. "One of the best decisions I've made was in convincing him to become my business associate. Ron develops relationships with many of the designers, while I spend my time sourcing the fabrics. It's a nice balance."

Current clients, including some of the most prestigious names in the apparel industry such as Carole Little, Jessica McClintock and Victoria's Secret, acquire Deane's fabrics, which originate in Germany, Belgium, France, Asia and the United States.

In 1992, Deane's vision and eye for the unusual led her to bring a number of Eastern novelty fabrics from Korea, China and India into her thriving Western business.

"The future of the market is in novelty fabrics," says Deane. "It just so happens that's what I've been doing all these years. I think the key to my success in this industry is that I really care about providing my clients with a high quality product and an unparalleled level of customer service. I think of clothing design and the fabrics that are chosen as an art form and I enjoy the challenge of keeping one step ahead of the latest trend."

KAREN KANE, INC.

Success in the highly competitive world of fashion is a rare and elusive commodity. New labels appear on the runway in the fall and are distant memories when it's time for the spring showings. It's a tough business and nearly 20 years of growth and profit are considered exceptional.

That's especially true when a designer starts in a garage with little more than a dream and a wealth of talent. That was the situation in 1979 when Karen Kane and her husband, Lonnie, founded the company that bears her name. Today, Karen Kane has a 100,000-square-foot, state-of-the-art facility, four free standing California stores and more than 350 employees.

That's quite an impressive feat for this wife, mother and professional who has a basic belief that underpins all her creations.

"Comfort, ease, luxury, longevity; that's my fashion philosophy and I repeat it every time I design a new collection," said Kane. "A woman needs simple, stylish clothing, because life is complicated. I need to know my clothes are polished enough for work and relaxed enough for weekends, are easy to maintain, can travel with ease and have the integrity to last a long time; not just a season or two."

Those motivations grew from Kane's own life experiences. In the beginning she envisioned a collection of easy shapes in solids and prints that could be pulled together in many ways and her Sportswear group was born. That group is about mixing rich colors and patterns in a variety of fabrics.

Over the next few years, the pace of her life increased and so did the appreciation for her private time. That led to the development of her Easywear Line, a collection designed to keep pace with women's weekend pursuits such as running, hiking, skiing and sailing. Easywear provides the perfect pieces to pursue the great outdoors.

When Kane's second son was born in 1991, and her creative energy turned into a personal quest for the "life saver," which led to her Lifestyle group, a collection of indispensable items. Faded jeans, wear-under-everything T-shirts, year-round jackets and sweater sets are all Lifestyle hallmarks.

Kane sees her success as an ongoing collaboration with her total environment. She continues to be inspired by the beauty of the California landscape, urban architecture, city streets, the women with whom she works and most of all her family. She is a keen observer of details and carries a notebook at all times.

Kane also believes that community outreach is an important aspect of who she is and what she wants her company to be. She uses the company's visibility and resources to support various philanthropic causes. Big Sisters of America is a particular favorite. Kane sees Big Sisters as an avenue for young women to be mentored and encouraged to reach their full potentials. Kane also works with the Fashion Industries Guild and has seen her dedicated efforts rewarded by being nominated for California Designer of the Year.

Her designs have evolved into four collections; Karen Kane Lifestyle, Karen Kane Sportswear, Karen Kane Golf and the Karen Kane Collection. Through them she makes a recurring statement about her passion for life and her boundless creativity, while adhering to her central theme of "simple clothing for women who lead complicated lives."

Karen Kane

PARTNERS IN LOS ANGELES
MANUFACTURING & DISTRIBUTING

In addition to providing an astounding variety of goods for individuals and industry, area manufacturing and distribution companies also provide employment for Los Angeles residents.

Western Bagel

n an era of mega mergers and corporate downsizing, it is remarkably refreshing to hear the President and CEO of a company declare that when he hires a new employee, "I want it to be that employee's last job." Building employee loyalty is one of the strategies behind the phenomenal growth of Western Bagel. (So is the fact that bagels from Western Bagel are very, very good.) And, so too, is the fact that Steve Ustin, owner and CEO of Western Bagel is a devoted family man who believes that other people's families are just as important as his own. Steve is the third generation bagel baker upholding the long tradition of his astonishingly successful family business. The story of Western Bagel is a family saga, and the story began long ago when Louis Ustin left his native country to escape the Russian Revolution.

The story of the bagel began long before that. The bagel was born during the Italian Renaissance. No one has determined whether Michelangelo had a bagel by his side when he painted the Sistine Chapel, but ever since those glorious days, Europeans agreed that life was better with a bagel. And so, they brought their bagel recipes with them to New York, home to hordes of new immigrants who arrived full of hopes and dreams but still nostalgic for a taste of the old country.

Louis Ustin was one of those immigrants. He made his way to the Bronx where he studied to be a rabbi. His home was a bakery, and, during his student days, he learned the baking trade. It was an imperative decision in the Ustin family history. His son Dave followed in his father's footsteps and went to work for the bakery when he was nine years old. For four hours every Sunday morning, Dave counted bagels in the back of a delivery truck. He was paid the grand sum of 25 cents per day.

But Dave was never one to think small change. By the time he was 13 years old, Dave was working full time in a Bronx bakery. Later, when he overheard a union representative bemoan the fact that there were no good bagels in California, Dave set his sights on the West Coast and never looked back. Dave Ustin and his wife Ethel arrived in Los Angeles in 1946. In that year, there were more orange trees in Southern California than people. But all that would soon change. World War II had just ended a year before. Soldiers and sailors who had begun their service from out West decided to come back and settle down. Young families arrived from all over the country and began the famous baby boom. They were ready for a new life, and that included new tastes in food. Dave Ustin was certain they were ready for bagels.

With two partners, he set up shop at 324 West Pico Street. That was in January, 1947, and Western Bagel was the first bagel bakery in Los Angeles. The tempting aroma of baking bagels drew in the customers. The first week, Dave Ustin sold 4,773 dozen bagels. The grand total was $1,145.90, an average of 24 cents per dozen bagels. In the beginning he baked the big three: water, egg and salt. Ironically, even with more than 20 varieties and growing, Western Bagel's best-selling bagel is still

Western Bagel's 85-foot bagel oven bakes bagels by the dozens and dozens and dozens.

the water bagel. Dave Ustin was on to something.

Back in those days, Dave Ustin faced a challenge and a choice. Bagels were an East Coast thing. And East Coasters, particularly New Yorkers, had a big thing for bagels. A bagel had to be baked one way, and that was the New York way. If it wasn't a New York bagel, well, according to the purists, it wasn't a bagel. Dave Ustin dared to try something new. New York bagels didn't set well out West. His customers thought they were too hard and heavy. So, Dave Ustin baked the bagel that appealed to his customers. They liked the soft touch.

The Western Bagel bagel is crusty on the outside and soft and chewy on the inside. It became the prototype for what is now described as the "West Coast" bagel. It became so successful that, over the years, the competition stepped in to create many versions of the soft bagel. But Western Bagel started the trend. There will always be those who clamor for what they claim is the real thing, but Western Bagel understands the secret of its own success. They bake the best they know how to bake and don't aim to please absolutely everyone. So far, the strategy has worked. They've pleased so many people that distribution, solid throughout Southern California, includes more than a dozen other states, and the company is going global.

That growth took time, big dreams and big plans. After a decade at the original shop, business was booming, and it was time to expand. In 1958 Western Bagel moved to the Valley and added the onion bagel to its lineup. The Western Bagel factory is still at the same address on Sepulveda Boulevard. Next door is the retail store which specializes in serving caterers and other food service outlets. In 1993, a new facility on Saticoy more than doubled the factory's capacity to an output of 5,000 dozen bagels per hour. Off-site retail stores, operating under the name of Western Bagel Too, are located throughout the Valley, the Westside and Orange County: Woodland Hills, Granada Hills, Chatsworth, Northridge, Studio City, Westlake Village, Encino, Valencia, Redondo Beach, West Los Angeles, Burbank and Tustin. The company's growth plan includes adding two or three new stores every year.

Western Bagel thinks big, but not so big that quality

Production managers at Western Bagel are vigilant in their pursuit of quality control.

gets out of control. To keep up its high standards, it keeps its business under tight scrutiny. Rather than succumb to the lure of massive expansion, the company plans to build its business slowly and steadily. The company can afford to chart its own course because, as a family-owned business, it does not need to impress investors or analysts. The executives aren't looking over their shoulders and wondering if the stockholders are happy, so they're free to make the decisions that are good for Western Bagel in the long run. It's this unique independence and flexibility that contribute greatly to its success.

The retail stores are a good example. They cater to a select customer base, but they're good for Western Bagel's long-term business plan, too. Western Bagel Too shops make it easy to test market new bagels with a minimum investment. Customers let the company know right away if a new bagel is a hit or a miss. If it's

treat. Western Bagel also bakes bagels in several sizes which range in weight from one-and-a-half to five ounces. The three-ounce bagel has been the standard, but in recent years, customers have been asking for bigger bagels, and so the four-ounce bagel is increasingly popular.

a hit, it goes into broader distribution, and if it's a miss, it disappears. Naturally, the shops provide a guaranteed volume for the plants, and, in turn, the presence of the retail shops is a constant reinforcement for customers who can also shop elsewhere for the brand because it is widely distributed in Southern California supermarkets. Perhaps most importantly, the customers at Western Bagel Too are upscale, quality-conscious consumers who appreciate the value of buying the best.

Western Bagel's two factories turn out an astonishing 5,000 dozen bagels an hour, 24 hours a day. Do the math and that adds up to 1.4 million bagels a day. Couple that with the fact that the factories are in production 24 hours a day, seven days a week, and that is an enormous number of bagels produced every year, well over 500 million. And Steve Ustin doesn't intend to stop there.

A lot of people in a lot of places are craving bigger and better bagels, and Western Bagel is happy to oblige. The variety just keeps growing, and it ranges from the plain to the piquant. Among the most tempting, in addition to the basic water, egg, salt and onion, are strawberry, cranberry, blueberry, pizza, cheese, jalapeño, garlic, poppy seed, sesame seed, sourdough, pumpernickel, rye, everything-cheese and sundried tomatoes. Holidays are times for specialty bagels. For St. Patrick's Day, bagels go green, while at Halloween and Thanksgiving, pumpkin bagels are a delicious

Bagel baking is a complex business. Just storing the flour is a monumental job. The bakery's silos range in capacity from 50,000 to 120,000 pounds. (The smaller sizes are mandated due to the plant's location in a seismic-prone area.) High-fructose corn syrup is stored in a 6,000-pound tank. Assembly begins when the flour, which is 13.5 percent to 13.8 percent protein flour, is sifted and transferred to mixers. Flour and water, in a ratio of 49 percent to 51 percent, are mixed for eight minutes. The dough receives an immediate proof and then travels down chutes to the formers. From there, 48 balls of dough are dropped at one time on to wooden peel boards dusted with rice flour. The next step is for the peel boards to be racked and placed in a proof box with high heat and humidity for one hour. Then they head to a 120-rack retarder where they rest until they are ready to bake. Next it's time for a quick 45-second

plunge into boiling water. Then it's into the oven where they bake for eight to eleven minutes. Finally, the bagels go into packages of four or six, and they're ready for shipping.

All this activity requires the close scrutiny of a large staff dedicated to perfection. Western Bagel is now in its second generation of management, but President and CEO Steve Ustin, Dave Ustin's son, prefers to call himself a third generation bagel baker, in honor of his grandfather. Steve came on board the family business at an early age when his mother would give him stale bagels instead of teething rings. In elementary school, Steve swept the factory floors, made dough and ran the ovens. He worked at the bakery all through high school and college. In 1972, Steve bought out his father's surviving partner, and eventually the management of Western Bagel passed from father to son. Steve has high hopes that his four children will choose to make Western Bagel their careers as well. So far, his two oldest have seized the opportunity to carry on the family tradition, Corie as Marketing Director and Jeff as Production Manager.

Steve Ustin is as proud of his family as he is of his business, and his management style reflects his belief that work and family can be mutually supportive. He believes it's important to take the time to watch kids grow up, and he doesn't reserve that privilege for himself alone. He is one CEO who really cares about his people, and he exemplifies the philosophy that it takes great people to produce a great product. He believes that his company is only as good as the people who work there, and he has created a work environment where attending a child's soccer game is as important as participating in a marketing meeting. In return, his employees are immensely loyal, and morale at the company is extremely high. The management team has been with Western Bagel for years and years, and their CEO has never had to fire anyone.

He is reluctant to publicize it, but the Chairman of Western Bagel cares for his neighborhood as well as for his employees. The company has adopted three local schools and is actively involved in the lives of the students. Many of them are from very low-income families, so distressed that siblings sometimes skip school because they have to share shoes and jackets. Steve and his team celebrate the holidays with the children, wrapping gift baskets and bringing breakfasts (bagels, of course, with cream cheese) for everyone. For select children who are truly in dire need, the company arranges an annual Christmas shopping trip to a local mall which opens early for their benefit. Older students interested in part-time work are invited to apply to Western Bagel. Many of them are bilingual, and they tutor Western Bagel employees who need to improve their English language skills.

Steve Ustin, Western Bagel's president and CEO, is standing next to his father, Dave Ustin, the company's founder.

Western Bagel has set an ambitious agenda for the future. In addition to rolling out the new retail outlets, the company is in distribution in Japan and Australia and is setting its sights on the European and Central American markets. With more than 50 years of remarkably steady growth to guide him, Steve Ustin is confidently leading his company into the next generation. He's proud to enroll his children in the family business, knowing that Western Bagel's more than half century of dedication to quality and service will be in good hands with the fourth generation of Ustin bagel bakers.

A-1 INTERNATIONAL FOODS

he A-1 International Foods history is rich in vision and dedication. The company was founded in 1964 when a group of investors led by Marvin Pearlman created a small distribution company. Recognizing the need for a company that delivers quality merchandise and outstanding service, Mr. Pearlman transformed the small company into a major supplier of specialty food products to the supermarket industry. He took control of the firm, and now, more than 30 years later, the Los Angeles-based company is a leader in the marketing and distribution of specialty food products.

Marvin's dedication to service continues through each of A-1's 600 employees, throughout ten Western states.

From the beginning, the company's mission has been "to provide excellence in sales, marketing and distribution services to the food industry, with passion, expertise and innovation." The company supports this mission with the philosophy that "Service not only means having enough people to do the job, but the best people with the right talents and experience in the proper positions."

(Left to right) Ross, Marvin and Mitch Pearlman.

A-1 International Foods Los Angeles office and main distribution center.

Ross and Mitch Pearlman, Marvin's sons, exemplify this philosophy. In 1976, Ross joined A-1's then half-dozen employees as a buyer and has worked his way up to his current position as company president. Mitch joined A-1 in 1984 as the purchasing manager and currently serves as the company's senior vice president of Marketing and Human Resources.

Through the years, the family business expanded and evolved to meet the challenges of an increasingly diverse and complex marketplace to become the largest privately-held specialty food distributor in the Western United States.

A-1 currently handles more than 13,000 items in over 700 product lines in all ethnic and specialty categories. The company emphasizes national and international brands, namely those that are recognized by consumers and that bring the maximum amount of marketing and promotional support to retailers. Understanding the need to be responsive to specific, local product requests, A-1 also carries a wide variety of regional lines.

A-1 International serves a variety of retail customers, from major Western chain stores such as Albertson's, Lucky, Ralphs and Vons, to one and two-store independent markets in Idaho, Utah and Montana. Large and small alike, A-1's customers demand a distributor that provides a complete selection of specialty and ethnic foods including natural, gourmet, organic and seasonal items.

Four of A-1's Senior Executives; Sandy Johnson, David Billings, Ken Croft and Peter Kalin.

Founder and C.E.O. Marvin Pearlman

President Ross Pearlman

Orders are palletized and prepared for delivery.

Automated order sortation system allows for next day delivery.

"We want to supply everything our customers need," says Marvin Pearlman. "If they want an item, we get it for them — no matter how difficult. We're a customer-driven company. We do everything that a full-service DSD distributor is known for, but we think we do it a little better and more efficiently than our competitors."

Marvin attributes the company's success to the industry's need for a service-oriented distributor.

"There was a real need for a company like ours in Southern California when we first started," says the company's chief executive officer. "We provided a service that saved labor for supermarkets and brought a higher level of expertise to specialty foods."

A-1 continues to be a Direct Service Distributor and, through its employees, maintains a high level of service.

"Our account executives work with supermarket headquarters to help retailers determine item selection based on demographic factors," says Ross Pearlman.

"Then a salesperson visits each location as often as three times per week to determine inventory needs and to transmit orders electronically to a centralized warehouse system. If an order comes in at 5 or 6 p.m., it leaves the warehouse before the sun comes up. That's what sets us apart from the competition."

Staying at the forefront of technology is a major factor contributing to the development of A-1's business. In 1992, A-1 outgrew its main 72,000-square-foot warehouse and three small satellite facilities. The company currently operates out of a state-of-the-art 260,000-square-foot warehouse and a nearby 115,000-square-foot satellite in Los Angeles.

A-1's automated order sortation system is one of the most sophisticated order fulfillment systems in the

specialty food business, with daily shipments exceeding 40,000 cases. As with all facets of A-1's business, however, quantity never supersedes quality: every customer order is guaranteed top-of-the-line handling.

"Technology is vital," observes Ross Pearlman. "A-1 is committed to remaining at the forefront of the industry's technological advances. We're known for the services we provide our customers, and our investment in technology allows us to do that better than our competitors."

Over the years, the role of the distributor has changed dramatically. While retailers continue to rely heavily on store-level services that distributors provide, they now require total marketing expertise. Despite rapid growth, A-1 has remained a family-owned business and has been able to retain a family atmosphere that permeates all aspects of the company's operation, especially its commitment to service. The bottom line for A-1 International Foods has always been, and continues to be, customer service.

"Service is the key word and the key element in the distributor business," says Marvin Pearlman. "As an industry, we provide a lot of labor and expertise to our retail customers. Studies show that direct store delivery is very profitable to supermarkets. We're confident that specialty food distributors will continue to play an important part in the supermarket industry and that A-1 International will maintain its current leadership position."

I.S. Director Rory Troglia

V.P. of Operations
Michael Ladisa ensures
that the fleet delivers.

ANGELUS SANITARY CAN MACHINE COMPANY

n 144 countries worldwide, a deceptively simple looking product, the can, affects the lifestyles of billions of people. Taken for granted by most of us, the unassuming can paradoxically requires an immensely precise technical and organizational expertise to produce. Without it, much of the convenience we enjoy of near endless foodstuffs, beverages, and many other products would not be possible. Responsible for the basic expertise producing the machinery to close approximately 65 percent of all finished cans is a fascinating Los Angeles-based business known by the somewhat sobering name of Angelus Sanitary Can Machine Company.

Angelus, founded in 1910 by inventor Henry L. Guenther, has based its reputation on perfecting Guenther's revolutionary machinery for closing or "seaming" ends on cans. Since food and beverage cans must be airtight to insure the safety of their contents, the process is vital, and closely regulated by governments and various international institutes. Guenther designed and patented machinery for producing what is known as double seams on cans, which satisfies today's stringent requirements of the European CE Marking and EU Directives, and is manufactured under an ISO9001 Quality Management System.

This photo shows assembly technician setting pin gauge height for can and adjusting machine's seaming rolls to proper can seam specifications.

The production of a gassing turret in process. It is being manufactured to specified close tolerance dimensions on a numerically controlled precision cutting machine tool.

Maury Koeberle, President of Angelus emphasizes how important such official approval is to the company's product refinements and continued preeminence in its field. Since expanding markets are predominantly international and have all started incorporating common technical standards of acceptance, Angelus knows that meeting these international specifications is fundamental. The level of engineering proficiency Angelus practices has actually helped define many of the specifications.

The company takes its work seriously, both technically and personally. As the dominant player in its industry, its products are used in most can manufacturing countries of the world. Formulating and administering its own set of operating guidelines, Angelus secures its position both as a technological leader and as an exemplary manager of people. The company is as proud of its workforce as of its products. The 500 company employees are unusually loyal, the average having worked for Angelus at least twelve years. This is due as

much to Angelus's commitment to its employees' job security as to the cordial relations it maintains with the workers' United Steel Workers Union.

As a practical matter, the wedding of precise technology to quality human relations is fundamental to the company's success. Starting in its Calibration Laboratory, where highly-trained specialists calibrate all company instruments to specific tolerances often as fine as .000020 (20 millionths) inch, training and servicing the needs of its employee's is uppermost in Angelus management's minds.

With over 282,000 square feet of plant on ten acres of land, and with thousands of separate design and manufacturing processes requiring constant and consistent coordination, satisfied teamworkers make the difference between competence and excellence. From research and design, where computers and trained engineers mutually inspire product innovation, to the shop floor, where trained machinists and mechanics create

All instruments used for measurement at Angelus are controlled and held to specified tolerances to ensure measurement of parts are correct.

industry-related associations dedicated to this sort of future watching, as well as by relating closely to its client base's changing needs.

Throughout the fifty United States, Europe, Asia, Canada, the Southern Hemisphere, and in all developing nations, Angelus attends to this daunting task of keeping the can up to date with a changing world. A seemingly innocuous endeavor, Angelus's work impacts positively upon human lives to an extent rarely considered by most of us. Its efforts help feed an endlessly increasing world population, without fanfare, perhaps, but with telling economic efficiency.

As world leaders in the design, manufacture, and service of Can Seaming Machinery, Angelus is a prime example of the vitality that creative technology and humanized industrial people power can bring to the evolution of a world on the cusp of the 21st century. It is also commendable that the company's own view of itself revolves around its perceived accomplishment of having provided stable and secure employment for its workers over the past 87 years. If ever the word symbiotic were appropriate, it is here in the activities of this quietly ubiquitous behemoth.

precision parts and assemble the final equipment, teamwork is essential.

What precisely is the final product that Angelus manufactures? It is large, intricately conceived manufacturing equipment which brings together the edge of a metal, plastic, or composite container to its metal top, rolling and binding the two thin gauges of material into an airtight connection. Accomplishing this requires that an intricate Angelus machine place a metal top on the upper edge of a can and form both metal edges around themselves — twice. This is done at the rate of up to 2,500 cans per minute. The result is an hermetically-sealed container, impervious to leakage or outside intrusion.

To achieve top quality control, Angelus designs and manufactures 90 percent of the hundreds of precision parts which comprise its final product. With an astute marketing perspective, the company constantly monitors and assesses emerging worldwide trends in food and beverage processing and packaging. This comes about by maintaining liaison with various

Shows service technician checking and analyzing final inspection of can seam. The physical and dimensional qualities of the seam must meet customer's specifications.

A machine operator at a laser machine which is capable of making precision cuts in steel, stainless and other materials to .001 inch accuracy and up to .625 inches in material thickness.

DUNN-EDWARDS

For over seven decades, Dunn-Edwards has built upon a legacy of painting industry leadership that began with the company's original owners.

What started as a small wallcovering store in 1925 has evolved into the largest family-owned paint corporation in the Southwest and the region's leading producer and supplier of paints and architectural coatings.

In the days when it was still deemed illegal to cook varnish within Los Angeles, Frank "Buddy" Dunn set up shop just beyond the city limits to manufacture his own line of paints in 1937.

Interior of manufacturing facility.

Accompanied by only two employees in a 5,000-square-foot factory, Dunn was joined a year later by his friend, Arthur Edwards, who bought out Dunn's partners to form the Dunn-Edwards Corporation. Previously a painting contractor and then top salesman for National Lead Company, Edwards brought a wealth of knowledge and expertise of the paint contracting business to the new venture.

During World War II, Dunn-Edwards began an ongoing expansion, opening the first in a string of full-service stores dedicated to serving professional painting contractors, architects and design professionals throughout Southern California, Arizona and Nevada.

Dozens of Dunn-Edwards full-service centers are currently conveniently located throughout the West. Each store is staffed with sales professionals who possess the in-depth knowledge necessary to help customers choose the right paint, color and application techniques for the demanding requirements of specific commercial, new residential or repaint projects.

Prior to his passing in the mid-1950s, Dunn sold his interest back to the corporation.

Bud Dunn and Arthur Edwards, Company founders.

Since that time, the Edwards family has maintained control of the privately-held paint company, handed down from father to sons.

It seems all three of Edwards' offspring were destined to follow in their father's footsteps. After graduating from Occidental College with a degree in chemistry, and the University of Michigan with an MS in Chemical Engineering, oldest son Ken immediately went to work for Battelle Memorial Institute as a principal chemist in the Organic Coatings Division before joining his father's firm in 1958.

Ed Edwards graduated from Occidental College with a degree in Physics in 1959, and after doing some graduate work at the University of Washington in the field of Physics, he obtained a teaching position in the City of Los Angeles school system where he taught for several years. He subsequently joined the Dunn-Edwards Corporation, worked as a store manager and ultimately became involved with the Corporation's Wallpaper Distribution and Sales division. He left Dunn-Edwards in 1973 to work as a wallcovering consultant and eventually purchased his own firm, Environmental Graphics Inc. He currently serves on the Dunn-Edwards Board of Directors and oversees special projects for the corporation, particularly those of a political or environmental nature.

Dozens of Dunn-Edwards full-service centers are currently conveniently located throughout the West.

Jim Edwards joined the corporation after high school working at various positions in the stores and then becoming a specialist in the development of spray equipment, brushes and rollers. He was for many years vice president in charge of sales and now, like his brothers, serves on the Board of Directors and directs projects for the Board.

Ken Edwards and his brothers, Ed and Jim, currently carry on the company tradition to "be a leader and innovator for producing the 'best' paint possible."

The key to company's success to date can be directly traced to its philosophy of "providing supreme customer service, supplying the highest quality of materials available for getting a job done and charging a fair price" as well as its understanding that "superior performing products spread further, look better, go on easier, cover better and last longer" than inferior products.

"Nothing can take the place of hard work in determining the success of a company," says Ken Edwards. "At Dunn-Edwards, we are structured and continually strive to produce the finest product on the market."

It seems many industry experts agree with Edward's simple philosophy: Dunn-Edwards' paints' protect and beautify some of the most recognized commercial, industrial and residential buildings in the Southwest, including Los Angeles historic Union Station. Its paints and colors can be found on such diverse projects as department stores, high-rise office buildings, apartment homes, hospitals, hotels, schools and even the most famous amusement theme parks in America.

Dunn-Edwards products have proven effective on all surfaces in a wide range of challenging climates, from desert heat to coastal moisture. To achieve this, they are willing to manufacturing different coatings for the various environments that they encounter.

Dunn-Edwards' growth over the years can also be attributed to the company's continued commitment to research and

Old Flower Street Store, Original Company Headquarters, Los Angeles.

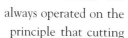

Historic photos of the early days of paint manufacturing.

development and manufacturing innovations.

The company's ability to manufacture the industry's finest paints stems from having the most technologically advanced research and development available. Chemists in the R&D group at Dunn-Edwards have been drawn together from around the world to challenge the leading edge of technology to achieve product excellence. Beyond research and development, these scientists meticulously monitor new paint products for quality and performance and redevelop existing products to meet current environmental standards.

The Dunn-Edwards manufacturing plants, located in California, Arizona and New Mexico, produce high quantities of paint without compromising quality or flexibility. Among the finest in the industry, the company's factory mixers and tinters produce paints and coatings of unequaled quality that remain constant over time.

Quality assurance programs are implemented to monitor incoming raw materials, paint in progress and finished products to "make a complex production as trouble-free as possible."

Dunn-Edwards has always operated on the principle that cutting

corners in ingredients, formulations or production will negatively impact the quality of paint.

The company does, however, believe in being on the "cutting-edge" of technology. The Quik-Tint store and factory color computer systems are unrivaled in reproducing any color placed in its memory with absolute accuracy day after day, in quantities ranging from a single one-gallon container to hundreds of five-gallon buckets.

The industry's greatest precision, predictability and control of color are central to the Dunn-Edwards proprietary Galax-Z color system. Synchronized with the company's state-of-the-art manufacturing process, the Galaz-Z system was developed exclusively for the painting industry's unique need for a infinite range of color options.

The key to this cutting-edge color system is its computerized mathematical paint formulations and even allows a customized subtle shade between the system's standard hues with equal precision.

Additionally, Dunn-Edwards is the only paint manufacturer that offers factory-quality color consistency for small batches mixed and tinted in its stores. Because its store colorants and formulations are identical to Dunn-Edwards' quality-controlled factory colorants and formulations, the customer can always be assured of consistency in all aspects of oil and water-based paint performance.

Since performance also relies heavily on the proper application, Dunn-Edwards manufactures its own line of synthetic roller covers and premium quality brushes. Handcrafted to maximize application control and efficiency, these brushes bear a distinction its competitors can't claim: Dunn-Edwards thoroughly tests its brushes in high-performance paints by Committees of Professionals Painting Contractors. Brother Jim has purchased the brush and roller division from Dunn-Edwards and is expanding it to provide the entire coatings industry with the finest brushes and rollers.

The principals at Dunn-Edwards extend the same commitment to members of its "extended family." Since 1992, the company's employees have implemented a "Unity in the Community" vocational training program to give Los Angeles residents a chance to begin productive careers by learning painting skills.

This commitment to community, customer service and quality products have always been the cornerstone of Dunn-Edwards' business philosophy.

The Twenty-Year Club, established in the 1950s, provides that every two years, employees who have worked for the company for 20 years or more are treated to an all-expense paid weekend at an out-of-town location to enjoy golf, tennis, fishing or sightseeing. An awards banquet, held on a Saturday evening, includes a brief biography of each new inductee accompanied by the presentation of a specially engraved 20-year watch.

Future plans include continued research and development of innovative specialty products, manufacturing technologies, quality control techniques, distribution processes and sales-support systems.

Dunn-Edwards' resources, manufacturing technologies, research and development efforts, sales and marketing initiatives and quality products create a distinct competitive advantage as the company enters into the new millennium.

Interior of manufacturing facility.

Dunn-Edward's Galaz-Z system was developed exclusively for the painting industry's unique need for a infinite range of color options. (Top left)

TOMCO AUTO PRODUCTS, INC.

For more than 50 years, Tomco Auto Products, Inc. has succeeded because of its commitment to keep ahead of automotive changes and trends. It was vision that enabled Tomco to become the world's leader in carburetor remanufacturing and supply. It is foresight that will drive the company in new directions as the last remaining cars and trucks equipped with carburetors gradually disappear from freeways and roads.

The Grumet brothers established Tomco in 1946 as one of the original "green" businesses, recycling used automobile parts by remanufacturing and reselling them. They opened their shop on Georgia Street, near the present site of the Convention Center. Their business grew to the point where they needed larger facilities, and in 1963, they moved to a 30,000-square-foot facility on Santa Fe Avenue.

When Victor Moss bought the company in 1976, Tomco Auto Electric Co., its name at the time, was a struggling local auto parts remanufacturer. Although Tomco had been in business for 30 years, the competition and high interest rates had become too much for the Grumets, who had taken Tomco as far as they could. Tomco had annual sales of $500,000 with 20 employees and customers limited to California, Arizona and Nevada.

Richard Smith, who was a friend and supplier to the Grumets, was working for Maremont Corporation at this time. The Grumets knew that Moss, new to the automotive aftermarket, would need some sales help, so they arranged a meeting between the two. Moss immediately hired Smith as vice president of sales and head of marketing.

Moss and Smith recognized the need to expand the business. They decided to concentrate on filling the vacuum in the market for remanufactured carburetors. Imported cars were increasing in popularity and the demand was especially great for Japanese carburetors. Although Tomco still offered a wide range of remanufactured auto parts, such as fuel pumps, distributors, alternators, generators, starters and water pumps, the emphasis on carburetors would prove to be a crucial one.

Because of an industry-wide lack of organization, carburetor orders were the most difficult to fill for all remanufacturers. A 60 percent order fill rate was considered excellent, meaning almost half of all the cars in the country, especially Japanese imports, were waiting as long as four to five weeks to be serviced. For the Volkswagen Beetle, an American company manufactured a unit called the Bug Spray, a modified domestic carburetor to replace the original part. Although some mechanics tried to do the same for Japanese cars, these parts never quite measured up to the original

them in such a way that order fill rates would rise beyond 90 percent.

The key was the new information system developed by Moss, Maltzman and Smith. In addition to reorganizing carburetor remanufacturing, Tomco had to educate the core suppliers, mechanics and parts stores they supplied. This was a monumental task because there was no standard catalog for carburetors. Each original equipment carburetor manufacturer had their own designs, specifications and parts, usually by vehicle model produced, so Tomco had to buy as many available cores as possible, carefully organizing and categorizing them.

In the early days, it was common practice for core suppliers to bring a truckload of cores to the factory, only to find that Tomco was overstocked on the type of cores they had on the truck that day. The contents of the truck was always a mystery, as the suppliers simply brought whatever they had to sell to Tomco. These purchasing methods were a poor use of time and resources, so Moss designed a unique catalog and numbering system to identify all cores, supported by information systems that determined which cores were needed. This, in turn, forced the core suppliers to learn exactly what they were selling. Eventually, the Tomco catalog would become the industry standard by which core suppliers worked.

Japanese parts. Japanese carburetors were more complicated than domestic models and the conversion of mass quantities was not a viable option.

Smith had many years of experience with imported cars and parts, as well as a connection to Nikki Carburetor Co., one of Japan's largest carburetor manufacturers. He managed to attend a board meeting in Japan and convinced the president of the company that if the aftermarket, which included auto parts stores as well as independent repair shops, could not get replacement parts for Japanese cars, those cars would eventually become extinct in the United States. Smith made such a strong argument for a working agreement between Tomco and the Japanese company that he was immediately declared the first American VIP in the company and was given carte blanche and access to all of the Japanese plants.

Smith had opened the door for Tomco's nationwide expansion, but he also created a whole new set of obstacles to overcome. Tomco needed capital and a marketing plan. Donald Maltzman joined Tomco as Moss' partner in 1977 and this new team increased the company size to more than 30 employees.

In February, 1980, Tomco decided to discontinue its other product lines and offer a complete line of carburetors, backed by its new relationship with Japan and a new system of organizing carburetor cores (used carburetors which can be remanufactured). Tomco was steadily building a healthy supply of cores, organizing

In the immaculate assembly plant, import carburetor remanufacturing was perfected utilizing the core inventory

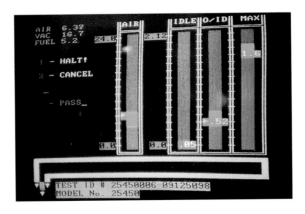

and new component parts. This was no easy task, since carburetors were at their peak of development, becoming more complicated and intricate in design to satisfy fuel economy and emission control requirements. Once the import carburetors were perfected, Tomco expanded its focus on domestic units. Armed with its new information systems, the highest quality component parts and a growing inventory of cores, Tomco was changing the world of carburetor remanufacturing as it expanded its distribution throughout the United States.

Change did not come easily to the automotive aftermarket. Although it was universally recognized that carburetor remanufacturing was in need of a revolution of sorts, not all of Tomco's customers and suppliers wanted to learn new ways to distribute product and process cores. But, Moss made it difficult not to learn. He'd pay $25 for a core instead of the usual $10, if it was the core he was looking for. This allowed him to get the cores he really needed to offer a complete domestic and import line of carburetors. There are more than 1,600 part numbers in the Tomco catalog, covering domestic and import units, governor controlled units for trucks and throttle body fuel injection (TBI) units. Since 1987, Tomco has maintained a stock of more than 500,000 cores, a significant portion of the United States supply of cores.

As a service leader in the industry, Tomco established training programs for jobbers having difficulty selling the right parts. Smith did much of the training himself, eventually establishing formal training clinics for technicians, which continue today. Later, Tomco added 1-800 toll free troubleshooting hotlines. This put certified technicians just a phone call away to answer any questions regarding the installation or selection of Tomco's carburetors.

Rounding out the education program were the famous flyers and instruction manuals featuring Tommy Tomco, the cat. The instruction manual, which is included with each carburetor shipped, was illustrated by a Disney trained artist. In the manual, Tommy Tomco and his sidekick, a bird named Hi-Octane, illustrate the proper installation procedures and well as solutions to common installation problems. A companion brochure, "10 Ways to Avoid Buying a Carburetor," illustrates troubleshooting procedures to be certain the carburetor actually needs replacement.

In 1987, most new vehicle production shifted from carburetion to fuel injection, thus bringing an end to an era of automotive fuel delivery. This created a tremendous opportunity as tens of millions of carbureted vehicles would need quality remanufactured carburetors to extend the service life of the vehicle because new carburetors would no longer be available in the marketplace. A decade after the elimination of carbu-

retors from new vehicle production, Tomco continues to thrive. In 1989 Tomco was named "Remanufacturer of the Year" by the prestigious Automotive Service Industry Association (ASIA). The obvious question arises as to how and why a company which remanufactures a part which is no longer made can keep growing.

Richard Schoenfeld served as Tomco's outside CPA for eight years before he joined the company in 1986. Named executive vice president in 1993, he assumed daily operating responsibilities, building on the successes of Moss, Maltzman and Smith. Tomco increased its profitability through teamwork and operating improvements, enabling the company to establish an ESOP program and begin the transition to employee ownership.

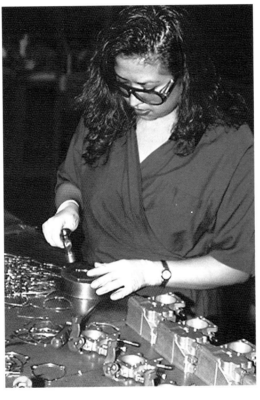

Schoenfeld estimates that there are approximately 180 million cars and light trucks in the United States of which 80 million use carburetors or TBI units for fuel delivery. The decline in the number of vehicles using carburetors has been steady, but slow, leaving Tomco as one of the few national suppliers of remanufactured carburetors for those 80 million vehicles. If one considers that the average age of cars and trucks on the road is steadily rising each year, it is not hard to see that the need for remanufactured carburetors will continue to create viable business for Tomco for many years.

But Tomco isn't waiting around for the last car with a carburetor to die. Just as Moss and Maltzman, still the principal shareholders, and Smith found a niche for their fledgling company, Schoenfeld is planning to take Tomco, a national remanufacturer with 350 employees, into expanding areas of fuel delivery. As they continue to supply the nation with the highest quality remanufactured carburetors, Tomco plans on becoming the leader in remanufactured diesel fuel delivery systems.

That's right. Diesel.

Every American on the road imagines those huge trucks and buses belching thick black smoke as they clog up highways and the atmosphere. The reality is that diesel technology has advanced dramatically since those trucks and buses were built. Diesel engine builders continue to develop better catalytic converters, inter-coolers, turbochargers and injection systems for modern diesel engines. These newly designed engines are more fuel efficient and produce less (in quantity and toxicity) harmful emissions than conventional gasoline engines.

Tomco has recognized that diesel engines are built to last a long time, running relatively maintenance free. Those old trucks and buses are just getting broken in when they reach 250,000 miles. The new diesel technology is being adapted to and retrofitted in some of the older equipment as it enters the repair cycle. The newly designed engines have quietly entered the United States market in airport shuttles, hotel shuttles and rental car shuttles around our airports as well as pickup trucks and small delivery vans. This is merely the tip of the iceberg. The technology is here and Tomco will become a dominant player in this industry.

While this market develops, Tomco will continue to service the 80 million vehicles in its target market. When one of those vehicles needs a remanufactured carburetor, it will most likely be Tomco who supplies that mechanic or parts store with the same high quality parts as it has since 1946.

ULTRAMAR DIAMOND SHAMROCK CORPORATION

Much of Southern California's automobile-driven economy runs on gasoline produced at the Wilmington refinery of Ultramar Diamond Shamrock Corporation. Situated next to the Port of Long Beach, the 137-acre Ultramar facility produces more than 115,000 barrels of gasoline, diesel fuel and jet fuel every day. More importantly, as of 1996, Ultramar became the first refinery in the state to produce 100 percent of its gasoline to comply with cleaner-burning standards mandated by the California Air Resources Board (CARB).

Ultramar's roots date back to the 1920s, when the Union Pacific Railroad found oil and installed "grasshopper" production pumps on easements on either side of their railway tracks in Wilmington and Long Beach. The company then sent the unrefined crude oil directly to other nearby refineries to be processed into gasoline.

Southern California sits on deposits of a very heavy, high sulfur crude oil referred to as "sour" crude. The impurities make it more difficult to refine than oil pumped anywhere else. A Southern California refinery needs to take many more steps than are necessary with lighter crude oils in order to make each barrel into the largest amount of fuel-grade gasoline. Each step in the refining process increases the value of the product, as

well as its cost to produce. The fact that California crude oil, while heavy with impurities, is also among the most inexpensive oils in the world makes this extensive refining process cost-effective.

In 1969, under the name Union Pacific Benefaction Project (UPBP), the Union Pacific Railroad built a topping plant to begin the process of refining oil and add to the company's revenue stream. The company installed one crude unit, a vacuum unit to take out gas oils, a sulfur train, and a coker unit to remove the coke, a coal-like material. Topping is one of the first steps in refining required to upgrade crude oil to higher value products.

UPBP began operations processing the crude pumped from their local land plus quantities brought in by pipeline from nearby oil fields in Long Beach, the San Joaquin Valley and offshore at Santa Maria. The resulting oil was not yet at gasoline grade. The company sold this partially refined oil, called intermediate feed stock, to other Long Beach area refineries such as Unocal, which in turn manufactured fuel grade gasoline.

Union Pacific officials quickly realized that operating railroads did not prepare them for running an oil refinery. To secure knowledgeable management, in late 1969 Union Pacific bought Champlin Petroleum, a well established company with refineries in Oklahoma and Texas. They changed UPBP's name to Champlin to align it with the older company and brought in Champlin's experienced managers to run the Wilmington facility.

By the late 1970s, the continuous expansion of Los Angeles created an ever increasing demand for gasoline. With a captive crude supply and minimal transportation costs, Champlin found itself perfectly positioned to expand into gasoline refining. In 1979, the company doubled in size by installing a second crude unit and coker. They added naphtha and gas oil hydrotreaters to remove further impurities from the crude. In oil

The Wilmington refinery of Ultramar Diamond Shamrock Corporation

ing into retailing. They supplied product to their stations and sold the rest to other oil companies.

Champlin closed the Oklahoma refinery in 1987 and sold the Texas refinery in 1988. The Venezuelan company which purchased the Texas refinery and retained the Champlin name, and the company managing the Wilmington refinery changed its name to Union Pacific Resources Company (UPRC).

A short time later, UPRC decided that while pulling oil out of the ground was not difficult, they didn't want to continue operating refineries. In late 1989 UPRC was sold to Ultramar PLC, a British petroleum company with refineries and exploration facilities all over the world.

Lasmo, Ltd., another British company, engineered a hostile takeover of Ultramar PLC in 1991. Lasmo made it known from the outset that they were not interested in refining or other downstream operations; they bought the company solely for its oil leases and exploration rights. When Lasmo tried to sell off the Ultramar Wilmington and Quebec City refineries, the people running those plants offered to buy them, saying that they could raise more money as a new company than Lasmo could by selling them individually.

Ultramar Corporation was formed in April of 1991 to acquire Ultramar Inc. in California and Ultramar Canada Inc. Through the merger acquisitions firm of Goldman Sachs, an Initial Public Offering was made on the New York Stock Exchange. Enough money was raised through the stock sale to buy the company from Lasmo, and Ultramar was now an independent, privately owned company consisting of refineries in Wilmington and Quebec City, Canada.

During the last quarter of 1996, Ultramar underwent a friendly "merger of equals" with Diamond Shamrock, a company with two refineries in Texas. Under the name Ultramar Diamond Shamrock, the

A Beacon gas station in Sand City, California, one of 166 Ultramar Diamond Shamrock outlets in California supplied by the Wilmington refinery.

refining, hydrogen works as a "magic bullet" to help desulfurize crudes. The product which results from this process, naphtha, is gasoline-range, though not yet at the quality required for running automobiles. Again, Champlin sold this intermediate feed stock to Unocal's refinery in Wilmington.

From the manufacture of naphtha, it was only a short step for Champlin to expand into refining gasoline. In early 1982, the company installed a fluid catalytic cracker, an alkylation unit and a butamer unit to maximize gasoline production. This placed the Wilmington facility on par with other Long Beach area refineries such as Unocal, Chevron and Mobil in creating the gasoline that runs Los Angeles.

The process of refining crude oil into gasoline consists of linking the right number of hydrocarbons into molecule chains. Hydrocarbon chains of varying lengths form different kinds of products. A string of two carbon molecules results in ethane, three in propane, four in butane. Gasoline range molecular chains consist of five to nine linked carbon molecules. In the manufacturing process, shorter chains must be spliced together and longer chains must be broken apart and recombined to create as much gasoline as possible.

Champlin entered the retail market in California by acquiring 300 Beacon Oil stations in 1981. This allowed the company to move from gasoline wholesal-

company acquired Total Petroleum North America in 1997 and with it three more refineries in Oklahoma, Colorado and Michigan.

The combined Ultramar Diamond Shamrock ranks as one of the largest independent refining and marketing companies in North America, with assets of over $5 billion and 23,000 employees. Its seven refineries have a combined capacity of 650,000 barrels per day, sold through approximately 6,300 retail gasoline outlets in 21 states and six Canadian provinces.

Every day, the Wilmington refinery throughputs 125,000 barrels of crude oil and intermediate feedstocks, and produces 65,000 barrels of CARB gasoline, 30,000 barrels of diesel fuel and 14,000 barrels of jet fuel. The 1,500 tons of coke produced each day are sold for heating and steel manufacture. The daily 250 tons of sulfur removed from the oil is sold for pharmaceutical and fertilizer uses. What's left when the refining process ends, a sludge called slurry oil, is sold for use in asphalt. Nothing is wasted and nothing is casually dumped back into the environment.

There's a large marketplace unseen by the public where gasoline manufacturing companies provide for each other's needs. When consumers buy a particular brand of gasoline, there is no guarantee which company has manufactured it. Additive products differentiate the brands and any refinery can make specific formula-

tions. Thus if the Mobil refinery goes down, Ultramar might provide their gasoline for a while, or Chevron might supply Arco's needs. Southern Californians demand so much gasoline in the course of the year, most brands must supplement their local production by buying gasoline from other companies. Ultramar regularly supplies gasoline to other companies as well as to their own retail outlets.

The greatest expense in marketing gasoline comes from transportation costs. Just because Ultramar has stations in Northern California does not mean that gasoline from the Wilmington refinery ever reaches there. To hold down the cost of transporting gasoline, refineries in different areas will trade barrels — create gasolines with identical formulations and then supply each other's areas on a quid pro quo basis. For example, when the Exxon refinery near Sacramento supplies gasoline to Ultramar stations in Northern California, Ultramar reciprocates by supplying an equivalent number of barrels to Exxon facilities in Southern California. The gas has been made available without incurring massive transportation costs, resulting in savings for the oil companies and consumers.

In 1996, Ultramar became the first refinery to produce commercial quantities of gasoline that meets the demanding standards set by the California Air Resources Board (CARB). The conversion to manufacturing CARB gasoline required the design, construction and start-up of seven new and a dozen modified refining units. The company spent approximately $300 million to lower the content of benzene, olefins, sulfur and aromatics in its gasolines, bringing it in line with California's standards — the toughest in the world.

Ultramar's Wilmington facility conforms to the highest standards set by the Environmental Protection Agency. There is no visible pollution, no noxious odors. Management likens their emissions control policy to placing a large envelope or bubble around the refinery. The company is the first in Southern California to reach reclaim status, which means they have in place the equipment necessary to monitor the refinery's pollutants, in compliance with the South Coast Air Quality Management District (SCAQMD). Ultramar installed 17 continuous emission monitoring stations (CEMS), small buildings containing sophisticated equipment for measuring pollutants, at a cost of $3 to 4 million each. The information gleaned by the CEMS is sent directly to SCAQMD in Diamond Bar, where the Wilmington facility's operations can be checked on 24 hours a day, 365 days a year.

Previously, oil refineries could be monitored by outside sources, which proved costly, time consuming and inefficient. Ultramar chose to install the CEMS to keep their emissions low and monitor their own pollution. While the move was not mandated by the government, it ultimately provided Ultramar with a cost effective way to maintain the highest standards of emission controls. Ultramar management saw it as an instance where environmental people and the petroleum industry worked together to accomplish something that's good for the environment and can be obtained without undue cost to businesses — a win-win situation.

Ultramar regularly offers training programs to its 400 Wilmington employees. The Power of Teams teaches five key concepts which align with the corporate values: safety, environmental and regulatory compliance, reliability, profitability and intellectual honesty. It trains employees in problem-solving skills and supports an open, honest work environment.

In addition, employees participate in a pay partnership, an incentive program where everyone shares in the success of the company. Bonuses are paid if targets are hit and the amount of money increases if targets are exceeded. Ultramar believes it's in everyone's best interests if employees have a stake in the company.

Ultramar Diamond Shamrock maintains a strong commitment to being a good neighbor. Employees are encouraged to participate in their many outreach programs. Managers and employees have sat on the board of the Boys & Girls Clubs for Long Beach and Wilmington. The company gave $50,000 to help build the Wilmington YMCA. During floods, they volunteer some of their vacuum trucks to unclog drains and sewers, and they hold joint drills with local fire departments using their own equipment. Ultramar holds regular meetings with homeowners to hear their concerns about the refinery and an annual open house where local people can tour the plant. Company policy is that people fear what they don't understand, and the time to develop a friendship is before problems arise.

According to Bill Haywood, refinery manager at the Ultramar Diamond Shamrock Wilmington facility, "We're very gung ho on the future of this business. California is the most environmentally aware area in the world, and our goal is to help drive the economy by manufacturing gasoline, jet fuel and diesel in an environmentally friendly way. What we manufacture is critical in the economic development of this area, and we plan to be here for a long time."

The Ultramar Wilmington refinery circa 1995, shown midway through construction of the gasoil hydrotreater and naphtha hydrotreater, part of the Ultramar Clean Fuels Project which was completed in 1996.

CAL WESTERN PAINTS

For more than 50 years, Cal Western Paint corporation has supplied quality paint products to residential, commercial, city, county, state and school systems in the greater southwestern region of California. Cal Western manufactures a multitude of specialty and specification coatings that offer the ultimate protection while meeting the requirements of various local, state and federal agencies.

The Cal Western success story began in the mid 1940s, when Edward Hey and John Kanavas opened a business supplying paint to commercial painters. They began with one store, but gradually increased that number to over a dozen stores throughout Southern California. In 1964, the pair decided to manufacture their own paint, rather than rely on other companies to make the paint for them.

The company's first manufacturing plant was on Sheila Street in the City of Commerce. One man — Bob Waltman — made the paint, canned the product, labeled the can and delivered the paint. After a few weeks, two more men were hired, and as orders grew, so did the number of employees. After five years, the company moved to a site on East Slauson Avenue in Santa Fe Springs and constructed a manufacturing plant, offices, a retail store and warehouse facility.

Eventually, Heys and Kanavas began selling their various retail locations to concentrate on their manufacturing business, until only one location remained — the current store on East Slauson. After Heys passed away in 1978, Kanavas offered to sell the entire operation to Bob Waltman, who agreed to take over the business and has been running it with his wife, Donna, ever since. Their children also work for Cal Western, and it's that family

Repairing the retail store after the earthquake.

Grand opening of Cal Western Paints, 1969

atmosphere that long time customers and newcomers alike really appreciate.

One prime reason for Cal Western's success is the quality of its products. Disneyland, Knott's Berry Farm, Magic Mountain and many movie studios all use Cal Western products. Both the City of Los Angeles and L.A. County have contracts with Cal Western paints, and a long list of satisfied customers means Cal Western is the paint product of choice for thousands of people.

According to Cal Western President Jerry Mulnix, manufacturing paint is similar to baking a cake, because

there is a specific recipe for each formula of paint. Whether it's water or solvent based paint, there are glues, resins and binders that make the paint stick to a surface. Pigmentation is added to give paint a particular color and texture. Other additives serve a variety of functions, including smoother flow, shinier paint, faster drying and ultimately making paint more user-friendly.

There are three main steps to making paint: the grind (where solid material is forced together with friction and heat), the let down (or dilution) and the tinting. After that, the paint is canned, a process that includes filtration to make sure that any particles not fully disbursed do not get into the finished product. Throughout this entire procedure, the product goes through a series of quality control measures to ensure that the finished product is of the highest possible quality.

About 85 percent of Cal Western business is custom blending. Customers can request a specific gloss, coat, color or texture in any size batch. Any color, no matter what size sample, can be custom matched. On-site bulk storage tanks hold myriad paint ingredients, ready for any special customer request.

An important aspect of Cal Western manufacturing procedure is the company's dedication to recycling. Pigment bags can be reused about two dozen times, and paint drums are also recycled for multiple use. Many customers prefer to purchase recycled products, thereby reducing cost and helping to keep landfills cleaner.

The entire manufacturing process is still a hands-on effort, much like it was many years ago. While there have been advancements in machinery and paint technology, the manufacturing process has changed very little. It is a straight-line process, so materials are not handled more than necessary.

Adjacent to the manufacturing area is the nerve center of Cal Western paints. Within a small cluster of offices several very important department, including batch scheduling, purchasing and procurement, research and development, quality control and testing. Key decision makers are in close proximity to one another for greater efficiency.

The company has installed computers to make communication with customers easier and provide a tool to chart and track various aspects of the business. The company has the ability to do material resource planning and computer modeling. They can project what would happen if they assembled a set of ingredients a particular way, and then receive a prediction, which could change based on new input. The computerization also provides the company with greater ability to make custom paints.

Cal Western had the ability to manufacture over 2,000 products, including a growing niche market of specialty products such as special effects paints that achieve an older cracked paint look when dry, and liquid duct tape that has the ability to conform to the shape of duct work. New developments at Cal Western include manufacturing paint that is less toxic for people who are sensitive to the fumes or chemical makeup of regular paints.

In addition to paint, Cal Western also makes industrial coatings, adhesives, cleaners, sealers, preparation agents and additives for other products, but most of the company's focus is on the architectural construction building products market.

Popular Cal Western paints include vinyl-acrylic flat, 100 percent acrylic, wonder glide velveteen, acrylic semi-gloss enamel, durasheen semi-gloss enamel and wonder glide aquasheen. Special paints available through Cal Western include nonskid coatings, roof, elastomeric, water barrier coatings and government specification coatings.

Even with all that specialized paint, there is still one force of nature that Cal Western paints cannot withstand—earthquakes. In 1984, the 5.0 Whittier Narrows earthquake shook the Cal Western building, dumping 5,000 gallons of paint throughout the store and factory. Cleanup crews had to slog through nearly three feet of paint in their efforts to remove the mess. It took Cal Western almost a month to repair the facilities and replace broken items, but the store bounced back better than ever.

Cal Western Paints believes in giving back to their community. The company supports many local outreach programs aimed at disadvantaged youth by providing paint products to create community art projects.

Thousands of gallons of paint were lost during the earthquake.

DAVALAN SALES

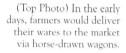

As midnight falls on Los Angeles and downtown's skyscrapers and streets are dark and empty, just a few blocks away the Los Angeles Produce Market is alive with activity, preparing to feed the city's millions for another day.

The way business is done at the market is nearly the same today as 100 years ago. Solid relationships and a reputation for fairness bring success in this environment where thousands of dollars in product are bought and sold on a handshake or conversation. In many cases, the same families run the business, having passed on knowledge and relationships from father to son, to grandsons and nephews.

(Top Photo) In the early days, farmers would deliver their wares to the market via horse-drawn wagons.

(Bottom Photo) Davalan maintains a fleet of trucks.

In 1983, a couple of young upstarts with just a handful of years in the produce business bucked this family tradition by starting Davalan Sales from scratch. Through a combination of traditional business values and modern techniques, Davalan has grown into one of the largest produce companies in Los Angeles.

Founders and owners Dave Bouton and Alan Frick met at their first job, right out of college. They spent a few short years learning the business at C.H. Robinson, one of the world's largest produce brokerage companies. Still in their mid-20s, they left C.H. Robinson on a Friday and started Davalan Sales on the following Monday with one employee and zero customers. Having yet to establish credit for their company and being unknown to the produce community, Bouton and Frick initially walked the market with cash in their pockets to fill the first orders for their infant company.

From a warehouse in Vernon, just blocks from the main Los Angeles produce market, Davalan focused on the consolidating and shipping aspects of the business. They combined produce loads from small farms and other sellers, and sold and shipped them to distributors at competitive wholesale prices. Just five years later, Davalan bought space in the Los Angeles Produce Market, which was opened in 1986. The relocation allowed the company to expand its operations into wholesaling in addition to increasing its shipping and consolidation activities.

The Los Angeles Produce Market is the hub of the region's produce business. The 530,000-square-foot facility, located southeast of downtown at Olympic and Alameda, is owned by its major member companies. It is the largest privately owned wholesale market in North America, with sales in excess of $1.1 billion. This facility augments the older produce market, located several blocks away. It's proximity to California's Central Valley, one of the nation's largest growing areas, as well as two ports, rail and multiple airports, makes this market a hub of average and exotic products from around the world. Produce markets throughout the country rely on these Southern California merchants to select and ship the more unusual items that are commonly found in the Los Angeles market.

In this environment, Davalan quickly became one of Southern California's leading wholesalers. Shipping operations were even shut down in 1991 to devote more of the company's resources to the wholesale business. In 1992, Davalan was able to expand its space in the market to accommodate the company's phenomenal growth.

Over the years, Davalan developed strong relationships with growers, buyers and other wholesalers as the company's reputation for reliability and responsiveness grew. As expansion continued, Bouton and Frick sought out the most experienced produce specialists in Los Angeles. All of Davalan's department heads have 15 to 20 years of industry experience, and many come from families whose involvement in the produce industry dates back several generations. A case in point is The Banana Company, a division of Davalan Sales which is operated by a family now in its fourth generation in the business. Davalan Sales also takes advantage of technology to manage the business better. For example, the ripening rooms at The Banana Company are state of the art, allowing a high level of responsiveness to market demands.

In 1995, Davalan returned to the shipping business and opened a produce brokerage office in San Francisco, and in 1998, the company moved into a larger space on the market. The company maintains extensive refrigeration and dock facilities as well as a 62,000-square-foot shipping operation where trucks can load and unload 24 hours a day. Within a two-mile radius of the Los Angeles Produce Market, Davalan has 120,000 square feet of warehouse storage.

Today Davalan deals in hundreds of types of produce, ranging from baby vegetables and purple wax beans for upscale restaurants, to apples and oranges for the average American family. Reflecting the city's tremendous ethnic richness, Davalan also deals with more exotic items such as lychee nuts, taro root, tomatillos and star fruit.

Undoubtedly, Davalan Sales will continue to grow over the coming years. As the population of Los Angeles continues to expand and diversify, so will the area's produce industry. Davalan's flexibility and experience ensure it a vital place in Southern California's economy for years to come.

Just a few of the produce items that Davalan stocks.

FLANIGAN FARMS, INC.

lanigan Farms is a company with an ambitious goal: good health for everyone. Following this simple philosophy has made them one of Southern California's leading pioneers in the natural foods industry. In fact, when Patsy and Owen Flanigan first started their business in 1970, it was just the beginning of the health movement that California was later to become known for. Patsy, a food technologist and mother of four daughters, and Owen, a mechanical engineer, felt a business of their own would ensure the family's financial future. Since both were health enthusiasts who recognized the need for more natural products in supermarkets, a healthy foods company seemed obvious. "So many people spend the first half of their life trading health for wealth, only to spend the second half trading wealth for health," Patsy explains. "We wanted people to know there was an alternative."

Granola was the couple's first product, which was very well received. They began selling to smaller independent markets. Without automated equipment,

Fuyu Persimmons in the Fall at Flanigan's certified organic "Little Farm."

orders were originally filled manually. Owen soon designed equipment to mechanize Flanigan Farms' production. He also handled the sales for the young company. Patsy developed new products and packaging, and made sure the office ran smoothly. As business increased, unsalted nuts and trail mixes were added. When Owen passed away in 1992, Patsy took over responsibility for the entire company.

This history of Flanigan Farms very much parallels the growth of Los Angeles itself. The early 90s were a considerable challenge for both the City of Angels and Flanigan Farms. The Los Angeles riots and the Northridge earthquake also affected business dramatically. The loss of stores directly following the riots hurt Flanigan Farms immediately. In 1993, orders dropped by 15 percent due to people leaving the area for places like Colorado, Arizona and Washington. Before these events, the company's sales territory was mostly from Los Angeles south to San Diego. As people left Los Angeles, Flanigan Farms expanded its sales north to include Bakersfield, Fresno and the central coast areas. They also added packages as small as 1 1/2 ounces to meet the growing consumer demand for healthy snacks.

Owen and Patsy's daughter, Catherine, joined the family business in 1992. A business management consultant with an Economics degree from UCLA and an MBA from Loyola Marymount University, Catherine is the Vice President of Operations. Her duties include management of the manufacturing, information systems, human resources and accounting/finance areas. She also takes a special interest in international sales and marketing. Flanigan Farms regularly hosts groups from other countries, as well as providing tours for nearby schools to complement lessons on business and/or nutrition.

Another daughter, Monica Flanigan Heeren, rejoined the company in 1997 after managing her own design firm out of state for a few years. Monica has special talents in graphics, marketing and merchandising.

She designs packaging, marketing and promotional material, and is currently Merchandising Manager. Working with Distributors and Market Merchandisers, Monica's enthusiasm, motivating influence and efficiency have developed increased stability in Flanigan Farms service to markets.

For their 20th anniversary, Flanigan Farms sponsored a "Fitness Is Fun" program for the Culver City schools. The event concentrated on the joy of healthy food and the fun of participating in vigorous activities. It produced a half-hour video of the students, which was shown on cable television. The company also sponsors various American Heart Association activities. Additionally, Flanigan Farms is an active member of the Culver City and Los Angeles Chambers of Commerce. Patsy, a Southern California delegate to the White House Conference of Small Business and a member of the National Association of Women Business Owners, enjoys the opportunity to meet with other business owners and to stay in touch with the community.

Flanigan Farms isn't just about natural foods — it's also about people. Both employees and distributors participate in taste tests and contribute to many of the collective marketing decisions. Reflecting the multi-cultural population of Los Angeles, the company employees through the years have represented a diverse mix of cultural heritages including Tanzania, Costa Rica, India, Mexico, Fiji, Scotland and Vietnam. In fact, when a Flanigan Farms employee gains citizenship, it is cause for celebration. The entire office throws a party and presents that person with an American flag. "We think this is welcoming," says Patsy. "If we Americans did this for everybody, had some kind of ceremony for people when they become old enough to vote, then maybe people would take their citizenship more seriously."

Patsy Flanigan has devoted a great deal of her life to promoting healthy eating habits and providing nutritious snacks. She is a board member of Santa Monica Chapter of the American Heart Association and the Didi Hirsch Community Mental Health Center, and serves on the Nutrition and Health Council of America. It was her desire to spread the word on good nutrition that inspired Flanigan Farms' monthly newsletter. Informative articles provide insight into the challenges of selecting a nutritious diet. Ironically, the health-conscious company faced a marketing challenge because of the emphasis on fat content in foods. Nuts do have lots of fat, but it is the "good" polyunsaturated and monounsaturated fat, not the "bad" saturated fat. To get the point across, Flanigan Farms includes a breakdown of fat on its labels.

Flanigan Farms, located in Culver City, is now in more than 600 markets, including Ralphs, Vons, Pavilions, Hughes, Food 4 Less, Gelson's, Bristol Farms and many independent markets. Although nuts and their classic trail mixes are the core products of Flanigan Farms, the company also sells dried Fuyu persimmons which are grown on its certified organic farm in San Diego County. The family-owned farm has over 500 persimmon trees and also grows macadamia nuts.

Some people would consider starting your own business from scratch to be just plain nuts. But Flanigan Farms caught the early wave of the natural foods business and has ridden it to success with a personal vision, hard work and perseverance. More that 25 years later, the health-conscious company is one of the leading packagers and distributors of natural unsalted nuts in Southern California. Perhaps their company philosophy states it best: "Our mission is to be a united team, leading in the field of natural foods. We encourage good health and fitness for all."

Patsy Flanigan with Flanigan Farms "shipper" display of nuts, trail mix and dried persimmons.

Machine Operator checks packages of cashews coming off automatic machine.

GOLDBERG AND SOLOVY FOODS

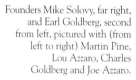

stablished in 1974 by Mike Solovy and Earl Goldberg, Goldberg and Solovy Foods, Inc., is a broadline institutional food service distributor — one of the largest food distribution companies in southern California. The company provides the Southland's food service industry with a full line of products including fresh meat, pork, seafood, poultry, canned foods, frozen foods, paper goods, imported cheese, disposables and smallwares and equipment. Goldberg and Solovy CEO Mike Solovy and President Earl Goldberg have worked together for over 35 years. It's their hard work and dedication, and that of their employees, that has made Goldberg and Solovy prosper and grow into one of the top 50 broadline distributors in the United States. The company was also named as one of the *Los Angeles Business Journal's 100 Fastest Growing Companies* in 1997.

Goldberg and Solovy's roots can be traced back to 1919, when Earl Goldberg's grandfather opened "Goldberg's Live Chicken Market" in Los Angeles and Mike Solovy's grandparents started a "Live Poultry Market" in Boyle Heights. Earl's father, Charles, and Mike's father, Joe, were longtime friends who entered into the food distribution business when they purchased Warner Poultry (later Warner Foods) in the late 1940s in Pasadena. In 1952 they moved the company to the city of Vernon, where they continued to process live chickens, turkeys and ducks.

Earl and Mike went to work for Warner Foods in 1963. Warner Foods partners, Charles and Joe (along with partners Hal Michaels and Sam Dubin) sold the company in 1969. Early in 1974 Mike Solovy started Mike Solovy Foods; a few months later Earl

Goldberg joined him, and Goldberg and Solovy Foods Inc. was formed. Joe Azzaro and Lou Azzaro joined the company as partners later that year. Martin Pine became a partner in 1977, and is the company's Vice President directing the company's meat department.

Armed with plenty of experience and industry contacts, but little in the way of inventory or warehouse space, the founders guided Goldberg and Solovy Foods, Inc. to sales of $9 million in the first year of existence. Warehouse space, employees and trucks were initially provided by U.S. Growers Cold Storage in the city of Vernon, and in 1977, Goldberg and Solovy took out a long-term lease on their own plant. By 1987, Goldberg and Solovy had outgrown their facility, and after securing an Industrial Development Bond, they built in Vernon, the most modern food distribution and processing plant in Southern California. With more than 1.5 million cubic feet of space, Goldberg and Solovy's facility is large enough to store over 12,000 items. The warehouse is busy 24 hours a day servicing thousands of accounts six days a week.

Perhaps the most important element of Goldberg and Solovy is revealed in their company slogan: "Service, Service and more Service." Southern

Goldberg and Solovy building.

Founders Mike Solovy, far right, and Earl Goldberg, second from left, pictured with (from left to right) Martin Pine, Lou Azzaro, Charles Goldberg and Joe Azzaro.

California's fast-paced, competitive food service business demands new solutions and greater service than ever before. One company answers that need with a state-of-the-art distribution plant, full-service capabilities, and attention to detail — Goldberg and Solovy Foods, Inc.

In the past few years, the press has carried dramatic stories on contamination outbreaks. These events have caused government agencies to strengthen laws concerning sanitation. Goldberg and Solovy has always considered sanitation to be a critical issue for distributors and consumers alike. The entire Goldberg and Solovy building is under continuous United States Department of Agriculture inspection with on-site USDA inspectors checking all products and shipments 24 hours a day. Seafood, poultry and beef are stored and processed in separate areas to avoid cross contamination. When an order comes in from a restaurant stating the item and type of cut, it is processed that day, shipped at night, and arrives at the restaurant the next morning. Whole fish is filleted, chicken is deboned and portioned, and beef is aged and cut to order. The warehouse boasts state-of-the-art amenities, including a refrigerated dock for receiving and shipping product to maintain proper temperature levels. Storage coolers and freezers hold millions of pounds of product, which are monitored by alarms to ensure temperatures are held in a safe range. Not only has Goldberg and Solovy always been a federally inspected facility, but is currently providing industry leadership with compliance to the federally mandated HACCP (Hazard Analysis Critical Control Point) legislation guidelines. The HACCP system is one of the many steps the government and the meat industry have taken to further enhance the safety of today's meat products. Meat, poultry and fish plants must examine the way they make their product, determine where problems are likely to occur and take adequate steps to prevent those problems from actually occurring. Every day and on every shift, the processing and warehouse facilities are cleaned and sanitized.

Originally a fresh and frozen center of the plate distributor (meats, poultry and seafood), Goldberg and Solovy gradually added dry grocery goods to broaden their service capability. Today, the company finds itself distributing all institutional foodservice needs. The addition of new food categories, along with disposable, janitorial, and smallwares and equipment has made Goldberg and Solovy both a niche supplier and a broadliner. The company's ability to provide customers both "broadline" goods and niche items gives Goldberg a unique position in the food industry.

Although the company is one of the larger food distributors in the United States (over $75 million in annual sales), Goldberg and Solovy is still very much a family owned and operated business. Many of their 270 employees have worked for the company for more than 20 years, and some have brought their children or other relatives into the business. Erin Solovy, Mike's daughter, has been with the company for 14 years; other relatives who have worked for G&S over the years are Marc Solovy, Josh Solovy, Charles Goldberg, Sarah Goldberg, Don Goldberg and Margaret Azzaro. The company has embraced the computer technology age, yet retains a positive family atmosphere.

(Left) Earl Goldberg's grandparents in "Goldberg's Live Chicken Market" circa 1919, Los Angeles. Second from right is grandmother and third from right is grandfather.

Parents of Earl Goldberg and Mike Solovy, c. 1967 (Left to right) Charles Goldberg and Joe Solovy, owners of Warner Foods, Vernon, California.

Mike Solovy's grandparents, toward the back, in their "Live Poultry Market" in Boyle Heights.

IMPERIAL TOY CORPORATION

Of all the toy companies in the world, one company sells more individual toy units each year than any other. Imperial Toy Corporation near downtown Los Angeles for nearly 30 years and now for over 20 years on East 7th Street has manufactured and distributed a variety of toys throughout the United States and the world. The company makes over 800 different toy items, although when Fred Kort started the business in 1969, he began with one item called the Teeny Bouncer, a small high-bounce ball that when dropped without force to the ground would bounce 80 percent of its original height. The toy was a hit with children, and Kort soon found himself overwhelmed with orders.

Fred Kort

Kort began adding more toy items and soon showed his variety in his own toy catalogs which are published twice a year. Kort added more employees and toy items until he began to outgrow his original 20,000-square-foot facility. In his search for a new location, Kort found a large building on East 7th Street that had been built by Henry Ford in 1914 to be used as Ford's and the West Coast's first automobile factory. In 1932, Ford moved his plant to a larger facility, and the building was purchased by Lockheed Aircraft, who had 4,500 workers manufacturing aircraft parts during World War II. After the war, Lockheed moved out and Bullock's Department Store moved in. After many years, Bullock's also moved. In 1976, Kort purchased the building and relocated Imperial Toy Company to its current facility — the company's worldwide headquarters.

Over the years, Kort has renovated and expanded the building to its current 400,000 square feet. Imperial Toy Company now has close to 500 employees working in the company's manufacturing, warehouse, shipping, and office facilities in Los Angeles. Another 350 employees are scattered throughout Tijuana, Mexico, Toronto, Canada and Hong Kong. In excess of 3,000 manufacturing and assembly workers produce toys in various facilities throughout China. Total worldwide footage for all Imperial Toy locations is over one million square feet. The company also has a sales office and showroom in New York City, and a distribution center in Memphis, Tennesse.

Imperial Toy Corporation ships toys to over 50 countries throughout the world, but the largest customer base is still right here in the United States. Due to the company's basic toy category, Imperial Toy sells more toy units than any other toy company. The company sells to major retailers such as Kmart, Wal-Mart, Target, Toys 'R' Us, Kay-Bee, Walgreens, CVS and most supermarkets and drugstore chains. Virtually anywhere toys are sold, Imperial Toy items can be found.

About 60 to 80 new toy items are introduced twice a year — spring and fall. A similar number of toys are discontinued to balance the merchandise. Some items, such as the Teeny Bouncer and bubble blowing toys, remain popular forever, but they get a new twist that keeps them fresh for each season.

Imperial Toy Corporation's catalog includes many traditional toy items such as bubble makers, jump ropes, paddle balls, toy animals (including the ever-popular Jurassic dinosaurs), small stuffed animals, yo-yo's, marbles and flying disks. Other toy items include dress-up fashion accessories, removable tattoos, dolls, die-cast cars and micro cities, candy toys (toys filled with candy), miniature figure assortments, the highly successful Petite Miss, first makeup kits for girls and many more.

Kort's three sons work with him at Imperial Toy headquarters, but he remains active in his business and mindful of what led to his success. Kort is one of only nine people in the world to have survived the

Treblinka death camp in eastern Poland, where more than one million people were murdered in little more than a year. Born in Germany just before Adolph Hitler came to power, Kort lived in both Vienna and southern Germany before his family was deported to Poland in 1938.

Kort was forced into the Lodz ghetto and later escaped. The young Kort was then captured and taken by German soldiers to a forced labor camp under the jurisdiction of the German SS near Warsaw where he stayed for nearly two years. After escaping from there and being recaptured, Kort was taken to the Kawenczyn labor camp. Shortly thereafter, the camp's entire labor force of approximately 2,000 was transferred to Treblinka where 90 percent of the men, women and children were immediately exterminated. Kort managed to survive Treblinka for the next year until July 1944 when he escaped.

After spending three weeks in the Polish forest, Kort joined the Polish underground and then was inducted into the Polish Army. A year later, he returned to Germany and was reunited with his mother and sister who had returned safely from Russia. Kort's father, and brother perished in the Holocaust.

In 1947, Fred Kort left Europe to begin a new life in America. He landed a position as a technician with General Electric, while at the same time attending night school and studying the electrical trade. He later received a transfer to Los Angeles, where he soon left GE and obtained a position as an assistant electrician at the Los Angeles Biltmore Hotel. One day while working at the hotel, a guest approached him and asked if he knew of anyone who could help him set up a toy factory. Kort said he did — himself.

After spending the next five years learning the toy business, Kort started his own fledgling toy factory. Timing was not right and three years later in 1957 Kort gave up his company. He then established an independent sales firm representing a number of different toy companies. However, the desire to have his own tory manufacturing company was a dream which was still alive inside of him. In 1969, Fred Kort fulfilled that dream when he created the Imperial Toy Corporation.

Fred Kort has never forgotten his past and what it was like to struggle to survive. The Kort family and Imperial Toy are major philanthropists donating to many charities, the remembrance of the Holocaust and children in need. In 1993 Kort was appointed Honorary Ambassador to the Tel Aviv Foundation. He is also one of the original founders of the United States Holocaust Memorial Museum in Washington, D.C., and a major benefactor of the Los Angeles Holocaust Monument. He has received the Anti-Defamation League's Achievement and Community Service Award, as well as the United Jewish Fund's Humanitarian of the Year Award and the Holocaust Survivors Division of State of Israel Bonds' 1997 Holocaust Remembrance Award. Steven Spielberg asked Kort to share in his partnership in history, and he is now fully involved in the Survivors of the Shoah Visual History Foundation. Recently, Kort was presented a doctorate degree, Honoris Causa, from the Bar-Ilan University for his commitment to many and varied humanitarian causes.

Imperial Toy has sponsored three exhibits at the Los Angeles Museum of Natural History, including the "Remember the Children" exhibit on the Holocaust. Imperial continuously donates toys and money to a wide variety of charities assisting children who have been victims of violence and natural disasters. Additionally, Imperial Toy regularly supports Toys for Tots, City of Hope, Cedars Sinai Hospital, D.A.R.E. America and many other important organizations.

Kort is very involved in the civic concerns of Los Angeles. The mayor's office regularly calls him for advice on import/export matters, and he has many citations from the City and State of California thanking him for his involvement with civic organizations.

"It's very important to remember where you came from," says Kort. "I appreciate my newfound home." And millions of children throughout the world appreciate Kort for the countless hours of joy his toys bring to their lives.

Imperial Toy Showroom

INDUSTRIAL DYNAMICS

ndustrial Dynamics was formed in 1958 by Fred L. Calhoun to develop and manufacture inspection equipment for the beverage industry utilizing advanced technologies acquired from the guided missile industry.

Since that date, it has grown into a high technology multi-national organization headquartered in Torrance, California with approximately 450 employees in its modern 190,000-square-foot complex. Another 75 employees are located in its foreign subsidiaries. Its products include state-of-the-art inspection systems and laser coding equipment for the food, beverage, brewing and various other packaging industries. The company has ten wholly owned subsidiaries that sell and service its equipment worldwide.

Industrial Dynamics' customer roster reads like a who's who of multinational beverage producers and includes Anheuser-Busch, Coca-Cola, Proctor & Gamble, Heineken, South African Brewery, Pepsi-Cola, Coors Brewery, Lever Brothers, Miller Brewing Company and Philip Morris, to name just a few.

The company takes pride in its fully integrated manufacturing facilities utilizing Demand Flow Technology and advanced Research and Development Laboratories. It is the world's most prolific manufacturer

The assembly floor where 95 percent of all Industrial Dynamics' manufactured components are made.

The Braintrust at Industrial Dynamics is led by President and CEO Fred Calhoun, his daughter, Worldwide Sales Promotion Manager Joanie M. Calhoun and his son, Executive Vice President Steve M. Calhoun.

of inspection equipment in terms of market share, dollar and unit volume. Industrial Dynamics offers a complete line of empty bottle inspectors, fill level inspectors, filler management systems, case inspectors and a wide range of rejection systems and laser coding equipment. Most of these products were pioneered by Industrial Dynamics.

The company is a privately held corporation owned by the Calhoun family. President and CEO Fred L. Calhoun continues to oversee most of the research projects and is assisted by his son, Steve M. Calhoun, who is the Executive Vice President and heads up operations and other vital sectors of the company such as personnel, foreign sales, etc. Joan M. Calhoun, Fred's daughter, works in the Customer Services and Sales Promotions divisions and assists her Father with various other company functions.

The focus on in-house development and production translates into having 95 percent of all of Industrial Dynamics' manufactured components made at the company's facilities and results in a six-to-eight-month development cycle on most products. The delivery lead time on their complex electronic equipment ranges from three to eight weeks.

The list of technological breakthroughs for Industrial Dynamics is a long one and ranges from the introduction of the world's s first Empty Bottle Inspector in 1958 to the first true All Surface Empty Bottle Inspector in 1991.

The company is perhaps best known, however, for fill level equipment using gamma technology that is marketed under the name "filtec." With more than 10,000 inspection system installations worldwide, filtec has become the industry standard. Many large OEMs that make and sell competitive equipment buy filtec equipment for installations in remote locations throughout the world where they are unable to technically support complicated inspection systems.

This worldwide reputation for technical support, as well as outstanding quality, is behind the push by Industrial Dynamics to accelerate its international growth through the development of a global service network. Independent Distributors are a part of this network.

"In the markets where we cannot locate compatible, qualified distributors who are willing to make a high level commitment to customer service and spare parts, we will go in and establish a wholly-owned subsidiary," said President and CEO Fred L. Calhoun. "Our mission is to supply and support our customers with the world's best and most innovative automated inspection equipment to increase their production efficiency and improve their product quality. We will not sell any equipment in a market we cannot service."

Major population centers are being targeted, especially in South America and the Asia-Pacific area, because that is where the global beverage industry is concentrating its efforts. The strategy for Industrial Dynamics is to open up a new market with service and then move into new product sales. Service centers are opened first so that customers have local support in their own time zone and their own language and can get parts, training and equipment maintenance quickly.

Company officials call it their "Big Mac" approach to customer service and are incorporating a system that provides a standard of quality service that is identical regardless of the location. In the United States, Industrial Dynamics offers 24-hour turnaround on all parts delivery and service calls from the time the order is placed and one-week turnaround on all factory repairs. The goal is to provide the same level of service on a global basis.

To achieve such desired levels of synergy and consistency, Industrial Dynamics has a vast customer service initiative in which training is a vital component. A complete, modern training facility has been established at the industrial complex in Torrance and fully-staffed and fully-equipped training centers are in operation in Mexico City, Hamburg and Brussels. Sites are also being developed in Medellin, Columbia; São Paulo, Brazil; Singapore and South Africa.

The customer training centers feature current technology including the range of Industrial Dynamics equipment, as well as actual bottling conveyor loops and hands-on training. The comprehensive course runs for a minimum of one week and may run for up to two weeks. Customers are also offered on-site training once equipment has been installed and the customer has been trained at Industrial Dynamics' dedicated facilities.

With many countries around the globe only in the initial stages of utilizing cans, non-returnable bottles and returnable PET, there appears to be unlimited potential for major players in the international beverage arena and Industrial Dynamics aptly fits that description.

This privately held company has shown the vision, innovation and dedication to become the leader in a fiercely competitive market. Armed with an aggressive plan for expansion that is based on a solid history of quality, service and dedication to customer satisfaction, Industrial Dynamics prepares for the next millennium.

Industrial Dynamics' newest All Surface Empty Bottle Inspector.

KOPPL COMPANY

S ince its inception, Koppl Company has built a reputation as an industry leader providing quality engineered specialty products and services to the water, gas and electric utilities and to the petroleum, pipeline, pulp and paper and plumbing industries.

Founded by Leo T. Koppl in 1925, this environmental systems company began as a family business when Koppl, his brother and a cousin opened a blacksmith and machine shop in Huntington Beach. They built tools and welded for the growing Southern California oil industry.

Koppl work crew, 1955.

In 1929, Koppl struck out on his own, following the oil boom to Santa Fe Springs and then to Montebello where he built his machine shop at the corner of Poplar and Beverly Boulevard. From here he continued to build equipment and provide services in the local oil fields. It was during the slow times of the Great Depression that Mr. Koppl developed and patented his Hot Tap machine.

Founders, Leo T. and Effie Koppl

During World War II, Mr. Koppl supported the war effort by providing welding services to the shipyards in Long Beach by day and the local oil refineries by night. It was during this time that the importance of his tools became apparent to the refineries and their demand for his services increased.

The housing boom in Southern California after the war brought Koppl to the forefront in the water industry. As housing developments grew and the need for expanded water services increased, Mr. Koppl put his hot tap equipment to a new use. Using his patented machines, new pipeline systems could be connected to the existing lines without interrupting service to residents. In conjunction with the growing water industry, in 1958, American Pipe asked Koppl to build and install their specially engineered tapping saddle for their concrete cylinder pipe which had been used throughout Southern California.

As the company continued to thrive, it remained a family run business. Leo's wife, Effie, and later his daughter, Jean, worked beside him in the office while his son-in-law, Melvin, worked for him as a welder. As

his grandchildren, Hazel and Douglas, grew up, they also worked beside their grandfather in the company.

In the years since its inception, Koppl Company has continued to expand its operations. Currently headquartered in Montebello, the firm has service centers throughout the United States with locations in Northern and Southern California, Washington state, Nevada, Arizona, Texas, Kansas, Georgia and Florida.

Upon Mr. Koppl's death in 1981, his grandson, M. Douglas Coker, took over the helm as president and CEO while his wife, Sue, handled the administrative aspects of the business.

"We consider ourselves a big, extended family here," says Coker. "Koppl Company has provided many job opportunities and has often been the first and only work experience for many of its employees. Many of the employees currently working at Koppl Company have been here for over 20 years. The success of the company to date can be directly traced to my grandfather's influence and reputation in the industry and the commitment of its employees."

Although the company has recently been sold to Innovative Valve Technologies, Inc., Coker hopes to "help preserve the integrity of the company and grow the firm into the future."

Koppl Company corporate headquarters.

(Top left)
Finished 36" hot tap at Union Carbide.

Forty-eight inch hot tap on a 52" water main for a city of Tucson water project.

L.A. DYE & PRINT WORKS

ince 1983, L.A. Dye & Print Works has been serving the textile and apparel industries with competitively-priced, high-quality product. Using a large scope of state-of-the-art equipment, this innovator has carved itself a niche into today's fabric business. As a result, the industry giant houses over one million square feet under one roof, with 1,600 employees throughout Los Angeles County.

Helmut Ackermann and two partners, Bruno Lamprecht and Morris Latt, were the successful bidders on a then-bankrupt dye house in 1983. Helmut had been in the textile industry previously, and had more than 20 years of experience in both administrative and financial areas. Ackermann also had background in both men's and women's apparel manufacturing, including 11 years in textile fabric production.

The company's mission is simple: to quickly produce a large amount of fabric at the highest standard, best-quality and most reasonable price. Based in Los Angeles, L.A. Dye & Print Works has grown to become the largest textile company west of the Mississippi River. The company maintains numerous warehouses and production facilities throughout Southern California which handle various production phases for its fabrics.

L.A. Dye & Print Works uses two kinds of basic fabrics, knits and woven.

The process starts with the purchase of yarn from spinners, which are knitted into fabrics by the company's knitting operation. L.A. Dye & Print Works' knitting operation produces approximately four and a half the five million pounds each month, or the equivalent of nine million yards of knits. After producing knits and purchasing woven fabric from a weaver, the company moves its product to one of its two dye houses. The knit dye house averages 10 to 12 million yards of fabric each month; the woven dye house averages three and a half to four million. Once fabric has been dyed or bleached, some of it is sent to the company's printing operation, which can print as many as ten colors on a single pattern. The print operations present capacity is between seven and eight million yards per month. After dyeing and printing, some fabrics are sent to the company's finishing operation, which adds special finishes such as being laundered, chintzed or sueded.

L.A. Dye & Print Works uses the latest high-tech equipment in each of its facilities. In fact, it has made a sizeable investment in equipment in order to produce fabrics that are traditionally only handled on the East Coast. For example, the mercerizing machine both cleans and adds depth to woven fabric. This gives L.A. Dye & Print Works an edge and raises the standard of quality. Both staff and employees are committed to the highest standard of quality throughout all operations. All divisions synergistically act together for total Quality Assurance and Quality Control. That's why they continually work toward re-inventing themselves in the never-ending pursuit of excellence.

The future holds a completely different action plan. Garment manufacturing is gradually moving offshore into low-labor, underdeveloped countries such as China, India and Eastern Europe. NAFTA is encouraging that movement into Latin American countries. Sooner or later, textile mills will have to follow.

Ackermann believes in looking toward the future to catch the next wave of opportunities. California is critically positioned for new biotech breakthroughs in agriculture due to its location, climate and educational opportunities. California Universities are excellent for basic research in fruits, vegetables and live stock. Ackermann believes that, in the near future, California will be producing fruits and vegetables that don't exist yet. These foods will be tastier, more pest resistant, have a longer shelf-life, etc. "We are therefore purchasing land

throughout the state for the purpose of creating new food-based products to support the future growing global community." Specialty food is a growth industry with an unlimited growth potential.

"Nothing lasts forever," observes Ackermann. "The key is that while you're being successful in catching current trends, always keep an eye open for the next opportunity." As a larger and larger portion of the global population enters the middle class, more people will be shopping for various products via their personal computers and the Internet. The days of being physically limited to just shopping across the street are numbered. So, what does the future hold? "Our long-term goal is to continue to provide the best quality products at the lowest possible cost to a global customer."

NORMAN, FOX & CO.

os Angeles-based Norman, Fox & Co. manufactures and distributes specialty chemical product swhich intimately touch our daily lives in personal care products, cosmetics, food, household and janitorial cleaners, pharmaceuticals, automotive products, paint and plastics, metalworking and construction materials, and textiles. Proprietary ingredients sold by the company are part of the recipes for nationally recognized brands, boutique products and industrial processing aids.

Herbert Norman and Fred Fox formed the company in 1971 when their employer, Swift & Company, decided to get out of the chemical business. Suddenly unemployed, Norman, the division's western general manager, and Fox, its marketing director, joined forces to see if they could salvage the business they had built for Swift. Starting in a tiny office equipped with two desks, two phones and their contact sheets, they tried to sustain as much of the line of chemical ingredients as possible through distribution of similar products. Norman and Fox were joined by three former Swift salesmen who

An aerial view of Norman, Fox & Co. headquarters in Vernon, California, just east of downtown Los Angeles.

agreed to work on straight commission because the company couldn't afford to pay salaries.

Within one year, the burgeoning company purchased Swift's industrial soap manufacturing equipment and moved it to its present site in the city of Vernon, just east of downtown Los Angeles. They began making industrial soap in 1972. To expand their product line, Norman, Fox & Co. soon represented three categories of products: those they manufactured in Vernon; those other companies manufactured; and products made especially for them which they sold under their brand name, Norfox®.

The natural route for company expansion was to build on products made from existing raw materials, which were mostly derived from renewable resources such as tallow and coconut oil. Ultimately this worked to their advantage when Americans became concerned with environmental issues, especially the biodegradability of soaps and detergents. Norman, Fox and Co. also aligned itself with leading national and international manufacturers of related materials to provide a complete line of specialty chemical ingredients to their growing customer base.

Trade secrets and proprietary formulas are jealously guarded by the soap and cosmetic industry. In the Middle Ages, candle and soap makers zealously protected their secret recipes. To this day, ingredient sourcing, formulation techniques and other aspects of production are viewed as proprietary by many manufacturers. For that reason, Norman, Fox & Co. employees refrain from mentioning the companies they supply

Norman, Fox & Co. is the only company west of the Mississippi still manufacturing natural soap flakes and granules. The recipes they follow hearken back to old-fashioned kitchen soap making, only on a much larger scale. In 15,000 gallon cauldrons, they cook up soap using fat, caustic soda (also known as lye) by boiling with steam to a lava-like consistency. Next, it is washed with water and salt solution to remove glycerin and impurities. The hot slurry is mixed with preservatives and antioxidant agents to prevent rancidity, then cooled and converted to long flat ribbons that look like wet pasta. It then travels through a drying oven, and the dried soap is ground into flakes or granules and packaged for transport. The process takes one week for each kettle, and the six kettles are kept in constant production. The Vernon factory produces between five and six million pounds of industrial soap per year. The company does not manufacture finished products for consumers, as that would put them in direct competition with their customers.

While many of the materials the company processes are derived from natural sources, the government still considers these products to be chemicals subject to a myriad of regulations and restrictions. As members of the National Association of Chemical Distributors and other trade groups, Norman, Fox & Co. has pledged to comply with the industry's Responsible Distribution Process in the manufacturing, handling and selling of their products. This stewardship initiative ensures a continuous, uninterrupted chain of custody from producer to qualified end user.

Before someone is allowed to make a purchase, the company makes certain they are qualified to work with chemicals and hazardous materials. They require that customers know how to handle the products safely and that they're not operating in an area which might be exposed to unqualified individuals or children. The company's Web site specifically targets professional manufacturers as opposed to consumers, and they discourage individuals from contacting them directly to buy a bag of industrial soap.

Today, Norman, Fox & Co.'s list of clients spans the Western United States, Hawaii, the Pacific Rim, Central and South America, to countries as diverse as Pakistan, China, the Czech Republic, Ghana, Egypt, South Africa and the Republic of Belarus. Their product line ranges from soap flakes to rust inhibitors, almond meal to concrete waterproofing, chemicals that help condition hair, grease underwater pipe joints, create or destroy foam. This presents clients with a full range of ingredients from which to formulate products.

Ecological concerns have led them to package dry soap in 1,000-pound returnable "super-sacks" instead of 50-pound bags, and ship liquids in 330-gallon recyclable totes rather than one-way 55-gallon drums.

In 1976, the company expanded its capabilities to manufacture products derived from natural sources by adding a sophisticated chemical reactor to its manufacturing activities. The success of this line of products caused them to institute a significant further expansion in 1998. This new venture allows them to create formulas for ingredients which still emphasize renewable resources but allow for a wider variety of products.

Helping new entrepreneurs plays a key role in building Norman, Fox & Co.'s future. Some clients are individuals who got an idea for filling a marketing niche and held their first meetings with company representatives in a home kitchen while stirring up a new formula. Many of these entrepreneurs have gone on to become major factors in the soap and cosmetics market. Companies needing advice to solve problems or create new formulas can freely consult with in-house experts. The Norman, Fox & Co. Technical Service Department sends out samples of ingredients to prospective customers, and has access to the research and development departments of the many U.S. manufacturers for whom they distribute.

Fred Fox passed away in 1988, but Herb Norman continues to lead the company as Chairman and CEO. In 1996, Norman, Fox & Co. began a process to become employee-owned, allowing the staff of 42 a stake in the company's future. For the company's 25th anniversary, Norman, Fox & Co. commissioned the production of premium quality bars of soap made from ingredients they either manufacture or supply. Boxed with the Norfox® logo and the company's contact information, these samples serve as a memorable calling card for a competent and well-respected company.

An operator checks the quality of the dried soap before it is processed into flakes or powder.

O.E. CLARK PAPER BOX COMPANY

ew family-owned Los Angeles businesses can boast a history that dates back to the days when the land that would eventually evolve into a major metropolitan city was still largely made up of farms, meat packing houses and power plants.

Ten years before buying his own company, Oliver Estes Clark worked in the paper box industry. At that time, he could see the future of the paper box industry.

In 1926, Oliver E. Clark bought out an existing box manufacturer for $800, which included all existing machinery and equipment. Then a one-man operation, Clark assembled and delivered orders of 50 to 100 rigid boxes to area retail stores and industrial companies.

He moved to 417 Wall Street in the early 30s. Before long, Clark's fledgling business grew to incorporate the building's third and fourth floors. In 1936, he passed away, leaving the thriving business to his son Oliver E. Clark Jr.

After World War II, Boyce Tolliver, Mr. Clark's brother-in-law, joined O.E. Clark employees as a plant superintendent, a position he held until his retirement in 1981.

By 1947, Oliver E. Clark Jr. built an 18,000-square-foot facility in Vernon to accommodate the booming business. By the late 60s, the operation included converting paper board into "folding" paper boxes which serve as containers for a wide variety of merchandise such as dry food, laundry detergent and computer software.

By 1960, Clark Jr. was grooming his own son to one day oversee the company's operation. Oliver "Robin" E. Clark III began by sweeping the floors and learned every aspect of the business by working in the various divisions from manufacturing to administration.

The family firm branched off and introduced the "Specialties Folding Box" division in 1957 and Central City Box & Paper, a distribution arm a decade later.

The following companies were acquired by O.E. Clark: In 1962, J. V. Sparks of Long Beach, a paper box manufacturer; Marquisee Paper Co. in 1967; Maywood Industries in 1974; Frank L. Smith Stationery in 1977; Specialty Paper Box in 1981; American Paper Box in 1991; Alpine Paper in 1992; and the Herman Paper Co. in 1994.

Ranked among the top five rigid box manufacturers in California, the O.E. Clark Paper Box Company currently encompasses three separate structures totaling 185,000 square feet, all situated on the same street, which serve as the administrative offices, manufacturing facility and warehouses.

Today, the company turns out orders of 20,000 to 30,000 rigid and folding boxes for clientele in the software, retail, manufacturing, construction and pharmaceutical industries. Many national clients contribute to the company's success.

The Pacific Coast Box Maker's Association and National Paper Box Association has bestowed a number of safety and packaging awards to the company, which continually strives to remain competitive by keeping abreast of industry changes.

"In recent years, the company's growth has really revolved around updating to modern equipment and

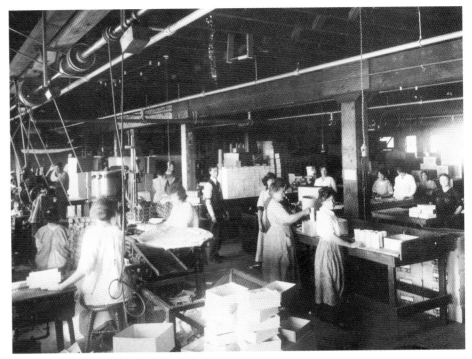

implementing the technological advances into the operation," says Clark. "The advent of computer graphics has significantly impacted the industry in such a way that folding boxes can look almost as good as rigid boxes and in larger quantities are much more competitive and economical. We shine because we go out with a better product, and our prices are always competitive."

The Clark family tradition continues with Robin's wife Jean as the company's secretary treasurer. Brother-in-law Carlos Harrison works in sales and daughter Cheryl Bocksnick handles customer service while his sons Oliver E. Clark IV and Mark Bocksnick serve as production and maintenance manager and graphics manager, respectively. Eleanor Clark is the assistant production manager.

"Although so many members of my immediate family work here, the O.E. Clark Paper Box Company is truly a family operation in the sense that many of our employees and their relatives have been working here for years and have really become an extended family for us," says Company President Oliver "Robin" E. Clark III. "The independent paper box industry as a whole really lends itself to family. I guess paper dust just gets into the blood from birth."

Founder Oliver Estes Clark

TAPATIO HOT SAUCE COMPANY

When entering the front office of the Tapatio Hot Sauce Company, the sweet, spicy smell of hot sauce engulfs every sense. Jose-Luis Saavedra Sr. started the Tapatio Hot Sauce Company in 1971 as a family business and continues to keep it that way. Incidentally, the product's name "Tapatio" means a person born in Guadalajara, capital of the state of Jalisco in Mexico, which is the town where all of his children were born.

From the start, Jose-Luis Saavedra Sr. and his wife Lolita Cuervo, knew they were on to something special when they noticed that their friends would drive from as far as Orange County, nearly 40 miles away, just to

The Saavedra family is surrounded by boxes of hot sauce in the warehouse of the company's new Vernon location. From left: Dolores, Jose Luis Jr., Jacquie, and CEO Jose Luis Sr.

get a bottle of their one-of-a-kind specialty hot sauce. When the recession hit the aircraft industry and the plant where Saavedra worked closed, he interpreted the incident as divine intervention and went shopping for a small business loan. After numerous rejections from his bank, he was finally approved for a $4,000 home improvement loan. He bought a couple of stainless steel tables, a scale, blender and some raw materials to begin manufacturing. He also rented a 485-square-foot building in Maywood and figured now was as good a time as any to fulfill his dream and start his own business. At 42 years old, with no formal business education or even a business plan, Saavedra started the Tapatio Hot Sauce Company.

Saavedra began manufacturing and distributing his popular hot sauce in the small industrial warehouse and continued to work out of that site for the next 14 years. For the first five years, he struggled to make ends meet and worked two additional jobs. The Tapatio Hot Sauce Company's humble beginnings were tumultuous to say the least, and Saavedra had several obstacles to overcome. He was forced to rent a U-Haul truck and make trips to Mexico to buy glassware because none of the big Los Angeles glass manufacturers would sell him bottles in such a small quantity. He would make the long drive to Mexico and then come back to his plant, mix his secret blend of herbs and spices to produce huge batches of his signature hot sauce. Each bottle was filled, labeled and capped by hand. Once complete, he would put the finished bottles in the cardboard shipping box that he stenciled, assembled and taped by hand. On a good day, he produced several cases a day; Saavedra would then pack the boxes into his car and begin delivering to his customers. At this stage in his operation, he bought just enough supplies to fill orders because his small quarters did not have enough room to store ingredients or boxes.

As the case with most small businesses just starting out, Saavedra struggled to make ends meet. It took a

good five years of hard work before the Tapatio Hot Sauce broke even and it took another five years for the business to show a steady growth. As a result, his customers demanded more hot sauce and larger quantities.

As sales increased, Saavedra became overwhelmed with the daily operation of the business. No sooner did he put out the call for help, did his family respond. Saavedra's son Jose-Luis Saavedra Jr., gave up his profession as a physician to become general manager. Saavedra Sr. knew his present facility was too small, so he moved the company to a new 7,800-square-foot location in Vernon, California, just east of Los Angeles. Saavedra began manufacturing three different bottle sizes to accommodate his customers requirements. He soon ran into problems with receiving supplies and shipping his product. The building was much bigger, but it had only a single loading dock and limited storage space. Loading trucks were tying up traffic on the street since they were forced to wait in long lines in order to pickup and deliver shipments. In addition, production workers had to frequently retool the line to meet the daily demand for the three bottle sizes. Saavedra decided that it was again time to look for a larger facility. Upon advice from his daughter Jacquie, he began his search for a building that would provide enough space to meet the company's current requirements and anticipated growth in the years to come.

After a long search, Saavedra found a site where the developer would build to suit. The spacious new 30,000-square-foot facility that the Tapatio Hot Sauce Company presently occupies, is just two miles from their old Vernon plant. They now have a brand new state-of-the-art facility with several loading docks and a fully-automated production line.

The company that Saavedra founded in 1971, has evolved into a modern plant, yet it keeps the warmth of a small, family-run business. With the addition of customized machinery and operation streamlining, Saavedra Sr. is able to produce in two hours what took him a year to produce in 1971. In addition, he now has added help from his daughter Dolores. Jacquie runs the business office and Dolores uses her law degree to handle all of the company's legal matters. The new facility has offices, a warehouse and a processing area, with enough room for future growth. For the first time, the company is able to store both ingredients and finished products. And now Tapatio gears its bottling line for one size for several days without stopping to change bottles, caps and packing boxes.

Tapatio is now benefiting from the hot sauce craze and each year the company continues to flourish. The company currently distributes nationally and has begun exporting to Mexico, Canada, Central America, and some countries in Europe. Saavedra hopes to heat up sales and someday be right next to the salt and pepper shakers at restaurants and homes worldwide.

Tapatio's 30,000-square-foot facility.

TOYOTA MOTOR SALES
Toyota/Everyday

When Toyota decided to come to America more than 40 years ago, Los Angeles was considered one of the premier automotive markets in the United States. That hasn't changed. And since its humble beginnings in a Hollywood dealership, Toyota has grown to become America's fourth largest automobile manufacturer. Led by Camry, America's favorite car, Toyota's 1997 sales surpassed one million units for the eighth consecutive year.

With its U.S. headquarters now established just south of Los Angeles in Torrance, Toyota has maintained a key presence in the city. Toyota's total American investment has grown to nearly $8 billion. In Southern California, Toyota directly employs 4,700 people with a payroll of more than $297 million.

Toyota has diverse operations in Southern California. U.S. sales and marketing activities for Toyota and Lexus, its luxury division, take place in Torrance. Toyota Motor Credit Corporation, Lexus Financial Services and Toyota Motor Insurance Services also call Torrance home. Offering financial and insurance packages, these divisions provide valuable support services to Toyota and Lexus customers.

An important facet of selling cars in America is designing them with American drivers in mind.

The lifeblood of any organization is its employees, and at Toyota, employees share the commitment to give back to the community. Here, employees cheer athletes in the Southern California Special Olympics Athletes' Village.

Toyota's Calty Design Research facility in Newport Beach was the first design studio established by a major automaker in California and celebrated its 25th anniversary in 1998. Calty contributed ideas and concepts for the Tacoma compact pickup truck, Previa van, Toyota Celica and Lexus SC 300/400 sport coupe.

The Los Angeles area also is home to Toyota's state-of-the-art research and development facilities. Toyota Technical Center, U.S.A. (TTC) has offices in Gardena, as well as other locations across the country. This division of Toyota supports North American manufacturing operations with engineering design and development; parts, materials and engine evaluation; technical and environmental research; and vehicle performance evaluations.

Toyota doesn't just design, test and market vehicles here in America. It builds vehicles here as well. In 1997, more than 60 percent of the Toyota vehicles sold in the United States were built in

With a sportier new look, the Toyota Camry earned acclaim as America's Favorite Car in 1997. Camry is one of five Toyota models assembled in North America.

North America. One of Toyota's facilities, TABC, Inc. in Long Beach, manufactures truck beds for Tacoma trucks as well as catalytic converters and substrates for other vehicles.

The Inland Empire is home to the Ontario Parts Center, Toyota's largest parts procurement center in the world. This facility handles parts processing and orders for Toyota's North American parts distribution centers and represents a $75 million investment in the local community.

The Port of Los Angeles is a crucial lifeline to Toyota's distribution system to dealerships across the country. It also is an import and export point for the company. In

Steel is welded during Toyota Tacoma truck bed production at TABC in Long Beach. TABC also assembles steering columns for Toyota Tacomas.

1997, Toyota exported $654 million worth of goods to several major markets throughout the world, including Japan, Europe and the Middle East. Export sales are expected to reach $900 million in calendar year 1998.

Toyota also believes in giving back to the communities in which it does business. Over the last seven years, Toyota has provided more than $90 million to support education, health and human services, community development, the arts and to provide humanitarian aid across the country. In Southern California, Toyota employees can be found refurbishing homes and nonprofit facilities in Long Beach and Orange County each year during the "Christmas in April" volunteer program. They also run the Athletes' Village during the Southern California Special Olympics at UCLA, participate in AIDS Walk Los Angeles; and run in the Jimmy Stewart Relay Marathon benefiting St. John's Hospital.

Toyota believes an auto company can be a vehicle for change in local communities. For more than 40 years, the company has worked to demostrate that belief. Toyota is proud of its American heritage, and continues to strive to meet the evolving needs of its customers and its community.

Toyota's Calty design studio in Newport Beach brings Southern California flair to cutting-edge automobile designs. Concepts for several Toyota models take shape here.

TROPICAL PRESERVING CO. INC.

he Tropical Preserving Co. may be small by comparison to the corporations that make up the nation's largest jam and jelly manufacturers. But this family-run operation has a much stronger heritage and colorful history than many of its competitors.

When Tropical Preserving Co. opened its doors in 1928 in the then-largely residential neighborhood it currently occupies, women from the surrounding homes arrived at the plant to help clean, pit, peel and prepare apricots, peaches and plums for processing.

Tropical continues this tradition today by hiring employees "from the immediate area," many of whom have been with the company for over two decades and who have subsequently made Tropical their own family operation by bringing their relatives on board over the years.

In the early days, Tropical's preserves were packaged in pottery crocks, sealed with paraffin and secured with string. The original preserves contained only pure fruit and sugar, slow cooked in open steam jacketed copper kettles to a thick consistency before packaging. Each container was then covered with wax paper and shipped in wooden crates throughout the West.

The operation changed hands in 1934 from Dan Reed to the Randall Family, who continues Tropical's tradition to the present day. Along the way, Tropical joined forces with Sunkist to test and use citrus pectin in the production of its jams and jellies. The

In the 1950s, Tropical Preserving Co., Inc. set an industry trend by replacing these antiquated copper kettles with steam-jacketed stainless steel kettles.

successful result led to the thick, delicious preserves produced today.

By the 1950s, Tropical again set a trend by replacing the antiquated copper kettles with steam-jacketed stainless steel kettles and led the industry in field testing vacuum seal capping. This testing met with so much success that Tropical became the first West Coast processor to use vacuum sealed lids.

Despite the onslaught of orders from retail stores during WWII, the Los Angeles-based family firm was forced to ration its preserves and distribute its product in assorted cases rather than by the case.

During this downtime, Tropical gradually upgraded their production facility, a process that culminated in the current 30,000-square-foot processing plant and on-site administrative offices.

In the 1980s, the company completely renovated its equipment again. This time, replacing the stainless

steel kettles with state-of-the-art 250-gallon stainless steel vacuum cookers which allow the product to be processed at extremely low temperatures to retain the maximum amount of flavor and color.

Tropical also purchased a new high-speed piston filler and an automatic case packer and sealer in order to keep up with the new cookers. This equipment allows Tropical to consistently increase its production of the 100-plus items currently shipped to the shelves of nearly every major grocery store chain in the western United States and Hawaii.

Tropical's family of products range from 20 different flavored signature preserves and four private label brands to pancake syrup.

"I think the success of our company over the years can largely be attributed to the fact that we've paid close attention to every aspect of the business and we take a very 'hands-on' approach," says Company President Ronald Randall. "At Tropical, our philosophy has always been to supply quality product at an affordable price. We are a smaller, leaner organization than some of the larger corporations, but it is for that very reason that we are proud to be able to pass those savings on to the customer."

Lee Randall, CEO and Ron Randall, President.

A view of the processing plant in the company's early days.

U.S. FOODSERVICE INC.™

For almost 100 years, U.S. FOODSERVICE,™ originally known as S.E. Rykoff & Co., has provided top quality value-added products and services to customers throughout the United States and is recognized as a distributor who listens and cares.

The company's roots go back to 1911 and a neighborhood grocery store in Los Angeles. The Rykoff family came to California from New London, Connecticut and bought a small grocery. It was hard times, but they supported themselves by selling produce and meat to railroad workers. Saul Rykoff, his brother and five sisters grew up working in the family business. As a result, the store became Saul's lifetime commitment.

People's lives are frequently changed by seemingly small events. Such was the case with Saul when a customer made an unusual request for a 100 pound bag of potatoes. Saul was curious and soon learned the man was a buyer from the county health institution, located just a block from the store. Realizing he could pass the benefits of quantity buying directly on to his customers, Saul devised a plan to tackle the high cost of beef. Under the guidance of a butcher who worked at the store, Saul purchased sides of beef and sold portions to both regular customers and the county institution's buyer. This was Rykoff's introduction to quantity wholesale buying and selling. The system worked so well that the family store grew and ultimately became S.E. Rykoff & Co., named after Saul.

Meanwhile, across the country in Chicago, another family was busy creating the canning process. John Sexton, Sr. pioneered canning and invented the institutional #10 size can. Years ago, customers referred to it

U.S. FOODSERVICE™
Southern California Division.

as the "gallon can." Eventually, the Sexton's family business became known as the "Home of the Gallon Goods." The Rykoffs became increasingly interested in food preservation methods, specifically those utilized by the canning industry. Young Saul Rykoff had never seen food in cans before. He was so fascinated by the potential of these new preserving methods that it motivated him to establish better canned food packing standards.

Saul Rykoff made his greatest contribution to the food service industry with the concept of "value-added," a term which is now a buzz word for many successful businesses. "Value-added" actually means consistently adding extra useable ounces of product into each container. The company still maintains strict adherence to these "value-added" concepts regarding products and services. This simple, honest philosophy of Saul Rykoff's was well received by the industry and became the basis for the company's continued growth through the years.

In 1967, Saul Rykoff died after leading the company for 56 years. The foodservice industry was virtually exploding. Rykoff's sales more than quadrupled, from $18 million in 1962 to $75 million in 1972, the same year the company went public.

By the 1980s, Rykoff was uniquely poised for growth. The company was financially strong and had no long-term debt. Most importantly, Rykoff had mastered the controls it needed to manage rapid growth. In 1982, Rykoff was listed on the American Stock Exchange and the acquisitions continued. The most significant of these was the purchase of John Sexton & Company in 1983. Rykoff acquired Sexton for a lot of reasons, not the least of which was the chance to expand nationally with just a single pen stroke. Rykoff and Sexton were a perfect fit, both possessing a quality image and extensive manufacturing capabilities. The companies joined under a new name and Rykoff-Sexton Inc. was born.

In May of 1996, Rykoff-Sexton Inc. merged with U.S. FOODSERVICE, Inc.™ to become the third largest national foodservice distributor in the country. In December of 1997, U.S. FOODSERVICE, Inc.™ merged with J.P. FOODSERVICE to become the second

From soup to nuts, U.S. FOODSERVICE™'s well-stocked Southern California warehouse is duplicated by a widespread network of branches and distribution centers.

largest foodservice distribution company in the nation. Each company has a long history of commitment and service in the finest traditions of foodservice distribution. And each company began decades ago as a local distributor, dedicated to serving the special needs of foodservice operators in its district market. The company is now operated under the name U.S. FOODSERVICE™.

Today, U.S. FOODSERVICE™ continues with the highest standards of Quality, Service and Integrity. Providing turnkey sourcing solution, U.S. FOODSERVICE™ is more than just a supplier. The company is a resource for consumer trends, market data, menu analysis and labor-saving options. Sales people are trained consultants who emphasize listening instead of dictating. U.S. FOODSERVICE™ consists of a wide-spread network of divisions and distribution centers across the nation. The immense product line now includes frozen and refrigerated foods, center-of-the-plate items, imports and specialty foods, beverages, paper, produce and janitorial supplies and a selection of equipment. The company offers a full line of both private label and national brands, produced domestically and imported from 31 countries around the world.

At U.S. FOODSERVICE™ the goal is to become its customers partner by delivering success from the service line to the bottom line.

VENTURA FOODS

The merger of the packaged edible oil and related food products businesses of Mitsui Company Ltd. of Tokyo and Mitsui and Company (U.S.A.) with Harvest States Cooperative formed the largest company of its kind in the United States, Ventura Foods, LLC. This union, completed in 1996, has produced a company with formidable combined assets that offers unparalleled value and service to the marketplace. The roots of the company's success can be traced back to the humble origins of two small businesses. The story of these two businesses is an enlightening picture of the values and hard work that have led to Ventura's present position as an industry leader.

In 1919, Hayes Wilsey began an egg business in Petaluma, California. During the adverse years of the Great Depression, a time when thousands of businesses throughout the United States were closing or cutting back operations, the then Wilsey Bennett Company diversified by starting a butter packaging business.

Through the following years, the company continued to expand while focusing on the emerging food service industry. During the 1980s, the growth of Wilsey Foods led to the establishment of production and sales facilities in the Western, Southwestern and Southeastern United States. In addition, the company began servicing many of the nation's largest restaurant chains. In 1989, Mitsui & Company, Ltd., a leading Tokyo-based international trading corporation, along with Mitsui (U.S.A.), Inc., acquired Wilsey Foods as the U.S. flagship company for their value-added food business. This acquisition afforded Wilsey dramatic new opportunities to expand its domestic and international business activities.

Holsum Foods, the eventual partner of Wilsey Foods, began in 1867 as the Jewett & Sherman Company. It manufactured and marketed a line of food products that included dressings, pickles, coffee and other specialty items. With its origins in the American heartland, Holsum succeeded in the following years with its traditional values of quality products, hard work, and a respect and concern for their customer's needs. In 1967, Holsum became a division of Harvest States, the largest U.S. grower's co-op and a major soybean processor. With the belief that specialization was a key to the company's future success, Holsum focused on a select number of edible oil, dressing and sauce products. At the same time, the company managed to combine the buying power and expertise of a large company with the flexibility, quick response time and attentiveness to customer needs of a small business. These factors produced a classic American success story.

As a prelude to a merger, the two companies entered into a joint venture that involved purchasing a production

Part of the distribution network that spans the country.

facility in Chambersburg, Pennsylvania. This facility produced a variety of condiment items. The venture also involved the sharing of contracts for the production of private label mayonnaise, salad dressing, sauces and soup bases. With the success of this initial venture in hand, the companies decided to merge their resources to form Ventura Foods, LLC.

The resulting corporation has capitalized on the strengths and abilities of the two companies. The combined production and distribution capabilities have put Ventura Foods in a position to provide customers with quality food products and outstanding service in every U.S. market. Wilsey's reputation as a strong marketer, together with Holsum's consumer and distribution expertise illustrate Ventura's ability to better serve retail and foodservice customers in domestic as well as international markets.

With 12 manufacturing plants strategically located throughout the United States, Ventura Foods has ably positioned itself to meet its customer's needs. These facilities have enabled the company to quickly respond to the specific situations and requirements of its customers in the foodservice, bakery and retail fields, as well as produce a wide range of products to meet the diverse needs of customers. The products include shortenings and oils, mayonnaise, flavored dressings, sauces, syrups and bakery ingredients. These facilities each play a unique and integral role within the company. The City of Industry, California facility, for example, produces a full line of branded and private label mayonnaise and dressings products for the foodservice market, as well as shortenings and margarine. The plant in Waukesha, Wisconsin specializes in contract packaging for retail and foodservice accounts; and in the east, the 435,000-square-foot Chambersburg, Pennsylvania, facility brings full lines of Ventura brands and private label products to retail and foodservice customers.

A key component of the company's continuing growth has been its devotion to quality assurance and product development. Ventura controls quality and cost from harvest to refining, processing, packaging and distribution. The company has implemented an advanced quality assurance program that focuses on

The facilities that allow Ventura Foods to meet the needs of its customers across the nation and the world.

product safety, consistency and performance. Quality control managers at each facility conduct performance and specification tests, as well as thorough sensory evaluations on all Ventura and customer brands. Ventura's product development group is a key asset in meeting the demands of the customer. When a customer requires a product to cater to changing taste preferences, performance or function, the group is able to respond quickly. The company's emphasis on quality control and its ability to adapt to customer requirements are considered crucial to the continued growth of both the company and its clients.

The company controls all aspects of quality and cost from harvest to refining, processing, packaging and distribution. Since Ventura provides its customers with valuable commodity market information and risk management services, the company is able to offer a variety of high-quality products at a lower cost. All of the company's customers benefit from the strategic location of Ventura's manufacturing and distribution facilities, and because the company offers its own brands of specialty products, as well as a broad range of private label brands and custom-made items, customers are able to consolidate a variety of product requirements with one key supplier.

Ventura foods has grown from humble origins to its present position as a titan in the food service industry. A background of marketing expertise, manufacturing and logistics expertise provides Ventura's customers with exceptional value at the lowest possible cost. And with ongoing, changing customer needs, Ventura is poised to continue in its role as a major growing resource for the food industry into the 21st century.

WESTERN TUBE AND CONDUIT CORPORATION

stablished in 1964, Western Tube & Conduit Corporation began operations out of a small facility in Oakland, California, and expanded to Vernon, California, in 1965 with a single tube mill to produce conduit.

Originally founded by a joint venture between C. Duane Erikson and International Tube Corporation in Illinois, the majority share was subsequently acquired by Sumitomo Metal Industries, Ltd. in 1968. Sumitomo Metal is an integrated steel manufacturer in Japan, distinctly characterized as a premier leading manufacturer of pipe and tube.

Since that time, the operation has expanded and evolved with the technical expertise of Sumitomo Metal and customer relations skills of its employees, which currently number over 240.

By 1975, the firm opened the doors of its present location in Long Beach, California. Spread over 20 acres, Western Tube & Conduit Corporation currently boasts five high-speed tube mills, a steel slitting line and facilities for finishing.

Western Tube & Conduit Corporation is currently the largest manufacturer west of the Rockies making electrical metal conduit, fence post and mechanical tubing.

Unique Production Capabilities

Over the years, Western Tube & Conduit has emerged as a major player in the production of electrical metal conduit (EMT), intermediate metal conduit (IMC), rigid conduit, fence posts and mechanical tubing.

The company's on-line galvanizing process is uniquely designed with distinct technology incorporated, which is a high-speed and fully continuous production line forming through galvanizing and coating. Because of its extremely high productivity with a high quality controlled surface, galvanized tubing has become core component products that are now difficult to be challenged.

Western Tube's mechanical tubing, which includes carbon steel, galvanized, aluminized, alloy steel and stainless, is found in some of the most demanding applications which range from structural and decorative portions of furniture to hundreds of various components for commercial, automotive and industrial uses.

The company doesn't just stop with making a high-quality product. Western Tube & Conduit Corporation also maintains a computerized inventory control that can quickly pinpoint the availability of all the mechanical tubing in stock. The company owns, controls and maintains a fleet of trucks to ensure quick delivery.

Much of the company's success to date can be directly traced to its original concept and company culture, defined by a combination of "strong ethics and discipline, result orientation, competitive prices, quality products and unparalleled customer service."

Since its inception, the company's philosophy has been to make Western Tube & Conduit, first and foremost, a service organization as a manufacturing extension of a client's own production facilities. The firm's production engineers work directly from client input to develop the specific ways in which Western's tubing products and services can most effectively match its client's needs.

Corporate Culture and Direction

This company's culture is characteristically different from its competition in the pipe and tube manufacturing industry. The atmosphere at Western Tube & Conduit is distinctly rooted in both customer relations and a tightly knit team operation.

All of the company's marketing forces from engineering to technical maintenance and customer service are housed under the same roof, unlike most of the other manufacturers which lose the personal touch and level of teamwork by having offices and plants spread across the nation.

Because everything happens from this single location, Western Tube & Conduit is able to respond to its customers' needs with exceptional speed and agility to deliver the highest quality products and services in the industry today.

"Our growing success in sales volume and profit is a result of the company's strong market presence, our commitment to technical innovation and enhanced ability to quickly deliver quality products to our clients," says President and CEO Takeshi

Ogata. "We value five principles as the company's goal: strong ethics and discipline, result orientation, customer orientation, competitiveness in cost and quality, and a great place to work. Adhering to these principles, the company can be a more proactive, slim and nimble organization."

The company's position in the industry certainly stands as testament to the success of its innovative ideas and unique business philosophy. The reason for the company's recent rapid rise was a carefully orchestrated effort to do things differently from its competition. The company is vigorously pursuing corporate growth through niching, partnering and acquisition. As to ensure long-term corporate growth, it also emphasizes environmental consciousness, compliance with laws and contribution to society.

BRIGHT GLOW CANDLE COMPANY

When it comes to candles, one company shines brighter than the rest: Bright Glow Candle Company in Vernon. Founded in 1982 by Richard Alcedo, Bright Glow Candle Company sells millions of candles every year, making the company one of the top manufacturers and distributors of candles in the United States.

Alcedo, a native of Peru, was not raised as a maker of candles. After immigrating to the United States, he met a gentleman who was closing his candle manufacturing business because of poor health, thereby putting several candle makers out of business. One of those men offered to teach Alcedo — who knew nothing about the candle business — how to make candles. Alcedo agreed, and the two men set up a rudimentary candle-making shop in Alcedo's small garage in El Monte.

After two months the candle expert departed, leaving Alcedo to make them on his own. He would heat a large pot full of wax, and using a piece of hose and simple valve, fill his empty glass containers two at a time. His equipment was crude and his progress slow, but Alcedo persevered. He would take orders in the afternoon, manufacture the candles at night, and deliver them the next morning. Slowly, his business grew, until in 1987 Alcedo was able to move out of his garage into an actual warehouse. His business continued to grow, and Alcedo moved into his current 40,000-square-foot facility in the City of Vernon in 1990.

Now, Bright Glow Candle Company has 50 employees in the Vernon facility who manufacture and distribute about 5,000 dozen candles every day. And because of the demand for Bright Glow candles, the company opened a second manufacturing plant in Miami, Florida in 1998.

The most popular items at Bright Glow Candle Company are the votive candles and the larger decorative candles, which feature religious designs popular with the Hispanic population. Bright Glow also makes and sells birthday candles, household candles, scented candles and special occasion candles, many featuring holiday designs such as Santa Claus and the menorah. Some candles are geared toward other ethnic markets, including Portuguese and Italian. Alcedo stands behind his candles. His company promises quality merchandise, and delivers on that promise. All Bright Glow candles are designed to be smoke free and odorless, and guaranteed to burn clean to the bottom of the glass while leaving no residue.

Company sales reps go to stores that carry Bright Glow products and clean shelves, merchandise the stock, and do whatever they can to ensure complete customer satisfaction. Service is important, because competition in the billion-dollar candle industry is fierce. To stay competitive, Alcedo buys his material in large volumes. His company purchases about 10 million pounds of wax every year, and about one million cases of glass.

Although Alcedo is the only member of his family involved in Bright Glow, the business still has a family feel to it. Some of his employees have been with Bright Glow for many years, and will be for years to come.

Alcedo does charity work with the local Chamber of Commerce, because he believes you have to share what you make in order for it to come back. He also believes that anyone can fulfill their dreams if they give them a fighting chance.

"Too many people get discouraged too soon," says Alcedo. "If you see something, latch on and do the best you can. You have to look for different angles to be successful. And don't forget to service your customers as best you can."

As a self-made, successful Hispanic business owner, Alcedo has practiced what he preaches. Through Bright Glow, he is lighting the way for other would-be entrepreneurs who want to turn their business dreams into reality.

LA REINA, INC.

When Los Angelenos bite into a burrito, quesadilla or any dish made with wheat tortillas, they're tasting a product first popularized and made available by one man and one company — Mauro Robles and La Reina, Inc. From an immigrant's dream, hard work and innovative planning, La Reina has grown into the second largest minority-owned business in Los Angeles and one of the top 60 Latino-owned companies in the country.

The founding of this family-owned East Los Angeles business reads like The American Dream. Mauro Robles immigrated from Mexico to Los Angeles in 1951 and worked at a small factory which produced handmade corn tortillas. At that time, large-scale tortilla factories did not exist, wheat tortillas were a homemade rarity, and handmade corn tortillas were available only in Mexican restaurants or markets.

Robles noticed the American preference for the taste of wheat and saw tremendous potential for flour tortillas. He investigated methods for speeding production and discovered the union rounder, a machine used by commercial bread companies to cut vats of dough into smaller units of uniform size and weight. This machine offered Robles a production shortcut never before used by tortilla makers.

On May 4, 1958, Robles opened a small tortilla factory at Sixth and Indiana streets in East Los Angeles. By modifying corn tortilla ovens and utilizing the union rounder, he could produce tortillas faster and less expensively than all the other tortilla factories. When markets and restaurants learned it was cheaper to buy from La Reina than make tortillas themselves, business boomed.

For nearly a decade, the company experienced vertical growth. In 1978, Robles diversified by purchasing Anita's Foods in San Bernardino and expanding his product line to include corn tortillas, taco shells, tostada shells and tortilla chips. Eventually that division branched out into low-fat snacks and organic blue corn chips.

Also in the late 70s, Robles started a division in Monterey Park to produce a line of frozen foods. Today, that division produces a full line of Mexican frozen foods including burritos and taquitos, frozen pizzas, and Chinese and Italian noodle entrees.

In 1960, La Reina moved to a 12,000-square-foot building at its present location. Coincidentally, the facility opened the same day as the adjacent Long Beach Freeway, providing easy access for distribution. Through the years, the company's factory expanded to its current 65,000 square feet.

La Reina maintains operations 24 hours a day, six days a week, manufacturing in excess of 100,000 pounds a day — 90,000 to 120,000 dozen — of pressed and hand-stretched flour tortillas. These are marketed under the La Reina, Anita's, or Villa Victoria names, or as private labels for other companies. They also produce gourmet flavored wraps, Indian chapatis and naan. The company ships tortillas to Western Europe, Australia, Korea, Canada, Japan and 44 states — including Texas.

Today, La Reina's combined companies sell over $55 million annually. Mauro Robles continues as CEO, with each division headed by a family member. Ricardo Robles, president of La Reina and Mauro's son, states the philosophy which fuels their success: "This is a family owned and operated business," he says, "so we take a lot of pride in what we do here. We want to always create a quality product that we can be proud to take home to our families."

Mauro Robles, founder and CEO of La Reina, Inc.

A rainbow of corn tortilla chips, from standard to exotic varieties such as blue and red corn and chili & lime, a few of the many products produced by La Reina, Inc. and its divisions.

PACO STEEL & ENGINEERING

Steel, both durable and strong, is the primary structural building material throughout the world. Millions of tons of steel beams are consumed annually, and nothing is more cost-efficient and versatile than the "Lightweight" I Beam.

In 1980, Paik invented and patented the extremely light-weight Corrugated I Beam.

The proper application of steel in projects requires years of experience and training. Founded as an engineering firm in 1974, PACO Steel and Engineering has always had knowledgeable experts on hand to assist in the design and utilization of steel products. The company holds numerous patents including the PAIK Knee Joint, a column and rafter connection that facilitated the rapid construction of military facilities in Vietnam without the use of welding, heavy equipment or experience.

Since its inception, PACO Steel & Engineering has grown to become the largest worldwide distributor of lightweight beams and offers the largest selection of mini, light and corrugated beams in both welded and hot-rolled configurations.

Pioneered initially for the manufactured home industry, lightweights have found their way into new applications that range from recreational vehicles and home construction to freight containers and truck chassis.

A graduate of the Indiana Institute of Technology, the University of Oregon and the Yense University in his native Seoul, Korea, company founder and president Young J. Paik stands at the forefront of innovation in the steel industry.

Company founder and president Young J. Paik stands at the forefront of innovation in the steel industry.

Shortly after he founded PACO Steel & Engineering, Paik worked with a Japanese steel manufacturer to develop new technology and faster production of lightweight welded steel beams.

In 1980, he invented and patented the extremely lightweight Corrugated I Beam, which enabled the company to expand into national markets.

As the industry leader in the distribution of lightweight beams, PACO offers substantial advantages to its customers. The firm provides the highest quality product with every beam being subjected to extensive quality control checks before leaving the mill. PACO also has the largest inventory of lightweight beams with stock locations throughout the country.

In early 1996 PACO began building a manufacturing facility adjacent to the Mississippi River in Arkansas. This mid-United States location is convenient for both in and outbound shipments nationwide. The plant is now in operation and utilizes the latest in high speed, super efficient welded beam technology featuring solid state electric resistance welders, accumulators, automated bundlers and slitting line. Manufacturing its own beam permits PACO to be more flexible and responsive to customer needs and allows development of custom designed products.

As a result of advances in steel technologies and new applications, steel consumption is increasing worldwide. PACO Steel & Engineering is committed to leading the way to the future. Mr. Paik and his staff strive to offer more value to their customers: with PACO, steel customers receive the highest quality product along with unparalleled support to successfully accomplish their goals.

ROSCOE MOSS COMPANY
Making Water Work For Los Angeles

The early migration of settlers to the West brought a need for assured water supplies in this vast, largely arid region. Water for agriculture, mining and transportation, coupled with an exploding population, required deep wells and the development of products of unusual strength and capacity.

By the turn of the century, the Roscoe Moss Company had already established itself as an industry leader in ground water development in Los Angeles and the southwestern United States. Founder Roscoe Moss incorporated his expanding company in 1927 and transformed the water well drilling firm into an innovative, well-equipped and highly-skilled contracting business. In the years since its inception, Roscoe Moss Company has greatly contributed to the ground water development industry in the Southwest, across this continent and around the world.

In 1926, Roscoe Moss Company began production of steel tubular products as a natural extension to their traditional role as water well drilling contractors. That same year, the firm moved into its present facility and built a factory for the manufacture of well casing. The addition of new product lines and further expansion have placed the company in a unique position as a state-of-the-art premier provider of steel water pipes serving the western United States.

(Left photo)
450' Irrigation Well, 1918

Current production centers around spiral weld technology, a flexible process noted for manufacturing a round, straight and uniform product with the capability of producing a variety of lengths, diameters and wall thicknesses. Water well casing and screen are manufactured from a variety of steel material including several grades of stainless steel.

For over half a century, Roscoe Moss Company has manufactured the well casing and screen used in its drilling operations. Today, many domestic and international contractors, municipalities, industrial and agricultural users are among the firm's customers.

Since its inception, Roscoe Moss Company has recognized and filled the need for successful development of ground water at home and abroad. Whether through its own contracting and consulting services, pipe, well casing and screen production or through publication and dissemination of its expertise in all of these fields, Roscoe Moss Company has made water work for Los Angeles and worldwide.

PARTNERS IN LOS ANGELES
MARKETPLACE

Los Angeles retail establishments, service industries and
leisure/convention facilities offer an impressive variety of choices for
Los Angeles residents and visitors alike.

ABLE FREIGHT SERVICES, INC.

Oxnard strawberries in Amsterdam, Visalia onions in Chile, lettuce in Kuwait, grapes in London, cherries in Japan — when the world feasts on California's agricultural bounty, Able Freight Services, Inc. is the company that makes it possible. This Los Angeles-based freight forwarder specializes in shipping highly perishable commodities to markets across the country and around the world.

Since its founding in 1992, Able Freight has rapidly become one of the largest forwarders of fresh fruits, vegetables and flowers on the West Coast. The company confines itself to transportation; they do not buy and sell produce. According to company President and Founder Scott I. Murray, "Everyone in the business of getting food to your table has a special function that they perform better than anyone else. Ours is transportation."

Able Freight serves West Coast growers through an 8,000-square-foot main office and warehouse in Los Angeles, as well as an office/warehouse in San Francisco, and an office in Seattle. Operations continue 24 hours a day, 365 days a year.

One of the United Airlines jets which transports Able Freight's produce around the world.

Able's customers are always able to communicate with somebody at the company. Murray wears a beeper and is always on call. Able's philosophy is simple: "The customer comes first," he says, "then the employee, then myself, and I take care of people in that order.

Murray never planned to run a freight forwarding business. After his graduation from The American Graduate School of International Management, he moved to California without a job. Having made letter of credit presentations to banks on behalf of a freight forwarder, Murray was familiar with the business. Upon arriving in San Francisco, he checked the phone directory under Freight Forwarders to find a company which would allow him to work part-time while conducting his "real" job search. The company which hired him handled fresh produce, and Murray worked there for four and a half years. When his employer balked at giving him a raise, Murray left. He now laughs, "If they'd given me what I asked for, Able would not be here today."

He was hired by another freight forwarding firm to develop their perishables market. One day a close friend, Rosalba Gil, said to him, "Why are you doing that research for somebody else? You could open a business on your own." The idea took hold. At the time, not many companies handled the often difficult logistics of shipping fresh produce. Murray saw this as an opportunity to serve a niche market.

Every freight forwarding company must obtain a license from the International Air Transport Association (IATA). Before acquiring his own license, Murray needed to prove to IATA that he had the experience and knowledge to run a freight forwarding company, and thus operated Able Freight for one year using his friend Rosalba's license. Simultaneously, he acquired a small line of credit with the airlines. He worked from a desk and phone in his friend's office.

Murray chose to focus his business whenever possible with United Airlines. "I picked a carrier that gave me a lot of options and destinations," he says, "and I started to give them my business as much as I could." When he began the company in 1992, United gave Murray $2,500 per month in credit. As of 1997, Able Freight became one of United's largest cargo customer in the State of California.

The Los Angeles warehouse bustles with activity 24 hours a day. The building contains four individual refrigerated coolers, each kept at a constant 33 to 34 degrees Fahrenheit. One unit contains a hydro precooler, which removes hot air from the produce and provides a fine mist of water from above to rehydrate commodities which need moisture, such as asparagus. The damp air circulates constantly and within minutes, the produce is cooled to its ideal temperature.

Able then packs the produce into airline shipping containers capable of holding 3,500 pounds, or stacks cookie sheet-type pallets which hold up to 10,000 pounds. These are then loaded onto cargo planes or in the belly of passenger planes. The company does not warehouse the produce; rarely is any commodity held for 24 hours.

Getting fresh produce from the farmer's field to a dinner table is far more complex than the average person considers. The process starts with a market or restaurant determining its need for premium fresh produce. The buyer or chef places an order with a produce broker, the person who deals directly with farmers. The broker then calls Able Freight to list the amount and type of produce that needs to be shipped, and by what time it must be moved.

The contact at Able checks the airlines to determine which flights have space to handle the shipment, the pricing options and how soon they'll need to have the produce on hand in order to ship on time. Variables to be considered include whether the flight is direct or requires a connection; reliability of the carrier; and what time the produce is off-loaded at the destination. For example, a flight that gets in earlier and unloads during midday heat may be less desirable than one that lands a few hours later when the temperature cools down. The commodities being shipped are so perishable and consumer pricing so competitive, every precaution must be taken to guarantee the highest quality at the lowest cost.

Once the broker decides upon the carrier, Able books space on the flight and sets the time by which the commodity needs to be available in Los Angeles. The broker contacts the grower and has the produce loaded from fields onto trucks and driven to the Able Freight warehouse. A small padding of time is worked into the

The Los Angeles headquarters for Able Freight, located just five minutes from the loading docks at LAX.

process to accommodate heavy traffic, bad weather, or human error on the road. Once the produce arrives, it is unloaded, packed into the appropriate airline container, and loaded into one of Able's refrigerated trucks.

The company's Los Angeles facility is located only five minutes from LAX airport terminal, and Able must deliver product to the airline between two and four hours before flight time. Timing is everything, and containers delivered to an airline 90-minutes before a flight are probably too late to be loaded. Able ships about 40 to 50,000 pounds of produce a day to New York's JFK airport alone, and during peak season might move 500,000 pounds of California's harvest worldwide in a single day.

While in transit, Able Freight tracks the location of the product by a direct link to the airline's computer system. They keep both broker and customer advised as to when the product will be available at destination. Once it arrives, the order is off-loaded, sorted for delivery to specific sites, and shipped by local truckers to their destinations.

Able Freight ships less perishable produce, such as apples and broccoli, via ocean freighters.

International shipments proceed in much the same way, with Able handling the extensive paperwork required by the U.S. Department of Agriculture and Customs.

The company ships via air and ocean. For ocean shipments, produce is placed in 20-foot or 40-foot containers which may be loaded directly at the packing houses. Modern technology allows the contents of these containers to be refrigerated and gassed, which "puts the produce to sleep," preventing spoilage.

Able Freight does not advertise its services; clients come to them based on word-of-mouth or prior business dealings with one of the company's employees. Murray noted, "Freight forwarding is a very person-based business. Customers will call an agent whether they're with ABC company or XYZ company, because as far as the customer is concerned it's the person that makes it happen, not the company."

When Murray began Able Freight, many of his clients followed him from his previous employer. As operations expanded, he hired people who were well-known in the industry. Through their networks they brought in additional clients. Murray built his client base selectively, concentrating on stable customers which would afford the company a good cash flow. Murray attributes Able Freight's success to his coworkers, notably Orlando Wong, Alberto Jauregui, Ben-Hur Felix, Say-Wei Lee, Cathy Thalmann, Maria Hofilena and So Young Park in Los Angeles; Anita Koch in San Francisco; and Sara Barnes in Seattle.

Though the West Coast's harvest continues year-round, production of much of the world's seasonal fruits shifts south of the equator during colder months. To expand its operations, in 1997 Able Freight began handling imported produce sent from California's "geographical partners" — Chile, Australia and New Zealand. These countries produce and ship the same commodities as the West Coast, but at different times of the year. In essence, the countries take turns at providing the world's fruits and vegetables.

As an importing freight forwarder, Able reverses its usual shipping process. The company is contacted by freight forwarders in other countries and authorized to handle deliveries. According to Murray,

"Now it's our turn to worry about where the produce is, whether the planes will be on time, whether quality has been maintained."

International shipments to this country require approval from the U.S. Department of Agriculture inspectors before fresh produce can be imported and distributed. As a bonded freight forwarder, Able can pick up cargo at the airport, bring it to the warehouse and start cooling the product before inspection. Without bonding, a freight company's shipment must stay in the airline's hangar until after inspection. Given the delicacy of fresh produce and the ease with which it spoils, timeliness is essential.

Once shipments clear Customs and Deptartment of Agriculture inspectors, Able Freight breaks down the containers for delivery. Some get rerouted to other American cities, and Able ships via the most appropriate flight. For local delivery, each grocery chain, market or restaurant sends its truck to pick up the produce. Able's loading dock can handle up to eight 40-foot trucks at the same time. If the customer doesn't have a truck available, the company calls freight haulers who specialize in local deliveries to get the order to its destination.

What makes shipping fresh produce at great expense all over the world worth it is consumer expectation and demand. Travelers in distant countries expect to find a wide variety of fresh fruits and vegetables available, even if they're not in season locally. Consumer willingness to pay for quality fresh produce makes it profitable for merchants to have these products available. Everything has to be sold

in season; markets and restaurants can't hold onto large inventories because the commodities will go bad. The supply of nonlocal produce must be constantly replenished. That puts Able's services in constant demand. While the shipping process is costly, end-user demand and satisfaction make the entire process of supplying fresh produce a win-win situation.

Scott Murray continues to build Able Freight, planning future locations for offices and warehouses, and traveling south of the Equator to secure new clients for the import side of his business. His choice of the company's name demonstrates the thoroughness of thought he puts into every aspect of his business:

"I chose 'Able Freight' for several reasons," Murray explains. "It's at the beginning of the alphabet, which makes people likely to see it in a directory or list. Airlines often load containers in alphabetical order, so we have an advantage there. But just as important is the connotation the name conveys. Quite frankly, whatever the job, Able is able to do it."

One of the many refrigeration units where the fresh produce is held before shipping.

SMART & FINAL

he history of Smart & Final, the largest non-membership grocery warehouse chain in the United States, began in an era when the notion of packaged goods was unheard of. Grocers received huge casks of prunes and pickles, barrels of rice, flour and sugar and patent medicines in bulk quantities, and sold them by weight to eager customers.

It was 1871 and 16-year-old Abraham Haas had just arrived in the small, dusty ranching town of Los Angeles after the long journey by boat and railroad from his home in Bavaria.

Along with his brother, Jacob, and partners, Bernard Cohn and Herman Hellman, Haas opened the Hellman-Haas Grocery Co. in a two-story brick building on Los Angeles Street. From there, they administered to the food and sundry needs of the 6,000 people who lived in this broad expanse of cattle, sheep, unpaved streets and squat wood and adobe buildings.

The business grew, some of the original partners went on to other endeavors and new partners were acquired. By 1889, the sole owners were Abraham Haas and Jacob Baruch. They changed the company name to Haas, Baruch & Co. and introduced a private Iris label of canned tomatoes that amassed sales of $2 million by 1895.

When Haas left Los Angeles in 1900 to found Haas Wholesale Foods in San Francisco, Haas, Baruch & Co. was the largest wholesale grocer in Los Angeles, which now boasted a population of almost one million people.

It was still the leading wholesaler in 1914 when the two-year-old Santa Ana Wholesale Company was sold to a banker from Saginaw, Michigan named J. S. "Jim" Smart. When H. D. Final came onboard as his partner, the company became Smart & Final Wholesale Grocers. It also became

(Right to left) J.S. Smart and H.D. Final, founders of Smart & Final, the largest non-membership grocery warehouse chain in the nation and the pioneers of the cash-and-carry concept on the West Coast.

extremely profitable after moving near the docks in San Pedro where supplies could easily be replenished. By 1919 gross sales at Smart & Final totaled $10 million.

Still, it was a tough time to be a grocery wholesaler. Competition from other wholesalers was stiff and many retail grocers negotiated their own deals with manufacturers, bypassing wholesalers. In 1923, Smart & Final debuted the novel "cash-and-carry" self-service concept in Long Beach, along with the highly successful innovation of locating stores near customers' businesses.

Previously, grocery stores — even at wholesale — required a clerk to collect goods for the customer. Smart & Final accurately figured that the chain could reduce overhead by introducing self-service, but still retain high-quality selection and service, pioneering cash-and-carry stores.

Smart & Final and Haas, Baruch merged in 1953, and ushered in an era of change. Smart & Final, the surviving company, was purchased by the Thriftimart supermarket chain in 1955 and grew to 83 stores. Then, in 1984, the Thriftimart stores were liquidated and corporate focus shifted to modernizing and expanding Smart & Final stores.

That expansion has resulted in over 5,000 employees and more than 200 stores in Arizona, California, Florida, Idaho, Nevada, Oregon, Washington and Mexico. Sales have increased in excess of 600 percent from $240 million in 1987 to more than $1.45 billion in 1997. Smart & Final is now also in the foodservice distribution business delivering food and related supplies directly to restaurants and other institutions via two subsidiary companies — Henry Lee Company in Miami, Florida and Smart & Final Foodservice Distributors in Stockton, California — which account for about 30 percent of Company revenues. The Company's private-label products, which shed the Iris name in 1996 for an updated "Smart & Final®" brand, now represent over 20 percent of store sales.

The success with which Smart & Final has met the challenges of the distribution and wholesaling industries has been attributed to visionary management. The Company has maintained a commitment to customer service and value and has become a vital resource to Los Angeles by supporting small businesses with conveniently located non-membership stores throughout the county.

Smart & Final stores are especially tailored to meet the needs of small businesses including independent restaurants, caterers, general businesses, clubs and organizations, as well as value-oriented consumers. Customers are offered low warehouse prices on more than 10,000 grocery items (including produce, delicatessen and frozen foods), paper supplies and janitorial goods in large sizes and quantities.

It is this mix of low prices, consistent product selection, convenient store locations and personalized services such as menu planning and ordering by fax that allows Smart & Final to deliver maximum customer satisfaction and value.

One vital Smart & Final philosophy is that a company's most important resources are the people who work there. Associate training and development is seen as a strategic corporate investment. To underscore that belief, Smart & Final has developed Smart University®, a company division that began as a unique in-house training facility. Based on the success of delivering superior training and professional programs to its 5,000 employees, Smart University has built campuses in Los Angeles and Stockton, California and in Miami, Florida that are open to outside clients as well.

The Company's private-label products have always represented consistently high quality and value. Today, more than 1,200 corporate brand products contribute over 20 percent of store sales, with new products constantly being added.

These campuses offer organizations throughout the United States innovative, high quality, cost-effective programs designed to enhance business strategy through focusing on human resource development. Custom consulting programs and pre-scheduled classes, ranging from strategic planning to computer skills and professional development are conducted on- and off-site by a flexible staff of training professionals and performance consultants.

Another ground-breaking innovation by Smart & Final was the 1997 opening of a Smart & Final Plus store in North Hollywood. The 30,000-square-foot facility is twice the size of the average Smart & Final store and utilizes the additional space to test new products, concepts and merchandising before introducing them to other stores in the chain.

The increased store size also accommodates wider aisles and deeper shelves and a designated Special Orders desk that connects shoppers via computer to 10,000 additional items available from the Smart & Final foodservice distribution warehouse and hundreds of suppliers.

Based on the tremendous success of the Smart & Final Plus concept, the Company launched a Smart & Final Plus Division with plans to open 35 Plus stores of 20,000 to 25,000 square feet by the year 2001.

The Smart & Final Plus store opened in North Hollywood in 1997 as a research and development facility to test new products, concepts and merchandising before they are introduced in other stores in the chain. The concept was so successful that the Company has launched a Plus Division.

complements Smart & Final's long tradition of service and excellence with the technological innovations needed to keep the Company competitive into the 21st century.

The new distribution center positions the Company for another growth opportunity; offering food-service delivery to customers throughout Southern California. Smart & Final's high name recognition and quality reputation in Los Angeles, the greatest foodservice market in America, provides a strong foundation for their expansion into this market.

The 1998 acquisition of 39 Cash & Carry stores in the Pacific Northwest expanded Smart & Final's territory to seven states and Mexico, with West Coast exposure from Baja to the Canadian border.

Smart & Final enters the new millennium with its stock listed on the New York Stock Exchange, trading under the symbol SMF, and sales nearing the $2 billion mark. In addition, Smart & Final has a website on the World Wide

Robert J. Emmons, Chairman and Chief Executive Officer, with Smart & Final Plus store manager, Jeff Bloks.

A move from their Vernon office and warehouse facility that housed the Company for more than 40 years to new facilities in nearby City of Commerce marks another significant milestone in 1998. The landmark Citadel Office Complex, a development as rich in history as the Smart & Final Company itself, provides a fitting new headquarters for the Company's 400 corporate associates. A state-of-the-art distribution center in a 445,000-square-foot facility near Washington Boulevard and Eastern Avenue

Web which includes "The Party Zone," where visitors can view menus for entertaining large groups, as well as features such as a directory of store locations, new products and promotions and company financial information or employment opportunities.

But nothing overrides the basic principles of providing small businesses with a consistent product selection at low warehouse prices and in convenient locations. With more than 125 years of superior service, growth and success, Smart & Final approaches the new century with a confidence rooted in a history of achievement.

FREDERICK'S OF HOLLYWOOD

n answer to the eternal question, "What do women want?" Frederick Mellinger figured he knew. He believed that women wanted to be curvaceous, audacious, saucy and sexy, so in 1946 he started a lingerie company that practically invented ultra racy and provocative undergarments for the general public. He deftly turned what was taboo in a cautious culture into something naughty, but still nice enough for the girl next door. The store he founded on Hollywood Boulevard became both an icon of glitz and glamour and a national retail success story. More than 50 years later, having evolved with the changing times, Frederick's is still giving women what they want, through its more than 200 stores in 39 states, a national catalog and an online e-commerce site.

Back in mid-century, saucy lingerie was the province of Paris boutiques. Frederick's imitated the French style and introduced American women to the peignoir, the push-up bra and the fancy girdle. Men loved them. Women liked the inventive underwear that thinned their waists and perked up their bosoms. (When bra-burning became the fashion, Mellinger predicted he'd prevail because the law of gravity was on his side.) The Captivator II bra was introduced in 1971, and it's been a favorite ever since. More firsts from Frederick's include front-hook bras, sculpted leg pads, bras with shoulder pads, bustiers and bosom-boosting demi pads.

Indeed, it was the bosom that inspired the world's first Bra Museum, located in the Frederick's flagship store. It evolved into the Celebrity Lingerie Museum which is visited by thousands of tourists every year. On display are pretty vintage petticoats worn by Jeannette MacDonald, Greta Garbo and Joan Crawford in movies from the 30s, the bra Marilyn Monroe wore in *Let's Make Love*, Ingrid Bergman's corset from *Cactus Flower*, Judy Garland's nightgown from *Presenting Lily Mars*, the boxer shorts Tom Hanks wore in *Forrest Gump*, the bustier that Madonna made famous, plus many, many more intimate underfashions worn by past and present stars of film and television.

Today, Frederick's of Hollywood is updating its image. In beauty language, it might be said that Frederick's has had a makeover. Gone are leering looks and heavy pancake makeup. In are sweet smiles and romance, even if the models are clad in see-through negligees. Soft seduction is the mood, and marketing directly to independent young women is the strategy. Oddly enough, for a company that succeeded so spectacularly by selling sex appeal, some of the catalog's hottest sellers are innocent dresses with modest necklines and puffy sleeves.

The fabulous facade of Frederick's of Hollywood's flagship store on Hollywood Boulevard.

By filling its stores with a wide range of merchandise, Frederick's is prepared to offer its customers everything they want. To make shopping simple and convenient, the retailer mails out a catalog, has stores in suburban malls and maintains a presence on the Web. Sportswear sells briskly through the catalog, while lingerie is the priority in the stores. The stores are staffed by expert bra fitters, a service which not many retailers do well, and that makes a great difference to women.

Making a difference in women's lives was Frederick Mellinger's founding principle. His strategy succeeded brilliantly and made Frederick's of Hollywood a household name. Today the business he founded more than half a century ago is poised to go global, having fine-tuned its merchandising philosophy with the understanding that what women want is probably everything.

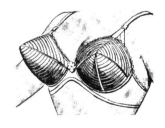

The original Frederick's of Hollywood push-up bra.

AMERICAN FISH & SEAFOOD COMPANY

Ernie Doizaki,
President & Owner

I t's hard to believe that there was a time, and it was not so long ago, when sushi wasn't chic and tuna mostly came out of cans. A generation ago, fish suffered from a serious image problem — it was generally associated with deprivation, eaten either because people were poor or doing penance. Fish could be found, of course, (every Friday in lots of households) but most people wanted ways to make it taste, well, less fishy. Home cooks generally overcooked it, much the way they boiled vegetables to death, or took the saturate-it-in-sauce route. Gradually, as American food tastes grew ever more adventurous and health conscious, fish finally came into its own. And so did American Fish & Seafood Company.

The story of American Fish spans more than half a century, beginning back in the days of World War II. George Doizaki, a Japanese-American living on the West Coast, had relatives in rural Colorado, and with their sponsorship, he was able to voluntarily relocate to the interior of the United States and avoid the fate of forced internment. He and his family spent the war years farming, but farming wasn't for him, and when the war ended, he drove back home to Los Angeles. On the way, the family stopped by a lake in Utah where he watched a group of fishermen. Call it luck or inspiration, but then and there, George Doizaki decided that fish were his future.

He acted fast. In 1947 he founded American Fish & Seafood Company with his partner, Masuro Okamoto. It was an uphill effort. Fish wasn't fashionable, and customers weren't plentiful. But they were loyal, and American Fish grew slowly and steadily. The company's first processing facility was primitive by today's standards, and deliveries were made on old flatbed trucks. Early on, the partners pledged to dependably deliver the freshest fish of the finest quality, and it is this commitment to customer service and reliable availability that keeps American Fish on its steady growth track. After 50 years in business, the company delivers half a million pounds of fish a week to retail and food-service customers.

American Fish got its first big break in the 1950s when a longtime family friend, Harry Fujino, joined as the firm's third partner. He had a background in produce and ties to the Vons supermarket chain. His connections landed American Fish its first major retail account, and the company was on its way. More and more supermarkets followed. So did restaurants, hotels, hospitals, caterers, airlines and cruise lines. Now customers from Newport Beach to New York regularly order from American Fish, and while local delivery is a round-the-clock process, even diners in America's heartland can enjoy an order of fresh fish the day after the order is placed.

Back in the 50s, a grocery store's seafood selection was limited, usually rock cod, red snapper, ocean perch, sole and oysters. Today, the list of fish sold by American Fish is much, much longer, with more than one hundred varieties, ranging from abalone to yellowtail. The shrimp category alone offers 400 different options. The most popular seafood are salmon, shrimp and tuna, but demand is high for fish of all kinds. Invoices for each of the company's supermarket clients average 800 to 1,000 every day, and the company ships both fresh and frozen fish locally and across the country.

While customer demand is instrumental in the surge of its business, American Fish is committed to creating partnerships with its clients, working directly with retailers and encouraging them to expand by introducing new items. Experimenting is part of the process. So is staying attuned to the evolving ethnicity of Southern California. By keeping abreast of changing consumer trends, American Fish offers its clients new opportunities for profits. Sending out its own merchandisers, the company also provides training programs for retailers in the handling and presentation of its products, and it encourages the use of in-store demonstrations to introduce customers to new tastes.

American Fish & Seafood Company has seen its greatest growth under the leadership of Ernie Doizaki, George Doizaki's son. He became president of the company in 1982, but his entry into the family firm was a reluctant one, delayed due to his early aversion to fish. He went to business school and afterward visited Japan. (His Japanese heritage is important to him, leading not only to his lifetime career but to his current involvement in Japanese-American cultural institutions back home in Los Angeles.) In Japan, Ernie Doizaki discovered a new appreciation of fish and a newfound respect for the opportunity back home in Los Angeles. He spent 12 years learning the fish business, from the hands-on handling of fish to receiving, dispatching and delivering. When George Doizaki died, his son was ready. He took charge of American Fish in partnership with George M. Cohan, his father's longtime friend, as chairman of the board.

Headquarters of American Fish are in Downtown Los Angeles, but operations have expanded across the country to Miami, Phoenix, Las Vegas, Reno, Sacramento, Palm Springs and New Jersey. Fish arrive from such far-flung locales as Canada, Chile, Costa Rica, Japan and China. Lobster (15,000 pounds at a time) is processed from a facility in nearby Sunset Beach, while the company's subsidiary, Los Angeles Fish Co. specializes in serving more than 300 Japanese restaurants with more than 60 varieties of fish for sushi and sashimi.

The future of the fish business lies in the hands of the very small or the very large providers. Doizaki is determined to make sure that American Fish & Seafood Company is the best of the biggest. The company's first commitment is to service: Its customers can rely on American Fish to have all the fish they want when they want it. The quality of its fish is always the highest, guaranteed because American Fish voluntarily employs its own federal inspectors who are on duty seven days a week. To get the orders in and the fish out, Doizaki has invested in the most advanced equipment, from the 17,500-square-foot plant which was built in Little Tokyo in 1982 to modern computers and communications tools to give his sales force instant access to over 350 resources. Keeping abreast of weather conditions, market trends, seafood availability and pricing are all elements in a sophisticated network of information, enabling the processing of fish to go on almost every hour of the week. With the exception of midnight to eight on Sunday morning, American Fish & Seafood Company is buzzing day and night, keeping abreast with its fish-friendly clients.

CENTURY WILSHIRE HOTEL

estled between high rise apartment buildings and office complexes along the exclusive Wilshire Corridor in Westwood is a three story white building with blue awnings. This modest structure houses one of Los Angeles' most endearing European-flavored boutique hotels: the Century Wilshire Hotel on Wilshire Boulevard.

Entrance to Century
Wilshire Hotel

Built in the 1940s, the Century Wilshire Hotel is a charming throwback to the past. It is one of the first three story wooden structures in Westwood, and through the years has been a home-away-from-home for VIP's, entertainment industry executives, reclusive movie stars and vacationing families. Traditional European furnishings give the hotel a comfortable ambiance and personality all its own.

The Century Wilshire Hotel is built around a garden courtyard, where guests may enjoy a complimentary continental breakfast while basking in the sun. A sunny breakfast room is also available in which to enjoy the daily repast of fresh fruit, toast, muffins, cereal and beverages.

Another feature of the hotel is the large pool area. Chaise lounges, tables with umbrellas and palm trees surround the pool, which offers a shallow area for children

Living room of a Century
Wilshire suite.

yet is perfect for lap swimming. Many movies and TV series have used the Century Wilshire Hotel pool area and exteriors as set pieces for filming.

The 99 European-style rooms offer old-fashioned class and comfort. Many rooms have balconies with garden courtyard or poolside views. All have showers, and some have traditional-style bathtubs next to the showers. The individually decorated rooms offer modern amenities such as telephones and color televisions. Standard rooms with two beds are spacious and can accommodate up to four people, while the junior suites are perfect for business travelers and come with fully equipped kitchens. The one-bedroom suites also offer kitchens, as well as separate living, dining and bedroom areas — perfect for extended stays.

The basic room design has changed little in 50 years. Many of the original doors with distinctive knockers are still in place. Some rooms have been remodeled, but the original architecture and style have been proudly restored. Many rooms even have the original mail slots, located a few inches from the ground against a hallway wall.

If the walls of the Century Wilshire Hotel could talk, what stories they'd tell. It is said that one of Amer-

Century Wilshire courtyard,
perfect for dining or relaxing.

ica's most famous redheaded comedians had an apartment there in the 1950s so she would have a place to stay when she and her husband had one of their famous quarrels. Other stars have slipped into the hotel incognito to escape the glare of stardom. Many aspiring actors have stayed in the hotel while working their way into the glamour of Hollywood, while established showbiz types enjoy the hotel's relaxing atmosphere when they are in town. The hotel staff respects the privacy of their guests, and does their best to see that every guest receives personal yet discrete service.

The Century Wilshire Hotel has had its share of long time guests. "People check in for a day or two, and end up staying here for years," says Ken "Gee" Giurdanella, the hotel's Director of Sales. "We have had people here for as long as 15 years. Other people come back year after year, and they want the same room. To them, it is 'their room.'"

Asha Mallick has owned the hotel since the early 1970s. She established a family feel to the hotel, and the employees (including the owner's children) have become more of an extended family than simply hotel staff. That family-run atmosphere rubs off on the guests.

Problems are solved quickly and easily, information is provided on a moment's notice, and special requests are handled with ease. It's that family feeling that turns first time guests into repeat customers. The multilingual staff takes pleasure in helping arrange tours, rental cars, limos, or anything else guests may need — even the birth of a baby, which has in fact happened...

The Century Wilshire Hotel is located just minutes away from favorite Los Angeles destinations. Westwood Village is a three-minute walk, and offers a variety of shops, restaurants and movie theaters. Just beyond Westwood Village is the campus of the University of California at Los Angeles (UCLA), home of the Bruins. Famed Rodeo Drive in Beverly Hills is a five-minute drive, while the infamous beaches at Venice, Malibu and Santa Monica are a 15-minute drive. Hollywood, Universal Studios and other attractions are also just a short distance from the hotel.

The Century Wilshire Hotel — a great place to stay while you're away.

Enjoy a sunny day in L.A.
by lounging at the pool.

BRIDGESTONE/FIRESTONE, INC.

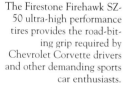

As early as 1919, Harvey S. Firestone began looking for sites to build a tire manufacturing facility on the West Coast — to save freight costs on shipping finished products. At that time, The Firestone Tire & Rubber Company, which was founded in 1900, had only one manufacturing site in the US, located in Akron, Ohio.

In 1927, The Firestone Tire & Rubber Company made surveys of several sites in Southern California and selected a 40-acre tract (then used as a bean field) in Los Angeles. At a luncheon meeting in August of that year, hosted by the Los Angeles Chamber of Commerce in recognition of Firestone coming to Los Angeles, Russell A. Firestone, member of the Board of Directors and second son of the company's founder, presented a purchase check to the land owner's representative.

Russell Firestone provided insight about the company's decision to move to California: "We have chosen the West Coast site as our first plant outside of Akron because crude rubber can be shipped directly from the Far East and because of Los Angeles' transportation facilities, its increasing population and industrial growth."

Ground-breaking ceremonies for the Los Angeles facility were conducted on December 15, 1927. It was announced the new facility

The Firestone Firehawk SZ-50 ultra-high performance tires provides the road-biting grip required by Chevrolet Corvette drivers and other demanding sports car enthusiasts.

would have a capacity to produce 5,000 tires and 7,000 tubes a day.

In only six months, the facility was far enough along in the construction process that equipment was installed to permit the production of the first tire the following June. Company founder Harvey Firestone rolled up his sleeves to make that first tire.

A formal open house for the plant was conducted on December 4, 1928, and some 60,000 visitors toured the plant. Prior to the formal opening, it was decided the plant needed additional room. This addition was dedicated on June 5, 1929. The original plant provided 408,000 square feet plus the administration building, the power house and the machine shop. The 1929 addition provided another 400,000 square feet of manufacturing space.

The plant produced the most popular tire for passenger cars at the time — the 4.50x21 which had just replaced the 30x3.5. The average price of a tire was $12.30, and a $1.85 tube was also required.

A separate 72,500-square-foot facility was constructed in 1929 for use by the company's Xylos Division in reclaiming rubber. The next major addition came in 1942 when the company expanded again to produce fuel cells and industrial products. The new manufacturing area for this expansion created an additional 104,790 square feet of space.

In 1951, the facility expanded again, this time adding 217,000 square feet for warehousing and shipping operations. That same year, the company entered an entirely new field — the production of missiles. The Guided Missile Division engaged in engineering and manufacturing of the Corporal guided missile and its ground handling equipment. In 1954 the facility grew again, this time adding another 350,000 square feet of manufacturing space.

In 1958, the plant observed its 30th anniversary by also celebrating the production

League, Bridgestone/Firestone Inc. provides many contributions affecting the lives of many L.A. residents.

Bridgestone/Firestone Inc., headquartered in Nashville, Tennessee, produces a variety of tire, automotive, roofing and industrial products. The Firestone Racing program, one of the company's more visible efforts, has a large number of fans in the Los Angeles area who attend the annual Indy car race in Long Beach. Firestone-equipped drivers won that race in both 1996 and '97 and Firestone is the official tire of the Long Beach race.

At auto events in Southern California, including the prestigious Los Angeles Auto Show, Bridgestone/Firestone Inc. has had a very visible presence. And since many internationally-recognized automotive journalists call the L.A. area home, the company has conducted ride & drive and product demonstrations in and around the city.

Products showcased in recent L.A. area events include the popular Firestone Firehawk SZ-50 and Bridgestone Potenza S-02 ultra-high performance tires. The Firestone SZ-50 is born of Indy racing technology and features a water-evacuating tread pattern very similar to the successful Firestone Firehawk racing radial used in Indy car races. The Bridgestone Potenza SZ-50 is found as original and replacement equipment on some of the world's finest high-performance vehicles. Both feature the patented UNI-T™ technologies.

By 1954, the Firestone plant in Los Angeles, located at Firestone Boulevard, Santa Fe Avenue and Alameda Street, covered more than 50 acres.

of its 55 millionth automobile tire. In addition to auto tires, the plant also produced truck, tractor and off-the-highway tires. In its peak years, the South Gate plant employed more than 3,100 men and women.

In 1979, the plant stopped production of bias-ply passenger tires as the radial tire took an increasing share of the market. The plant continued to produce bias truck tires until it was announced in March of 1980 that the facility was one of six to be closed under a restructuring of the company. A year later, the 51-acre complex was sold to HON Industries, an Iowa-based manufacturer of metal and wood office furniture and materials handling equipment.

In 1988, Bridgestone Corporation acquired The Firestone Tire & Rubber Company for $2.6 billion. In 1990, Bridgestone and Firestone operations in the Americas were consolidated as Bridgestone/Firestone, Inc.

Although Bridgestone/Firestone no longer has manufacturing facilities in Los Angeles, the company is still very active in the city, having 78 retail outlets in the greater Los Angeles metropolitan area, employing more than 700 people. It also has more than 600,000 square feet of warehousing operations in nearby Ontario.

As it does in communities across the US, Bridgestone/Firestone Inc. contributes in many ways to Los Angeles' corporate, cultural and civic efforts. In projects ranging from financial support to the Music Center of Los Angeles to creating minority employment opportunities through the Los Angeles Urban

Drivers on Firestone tires finished 1-2-3 in the 1997 Grand Prix of Long Beach. Alex Zanardi, center, finished first while Mauricio Gugelmin (R), finished second and Scott Pruett came in third.

FORMOSA CAFÉ

It's hard to believe that a little red restaurant could stand up to one of Hollywood's biggest studios, but that is quite literally what the Formosa Café did in 1991. When the Warner Brother's Hollywood Studio across the street wanted to raze the restaurant, its long-time patrons raised a ruckus and got it declared a historic landmark. Getting things done is often easier when you're famous, and lots of the Formosa's patrons happen to have a secure standing in the list of who's who in Hollywood. They weren't about to see their classic little hangout be paved over as part of some parking lot.

The big stars have always hung out at the Formosa. The café was hot back in the 40s and 50s, and it's still a hip place to party at night. The famous faces have changed over the decades, but the Formosa Café hasn't. Somehow, it stays the same, and new generations of the cool and the trend-setting find that irresistible. The Formosa Café has always been a place to see and be seen.

Santa Monica Boulevard is full of fast traffic, and the distracted eye could easily miss the little restaurant except for its distinctive red color. The Formosa sits demurely on the southeast corner at Formosa Street, a small, narrow structure that looks like it's been there forever. Actually it's been there since 1925 when it was built and operated as Jack's Steakhouse. Fourteen years later, the stepgrandfather of the current owner took it over, renamed it the Formosa Café and began serving Chinese-inspired food.

Walking inside is like going back 40 or 50 years in time. It's dim, just like an old bar is supposed to be, and feels worlds away from the rush of traffic right outside. The color scheme is red and black, a somewhat faded red and black as opposed to a polished Chinese lacquer red and black. The bar is an expansive sweep that takes up half the space in the front room. The booths opposite are deep, round and welcoming, the kind people really have to sink down and slide into. The bamboo-themed wall covering is original. The back rooms are as thin as a railroad train (before they hooked up with the

Formosa, they were a Pacific Dining Car) with tables packed in tightly. Here and there, seat covers have been slashed. It's all part of the atmosphere. And the memories.

Memorabilia are everywhere. The "Guys" and "Dolls" on the restroom doors are souvenirs from the movie. Famous faces, most autographed, are lined up frame-to-frame on the narrow strips of walls above the low-slung windows and over the tables in the back rooms. The portraits are instantly recognizable, and their presence makes a visitor feel on intimate terms with them. It's like stumbling onto someone's private family photo album, except these pictures are all of people who were the biggest stars in the whole world. They all walked into the Formosa at one time or another, movie stars and mobsters, too. In the old days, they'd stop by after a day's work at one of the nine studios within a two-mile radius of the place. They knew they could eat, have a drink and run into their friends.

For almost as long as it's been the Formosa Café, they probably ran into Pat Edie. She's worked at the Formosa since 1950, and she's served them all. She recalls that movie stars tip pretty much like everyone else and that the mobsters, like Mickey Cohen and Bugsy Siegel, behaved themselves. They liked the Formosa's back room as a private place to play cards and hold meetings. (If those walls could talk! Or maybe

The Formosa Cafe, built in 1925 and now a landmark, has played host to Hollywood's elite for half a century.

they talked to the IRS and got Cohen in big trouble.) Pat remembers lots of people. Peter Lorre and Burt Lancaster. George Burns, who never made a fuss when the hamburger she served him slid off the plate. Roy Rogers and Dale Evans. Even The King himself. When he was in town recording, Elvis preferred a booth near the front door, and many times he'd have the place locked up after hours and party all night with his pals.

Not to name drop, but the list goes on: Charlie Chaplin, Mae West and W.C. Fields from the old, old days. Samuel Goldwyn had a favorite booth where he liked to work. Clark Gable, Humphrey Bogart, and John Wayne. One night Howard Hughes had to borrow $20 off one of the bartenders, and one of his ex-wives is still a frequent patron. Dean Martin and Jerry Lewis. Ginger Rogers, Edward G. Robinson and Marlon Brando. During the shoot of *Some Like It Hot*, Marilyn Monroe was a regular. Lucille Ball came in with Desi Arnaz, and Lana Turner liked to bring her infamous gangster boyfriend, Johnny Stompanato.

And lately, it was the film crew of *L.A. Confidential*. The film's production designer had a dream location, because the Formosa Café is so authentic, there was no need to alter a thing inside. Only the outside shots had to be doctored, like covering up the walk/don't walk signs that weren't part of the landscape in the 50s. Inside, all the crew had to do was close the restaurant for three days and roll the cameras.

The Formosa Café has put in an appearance in other films and television commercials. The opening scene of *Beverly Hills Cop II* was shot at the Formosa bar. Schlitz Malt Liquor put a bull in the bar area, and Macintosh Computers set up a shoot in the back room. The Formosa is just one of those places that's so real and unique that art directors can't possibly improve on it.

The Formosa Café was never designed. It just evolved, and its evolution is continuing as ownership passes from father to son. William Jung, who has owned the Formosa since 1978, inherited the restaurant from his stepfather, Lem Quon, who co-founded the Formosa in 1939. William Jung's son Vincent will continue the family dynasty. Vincent began washing dishes at the restaurant when he was seven, and he knows it's the atmosphere his patrons love. But Vincent has some subtle changes in mind, much to the consternation of his regular customers who don't want to see anything changed. Even if it's for the better.

Some of those changes include a revamped kitchen with modern equipment, the better to handle the new, upscale Pan-Asian menu. There is also a new patio with a smoking deck. Wear and tear have taken their toll throughout the interior, and a little cleanup is in the plans. No major design changes can happen inside, though, because of the café's historic status. History and comfort will still prevail, just as they always have. It's the way everyone wants it. That's why they keep coming back.

FRUIT DISTRIBUTING CORPORATION

Whenever you purchase fruits or vegetables from a grocery store in Los Angeles, chances are pretty good that Fruit Distributing Corporation was responsible for getting that produce to the store. Since 1958, Fruit Distributing Corporation — one of the oldest produce brokerage companies in Southern California — has built its reputation on providing fresh produce to Southland supermarkets and grocers in a timely, reliable manner.

Over the past four decades, owners Harold Weisfeld and his son Jeff have developed Fruit Distributing Corporation from a small produce importer into a strong, independent, customer-oriented produce distributor. Harold Weisfeld began his business by importing grapefruit into California from his native Texas. Harold then began buying mixed loads of produce from local Los Angeles growers to ship to the midwestern and southern states. At that time, local growers would bring their crops to a large, communal farmers market where local shippers would purchase the goods for distribution throughout the country.

The shifting economic landscape and changing demographics eventually led to the demise of the farmers market. Instead, Harold went straight to the growers, obtaining fruits and vegetables from other states, and other

The pride that the Weisfelds take in their work is equaled only by the pride they take in Los Angeles. The longevity of their company is a testament to their commitment to the region, and they hope to continue supplying produce for generations to come.

countries, to sell in Southern California. Business grew rapidly, so Harold's son, Jeff — a native of Los Angeles — came on board in 1985 to help run the organization.

Fruit Distributing Corporation's day begins at five o'clock every morning in a small suite of offices on Short Street near the Sears Tower. While most of Los Angeles sleeps, Jeff Weisfeld and his team of buyers are on the phone to growers throughout the country, discovering what produce is available that day, and at what price. The buyers then call customers to determine their produce needs and buying price. The goal: negotiate the best value for the customer and the highest margin of profit for the shipper. Once the orders are set, Weisfeld arranges transportation through truck brokers and provides truckers with their destination.

Fruit Distributing Corporation prides itself on being a manageably small, yet profitable father-son operation. The company distributes $15 million of fresh produce every year to the Southern California market. Three to four million packages of fruits and vegetables are shipped annually to major supermarket chains like Ralphs and Lucky, and to smaller, independent grocers.

The Weisfelds have learned to take advantage of the global marketplace. In order to ensure that Southern Californians get a variety of fresh produce year around, Fruit Distributing Corporation works closely with growers and shippers from countries throughout the world. For example, during certain months local markets may get their peaches and plums from California, but as seasons shift the same products may be imported from Southern Hemisphere countries like Chile, Guatemala, or South Africa. Summer and fall are prime tomato growing seasons in Southern California, but during the winter months, tomatoes are imported from Mexico.

"The entire business has changed to where there are no borders anymore," says Harold. "And with today's fast transportation, the produce stays fresh from grower to consumer."

Fruit Distributing Corporation was one of the pioneers in the fresh produce craze that erupted over the last decade. Most grocery stores have evolved from stocking 15 to 20 items in their produce section to nearly 200 items. The Weisfelds attribute this phenomenon to a variety of factors, including increased demand for prepackaged produce, such as salad mixes and organic merchandise. Also contributing to the demand for fresh produce is the rise of the Asian and Latino populations in Southern California. This growth of ethnic diversity has led to a wider variety of produce in local markets.

Focus on quality is essential in an industry that requires the product to be moved fast and fresh. Produce is ready to go the moment it is harvested, so there is a limited window of opportunity in shipping and distributing that produce. Fruit Distributing Corporation takes advantage of their industry knowledge, experience and contacts to make not just a good deal,

but the best deal for all parties — grower, shipper, distributor, grocer, and consumer.

If there is a golden rule in the business, it is the concept that all parties must be treated with care. Weisfeld is on call to his customers 24 hours a day, ready to troubleshoot any problem or back a produce deal. For 40 years, Fruit Distributing Corporation has relied on a verbal handshake so close every deal. Unlike most large corporations, the Weisfelds operate without lawyers and without any legal contracts; they simply take a person at his word. The growers are treated with the same care. Fruit Distributing Corporation recognizes the blood, sweat, and tears that the growers pour into their product and respond to that commitment with their own promise of satisfaction.

... Fruit Distributing Corporation — one of the oldest produce brokerage companies in Southern California — has built its reputation on providing fresh produce to Southland supermarkets and grocers in a timely, reliable manner.

The pride that the Weisfelds take in their work is equaled only by the pride they take in Los Angeles. The longevity of their company is a testament to their commitment to the region, and they hope to continue supplying produce for generations to come. In tracing the evolution of the business, it becomes clear why Fruit Distributing Corporation has been able to establish such a stronghold in the area. Their knowledge of the three major avenues of the produce industry — growers, customers, and truckers — is the key to their success.

So, the next time you take a bite of an apple or slice a tomato, remember the team effort that went into getting that produce to your store. Fruit Distributing Corporation is proud to be a leader of that team.

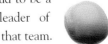

GEM TECH JEWELRY CORP.

arrying art and commerce is a delicate balance. One must apply skill, craftsmanship and marketing savvy. It's not an easy thing to pull off. Yet, Los Angeles-based jewelry manufacturer Gem Tech has done just that since 1974. Established by Korean immigrant Seun Lee, Gem Tech specializes in designing rings for thousands of business customers both domestically and abroad.

In 1988, Seun's brother Andrew, a former banker, took over the business. To add to his acumen, Andrew studied at the Gemological Institute of America in San Diego, an experience that helped train him for his role in selecting Gem Tech's precious, semiprecious and synthetic stone designs. Andrew Lee has trained his eye for detail, which means looking for what is called in the jewelry trade as "the four Cs" — carat (for weight), clarity, color, and cut.

To stay competitive — perhaps the fifth "C" — Lee and his staff attend trade shows, advertise in wholesale and jewelry magazines, and participate in Manufacturing Jewelers and Silversmiths of America ("MJSA"), which is based in Rhode Island. The company also attends industry trade shows where it exhibits along with a variety of manufacturers, wholesalers and marketing companies. Sponsored by the the top jewelry publications, potential buyers come from major department stores, small retail shops and what are called "multiples" or multiple-buying outfits such as at-home shopping networks.

Industry shows are held throughout the United States, particularly in Los Angeles, New York, Las Vegas and Miami, as well as abroad. Switzerland's Basel Fair is an annual stop for Gem Tech's executives. As the name implies, at a "fair," Gem Tech joins its competitors by establishing an exhibitor booth and "crossing its fingers" that word-of-mouth will attract traffic to its site.

After the show, it's always back to business. That means producing 1,700 to 2,000 items each day, 75 percent of which are rings, and the other 25 percent earrings and pendants. To process such volume, Gem Tech must adhere to strict quality standards and a detailed tracking process. Before an item can be shipped, it must go through several departments: after being processed in the computer, the item goes to design, original molding, waxing, casting, setting, prepolishing, polishing and steaming. Each item is given a number, and at each stage, the piece is rerouted back to the ordering department where it is carefully tracked.

Each stage of design is a little world unto itself and each employee is an experienced artisan who understands his or her role in the process. In the waxing department, for instance, workers pour a wax mixture over the jewelry and mold it into a wax "tree" in rubber books. When the rubber is opened, out comes the tree, into which the item is set. The tree will be sent to the next stage, casting, where it will be baked in a 1,050-degree oven before advancing

to a 1,850-degree vacuum machine to melt the gold.

When the item reaches the setting department, stones are meticulously set into the ring, pendant or earring encasement. Here, the focus is palpable. Workers concentrate on one item at a time, separating each piece by number before advancing it to prepolishing. Once an item has gone to pol-

ishing, it goes through an ultra-sound machine that looks for defects. If any defect is found, it is immediately rerouted through the various departments until perfected.

The company prides itself not only on such quality, but innovation. Andrew Lee selects or creates as many as 50 new designs each month, choosing creations from the likes of magazines, shows or his own imagination. Lee also considers the total weight and what is called the "price point" of each item. The most popular designs he sells are made of 14-karat gold (24-karat gold is considered too soft). While $500 is a minimum order, there is no minimum or maximum number of items the company will ship. They have been known to ship 5,000 pieces off to England one day, while mailing another three items to small family-owned shop the next.

Gem Tech executive Sue Yi says that most jewelry manufacturers specialize in one item. While Gem Tech primarily manufactures rings, the company boasts hundreds of different lines. Customers can choose from something simple and nondescript or a bolder, flashier, trendier ring. Yi points out that women abroad are still purchasing some of the flashier designs, which women in New York may have abandoned long ago. Los Angeles, Yi says, is a better market than New York for the flashier designs, where women seem to prefer more personality in their rings.

To service these women, the company is expanding in California, building a number of factory outlets throughout the state. Such expansion is key if the company wants to keep pace in the more competitive U.S. market. According to Yi, countries such as China, Turkey and Spain have brought down the price of jewelry on a global level. The mid-1990s were challenging times for Gem Tech, which was able to rebound in the latter half of the decade. Its peak order topped the $1.8 million mark.

Of course, Andrew Lee isn't just in it for the money. He is involved with a lot of missionary work and consistently donates a percentage of profits to Protestant missionaries overseas. He also donates to the local Protestant charities and is involved in the Los Angeles Chamber of Commerce.

Yi praises the community that has allowed the Lee brothers and herself to thrive. She points out that company notices are always posted in three to four languages. "Everyone here came from somewhere else," she says. "It's more acceptable here to have multiple cultures than it is in some other areas of the US. Also, New York and Los Angeles are the best cities in the States for wholesale manufacturing."

KOONTZ HARDWARE
More Than You Expect in a Hardware Store

Koontz Hardware, owned by Russ Wilson with wife Judy and operated with brother Dean, is a West Hollywood landmark, representing to many the heart of the American Dream: the opportunity to build something out of nothing with one's own two hands. Even people who can afford to pay someone else to do construction and repairs take pleasure in not only doing such jobs themselves but also personally shopping for the odds and ends that are integral to their projects. Koontz has, over the years, attracted a vast celebrity clientele. TV's well-known tool man is just one of the Hollywood luminaries who, when it comes down to brass tacks, chooses Koontz Hardware. But the Wilsons pride themselves on the relationships they've developed with all their customers, famous or not. The friendly, well-informed Koontz staff members, whose heritages reflect the multiethnic, multilingual surrounding communities, help people feel comfortable and confident with the store; anyone with questions about the product they're buying will not leave without being informed how to install or assemble it.

Loyal customers from all over Los Angeles come to West Hollywood's Koontz Hardware for its renowned selection and service.

But Koontz's real stock is its stock. Koontz Hardware was founded by Art Koontz with his wife Trudie in 1938. "At that time, they made a commitment to breadth of inventory," says Russ. "When I bought [Koontz] in 1977, we tripled the selection. And it made an immediate impact." Entering Koontz Hardware, one is surrounded by towering shelves jam-packed with innumerable items invaluable to professional and amateur handypersons alike. Employees use library ladders to retrieve objects from the top shelves.

"The thing that makes people come back here is if they need a plumbing part, we've got that plumbing part. And then [a customer might] say, 'Let's look at kitchen cabinet knobs while we're here.' We've got a larger selection in stock than anyplace else. You want a specialty bulb to light that little alcove — we have it. We've got 100,000 items, 100,000 discrete, different items, whereas [other stores generally] carry 35,000. So we've got three times as many items as places that are 20 times as big.

"Every store has an eighth inch, a quarter inch, a half inch, a three-quarter inch and an inch. But how many of them have a seven-sixteenths or a fifteen-thirty-second? That's the kind of thing that makes our reputation."

Koontz's policy is to try to offer three options in pricing to meet everyone's needs. There will often be inexpensive, moderate and high-end versions of many items, to correlate with individual

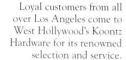

budgetary and quality requirements. "If you want to spend $10
for it or if you want to spend $300,
we've got something that will
work," says Russ.

The nuts and bolts of
Koontz's success is not just nuts
and bolts. Alongside the ham-
mers, nails and flanges you'll find
such items as elegant picture
frames, beaded candle holders,
gourmet cookware and even a
wide selection of wind chimes.
Unique inventory is a priority.

Koontz's buyers travel nationwide and internationally to find
the latest products, attending
major hardware and houseware
fairs around the globe. They go to great lengths to make
sure they offer their customers everything they need for
maintenance, construction and repair. Sensitive to the
specific needs of the Southern California market, Koontz
was among the first in Los Angeles to sell a product
known as Quake Wax, a putty used by the Getty Museum
to keep their valuable antiquities in place during tremors.

The region's tendency toward temblors has proven
Koontz's commitment to its community in other ways
as well. The day of the 1994 Northridge earthquake,
Koontz was one of the only stores in the L.A. basin
open for business. Though they didn't have any electricity, they simply used some of their stock of flash-
lights and did business out of cigar boxes. Somehow the
word got out that Koontz was open, and people drove
from all corners of Southern California, knowing
Koontz would have what they needed. "We weren't trying
to make money; we just didn't want to disappoint
anybody," says Russ. "And we certainly want to be
there when they're having a problem. People know
we're always going to be here."

There was a time when the possibility arose that
Koontz wasn't always going to be here. In 1982, just five
years after the Wilsons bought Koontz from its retiring
founder, an arsonist setting random fires around the city

burned Koontz Hardware to
the ground. Russ recalls that as
he and Dean stood outside the
blazing building, people from
the community came in droves
to express their condolences
and their personal devastation
at the loss. It was then that
Russ realized that he'd become
the keeper of a heritage. News
anchorwoman Connie Chung,
a regular customer at Koontz,
went on the air with a touch-
ing segment about the tragedy.
Russ laughs as he recalls being
quoted on the news segment
over optimistically predicting
that Koontz would be back in
business on the same site in a couple of months.
Operating in the interim out of an old abandoned factory
around the corner, the Wilsons found that it took six and
a half years to restore Koontz to its former grandeur.

According to Dean, upon discovering that Koontz
had reopened, an enthusiastic longtime customer burst
into the nearby (now-defunct) Ma Maison (at one time
one of the most popular, celebrity-laden restaurants on
the west side) and announced, "Koontz is open again!"
Practically all of Ma Maison's diners hurriedly abandoned
their meals and came running over to Koontz.

Russ says Koontz might never have been rebuilt at
all were it not for a stroke of serendipity. The insurance
company was skeptical about Koontz's loss claims, due
to the tremendous amount of inventory they cited;
however, it so happened that the adjuster assigned to
the case had patronized the shop the day before the fire
and could confirm Koontz's mind-boggling quantity of
stock. "If he hadn't been there, we might not have
survived," Russ muses.

Fortunately, Koontz is here for present and future
generations. As Dean overheard one longtime customer
telling her 10-year-old grandson on his first visit to the
store, "This is Koontz Hardware. This is where you
come when you have a problem."

Koontz Hardware has
100,000 items in stock at a
time, from hardware to
knickknacks to earthquake
emergency supplies. "We've
got three times as many
items as places that are 20
times as big," says owner
Russ Wilson.

LOS ANGELES MARRIOTT DOWNTOWN

The Los Angeles Marriott Downtown rises like a 14-story mirrored jewel in the heart of downtown Los Angeles. At home on South Figueroa Street, the Marriott has become one of the City's premiere business addresses and occasional home to business travelers, musicians, professional sports teams and tourists alike.

An integral part of the local scene, the Marriott is convenient to all major freeways and within minutes of all major downtown attractions such as the LA County Music Center — home of the Dorothy Chandler Pavilion and the Oscars — the Museum of Contemporary Art, Dodger Stadium, the Los Angeles Central Library, the Garment District, the Los Angeles County Courthouse, the Coliseum, the Mark Taper Forum and Ahmanson Theatre and the downtown Macy's Plaza Mall. In addition, the Marriott is within close proximity to Universal Studios, Beverly Hills' Rodeo Drive, the Hollywood Walk of Fame, Santa Monica's Third Street Promenade and Venice Beach.

Heralded as a centerpiece of the revitalization of downtown Los Angeles, the groundbreaking of the hotel was greeted with gala receptions at the Dorothy Chandler Pavilion and Security Pacific National Bank Plaza as early as a year before its construction was completed. Dignitaries, like then-mayor Tom Bradley and others, enthusiastically welcomed the arrival of a first-class hotel in the downtown area, at a time when most of the luxury hotel business was going to the surrounding suburbs. The hotel officially opened its doors in June of 1983, touting 469 guest rooms and suites, 23,000 feet of meeting space and four separate cocktail lounges and restaurants. In February 1998, the Grande was reflagged as the Los Angeles Marriott Downtown.

The Marriott's elegant guest rooms have spacious living areas with appropriately designed work areas, dual-line telephones with a complete personalized voice message system, computer modem and facsimile hook-up capabilities, fully stocked mini-bars and personal safes in every guest room. There are 400 deluxe oversized rooms, 69 suites, including 49 Executive suites, 16-one-bedroom Vista suites with spectacular views, two Marriott two-story suites and a remarkable California Suite that has hosted government and political leaders, captains of industry and the biggest names in entertainment.

The focal point of the Marriott is its elegant lobby which houses a monumental 18-by 22-foot original renaissance oil painting. Designed specifically for the hotel, and titled "In Absence of Paradise: to Church and Vermeer," this masterpiece is one painting in a collection by Canadian artist David Bierk, which he calls "Painting in Absence of Paradise." The painting, which was completed in Bierk's studio in ten weeks on ten separate canvasses, was hung by the artist himself in the hotel's lobby over a period of three days.

On the lobby level are all of the hotel's three distinct restaurants. Moody's Bar & Grille, with its forest green walls, ivory- and black-checkered marble floors, rich oak woodwork and polished brass accents, creates

The Los Angeles Marriott rises like a 14-story mirrored jewel in heart of downtown Los Angeles and has become one of the City's premiere business addresses.

a New York bar atmosphere in the heart of Southern California. Sofas, tables and overstuffed chairs dot the perimeter creating cozy conversational niches where guests can sit back and watch a sporting event, monitor the stock reports or catch up on the news of the day on one of the bar's several television sets. The restaurant Three Thirty Three, which utilizes the hotel's address as its name, offers a more intimate fine dining experience, serving contemporary American cuisine in an elegant yet friendly atmosphere. Many guests begin their evening at 333 before heading off to the theater or a concert. For breakfast and lunch The Back Porch is a guest favorite. Open and airy, a glass atrium surrounding the entire west side of the restaurant allows its guests to enjoy their morning coffee in the sunshine. For those who prefer dining outdoors, tables and chairs overlook the pool.

California greenery outside the hotel creates an oasis amid the bustling city sidewalks, and this oasis-like atmosphere is well captured in the outdoor recreation area. Possibly one of the most popular features of the hotel is the Marriott's outdoor swimming pool. Guests looking to take a break from their day can enjoy a swim in the pool's heated waters or simply kick back and soak up the warm California sun on the poolside terrace. Surrounded by a lush tranquil garden, the setting defies the hotel's downtown location. And for those simply looking to relax there is also a lobby lounge that serves cappuccino and has a piano player in the evening.

In keeping with the hotel's commitment to providing business travelers and corporate clients the services and amenities demanded in today's business world, the Marriott offers a full-service Business Center. The Center offers copying services, fax machines, computer and typewriter rental and individual work stations with desks and chairs. Guests may also purchase business supplies in the center, which is staffed by a communications' professional and offers a full range of communications and secretarial services.

Also unique to the Marriott are the executive boardroom and the Marriott's securable conference registration areas (on the second floor), as well as its Conference Support Center, and a complete

The Marriott has 22 superbly appointed meeting rooms, state-of-the-art A/V, exquisite on-site catering and meticulous attention to detail.

audio visual department that handles all AV needs, and provides state-of-the-art sound, video and lighting equipment.

Dedicated to providing superior service at competitive prices, the Marriott catering department offers packages for weddings, proms, reunions, bar mitzvahs, office and holiday parties, picnics and other events where elegance and affordability are the main concern. Catering professionals can design personally-tailored events to meet the individual needs of those planning parties and special functions. From themed, sit-down dinners for 800, to festive poolside events or intimate gatherings in private rooms, the Marriott delivers the highest service at value prices.

Here in the City of Angels, where trends are started and the eyes of the world are often focused, the Marriott stands out with a reputation for superb, personal service and luxury. It is a premiere destination in a region that is itself a premiere destination. As the Los Angeles Marriott Downtown prepares to enter the 21st century, it continues its proud tradition of excellence and dedication to detail.

The Grande's elegant lobby sets the stage for impeccable service from an attentive staff and features a lobby lounge with nightly entertainment.

PARKING COMPANY OF AMERICA

here are two things that are commonplace at Parking Company of America's (PCA) headquarters office. A big, welcoming smile and the same last name, Chaves.

Formed in 1965 by Alex Chaves, the son of a New Mexico farmer, PCA is a multi-million dollar, 1,000 plus employee company, owned and operated by the Chaves family. Alex Chaves' wife Nadine, their two sons, Alex Martin Chaves and Eric Chaves, and their sister, Renee Chaves Valdes, operate the company, handling day-to-day operations.

Today, the Chaves family works the land as did their ancestors. The landscape, however, is different. Instead of growing apples in New Mexico's arid climate on a 20-acre orchard, they continue to expand their $50 million operation running over 200 nationwide parking lots, airport parking facilities and fixed-route shuttle systems in Pittsburgh, Houston, Dallas, Memphis, Albuquerque, Denver, Phoenix, Oakland, San Francisco, San Diego and Los Angeles. Since 1967, PCA has made Los Angeles the company's corporate headquarters. PCA manages over 100 locations in L.A., including LAX, Van Nuys Airport, Ontario Airport and Union Station.

PCA is one of the largest privately owned parking and shuttle businesses in the country.

Chaves' father would have been proud. Alex Chaves remembers, "My father told me the day I had come home with a bloody nose after fighting at school that he was not impressed, but what would impress him would be that I go into business. 'That,' he said, 'takes guts.'" A photograph of his father, a handsome man attired in a cowboy hat and a suit coat, now rests in a frame on Alex Chaves' desk. Nick Chaves passed away in 1971, at the age of 75.

From a family of nine brothers and one sister, Alex Chaves set out to meet his father's challenge and to go into business. Chaves and his brother Richard leased their first parking lot in Albuquerque more than 35 years ago. From here, more lots were purchased. Alex remembers telling his brother, "If we're going to be millionaires, we not only have to get that parking lot, but we have to get the next one, the next one and the next one..." It seems he was right.

Today, PCA provides a variety of services for its clients. PCA owns and manages both on-site and off-site airport parking at Los Angeles, Van Nuys, Ontario, Memphis, Denver, San Francisco, Oakland, Phoenix, Houston, Dallas and Pittsburgh airports. As a transportation specialist, PCA also manages and develops fixed-route and special event centers, business parks, stadiums and events of all sizes. Furthermore, PCA provides first class attendant valet, metered, controlled permit and special event parking facility management and development services to both private and public entities throughout the Western United States.

Every Chaves family member has a strong hand in the company's success. They work together diligently, efficiently and very happily. Responsibilities are carved out to suit everyone's talents. Alex Chaves Sr. is, appropriately, PCA's CEO and sets the company policy decisions. Alex Martin Chaves acts as PCA's president, in charge of operations, while Eric Chaves Esq., the younger son, takes the role of vice president, general counsel in charge of all acquisitions, finance and legal issues. As the head of marketing, Nadine Chaves' responsibilities include setting and orchestrating the company's nationwide marketing efforts, while Renee Chaves Valdes is the vice president in charge of all quality control issues. The family's commitment to each other and PCA has enabled PCA to thrive, enjoying unparalleled success and growth for three decades.

According to Eric Chaves, one of the biggest changes in the parking business is that it has become much more service oriented. "When my Dad started the business," Eric says, "there weren't many employees, just parking meters. Today, we at PCA are highly service directed, providing our clients with experienced management and dependable personnel, which in turn, enables us to provide superior service, dedication, integrity and commitment to service." He continues, "Uniformed attendants, luggage services, electronic ticketing and 24-hour security, are just some of the services PCA has instilled."

"Today, we at PCA are highly service directed, providing our clients with experienced management and dependable personnel, which in turn, enables us to provide superior service, dedication, integrity and commitment to service," says Eric Chaves.

PCA is one of the largest privately-owned parking and shuttle businesses in the country. Financing, however, says Eric Chaves, "is the biggest obstacle to overcome." He continues, "Due to PCA's longevity and consistent delivery of the right combination of expert management, competitive pricing and commitment to client satisfaction, institutions such as banks have attributed to PCA's continued prosperity." Unlike other parking companies, PCA develops parking facilities, as well as operating them. PCA's most recent developments include Oakland, Dallas, Pittsburgh and Memphis long-term airport parking facilities. With PCA still set to grow, Eric Chaves sets out to secure more locations and financing, brother Alex Martin is focused on expanding the leasing business, while Alex Chaves Sr. targets buying properties.

The Chaves success story is one that will inspire others. Raised in a devout Catholic family, Alex Sr. met his wife Nadine, a cheerleader and straight-A student, in school. He married her two years later. Chaves left

school at 21 stating, "It (school) never really interested me. I was just killing time before I went into business." After leaving the world of real estate sales, Chaves secured his first parking lot contract for $7,000 with the funds being put up by his father. The very next day, Chaves was parking cars. Within two years, Parking Company of America — Chaves' big vision for the company — had about 35 lots under lease. From Albuquerque, Chaves decided to live up to the company name and expand nationwide. By 1968 PCA had sold 35 franchises in Colorado, Nebraska and California. Chaves moved to California, packing up the family car and driving with Nadine and their three children: Alex, four; Renee, two; and Eric, two months, to Los Angeles.

Then came airport parking. From a small, 200-stall lot near San Francisco airport, the satellite airport parking services — parking cars outside the airport and then shuttling the passengers to and from the terminal — was a new concept and Chaves saw its future potential. He spent 16-hour days doing everything from cashiering to driving and parking cars. Renee, just 13, handled the money, while Alex Martin, not yet 15, dealt with the lot's 10 employees. Chaves recalls, "My kids grew up in parking. Those were some of the cherished times we spent as a family." Today, the San Francisco airport facility has been expanded to a capacity of 2,000 cars.

PCA predicts continued growth and success. Plans include the expansion of airport parking facilities across the country, with the addition of parking in 10 to 15 cities as its current goal. Meanwhile, PCA is pursuing other companies and properties for acquisition. PCA also intends to continue its successful expansion through word of mouth and its sales force. Based upon its past performance, PCA expects to triple the size of its holdings and market share by the end of 1998. United by the strength of generations, PCA and the Chaves family is committed to the tradition of customer service and business excellence in Los Angeles, and throughout the United States. PCA is proud to be a part of Los Angeles' rich history and thanks the people and the city for its success.

PUBLIC STORAGE INC.

California has a reputation for being fast-moving, trend-setting and forward-thinking. The same things could be said about Public Storage. Celebrating over 25 years of California tradition, Public Storage is one hot enterprise with a very sunny future.

Public Storage was founded in 1972 by real estate developers B. Wayne Hughes and Kenneth Q. Volk. Both visionaries were attracted to the idea of forming a real estate company that would build, but not own mini-warehouses. Hughes, a USC graduate, saw potential for opening the business in California. Together, he and Volk built a mini-warehouse in El Cajon and started their own self-storage-based real estate empire. Offering easy month-to-month rentals, the consumer response was tremendous — and at a low break even point, so were the profits. At the time, the per square rate for storage space and garden apartments were the same, but construction costs were about 35 percent to 40 percent less. Much like the excitement of California's early miners at the sight of that first sparkling nugget, Hughes and Volk were indeed convinced there was "gold in them there hills."

They couldn't have been more right. Public Storage has been so successful, it's become a generic name for all self-storage space. The large orange Public Storage umbrella today covers four closely related business lines: self-storage, portable self-storage, truck rentals and retail store businesses. Truly a "One Stop Shop," Public Storage offers professionally managed,

Pubic Storage Pickup & Delivery℠ is a premium service to deliver portable self-storage containers directly to the home or business — perfectly engineered for California's quick-change, mobile, full-service needs.

Public Storage also offers truck rentals in a variety of sizes.

clean, quality self-storage space in a variety of metropolitan markets. Each facility has similar features for easy recognition — bright orange doors, with a big bright orange sign. In fact, the orange color has become a distinguishing trademark for Public Storage.

"Seventy percent of our customers come to us because of an event in their life," says Hughes. More than 46,000 American households move every day. The average city dweller relocates every 7.5 years and, according to the US Postal Service, will move an average of 12 times in a lifetime. Moving, marriage, divorce, job loss and attending college are just a few of the events that trigger an individual's demand for self-storage space. Commercial users such as regional salesmen, small corporations and retailers use self-storage properties to meet a multitude of record keeping and inventory storage needs. Customers come from all walks of life, but the majority can be categorized as residential, commercial, military and students. Whereas their reasons for coming to Public Storage may vary, they all come for the value, service and location.

Originally, Public Storage located property, designed and built the facility, and then sold it outright. During this early period, the company averaged $300 million to $400 million in annual construction costs.

However, in 1976, Public Storage changed its direction and decided to manage its own facilities. Hughes and Volk raised $2.8 billion through a wide variety of small and large investors, including the Queen of England. The result was an investment group which bought land and funded an aggressive push for construction. It was a positive move and by the 1980s, a new Public Storage facility opened somewhere in the United States every seven days. That's an impressive pace.

By 1997, Public Storage had over 1,100 facilities and 600,000 spaces in 38 states, coast to coast. The company was already in 81 markets, with more than 3,500 employees worldwide. In fact, based on capitalized market value, Public Storage had become one of the largest real estate investment trusts in the US, owning and operating more self-storage industry helped enable the company to provide continuity from one rental experience to the next. This encouraged repeat business, as customers were able to expect the same level of quality and professionalism regardless of the Public Storage location.

A National Reservation Call Center organizes the high volume of consumer phone traffic and contributes to Public Storage's ability to offer "One Stop Shop" convenience. Indeed, a goal of the Center is to provide customers with a single point of contact for all their storage-related needs. In other words, make it easy for people to find storage space without the hassle of leaving their home. Using an integrated telephone and computer system, staff access current information about space availability and rates for the majority of Public Storage's properties. The center has received as many as 200,000 calls per month. If customers prefer, they can also complete rental applications and find convenient locations through the company's internet site.

Public Storage, which is listed on the New York Stock Exchange (PSA), achieved another milestone in 1996. Just after celebrating 25 years in business, Public Storage expanded many of its self-storage facilities to include complete storage-related retail centers at locations in major cities, including Southern California. This provided tenants and other customers with the ability to purchase a variety of move-related merchandise, including corrugated boxes in a range of sizes, locks, packing supplies and furniture covers. Around the same time period, Public Storage and HFS Inc., the world's largest franchisor of residential real estate brokerage offices, entered into a three-year preferred alliance to co-market rental storage space to CENTURY 21®, Coldwell Banker® and ERA® brokerages and their customers.

Moving into the fast lane to match speed with the fast-paced California lifestyle, Public Storage zoomed into first place again by developing a unique storage system on wheels. In late 1996, the innovative company rolled out Public Storage Pickup & Delivery℠ — a premium service to deliver portable self-storage containers directly to the home or business. Big purple containers are delivered and then filled by the customer. Public Storage Pickup & Delivery℠ drivers pick up the containers for storage in a central warehouse. The entire system is perfectly engineered for California's quick change, mobile, full-service needs. To launch the program, facilities were opened in metropolitan areas through-out California and then in other parts of the country. Public Storage Pickup & Delivery℠ customers don't need to rent a truck or even unload their possessions. The container, made of wood, holds all of the items found in a typical home or office. Filling containers is easy; they even feature removable center posts for easier access and locking hasps. Customers simply pack their items, lock the container and retain the key. Public Storage can also provide any needed boxes and packing supplies. Customers can access their containers at the storage center any time during regular business hours, or a driver will deliver the container to their home or business.

Whether it's private storage space, professionally managed commercial properties, truck rentals, moving-related products or portable storage — Public Storage has it all. And with plans for continued growth, this California-based business' future is definitely rolling in the right direction.

Truly a "One Stop Shop," Public Storage offers professionally managed, clean, quality self-storage space in a variety of metropolitan markets.

RADISSON WILSHIRE PLAZA HOTEL LOS ANGELES

estled in the heart of the bustling Mid-Wilshire Business District, the Radisson Wilshire Plaza Hotel is conveniently located near Downtown, Beverly Hills and Hollywood.

A recent multimillion dollar renovation of guest sleeping rooms, suites and guest hallways includes new furniture, soft furnishings, upgraded bathrooms and a host of exciting new features carefully selected with the comfort and convenience of hotel guests in mind.

Refurbishment efforts also extend to luxurious appointments, award-winning restaurants, a host of meeting and hospitality rooms, conference and business center, gift shop and Grand Ballroom.

The arched picture windows and marble columns in the lobby only hint at the elegance of the 380 guest rooms, including 14 spacious suites, each defined by floor-to-ceiling windows and many offering panoramic views of the nearby Hollywood Hills.

The Wilshire Business Plus Floor has been designed exclusively to meet the needs of today's discerning corporate traveler. Each room offers corporate guests superior comfort combined with a myriad of upgraded amenities including a laser printer/copier/facsimile machine with direct line access, two 2-line speakerphones with data ports and voicemail, ergonomically designed desk chairs, bottled water, robes, coffee makers, hair dryers, iron and ironing boards and a nightly turndown service. Additionally, all rooms feature mini bars, phones with dataports, comfortable work desks and clock radios.

A recent multimillion dollar renovation of guest sleeping rooms, suites and guest hallways includes a host of exciting new features carefully chosen with the comfort and convenience of hotel guests in mind.

Guests of the Business Floor are also invited to enjoy the hotel's Plaza Level Lounge featuring complimentary continental breakfast and evening hors d'oeuvres.

Additional amenities and services include an outdoor heated swimming pool, sun deck and state-of-the-art fitness center as well as an on-site concierge, room service, same-day valet and video check-out. A daily shuttle is available to Universal Studios, Rodeo Drive in Beverly Hills and Santa Monica's renowned Third Street Promenade. Evening shuttle service to Hollywood is also available.

Guests of the Radisson are ideally situated to explore the numerous recreational and dining opportunities within easy reach of the hotel. Universal Studios and Universal City Walk are just a few miles to the north and offer a unique selection of stores, restaurants and all the incredible rides available inside Universal Studios.

Hollywood, with the famous Boulevard, Walk of Fame and Graumann's Chinese Theater are just a ten-minute drive away. To the west, guests may enjoy a selection of cultural experiences ranging from the L.A. County Museum of Arts to the Museum of Miniatures, located on Museum Row. Further west, guests can browse through some of the most prestigious stores in the world on Rodeo Drive, Beverly Hills, or choose from an exceptional array of casual or fine dining experiences.

While at the hotel, guests may choose from three distinct dining experiences. The Tulips Garden Restaurant serves a selection of continental cuisine created with a California flair while more exotic and authentic Asian cuisine, such as sushi, teppanyaki and tempura, can be found at the award-winning Saka-E Japanese Restaurant. For more informal options, guests can sip Starbucks coffee or enjoy Ben & Jerry's ice cream, made-to-order sandwiches and tempting desserts at The Boulevard Cafe located in the lobby.

With over 12,500 square feet of multifunctional facilities, the luxury high-rise hotel easily accommodates up to 400 people in the Grand Ballroom. This stunning room has been completely recreated as part of the hotel renovation and is the ideal location for any type of corporate meeting, banquet, wedding or personal celebration. The in-house catering staff welcome the

opportunity to create a personalized menu to ensure a memorable event.

The Radisson Wilshire Plaza Hotel strives to not only meet, but exceed the needs and expectations of the business traveler. With everything under one roof, there's no need to leave. But guests who wish to explore Los Angeles at their leisure will find numerous recreational and fine dining opportunities all within easy reach of the hotel.

The arched picture windows and marble columns in the lobby only hint at the elegance of the 380 guest rooms and suites.

RENÉE STRAUSS FOR THE BRIDE

The phrase "the most important day in a woman's life" has long been used to describe the wedding day. Even in today's politically correct, equality-focused society, few would deny the momentous personal significance of this occasion. It's still the day every little girl dreams of, with many having already imagined their ideal gown, figured out the color scheme and decided who to invite before they're out of kindergarten.

"My philosophy is it's much more important to listen than to talk. So I keep my ears and eyes open to find out 'What are people asking for, what would enhance our selection, what's the need, let's create it for our own inventory.'"

Renée Strauss, owner of the Renée Strauss for the Bride wedding salon in Beverly Hills, relishes the opportunity to play "fairy godmother" to excited brides-to-be every day. Her two-level boutique, a fantasy world of silk-satin and tulle, contains hundreds of gorgeous, dream-come-true designs, many of which are one-of-a-kind. Brides — often accompanied by an entourage of family and friends, whom Strauss jokingly calls "the judge and jury" — select samples under the guidance of Renée or one of her associates. Personal attention is a top priority. Strauss' company slogan is "Your wedding. Your style." And that means finding out what the customer wants — even when she's not sure herself.

"My philosophy is it's much more important to listen than to talk. So I keep my ears and eyes open to find out 'What are people asking for, what would enhance our selection, what's the need, let's create it for our own inventory.' While in the design studio, we'll be gathered around a mannequin and we'll say 'That looks good. This sleeve is popular, this beading is beautiful,

let's drape it.' And then the creative process turns into a reality, fueled by consumer need."

Another of Strauss' philosophies is "We never say no, we say no problem." This reflects some of the lengths to which she'll go to make her customers happy, like the time she and her employees worked tirelessly to sew hundreds of heirloom pearls onto one bride's gown, or the occasions when she'll open her shop in the middle of the night to accommodate families flying in from foreign countries who are accustomed to a different time zone. "We don't watch the clock. People ask, 'What time do you close?' and I answer 'When the last person's needs have been met.'"

Renée Strauss for the Bride also offers a full selection of bridal accessories, including an extensive variety of elegant veils, tiaras, gloves and shoes from designer collections worldwide, as well as the most expansive collection of bridesmaid and flower girl dresses on the West Coast. Another unique element is a Lady-In-Waiting service, which provides a dresser for the wedding who helps the bride prepare for the big moment. Also offered is a complimentary directory listing exclusive matrimony-related professionals in the area, such as florists, photographers, caterers and entertainers whose work Strauss holds in high esteem. Amenities like these are what have made Strauss' dream-turned-reality a success.

Strauss grew up in Chicago, Illinois, and was involved from an early age with the family catering business. She was entranced by these elaborate parties, many of which were weddings, anniversaries or other grand, but at their heart familial, celebrations. "I loved the wardrobe, and I loved the glamour," says Strauss. "I always knew I had a creative side to me, but I never really quite understood how it could manifest itself professionally." Little did she know that while working for her family as a coat-check girl, she was absorbing information that would lead her to a career in wedding fashion, making the nuptial dreams of some of Beverly Hills' brightest stars come true. Most importantly, she learned the caliber of service required to make lavish events a success.

After managing departments in such world-class stores as Saks Fifth Avenue, then meeting her husband with whom she opened a men's wear store, Strauss realized that fashion was her true calling, and, in 1984, decided to merge her complementary passions and experience by servicing the grandest occasion of them all, the wedding, through her bridal salon.

Strauss' husband was very supportive of her plans, saying "Let's go for it!" "And we did!" says Strauss. She landed her first big account the first week she was in business: a costumer who was wardrobing a wedding-themed television commercial. "She came in and just went crazy in the store and picked everything in sight. It was an enormous order. We pulled the whole thing together in three days. It was challenging and exciting. The very first week I went into business! It was amazing. It put us on the map.

"And the advertising executive that was in charge of the account eventually moved up to become the president of the agency, and has sent me so much business over the years. Not only that, but when he got married five years later, his wife traveled across the U.S. to select her gown at our salon!"

Strauss feels great satisfaction about the relationships she's developed — with costumers, production companies and, of course, families, who often become generational customers. "We've taken care of families where we've had five daughters get married — they scatter all over the world but they all come back for their wedding gowns! The confidence and trust that has been built over the years has brought us tremendous repeat business. And that has just been the most fabulous part of it. You develop so many personal relationships. The best thing about this business is that you can touch people's lives on a personal level. It is so rewarding."

The secret is service and selection. "We have a real Beverly Hills salon—an international selection, but with an ambiance of warmth," says Strauss. "You walk into our store and it's a salon environment, but it's very homey. And that's so important to me. Everybody that walks into the front door is a guest in my home."

Renée Strauss, founder and owner of Renée Strauss for the Bride, says that the best thing about being a professional in the bridal industry is that "you can touch people's lives on a personal level." *Photo by Jack Caputo*

Still, that home is Beverly Hills, one of the world's most glamorous, style-setting cities. Strauss has worked hard to establish her renowned reputation in this district that boasts the world's densest square footage of Hollywood's top glitterati. As a result, Strauss' clientele has included such celebrities as Heather Locklear, Kathy Ireland, Raquel Welch, Shannen Doherty, Jennie Garth, Victoria Principal, Valerie Bertinelli, Delta Burke, Kelly LeBrock, Kelly Preston, Vendela and Roseanne, and she's provided gowns for numerous film and television productions including *Father of the Bride, Mr. Magoo, Wayne's World II*, "ER," "Beverly Hills 90210," "Melrose Place," "L.A. Law," "NYPD Blue," "Dallas," "The Fresh Prince of Bel Air," "The Young and the Restless," "Days of Our Lives" and "General Hospital." But Strauss gives all her clientele the same star treatment. "It doesn't matter who comes through our doors. Everyone is a bride-to-be. And every bride is treated with the same love and care I look forward to providing my own daughter with."

THE SHAMMAS GROUP

ust about everybody who lived in Los Angeles in the 1960s knew about Felix Chevrolet. Everybody knew about Felix Chevrolet partly because of Felix the Cat, the cartoon sensation perched atop the dealership on a huge sign that was a hugely popular LA landmark. Felix Chevrolet was very famous. It was famous all across the country because it was the dealership that moved more cars than any other car business west of the Mississippi. Having Felix the Cat helped. So did the innovative use of radio and television advertising, with live, three-minute commercials featuring noted personalities. But what really made Felix Chevrolet famous was the vision and the strategy and the drive of Nick Shammas.

Nickolas N. Shammas is the founder of The Shammas Group. He's been an entrepreneur since his student years at Fairfax High back in the 1930s when he began refurbishing and selling used cars. From there Mr. Shammas went on to create several successful used car operations in the Valley. But it was his purchase of Downtown's Felix Chevrolet in 1955 that started his astonishingly successful run as a leading car dealer in Southern California. In 1958 Mr. Shammas moved Felix Chevrolet from its original location at Twelfth and Grand to join the string of auto businesses which

Felix Chevrolet sales force in 1956, one year anniversary. Mr. Shammas is in row two from bottom center (5th person in).

stretched for 30 miles along Figueroa Street. Years ago, Figueroa Street, just south of the central city, could have been renamed Auto Row. From Downtown to the harbor, car dealerships and auto-related businesses were the prime presence on the boulevard. When Angelenos wanted to buy a car, they went to Figueroa Street. And very likely they went to a dealership owned by Nick Shammas.

Over the years, Nick Shammas' Felix Chevrolet (Cadillac was included in 1995) was joined by Downtown LA Mercedes-Benz, Dodge of Downtown LA, Nissan of Downtown LA, Volkswagen of Downtown LA, Porsche of Downtown LA and Audi of Downtown LA. While acquiring auto dealerships, Nick Shammas continued to expand his holdings. He purchased 20 acres of commercial property in Los Angeles. And he acquired the Petroleum Building at Olympic and Flower. It houses the company's executive offices as well as Workmen's Auto Insurance and Life Insurance, also part of The Shammas Group. The Petroleum Building has its own curious history as its top floor was the site of the notorious Teapot Dome Scandal back in the Roaring Twenties.

The Shammas Group actively contributes to the revitalization of the south Downtown district. The Figueroa Corridor Partnership, chaired by Darryl Holter, Chief Administrative Officer of The Shammas Group, is a coalition of local business owners working together to keep the area clean and safe. As part of its interest in the welfare of the area, the Partnership participates actively in community-based policing. Patrol officers are always welcome at the dealerships. When the LAPD's bicycle patrol was two bicycles short for the eight officers assigned, The Shammas Group donated two more bikes so that the patrol could be at full force. The Shammas Group is also involved in the Business Improvement District, The Central City Association, and the Community Redevelopment Agency's Strategic Plan for the Figueroa Corridor.

Throughout more than 40 years of growth and social change, The Shammas Group has focused its business strategy on the more than 300,000 people who commute to work in Downtown Los Angeles every day. Downtown Los Angeles Motors Mercedes Benz illustrates this commitment with a track record of success and innovation. Founded by Nick Shammas in 1970, the dealership thrived throughout the 1980s. During those years it was number one in sales of Mercedes Benz automobiles in the United States. But the 1990s brought problems. Competition in the suburbs drew customers away, and the civil disturbance in the midcity contributed to the perception that Downtown was a place to avoid. Rather than succumb to these pressures, The Shammas Group devised successful strategies to surmount them.

The Shammas Group reinvigorated its Mercedes business by redesigning its entire business approach. Customer loyalty and satisfaction came first. The dealership was remodeled, and the attractive new showroom welcomed customers into an environment that was comfortable and service-oriented. Managers were invested with more authority. Close attention was paid to the development of sales associates. Marketing strategies included broadening the advertising base and reaching out to the many ethnic groups throughout the area. The Downtown LA Motors Advantage Club was created to provide exclusive benefits in sales, service and parts. The strategy worked. In 1995, DTLA Motors was number 12 in the country. Two years later, it regained its national prominence and finished the year fifth among the nation's Mercedes dealers.

The Shammas Group understands that public perception is key to the success of a city and a business. By linking its future to that of Downtown Los Angeles, The Shammas Group has made a significant investment in its surrounding neighborhood. Figueroa Street links Downtown to the USC campus and the museums in Exposition Park. Nearby are such noted landmarks as The Shrine Auditorium and Orthopaedic Hospital. With these institutions and the many automobile businesses on Figueroa Street, The Shammas Group is engaged in an active partnership to reinvigorate an area which has

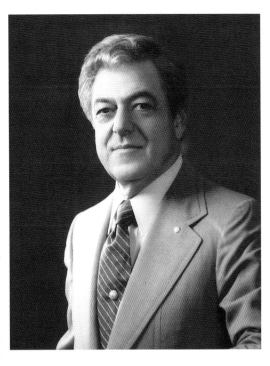

extraordinary potential to serve a vast population of employees, shoppers, visitors and tourists.

Los Angeles has many reasons to be proud of the achievements of Nick Shammas. Throughout his long and distinguished career he has addressed the important social and economic problems of the city, and he has engaged in national politics, too. In 1960 he was a leader in the campaign to elect John F. Kennedy as President of the United States and was a member of the Democratic Party Finance Committee. He is a well-respected leader in the Lebanese-American community and an early sponsor of the Mexican American Political Association. Mr. Shammas is also a longtime member of the Rotary Club, first in Studio City and currently in the Southwest Rotary Club located near USC.

As important as his community contributions have been, Nick Shammas is equally proud of the part that his business has played in the lives of his employees. Nearly 600 people are employed by The Shammas Group, and Mr. Shammas has worked hard to create a work environment where energy, initiative, pride and service flourish. He has nurtured a tradition of excellence throughout good times and bad, so that The Shammas Group will continue to confront all future challenges with energy and enthusiasm.

Nick Shammas has always been an ardent supporter of Los Angeles. LA has been his city since childhood, and his faith in the future of Downtown has helped enhance the business climate in an area that has experienced both triumph and turbulence. From his initial foray into Downtown, when he and Felix the Cat reinvigorated the auto business, Nick Shammas has persevered, determined to preserve the importance of Downtown Los Angeles as a business center of preeminent importance.

Nickolas N. Shammas has been a successful automobile dealer since 1955 when he signed his first dealer agreement with Chevrolet.

STILLWELL HOTEL

f one can't always judge a book by its cover, the same could be said of a building. Behind a classic and understated exterior, an interior of muted, old-world elegance may await the adventurous traveler. This is precisely the unique character of the Stillwell Hotel, located in the South Park area of Downtown Los Angeles. Built in 1912, the ten-story edifice presides over its somewhat barren stretch of Grand Avenue between 8th and 9th with a modest, but welcoming demeanor that recalls a bygone era of grace and gentility. Downtown Los Angeles has erected many glamorous, intimidating high rises, but the old-style Stillwell Hotel will make a visitor feel immediately at home.

The Stillwell Hotel is a small gem. It was fully restored in the late 1980s by the owners, Telikjan and Harpal Gill. The renovation was so successful that it was honored by the Los Angeles Conservancy with one of its first Preservation Awards. An old architectural rendering portrays a front facade with elegant arches and calm, classical proportions. The upper stories display real magnificence, with two rounded towers at either side and a wealth of decorative applique. Today, while some of the more elaborate details are no longer in place, ease and elegance still prevail.

The quiet, elegant lobby of the Stillwell Hotel is a congenial meeting place for guests.

The Stillwell Hotel was built during the first of Downtown Los Angeles' three major building booms. That period spanned the years at the beginning of the 20th century, from 1900 to 1917. (The second was a brief, ten-year burst during the 20s; the third began in the late 60s and has continued unabated ever since.) The architectural style of the first period was the Classical Beaux Arts, modeled after the Ecole des Beaux Arts in Paris, and, indeed, many prominent architectural firms employed French-trained architects who imported the panache of Paris to satisfy the conservative tastes of their financial and business clients. During that early era, many ten- to 12-story buildings were built, among them the Stillwell Hotel. The architect of the Stillwell Hotel, Frederic Noonan, also designed a hotel on Spring Street, similar in style to the Stillwell and built one year later.

The South Park community of Downtown has escaped the encroaches of skyscrapers. Many of the buildings in the area are old and substantial and go unappreciated by a public that associated prosperity with shiny new glass and steel. But these are buildings full of character inside and adorned with intricate ornamentation on the outside. When they are preserved, their distinctive design and human-scale proportions are both exciting and comforting. When such a building's owners have the courage to retain and restore it, they display both a reverence for the past and the courage to buck the prevailing trend.

The Stillwell Hotel offers its guests 250 rooms, all recently redesigned. It also features 4,000 square feet of

meeting space, banquet facilities and a full catering service. The hotel is proud to describe itself as offering luxurious suites at moderate prices. For the traveler on a budget, the Stillwell is an affordable opportunity to stay close to Downtown's business and cultural attractions. So much that Downtown has to offer is within an easy walk from the Stillwell. The Convention Center is just minutes to the south. The Music Center is directly up the hill. Two major shopping centers are a couple of blocks away, and the corporate and financial center is easily accessed by foot. Little Tokyo and

of nan, the traditional Indian leavened-dough bread. Chicken, lamb, seafood and vegetarian entrees round out the menu. Rice dishes, desserts and favorite Indian beverages are also available.

Indian cuisine is highly spiced, but the menu at Gill's has been tempered to suit the American palate which is often intimidated by extremely hot food. This temperance allows the diner to fully experience the elusive medley of flavorings, both herbs and spices, which infuse all the selections. However, if a diner should request more fiery flavorings, Gill's will be happy to oblige.

Guests who prefer a more familiar American ambience can relax at Hank's New York Bar for cocktails and traditional grill fare. Decorated in typical bar style, the dark wood walls and fully stocked bar invite the visitor to sit back and stay awhile. And, this being Los Angeles, a Mexican restaurant occupies the front of the Stillwell's lobby. Lily's Grill serves traditional Mexican dinners and south-of-the-border combinations. Lily's aims to please all comers: Early diners can order from a menu of breakfast items, while sandwiches and burgers will satisfy any cravings for all-American cooking.

Chinatown, the Garment District and the Jewelry Center are all close by. And, of course, there are Downtown's many exciting restaurants.

But no restaurant has quite the delicious character of Gill's, located in the rear of the lobby of the Stillwell Hotel. The restaurant advertises itself as specializing in exotic Indian food, and a first-time visitor will be impressed with the enticing aromas which greet all the guests. The cuisine is authentic, which is not a surprise, as the owners of the Stillwell are originally from India. The restaurant specializes in food cooked in India's famous tandoors, the clay ovens which concentrate the seductive and tantalizing flavors of the food. An expert on Indian cuisine would advise the novice to be wary of a restaurant that has no aroma; the nose is the guide when taking a first impression.

The first impression of Gill's is very promising. A sumptuous, savory smell fills the room which is decorated in the warm and colorful Indian style. Beautiful tapestries, mounted under glass, line the walls. Carved wood, brass trays and Indian dolls complete the exotic environment. The reasonably priced menu offers an array of appetizers, half a dozen tandoori specialties and an equal number of tandoori breads, including various versions

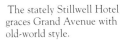

The interior of the Stillwell is serene and tranquil. Exquisite embroidered tapestries adorn the walls of the lobby where small seating areas encourage relaxation and conversation. Service is friendly, and a warm welcome is extended by all the staff. The effect is one of timelessness, a quiet refuge from the buzz and business of the enormous Los Angeles metropolis of which Downtown is the hub. If, after nearly a century, the Beaux Arts architects were to return to LA, chances are, they would feel right at home at the Stillwell Hotel.

SYSTEMATIC OFFICE SUPPLY

I n the summer of 1928, Spring Street came alive at 8:30 every weekday morning when office workers stepped off the crowded streetcars and scurried into the buildings that made up the main street of L.A.'s financial district. It was on Spring, between Third and Fourth Street, that Stationery Exchange was born. This thriving business, now spanning more than seventy years, was all started by a blind man with a vision of the future.

Eddie and Lena Rosenblum with their employee, Helen. Old timers still remember how the blind Eddie would personally greet each customer by name, correctly recognizing them by the sound of their footsteps.

Eddie Rosenblum, a thirty year-old blind gentleman, had recently married Lena Weisman, a widow with two children. He took on the responsibility of raising Lena's two children, Sid and Mildred, as his own. To support his new family, Eddie opened Stationery Exchange and installed a hand-fed printing press in the back of the 5000-foot building. The store stocked a variety of office supplies to service the surrounding downtown business community. Old timers still remember how the blind Eddie would personally greet each customer by name, correctly recognizing them by the sound of their footsteps.

When Sid was fifteen, he started helping his parents in the store by filling orders, making local deliveries and learning the ins and outs of the business. In 1937, Sid married his childhood sweetheart, Thelma Kobey. Two years later, Thelma gave birth to Marvin, the first of their four children. The day Marvin was born, his grandfather sold Stationery Exchange to Sid for $1,000. Eddie used that $1,000 to buy a high-speed envelope press and start a company called Envelope Printers. Marvin spent summer vacations working in the store, learning from his father. In 1970, Marvin became his father's partner in the then $300,000 per year company. In 1975, Sid and Marvin purchased another local office supply company, Systematic Office Supply (SOS). They incorporated in 1976 and Sid-Mar Inc. was created.

Today, Marvin's two sons, Brian and Craig, continue the family tradition by working along side their father. This fourth generation multi-million dollar cor-poration has become one of the largest independent office supply dealers in Los Angeles and Orange Counties. After several moves, SOS purchased a building on Mateo Street with 14000 square feet of offices, warehouse space and a print shop. A subsidiary of Systematic Office Supply, S.O.S. Printing Company is the home of eight offset presses, including a Webb Offset Press that produces 25,000 copies per hour and can print either one-color two sides or two-color one side. With the most up-to-date camera equipment, S.O.S. Printing Company has the capability to photograph both half tones and line text. In-house designers work one-on-one with customers to create letterhead, envelopes, brochures and catalogs. SOS may be the last of a dying breed of independent office supply dealers. In the 1980s, office supply "superstores" started to appear. Since then, stores such as Staples and Office Depot have greatly changed the office supply industry. Many small and medium sized dealers have closed their doors, unable to compete with the massive super stores. Others, such as SOS, joined a nation-wide buying group to give themselves an edge. As a member of National Office Buyers Group, SOS can offer customers an endless variety of products at very competitive prices. National Office Buyers Group has over 300 members throughout the United States. Independents, like SOS use buying groups to allow them to compete with the less personal superstores.

One way SOS distinguishes itself from the competition is through its knowledgeable order department. Customers receive personal service in locating the exact products they need. At superstores, consumers can be stuck roaming endless aisles in search of supplies. But SOS's friendly order desk will spend whatever time it takes to locate every item — even specialty supplies. SOS even assembles all furniture before it's delivered. And most orders are delivered the next day. Customers may order electronically as well, via personal computer. Many fax their orders, selecting products from one of SOS' many catalogs. SOS has a main catalog with over 25,000 items, a smaller catalog with about 3,000 frequently used items, and an assortment of niche catalogs from furniture to cleaning supplies. SOS also mails quarterly flyers with special products and prices.

SOS' philosophy is simple: build a strong internal service team and keep the customer happy. That's why SOS has dedicated itself to fulfilling client needs through excellent service and quality. Each area of the company is designed and managed with customer service in mind. Delivery trucks are radio dispatched, allowing greater flexibility. If a customer urgently needs a product delivered, the closest driver can be called back to handle the emergency. Customers are also given the option of either morning or afternoon deliveries. The idea is to give the customer exactly what they want, as quickly as they need it.

What is SOS' management style? Definitely easy going. They resisted using time clocks for years. According to Marvin Rosenblum, "old fashioned trust and flexibility" is the secret to the company's low employee turnover. Or maybe its the Christmas parties. The break room walls at SOS are covered with hundreds of color photos on pasted poster board — photos of Christmas parties past. The Kodachrome smiles of co-workers make it clear there's a special, family-like relationship at SOS that everyone enjoys. The face of SOS has changed over the years, as a result of going head-to-head with competing superstores and growing with the computer age to meet the needs of a new generation of office supply buyers. But the heart of the company still beats with the desire to provide the same old fashioned service Eddie gave all those years ago.

The Stationery Exchange was born in 1928 on Spring, between Third and Fourth Street, right in the heart of L.A.'s financial district.

W.I. Simonson Inc.

.I. Simonson, Inc. is one of the original Mercedes-Benz dealerships in the United States. Three generations of the same family have owned and operated this service-oriented business for more than 60 years.

William I. "Bill" Simonson was born in Wolf City, Texas. He moved to Dallas and began a career of selling luxury items at Titche-Getinger Co., the fanciest department store in town. In 1926, he moved his wife Alma and six-year-old daughter Mary to Santa Monica. His uncle Will lived there and believed career possibilities existed for Bill at the local Packard dealership.

The Packard was the "crème de la crème" of the automobile world at that time and Bill Simonson rapidly earned a reputation for being the nation's top salesman of these magnificent motor cars. His favorite saying was, "If you treat your customers fairly, they'll always come back." It was the philosophy on which he built his business.

He held the title of Master Salesman when the Great Depression hit and selling cars became virtually impossible. Simonson refused to be deterred. He obtained a line of credit from a local banker, rented a warehouse and operated a modified taxi and touring service, thus surviving the Depression without having to liquidate his property. By 1934, people were buying cars again and in 1937, Simonson and fellow Packard salesman Leo Schactmayer purchased the Santa Monica dealership.

Within ten years, Simonson had gone from salesman to co-owner of the thriving Packard dealership. His acumen with employees and customers earned the company a loyal following that included the likes of Will Rogers and Mary Pickford.

After World War II, the popularity of the Packard declined. Studebaker merged with Packard and then became the U.S. distributor for Mercedes-Benz. On June 13, 1957, Bill signed on with Mercedes-Benz thus becoming one of the first 20 dealerships in the nation. It remains one of a handful of U.S. Mercedes dealerships still run by those original families and one of only two still owned in California.

In 1969, W.I. Simonson became sole owner of the company. However, challenges faced by the company and the family were not over. After Simonson passed away in 1976, his daughter Mary Simonson Rehwald assumed the Presidency. It was a time when very few women were in business for themselves, let alone owning and operating an automobile dealership. "But my father believed I could do it and I had confidence in myself," said Mary Rehwald.

That confidence was well founded. The dealership thrived for a decade under her leadership. In 1986, a year before the anniversary of 50 years in business, tragedy struck. A cigarette is believed to have started a fast-moving fire that destroyed the showroom, service department, reception and quick service area and business offices. No one was injured and all customer cars in for service were removed before sustaining any damage, but all the company records and 21 new cars on the showroom floor were destroyed.

William I. "Bill" Simonson (left) and his partner Leo Schactmayer after they purchased the Santa Monica Packard dealership in 1937. Simonson became sole owner in 1969.

Miraculously, W.I. Simonson was open for business the very next day and every employee was on the job. Mary Rehwald credits then-general manager Elvira Reed with having the forethought on the night of the fire to make arrangements to rent trailers for office space and to make sure phones would be in operation.

It was difficult over the next year-and-a-half with cramped quarters and major construction. Seven months after the fire, Mary Rehwald hosted a groundbreaking celebration for a $2.2 million reconstruction project. By now, all three Rehwald children worked full time at the dealership, and the family made the decision to replicate the 1922 Spanish Revival style building as close to the original as possible.

The task was enormous since plans of the building no longer existed. To aid in the process, photographs were supplied by the niece of the original builder. The rebuilding was completed in February of 1988 and included attention to historic details. Exact reproductions of the ceramic tiles were manufactured by the Malibu Tile Company, the same firm that made the original tiles.

The restored 29,000-square-foot building has won numerous awards including: The Los Angeles Conservancy Preservation Award, The California Historical Society Award of Merit, resolutions of commendation from the City of Santa Monica Landmarks Commission and the City of Los Angeles, and the Annual Preservation Award from the Santa Monica Historical Society.

In June 1997, W. I. Simonson celebrated 60 years in business and 40 years as a Mercedes-Benz dealer. That might seem like the epitome of success when coupled with the fact that W.I. Simonson has consistently been ranked one of the top ten Mercedes dealerships in the United States. But true success, according to Mary Simonson Rehwald, came in 1994.

"That was when I told my three children that I wanted them to run the business," said Rehwald. "My father gave it to me and I wanted to be able to do the same for my children."

Today, the three manage day-to-day operations. William Rehwald serves as chief financial officer. His two sisters Judy Richards and Frances Rehwald share the title of general manager. One sister holds the actual position for three months, then the other takes over for three months. Frances is also in charge of marketing and advertising, while Judy oversees human resources and personnel. It is a unique arrangement that Mary Rehwald says serves the company well and takes advantage of the strengths of each of her children.

One strength of a company where three-fourths of the leadership is female has been recognizing that more and more women are buying cars and there is a need to ensure that all personnel treat Simonson's customers with equality. Women's service clinics have been developed to inform women customers about engines, auto components and servicing requirements. "We believe an educated automotive consumer is a better consumer," said Frances Rehwald.

That level of concern extends to active involvement in the Santa Monica community where they have been significant contributors to the YMCA, the Westside Women's Health Center, the Santa Monica UCLA Medical Center, the Santa Monica Historical Society, the Santa Monica Symphony, L.A. Baroque Orchestra, Carlthorpe School, various environmental concerns and Santa Monica High School and Santa Monica College where three generations of the family have attended.

As a fourth generation prepares to assume the mantle of leadership, the dealership is expanding to accommodate the customers and vehicles of the future and the family of W. I. Simonson stands ready to meet the challenges of 21st Century.

Mary Simonson Rehwald (front) inherited the dealership after the death of her father. She has passed the reins of management to her three children; (left to right) William Rehwald, chief financial officer, Frances Rehwald, co-general manager and Judy Richards, co-general manager.

ARGYLE HOTEL

From the moment the Sunset Tower opened its doors in 1925, the Leland A. Bryant-designed hotel was destined to become a Los Angeles landmark.

Situated on the legendary Sunset Strip, the elegant Art Deco style structure boasted the same prestigious zip code as many of the era's most popular nightclubs and famous restaurants.

West Hollywood has always catered to celebrities and since its inception, the Sunset Tower has embodied all that Hollywood-ites aspired to be. Former residents include Howard Hughes, John Wayne and even gangster Bugsy Siegel.

To attract a demanding clientele, the building incorporated the latest in both technology and design. Modern conveniences in those early days included electrical outlets in every bathroom for electric shavers and windows were found everywhere to afford residents spectacular panoramic views.

From an architectural standpoint, the Argyle Hotel represents the moment when Los Angeles, Art Deco and Hollywood came together, their combined qualities producing elegance, sophistication and fantasy.

In recent years, the structure itself appeared on the silver screen in *Wayne's World II*, *Get Shorty*, and Robert Altman's *The Player*. Former Beatle Ringo Starr was interviewed on site for "The Beatles Reunion" television special and famed local novelist Raymond Chandler gave the building its first literary mention in the early 1940s.

Architect Leland Bryant specialized in luxury apartments, but the Sunset Tower was easily his crowning achievement. Although his previous work predominantly comprised Period Revival styles, the Tower's pure Art Deco design proved his ability to work with modern idioms and made a statement of "joyous rebellion and prosperity."

Most of the exterior surface is smooth concrete, the windows forming a pattern of vertical bands which draw the eye upward and emphasize the structure's height. Faceted windows accent the corners of the building while flora, fauna, mythological creatures, zepplelins and even Adam and Eve comfortably coexist in the space.

From an architectural standpoint, the Sunset Tower represents the moment when Los Angeles, Art Deco and Hollywood came together, their combined qualities producing elegance, sophistication and fantasy.

After several failed attempts to demolish the structure in the 1970s and early 80s, the building sat derelict for many years until it was purchased by the St. James Club of Great Britain in 1986. A subsequent renovation and restoration project ensued, including a pool area and full service restaurant.

Apartments were reconfigured to create suites and furnished with made-to-order reproductions of original Art Deco pieces. Public rooms feature exquisite copies of French Deco furnishings and object d'art and carpets woven-to-order from Europe.

The Argyle Corporation purchased the hotel and the Denver-based Richfield Hospitality Inc. currently manages the Argyle. With great regard for the hotel's history and architectural significance, the new owners employed the services of architect Scott Field, whose innovative design style led to the creation of a separate entrance to the restaurant, "fenix." Future plans include refurbishing the fabrics and carpets, as well as displays which focus on the hotel's history.

Sixty-five years since its inception, the hotel remains one of the most elegant, extravagant spaces in the City of Angels.

BIG TREE WINE DISTRIBUTORS

family business owned by Bill and Trudy Tom since 1979, Big Tree is a major wholesale "cash and carry" distributor of beer, wines, and alcoholic beverages. Bill, its healthy 73 year old owner, originally bought the business from an old friend, John Cascio, who had started it fifty years before. In the following 17 years, Bill and his wife Trudy have built up the business by more than fourfold.

Does this sound like the typical American success story? Well, it is — with one major exception: Bill's and Trudy's country of origin is not the United States, but China from where they emigrated as youths. "Bill came when he was thirteen and I was three," says Trudy. "But, we are Americans through and through and proud of it." Landing in San Francisco sixty years ago, Bill and his father headed immediately to Los Angeles, where he has lived ever since. He met and married Trudy here 43 years ago. Prior to buying Big Tree, Bill whetted his skills by owning and running another liquor business for 14 years. He and Trudy had their eyes on an early retirement until the Cascio's offered to sell their company to him.

Bill bought the business because he believed it was a good investment for his children. His two sons, Lawrence and Roger, developed other interests, however. Bill's daughter-in-law, Susan, liked the business and has stayed with it until today (1997). From one son and daughter, Linda, Bill and Trudy have three granddaughers: Stephanie, Lindsey, and Lauren.

The company is unique because it is open seven days a week, caters to all beverage licensees, including bars, restaurants, markets, and liquor stores who may be

in escrow, have limited capital, or find themselves out of stock on weekends and holidays. With a major inventory of all brands, Budweiser, Coors, Miller, Gallo, Bacardi, Smirnoff, Hennessey, and the like, Big Tree services primarily Los Angeles and Orange Counties. Smaller retail outlets like doing business with Big Tree because they can buy daily if necessary, and may buy smaller quanties than from other distributors, thereby controlling their cashflow.

Big Tree's first milestone was adding 10,000 square feet of warehouse to its original storage facilities. Liquor products were added to beer and wine to enable licensees to purchase individual bottles instead of full cases. Bill is now planning to expand into wholesale grocery products, which are essential to his customers. Big Tree's present warehouse space is comprised of 50,000 square feet.

Twenty-three employees help Trudy and Bill manage the operation. When orders are received, workers load them onto four-wheeled, flatbed carts, which the customers themselves pick up. Big Tree makes no deliveries itself, but when inventory is delivered to it, it is in quantity. Beer is delivered in trailer loads of twenty-six pallets to a load, about 2,000 cases. Major regional companies who distribute for breweries and distillers are Big Tree's suppliers. Big Tree is a direct distributor of Gallo and Monarch Wines.

There seems to be no end to the energy and the entrepeneurial enterprise of Bill Tom and his wife Trudy. An example of American opportunity fulfilled, Big Tree heads into the coming millenium with a head of steam any company would be proud to possess.

Bill & Trudy Tom, partners in business and in life.

HOLIDAY INN DOWNTOWN

All of the excitement of Los Angeles and the best in Southern California attractions are only a stone's throw away for guests of the Holiday Inn Downtown. Ideally situated in the heart of the city, the Holiday Inn Downtown offers something for everyone from the corporate or business traveler to vacationing couples or families.

Corporate guests appreciate the hotel's proximity to L.A.'s Convention Center and Financial District while travelers in town for government business are within walking distance to State and Federal offices.

Holiday Inn Downtown offers something for everyone from the corporate or business traveler to vacationing couples or families.

Those in town to take in a little fun and sun find an abundance of area attractions and sightseeing destinations within a 20 mile radius, including Disneyland, Universal Studios, Dodger Stadium, Little Tokyo, the landmark Griffith Park Observatory, Mann's Chinese Theatre, the Hollywood Walk of Fame and the upcoming Staples center.

Guests enjoy the hotel's sparkling outdoor pool.

Conveniently located just 12 miles from the Los Angeles International Airport, the Holiday Inn Downtown originally opened its doors in 1968. The current owner, L.A. Hospitality Inc., has successfully managed the hotel since 1989. The hotel features 204 newly-decorated guest rooms, each equipped with air-conditioning, clock-radios, remote control 25 inch color cable televisions with pay-per-view first run feature films, in-room coffee makers and hair dryers. Each room features an electronic safe for individual guest use. Other amenities include a same day laundry valet service, a lounge complete with a billiards table and video games, complimentary covered parking and a cocktail lounge with complimentary hors d'oeuvres on weeknights from 5 to 7 p.m.

The Garland Café, known for its American cuisine with a Mexican flavor, has earned a reputation for quality, service, ambiance and excellent prices.

Guests soak in some sun at the hotel's sparkling outdoor pool or head to the white sand beaches of the nearby Pacific Ocean. Guest privileges to fully equipped new fitness center offer hotel patrons the option of an invigorating workout.

Business travelers can take advantage of the hotel's multi-lingual translation services, 24-hour Business Center, private parlor meeting rooms for intimate business functions or board meetings and banquet facilities which serve as the perfect setting for functions from sales presentations to elaborate sit-down dinners.

General Manager Sabir S. Jaffer cordially invites you to experience the comfort and hospitality of the Holiday Inn Downtown. Whatever your pleasure, this hotel offers the perfect site from which to experience the sunny weather, sparkling water and white sand beaches, sporting events, amusement parks, shopping, dining and entertainment of the cultural mecca that is Los Angeles.

HOLLYWOOD ROOSEVELT HOTEL

n 1927, the Hollywood Roosevelt Hotel opened her doors to a glamorous throng. Local real estate baron Charles E. Toberman dreamed of creating a hotel befitting the film world and its attendant circles. But the inevitable design of the classic Spanish revival building exceeded even Toberman's expectations.

Named for the exuberant 26th President of the United States, Theodore Roosevelt, this new hotel matched his spirit and the buoyant mood of Hollywood in its heyday.

The founding members of the Hollywood Holding Company and the first owners of the hotel, Louis B. Mayer, Marcus Loew, Joseph Schenck, Douglas Fairbanks, Toberman and Mary Pickford celebrated the historic opening of the "Home of the Stars."

The hotel's now famous "Blossom Room" was the site of the first Academy Awards presentation presided over by Douglas Fairbanks. Oscars that night were given to Janet Gaynor, Emil Jannings and Victor Fleming. The hotel's legendary Cinegrill became a haven for writers such as Hemingway and Fitzgerald and was a favorite romantic rendezvous for Clark Gable and Carole Lombard. Errol Flynn invented his own gin cocktail behind the barber shop and David Niven was once given a room in the servants' quarters at the start of his acting career.

In 1984, a group of investors bought the hotel and temporarily closed her doors. Almost two years were spent restoring the hand-painted ceilings and Spanish wrought-iron grill work that distinguished the handsome architecture. Her dignity regained, the Hollywood Roosevelt was toasted by more than 1,500 civic and film leaders at the reopening on March 7, 1986.

Today, the hotel features 335 beautifully-appointed rooms, including 20 luxury suites. Among the suites are a Grand Suite, the "Celebrity Suite," 10 movie-themed suites and nine three-room Hollywood suites. There are also 65 Cabana rooms in a tropical garden setting bordering an Olympic swimming pool, Jacuzzi and Tropicana Bar.

The Roosevelt offers as standard amenities voice mail service, hair dryers, coffee makers and irons/ironing boards in every room while the Business Class floor features 2-line phones, modems, data ports, office supplies and additional workspace in each room.

The glamorous reputation of the Roosevelt has endured as long as the legendary artists whose names decorate the "Walk of Fame" outside: Errol Flynn, Douglas Fairbanks, John Barrymore and Maureen O'Hara.

Today, hotel guests see film and musical performers continuing to be immortalized in the pink granite stars along Hollywood Boulevard. In addition to the excitement of the "Walk of Fame," visitors also find the renowned Mann's Chinese Theatre at their doorstep and major attractions, such as Universal Studios, Disneyland, Beverly Hills, the Hollywood Bowl, sports stadiums and area beaches within easy reach.

The Roosevelt is now the hottest and most popular spot for live cabaret in the Cinegrill lounge. Theodore's elegant dining room is perfect for business luncheons or late-night dinners after the show. The superb classic cuisine and charming European atmosphere provide a setting appropriate for any occasion.

Once again, the restored Hollywood Roosevelt is the place for a star-studded night on the town.

Named for Teddy Roosevelt, the classic Spanish revival hotel matches the exuberant spirit of the 26th President.

Hand-painted ceilings and Spanish wrought-iron grill work distinguishes the handsome architecture of this historic hotel.

Irèna's Photographic Rental Service Inc.

Irèna's Photographic Rental Service Inc. (PRS) allows photographers to turn their creative dreams into reality.

Founded in 1979 by still and film photographer Irèna (one name only), PRS rents and sells cutting edge cameras and accessories, lighting, grip equipment, electronic imaging, video and audio-visual systems to provide for virtually all types of photographic needs.

Since no other similar services existed at the time, Irèna essentially blazed a trail for competitors to follow. But even today, the competition has trouble keeping up as Irèna purchases and stocks her shelves with the most advanced merchandise on the market.

This one-stop shop allows fans of all skill levels of photography access to state-of-the-art equipment that may otherwise be out of their financial reach.

"PRS really allows photographers to be creative with the advent of new technology and the most advanced equipment available today," said CEO and Owner Irèna. "This service has allowed us to make a major impact in the industry."

What began as a one-woman entrepreneurial endeavor grew to encompass 36 employees at two rental facilities and a PRS Grip House, located adjacent to the original rental and sales location.

Currently the largest camera and equipment rental house in the United States, PRS caters to customers across the country and around the world.

Irèna counts among her clients everyone from amateur shutterbugs to renowned photographers like Annie Leibowitz and Herb Ritts, who rent her equipment for magazine shoots and commercial advertising photography. Although she doesn't "do" cinema, many of Hollywood's motion picture houses also call on Irèna's services.

The business of photography has changed even if the "basic" technology remains somewhat the same. Although photographers today still need to work with the same principles of light, film and cameras as their predecessors, they must now react much more quickly. And PRS is uniquely suited to meet the need for speed.

With the advent of digital, or filmless, photography, Irèna was able to supply photographers covering the Academy Awards with the equipment necesssary for them to instantly capture images and upload them to the wire services in record time.

Digital technology currently accounts for 15 percent of Irèna's business, but she expects that figure to grow exponentially as technology becomes more refined. PRS supplied the U.S. Army with digital cameras for the Persian Gulf War. Today, the same state-of-the-art equipment can be rented or purchased from PRS at very reasonable prices.

For top-of-the-line technology and competitive prices on all product lines including film, electronic imaging equipment and supplies, PRS makes all things possible.

Irèna's Photographic Rental Service Inc. (PRS) has helped photographers turn their creative dreams into reality since 1979.

Irèna continues to oversee operations at the nation's largest camera and equipment rental house.

L.A. MART

The L.A. Mart has evolved during more than half a century from a trade cooperative to furniture mart, and then to general merchandise mart. By keeping pace with the changing economy, the L.A. Mart has remained a major force in the economic fabric of Los Angeles.

Beginning in 1928, the current L.A. Mart evolved from a cooperative of furniture manufacturers, manufacturer's representatives and large retailers known as the Los Angeles Home Furnishing Mart (LAHFM). Similar to a trade association, these groups operated a furniture mart designed to display and serve as a marketing center for their products.

In 1958, the furniture mart moved into its present 900,000-square-foot facility where tenants prospered into the 60s and 70s until structural changes in furniture distribution methods caused an industry-wide decline.

In 1978, the LAHFM sold the structure and its related parking lots to the International Fastener Research Corp. (IFR), a diversified investment company.

IFR principals David Weisz, Stanley Kleeman and Richard Miller worked together to transform the then-struggling furniture mart into a thriving new business.

The trio expanded the operation to a general merchandise mart that, in addition to furniture, features gift, decorative accessories, home accents and other related items to a large base of retailers and interior designers.

Renamed the L.A. Mart in 1979, the business continues to thrive as a wholesale mart offering a tremendous product selection. The L.A. Mart currently has over 550 tenants representing virtually every line in the gift and decorative accessories arena as well as offerings from the most popular furniture manufacturers and unique custom design.

Although it also caters to international clients, the L.A. Mart primarily serves the geographic areas west of the Mississippi, with particular emphasis on Utah, Nevada, Arizona, Idaho, New Mexico, Colorado, Oregon, Washington and all of California.

One of the L.A. Mart's most significant strengths, in addition to its vast product selection, is that over 25,000 buying units — all potential customers of L.A. Mart's tenants — are situated within a two hour driving radius.

The L.A. Mart continues to aggressively seek out and identify new products for building business in addition to attracting new and established tenants in the area it serves.

A vast selection of products, innovative marketing programs and highly successful trade shows held at the site throughout the year contribute to the L.A. Mart's industry-wide reputation as one of the nation's premier merchandise marts.

In addition to the immensely popular January and July gift shows, the L.A. Mart promotes specialized programs and promotions created to help its customers better merchandise their products. Extensive seminars feature industry leaders who impart innovative and helpful information which these customers can put into practice to further build their individual businesses.

Mr. Weisz and Mr. Miller have since passed away, but the L.A. Mart continues to be owned and operated by the Weisz, Miller and Kleeman families.

This 900,000-square-foot facility is home to a general merchandise mart and features furniture, gifts, decorative accessories, home accents and other related items to a large base of retailers and interior designers.

MARRIOTT HOTELS

A classic American dream come true, that's the story of the Marriott Corporation. What all started with just a nine-seat root beer stand has grown into a multibillion dollar enterprise that is a world leader in today's lodging industry.

On the same day that Charles Lindbergh made the first flight across the Atlantic — May 20, 1927 — J. Willard Marriott introduced the people of Washington D.C. to A&W root beer. Alice and Willard married and began working side-by-side in their new business. Soon hot entrees were added with the name "Hot Shoppe" and the Marriotts had seven outlets in the nation's capitol by 1932. Over the next several years, Willard added in-flight catering and food service management to the company's operations. In 1953, Hot Shoppes' stock was first offered to the public. Their first hotel, the Twin Bridges Marriott, opened four years later near Washington's National Airport and was a tremendous success. Other hotels followed in Dallas and Philadelphia in 1964.

Marriott was just 27 years old when he sold his first five-cent mug of root beer. Forty-six years later in July of 1973, he celebrated the opening of his 31st hotel, the Los Angeles Airport Marriott. In true J. Willard style, the dedication ceremonies were impressive for this 1,020-room luxury hotel located on 14 acres across from Los Angeles' busy International Airport. At the time, the $52 million Century Boulevard facility was the most costly project the company had undertaken. The highlight of the event was the cutting of a 200-foot ribbon, which released 2,000 red, white and blue balloons from the top of the hotel's roof. Both

The Los Angeles Airport Marriott Hotel.

Marriott and eldest son J.W., Jr. were in attendance. That same night, Bob Hope chaired a dinner to honor the Marriotts which included Mr. and Mrs. John Wayne, Former Governor and Mrs. Edmond G. Brown, Mayor and Mrs. Tom Bradley and many others. The Los Angeles facility was only the second Marriott Hotel to be built in California; the Berkeley Marriott on San Francisco's Bay was the first.

Since its auspicious opening, the Los Angeles Airport Marriott has been an active participant in the fast-changing history of its community. Because it was designed for great flexibility, it easily accommodates a convention one day and a beautiful wedding the next. The facility has hosted numerous local and national political events. Sporting events frequently serve as decade markers, and the grand Hotel has housed more than its share of landmark athletics, from World Soccer Cups to Super Bowls. In fact, the Los Angeles Marriott Hotel was the press headquarters for the 1984 Super Bowl, when the L.A. Raiders beat the Washington Redskins 38-9. Perhaps one of the most exciting events to be hosted at the celebrated Hotel was the 1984 Olympics, where it served as the processing site for all of the participating athletes. It was at the 1984 Olympics that Carl Lewis became the first athlete to win gold medals in the 100- and 200-meter dash, the 400-meter relay and the long jump.

J. Willard died in 1985, at the age of 84, and was succeeded by his son, J.W. Marriott Jr. Associates mourned the death of this great man, but his values and traditions remain as the foundation of today's Marriott International Inc. Currently, the Los Angeles Airport Marriott Hotel continues to operate with the same old-fashioned good values that J. Willard practices. This on-going pursuit of excellence is based on a lasting heritage — the innovative and aggressive spirit that characterized J. Willard Marriott's modest business beginnings over 70 years ago.

PACIFIC DESIGN CENTER

aking a resounding architectural design statement with brilliant blue and green structures on Melrose Avenue and San Vicente Boulevard, Pacific Design Center (PDC) makes no less a statement with its products and services. As the West Coast's largest resource for fine traditional and contemporary furnishings for the home and office, its 150+ showrooms feature an eclectic array of fabrics, floor coverings, fine arts, lighting, wallcoverings, antiques, furniture, and kitchen and bath products.

Center Blue, a 750,000-square-foot building, was constructed in 1975 and Center Green, containing 450,000 square feet, arrived in 1988.

In addition to fine showrooms, PDC incorporates a 200-seat conference center, a 382-seat state-of-the-art theater, meeting rooms, food services, a 1900-car parking structure, and office spaces for design-related tenants.

With a total of 1.2 million square feet, PDC's showrooms display and sell over 2,100 product lines, primarily to buyers from the western 13 states and Pacific Rim countries. Designed by world-renowned architect Cesar Pelli, the physical structure portends the imagination inherent in the business: its stock in trade is design excellence.

This is promoted by utilizing the building as a major venue for design-related events. An annual three-day international market event entitled WestWeek is sponsored by PDC. Attended by more than 20,000 members of the design community, it includes symposia, conferences, special events, exhibitions, and awards.

The Feldman Gallery, a 3,000-square-foot gallery on the PDC Plaza, has featured such diverse exhibitions as Woman in Architecture, New Italian Expressionist Color and Fabric, Frank Lloyd Wright: Decorative Designs Today and California Projects, Rhythm and Line, and Chairmania: Fantastic Miniatures.

Throughout the center, more than 300 special events, meetings, lectures, screenings, programs, and photography shoots occur annually. Organizations using the facilities have included the American Cinema Foundation, British Academy of Film and Television Arts, Chrysler, Christie's, HBO, Price Waterhouse, Turner Network Television, and the Thai Chamber of Commerce.

The 16-acre site and buildings are indeed a magnet for the many design disciplines. The dramatic appearance establishes a standard which inspires a designer to develop his or her craft to the fullest. Acknowledging that "how consumers are served is the most important challenge to face in the future," Pacific Design Center meets that challenge with style and sophistication.

The West Coast's largest resource for fine traditional and contemporary furnishings for the home and office.

PASSIONFRUIT

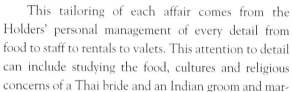

"We love creating food for the body that's also a pleasure for the heart and mind," say Lynne and Jeff Holder, partners and husband/wife team of the catering company, Passionfruit. "Food that's wholesome, while appealing both to the eye and the taste buds is the key to health and happiness and to our business."

Lynne and Jeff pursue this philosophy with a passion that comes from their in-depth experience and training and the belief that true culinary artistry can be truly memorable.

"One of the main ingredients in all our catering business is the way we customize each affair specifically for each client. We make it unique, so that no two affairs are ever the same, even for repeat clients," say the Holders. "That's why we'll show a client our extensive range of menus, but no brochure — we don't have one."

This tailoring of each affair comes from the Holders' personal management of every detail from food to staff to rentals to valets. This attention to detail can include studying the food, cultures and religious concerns of a Thai bride and an Indian groom and marrying the cuisine and the reception into a festive occasion that honors both Buddhist and Hindu customs while looking and tasting as if it were made by natives.

Steeped in the East Coast cooking tradition, Jeff Holder grew up in New Jersey, attended the New York Restaurant School and spent 15 years in New York City working his way from bartender to chef to food manager at establishments such as Adams Rib, Garvins, The Village Green, The Custom House, The Orchid Restaurant and Donald Sacks. His trek westward began with a notable tenure at La

Food that looks good and tastes great!

Casa Sena Restaurant in Santa Fe, New Mexico where he rose from cook to executive chef to assistant general manager. Continued successes led to executive positions in Albuquerque and finally, in 1989, in Los Angeles.

Lynne Holder studied under executive chef Gordon Hopkins of Michel's at The Colony Surf, a five-star establishment in her native Hawaii. She credits that experience with honing her management skills and intensifying her dedication to perfection. Since arriving in Los Angeles in 1981, she has managed food service operations at Los Angeles International Airport, the Los Angles Music Center, the Los Angeles Chamber of Commerce and the 1984 Los Angeles Olympics.

Lynne and Jeff met in 1989 while working for a nationwide catering company. Less than a year later, they married, invested their savings in equipment and a van and established Passionfruit under the Women and Minority Business Enterprise Act. Their first jobs came from friends who then passed the word around. Recommendations followed rapidly, as did referrals and repeat customers. And not long after celebrating their first year anniversary in business, they were rewarded with

a major coup: being named primary caterer for the Los Angeles Chamber of Commerce in 1991.

Passionfruit creates unique, individualized menus with a special flair for spicy, ethnic cuisine that consistently delights a list of prestigious clients that includes The Los Angeles Area Chamber of Commerce, ARAMARK, Southern California Gas Company, Texaco, UCLA, Sanwa Bank and the State Bar of California. The way the Holders see it, they put their passion in more than just the food they serve — it's in every aspect of their business.

PEDUS SERVICE

s the new millennium approaches, more and more companies are responding to changing economic conditions and increased competition by turning to selective outsourcing. Pedus Service is ready to meet those outsourcing needs by spanning the globe with an impressive range of high-quality services, from preparing delicious, economical food in company restaurants and school cafeterias to checking in passengers and handling baggage at major airports.

The external service specialists at Pedus have an impressive history of providing alternatives to in-house support functions so that businesses can focus their energies on their core competencies. The company began in Germany in 1963 with ten employees and by 1998 had established its first foreign subsidiary in Austria. The year 1970 saw the addition of a subsidiary in Italy, followed by subsidiaries in Italy and the United States in 1978.

The establishment of a Swiss subsidiary in 1989, in preparation for expansion into newly opened markets in Eastern Europe, paved the way for the opening of 14 branches in East Germany in 1990, subsidiaries in Hungary and the Czech Republic in 1994, and in Russia, Bulgaria and Slovakia in 1995. Expansion into China, Vietnam and the United Kingdom came in 1995. By 1998 Pedus employed more than 37,000 staff members in 22 countries.

Pedus' unprecedented growth has been driven by the company's philosophy of "synergy through networked services." The company's phenomenal success is based on its ability to help other businesses reduce nonproductive expenditures by offering selective outsourcing.

Creating a network of interconnected services, Pedus has relied on central purchasing, process management, quality assurance and intensive employee training and motivation to offer an ever-increasing array of services. The net effect for Pedus' clients has been cost savings, enhanced flexibility and profits, streamlined organizational and operational structures, increased competitiveness and a reduction in workload.

Pedus' leadership in service outsourcing is reflected in the quality of its divisions.

Pedus Service Facility Management offers a full array of janitorial, engineering, security, food preparation and concierge services. The result for property managers: satisfied tenants in safe, comfortable surroundings.

Pedus Service delivers professional food services with an emphasis on taste, value, nutrition and individual preference. Its philosophy of combining individuality with cost-consciousness means customized food service solutions for every occasion and every institution.

Pedus Aviation Service helps airlines and airports cope with an increasingly competitive environment, expanding numbers of passengers and ever-more-stringent security requirements. Clients using Pedus' passenger check-in security, baggage handling and aircraft washing and cleaning services realize lower operational costs and improved quality, safety and efficiency.

Pedus Office is grounded in the philosophy that flexibility means freedom for new and expanding businesses and freelance professionals. It offers business premises in major U.S. and European cities in custom sizes and configurations with business support from telephone connections to full secretarial, computer and communication services, all without capital investment or risk.

Pedus' corporate philosophy of consistency, innovation and awareness of clients' needs resulted in total sales worldwide on one billion dollars in 1998. By anticipating new areas of demand and by responding to a growing preference for outsourcing, Pedus' management is both poised and committed to help its clients grow prosperously into the 21st century.

Pedus Service Facility Management provides property managers with reliable and cost-effective alternatives for support services.

SUNKIST GROWERS

Sunkist. A name known worldwide. A name that stands for the very best in citrus.

Sunkist Growers had its beginnings in 1893, when 60 orange growers responded to unscrupulous fruit brokers by forming a marketing cooperative. The growers shared the expenses of packing and marketing, and every co-op member received a share of the proceeds according to the amount and grade of the fruit they shipped.

With more than 6,500 family farmers throughout California and Arizona, Sunkist is the largest American cooperative in the fruit and vegetable industry and the tenth largest overall. Sunkist member-growers own the cooperative. The business proceeds, less the cost of operation, are all returned to the member-growers.

People around the world know and trust the name Sunkist. It stands for quality, service and dependability. The Sunkist name is the cooperative's greatest asset. It is the 43rd most recognized trademark in the United States, and the 47th most recognized in the world.

Sunkist is unique because it offers a year-round supply of fruit, unlike many of its competitors. Sunkist also offers a wide variety of citrus: two types of oranges — Navel and Valencia; lemons; grapefruit; six types of tangerines; and seasonally, pummelos and blood oranges.

While Sunkist's headquarters are in Southern California where the business started, Sunkist growers farm throughout the states of California and Arizona, from San Bernardino to Ventura to Central California to Yuma, Arizona.

Visitors to the Sunkist building are greeted by a vibrant logo and grove scene and walls dotted with historic photos. The spacious, multi-level headquarters has its own ample parking as well as a shady outdoor patio. Employees seem genuinely happy to be there, perhaps because they are.

Sunkist has a record of employee loyalty and long-term association.

Sunkist is an active supporter of the Los Angeles community. For example, it is a founding member of the Los Angeles Chamber of Commerce and its employees are quite actively involved in community matters.

For the past 20 years, the cooperative has been headed by President Russell L. Hanlin. His is a true American success story. He started as a mailroom clerk

in 1951 and rose through the ranks to President and CEO. During his 20 years in office, Sunkist has grown from a $150 million cooperative to a billion-dollar cooperative.

For the past century, Sunkist's famous oranges and lemons have symbolized the sunshine of California to millions of people in the United States and around the world. Today, Sunkist is one of the most powerful, most recognized brands anywhere. Its name stands for quality and service worldwide.

VOGUE TYRE AND RUBBER COMPANY

arry Hower married into the tire business in 1919. His new bride Margaret had a brother in the business whom Harry joined forces with to manufacture a new design tire — the whitewall, a unique wider whitewall tire they hoped would attract the business of chauffeur-driven cars.

Hower and Woodbury successfully promoted the new "Vogue Custom Built" tires to that particular market in the Chicago area until 1928, when Loyd O. Dodson took these trendy tires to the Los Angeles market to expand the company's sales.

The trio of tire sellers weathered the Depression years by marketing Vogue Tyre to Hollywood legends like Clark Gable and Bob Hope. Although the business began back East, the tire's popularity grew as a result of exposure to the entertainment industry in LA.

Beginning in 1937, Vogue Tyres were manufactured by The Kelly-Springfield Tire Co. in Cumberland, Maryland and continued until 1942, when the plant was converted to manufacture munitions for the military at the start of WWII.

In December of 1942, Hower sold his interests to Dodson, who kept the operation going during these lean years with a skeleton crew.

The year 1943 saw the development of synthetic rubber, which eventually spawned a limited industry of synthetic rubber passenger tires. Dodson met with executives from the Goodyear Tire & Rubber Co. to discuss the manufacture of synthetic tires for Vogue in 1943. The result of this meeting put Vogue Tyre back on the map after the Depression.

When Loyd Dodson passed away in March of 1996, his son Warren took over as chairman of the board of directors of the highly successful company.

This 1998 Cadillac Eldorado is equipped with Vogue Custom Built Tyres.

For over 78 years, Vogue has designed and built custom tires for demanding driving conditions and discriminating customers who want only the best. Over the years, The Custom Built Vogue Tyre has become distinctly recognizable due largely to its prismatic whitewall design and gold stripe.

Today, Vogue has broken through the industry barrier of tire standards with the introduction of the Custom Built Wide Trac Touring Tyre. This new touring tire, with its futuristic tread and sweeping shoulder design, has earned the industry honor of *Consumer's Digest* "Best Buy" designation beginning in 1993.

This 1928 Lincoln Phaeton sports the innovative "Vogue Custom Tyres."

PARTNERS IN LOS ANGELES

NETWORKS

Los Angeles transportation, communications and energy companies keep people, information and power circulating throughout the region.

SOUTHERN CALIFORNIA GAS COMPANY

The 130-year history of Southern California Gas Company reads remarkably like the story of the vibrant region it serves. Both have faced the challenges of unparalleled growth, fierce competing interests, politics, war, depression and the dramatic economic impact these forces bring to bear. It is a history that intertwines the life experiences of a company, a city and an entire region.

Today, Southern California Gas Company, which uses the registered trademark, The Gas Company, is the largest natural gas distribution utility in the nation. First and foremost, it is a Southern California entity that adheres to the company philosophy: "our roots run deep." It operates in 535 cities and communities throughout a 23,000-square-mile territory with a population of almost 18 million people, serving residential, commercial, industrial, electric generation and wholesale customers.

The Early Years

In 1860, there were fewer than 50,000 people in all of Southern California and less than 5,000 lived in Los Angeles. There were no organized police or fire departments, no banks, no public transportation, no paved roads or sidewalks and no street lights. There was, however, a citizen hue and cry for the installation of street lights to reduce the criminal activity that made it dangerous to venture onto the Los Angeles Plaza after dark.

On June 28, 1867, a blacksmith, two partners in a sawmill, the town postmaster and a lone gas engineer formed the Los Angeles Gas Company, the forerunner of The Gas Company. It became the first gas supplier in Southern California and signed a contract with the city to install 25 gas street lamps.

The new company had difficulty meeting demand. There were rate disputes and complaints about smoky, bad smelling manufactured gas lamps that never burned brightly enough. Those complaints continued until 1913, when the company converted from manufacturing gas to providing a cleaner, far superior product, natural

gas. But the real threat to the company came in 1879 when Thomas Edison invented the incandescent electric light and The California Electric Light Company was founded. In 1882 the Los Angeles City Council voted to replace gas street lights with electric lights.

By 1889, the emergence of more than 50 energy utilities had created a cutthroat competitive environment in Los Angeles. It is understandable that Charles H. Simpkins, owner of Los Angeles Gas Company, was receptive when two, young San Francisco entrepreneurs offered to buy him out. They were Christian Otto Gerberding (C.O.G.) Miller and Walter Cline, both in their 20s, who founded Pacific Lighting Company in the Bay area in 1886 and were attracted to the business potential of Southern California.

The two men acquired interests in several regional gas companies and, in 1889, purchased Los Angeles Gas Company to form Los Angeles Lighting. Cline

A turn-of-the-century gas street light being lit by hand.

moved to Los Angeles to head the new company, while Miller remained in San Francisco to run the parent company. In 1904, combining their gas and electric utilities in the area and changing the utility's name to Los Angeles Gas and Electric Company, they set out to conquer the market.

But major gas shortages during the winter "Gas Famine" of 1906-1907 resulted in a rival gas company being formed with the backing of prominent Los Angeles business people. The new company eventually failed and was sold to a company owned by William G. Kerckhoff and Allan C. Balch. In 1910, Kerckhoff and Balch combined their holdings and formed Southern California Gas Company, which became one of the chief rivals of Los Angeles Gas and Electric until it was acquired by Pacific Lighting Corporation in 1929.

Throughout this era, there was a great debate over municipal ownership of utilities. Campaigns were waged in newspapers, courtrooms and local elections. Finally, in 1937, Los Angeles Gas and Electric sold its

electric properties to the City of Los Angeles. That's when both affiliates of Pacific Lighting adopted the sister company's name, Southern California Gas Company. But the regional popularity of gas continued and by the end of the 1930s, Southern Californians were using more gas and paying lower rates than anywhere in the nation.

Expansion, Exploration And Conservation

With that backdrop, The Gas Company entered the 1940s with great expectations. There were ongoing concerns, however, about seasonal fluctuations in consumer demand that could be seven times greater in the winter than during the summer. With supply sources as far away as Texas and Canada, those fluctuations could mean not having gas when customers needed it. There was a need to develop a system to ensure adequate supplies of natural gas, while meeting The Gas Company's rigid safety standards.

In 1940, The Gas Company already had numerous above-ground natural gas storage containers, but introduced a new system based on the premise that if underground rock formations held natural gas securely for millions of years, they could continue to do so under controlled conditions.

California's depleted oil and gas fields offer ideal storage, and today The Gas Company operates five underground storage fields in the greater Los Angeles area. Natural gas can be withdrawn to meet heavy

With pipewrapping equipment in the background, construction continues in 1947 on the "biggest inch." It was the largest and longest gas pipeline of its time and ensured Southern Californians with reliable supplies of natural gas.

1925 street crew extending The Gas Company's roots into the Los Angeles infrastructure.

Natural gas was once stored in above-ground containers like the one pictured at Scallion Avenue and Santa Fe in Los Angeles, in 1947.

Today, a new and improved underground storage system provides a safer, more efficient method of ensuring ample supplies of natural gas for Southern California. This modern pipe design leads to the Aliso Canyon gas storage fields. It was built in the 1970s and is the largest in the Western Hemisphere.

demand, or surplus gas can be injected into the storage fields when demand is light.

On December 7, 1941, the Japanese attacked Pearl Harbor and the nation was plunged into war. The need for a consistent flow of energy for the war effort was a primary concern. Conservation became a watchword, voluntary measures were encouraged, and there were involuntary cutbacks in service when the demands of war industries dictated.

Women played a vital role with The Gas Company during the war years. With men making up the majority of workers on military leave, women employees took over the drafting department, dominated the messenger service, became punch card operators, and learned other necessary technical and mechanical skills. Advances continued after the war and The Gas Company became a pioneer in adopting equal pay for women performing the same jobs as men.

Natural gas usage hit all-time highs during World War II, and the energy demands created by Southern California's huge post-war population boom, and growth in the area of industries such as aircraft manufacturing, prompted concerns about reliable sources of gas for the future and the search for new natural gas resources.

The result of those concerns was an agreement between The Gas Company, Pacific Gas and Electric Company and the El Paso Natural Gas Company for construction of the largest long-distance gas pipeline built up to that time. The pipeline — nicknamed "the biggest inch," because of its 30-inch diameter — stretched 1,200 miles, connecting the natural gas fields of Oklahoma and Texas to Southern California. Construction began in November 1946 and was completed in October 1947, in a massive undertaking that severely tested the best engineering technology of that era.

With ample availability, gas promotion efforts were accelerated with an astounding success rate. By the end of the 1950s, 90 percent of all cooking ranges in Southern California were gas fueled. Gas stove sales were six times the national rate in comparison to electric ranges, and more than 98 percent of all water heaters and home heating systems were fueled by natural gas.

But in the 1970s, oil shortages and government pricing regulations signaled an impending energy crisis and energy conservation became a mandate for the decade and beyond. The Gas Company actively encouraged more efficient gas usage and developed conservation programs that encouraged energy-saving features in new construction long before required by law. Those programs included extensive home insulation efforts and rebates, enabling one out of every four homes in Southern California to be weatherized.

Throughout the 1980s, use per meter went down continuously in Southern California. The Gas Company's conservation programs enabled residential customers to realize approximately $550 million in savings from lower energy bills. Innovative advertising campaigns encouraged consumer conservation and vigorously promoted gas-efficient appliances and incentives for consumers to install solar energy systems, as well as insulation.

A History Of Community Responsibility

This ongoing dedication to customer service is another aspect of the "our roots run deep" philosophy

that is part of The Gas Company's commitment as a responsible, involved corporate citizen of Southern California.

In 1992, when violent civil disturbances in Los Angeles made national headlines, The Gas Company joined the "Rebuild L.A." effort, committing $40 million in cash and in-kind services to help make a difference. More than 350 company volunteers distributed food, removed graffiti, and found shelters for people displaced by the disturbances. The Gas Company also worked directly with many community institutions as a concerned corporate citizen.

When a massive earthquake devastated parts of Los Angeles and the San Fernando, Simi, and San Clarita valleys in 1994, The Gas Company was there. With an impact area equivalent to the sixth largest city in the world, the largest mobilization of personnel in the history of Southern California was required. Gas Company employees worked around the clock, set up command centers within communities in the impact area, and restored service to more than 150,000 customers. Among the many volunteers, The Gas Company also received a great deal of help from many neighboring utility companies.

But it's not just in emergencies that The Gas Company acknowledges its role as an integral part of the Southern California community. It has a long history of civic involvement in initiatives, such as The Gas Company-instituted Community Advisory Panels that regularly discuss emerging issues and trends with various community leaders.

This proactive approach keeps The Gas Company in touch with the pulse of the community and better informed when asked to support local policies, worthy projects, or respond in times of crises. The Gas Company remains actively involved with numerous local causes and provides support to many diverse organizations.

Realizing that its greatest strength is its nearly 7,000 employees, The Gas Company is committed to maintaining a diverse workforce that represents and reflects the communities it serves. Those employees, in turn, often provide financial support and hands-on assistance to hundreds of community-based organizations.

Through the company-sponsored Volunteer Incentive Program, Gas Company employees provide human and financial resources to nonprofit groups of their choice by volunteering their time and money.

Whether it is assisting in a low-income housing unit in Koreatown or a clothing designer's expansion to create 800 new inner-city jobs or adopting schools or contributing computers to the African American Unity Center so students can develop office skills, The Gas Company continues to sink deep roots into the Southern California community.

A Challenging Future

While community outreach efforts and dedication to customer service are constants, the business environment in which The Gas Company operates continues to be volatile. Deregulation of the U.S. natural gas industry began in 1978, continued through the 1990s and injected competition into what had basically been a regulated monopoly market.

Competitors, including interstate pipelines, gas brokers, and even municipalities, raised the ante for The Gas Company by attempting to serve its customers directly or offer traditional utility services, such as gas procurement and storage, gas service line extensions, or even customer billing. Additional market uncertainty was caused by state and federal plans to restructure the electric industry.

This competition has led to dramatic changes in the way The Gas Company and other gas utilities across the nation do business. A utility's economic strength in the future will depend on its ability to develop new strategies in order to keep prices competitive while maintaining high levels of customer service.

The Gas Company stands ready to meet those challenges. It takes with it a history of more than a century of change bolstered by strong management, customer service, and civic responsibility as it enters the 21st century still deeply rooted in the destiny of Southern California and the people who call it home.

Today's Gas Company meter readers are still "glad to be of service."

SOUTHERN CALIFORNIA EDISON

*At the Dawn of a New Era, SCE Builds on its
History and Tradition of Community Service.*

or more than 110 years Edison International has been a leader in the growth and development of Southern California. From its early days as the first electric company to bring power to Southern California, to its transformation into the dynamic affiliates that now make up Edison International, the Edison name has always been synonymous with innovation and reliability. Over the decades, Edison International has proven to be more than just an energy partner for its customers. Throughout its history, the corporation and its affiliated businesses have worked behind the scenes to bolster the region's economy and to increase the overall quality of life for the residents of all the communities they serve.

Edison International and
SCE Chairman and CEO
John E. Bryson, and
Southern California Edison
employees volunteer for
Follow Your Heart Day tree
planting at Whittier Narrows
facility, South El Monte.

Southern California Edison
volunteers at Oceanside
cleaning site at "Follow
Your Heart" project.

Regardless of the boundaries of local utility service, Southern California Edison (SCE) and Edison International have devoted resources — both physical and financial — to improve Southern California.

Because its communities are so interconnected, all residents of the area are likely to have benefitted from SCE's community involvement, regardless of which utility provides their electric service.

Simply put, despite the changing energy marketplace, SCE remains committed to the economic, educational and community enrichment of Southern California. To support that pledge, Edison International has continually utilized its vast financial resources to bring hope and new skills to businesses, organizations and individuals in Southern California. Since 1991, SCE has donated more than $67 million in contributions and programs to support the economic and social vitality of the region. Of that, more than $35 million was dedicated to community renewal following the civil unrest in 1992. A significant portion of this commitment assisted the Los Angeles area specifically.

To manage its resources most effectively, SCE implemented a successful plan for its corporate contributions that targets four primary areas: education, economic and business development, job training and community support.

Helping Business Prosper

In the last six years, direct economic and business development efforts on the part of Southern California Edison have helped retain more than 570 companies and more than 127,000 jobs in the region — businesses and jobs that would have left the state or the country without intervention. In working with these firms, experts from SCE helped identify government, private-sector and utility resources, including flexible pricing options for their electric service, to make doing business in Southern California both attractive and profitable.

SCE's economics and business development experts also work with start-up companies and entrepreneurs to identify sources of venture capital. This is achieved primarily through the utility's sponsorship of unique investor forums that bring companies in need of funding together with leading investors and venture capitalists. SCE also helps existing businesses identify new technologies that can help reduce operating costs and streamline production. SCE does all these things, because it knows that when its customers succeed, it does too.

Investing in the Future

Like its namesake, Thomas Alva Edison, Edison International believes in the importance of learning and education. For this reason, Edison has been a supporter — with financial, human and in-kind resources — of Los Angeles' educational reform initiative, LEARN, since its inception. This support includes SCE's parent-involvement program, Parents for Student Success, as well as a technology project to bring computers to local schools. Edison also provides more than half a million dollars each year to deserving students through its New Era Scholarship Awards. Recently, Edison International continued this long tradition of supporting regional educational initiatives by awarding $50,000 grants to three southland institutions of higher learning. The grants will support collaborative efforts to motivate and prepare at-risk students for higher education.

SCE also has forged one-of-a-kind partnerships with leading job-training programs in the region in order to give individuals new skills for success. The

Panasonic's DVD Disc Manufacturing facility in Torrance, California.

Regional Job Training Center in Compton stems from a unique partnership between Southern California Edison and the surrounding communities. At the center, young adults from the South Central Los Angeles community train and prepare for the workplace. In addition, SCE is a long-time supporter of the Los Angeles and Long Beach Conservation Corps. These organizations help train and place young people in jobs that protect and restore natural resources in both urban and surrounding areas.

In Partnership with the Community

In the past five years, SCE has given approximately $12 million through the United Way to more than 22 agencies that help worthy nonprofit organizations in Southern California. In the City of Los Angeles alone, SCE has contributed more than $4.3 million through the United Way to hundreds of organizations. SCE also supports many community-based organizations through corporate donations and developmental training, in an effort to make them self-sustaining.

In late 1997, Edison International announced the creation of a $4 million, three-year "Arts for the Community" program, designed to support regional grassroots arts organizations and to create affordable access to the arts for the community-at-large . The program involves two broad components: operational assistance for organizations that focus on under-served communities, and capital grants to expand and upgrade fine arts and performing arts facilities. Recognizing the importance of the Los Angeles Philharmonic Orchestra, the capital grant component includes a $1 million contribution to help construct Disney Hall at the Los Angeles Music Center.

This corporate support does not include the millions of dollars SCE employees contribute to the community through their personal donations and volunteer hours. For example, SCE employees have given approximately $900,000 per year to Los Angeles-area organizations through the United Way. In addition, employees donate more than 276,000 hours per year in volunteer time for projects, leadership and support of community-based organizations in Southern California.

A Rich History

Today, Edison International is made up of eight diverse companies with global resources and financial strength. Born out of the pioneering spirit that first brought electricity to Southern California, SCE wasn't always the global force it is now. More than a century ago, a fledgling utility that would one day become SCE provided rudimentary electric service to just a few dozen customers. It was the late 1800s and Thomas Edison had just invented the incandescent light bulb. The growth of rail lines and improvements to power generation and distribution systems were the building blocks of the early power industry — and Southern California Edison's predecessor companies were at the forefront of new developments. By 1893, SCE built what was then a state-of-the-art AC generator plant at Mill Creek, California. Coupled with new transformers, electricity could, for the first time, be transmitted across unlimited distances. Until that time, power had been a luxury for residents of cities. Even then, just as it is today, SCE was at the forefront of developing new ideas for a new era.

As we near the millennium, investor-owned and publicly traded Edison International (NYSE:EIX) is the parent corporation of Southern California Edison and six related businesses, including:

- Edison Mission Energy, which owns, develops and operates independent power facilities, and

- Edison Capital, which provides capital and financial services for energy and infrastructure projects.

Additionally, the following Edison International companies operate under the retail entity Edison Enterprises:

- Edison Source, which provides energy-related products and services to business and residential customers in newly restructured markets;

- Edison Select, which markets consumer products designed to enhance customer comfort and security, including in-home appliance repair, residential and small commercial security and monitoring services, computer repair and Internet access;

- Edison Utility Services, which offers billing, transmission and distribution outsourcing to electric companies in the United States and Canada, and

- Edison Technology Solutions, which develops and markets new technologies, products and services for the global energy and electricity marketplace.

For SCE, it has been a long and winding journey from building the first streetlights in Southern California, to where it stands today — the nation's second-largest investor-owned electric utility, serving more than 4.2 million customers within a 50,000-square-mile service territory in central, coastal and Southern California. Known around the nation for its

reliable service, SCE is proud to provide its residential, business, commercial, industrial and agricultural customers with the power behind peace of mind.

And like the utility, Edison International is poised to build on its history of reliability, quality and service as Californians face new choices in the emerging marketplace. With their dynamic, international approach to energy related issues, infrastructure development and innovative services, Edison International and its affiliate companies stand ready to take advantage of new opportunities — ever mindful of their longstanding responsibility to enrich the communities first served by their founders so many years ago.

John Salinas (center), George Hunnel (left), and Sam Tejeda are part of SCE's Distribution Business Unit. They and their 4,400 teammates prove each day that SCE's service knows no boundaries.

SCE employee, Eric Perrine, in front of a Santa Ana home where he discovered a woman and her dog in need of monetary assistance during his daily rounds. After purchasing groceries, he contacted relatives that were unaware of the resident's situation.

CLAY LACY AVIATION

While the name Clay Lacy may be unfamiliar to the average person, his work is not.

With his Astrovision® photography, Lacy has done aerial filming for such movies as *Top Gun*, *The Great Santini*, *Superman*, and *Capricorn One*, as well as virtually every airline commercial ever made, worldwide.

Clay Lacy Aviation, at the Van Nuys Airport, has been in operation since 1968. It is the oldest jet charter company on the West Coast, and is the only all-turbine Fixed Base Operation (FBO) airport in the country.

Lacy, a jovial and enthusiastic former pilot for United Airlines, has logged over 46,000 hours in the air, a world record. Additionally, he holds an Airline Transport license with 30 types of ratings, as well as helicopter, sea plane, flight instruction and flight engineer designations. When he retired from United Airlines on August 31, 1992 after 40 years and seven months, he ranked Seniority Number One. At the time of his retirement, Lacy was flying the Boeing 747-400 from Los Angeles to the Orient.

Chartering a plane at Clay Lacy could run you $38,000 if you fancied a round-trip ticket to New York.

Born in Wichita, Kansas, Lacy began flying at the age of 12 at Orville Sanders Cannonball Airport. In 1952, he left Wichita to work as a co-pilot for United Airlines on its DC-3 aircraft. In 1954, he took military leave from United to attend Air Force pilot training. After completion of the F-86 gunnery school in 1955, he returned to United Airlines and continued flying military fighters and other aircraft with the California Air National Guard.

In 1964, Lacy was one of the first pilots ever to receive a Learjet Type rating. At the time, he was manager of Learjet sales in 11 Western States for California Airmotive. From 1964 through 1972, Lacy flew a purple Mustang in every Unlimited Air Race and was the 1970 national champion.

Until 1965, airlines and manufacturers were still using WWII B-25 aircraft for photography, with marginal results — due to the great speed difference between jet and propeller aircraft.

Lacy did a trial photo flight for Douglas Aircraft in Long Beach and the world of aerial photography changed that day. Since then, Lacy has dominated air-to-air photography and has flown over 2,500 air-to-air photo flights, including 2,000 specifically for airline commercials.

Lacy has very few competitors in the aerial photography business; probably his chief competitor is the computer, which did all the "aerial photography" in the film *Air Force One*. However, Lacy explains that a computer will never be able to accurately recreate air flight to the trained eye.

As glamorous as it is working for movies and television — Lacy concedes with a grin that it's a personal passion — it's not the bread and butter of his business. Clay Lacy Aviation is primarily a management and charter operation, which comprises 60 percent of its business. Maintenance takes up another 20 percent. The fixed base operation and storage comprises 15 percent, and the movie and airline commercial business accounts for five percent.

To charter a plane at Clay Lacy Aviation, be prepared to spend upwards of $1,200 per hour. Movie studio heads and corporate executives shell out as much as $12,000 (for a smaller airplane) to $38,000 (for a Gulf Stream) to fly round-trip to New York. The ride is worth it: Lacy's planes boast plush, colorful interiors and often include a fancy lavatory, wet bars, movie screens and a selection of videos. One of his planes even has a separate bedroom, complete with four-poster bed and color television.

Some people, however, just enjoy parking their planes at Clay Lacy Aviation. Celebrities such as Larry Flynt have planes there, while Jay Leno often charters a plane for personal appearances.

Lacy likes being located in Van Nuys, which he explains, is a reliever airport for LAX. Some 56 big cities in the U.S. have their own reliever airports. Van Nuys airport has become the largest employer in the San Fernando Valley, and is becoming increasingly popular as an alternative location for travelers. Lacy points out that each aircraft at Van Nuys pumps approximately $1 billion into the local economy.

Of course, Van Nuys is a long way from Clay's roots in Kansas. While he still has the down-to-earth quality Midwesterners are known for, he is clearly a sophisticate. He likes the diversity of the Los Angeles area, and the fact that people aren't afraid to try new things. "People are doers in California, and it's in the culture to travel and go a lot of places," Lacy says.

Lacy is one of those who does go places. It is not unusual to find him flying to Las Vegas for a lunch meeting, and returning to Van Nuys by two o'clock. It is also not unusual for this gregarious man to invite a huge group of friends and associates for an exotic trip around the world to set records.

He also enjoys raising money for charities. In 1988, Lacy flew a Boeing 747SP around the world, establishing a New Around the World Speed Record and, in so doing, raised over $5 million for children's charities.

Clay Lacy Aviation is highly regulated by the Federal Aviation Administration (FAA). All Lacy's pilots are captain rated. Crews fly company-owned and managed aircraft and usually log 50 to 65 flight hours each month. Recurrent training is done at FlightSafety or Simuflight and Lacy requires all company pilots to take some basic aerobatics and unusual altitude training to improve situational awareness.

Lacy's crème de la crème plane is his Gulf Stream jet. He says that is what Corporate America has fallen in love with. He also has Boeing 727s and Learjets on the premises, in addition to a collection of retro planes from World War II, refurbished for the 90s, naturally.

On a tour of his grounds, Lacy is apt to take you on a jet, then spin wonderful tales about everything from his friends to his behind-the-scenes flying adventures. "People in aviation are the happiest people in the world," Lacy says. And he means it.

"People in aviation are the happiest people in the world," says pilot Clay Lacy, who has logged a record 46,000 hours in the air.

Clay Lacy Aviation in Van Nuys is home to both its own jets and others'. Larry Flynt stores a plane there, and Jay Leno charters a plane for personal appearances.

LOS ANGELES
INTERNATIONAL AIRPORT

n the 1920s, airplanes were still a novelty. With tremendous foresight, the Los Angeles Chamber of Commerce accepted the responsibility and vigorously promoted the idea of a municipally-owned and operated airport.

Considering a variety of sites, the Chamber eventually settled on Mines Field, an area which had originally been part of a Mexican land grant that had changed hands numerous times after California was taken over by the United States. The field had been utilized by tenant farmers until it was leased to the city and selected as the site of the 1928 National Air Races.

The races attracted 200,000 people who came to see daring aviators perform. After the races, the City of Los Angeles took over airport operations, created the Department of Airports and officially christened it Los Angeles Municipal Airport.

In the years that followed, the first permanent hangars and runways were constructed. But as the Great Depression set in, the city was unable to finance additional growth. Many citizens actually considered the airport to be a "white elephant" during the 1930s as it continued to operate at a loss.

As the Depression continued, aircraft manufacturers were attracted to the vicinity of the airport. Los Angeles continued to host additional National Air Races in 1933 and 1936.

As part of the federal government's plan to employ Americans in public works projects to stimulate economic growth and effectively bring an end to the Depression, the airport was granted federal funds for the first time, which facilitated many much-needed improvements. Additional funds were allotted after the city acquired the title to the airport in 1937.

In ensuing years, extensive improvements were made possible through federal funding and the passage of airport bond issues. City ordinances established a Board of Municipal Airport Commissioners in 1940 and officially changed the name to Los Angeles Airport in 1941.

At the onset of World War II, development came to an abrupt halt as military operations dominated the activities of the airport. These operations climaxed with the City turning operation of the airport over to the federal government "for the duration." Military activity required full camouflage of the site so that from the air it appeared to be a large farm.

In 1944, a master plan was developed for the postwar years which provided for the two-stage expansion of the airport, eventually resulting in the expansion and construction of massive new terminal facilities and the acquisition of 2,000 additional acres of land.

At the war's end, work began on the plan and by 1946, all five existing major airlines signed on to the airport, moving from Burbank Airport to transform the Los Angeles Airport overnight into the region's single major airport terminal. Three years later, plans soon began to link all of the regional airports into a system, beginning with the Van Nuys Airport.

In 1929, the L.A. Municipal Airport consisted of 640 acres, a 2,000-foot oiled strip (for "landing only") and a parallel dirt strip (for "take-off").
Courtesy Los Angeles World of Airports

The airport's name was changed in 1949 to the Los Angeles International Airport (LAX) in recognition of its status as a major world transportation center. LAX finally began to operate in the black in 1952, as passenger traffic reached an all-time high of over two million persons in one year.

Over the course of the next decade, the people of Los Angeles supported the airport's growth and development through bond measures. Revolutions in aviation, such as the introduction of the jet, further contributed to the airport's success while also necessitating additional construction.

LAX gained financial self-sufficiency and a vote of confidence from the voters in 1963. Passenger travel continued to grow, and air cargo rose at an incredible rate. In response to this growth, the Department of Airports acquired Ontario International Airport, devised a plan for an airport in Palmdale and began responding to issues of noise and air pollution and traffic congestion.

In the 1970s, the terminal at Palmdale conducted air service, technology continued to advance and LAX continued construction. The Los Angeles International Airport, Van Nuys and Ontario airports celebrated their 50th anniversary in 1978.

Groundbreaking began in 1981 for a $700 million improvement program, which resulted in the new Tom Bradley International Terminal and domestic Terminal One, the second level roadway and three new parking structures. These projects were completed for the 1984 Olympic Games.

In the next few years a multitude of projects were completed, which included the completion of the Gateway Cargo Center, The Centinela Hospital Airport Medical Clinic, runway reconstruction, a new Terminal Two, Connector buildings for Terminals Five and Six, and a joint-use agreement with the U.S. Air Force in Palmdale.

In 1990, LAX was officially deemed a "good investment" for the City of Los Angeles: an economic impact study showed that the airport was responsible for $28.6 billion dollars annually, a figure which increased to $37 billion by 1992 and $42 billion in 1994.

Today, LAX is ranked fourth in the world and third in the U.S. for number of passengers handled. More than 60 million people and two million tons of goods pass through LAX annually. Continuing its mission to meet ever-increasing demands and plan for the future, LAX recently began another stage of change designed to guarantee the continuance of the airport's vital role as an international gateway and contributor to the Los Angeles community.

Tn'T Auto Transport

An employee is looking forward to his or her relocation. They are busy focusing on their new job, the new promotion, coming back home or testing new waters. They want to enjoy the upcoming transition and have turned to their company to handle the details. They want their company to relieve them of the stress of the move and ensure the safety of their possessions. Their company wants the move to be efficient and uneventful, and Tn'T wants to help that company succeed.

Tn'T Claims Representative

When it comes to shipping a customer's vehicle across the state or across the nation, Tn'T is the acknowledged leader in the industry. Tn'T's dedication to the customer's perception of unequaled performance makes it the premiere service provider to the Relocation market. Tn'T measures its success by the support and goodwill of its customer base; this is the crucial element of the Tn'T operational plan.

Since 1969, Tn'T has provided a highly professional, and eminently reliable, motor vehicle transport service for corporations and individuals. Tn'T provides door-to-door service with full value, no deductible,

Tn'T Dispatcher

insurance protection. Present in all 50 states, and most major cities, Tn'T's network of over 80 qualified agent locations are positioned to deliver fast and flexible solutions to employee's needs. This network maintains its own local fleets, therefore a truck is always in the area allowing for a four hour pickup window. This premium service promise is standard, and is in stark contrast to the three day pick up window of most of their competitors.

Founded in Indiana, transporting vehicles for government agencies, the company's growth was fueled by customer satisfaction. Tn'T's reputation grew by word of

mouth and soon they branched out into corporate and private sector moves. Their attention to detail and market place innovations would eventually cause them to outgrow their facilities and propel them to Los Angeles. So, true to their rallying cry of "We're on the move for you," they established their Corporate Headquarters in Southern California to better serve their rapidly growing customer base.

Tn'T understands the Relocation industry and the challenges it must meet everyday. About 60 percent of their moves are corporate relocation of employees. Many of their clients are Fortune 500 companies with critical time and logistical issues, that is why they choose the Tn'T advantage. Tn'T's preeminent level of customer care, high on-time percentage, and low claims ratio make it the best choice for the relocation professional.

The other 40 percent of their moves are with private shippers that are looking for the same protection and efficiency that Tn'T offers its largest customers. This primarily personal reference business is the fastest growing segment of Tn'T's market share. Many of the private customers are repeat shippers and recommend Tn'T to their friends, relatives and coworkers. The red carpet is always rolled out and is available to every shipper, corporate or individual.

Tn'T continues to grow because it delivers what the customer needs and on what it promises. They offer a guaranteed pick–up and delivery date. If for any transportation related reason a vehicle is not delivered on time, a rental car will be provided at no cost to the shipper until the vehicle does arrive.

Tn'T includes peace of mind with every shipment, acknowledging that shippers have a personal attachment to their vehicle. Unlike most of their competitors, Tn'T is insured as well as their contracted carriers. If anything were to happen to a vehicle while in transport, this double protection forms a rock solid safety net.

Tn'T's capacity is built on fulfilling requirements during the peak May to November shipping season. Networking over 300 carriers, and enlisting more every month, ensures that there is always a slot available for a move, to any state in the nation most any day of the year. The safe and timely transport of nearly 20,000 vehicles a year is testament to the reliability and security of this nationally trusted company.

In addition to its Corporate Offices in Los Angeles, Tn'T has offices in Baltimore and Oakland. Tn'T operates its own terminal and offices in Chicago as well. Forty vigorous, innovative and resourceful relocation professionals provide the muscle behind this, the best auto transport company in the country. All Tn'T employees are trained to respond to any customer inquiry and assist in the coordination of their move. This prevents delays in customer service, one of the many valuable benefits of shipping with Tn'T.

Tn'T Quality Assurance Manager

The employees make the Tn'T advantage a reality. They ship for businessmen, families and celebrities with the personal care and customized service that each individual shipment requires. Each shipper is assigned a personal Tn'T contact who monitors their shipment daily and defends against any potential obstacles to a smooth shipment cycle. They apply skills daily that have been tempered by years of experience. With an average employee tenure of 12 years, there is nothing these seasoned professionals are not equipped to deal with.

With Tn'T's aggressive approach to customer satisfaction, its future remains bright.

Tn'T offices

VIRTUAL VOICE

imely delivery of complete and accurate information is essential to business and the key to success in any industry. Unfortunately, the progressive flow of information is often reduced to a trickle. Important messages are often delivered incomplete or not at all. Business contacts may not be available when called and a game of "telephone tag" ensues. Branch offices are frequently hours, often days, behind the information flow and field sales personnel may be unaware of recent announcements or changes.

When the flow of information slows, the windows of business opportunity close.

Virtual Voice Corporation's cutting-edge information processing system offers exciting state-of-the-art solutions to these common business problems. Using any touch-tone telephone, 24 hours a day, seven days a week nationwide, corporate clients or individuals can send and receive detailed messages instantaneously without having to buy or install any equipment.

Virtual Voice technology "makes every call count" and affords clients the ability to send group broadcasts, redirect messages with personalized introductory comments, as well as receive pager notification of urgent messages that have been received. This technology includes innovative products and services that combine voice messaging and fax processing to handle all areas of business communications — voice, image, data and text. Communication, precise and accurate, is simplified.

The company's sales and marketing team develop customized applications for a broad range of clientele — both large and small firms with a geographically dispersed work force, multi-level marketing organizations and companies with branch offices or multiple locations.

While traditional voice mail serves as an answering machine, Virtual Voice's Voice Messaging is a nationwide network of people sharing the same business interests and communicating through a single large system.

Founded in 1986 as a Voice Mail Service Bureau, the Los Angeles-based organization officially changed its name to Virtual Voice Corporation in 1993. *Business Week* magazine describes "virtual corporations" as "strategic alliances between organizations for the purpose of taking advantage of fast changing opportunities." These groups bring together specific areas of expertise to form an organization where every function and process is first class — something no single company can achieve.

Virtual Voice actively embraces this philosophy. Since its inception, the firm's goal has been to help clients "streamline their communications" through its strategic alliances with the world's premiere telecommunications providers: Octel/Lucent Technologies for its expertise in Voice Messaging communications hardware and software, Bell Labs for research and development, and AT & T for its unsurpassed quality and reliability in communication networks.

Virtual Voice also bears a distinction that few, if any, of its competitors can claim. Since its inception,

Management Team: (L-R, Back Row) Monte Stern, President & CEO; Sandra Hand, Vice President of Sales and Marketing (L-R, Front Row): Gerritt Beatty, Director of Operations; Jennifer Stern, Customer Service Manager; Terena Wollons, Octel Systems Manager; Emy Castillo, CFO & Human Resources.

the company's steady growth in the industry has been achieved "solely through word of mouth" from satisfied customers. "We have no outside sales force and we don't advertise," comments president and owner, Monte Stern. "The majority of our current customers come to us, which speaks for the quality, professionalism and customized applications that we develop combined with outstanding customer service."

Stern attributes the company's success to a combination of its employees' "attitude, skills and effort." This philosophy is one that was learned during his 25 years with IBM and subsequent years of experience with NYNEX and Com Systems.

Guided by the vision and experience of its management team, Virtual Voice strives to provide its clients with the finest personalized customer service, customized products and competitive pricing. Combined

with the assurance and reliability of its strategic alliances, Virtual Voice clearly represents the best value in information processing available today.

Customer Service Supervisors: Deborah Hutchens, Linda Afferino, Darrell Evans, Amber Voshall

WILLIAMS SERVICE CORPORATION

he founding of the city of Los Angeles and Williams share a common bond — highways. Los Angeles can trace its roots back to when Spain began to colonize California in the late 18th century. At that time, an expedition that included Father Junipero Serra set off on a 600-mile-long journey from San Diego to Sonoma. Along this route — which would become the El Camino Real or the King's Highway — Father Serra founded a system of missions that ultimately led to the founding of Los Angeles as it is known today.

Nearly 150 years later, multi-faceted Williams Service Corporation (WSC) had its beginnings in Los Angeles' massive highway system. The company was founded as Williams Transfer and Storage Co. in 1922 by John Williams, who operated his local trucking company from Ventura to San Diego. This family-owned business operated successfully for many years and eventually mirrored the growth that was steadily occurring in Los Angeles. Other family members eventually joined the company and helped it expand and diversify.

When the third generation of Williams', Douglas and Mark, joined the company in the 1970s, they worked on transforming it from a business that served the industrial community to one that serviced those in the professional, technical and service-based industries. Since the company was already involved in warehousing, it was an easy transformation to the records storage and management business. This evolution began what is today Williams Records Management.

Since the Internal Revenue Service and state agencies require certain types of records be maintained for specific lengths of time, often it is not feasible for companies to either take up valuable office space or put their records into self-storage units. This is especially true for record-intensive industries such as banks, legal and accounting firms and hospitals and medical offices. Because of this, the Williams' saw a need for a service that could not only store records, but could retrieve information as needed — so they converted their storage facility to one that specializes in records management.

Williams Records Management today services the entire state of California. It operates within a reinforced concrete and steel building with 450,000 square feet of storage space and is centrally monitored for fire, smoke, heat, motion, water and burglary 24 hours a day,

Today, WSC is run by the third generation — Mark and Douglas Williams.

WSC got its start as Williams Transfer Co. in 1922 by John Williams, who operated his local trucking company from Ventura to San Diego.

365 days a year with access strictly limited to authorized personnel. The company also has a written disaster preparedness and recovery plan in place. As a result of this plan, the owners have spoken on this topic to groups such as the Century City/Beverly Hills and Downtown L.A.-Law Records Management Association, California Medical Record Association, Century City Chamber of Commerce and many Rotary Clubs around Los Angeles County.

Records management is more involved than just storage. Additional services allow clients the ability to quickly and easily retrieve any information necessary. Company staff use a computerized bar code system that enables them to track and retrieve information, additionally they offer client and PIN numbers so only authorized personnel can view records. Other services include file preparation, inventory and indexing of files, pick up and delivery by bonded personnel, 24-hour access to records, private reference rooms for clients, remote access and certified document destruction.

Under the direction of Douglas and Mark, the company began to diversify. They took over management of American Driver Leasing, Inc. (ADL) — a company that had been a division of the family business run by their father, David, and uncle, Herb. ADL leases D.O.T.-qualified drivers both permanently and temporarily to drive clients' vehicles with 24-hour dispatch. The company not only provides on-the-road testing, drug testing and holds mandatory safety meetings, but it takes care of all of the necessary paperwork as well. ADL pays the drivers, keeps all payroll records, provides medical and dental health plans and retirement benefits. The company also provides driver safety programs for businesses, even if they don't lease drivers from ADL.

With this background in human resources management, the next step was to form Ideal Employee Management, Inc. This Professional Employer Organization (PEO) handles human resources management, employee benefits administration, workers' compensation management, safety and risk management, and payroll processing services for business firms and professional corporations. By using this PEO, a business only has to issue one check per payroll period. Other WSC ventures include Alameda Self Storage and truck rentals.

The unique combination of companies within WSC offers opportunities for clients to get a variety of their needs met from only one vendor so they can concentrate on their core business. "What makes our company stand out is the fact that we live and breathe the business. Our clients get more personalized service from us because we know our name and reputation is riding on everything we do," admits Mark Williams. The majority of competitors to WSC are large, national corporations that have many thousands of clients. Since WSC is much smaller and operates locally, clients always have access to the family so they can make sure their needs are met. Even though WSC and its subsidiaries continue to be family owned, the Williams' have assembled management teams for each of the companies to ensure they run as smoothly as possible — something that doesn't always happen on the L.A. highways!

Williams Service Corporation has long been a family business. From left are David, Herb, company founder John Williams.

To ensure the various divisions of WSC run as smoothly as possible, the Williams' have assembled management teams for each of the companies they operate.

ARCO

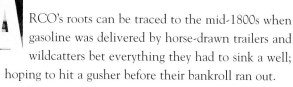

ARCO's roots can be traced to the mid-1800s when gasoline was delivered by horse-drawn trailers and wildcatters bet everything they had to sink a well; hoping to hit a gusher before their bankroll ran out.

It was a time of risk-taking and exploration; imbued with a spirit that is still alive in the West and in the men and women who make ARCO the leading gasoline retailer in the region.

That spirit was there in the 1960s when every other company had given up prospecting for oil on Alaska's North Slope. ARCO forged ahead and, in 1968, discovered North America's largest oil field at Prudhoe Bay.

But finding oil and getting oil to market are two decidedly different tasks. To move much-needed oil to the lower 48 states, ARCO and its partners undertook one of the greatest engineering feats of the 20th Century. They built the Trans-Alaska Pipeline, an 800 mile state-of-the-art construction through one of the harshest environments on the planet.

Equally remarkable is the fact that the project met strict environmental standards and intense scrutiny by government agencies and conservation groups.

ARCO's Alaskan gamble is still paying off. The 13-billion barrel Prudhoe Bay oil field, and other Alaskan oil fields discovered later, account about 20 percent of U.S. oil productions.

Four years after the Prudhoe Bay discovery, ARCO moved its corporate headquarters from New York to Los Angeles to be closer to its biggest market. Then, in 1982, in another controversial marketing move, ARCO did away with its credit card and lowered its gas prices. It redefined the gas station concept and created the AM/PM mini market. These big, bright, customer-friendly operations have become the national standard and offer self-service food and convenience items, as well as gasoline.

But more challenges lay ahead, as oil companies, and especially those firms doing business in California, were faced with reducing air pollution.

Mike R. Bowlin, Chairman & CEO

State and federal regulators developed plans to eventually replace gasoline with costly, unproven alternative fuels. Others in the industry debated the merits of these actions. ARCO took action and developed EC-1 the nation's first cleaner-burning gasoline. The idea was not only revolutionary; it worked. Reformulated gasoline is now the only gasoline sold in California.

Being a good neighbor is also part of the ARCO tradition. The ARCO Foundation has aided many deserving groups and organizations over the years. Singularly significant was the 1997 decision to contribute $10 million to build the Walt Disney Concert Hall.

ARCO was proud to play a major role in a project the company believes will allow generations of young people to study and enjoy music and will anchor the northern end of a dramatically changed and invigorated Central City.

The wildcatters at ARCO are still expanding horizons and looking overseas to augment U.S. production. ARCO was the first Western oil firm to explore for oil in China and developed China's largest natural gas field. It has entered into a long-term partnership with Russia's largest oil company and is active in Indonesia, the United Kingdom North Sea, Algeria, Ecuador, Venezuela, Tunisia and the Middle East. At the same time, ARCO is finding more oil in Alaska and growing its oil and gas business in the Gulf Coast. Once again, ARCO is reinventing itself and staying true to its pioneer roots, while preparing for a new set of challenges in the 21st Century.

PORT OF LOS ANGELES

Southern California boasts both the fundamental and philosophical ingredients to maximize every conceivable business opportunity and partnership. As the centerpiece for the region, the 7,500-acre Port of Los Angeles sets the standards for global commerce and transportation access. The Port's remarkable facilities, strong financial capability and strategic planning efforts have positioned this premier seaport in an undeniable leadership role for the next century.

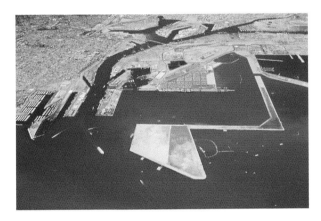

Founded in 1907, the Port once bustled with longshore gangs, thousands of commercial fisherman and workers in a dozen canneries, ship builders and ship crews.

The Port today may seem serene by comparison, but this independent, self-supporting department of the City of Los Angeles is one of the world's largest trade gateways and holds a reputation as the premier hub for oceanborne cargo destined for the entire country.

The Port of Los Angeles currently boasts a bond rating of "AA" from three credit rating agencies — the highest rating assigned to any non-tax supported seaport in the U.S. The Port industry accounts for more than one million jobs nationwide, including 259,000 jobs in Southern California (one out of every 24) and provides $8.4 billion in wages.

Adding to this economic impact is the Port's far-reaching capital development program which encom-

passes the nationally recognized two billion dollar Alameda Corridor and the Pier 300/400 Implementation Program, representing the largest capital improvement undertaking of any U.S. seaport.

A gateway for international commerce and an economic engine for the region, the Port is part of the largest container complex in the country. For the fiscal years 1991-97, this record-setting seaport handled nearly 15 million TEUs, welcomed nearly six million passengers at its World Cruise Center and handled a daily average of eight ships — some of which transport 5,000 cargo containers each voyage.

Such a record doesn't occur through pure happenstance. Around the world, the Port's marketing offices act as the "eyes and ears" in virtually every major trade center to provide firsthand perspectives on trends and to gather local market intelligence with which critical decisions in the volatile and high stakes international trade arena are made.

The Port of Los Angeles has achieved significant success in recent years to garner West Coast market share in a number of areas. This dominance is expected to grow as the new construction, cargo performance, financial strength and environmental leadership that have characterized the Port continues in the coming decades.

As the centerpiece for the region, the 7,500-acre Port of Los Angeles sets the standards for global commerce and transportation access.

The Port of Los Angeles is one of the world's largest trade gateways and holds a reputation as the premiere hub for oceanborne cargo destined for the entire country.

DEPARTMENT OF WATER & POWER

The story of Los Angeles is the story of water, because today's 3.6 million city residents could not live and work in the semi-arid Southern California area without the visionary projects bringing water hundreds of miles to the city and surrounding region.

The possibility of today's vibrant Los Angeles began in 1886, when a fast-rising 31-year old received another promotion from his company. The man was William Mulholland, and the post that he assumed was Superintendent of the Los Angeles City Water Company.

Under Mulholland, the water company kept pace with a growing Los Angeles, and when the city purchased the water company's assets in 1902, the highly regarded Superintendent began working for the city. The new city water department eventually evolved into the Los Angeles Department of Water and Power (DWP), the country's largest municipal utility today.

After the turn of the century, city growth overtook the local Los Angeles River water supply, requiring a critical decision to seek more water. By 1905, the city voted to construct a $26 million aqueduct 233 miles over the Mojave Desert and mountains to bring Owens River water to Los Angeles.

In 1907, work under Mulholland's direction began on the Los Angeles Owens River Aqueduct, an engineering marvel for its time. It was completed in 1913 and celebrated at a November 5th ceremony where

William Mulholland, 1855-1935.

DWP is helping Los Angeles to confidently face the future.

Mulholland proclaimed to the crowd, "There it is, take it." A byproduct of the aqueduct was electricity. In 1910, Mulholland selected Ezra Scattergood to head the city's power system, which began using the aqueduct flow to generate power for delivery to the city in 1917.

During the 1920s, additional water and electricity resources were conceived, including tapping the Colorado River for both water and power. By 1936, Hoover Dam was producing power for the city, delivered over the then world's longest electrical transmission lines, supplying up to 97 percent of the city's electricity needs. Four years later, the Mono Basin Project was completed, extending the city's aqueduct to 338 miles to utilize the waters of the Mono Basin in the Eastern Sierra. A year later in 1941, the Colorado River Aqueduct began delivering water to the Los Angeles region.

The 1940s through the 1960s saw exponential growth in Los Angeles, and the DWP kept pace with construction of four thermal generating stations in the Los Angeles Basin.

The 1970s and 1980s were the decades for development of long distance power resources delivered by new direct-current technology, linking the city with the Pacific Northwest and Intermountain regions. During this period electrical stations and dams were seismically upgraded or replaced, resulting in a more reliable utility system which aided in the city's recovery following the damaging 1994 Northridge earthquake.

Whether it's earthquakes, drought, conservation or deregulation, the DWP is looking forward to a competitive marketplace as an opportunity to renew itself as the city's "utility provider of choice" serving all who live and work in Los Angeles. A young, self-taught engineer once observed, "Whoever brings the water will bring the people." William Mulholland was right. He brought the water, the people came, and the present-day DWP continues to serve the city it has helped make possible.

METROPOLITAN WATER DISTRICT OF SOUTHERN CALIFORNIA

istory shows that maintaining Southern California's strong economy and quality of life requires dependable supplies of water.

No agency understands that better than the Metropolitan Water District of Southern California.

Created by an act of the state Legislature in 1928, Metropolitan wholesales imported water supplies to member city and water districts in six Southern California counties.

Each year, Metropolitan imports as much as two million acre feet — more than 650 billion gallons — from the Colorado River and Northern California. That's nearly 1.7 billion gallons a day, nearly 60 percent the amount used in the Southland.

Metropolitan's 5,200-square-mile service area stretches 200 miles from Oxnard to the Mexican border, and inland 70 miles, covering portions of Los Angeles, Orange, Riverside, San Bernardino, San Diego and Ventura counties.

When Los Angeles began importing water from the Owens Valley early in the century, other Southern California cities relied on meager runoff from nearby mountains and limited groundwater.

Voters changed that in 1931 when, in the depths of the Great Depression, they approved a $220 million bond issue to tap into the Colorado River. Metropolitan then built the aqueduct that would bring water to 13 cities.

Four dams had to be built; 29 tunnels drilled; five pumping plants constructed to lift water more than 1,600 feet; 242 miles of channels had to be dug, dredged and lined before the Colorado River Aqueduct was completed in 1941.

In the years following the aqueduct construction, five water filtration plants, a 700-mile Southern California distribution network and facilities to connect with California's State Water Project were built.

As urban Southern California's population exploded during the 1950s, it became apparent that another source of water would be needed. The state Legislature authorized the State Water Project to provide water to the San Francisco Bay area, Northern and Central California, and the Southland. In 1960, California voters authorized $1.75 billion in bonds to help finance the construction of the largest aqueduct system in history.

Water now comes to Southern California from the delta of the Sacramento and San Joaquin rivers through the State Water Project's network of dams, reservoirs, power plants and aqueducts, as well as the 444-mile Governor Edmund G. Brown California Aqueduct.

Metropolitan continues to meet the challenge of planning for the region's future. The foundation of that plan is the Eastside Reservoir Project in southwest Riverside County. When completed just after the turn of the century, the massive reservoir will nearly double the region's surface water storage for drought protection and emergency reserves.

The district also has initiated programs to enhance water supplies and reduce demands. In the early 1990s, Metropolitan and its member agencies developed Metropolitan's innovative Integrated Resources Plan (IRP) which identifies new sources of water to provide the region with supply reliability for the next ten years. This means 100 percent reliability even under a worst-case drought. Conservation, recycling, desalination, water transfers and local groundwater will all help to meet Southern California's growing demands.

Water is vital to Southern California's way of life. Nature made the Southland a desert. Man's ingenuity made it possible to build a comfortable lifestyle, and Metropolitan plans to ensure that lifestyle continues.

The Gene Pumping Plant along the Colorado River Aqueduct.

Metropolitan's Colorado River Aqueduct.

PACIFIC BELL

Who maintains 123 million miles of underground cable, 28 million miles of aerial wire and 1.2 million telephone poles? Pacific Bell, of course! The company also maintains a fleet of more than 12,000 vehicles, answers 2.5 million directory assistance calls every day and is the highest-productivity phone company in America.

The company started out on a considerably smaller scale in 1880, just four years after Alexander Graham Bell invented the telephone. That was the year the National Bell Telephone Company of San Francisco and the Gold and Stock Telegraph Company consolidated to serve the Bay area. It was also the year the first telephone exchange in Los Angeles was inaugurated by the Los Angeles Telephone Company to serve seven telephones.

By 1883, the need for interconnected long distance service became apparent and the Sunset Telephone-Telegraph Company was formed to construct and operate long distance lines throughout the far West. By 1884, the lines were put to use for the first overland long-distance call between San Francisco and Los Angeles.

The inauguration of the Pacific Company's "kitchen telephone" service began in 1896. This 50 cents per month plan was designed for the housewife to use in ordering household supplies. By 1900, telephones had spread far beyond the kitchen, and California boasted more phones per capita than any other region in the United States.

The Pacific Telephone and Telegraph Company incorporated in the fateful year of 1906, when an earthquake and fire devastated San Francisco and wiped out phone service. That was also the year that directory assistance was first offered, when New York Telephone Company directory included a paragraph about "Information Service."

The car and the telephone began their long relationship in 1912, when the Automobile Emergency Service Company of Los Angeles affixed the first emergency roadside phones to Pacific Telephone poles. Evidently phones themselves were in need of assistance, as well. The San Francisco Board of Supervisors passed an ordinance that year making it a misdemeanor for a person to "beat" a telephone.

The "coin-box booth" made its appearance in 1928, when 24-hour phones were installed along highways in California. Drive-up phones made their debut in 1959, where else but in Los Angeles? Mobile telecommunications took another giant step forward in 1961 with the creation of the"Bell-boy" pager by Bell Labs. The break-up of AT&T in 1981 paved the way for the formation of Pacific Telesis in 1984. That year, during the Olympics, a company subsidiary inaugurated cellular phone service in California. The next year saw the introduction of SMART Yellow Pages.

In 1997, Pacific Telesis merged with SBC Communications, which has been ranked by *Fortune* as the world's most admired telecommunications company. With more than 500,000 strand miles of fiber optic cable deployed, Pacific Bell has the most sophisticated fiber network in the world. They stand ready to move into the 21st century with an advanced telecommunications network backed by unparalleled reliability, flexibility and customer service.

The Princess phone, with its lighted dial and modern design, was the ultimate in telephone sophistication.

Pac Bell's worldwide fiber optic network demonstrates the unlimited future of telecommunications.

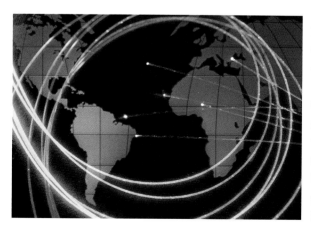

PRO EXPRESS

t might seem like a long way from crashing into opposing 300-pound linemen on a football field to running the largest exclusively local trucking company in Southern California. But that's the route George Strugar took when he founded Pro Express, a freight trucking company, while he was a defensive lineman for the then Los Angeles Rams of the National Football League.

In 1961, Strugar and two teammates, Will Sherman and Don Burroughs, decided to go into business together. Each had experience working with area trucking companies during the off-season and decided that a small, specialized trucking concern might be a profitable venture.

They started Ram Express with just three trucks. Burroughs soon left and Strugar and Sherman worked together until 1975 when they ended the partnership. The business had grown to a fleet of 40 trucks. Strugar left with 20 trucks and founded Pro Express.

Today, Pro Express has three sites just east of Los Angeles; a 106-door terminal on 15 acres in Monetbello, a 20-door satellite terminal on 2.5 acres in Fontana and a 150,000-square-foot public warehouse in The City of Commerce. The warehouse allows Pro Express to perform assembly, distribution, storage, handling, order picking and transportation of goods.

The transporting is handled by the company-operated fleet of more than 100 radio-dispatched trucks and more than 200 trailers, including stepvans, bobtails, two-axle and three-axle tractors and a variety of dry vans varying in length from 27 to 48 feet. All Pro Express bobtails and nearly all of the company trailers are equipped with hydraulic liftgates, with capacities that rage from 2,000 to 4,000 pounds.

The company maintains an on-site repair facility to minimize downtime in the event of road hazards or breakdowns and has a centralized dispatching system that handles most service inquires with a single call. State-of-the-art computerized vehicle location devices allow Pro Express staff to monitor vehicles within 150 feet of their actual location.

George Strugar passed away in 1997. His son, Douglas, is president of the company and handles the day-to-day operation of Pro Express. The operating philosophy, however, has not changed. There is an ongoing commitment to customer service; evidenced by a 99 percent efficiency rate for overnight deliveries that do not require appointment scheduling.

There is also a serious commitment to Southern California. The Pro Express service area includes zip codes from 90000 through 93700 continuously and pick-up and delivery is provided in Los Angeles, Orange, Ventura, Santa Barbara, Fresno, Kern, Riverside, San Bernardino, San Diego, San Louis Obispo and Imperial counties.

"It is our aim to provide an unparalleled level of service throughout the Southern California region," said Douglas Strugar. "This is our base. It always has been. It always will be."

That attitude has helped create a sustained annual growth rate for Pro Express and made it the leading (strictly local) common carrier in Southern California. With 35 years of experience and an earned reputation for fast, fair, thorough service, it's easy to see why this company has turned into such a winning proposition.

One of the more than 100 trucks that make up the fleet of Pro Express, the leading (strictly local) common carrier in Southern California; with a sincere commitment to the region and its customers.

THE RENDIC CORPORATION

n just ten years The Rendic Corporation grew from a three-person operation based in a garage in Woodland Hills to a respected $14 million freight-forwarding company with over 30 full-time employees, offices in four U.S. cities and an international network of agents.

Handling and Shipping of unusual and oversized cargo is a specialty of Rendic, and here a Corsair WWII aircraft is being shipped to New Zealand.

That remarkable growth rate is the direct result of finding an important business niche and becoming the very best at ensuring the safe, on-time delivery of items that often require meticulous attention to handling and intricate financial and government negotiations.

When Rendic was founded in 1988, the company primarily offered air export of perishable goods. A receptive market necessitated the move to larger quarters in Sherman Oaks in less than a year. Hard freight air import and export service was started in 1989 and ocean freight operations began in 1991. The staff had increased to seven by the time new, larger headquarters were found near Los Angeles International Airport (LAX) in 1992.

There is also a division for importers of perishable foodstuffs. Rendic will arrange U.S. Customs clearance, U.S. Department of Agriculture (USDA) inspection, pick-up from LAX, pre-cooling, delivery within Southern California and air-freight services within North America and beyond.

In 1995, Rendic moved to its current location. It is a 7,500-square-foot warehouse, just two miles from

View of a huge racing yacht as it is being lifted out of the water onto a vessel taking it home.

LAX, that operates 24 hours a day, seven days a week, and has two coolers with an area of 180 square meters. Rendic is bonded by the USDA and is therefore able to rapidly retrieve perishable freight and schedule prompt inspections at the company's facility.

Rendic has evolved into a full-service operation that includes import and export services of any size package or container through its general freight division. Included are a complete range of necessary international transportation services such as insurance, dangerous goods documentation and packaging, letter of credit negotiation, legalization of documents and registration with government customs agencies.

It was also in 1995 that Rendic opened its Chicago Office and separately, in association with The Visbeen Company in Amsterdam, formed Quality Handling, a handling facility for perishables at LAX that specializes in the worldwide distribution of flowers. Quality Handling oversees airline pick-up and drop-off, ensures shipment temperature control with state-of-the-art Dutch pre-coolers and maintains a 250-square-meter cooler dedicated solely to the storage and handling of flowers.

The ocean freight division rounds out the impressive list of Rendic services. It is able to assist in full and less than full container shipments, reefer containers, over-sized shipments, break bulk shipments, automobile exports, storage and distribution, export crating, banking, legalization and customs clearance services.

With the opening of a San Francisco office in 1996, a New York office in 1997 and a Web site on the Internet, Rendic has firmly established itself as an expert in international transportation that offers the professionalism, flexibility and expertise to ensure customer satisfaction. Whether it is getting strawberries to Bangkok, tortillas to Berlin, artichokes to Israel or machinery to Mongolia, Rendic's knowledgeable, multi-lingual staff of professionals has the experience and the contacts necessary for a successful freight-forwarding partnership.

PARTNERS IN LOS ANGELES
PROFESSIONS

Attorneys, accountants, architects, engineers and advertising professionals provide essential services to the greater Los Angeles area.

GIBSON, DUNN & CRUTCHER LLP

How the West Was Won

When John Bicknell led a wagon train of pioneers to California in 1860, he dreamed only of making it safely across six states. He would later establish one of the largest and most prominent law firms in the world. The firm, today known as Gibson, Dunn & Crutcher, has 650 lawyers in 13 offices in the U.S. and abroad, and provides comprehensive expertise in every area of law that impacts its clients. *Forbes* magazine named the firm one of the top three in the country in defense of securities cases. In another survey, corporate counsel ranked Gibson, Dunn & Crutcher one of the top two firms both for mergers and acquisitions and for litigation excellence.

The early years of the firm, founded in Los Angeles in 1890, foreshadowed its role as a major player in shaping the growth of Los Angeles and California and later of the national and international economies.

Picture this: Los Angeles in the late 1800s. Electricity has just arrived, along with the Southern Pacific Railroad. Citrus growers need water. A real estate boom hits in 1886, demanding an infrastructure that includes power and transportation. Oil is discovered in 1892 and wells spring up in backyards across Los Angeles. All along, Gibson, Dunn & Crutcher is there, helping its clients lead California through the developments that would dominate the 20th century.

From the start, the firm represented the Southern Pacific Railroad in business, real estate and litigation. It helped transportation magnate Henry Huntington form the network of trains and trolleys that served the city for the next half century. James Gibson was instrumental in organizing construction of the dam that brought irrigation to thousands of acres of citrus groves.

From L.A. Law to Worldwide Practice

By 1903, the firm was the largest in Los Angeles. Its clients were soon to include the Southern California Edison Company, Los Angeles Railway, Huntington Land and Improvement Company, and Janss Investment Company, which developed much of West Los Angeles, including what is now Century City. William Dunn was on the committee that chose the site of UCLA on land donated by Janss. Dunn had formerly served as Los Angeles City Attorney with Albert Crutcher as his deputy.

Nearly a century later, Gibson, Dunn & Crutcher has more than 650 attorneys with offices in downtown Los Angeles, Century City, San Francisco, Palo Alto (in the heart of the Silicon Valley), Orange County, San Diego, Denver, Dallas, New York, Washington, D.C., London and Paris.

Over the years, Gibson, Dunn has served more than three quarters of the Fortune 100 companies. It has represented clients in every industry from the Boston Celtics to General Electric, from Intel to Proctor & Gamble, from Sony to Times Mirror, from Merrill Lynch to Northrop Grumman. Its lawyers are prominent litigators in high-profile cases, such as Sony's defense of a $3.2 billion

Gibson, Dunn's early practice involved it in the oil industry, as oil wells sprang up in backyards across Los Angeles when oil was discovered in 1892.

suit when it bought Columbia Pictures, Unocal's victory over T. Boone Pickens' attempted hostile takeover, the Lincoln Savings and Loan lawsuits and the Orange County bondholders litigation, the largest municipal bankruptcy ever filed.

Throughout the firm's history, Gibson, Dunn & Crutcher's lawyers have been breaking new ground. In the 1950s, they persuaded the U.S. Supreme Court that baseball should remain exempt from antitrust laws. To this day, baseball is the only exempt professional sport. More recently, the firm represented CIFRA, a Mexican retail chain, in its $4.1 billion merger with Wal-Mart — the first cross-border tender offer of its kind in Mexico — and helped Intel, the world's largest chip manufacturer, with its first acquisition of a public company.

No Holds Barred

The firm helped to defeat the largest hostile takeover bid in the history of the computer industry, when Computer Associates, a Goliath of software developers, tried to swallow Computer Sciences Corp. If you believed predictions by media and Wall Street analysts, it was a guaranteed first round knockout for Computer Associates, which was eager to pay $9.8 billion to take over Computer Sciences. The industry giant was even tempting stockholders with $108 a share, when the market price was $80.

Lawyers from Gibson, Dunn & Crutcher were able to stop the takeover with a creatively orchestrated legal, lobbying and media assault marshalling the firm's diverse lawyering and political talents on all fronts. Called "one of the most innovative defenses" by *The Washington Post*, the defense was both speedy and well organized.

In less than a month, Computer Associates dropped the hostile bid. *The New York Times* lauded Gibson, Dunn's approach as the "textbook perfect defense against a hostile offer." For Gibson, Dunn & Crutcher lawyers, the month-long battle was business as usual.

William Dunn and Albert Crutcher moved into the Bradbury Building to join their new partners in 1903. The firm was then the largest in Los Angeles with seven attorneys.

On the Leading Edge

Computer and high-tech companies frequently are the targets of takeovers and securities litigation. These industries, which make heavy use of intellectual property, are emerging as frequent targets for private and government antitrust actions: witness the government's cases against Microsoft and Intel. Intellectual property law is clearly emerging at the turn of the millennium as a new antitrust battleground. The creation of intellectual property and the use, licensing and enforcement of IP rights are all activities fraught with cutting-edge antitrust issues.

When *Business Week* warned about the surge in antitrust cases, it came as no surprise to Gibson, Dunn & Crutcher lawyers, who were already in action. In the

Gibson, Dunn represented the Janss Investment Company in developing much of West Los Angeles, including Westwood Village and what is now Century City.

past decade alone, the firm's lawyers have litigated more than 100 antitrust cases, in every industry from airlines to the airwaves. Gibson, Dunn successfully defended American Airlines at trial against predatory pricing claims of $3 billion. The firm won a jury verdict for Sony in a case with worldwide implications and potential liability of $500 million. It helped Pfizer survive tumultuous times, when the company was faced with a series of antitrust lawsuits. Representing Toyota, Gibson, Dunn antitrust lawyers convinced the California Supreme Court to overrule 50 years of precedent.

Gibson, Dunn & Crutcher is also one of the leading firms representing clients who face SEC investigations on charges involving antitrust and securities law issues, such as insider trading, fraud or money laundering. In the largest SEC investigation in recent memory, the firm represented the National Association of Securities Dealers in a two-year probe of the conduct of NASD members by the SEC and the Antitrust Division of the Department of Justice. Some presumed the investigation rang the death knell for the NASD. But subsequent to Gibson, Dunn's involvement in the matter, the NASD has flourished, with recent acqui-

sitions of the American Stock Exchange and the Philadelphia Stock Exchange.

On the national and international fronts, the wave of mergers and joint ventures, technological innovation and the globalization of business have spawned new legal issues. Gibson, Dunn & Crutcher has handled some of the most sophisticated business deals of the last decade. Transactions include Northrop's successful bid to acquire Grumman in the face of a competing offer by Martin Marietta Corp.; MGM's buyout from a French government agency; acquisitions and subsequent sales of Tiffany, Gucci and Saks for Investcorp, a multibillion dollar merchant bank; and the Boston Celtics reorganization.

A Higher Authority

The firm's Appellate and Constitutional Law Practice Group is renowned. Described as a cadre of lawyers with "considerable appellate muscle" (as reported by the *National Law Journal*), this group boasts a strong presence before the U.S. Supreme Court, where its lawyers have won landmark cases on issues ranging from excessive damage awards to freedom of the press.

Depth and Breadth

One of Gibson, Dunn & Crutcher's greatest strengths is the depth and breadth of expertise across every area of the law.

Among Gibson, Dunn & Crutcher lawyers are a former Reagan administration attorney general, two former SEC commissioners, a federal prosecutor involved in the Ruby Ridge investigation, former prosecutors in the U.S. Attorney's Office and the Antitrust Division of the Department of Justice; lawyers who served with the Federal Trade Commission; a DEA Administrator and U.S. District Court Judge; and a Congressman, who now heads Gibson, Dunn's legislative and government advocacy practice.

The firm is home to leading practitioners in such diverse areas of law as aerospace, arbitration and ADR, bankruptcy, white collar crime, communications, corporate transactions, customs and international trade, entertainment, employee benefits and employment law, environmental, financial institutions, government contracts, health care, insurance, intellectual property and high-technology, litigation, media and First Amendment law, mergers and acquisitions, project finance, real estate, securities and tax.

Gibson, Dunn & Crutcher carries its pioneering tradition into the 21st century. The firm remains at the epicenter of significant transactions and litigation, creating many ideas that others follow.

Photos of Ronald S. Beard (left), chairman of the firm and Wesley G. Howell, Jr., the firm's managing partner.

During the 1890s, Gibson, Dunn represented Henry Huntington in developing the Los Angeles Railway and the Pacific Electric, which established many of the routes of today's freeways.

AUTO CLUB OF SOUTHERN CALIFORNIA

History of Member Service and Public Advocacy for Growth

At the turn of the 20th century, Los Angeles car owners coped with impassable roads, unreliable automobiles and inconsistent traffic rules.

In spite of the driving challenges, ten men in Los Angeles recognized that the automobile would play a key role in the future and founded the Automobile Club of Southern California in December 1900. They wanted to promote the construction of good roads, protect the rights and privileges of motorists and provide travel services and social events for members.

Today, this organization's more than four million members have made it the largest American Automobile Association affiliate in the United States.

Among the Auto Club's social gatherings prior to 1910 were auto races in Los Angeles. The races provided exciting sport for thousands of Los Angelenos and attracted racing greats including Barney Oldfield and Eddie Rickenbacker. The races also were used to demonstrate the safety and reliability of cars which helped further the causes of more liberal speed laws and road construction.

One of the more popular services in the early years was "sign posting." As road touring became popular, good maps and direction signs were needed, so the Auto Club started posting signs in 1907. Over the years, about 400,000 Auto Club direction and safety signs were posted on hundreds of Southern California roads and as far east as New York City. The Club also produced maps and tour books that were noted for their accuracy. Later it joined the American Automobile Association (AAA), so members could reserve service throughout the nation.

Over the years, about 400,000 Auto Club direction and safety signs were posted on hundreds of Southern California roads and as far east as New York City on the National Old Trails Road.

In 1909, the first Auto Club Tour Book appeared. It featured 388 pages of maps, historical sites, hotels and tourist camps and brief notes on state and local traffic laws.

Later that year, the Club began publishing *Touring Topics* magazines which was looked upon as the "traveler's bible." By 1933, the magazine's subject matter ranged beyond the Club to many facets of Western living, and to reflect that widened scope, a search began for a new name. Hundreds were suggested before the winner was selected: *Westways*. Today *Westways* is an award-winning travel and entertainment magazine, and one of California's oldest continually circulated periodicals.

As the number of members increased, the Club outgrew a series of locations in downtown Los Angeles before settling into its present-day headquarters building in 1923. The structure, located at the southwest corner of Figueroa Street and Adams Boulevard, was designated a historic, cultural landmark by the city of Los Angeles in 1971. The building's many special features include a stone fountain created in colonial fashion by artisans, high-arched ceilings, bronze work and wood carvings in Spanish Renaissance decor. The patio is landscaped with native and seasonal plants and antique road signs that were first mounted around the country by the Club. The entry to the patio was built around a Moreton Bay Fig tree.

As more services were added, the Auto Club added offices throughout Southern California. Over the years, local Auto Club staff became leaders of local traffic safety committees, tourism bureaus and chambers of commerce by providing Auto Club engineering and travel expertise.

The Auto Club not only posted directions for travelers, it also provided school and safety signs for Southern California cities and counties.

Between 1900 and 1910, the Auto Club sponsored and sanctioned endurance runs and oval track auto races such as this one at Exposition Park in Los Angeles.

To help reduce auto accidents during the 1920s, the Auto Club began providing communities with no-cost crossing guard, alcohol education pedestrian and bicycle safety programs through its local offices. The Auto Club provided its traffic engineering expertise to Southern California cities, including Los Angeles, to help reduce growing traffic congestion and crashes. In 1937, Auto Club traffic engineers studied the Los Angeles area. They produced a master plan of elevated highways that resembled the freeways of today.

In 1974, the Auto Club helped found the city's first major carpooling effort, called "Commuter Computer," to reduce traffic congestion. Prior to the 1984 Olympics in Los Angeles, the Auto Club co-sponsored transportation seminars that helped ensure free-flowing traffic during the Games.

The organization's legacy of community involvement continues today. The Auto Club works with cities and the state to improve driver and vehicle safety, improve air quality and ensure adequate means of financial roads and mass transit projects. The Auto Club has also carried on research into development of alternative energy forms and has strongly supported development of cleaner-running cars.

As part of its ongoing alcohol education program, the Auto Club introduced in 1996 "You Drink. You Drive. You Lose." — an information program to increase awareness of the personal and financial consequences of being convicted of drinking and driving. The Club's Target Car program promotes car design modifications for improved fuel economy, safety, maneuverability and comfort. The Club conducts safety investigations for the U.S. Department of

Transportation for possible car recall campaigns. To encourage passenger safety, the Club has extensively promoted seat belt use and air bag safety, including placing young children in the back seat.

From car racing, sign posting and map making in the early days, Auto Club member services today include a travel agency; auto, home, life and boat insurance; vehicle pricing and purchasing and an array of financial products including an Auto Club MasterCard; home mortgages, vehicle and home equity loans and other financial services.

The Auto Club also returns to its car racing roots as a sponsor of race car driver Gary Densham and participant in National Hot Rod association career fairs for high school students.

Services to the 13 southern California counties is provided through the Auto Club's 69 offices, a 24-hour highly automated telephone service center or the Auto Club's web site.

Since 1900, the Auto Club has been an active, visible part of Southern California culture. As it prepares to celebrate a century of service, the Automobile Club of Southern California plans future growth by building on its rich history if community involvement and member service.

Designated a cultural landmark in 1971 by the City of Los Angeles, the Auto Club headquarters building has stood at the corner of Adams Boulevard and Figueroa Street since 1923.

ADMARKETING

ood advertising starts with a good marketing strategy, a philosophy that has made Admarketing one of the most successful advertising agencies in Los Angeles. Since its inception in 1971, Admarketing has grown from billings of $2 million to over $200 million a year. The company's growth has been fueled by an entrepreneurial spirit that emphasizes innovative and creative solutions to marketing problems. From airlines and electronics to clothing and food products, Admarketing has served some of the finest names in the retail industry. The May Co., AirCal, Public Storage, Circuit City, The Home Depot, Shasta Beverages, Kentucky Fried Chicken and Ross Stores

are just a few of the many well known clients Admarketing has handled in the past 25 years.

Admarketing is a full service agency, offering clients everything from strategic planning and research to creative, production and media buying. In fact, Admarketing is one of the few agencies to have its own in-house buying service as well as in-house production facilities and staff. Jack Roth, agency President/CEO explains it this way: "Our primary business is retail and direct response. To be successful, we must control costs. At Admarketing we watch every penny. Efficient production and media costs are the key."

Admarketing has been successful because its clients have enjoyed extraordinary success. Take OnTV. This pioneer pay TV company founded in 1976 by Jerry Perenchio and Norman Lear had only 30,000 subscribers after 14 months in business. Then Admarketing was hired. The subscribers more than doubled after 1 month! And that growth continued until OnTV had more than 360,000 subscribers — more than four times any other over-the-air pay TV service ever!

"Admarketing has achieved outstanding success like this over and over again. Like the amazing turn-around story of AirCal. The storied successes of category killer retailers like Home Depot and Circuit City.

The unmatched growth in profitability of off price retailer, Ross Stores. This is what we are most proud of. These are our greatest awards," says Mr. Roth.

Roth believes that what you say is more important than how you say it. If you give people a good reason to buy a product, they will respond. Too many agencies create advertising that is self-indulgent and aimed at showing the cleverness of the agency rather than finding the most efficient way to sell the product.

"Our job is to use our skills to realize the client's aims as effectively as possible," says Roth.

The agency is well known for its innovative marketing ideas. Concepts like "Single Call Service" for AirCal and "Express Tailoring" for C&R Clothiers have left their mark on their respective industries and have changed the way people now do business. Together with the new pricing strategies, effective comparison advertising and other new strategies Admarketing has made a substantial contribution to the success of its clients.

Admarketing's efforts have produced impressive results for clients and earned Admarketing numerous advertising industry awards including *Adweek's* prestigious "Best Agency In The West" in 1986.

Even with Admarketing's tremendous success, Roth is constantly looking for ways to improve his company's performance. "I am a perfectionist," he states. "I am our toughest critic. I am not satisfied with good. I want great." It's that attitude that has kept Admarketing at the top of the retail advertising world.

THE PAYROLL HR SPECIALISTS

Les Warner was never interested in building an empire. He simply recognized a market niche that needed to be filled and understood the importance of personalized service in a time when most companies were only interested in the bottom line.

In 1962, Mr. Warner worked as a salesman for Los Angeles-based APEX Steel Inc. In an era when computer technology was still in its infancy, Mr. Warner knew that the huge IBM 360 mainframe computer APEX Steel operated during the day could be utilized at night to provide clients with comprehensive accounting services.

He struck a deal with the owner of APEX Steel to use the computer in the company's off hours, put his accounting background to use and founded APEX Data Processing. Mr. Warner handled sales and marketing while his partner, Mr. Joe Guardino, operated the machinery.

Less than five years later, Mr. Warner and Mr. Guardino bought out APEX Steel's interest and not long after that Mr. Warner became the sole owner.

Mr. Warner knew that computers were in the business to stay, but he also saw that he had chosen an ever-changing industry in which to work. In 1985, the company name changed to Warner Information Systems and expanded its range of services. The Warner Information Systems logo, a dinosaur with the motto "Adapt or Die," recalls the days Mr. Warner had aspired to become a paleontologist (before he settled into a business major), even as it describes the ever-changing computer industry.

Today, Payroll HR Specialists, a subsidiary of Warner Information Systems, is very much a family operation. After Mr. Warner passed away in 1990, his son Bill and others continued to manage the operations until his youngest son Chuck took over the helm as president three years later.

A graduate of Cal Poly with a degree in Management Information Systems and Finance and a

Certified Payroll Professional, Chuck follows his father's philosophy for "growing the business slowly."

"We are growing at a pace which allows us to continue to offer our clients a highly-focused, customized service," says the current company president. "Many of our clients have been with us for over a decade. I believe that part of the reason is that we continually strive to offer a high level of personalized service and that's unfortunately not something many of our larger competitors can offer."

From small local businesses to national corporations, The Payroll HR Specialists provides a broad range of specialized services, including general ledger reporting and interfaces, labor distribution, time clock interfaces, vacation and sick pay accruals, tax filing and human resource management as well as many other complex payroll functions.

This successful Los Angeles-based firm recognizes that every company has its own unique requirements. The Payroll HR Specialists offers a service that is both flexible and tailored to meet each client's specific needs with an unparalleled level of personalized service for a long list of clients, including Burger King, BioSource International, Inc. and Bentley Mills Inc.

And "Adapt or Die" still rings true today.

Brothers Chuck (left) and Bill Warner continue to run the successful payroll processing firm founded by their father, Les Warner in 1962.

RAND

Origins

As World War II came to a close, forward-thinking members of the U.S. military, government and intellectual communities became aware of the need to retain the much-needed services of scientists and engineers who had aided in the war effort.

In 1946, Project RAND took shape at Douglas Aircraft Company under a special contract from the Army Air Forces (now the U.S. Air Force). Two years later, Project RAND separated both physically and legally from the Douglas Aircraft Company and moved to the corner of Fourth and Broadway in Santa Monica, incorporating itself as a non-profit organization.

The establishment of The RAND Corporation as an independent non-profit research organization was announced to the world press in November 1948, with particular emphasis on the originality of the RAND concept, on its independence and nonpartisan quality, on its civilian control and on the promise of broadly disseminated research findings.

This first prophetic press release, issued from the Department of the Air Force, was written with the vision of RAND giving scientists the "greatest freedom of initiative" and permitting the "highest type of scientific research in conjunction with the best industrial experience and knowledge."

James A. Thomson,
President and CEO.

Expansion

Nearly half a century later, RAND has increased in size, expanded its locations and broadened its scope of research. All the while, the organization has remained a dynamic, responsive policy research institution making a valuable contribution to the American social and military policy decision-making processes.

The company's current waffle-shaped Santa Monica facility, completed in 1952, was architecturally designed to promote frequent chance meetings of staff and serves as a physical reminder of the institution's dedication to interdisciplinary research.

In addition to its Santa Monica headquarters, RAND's research staff now operate from such diverse locales as Washington, D.C.; Delft, the Netherlands, which is home to RAND Europe; and New York City, where RAND's Council for Aid to Education is located.

Today, RAND researchers operate on a uniquely broad front, assisting public policy makers at all levels, private-sector leaders in many industries, and the public at large in efforts to strengthen the nation's economy, maintain its security, and improve its quality of life. They contribute to the policy making process by analyzing choices and developments in many areas, including national defense, education and training, health care, criminal and civil justice, labor and population, science and technology, community development, international relations and regional studies.

Resources

RAND's research is supported by a wide range of sources. Although U.S. government agencies provide the largest share of funding, charitable foundations, private sector firms, individuals and earnings from RAND's endowment furnish a steadily growing proportion of financial resources.

Recently, RAND has stepped up its efforts to raise funds from individual donors and is now working for private-sector firms on projects addressing issues in the public interest.

Over and above its client-based research, RAND has developed programs to address issues it has identified as being of critical concern to our nation, spending $4 million per year of its own money to support such research.

RAND employs some 600 research professionals and consultants who form a unique collection of individuals with areas of expertise ranging from statistics

The main RAND office in Santa Monica. *Photo by John F. Peterson*

and economics, the physical and behavioral sciences, and engineering, to medicine, law and business. Nearly 50 percent of the institution's multidisciplinary professional staff hold doctoral degrees.

Research Results

RAND was specifically founded to further scientific, education and charitable purposes for the public welfare and security of this country. In pursuit of these goals, high-quality, objective research became the institution's hallmark.

Its first report, published in 1946, detailed the feasibility of space satellites, or "world-circling space ships." Other groundbreaking research in the first few decades made inroads in game theory, systems theory and the development of one of the first "modern" computers.

In 1950, the Atomic Energy Commission asked RAND to perform a study of nuclear weapons effects, thereby becoming the first non-Air Force sponsor of research at RAND. In 1959, at the request of the House

Select Committee on Astronautics and Space Exploration, RAND produced *Space Handbook: Astronautics and Its Applications*. This guide to the uses and characteristics of space systems became a standard reference.

RAND began addressing major problems of domestic policy in the 1960s. Since then, studies have documented the inefficient allocation of water in California, assessed the future of cable television, investigated ways to help low-income families acquire decent housing and examined a multitude of other critical societal issues.

Two early domestic projects are particularly noteworthy: In 1968, RAND began a relationship with the city of New York (The New York City RAND Institute) to tackle problems of welfare, health services, housing, law enforcement and other municipal issues. Then, in 1971, RAND launched the Health Insurance Experiment, one of the largest controlled social experiments ever attempted in this country and the largest health policy study in history. This 15-year, $80 million study sought to determine the effects different methods of financing health care would have on the use of health care and on personal health.

Graduate Education

Part of RAND's mission is education. In 1970, what is now known as the RAND Graduate School (RGS) was established to train policy analysts and decision makers. RGS offers a select group of graduate fellows an exceptional interdisciplinary course of study and an opportunity, as part of their education, to work with RAND research professionals with real world problems. Today, RAND awards more Ph.D.s in policy analysis than any other school in the country and is highly regarded as a model for other graduate programs in the field.

Current Agenda

RAND's current policy research agenda focuses on a wide spectrum of national, state and local concerns, including violence and drug use, HIV/AIDS medical care, trends in the civil justice system, educational reform, the US labor market and a variety of national security issues. Recent archetypal studies of immigration address the mixed economic progress of immigrants nationwide and the effects of immigration on the State of California. Never relinquishing its earliest interests in space, RAND has also recently assessed national policies regarding power systems for space

RAND a nonprofit institution that helps improve policy and decisionmaking through research and analysis.

About RAND · Reaching RAND · Research Areas · Technical Capabilities · 50th Year Anniversary · Publications · Educational Opportunities · Hot Topics · Employment Opportunities

exploration, the global positioning system and commercial space activity.

RAND has three national security federally funded research and development centers. One, Project Air Force, is funded by the U.S. Air Force. Another, the Arroyo Center, is funded by the U.S. Army, and the third, the National Defense Research Institute is funded by the Office of the Secretary of Defense. The research areas of these centers focus on strategy, geopolitics, force modernization and employment, technology application and resource allocation and management.

RAND's special proficiencies are inevitably drawn beyond national borders, and RAND Europe's research agenda encompasses numerous major strategy and resource allocation issues facing the public and private sectors in Europe. Other RAND units focus on policy issues of other areas of the world.

RAND continues to confront the nation's most difficult problems with intellectual expertise and analytical precision. Its work provides guidance for public and private sector decisionmakers by making policy choices clear and addressing barriers to effective policy implementations. Its studies result in innovative solutions to complex problems by bringing together researchers in all relevant academic specialties who are dedicated to impartiality and the highest technical standards. And it serves the public interest by making its research findings available to a general and extensive audience.

THE PARKINSON FIRM
...Since 1894

When driving about in the Los Angeles metropolitan area, at least one edifice designed by the legendary Parkinson firm will always be in close proximity. Since 1894, this historically important architectural concern has been continually building the public face of the Southland. Currently known as *Parkinson Field Associates*, they are the oldest continually operating architectural firm to have been founded in Los Angels.

Englishman John Parkinson first office on Spring Street in the same building which housed the Los Angeles Athletic Club. His choice of location proved socially beneficial, as he began personal relationships with future business and civic leaders that would last a lifetime. Parkinson's first commercial commissions before the turn of the century included the Currier Building (now demolished) and the city's first Class A office building, the Homer Laughlin Building (aka Grand Central Market).

With the opening of the 1904 Braly Building on 4th and Spring, Parkinson secured his future success. Towering above the skyline at 175 feet tall, it gave the firm credit for the first skyscraper in Los Angeles. This impressive structure remained by far the tallest building in town until later surpassed by another Parkinson design — the Los Angeles City Hall. Parkinson took on as partner Edwin Bergstrom in 1905, and together they designed scores of successful projects, including the Alexandria Hotel, the Pacific Mutual Building, the Los Angeles Athletic Club, numerous department stores, and an impressive roster of important bank and major office buildings.

The Parkinson firm reached its zenith after M.I.T.-trained Donald B. Parkinson in 1920 became the elder Parkinson's new partner. Besides designing the original campus of USC, Parkinson & Parkinson became responsible for major landmark structures such as Bullocks-Wilshire, the Los Angeles City Hall (Lead Designer, Associated Architects), the Memorial Coliseum, the Banks-Huntley Building, the LA Branch of the Federal Reserve Bank, Title Insurance Building and Union Station — to name only a few.

Fifty major structures still standing in downtown LA bear the Parkinson design stamp. Not restricting itself locally, the firm also became responsible for buildings located throughout California, and in Texas, New Mexico, Utah, Nevada and Mexico.

After WWII, the firm continued to grow, designing nearly every telephone company building in Southern California. By early 1991, the firm sought to diversify its largely institutional client base. Formally trained preservation architect Wm. Scott Field, AIA, was retained as vice president in that year. By August 1992, Field became sole owner, reorganized the company under the name *Parkinson Field Associates* and relocated the offices back to the firm's roots on Spring Street.

In March of 1994, seeking to help create a broader public consciousness for preserving the historical built environment in Los Angeles, the company organized the successful 1994 Parkinson Centennial. Throughout the year, local preservation organizations and heritage-mined Angelenos joined together in celebrating the firm's previous achievements.

In February 1995, the company headquarters was relocated to Austin, Texas. Today, the firm maintains clients throughout California, Texas and Oregon. Parkinson Field Associates is currently organized into three divisions: Residential, Commercial and Preservation.

The Parkinson firm's historical drawings, rare photographs and associated project records have been catalogued and established separately as The Parkinson Archives, LLC. One of the largest privately held architectural collections in the nation, the Archives is available to students, scholars, historians and other design professionals for the perpetuation of the Parkinson Legacy.

John Parkinson
(1861-1935)

Original design sketch, Los Angeles City Hall.

Donald B. Parkinson
(1895-1945)

HOWARTH & SMITH

ince its founding in 1985, Howarth & Smith has gained a national reputation for its extraordinary success in a variety of high profile trials and appeals. This boutique law firm, which represents plaintiffs and defendants, is the only firm in the country ever to have been selected by the National Law Journal for both "Top 10" plaintiff's and defense verdicts in a single year.

Howarth & Smith represented the plaintiff in a 1996 fraud and breach-of-contract action against General Dynamics, winning a $107.4 million judgment — the largest verdict in California that year. The firm also was responsible for one of the year's most notable defense verdicts in a product liability action defending Suzuki Motor Corp. Opposing the same counsel who had obtained a $90 million verdict against Suzuki in a prior suit, Howarth & Smith's bold trial strategy led to a defense verdict after the jury deliberated for three hours.

Howarth & Smith specializes in complex civil actions, including business and commercial matters, antitrust cases, class actions, toxic torts and catastrophic personal injury cases. The firm's practice is focused on high-stakes trials and appeals, including "bet the

Founding partners Don Howarth and Suzelle Smith.

company" cases. Howarth & Smith is selective in its client representation, undertaking matters involving intellectual challenges, serious social concerns and the opportunity to address groundbreaking legal issues.

The firm typically refers routine litigation to other capable attorneys and firms, many of which it has worked with over the years. Howarth & Smith encourages close relationships with attorneys and law firms throughout the country, and many of its clients, which include individuals, corporations and nonprofit organizations, are referred by other lawyers. The firm also serves as designated trial counsel in significant cases, where the pretrial preparation is handled by other firms in co-counsel capacity.

A brief list of particularly prominent cases demonstrates Howarth & Smith's remarkable achievements:

The firm represented the late Doris Duke and played a leading role in the battle over the billion-dollar estate of the tobacco heiress, resulting in the removal of the opposing trustees, preliminary executor and a major banking institution and the appointment of the firm's client as a trustee of the Estate.

Howarth & Smith represents the wife and son of the original "Marlboro Man" in their suit against Philip Morris and is heavily involved in the landmark class-action cases against the tobacco industry.

Another high profile case involved an antitrust challenge to the National Football League by the firm's clients — 16 top professional football players.

The firm has handled a number of consumer class actions, including a price fixing class action on behalf of all purchasers of eggs in Southern California.

The firm filed suit against a Pasadena shopping mall, successfully arguing that the mall's deficient security allowed two criminals to rape and murder the wife of its client. The jury returned a $3.6 million verdict in favor of the husband and against the mall.

In a product liability case, the firm won a $7 million jury verdict for a man left paralyzed in connection

with the use of a Sears extension ladder sold with inadequate safety warnings.

In a breach of oral contract to transfer an equity interest to a corporate executive, Howarth & Smith obtained a $9 million jury verdict for the employee.

The firm represents 12 California cities and municipalities in an action against other municipalities for recovery of $30 million lost in a fraudulent investment scheme.

On the defense side, the firm has represented many corporations in multimillion dollar suits, including antitrust cases against vitamin, catfish, cement and glass container manufacturers, NBA and NFL stars, high net worth individuals, the Vatican Library (as custodian of Vatican artwork) and several prominent law firms.

Howarth & Smith's unique legal accomplishments stem from its partners' recognized ability to combine strategic thinking, high quality legal analysis and persuasive courtroom presence. What further distinguishes these lawyers is their ability to distill complex legal issues, technicalities and jargon into understandable and compelling arguments, enabling juries to grasp relevant issues and understand the client's position. Howarth & Smith's flair for crisp, concise communication — coupled with its analytical skills and mastery of trial strategy — are a potent combination that makes the firm a powerful force in the nation's courtrooms.

Howarth & Smith is led by four partners, Don Howarth, Suzelle Smith, David Ringwood and Brian Bubb. The partners are supported by ten associates, of counsel attorneys and a group of experienced paralegal assistants.

Mr. Howarth specializes in trials and appellate arguments. He holds three degrees from Harvard University, including a Master's from the Kennedy School of Government and a JD from the Harvard Law School. He is an elected Fellow of the American College of Trial Lawyers and of the International Academy of Trial Lawyers. He is a Visiting Fellow at Oxford University (England), a Visiting Scholar at Cambridge University (England), an adjunct professor of trial practice at Pepperdine University and a Distinguished Lecturer at Southwestern University. He is a frequently invited speaker at high-level conferences throughout the U.S. and abroad.

Ms. Smith, recognized by *The National Law Journal* as one the nation's 10 best litigators in 1996, graduated summa cum laude from Boston University and obtained a Master's degree in Philosophy from Oxford University in England. She earned her law degree from the University of Virginia, where she was Order of the Coif. She is now a member of the University of Virginia School of Law Board of Trustee, a member of the Pepperdine Law School Board of Visitors, a Visiting Fellow at Oxford University (England), a Visiting Scholar at Cambridge University (England) and an elected Fellow of the International Academy of Trial Lawyers.

Howarth & Smith has demonstrated that creative attorneys with the right approach and the right set of skills can provide what is necessary to succeed in today's legal arena: individualized trial and appellate advocacy so difficult to find in large firms with generic programs.

(Left to right) Kenneth Tune (of counsel) and partners, Don Howarth, Suzelle Smith, Brian D. Bubb and David K. Ringwood.

Suzelle M. Smith and Don Howarth at the Bridge of Sighs, Oxford.

BENCH INTERNATIONAL

enise (Dee Dee) DeMan has never been one to follow convention. In fact, as the founder of Bench
International, one of Los Angeles' most successful
specialized retained search firms, DeMan routinely
redefines the "headhunting" industry by implementing
a policy of unparalleled personalized service not found
in many of her competitor's corporations.

After graduating from San Diego State University's
Graduate School of Speech and Hearing in 1974, she
decided to bypass a career in pathology research and
opted instead to follow her entrepreneurial spirit.

The then 22-year-old fledgling businesswoman
recognized that specialized retained search firms, or
"headhunting companies," would become increasingly
valuable to international
businesses seeking savvy,
global-conscious profes-
sionals in the technology
driven fields of science,
health care and emerg-
ing businesses such as
biotechnology.

So she "aligned" her-
self with science, evolved
with the industry and
filled this growing market
niche. But it wasn't an
easy road, particularly for
one so young.

"As a young woman,
I found it difficult to gain
credibility with CEO's of
Fortune 100 companies,"
says DeMan. "I knew in
order to succeed, I would
have to differentiate
myself and my company
from competitors. I did
this by meeting with

Denise "Dee Dee" DeMan,
CEO and founder of Bench
International.

prospective clients and helping them tailor our services around their specific needs and expectations
rather than arrogantly assuming that I knew what
they wanted."

Over the years, this simple, innovative approach
has earned Bench International a reputation as one of
the nation's most effective, comprehensive search and
organizational healthcare consulting firms dedicated to
the fast growing fields of biotechnology, managed care,
pharmaceuticals, emerging technologies and the consumer products industries.

Bench International's recruitment efforts focus
throughout a clients' organization from the senior level
scientist involved in crafting early discovery research
through to corporate officers, science and medical advisory boards, as well as boards of directors. The company's
extensive client list has included many multi-national
corporations with US holdings, such as Exxon, UNOCAL,
Johnson & Johnson, IBM, Dow Corning, Merck-
Medco and has supported such companies as Amgen
and Genentech as they move into the arena of the big
drug company players.

The firm's two-pronged goals are to provide a
performance-driven retained search firm designed to
produce "outstanding fits" for its clients not only
through recruitment, but also by providing its
clients with extensive mentoring, training and consulting support.

To this end, Bench International utilizes the special skills of DeMan's partner Cathy Balin, a former
vice president of human resources for a major health
and benefits trust administrator.

Together, they along with another professional colleague, a nationally renowned communications expert,
Eileen McDargh, formed ALIGN (an acronym for
Action, Leadership, Innovation, Growth and Net
Results), a custom-designed management forum created
to address the critical interpersonal and business issues
that affect an organization's bottom line.

Strengthened by the most comprehensive candidate referral network in the industry and enhanced by a state-of-the-art computerized database, Bench International is in a position to do what most employers cannot do for themselves.

The company's method of thorough prescreening, in-depth interviews and reference checking enables Bench International to develop comprehensive profiles on each candidate. Attentive to personal issues and technical requisites, the firm takes pride in providing a service tailored to the specific needs of its clients.

Aside from traditional search methodology, the firm's professionals are members of and annually attend over 50 domestic and international medical and scientific conferences to develop substantive relationships with members of the scientific and medical communities.

Bench International's corporate capabilities also encompass over two decades of industry-based expertise in human resource consulting, including the design and development of human resource manuals and management tools.

As a founding member of a national organization of search firms whose sole purpose is to raise the level of ethical conduct in the recruiting industry, Bench International is committed to maintaining the highest standard of ethical conduct and confidentiality.

Committed to excellence in all aspects of recruitment, Bench International is dedicated to helping its clients grow in an ever-changing marketplace.

BOOZ · ALLEN & HAMILTON

Should a company compete based on cost, speed to market, customer care or innovation? How do you leverage the power of being global? How can you improve your products and enhance their value to consumers? How can you cut the cost of complexity?

These are real world issues that demand realistic strategies delivered comprehensively and quickly. For timely, results-oriented solutions to organizational, technological or operational change, businesses throughout the world turn to the oldest management consulting firm in the United States: Booz · Allen & Hamilton, Inc.

Founded in 1914 by Edwin Booz, Booz · Allen & Hamilton is an international management and technology consulting firm committed to helping senior management solve complex problems — a commitment that has shaped the company's values and professional practices for over 80 years. As pioneers in the field of management consulting, Booz · Allen & Hamilton has led the way by providing services in strategy, systems, operations and technology to clients in over 75 countries on six continents. The company has

offices located throughout the United States and the world, including Los Angeles.

With more than 7,000 employees worldwide generating sales of over $1 billion per year, Booz · Allen & Hamilton's client base includes a majority of the world's largest industrial and service corporations, as well as major institutions and government bodies around the world, including most U.S. federal departments and agencies. The company is organized into two major business sectors: the Worldwide Commercial Business (WCB) and the Worldwide Technology Business (WTB). WCB clients are primarily international corporations, while WTB generally serves governmental clients both in the U.S. and abroad.

Booz · Allen & Hamilton provides business solutions through its expertise in its practice groups:

Industry Groups:
- Energy, Chemicals & Pharmaceuticals
- Consumer & Engineered Products
- Financial and Health Services
- Communications, Media and Technology

Functional Groups:
- Operations Management
- Information Technology
- Strategic Leadership

Among the resources Booz · Allen & Hamilton brings to the table are four core capabilities: they make change happen quickly, efficiently and cost effectively; they deliver real-world insight, achievable solutions and tangible results; they offer global continuity and consistency; and they excel in managing the flow of breakthrough ideas and knowledge.

Booz · Allen & Hamilton meets clients' objectives in three ways. First, by bringing deep experience and knowledge to the full spectrum of issues and challenges facing clients, from the strategic to the tactical. Second,

Lockheed Martin F-117, made in Southern California.

by developing an array of proprietary insights and approaches tailored to the special needs of clients. Finally, by using these cross-functional capabilities and insights to help propel clients to new levels of growth and profitability. This is accomplished by challenging clients to push the envelope and envision fresh new agendas and approaches. Instead of asking, "What are the best practices and strategies today?" Booz • Allen & Hamilton asks "Where will the best practices and winning strategies of tomorrow emerge — and how do I get there first?"

The unmatched ability to stimulate meaningful change flows from Booz • Allen & Hamilton's full-service, integrated approach. The ability to bring technology and operational expertise to bear on strategic decisions and strategic insight to functional solutions is a rare and powerful capability, and one that Booz • Allen & Hamilton has worked diligently to achieve.

Most consulting firms talk about being global but are organized regionally. Booz • Allen & Hamilton thinks globally and operates globally. Dedicated partner teams, staffing approaches, knowledge-sharing programs and reward systems are managed on a global basis. The company transfers partners to different geographies to support ongoing client initiatives and to help transfer new approaches and best practices from one locale to another. Professionals are rotated from office to office and across borders to cross-fertilize ideas and maintain client relationships.

While the Los Angeles office of Booz • Allen & Hamilton incorporates global strategy and positioning within its client base, the company places an emphasis on the types of businesses that operate in the greater L.A. area, including aerospace, media, manufacturing, high technology, computers, electronics and energy. A large group of Booz • Allen & Hamilton transportation specialists have been assisting with the installation of train, subway, bus and rail line infrastructure by providing systems integration work to support those projects. Booz • Allen & Hamilton also has an impressive client roster of companies from the entertainment and aerospace industries. And the San Diego office of Booz • Allen & Hamilton, which grew from virtually nothing two years ago to over 100 professionals today, works primarily with the U.S. Navy Space Command.

As global business grows, so does Booz • Allen & Hamilton. The company has been growing at a rate of about 30 percent a year, the most the company can handle and still provide consistent, expert services for a wide client base.

The firm's top management includes William F. Stasior, Chairman and Chief Executive Officer; Daniel C. Lewis, President, Worldwide Commercial Business; and Ralph W. Shrader, President, Worldwide Technology Business.

Consistent with its position as a business thought leader, Booz • Allen & Hamilton publishes the quarterly journal, "Strategy & Business," which reports on the latest developments in global management techniques, competitive tactics and strategic thinking. The company is a founding co-sponsor of the annual Global Business Book Awards, GBBA, which recognizes the most innovative contributions to business literature and promotes worldwide readership of business books.

Innovation, knowledge, expertise — Booz • Allen & Hamilton is poised to bring the consulting industry into the new millennium.

Los Angeles Mass Transit.

John Harbison, managing partner for Los Angeles.

INTERNAL & EXTERNAL COMMUNICATION, INC.

n 1983, long before the corporate world awoke to the possibilities of the interactive multimedia market, Los Angeles entrepreneur Alexandra Rand founded Internal & External Communication, Inc. (IEC), with little more than a vision and a sturdy kitchen table.

Rand's vision was that personal computers and custom software would revolutionize corporate training. Instead of pouring resources into classroom instruction, corporations could install interactive job skills courses and performance support tools on each employee's desktop. By tapping the capabilities of emerging technology and blending educational content with engaging media, games, exercises and video simulations, these programs could even make on-the-job training fun and more effective.

And her kitchen table? That's where Rand developed the proposals that won IEC's pioneer clients — and where she researched and wrote, designed, programmed, produced and tested the earliest IEC programs.

Word of mouth soon won IEC bigger contracts, so Rand retired the table and moved the company, now a small, dedicated group of writers, programmers, graphic artists and project managers, to a tiny office suite in Venice Beach. For several years, the team worked long

hours side by side (before the days of e-mail, the Internet, or high-speed modems) to produce the work that set the standards for multimedia training.

In 1989, while IEC was working with Prodigy Services Company, Rand met Suzanne Biegel, a marketing manager there. Impressed by Biegel's creative approach to corporate challenges and extensive experience in multimedia, Rand soon invited her to help IEC identify new growth opportunities both internally and externally. When Biegel joined IEC in 1991, she and Rand embarked on an aggressive campaign to win top corporate clients while building a complete, vertically integrated, in-house development team, ready to staff demanding projects at a moment's notice.

Seven years later, Rand, CEO, and Biegel, now president, are still at the helm of what has indisputably become the industry's leading developer of custom interactive multimedia training applications. IEC, located in Marina del Rey, California, employs 175 specialists in multimedia and Web-based development who work in teams to produce hundreds of hours of interactive courseware each year.

Because Rand and Biegel work closely with their employee teams at every stage in the process, from kick-

With common goals and shared values, IEC Founder and CEO, Alexandra Rand (right) and President, Suzanne Biegel (left) have formed an exceptional business partnership based on trust, collaboration, and spirited innovation.

(Opposite page, bottom left) IEC's office adopts a comfortable, contemporary Southern California beach theme; a channel of sand runs along the "front deck" and a blue wave of drywall curls around the reception desk.

off to delivery, daily imparting the company's standards, values, and goals, each IEC program is a one-of-a-kind solution that upholds and even exceeds the company's original quality standards.

IEC's growth in the last few years has coincided with the production of its most acclaimed programs. The company's awards case displays a collection of top industry prizes. More and more companies are demanding computer-delivered courses, attracted by growing evidence that employees trained this way learn job skills faster, apply them more effectively and remember them longer — lending support to IEC's firmly held belief that everybody learns best while having fun.

Fun is still an essential ingredient of each IEC product, reflected in user-friendly writing, vivid art, entertaining creative environments, challenging games and video simulations, high production values, and innovative use of the latest technology. IEC promises to custom-design each client's program to teach required skills — anything from systems training, to management development, to sales strategies — through a blend of instructional, creative, interactive, and technological approaches carefully targeted to engage the end-user.

For example, Lexus sales consultants travel to a top-secret virtual training facility to master product features and hone their sales techniques. Anheuser-Busch wholesalers visit the Busch Learning Center to take computer-based courses such as beer selling basics and

total quality management. And FedEx managers learn statistical process control while investigating the "FedEX-Files."

Since clients' technology needs are growing and changing every day, IEC makes sure to stay on the technical cutting edge, developing programs for the increasingly diverse range of available platforms and operating systems, and delivering them via CD-ROM, private networks, corporate intranets, or the World Wide Web. IEC also develops electronic performance support systems, learning architectures and networks, training workshops, print-based materials and promotional items in all formats.

Rand and Biegel are looking forward to the next century, when they will work to sustain IEC's long-term client relationships and select new business opportunities that will showcase its custom multimedia development expertise, while adding a commercial, semi-custom curriculum that will reach a far broader group of client companies. Both principals challenge themselves daily to make IEC not only its clients' best partner, but also the best place for its employees to work.

That's why they have incorporated fun into the workplace, too. The office is a lively, team-oriented environment where a commitment to "brilliant work, smartly executed, in a spirit of fun and goodwill," the IEC mission statement, is evident in every aspect of corporate life. Team members are encouraged to go beyond strict job descriptions to support each other and to celebrate each other's successes and achievements. The dress code is relaxed — a particularly Californian perk — and the beach never feels very far away: The front lobby includes a strip of sand and a surfboard.

Although the original kitchen table isn't around anymore, the vision and the entrepreneurial spirit of IEC's beginnings are clearly very much alive. Even in Los Angeles, which is famous for success stories, IEC's high standards, innovative approach and continued success make it a standout.

(Top) The Virtual Showroom delivers Lexus product training and information through high-end 3-D graphics and animations, sound effects, music, and video

(Middle) At the Busch Learning Center there's even a Video Arcade where trainees can view classic Budweiser commercials.

(Bottom) FedEx managers investigate key components of statistical process control with virtual "FPI" agents Mullen and Shelby.

J.T. NAKAOKA ASSOCIATES

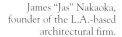

hroughout history, architecture has had the power to move people. The award-winning Los Angeles-based architectural firm of J.T. Nakaoka Associates Architects creates spaces and structures that also have the power to draw scores of customers and send sales figures through the roof for some of the world's leading retailers.

Founded by the firm's president James "Jas" Nakaoka in 1982, Nakaoka Associates has built an international reputation as a practice known for its environmental expertise, specializing in circulation planning, imaging, retail stores, museums and entertainment facilities for maximum impact. The firm, with work in the U.S., U.K. and Asia, recognizes the environment as a critical and contributing component in marketing and branding.

Nakaoka Associates is responsible for the quiet elegance and luxury of New York City's landmark Bergdorf Goodman men's store, the timeless image of the Monterey Bay Aquarium Gift and Book Shop set in the historic Cannery Row, the prestigious J. Paul Getty Center Book Store in Los Angeles, the innovative new image of Rampage, one of the nation's leading junior apparel retailers as well as various work for Pebble Beach, one of the country's premier golf courses.

J.T. Nakaoka Associates began by building educational facilities, movie theaters, major housing developments, high-end custom residential, planned office and commercial facilities. The firm further specialized over the years to serve as a consultant to many of the nation's major museums, including the Japanese-American National Museum located in downtown L.A.,

(Right and bottom of following page) Nakaoka Associates created an innovative yet subtle mix of styles and space for Rampage's flagship junior apparel store.

James "Jas" Nakaoka, founder of the L.A.-based architectural firm.

which has been honored with the city, state and national trust historic preservation awards.

The museum was built in 1925 as a Buddhist temple and used for storage by families interned during World War II, the site is currently a private, nonprofit repository for items documenting the Japanese-American experience. Working from photos taken of weddings, birthdays and funerals in the sanctuary, J.T. Nakaoka Associates painstakingly restored the interior, refurbished lanterns and replicated over 150 floral ceiling panels that were ruined beyond repair by years of incense burning.

"We shape buildings; thereafter they shape us," Winston Churchill once said. This observation extends beyond awe-inspiring architecture and also applies to the more pragmatic and commercial arena of store design and visual merchandising. Without visual merchandising, a store is simply a white room filled with racks of clothing; with it, a store can make a statement all its own.

When Rampage set out to make its own statement in 1994, the apparel manufacturer/retailer turned to the expertise of the award-winning retail, design and image company of J.T. Nakaoka Associates. The challenge for the then-13-year-old architectural firm was to develop a flagship store for a junior apparel manufacturer without creating a junior's store.

Unlike many of its competitors, J.T. Nakaoka Associates opts for a more "holistic" approach to architectural design. Rather than simply create a structure, the firm takes into consideration all aspects of the business from staff and sales analysis to back room operations and merchandise planning to design with long-term success in mind.

For Rampage, the result was an innovative yet subtle mix of styles and space. The store's facade reflects the timeless Art Deco designs of buildings on La Brea Boulevard, while the interior is similar to a warehouse with hardwood floors and track lighting. While simplicity may be the store's visual hallmark, it strikes a subliminal message of excitement from the industrial beige dress forms to the wooden display counters with their curling forged-steel legs, from the avant-garde diamond shaped, full-length mirror to the silk and metal woven sheers in the store window.

J.T. Nakaoka Associates considers itself a firm dedicated to "fashion, design and business...where architecture and interior comes into direct contact with people." The boutique firm's unparalleled success in this dynamic industry is largely due to its expertise, track record, personal service and surprisingly, its size.

"Our staff is comparatively smaller in number than other competing firms of equal international ranking," says Nakaoka. "As a result, we are selective in the projects we elect to take on because environmental marketing projects require total reevaluation and commitment from both the client and the design firm. Anyone can design a project, but it takes a certain talent to consistently reinvent the business and look at it in a fresh light and design architecture that will create a personality for our clients."

(Above) Nakaoka Associates is responsible for the quiet elegance and luxury of New York City's landmark Bergdorf Goodman men's store.

JOHN A. MARTIN & ASSOCIATES

Structural Engineering for the New Millennium.

Fox Plaza

Los Angeles
Convention Center

ohn A. "Jack" Martin formed John A. Martin & Associates, Inc. (JAMA) in 1953, when he was a young engineer with just a few years of experience. Forty-five years later, with Jack at the helm and continuing as CEO, JAMA has become the largest structural design company in the United States, with over 400 professionals and staff licensed to practice engineering in all 50 states and the province of Guam. Jack's son, nicknamed Trailer, has been president of JAMA and the head of all of JAMA operations for the past 20 years that he has been with the company.

JAMA engineering has, in essence, redefined the Los Angeles skyline. From soaring downtown skyscrapers to the condominiums in the Wilshire-Westwood corridor; from colleges and universities to the Los Angeles, Anaheim and Long Beach convention centers; from LAX to Disneyland, JAMA buildings can be found in nearly every neighborhood in the greater Los Angeles community.

The list of JAMA clients just in the Los Angeles area covers every conceivable aspect of structural design. Included are such notable buildings as the award-winning Los Angeles Convention Center expansion, the seismic retrofit of UCLA's historic Royce Hall, the Beverly Hills Hotel renovation, the Hyatt Century City Hotel, the landmark Fox Plaza office tower in Century City, the Museum of Contemporary Art (MOCA), Disney's corporate headquarters and the Disneyland Administration Building, downtown's 54-story "777 Tower," and the MTA/RTD Gateway Plaza.

While JAMA's practice has been most impressive in its hometown, it is by no means limited to the City of Angels. Have you been to Las Vegas lately? It is difficult to name a famous hotel/casino which is not a product of JAMA engineering. The Mirage, Treasure Island, MGM Grand, Bellagio, Venetian and Paris casinos are all designed by JAMA, including a striking half-scale Eiffel Tower under construction in front of the new Paris Casino. The firm has completed projects throughout the world.

In the highly specialized area of sports and entertainment venues, JAMA's impressive portfolio includes the new Staples Arena in downtown Los Angeles, Arizona's Bank One Ballpark with a retractable dome roof, the University of Nevada Las Vegas Thomas & Mack Center for Special Events, the Alamodome in San Antonio, Coors Field in Denver, the San Jose Arena, the Florida Suncoast Dome in St. Petersburg and the grandstand replacement at the Del Mar Racetrack.

The company's growth has been remarkable. The firm currently completes structural designs for more than 80 million square feet of construction each year. JAMA's practice encompasses high and low rise office buildings, airports, convention centers, stadiums, sports arenas and racetracks, theater and entertainment complexes, theme parks, university buildings, courts, police stations, jails and prisons, and military facilities.

JAMA's staff reflects Los Angeles' cultural diversity, warmth and appetite for new frontiers, with representatives from all ethnic backgrounds and many nationalities. With an average length of employment of 15 years, one reason for JAMA's extraordinary success is the family feeling and stability it provides to its employees.

JAMA and its personnel are known for being good team players in the design process, making them the preferred structural engineer of some of the most renowned architects in the world. State-of-the-art

UCLA Royce Hall

design techniques, computer applications and engineering concepts allow the firm to create structural systems based on their efficiency and economic feasibility, as well as consistency with each project's architectural theme.

While solid, time-honored engineering standards and minute attention to detail are what make JAMA a favorite structural engineer for architects and developers, the development of futuristic technologies makes JAMA appealing to universities and national research organizations.

Creative Artists Agency
Office Building

JAMA's Research & Development Division (the only such division in this industry in the United States) is respected in both the engineering and scientific communities worldwide. Under the leadership of internationally renowned earthquake engineer, Dr. Farzad Naeim, this division has been awarded research grants by diverse national and local agencies for studying earthquakes and their impact on seismic design practice. The State of California commissioned this division to develop the first multimedia earthquake encyclopedia. As well, the standard textbook on seismic design in nine out of the top ten engineering schools in the country is edited by Dr. Naeim.

JAMA considers global communication and the Internet as keys to success in the next millennium. To that end, it maintains a comprehensive world-wide-web presence which, in addition to company related information, features the largest collection of earthquake preparedness material on the Internet and is freely available to the public.

It is with a well-deserved sense of pride and accomplishment that John A. Martin & Associates enters the 21st century. The firm's history of stellar past achievements coupled with visionary leadership is a solid foundation from which JAMA will add significantly to the built environment of the next millennium.

MOFFATT & NICHOL ENGINEERS

ounded in 1945 by partners John Moffatt and Frank Nichol, Moffatt & Nichol Engineers is as much a local landmark as any created by the Long Beach-based firm.

Moffatt & Nichol is internationally recognized for its role in the evolution of the modern marina and small craft harbor design. To date, the company has designed well over 300 facilities servicing over 100,000 vessels worldwide, including the Cabrillo Marina at the Port of Los Angeles, San Francisco's Fisherman's Wharf, Marina del Rey in Los Angeles and Huntington Harbour in Huntington Beach.

The firm's unique expertise in this area enables it to develop innovative solutions to the problems confronting the maritime industry, including environmental compatibility, water quality, storm and ice protection, marina layout and dock system design.

The analysis of coastal processes and the planning and design of shore protection and enhancement systems have become important elements of the firm's waterfront work. Projects range from the modeling of future coastal conditions to the design of beach protection and erosion control systems.

Bob Nichol, president of the Long Beach-based Moffatt & Nichol Engineers.

Since its inception, this full service engineering firm has expanded its operations from traditional waterfront specialty areas to emerge as a multidiscipline engineering and planning firm providing a wide range of practices and expertise in the areas of high quality civil, structural, mechanical, electrical, coastal and construction engineering as well as design and planning services.

The firm's current areas of expertise extends to ports, harbors, marinas, coastal and shore protection, urban waterfronts, highways, bridges and grade separations, rail and transit, airports and public works to name just a few.

The firm has had a longstanding working relationship with the Port of Los Angeles, providing navigation and dredging improvements in the harbor, engineering design of maritime terminals and extensive involvement in container terminal planning.

Moffatt & Nichol Engineers, as part of a joint venture, was responsible for the design of Pier 400, one of the largest capital improvements projects undertaken by any U.S. seaport.

Moffatt & Nichol also provides comprehensive planning and design services for complex urban transportation problems. Projects range from local street improvements to major interstate interchanges and freeways.

Company president Bob Nichol is the project director leading the engineering team in planning and designing the $1.9 billion Alameda Corridor Project. The project is a 20-mile railroad freight expressway linking the Ports of Los Angeles and Long Beach (the nation's busiest seaports) to the transcontinental railhead near downtown Los Angeles.

The firm's highway structure services cover every aspect from inspection to design, with projects varying

The Pier 300/400 complex at the Port of Los Angeles is an example of the innovative design ideas the firm brings to the maritime industry. Courtesy Port of Los Angeles

from pedestrian crossings to major bridges, including the historic Arroyo Seco Bridge in Los Angeles. Constructed in 1896, this eight-span riveted steel plate girder bridge required that reconstruction efforts maintain the historic fabric and character of the original structure. The firm's successful design effort consisted of widening the existing bridge from a single-track structure to one which would carry both in-bound and out-bound light rail trains for the L.A. County Transportation Commission.

Moffatt & Nichol also works on a number of local projects, including earthquake retrofitting of the Gerald Desmond and Vincent Thomas bridges.

Each project undertaken by the firm is built upon its founders' philosophy of the importance of attention to detail and providing quality service to fulfill the diverse needs of their clients. The company's success can be traced to Moffatt & Nichol's commitment to client satisfaction.

The firm, which initially opened its doors in Long Beach, has now extended well beyond geographic boundaries with offices on both coasts and a client base in 35 countries and completed projects spanning six continents.

Even before there was a Moffatt & Nichol firm, its birth was preordained with the onset of WWII when founders John Moffatt and Frank Nichol worked together in 1940 on the engineering and construction of the Long Beach naval facilities.

Following the war, the young firm responded to other major events that became, like well placed stepping stones, a path for the company to follow. Civil engineering found a fertile environment for growth in the post-war era. The rapid growth and development of Southern California following the conclusion of the war, the expansion of international trade, the strengthening of naval installations, the burgeoning need for transportation facilities, the aftermath of natural phenomena such as earthquakes and the growing sensitivity to environmental issues and preservation of wetlands all demanded engineering skills the growing company could provide.

"I am constantly amazed at the level of development and investment that has been made in the Los Angeles region, yet it still seems to have enormous potential," said company President Bob Nichol. "Unlike other areas where you might go in and do one or two projects, California's economy is so vibrant and diversified that it is constantly growing and changing."

The diversity of work Moffatt & Nichol has tackled throughout its 50+ year history is one of the company's unique characteristics.

PDQ Personnel Services, Inc.

PDQ Personnel Services, Inc. prides itself on providing innovative staffing solutions for clients in business, industry and government throughout the greater Los Angeles area.

A recognized national leader in entrepreneurial and employment issues, Founder, President and CEO Patty DeDominic created the company with three simple principles in mind: to listen and respond to the

clients needs; to send clients only those candidates who can match PDQ's own exacting standards; and to always conduct PDQ business with honesty and integrity.

When DeDominic interviewed for jobs, she discovered a niche that needed to be filled. She began to develop a clear understanding for both sides of the employment fence. She saw what businesses needed as well as what workers were looking for.

Patty DeDominic, president and CEO of PDQ Personnel Services, Inc. spearheads a company that places hundreds of administrative support personnel.

The Glendale, California native enrolled in management courses at USC and UCLA before taking the plunge into business ownership. Armed only with an entrepreneurial spirit, two thousand dollars, a borrowed desk at an employment office, a single line telephone and "a shoebox filled with index cards" that served as her filing system, DeDominic started her fledgling personnel services firm in 1979.

Her first clients came by referral through the employment office where she had set up shop. But after the first month of well-placed workers, business began to roll in.

By offering clients the fastest response time and the best temporary employees in the business, PDQ quickly emerged as the premier provider of administrative and specialty staffing support in the city.

In her first year of business, DeDominic billed $136,000. Today, PDQ bills three times that amount each week! Over the years, her small entrepreneurial endeavor evolved into a highly profitable big business serving the staffing needs of some of the largest and most prestigious companies in the state.

PDQ Personnel Services, Inc. currently services Southern California,

Sacramento and San Jose. The firm employs more than 700 people, operates a client list of over 200 regular customers and has a database of 15,000 specialized applicants.

PDQ's administrative and clerical staff can handle any assignment from secretary to reception or file clerk. A cadre of trained professionals work in the accounting, payroll or billing departments and high-tech positions can be filled with data entry personnel, word processing and desktop publishing proficient temps, even nutritionists, graphic designers and financial officers.

Under DeDominic's creative and dynamic leadership, PDQ Personnel Services Inc. has grown from a one-woman operation into a multi-million dollar organization. DeDominic believes that the key to her success lies in asking applicants questions "several levels deeper" than her competitors.

"We go beyond how many words a minute they can type. We try to find out the reason they want to work — whether it's because they want to grow and develop, support the kids or be associated with a prestigious industry."

DeDominic's unique business philosophy has not gone unnoticed. This successful entrepreneur stands among a select group of professionals who advise political leaders at both the state and federal level. She has been recognized by Congress for her outstanding achievements in business, and by labor and business groups as a human resources expert.

At PDQ, no staffing project is too small, no challenge too daunting. Creating a successful, service-oriented, people-driven company has been the cornerstone of PDQ's success since its inception and DeDominic has never strayed from her original vision.

"We are professionals in the personnel business, dedicated to finding the right people for our clients. We believe that quality in service and referrals are the only way to operate a personnel service. The key to success in this business is to design custom-made solutions for our clients immediate needs without losing sight of their long-term goals."

PDQ Personnel Services, Inc. prides itself on the fastest response time and best temps in the business.

Ray Kappe, FAIA

The Kappe Residence

When does a building cease to be simply concrete and wood and become a treasured landmark? When does a house cease to be merely bricks and plaster and become a home? When viewed through the open-eyed imagination of a true master. Ray Kappe, FAIA, has been practicing his architectural art for almost half a century. This Renaissance man believes in blending function and form in not only his creations, but in his notable career as well, combining social and community advocacy, urban design and planning, and education. Kappe has authored publications, completed energy and advanced technology research, and pioneered one of the nation's most innovative and progressive design schools. And as an internationally acclaimed architect, his buildings have been recognized with the industry's highest achievement awards.

Ray Kappe began his architectural practice in the early 50s. He was committed to the ideals of the California lifestyle, which afforded the potential to live with nature. At the time, Southern California design was mostly led by such architects as Greene and Greene, Wright, Neutra and Schindler, followed by Ain, Soriano, and Harris. Kappe used these greats as the basis for his own work. Architect Hayahiko Takase once wrote in the Japanese journal *Toshi-Jutaku* that, "Ray Kappe is one of the few successors of the 'Great Tradition of California Housing.' His work has similar characteristics to the preceding California masters, such as open-mindedness, harmony with nature, clear systems, unostentatiousness and Japanese influence."

Since graduating from the University of California with Honors in Architecture in 1951, Kappe has been the recipient of numerous design awards. These include

six National American Institute of Architects (AIA) House & Home Awards, ten Southern California Chapter AIA Honor and Merit Awards, an AIA Sunset Honor Award, a National AIA Homes for Better Living Award, a Steel Institute Award, a Grand Prix Award from the City of Los Angeles, and the State of California Governor's Mansion Competition Award. His work has been published locally, nationally and internationally. In 1976, a retrospective of his residential work from 1966 to 1976 was published in GA *Houses*. His work from 1976 to 1985 explored solutions responsive to energy concerns, both passive and active. In 1987, he received the Neutra Award for Professional Excellence, followed in 1995 by the Maybeck Award for 45 years of outstanding architectural design. This is the highest state design award given by the AIA's California Council, and Kappe was the first recipient from Southern California. In 1996 he was awarded the Gold Medal from the American Institute of Architects/Los Angeles Chapter honoring him for his "lifetime achievements as an innovative designer, enlightened planner and inspired educator who has influenced generations of students and practitioners." The Kappe House was also named a Cultural Heritage Landmark in 1996 by the City of Los Angeles. The following year, the AIA/CC bestowed a Twenty-five Year award for the Kappe residence.

Ray Kappe describes his overriding design attitude as "total architecture" — the achievement of equality among the elements of user needs, the relationship of site and surrounding environment, the development of space through visual perception and the ordering of movement, the incorporation and recognition of natural and environmental factors, the exploration of construction techniques, and the ordering of structure and materials. Kappe attempts to counteract the impact upon the senses and the general lack of the obvious in his work by making the construction system and structure understandable. Although the structure and plan is measured, the spaces are not usually totally understood. Kappe chooses not to ignore any aspect of architecture in order to make a single point. Inclusive complexity within order is his attempt to reach the highest level of architectural experience.

Responding to his belief that everyone has a responsibility to the community, Kappe has contributed much time to advocacy planning work. Some of the projects undertaken by his firm include helping to save Watts Towers, master planning the Watts Community Arts Center, and the design of the recreational facilities for Ramona Gardens, a public housing neighborhood in East Los Angeles. He was also instrumental in establishing the Barrio Planners, which began with a group of students from Cal Poly, Pomona.

From 1953 to 1968, Ray Kappe was in private practice. During this period he completed 40 residential, nine multiple-unit, and eight commercial projects. He then formed the partnership of Kahn-Kappe-Lotery-Boccato. The partners came together through their work on the AIA Urban Design Committee and their shared concerns for improving the environment through good planning and urban design. The planning work of the partnership includes master planning for a new town in Valencia; downtown rehabilitation plans for the cities of Inglewood, Compton, Santa Monica and Watts-Willowbrook; open space and park planning for Charmlee Park, in the Santa Monica Mountains; a conservation and land use plan for the City of San Clemente; a low-income 255-unit development in Pasadena; and a Downtown People Mover Study for the City of Los Angeles. The partnership also produced civic and commercial buildings for Inglewood, Beverly Hills and Santa Monica, as well as residential work which was always prevalent in the practice. Since 1981, the practice has continued under the name of Kappe Architects Planners.

In 1969, Ray Kappe was selected to be founding chairman of the new Department of Architecture at California State Polytechnic University at Pomona. He later pioneered a private, tuition-funded school, which became known as SCI-ARC, the Southern California Institute of Architecture. Kappe served as director at the school from 1972 to 1987. Established in a recycled industrial building in Santa Monica, SCI-ARC is a private, tuition-funded program with both its graduate and undergraduate programs accredited by the NAAB. The combined 75-member faculty and 450 students make up the SCI-ARC community. A year-round campus for European study has also been established in Vico Morcote, Switzerland, accommodating thirty students per semester. In addition, SCI-ARC has reached out to the community with evening programs for working people, a Design Forum, and weekly public lectures featuring local, national and international speakers. Professional approval of SCI-ARC has come in many forms. Kappe received the Topaz Medallion in 1970, the United States' highest award for excellence in architecture education, presented by the AIA and the Association of Collegiate Schools of Architecture. Additionally, Kappe and SCI-ARC were recognized with the first California Council AIA Excellence in Education Award and the Southern California Chapter AIA Award of Honor for development of the school plant, both awarded in 1976. The Southern California Council AIA Awards Jury found the SCI-ARC building "a most notable example of transforming an existing building (made originally of recycled materials) into a most lively and stimulating teaching environment, created by a group of highly motivated teachers and students — an ongoing design cycle based on empirical use of exploration."

Still committed to the original ideals of his architectural art form, Ray Kappe continues to build Southern California's dreams.

The Santa Monica Bus Administration Building

Ridgway Associates

riedrich Von Schelling once said, "architecture is frozen music." If this is true, then Ridgway Associates — a well respected and award winning architectural interior design firm — is a composer of world class architectural symphonies. Since 1985, Ridgway Associates has provided complete, professional architectural interior planning, design services, real estate related consulting, project management and financial cost evaluation to hundreds of clients located in Southern California and selected cities throughout the United States.

The founding principal, Patricia Ridgway and her associates represent over 15 million square feet of professional architectural interior design, space planning and project management as well as consulting services related to the commercial real estate industry they represent.

Since the firm's inception, Ridgway Associates has offered a full range of professional real estate-related services for commercial office tenants, as well as entertainment facilities including telecine centers, sound and viewing rooms, editing rooms and animation studios. The company has provided professional services for developers of office buildings, mixed use tilt-up type buildings, regional mall conversions, power centers, and warehouse conversions and renovations. Ridgway Associates has represented many financial institutions (headquarters and branch offices), and venture capital groups whose acquisitions require third party management, design and documentation. As well, this group converts hotel property into time shares, renovates existing hotels or assists in new con-

cepts for hotels, sports clubs and resorts. The company is well versed in creative design solutions for entertainment companies, corporate office facilities, professional firms, retail concepts and retail mall renovations, the hospitality industry and many other specialty occupant needs.

Ridgway's success has been fueled by a combination of entrepreneurial spirit and artistic vision, traits that have made Ridgway one of the most respected interior-architectural design firms in Southern California. Many design firms are content to simply duplicate past success, but Ridgway strives to create a unique product for each client. Whether it's a Class A high-rise project in Century City or Downtown L.A., a campus-style environment for a studio in Burbank, or the conversion of retail space into office space in the suburbs of Los Angeles, Ridgway designs reflect the personality of each client. The company designs offices that are distinct yet functional, artistic yet efficient.

"One day we'll be working on a biotech or high-tech client's interior architecture within a tilt-up concrete building that's built or being built, and at the same time we're remodeling a chain of hotels and restaurants or sports clubs or medical suites," says Patricia Ridgway. "You never know what opportunity will come through the door."

Born and raised in Los Angeles, Patricia studied interior architecture, business and marketing at California State University, Long Beach and the Art Center College of Design in Pasadena. After spending several years in the architectural-interior design profession, she launched her own company, Ridgway Associates, becoming one of the youngest female owners in the business. Patricia approached her first client, 20th Century Fox, with an unusual proposal: complete satisfaction with her work or the project would be free. Fox awarded her a 40,000-square-foot architectural design project, which Patricia brought in on time and under budget. Her reputation as a creative force with an accountant discipline quickly increased her commissions, enabling Ridgway Associates to grow and prosper.

One of Ridgway Associates' many satisfied clients is the Los Angeles office of New York-based law firm Coudert Brothers. When the firm decided to relocate its office to the 19th and 20th floors of the Arco Center building in 1989, Coudert Brothers chose Ridgway Associates to design the new office. Ridgway was given creative license to develop a bold signature design for Coudert Brothers.

"We chose to retire the typically conservative law firm look and acquire distinction through proportions, lines, quality materials and contemporary artwork and furnishings," says Patricia. "We let the stairway set the tone." Indeed, the design's focal point is the striking custom-built anigre wood staircase — a harlequin pattern of light and dark contrasting veneer accented with etched glass panels. This theme is repeated throughout the office with custom flooring coverings and furnishings. Equally important in the design of Coudert Brothers offices was the overall "efficient functionality" necessary for an international law practice that is frequently open around the clock. Space planning took into account employee comfort and easy access to important functions such as the legal library, central filing and duplicating equipment.

The result of Ridgway Associates' efforts is an office that offers a well established look with contemporary style. And Ridgway brought the project in nearly $500,000 under budget, an impressive achievement.

Ridgway welcomes the challenge of working with a new client. With the ever-changing corporate landscape and technological advances, Ridgway Associates are experts at creating an environment that is both functional and aesthetically pleasing. And with today's workforce spending as much time at the office as they do at home, a friendly, inviting and comfortable work ambiance is essential to both productivity and employee moral. Ridgway strives to create that type of ambiance in every project.

Among the lengthy list of satisfied Ridgway clients are such companies as Alliance Insurance, U.S.A.; American Express Travel; the Bank of California; Brentwood Country Club; The California Endowment; Cineplex Odeon; Coopers & Lybrand; File-Net Services; Fulwider, Patton, Lee & Utecht; HomeBase,

Inc.; Jones, Lang, Wootton, U.S.A.; Kaye, Scholer; Los Angeles County Employee Retirement Services (LACERS); Metrolink; Metropolitan Life; Obayash Corporation; PacTel; The Prudential; Public Storage; Sakura Finetek, Inc.; Sullivan & Cromwell; Think New Ideas; Transamerica Occidental; Upper Crust Restaurant and Windswept Pacific. Ridgway projects range from multi million dollar entertainment facilities, hospitality chain expansions, corporate headquarters, law firms, accounting firms, educational facilities, State of California projects, City of Los Angeles projects, sports clubs and many others.

Ridgway Associates is consistently listed in the top Women Owned Businesses in Los Angeles, as well as in the Top Interior Architecture Design Firms. Patricia Ridgway is a contributor to the Downtown L.A. YMCA and the Los Angeles Area Council Boy Scouts of America. She is a member of Who's Who of Leading American Executives, the Jonathan Club, The City Club on Bunker Hill, and the California Certified Interior Design Council. She received the Distinguished Alumni of the Year Award for 1998 from California State University, Long Beach, and contributes regularly to a variety of charities, schools and churches.

Ridgway Associates — designing today's office for tomorrow's American-based businesses and their team members.

TROOP STEUBER PASICH
REDDICK & TOBEY, LLP

Preemptive Growth

Troop Steuber Pasich Reddick & Tobey, LLP is among the largest and fastest growing business law firms in California. The firm has an outstanding reputation for technical excellence and exceptional responsiveness, as well as for creating and implementing innovative solutions to complex transactions and business disputes.

Founded in 1975 by an entrepreneurial team of four attorneys, the firm's practice has grown to 156 lawyers offering expertise in 22 categories of business law. The firm's exceptional growth propelled a relocation in 1998 from its longstanding home in Westwood to its new 137,500-square-foot quarters in the Twin Towers in Century City, Los Angeles.

Driven by Clients' Needs

The key to the firm's success is pursuing a highly focused practice development strategy, concentrating on defined areas of business law that specifically address the needs of Troop's dynamic clientele; fast-tracking new ventures, high growth middle-market companies, and leading privately held and publicly traded companies. The firm serves Fortune 500 companies with its niche expertise in insurance coverage, entertainment finance and litigation, and specialty finance law.

Troop evaluates the quality of services rendered in terms of the contribution made to supporting client growth and meeting client objectives. Partners continually review their portfolio of offered services, and hone their expertise to address changing complex legal issues. They maintain close, ongoing dialogue with clients to learn and respond to client preferences for the delivery of needed services.

A paramount importance is placed on human resource development and management. The firm is well regarded for the academic credentials and highly focused expertise of its lawyers. Many of Troop's attorneys have graduated at or near the top of their classes from the nation's leading law

schools and were members of Law Review and/or Order of the Coif. To ensure the highest quality representation and work product, the firm supports an extensive continuing education program for its attorney staff.

The firm also invests heavily in support staff development and information technology to keep the entire organization efficiently instep with the latest changes in legal and corporate practices. Professionalism and teamwork are enhanced by having all members of the firm housed in one centralized location. The common workplace facilitates efficient, close interaction among all attorneys and support staff members critical in managing complex transactions and disputes.

Transactional Expertise

Long regarded as having one of the leading business-transaction law practices in Southern California, Troop's **Business Department** represents clients ranging from start-up companies to large, multinational corporations. The Department's *Corporate and Securities* practice designs creative approaches to capitalize or recapitalize ventures and established companies in diverse market settings during all stages of their development.

Corporate and Securities attorneys are skilled in structuring, negotiating, and documenting virtually every form of corporate finance transaction. Recently, the firm's Corporate and Securities attorneys successfully represented a major media corporation in a milestone acquisition merger valued at more than $1.9 billion. These attorneys also represent clients in a wide variety of international transactions, including financing, licensing and joint ventures.

Over the years, the Business Department has expanded its expertise into a wider range of practice areas including Financial Services; Specialty Finance; Intellectual Property; Technology; Bankruptcy and Insolvency; and Tax, Estate, Probate, and Compensation Planning.

The **Entertainment Department** represents many of the major entertainment production and distribution companies in Hollywood, having developed one of the most respected Entertainment transaction law practices in the United States. Entertainment attorneys also represent numerous independent production companies and other institutional entertainment and media entities.

Troop's **Real Estate Department** represents many domestic and foreign institutional and noninstitutional developers and investors in connection with transactions involving all major project types including: residential (tract and condominium), commercial office, retail, medical office, strip center, raw land, agricultural, mini-warehouse and hospitality. Typical Real Estate Department services include legal representation in connection with acquisitions and dispositions, financing, leasing, joint ventures, syndications and other equity formation activities, tax advice and structuring, land use and environmental issues, hazardous construction and waste materials, title issues, workouts, development entitlements, project management and operations and construction contracts.

Dispute Resolution Expertise

Client-specified objectives also determine how dispute resolution matters are handled by **Litigation Department** attorneys. These attorneys have successfully represented numerous clients in a variety of complex litigation and arbitration matters before courts, administrative agencies and arbitration panels. Throughout the United States they aggressively pursue negotiation and settlement approaches whenever such options meet client-specified goals, optimize recovery, and effectively contain litigation costs.

The Litigation Department's vast experience in the courtroom offers clients a distinct advantage when their cases come to trial in any California or federal venue. These attorneys handle contested issues in Insurance Coverage; Risk Management; Labor and Employment, Environmental, Intellectual Property, Product Liability, Securities, Toxic Torts, White-Collar Crime, as well as General Business law.

With Hollywood as one of Los Angeles' major centers of commercial activity, the Litigations Department's *Entertainment Litigation* practice concentrates on representing institutional entertainment companies across a full range of arbitration and litigation matters, through trial and appeal, in both state and federal courts. Entertainment Litigation attorneys provide preventive counseling and representation in disputes concerning motion picture and television program finance; development; production; domestic and international distribution; intellectual property (copyrights, trademarks, idea submission, and misappropriation, and licensing); mergers and acquisitions; tax; employment and labor; risk management; and insurance coverage.

Going into the next millennium, *Troop Steuber Pasich Reddick & Tobey, LLP* will continue to tailor its portfolio of services and pool of expertise to maximize the firm's key value proposition — business law counseling and representation to support client growth and strategic development needs.

WESTERN EXTERMINATOR COMPANY

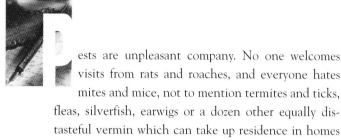

ests are unpleasant company. No one welcomes visits from rats and roaches, and everyone hates mites and mice, not to mention termites and ticks, fleas, silverfish, earwigs or a dozen other equally distasteful vermin which can take up residence in homes and commercial establishments. Getting rid of these unwelcome visitors isn't easy, and it's best to place the problem in the hands of an experienced expert. That's why more than 600,000 people a year call for help from The Little Man with the Hammer. He's been on the job since 1921.

The Little Man with the Hammer is the lovable logo representing Western Exterminator Company. The top-hatted, tailcoated gentleman with a mighty mallet hiding behind his back serves notice on a malicious mouse that its existence is about to be extinguished. The image may be quaint but the message is deadly serious. When it comes to pests, Western Exterminator means business. And business is booming for this family-owned company which started work when the 20s were just roaring in.

Back in 1921, Carl Strom was a scrappy young Swede, just 25 years old. He was born in Stockholm in 1896 and christened Romeo Alphonso Benedino Anselmo Zetterstrom, but Carl Strom worked better in America which is where the enterprising youth arrived in 1914 after four years at sea. He got a job in a Brooklyn ammunition factory and later joined the army, earning his citizenship from serving in World War I. After the war, he headed out West, stopping first in Akron, Ohio where he sold rubber goods for Firestone Rubber. He moved on to California and arrived in San Pedro with only one shoe to his name. Luckily, he found a job at Darby Pest Control.

Strom worked for Darby for a brief time before he decided he could do the job better on his own. He had $25 worth of chemicals and a headful of sound ideas: service, safety and efficiency. Strom believed passionately in personal service and made the concept the cornerstone of his business. His customers appreciated his polite and efficient eradication of their unwelcome guests, and soon his business was growing rapidly. By 1929, he had added employees and two partners: his brother-in-law, Guy Raymond Lovejoy and Ray's brother-in-law, Oscar William Dickens.

The Little Man became part of the team in 1931 when the Yellow Pages suggested that Western Exterminator advertise to increase its sales. Vaughn Kaufman worked for the telephone company and created the logo which became Western's registered trademark. The logo went through several names, from The Little Man with the Hammer to Kernel Kleenup to Inspector Holmes. But none of them caught on quite like The Little Man, and it's The Little Man who represents a very big exterminator company today.

During the decade of the 30s, Western Exterminator's business continued to grow, and in 1936 new headquarters were built on Beverly Boulevard. Nine years later, the company opened its first branch office in Oakland. The early 50s continued the firm's steady growth. In 1952 Western Exterminator became a privately held corporation and expanded its pest control services to include termite inspections, eradication and repair as well as construction services. That same year, having outgrown its previous office space, the company built its landmark headquarters on Temple Street with the Little Man occupying a large sign overlooking drivers on the busy Hollywood Freeway. Five years later, the first fleet of trademark bright yellow trucks was purchased.

The unexpected deaths of Western Exterminator partners Lovejoy and Dickens left Carl Strom in charge of the rapidly growing company. He continued to build the business and to emphasize his commitment to cus-

Pictured is Western's Flagship office on West Temple Street, Los Angeles, overlooking the Hollywood Freeway, taken in 1957.

tomer service and remained at the helm of Western Exterminator until his own untimely death in an airplane accident in 1961. Subsequently, his wife Daisy became chairman of the board, his nephew John Anderson became president, his son Robert Strom became vice president and his nephew Richard Lovejoy became secretary/treasurer.

During the 60s, nine more branch offices were added. By 1972, Western had expanded to Arizona and counted 350 people on its payroll. In 1973, having grown too large to concentrate all its operations in one location, Western separated the corporate headquarters from the service center office. The service center remained on the Hollywood Freeway in Los Angeles while the corporate staff moved to Orange County. During the 70s and 80s, Western's business doubled every five years. By the end of the 90s, the company employed more than 900 people in 30 separate locations in California, Arizona and Nevada.

All members of the Western Exterminator team work with a "we care" attitude which was inherited from its enthusiastic founder and continues to be the foundation of the company's solid reputation. Western's mission is to exceed its customers' expectations by focusing on their unique pest problems and making sure that the job is done properly. In a competitive market, Western keeps its edge by maintaining its commitment to satisfying the customer. It guarantees satisfaction or the customer doesn't pay, and Western makes it right. As a result, it is the largest family-owned pest control company in the West, and nationally it is ranked as one of the top companies within the industry. Standing behind its philosophy that service sells, Western has watched some customers defect to the competition, only to welcome them back when the service fell short.

In 1985, Western developed a unique Integrated Pest Eradication Program, designed especially for the food, beverage and hospitality industry. Its success has been the result of its high standard of service. Western works in compliance with county sanitation regulations and provides treatment procedures to keep restaurants free from pest infestations. In order that the client's business will not be disrupted, service is rendered after hours. The service includes immediate corrective measures, follow-up procedures and recommendations for further cleaning and repairs to reduce the risk of future problems.

Western gets the job done with its staff of highly trained technicians and a dedicated office staff. The training program is ongoing and extremely rigorous. The result is committed employees, many of them second and third generation, who make a significant contribution to customer satisfaction. In addition to its team of field technicians, Western Exterminator has a Training and Technical Division with staff entomologists and environmental health specialists who keep the company abreast of the development of treatment techniques and materials and in compliance with regulatory agencies.

Technology has changed dramatically since the days when Carl Strom began his business in a small store front with a handful of chemicals. However, customer expectations of quality service and satisfaction have not changed. Western Exterminator has grown and changed with the times but has never changed its simple, basic philosophy: The customer is always its first priority. Western is still owned and operated by the second and third generations of the family that founded it in 1921 and continues to live up to its tradition of delivering the best possible service at a competitive price. Among its employees, the family nurtures a spirit of pride and affection which is exceptional in today's business world. In return, Western Exterminator has earned an unprecedented degree of loyalty from both its employees and its customers. The Little Man has good reason to be proud.

Pictured is Western's Flagship Service Center on the Hollywood Freeway, taken in 1997 when their 75th Anniversary banner was displayed.

CAREER STRATEGIES

issatisfied with the way the employment industry was perceived by the public, Darin Rado and Michael Bourdon embarked on an entrepreneurial endeavor many believed was "against all odds" of succeeding.

Company founder Darin Rado (seated, L), believes that "no business is any better than the people who run it. For that reason, I believe our success lies in the fact that we have the best talent pool internally."

In 1989, the pair entered an already oversaturated market and started their own full-service personnel placement firm supporting clients with full time temporary and contract-to-hire personnel.

With a single employee and a small 1,100-square-foot office, Rado and Bourdon launched an "aggressive marketing campaign" to attract clients in a variety of different areas, including the administrative, financial, legal, long-term health care and information technology industries.

Their once fledgling firm has since emerged as an industry leader in employment solutions by working under a high ethical standard of providing the highest level of quality service, offering clients employment strategies with options and delivering the best qualified candidate for each client's individual employment needs.

Career Strategies understands that employment industry is built around people and prides itself on being a "personal personnel service."

Operating from a expansive 8,000-square-foot facility with 85 in-house employees, Career Strategies understands that employment industry is built around people and prides itself on being a "personal personnel service."

With offices in Los Angeles, West Los Angeles, Woodland Hills, Irvine, Westlake Village and Phoenix, Arizona, the company founders credit the firm's success to date to a team of "highly motivated, entrepreneurial men and women who recognize the responsibility of working with the careers of its candidates and the staffing objectives of its clients."

"I've always believed the best way to manage a business is from the bottom up rather than from the

top down," says Rado, company chairman and CEO. "No business is any better than the people who run it. For that reason, I believe our success lies in the fact that we have the best talent pool internally."

Career Strategies prides itself on offering its clients unparalleled customer service and productivity. The company's own employee turnover rate is nearly nonexistent, which means that clients will invariably deal with the same person, which in turn results in speed and accuracy of future searches.

The company's sophisticated QWIZ computer testing system analyzes a candidate's knowledge of a software package by the correct implementation of its functions. Other commonly administered evaluations range from speed typing, statistical typing, ten-key and data entry to a wide range of computer software programs.

Career Strategies' clients are guaranteed the best-qualified person for a particular position, rather than merely the best person reading the want ads.

With regard to regular hires, Career Strategies regularly networks for referrals with industry contacts and targets recruiting through prospective industries, locations and candidates while keeping in mind the nature, scope, responsibilities, accountabilities and interface relationships specific to each client.

Career Strategies Technical Services Group identifies and qualifies top-notch Information Technology professionals who consistently update and educate themselves on current technology trends and industry standards.

The fact that over 80 percent of the firm's sales comes from repeat business speaks volumes about its philosophy. At Career Strategies, the "personal" approach in the employment industry can make a tremendous difference in its client's business.

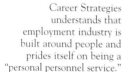

JOE ORTIZ & ASSOCIATES

s one of the first Latinos to emerge in both print and broadcast media, Joe Ortiz made a name for himself — not only in the Latino community, but throughout the entire Los Angeles area. He then parlayed this experience into a successful career in public relations, forming his own company in 1988.

Since opening a modest office in downtown Los Angeles, Joe Ortiz & Associates (JOA) has grown from a $1,500 per month company to a business that grosses $20,000 to $25,000 per month. Ortiz's client roster includes sports figures and celebrities, large corporations and small companies. He has developed and implemented major publicity campaigns for various authors and numerous community organizations, such as the Make-A-Wish Foundation, the Boy Scouts of America and the Manny Mota International Foundation.

Born in Southern California's Coachella Valley, Ortiz has always been ambitious. His drive, coupled with intelligence and a naturally effusive personality, led him into the heady worlds of politics, media and entertainment. Eventually, he'd work in broadcasting, but before that he held various community and public relations positions, including job agent for the California State Employment Development Department and administrative assistant to Los Angeles City Councilman John Ferraro.

"Mine has been kind of a dual career," Ortiz explains, "between social services and media, and the media I landed in by accident." In 1971, Ortiz fell into radio broadcasting. A friend had encouraged him to drop by KABC-AM 79. Assuming he'd be a guest, Ortiz inadvertently auditioned for the show, reading a short commercial that led to a position hosting the 9:00 a.m. to 2:00 p.m. show.

Ortiz left KABC in 1972 and pursued opportunities as a radio and television talk show host at KLOS-FM, KCBS (then KNXT) Television and KPFK-FM Radio. By the late 1980s he was hosting the "Prime Time with Joe Ortiz" show on KPPC-AM in Pasadena and KPZE-AM in Anaheim.

Along the way, Ortiz became involved in promoting a more positive image and lifestyle for Los Angeles Latinos, touting such causes as antidrug and antigang programs. He says he became an unofficial spokesperson for his community, meanwhile gaining clients as his network continued to broaden.

Joe Ortiz began his career at KABC TALK RADIO 79.

He secures clients through word-of-mouth and specializes in promoting campaigns that encourage corporate responsibility — either to the community, to education, or to social services. His client roster includes the Johnnie Walker Black Label, Miller Brewing Company and Southland Corp. (7-Eleven Stores).

Ortiz works smart by keeping overhead costs down. He works at home and largely subcontracts with a variety of caterers, graphic designers, photographers and web site specialists. He also employs a small staff to help him with JOA's myriad of media-related services.

As president of JOA, Ortiz can call on corporate entities to sponsor special events to raise funds for many community-based groups. He is often called upon by them to market their products and services to Latino and other ethnic markets throughout the world. He is likely to be found promoting special events such as golf tournaments featuring many celebrities and sports personalities like Tom Flores, Jim Plunkett and Manny Mota, or providing press for celebrities like Rita Moreno, Arnold Schwarzenegger and Milton Berle. Then again, he might be found coordinating media appearances and developing network and sponsorship packages for First Brother Roger Clinton, a close friend and current client.

When at KABC, Joe interviewed many celebrities, including the child stars of the television series, "Harry & The Hendersons."

CAROL HALL & ASSOCIATES

oday, when a client hires a public relations and event management company, that client expects professional, cost-effective and efficient results. Carol Hall & Associates provide more than results; they guarantee "peace of mind." Let Carol Hall worry about your public relations campaign or event, so you won't have to. It's the attention to detail and quest for quality that sets Carol Hall & Associates apart from other consulting firms. Much of the company's philosophy and culture stems from owner Carol Hall, who spent 16 years as a broadcast journalist in cities throughout the United States.

A St. Louis, Missouri native, Carol Hall spent most of her broadcasting career on the East Coast. She moved to Los Angeles in 1984, while working as a reporter for a nationally syndicated television news magazine show. The following year, Carol chose to capitalize on her broadcasting experience by opening her own boutique consulting agency, Carol Hall & Associates, specializing in corporate, public, community relations and marketing outreach services. The firm also provides corporate internal and external event management services, corporate publications, and presentations and speeches. Carol Hall & Associates functions as a virtual company, with a professional team of writers, photographers, meeting facilitators, audio/ video producers, graphic designers and other specialists on call for any client-need or size project.

Carol Hall
Photo By Pat Olear

Carol Hall focuses on corporate clients in traditional businesses, such as Sempra Energy-Southern California Gas Company, Shell Oil Company, Union Bank of California and Southwest Gas Corporation of Las Vegas. The firm specializes in issues of diversity and utility deregulation. Her company's varied client list also includes the Center Theatre Group, The Ahmanson and Mark Taper Forum, American Association of Blacks in Energy, Los Angeles Chapter and Bread for the World. Carol Hall's television news experience gives her special expertise and ability to synthesize complex information and to disseminate it creatively and effectively to consumers.

A longtime and regular client, Southern California Gas Company, uses Carol Hall for a number of special projects, including corporate newsletters, advertising and market consulting, and event planning and management. When a SCGC manager scheduled a board development session for the Southern California Regional Purchasing Council (SCRPC), Carol Hall was brought in to oversee the entire two-day event. From writing the invitation letter to the catered meals to drafting the opening remarks, Carol Hall's supervision ensured the event went off without a hitch. She produces events as if they were television news shows, audience-driven. Lighting, setting, words, audio and visual aspects of an event are plotted in script form, encompassing the entire day's speeches, remarks and activities. Carol Hall also provides special touches that often go unnoticed yet add to the success of any event. At a meeting site, Carol will inspect the facility, order decorative flowers, have carpets shampooed, paint touched up, even have trash picked up around the approach to a meeting site. Clients remember her attention to detail — most of Carol Hall & Associates' clients are repeat or referral customers.

An alumnus of Stephens College and graduate programs at Columbia University School of Journalism, UCLA Anderson School of Management and Dartmouth's Tuck School of Business, Carol Hall was named the SCRPC, Inc. 1997 Class One Supplier of the Year, and is a member of the 1997 Leadership California Issues Forum. Carol Hall holds membership in the Los Angeles Area Chamber of Commerce and the League of Allied Arts. A Girl Scout Co-Leader, Carol Hall is active in her church and in several community organizations.

HELLER EHRMAN WHITE & McAULIFFE

When Emanuel S. Heller opened his law offices in 1890 in the heart of San Francisco's financial district, Los Angeles was still considered a dusty ranching town.

During the next three decades, many things changed. Los Angeles became the second largest city in the country, Heller's practice and prestige grew and lawyers were added to the firm's roster. The name changed several times to reflect the addition or deletion of partners and, in 1921, the firm name became Heller Ehrman White & McAuliffe and has remained unchanged to this day.

The firm's long history in California has allowed it to grow side-by-side with some of the most important companies in the state and in the nation. Heller Ehrman's practice now reflects the extraordinary diversity of its clients who grew and prospered as California became a dominant force in manufacturing, financial services, retail, trade and technology.

From its historical base in Northern California, Heller Ehrman expanded into Southern California by opening a Los Angeles office in 1988. Starting with three locally prominent litigators, Heller Ehrman's Los Angeles office grew rapidly in the highly competitive environs of Southern California.

Today, areas of focus that continue to drive the expansion of the Los Angeles office include representation of accountants, financial institutions, and entrepreneurial entities such as high tech, life sciences, multimedia and entertainment companies of all sizes. The office's representation of clients ranges from corporate counseling, taking companies public, securities, selling and acquiring businesses, to labor and employment, insurance, and general corporate litigation.

Heller Ehrman's Los Angeles office is proud of its long tradition to communities and to those who need legal services, but cannot afford it. Recently, the firm has been involved with leading the charge to secure payment to Holocaust victims and their ancestors of

long-forgotten insurance policies. The office has also received several awards from organizations such as CARECEN in recognition of its work on behalf of the rights of Central American immigrants in the United States and United Way for raising a substantial amount of donations. Additionally, attorneys in the Los Angeles office and offices firm-wide, contribute thousands of hours each year to community, nonprofit and public interest organizations.

Consistently ranked as one of the 60 largest law firms in the United States, the firm has more than 400 attorneys practicing in eleven major commercial centers at home and abroad. The firm's vibrant, cutting-edge practice on behalf of its clients is matched by its exceptional record of service to the public.

As the firm moves forward through its second century, it looks ahead to expanding the service it provides and to continuing the tradition of excellent service begun over a century ago.

Pictured in Heller Ehrman's downtown Los Angeles office are (clockwise): Nancy Sher Cohen, managing partner of the firm's Los Angeles office; Wayne Braveman, partner; Raymond Fischer, former partner and current Associate Attorney General; and Victor Hebert, partner.

PARTNERS IN LOS ANGELES
QUALITY OF LIFE

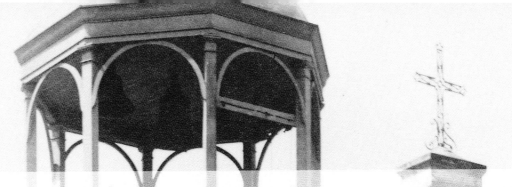

Medical, educational, social and religious institutions make significant contributions to the quality of life enjoyed by Los Angeles area residents and visitors.

t would be difficult to accurately depict the history of The City of Los Angeles without including the story of at least one other city. City of Hope National Medical Center and Beckman Research Institute is an integral part of Los Angeles and all of Southern California, as well as a compassionate innovator to the entire global medical community.

From humble and heroic beginnings, City of Hope has become one of the most advanced medical and research facilities in the world. The lives of millions of people around the globe are touched daily and made better by the activities that take place on this more than 100-acre campus.

City of Hope also has the distinction of being a National Cancer Institute-Designated Comprehensive Cancer Center. At these centers, physicians and scientists, who are among the finest in their fields, perform the latest diagnostic procedures and help set the pace nationally for overall cancer research, treatment, education and prevention.

Currently, full-time faculty members representing every department and division at the City of Hope National Medical Center and Beckman Research Institute comprise the City of Hope Cancer Center. Together, they are working to discover, develop and implement new strategies and treatments to fight cancer and were among the first in the nation to recognize the value of a multidisciplinary approach to patient care. This approach includes a full spectrum of services by clinical experts in hematology, oncology, surgery, diagnostic radiology, pathology, pediatrics and radiation oncology.

Every activity at City of Hope is guided by this credo that is enshrined on a gate within the rose garden in the International Garden of Meditation.

NCI-designated cancer centers are a select group of recognized leaders in the fight against cancer, each pledged to uphold the high standards set forth by the NCI. Recently, City of Hope's Cancer Center's core grant and designation were renewed by the NCI though the year 2000, representing continuous federal funding of cancer research programs at City of Hope since 1976.

The renowned City of Hope staff have created treatments for more than 200 forms of cancer, including leukemia, breast and prostrate cancer, as well as diabetes and other life-threatening illnesses. It is a world leader in the bone marrow transplant procedure and is engaged in ongoing research to unlock the secret of Alzheimer's disease, HIV/AIDS and many genetic and hereditary disorders.

Humble, Inspired Beginnings

City of Hope has risen to its current stature from humble beginnings that speak to the ongoing depth of its mission and commitment to outstanding, compassionate patient care.

Tuberculosis was the dreaded plague of the early 1900s and medical science had no cure. Many came to Southern California believing the hot dry climate would help them get better. They often came in vain and died sick and penniless on the streets because hospitals were full and would accept no more patients.

Some, who could find no aid and no shelter, took their own lives rather than suffer the slow, painful wasting away that is the nature of tuberculosis. One such victim was a tailor from St. Louis who was found on a summer morning in 1912 with only his watch, his thimble and a suicide note.

The soul of the downtown Los Angeles community was touched by this tragic death. It seemed to symbolize the hopelessness and desperation that were such a part of the times. A group of merchants and neighbors paid for the tailor's funeral and vowed to raise whatever funds were necessary to provide care for their brothers and sisters who could not afford to take care of themselves.

The vow promised to nurture and protect the right of people to health care regardless of race, creed or place of birth. That was the beginning of the Jewish Consumptive Relief Association of Southern California that held its first meeting on Sunday, September 28, 1912 in the Los Angeles Music Hall.

A gathering of City of Hope staff in the late 1940s.

Thirty-five men and women met and drafted a constitution that stated: *"We do hereby bond ourselves together and organize for the purpose of raising funds and establishing suitable quarters for the aid, cure and comfort of our brothers and sisters with tuberculosis."*

It was a month later when more than 100 people met and contributed a total of $136.06. A realtor came and told the group about 10 acres of land available for $5,000 in the Duarte desert, which was just 25 miles northeast of Los Angeles. A fund-raising party, on February 19, 1913, brought in the $2,400 needed to open escrow and the group, which had grown to more than 1,500 people, purchased the desert site.

On January 11, 1914, two tents were erected at Duarte. One housed the first three patients and the other, a nurse and medical supplies. Initially, food and water were brought in once a week by wagon and the actual sanatorium opened a few weeks before the ordinance went into effect.

Within a year, the sanatorium had a resident physician and the first of many wooden cottages to house patients and staff. The working men and women of Los Angeles — and their unions — were the prime early supporters of City of Hope.

Donations from the Workmen's Circle Branch 248, the Amalgamated Clothing Workers of America and the International Ladies Garment Workers helped move the sanatorium from tents to cottages to stucco buildings. So also did the donations that began coming in from other parts of the country from individuals who banded together to form auxiliaries in what has come to be called a "people's movement."

That movement has continued for more than eight decades and City of Hope has continued to adhere to the values of compassion, innovation, integrity, respect, teamwork and social responsibility in the quest for unequaled patient care and advancements in medical science.

An Outstanding, Ongoing Tradition in Research

A healing setting has been created for the more than 250 highly skilled and internationally respected physicians and scientists who work together at City of Hope. Their work is carried out by two unified, but separate, organizations — City of Hope National Medical Center and Beckman Research Institute — and is supported by a network of volunteer fund-raisers and donors in regional offices nationwide.

The Beckman Research Institute was established in 1983 in recognition of generous support from the Arnold and Mabel Beckman Foundation that brought together the numerous research groups that had evolved since 1951, when a laboratory research program was initiated.

The far-reaching influence of the Beckman Research Institute is legendary. Today, discoveries by City of Hope scientists continue to lay the groundwork for significant medical advances increasing the effectiveness of chemotherapy, bone marrow transplantation, radioimmunotherapy and potential gene therapy for cancer and other diseases. Among their many significant research landmarks are:

This nonsectarian facility underscores its philosophy in a formal mission statement: City of Hope, inspired and supported by a philanthropic volunteer movement, is dedicated to the prevention, treatment and cure of cancer and other life-threatening diseases through innovative research and patient care.

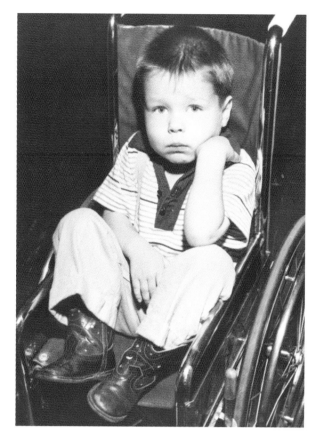

- *Developed Humulin, or human insulin* grown outside the human body, and ensured the production of unlimited quantities of synthetic insulin and reduced the costs for people with diabetes worldwide. It was the first product resulting from recombinant DNA research to be approved for use in the United States by the Food and Drug Administration and was an outgrowth of the collaboration of a City of Hope-Genetech, Inc. team

- *Developed a process* to produce human growth hormone outside the body from bacteria — helping to restore pituitary function in children who have undergone cancer treatments.

- *Developed the theory of evolution* by gene duplication, which explained how new genes develop and is the basis of much biological research.

- *Demonstrated that a unique chromosome* found only in females, was an inactivated X chromosome and helped to initiate the entire field of research on control of gene regulation.

- *Studying the combined use of high-dose chemotherapy and stem cell rescue* for the treatment of high-risk breast cancer — to date, reducing the chance of relapse by 50 percent.

- *Created an antibody* to detect a tumor-associated marker that can be detected in approximately 95 percent of all colon cancers, as well as cancers of the breast, lung, thyroid and ovary.

- *Devised a technique* that allows scientists to amplify and detect minute quantities of genetic material, significantly improving genetic research.

- *Developed a strategy* for minimizing the risk of CMV intestinal pneumonia in patients receiving donor-derived bone marrow transplantation (BMT). In the past, 15-25 percent of the individuals worldwide who underwent BMT developed this form of pneumonia and most died.

- *Developed genetic probes* that can distinguish between certain types of leukemia and aid in proper diagnosis by administering the proper treatment regimens.

- *Demonstrated how convulsive seizures* may be controlled chemically, which led to the use of a new agent for the treatment of epilepsy.

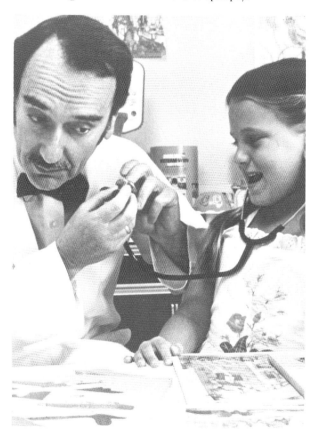

- *Designed a protector* for use with needles, thus shielding health care workers from accidental needle sticks with potentially infected needles.

A Vibrant People-Centered Philosophy

But whether it is a revolutionary research discovery or day-to-day business of providing unsurpassed patient care and treatment, at the heart of all City of Hope activities is the credo or philosophy of hope often expressed by Samuel H. Golter, who served as City of Hope executive director from 1926-1953.

That philosophy is inscribed on a gate leading to City of Hope's International Garden of Meditation and reads: There is no profit in curing the body, if in the process we destroy the soul.

Every activity at City of Hope is guided by that philosophy and driven by the belief that healing does not come about by a new treatment or drug alone, but also by the caring and compassion that a patient receives. City of Hope was one of the first medical centers to establish a dedicated social services department to address patients' emotional, spiritual and social well being in addition to their physical care.

Just a few examples of the human values that make City of Hope truly unique in the area of patient care include:

- The Positive Image Center that is designed to help individuals regain their confidence and cope with many of the stress factors resulting from surgery and the side effects of chemotherapy. In a private setting patients meet with hair and skin specialists to discuss options available to help them re-enter the world as they saw themselves before their disease.
- City of Hope's on-site residential communities Hope Village and Parsons Village were built to allow members of the patient's family to remain close to their loved ones undergoing extended treatment. They also house patients who need to be monitored before being completely discharged.
- City of Hope is a national leader in pain management and recognizes that pain is more than just a physical issue. The Pain Resource Nurse Training

Another testament to the longstanding efforts of City of Hope to eradicate cancer and in doing so, ease the plight of children victimized by the disease.

Program, the first of its kind in the United States, was developed by City of Hope and is now used in medical centers nationwide.

- A variety of extensive counseling and psychosocial support services are available through the department of Clinical Social Work. This team of highly trained oncology social workers provides short-term and crisis counseling, support groups, patient/family conferences, housing and other needs.

This focus on the total well-being of the individual requires a that a careful balance be maintained between advanced treatments and humanitarian values. These values are embodied in City of Hope's Torchbearer's Creed, written by Ben Horowitz who served as executive director from 1953-1986 and presented at a national meeting of volunteers.

Torchbearer's Creed

We bear witness to individual worth and human dignity. Our stress on the sacredness of man, formed in God's image, repudiates cynicism that "life is cheap." If our concept is fully accepted, could there be wars to snuff out lives, dictatorship to enslave people, bigotry, crimes of violence and greed?

We bear witness to the necessity of enhancing the personality of the human being. This is an age of conformity and everyone is being forced into a common mold. We reject the mass man and insist on bringing out the richness of genius, of dissent, of differences. The American heritage takes pride in the principle of "e pluribus Unum" — unity in diversity. In this fashion, we bring out the finest potential in every person. Self-realization and self-fulfillment will assure the maximum contribution to our culture and society.

We bear witness that democracy, properly organized and intelligently directed, can develop a large reservoir of leadership. Democracy is becoming a faceless thing, a mere matter of counting noses, which encourages the "one leader cult." Organizations like City of Hope must resist this trend, making it possible for people to be somebodies in a world of nobodies.

We bear witness to the responsibility of each of us to be out "brother's keeper." This means more than the social obligation of rescuing those plunged from the bright sunshine of health into the despairing darkness of disease. It involves a framework of social justice, emphasizing our larger social responsibility and man's humanity to man.

We bear witness that life can be lived to the full only by giving more fully of ourselves. Many people are lonely because they build walls around themselves, rather than brides to others. We affirm that to "love thy neighbor as thy self" is as important for the one who gives love as the one who receives it.

We bear witness that the resources of mankind be mobilized for constructive and not destructive purposes. "Atoms for life" has been a City of Hope theme for many years, and it symbolizes our conviction that the wealth and talents of man should be directed to the advancement of the sum total of human welfare.

We bear witness that spiritual values and humanitarian impulses must guide our everyday lives. Today, people have lost their moorings and drift aimlessly, living empty lives. City of Hope offers a creed that gives life a purpose and each day a meaning.

A Vision for the Future

This overall City of Hope philosophy — which includes a concern for quality of life for the entire person and his or her loved ones — takes into account diversity of culture and community and its importance in the healing process. It is an ideology that carries into the community, reaching out through support groups, chaplaincy training workshops, public and professional education seminars and ethical dialogues examining new directions being taken in health care, as well as in scientific research.

City of Hope has been called "the most democratic philanthropy in the world" and its volunteers the most essential group in the organization's structure. From the 35 founders to the 40 auxiliaries that existed in 1933 to the nearly 500 chapters in more than 200 cities in 32 states today, the growth and strength of City of Hope has been concentrated not in its organizational charts, but in the caliber of the men and women who serve as volunteers.

About 40 percent of City of Hope's annual operating budget is derived from volunteer efforts. Each auxiliary is autonomous, with no effort made by City of Hope to impose conformity. Each group sends delegates based on fund-raising quotas, to a biennial convention in Los Angeles. Between conventions, an elected board of directors, whose volunteer members are drawn from all parts of the country, oversees the organization's progress.

By fueling the efforts of cutting-edge research and treatment, these donors and volunteers are the backbone that helps City of Hope continue to turn laboratory discoveries into effective treatments that will save lives around the world. A unique quality of City of Hope is how research studies are translated into clinical research that quickly becomes innovative treatment.

City of Hope advancements attract people from around the world who are impressed by the compassionate caring of everyone they meet. All staff members possess that intangible spirit that contributes to a reputation as an institution that provides the highest level of progressive, quality patient care.

As City of Hope moves toward the millennium, it has developed a businesses-oriented operational plan that will guide future expansion to keep up with the ongoing needs of research and medical care. New and renovated facilities will make it possi-

ble to continue critical programs, as well as increase outpatient services to meet projected needs.

This vision will be accomplished through the same credo that built City of Hope from two tents in the desert into one of the leading medical institutions in the world: people helping people.

James E. Vaughn, Ph.D., Research Scientist and Chair, Division of Neurosciences (left), working with Robert Barber, senior research associate, Division of Neurosciences.

HEALTH NET

ccess to affordable, quality health care is of concern to everyone, and in California, more and more employers and consumers are choosing Health Net as their managed care provider. Since 1977, Health Net has grown from a small, nonprofit subsidiary to California's third largest managed care plan. Health Net's growth rate has been sure and steady, guided by its focused strategy aimed at offering its members access, affordability and accountability. Other health care plans talk about quality and availability. Health Net lives by them. It's a managed care company with a people point of view.

The company's human touch often begins with the reassuring voice at the other end of Health Net's Health Line. Whenever members are ill, troubled or confused about their health care options, they can make a telephone call that will be answered by a registered nurse who will listen and advise. From that initial call, a plan of action is put in place, and the appropriate care is determined. It might be as simple as taking an aspirin and checking in again the next morning or as complex as a visit to the emergency room. All options are considered, and members always receive the right kind of help right when they need it.

It's this easy and personal access to health care advisors that is part of the high degree of overall satisfaction expressed by Health Net members.

Although it maintains 33 offices throughout California, Health Net's corporate headquarters is in Woodland Hills.

Members report satisfaction with both the plan and its network of physicians and hospitals, and the highest degree of satisfaction is expressed by those patients with chronic illnesses. More than 90 percent of patients suffering from chronic conditions have indicated satisfaction with the treatment they receive through Health Net. Not only are they satisfied, but they recommend Health Net to their friends and family.

It's a position the company intends to strengthen. Part of its strategy is based on building partnerships with physicians and hospitals. Another factor is a commitment to hiring and investing in outstanding employees. And a major part is actively listening to the concerns of its members. President and Chief Executive Officer of Health Net, Arthur Southam, M.D., says of the company's philosophy, "If I have one guiding principal for Health Net going forward, it is that we put our members first in everything we do and provide the highest quality services available." Thus Health Net offers access to preventive care, physician and outpatient services, hospitalization, pharmacy, mental health, chiropractic and acupuncture services.

Superior service has been a guiding force throughout Health Net's history. Founded in 1977, it was originally formed as a nonprofit pubic benefit corporation under the auspices of Blue Cross of California. A year later, Health Net was allowed to operate throughout California as a nonprofit hospital service plan covering approximately 50,000 people. In 1986, Health Net became the first health plan to offer infant car seats as part of its prenatal program. After ten years, more than 60,000 free infant seats were installed in the cars owned by Health Net members.

In 1992, Health Net converted from a nonprofit to a for-profit business status and included 900,000 people as members. Two years later, Health Net merged with QualMed, a Colorado-based company, creating a new parent company, Health Systems International, Inc. In that year, HSI included 1.6 million members, more than 2,000 employees and a network of 36,000 physicians and nearly 450 hospitals.

Health Net's Quality Initiative Division was created in 1995 for the purpose of creating innovative programs to improve the overall quality of patient care. The initiative resulted in Health Net's being awarded the prestigious C. Everett Koop National Health Award for outstanding programs for improving member health. That same year, Health Net received a one-year accreditation from the National Committee for Quality Assurance (NCQA), the independent, non-profit organization established to review the quality of the care and service of managed care plans.

Another surge in growth for Health Net occurred in 1997. Health Systems International merged with Foundation Health Corporation to create Health Net's new parent company, Foundation Health Systems (FHS), the nation's fourth-largest publicly traded health care company. Trading of FHS shares began on the New York Stock Exchange. Financial success did not impair the success of patient service, and once again, Health Net received a one-year accreditation from NCQA in honor of its superior care and service delivery systems.

In 1998 Foundation Health Systems received approval to merge Health Net and Foundation Health, which had been operating as separate California operations, under the name Health Net. Health Net became a California powerhouse, from San Diego County in the south to Humbolt County near the Oregon border. Dr. Southam credits the move with enabling Health

WellSite, Health Net's award-winning web site, is easy to access and contains a wealth of information for members and nonmembers alike.

Net to meet the needs of a much broader consumer base through a new medical program and individual plans. It also enabled Health Net to expand its geographical coverage. The move increased Health Net's membership in California to 2.3 million members in 50 counties, employed 3,600 people and projected revenues approaching $4 billion. Its vast network is the broadest geographic coverage of any health plan in the state and offers the widest choice of primary physicians. That same year Health Net was voted as one of the top two California health plans by the large insurance purchasing cooperative, the Pacific Business Group on Health (PBGH).

With such a high-profile presence in California's medical industry, Health Net is able to offer a product list that is among the most comprehensive in the state. It includes an HMO, two fully insured Preferred Provider Organizations (PPO), two Point of Service (POS) options, Medicare and MediCal. The goal of the varied portfolio is to provide the highest quality care and affordable benefit plans and to improve the health of the community. Health Net's list of options includes a number of integrated programs.

Health Net SELECT is a three-tier, POS program that serves as three plans in one by offering the traditional HMO and indemnity-like programs in addition to a PPO-like program that allows members to self-refer to the physician of their choice within the network. Health Net ELECT is an innovative, two-tiered POS program that includes the features of an HMO and allows members to seek care at any time from other doctors and specialists who are Health Net providers. FLEX NET is targeted to executives and employees or dependents who live outside of Health Net's service area.

Seniors get special attention from Health Net. The Health Net Seniority Plus program is a Medicare HMO product offering more comprehensive benefits then Medicare alone. It includes coverage for prescription drugs and eyeglasses, plus wellness and social outreach programs which are designed to meet the unique needs of older adults.

Small businesses are eligible for Health Net Options. This is a PPO choice for small business groups with two to 50 employees. Under this program, members are allowed to self-refer to the Health Net PPO Network physician of their choice and access out-of-network benefits, including the privilege of self-referring to any licensed health care provider.

Health Net's award-winning Quality Initiatives Division (QID) has a mandate to constantly search for and implement innovative programs that will increase the quality of care and services available to its members. The division incorporates the best information technology to measure existing services and monitor their outcomes. In three years it advised Health Net to devise and implement wellness, risk reduction, prevention, member and physician education and care management programs. The QID interacts often with Health Net members and providers, soliciting feedback which it then uses to improve the delivery of care and service.

QID initiatives have resulted in several innovative programs which enhance the benefit of Health Net membership. Chronic conditions such as asthma and diabetes are targeted for the most up-to-date managed care programs with extra assistance given to members and primary care physicians. The latest treatment methods as well as prevention and self-monitoring are made available

so that the quality of chronic care is enhanced. Family medical care for all stages of life is a prime priority and includes prenatal programs, childhood immunizations and Seniority Plus for older members. In response to member demand, alternative treatments such as chiropractic and acupuncture services are available to members.

Another important initiative from Health Net's QID concentrated on the needs of large employer groups. They benefit greatly from Health Net's vast resources. Health Net is able to work individually with corporations to develop resources that pinpoint the special areas of concern for their members. One such program is the California Public Employees Retirement System's Cardiovascular Disease Assessment and Intervention which helpes the employer to identify the high rates of cardiovascular disease among its employees and implement a risk-management program. This flexibility and innovation enhance the value of membership in Health Net and contribute to its success in enrolling large businesses.

Health Net's QID has made wellness an integral part of Health Net's approach to medical care. Believing that a well-informed member will be a healthier person, Health Net offers a wide range of preventive programs. These programs offer access to health education programs, wellness resources and preventive care services. Members have a number of ways to interact with these programs.

Easy-to-access and always available, WellSite, the Health Net web site, offers tips on staying healthy (weight management, smoking cessation, parenting skills) and health threats (high blood pressure, diabetes). Health Net's registry of 36,000 physicians is available as are tools to make selecting a physician easier. Special member benefits are also part of the web site. In 1998 the web site received a Bronze National Winner in Health Promotion and Disease

Health Net's Worksite Wellness Program offers preventive monitoring services to employer groups through which employees have access to blood pressure screening, stress management and goal-setting. Health education workshops are offered through Health Net medical groups, and members are encouraged to attend in order for them to become better informed about their personal medical profile. Expectant parents are offered Early Bird Prenatal Programs and receive an infant car seat when they complete them. The WellWoman Women's Health Initiative focuses on continuing care through all the stages of a woman's life. Discounts to fitness clubs and other health programs are available through Health Net's Well Rewards program. And Health Net's newsletter *Health Net News* updates members regularly on the latest programs within the network as well as the newest developments in medical technology.

Health Net has responded to consumer's calls for easier access to alternative and complementary medical care benefits. Studies showing that one of every three Americans uses alternative medicine prompted Health Net to offer chiropractic as an optional rider to Health Net's employer groups. Since 1990, Health Net has provided chiropractic services and numbers 1400 practitioners on its list of providers.

Initiative and innovation have propelled Health Net to the forefront of California's health care providers. The company has succeeded by focusing on quality, service and value, always remembering that putting members first is the prime priority. Based in Woodland Hills, Health Net has achieved a predominant presence throughout California and is preparing to forge ahead as the foremost health plan in the state.

and Injury Prevention by a panel of experts in the National Health Information Awards.

People facing a health crisis need exceptional assistance in coping with the onset and duration of their illness, and Health Net does not abandon them when they are most vulnerable. The Care Management Program was designed to address their needs at the time when they undergo complex care. It steps in to ensure that they receive the care and comfort they require and acts as an advocate for them, guiding them through the health care system and making sure they are kept informed and involved.

THE SALVATION ARMY

n 1865, William and Catherine Booth founded The Salvation Army in an effort to fight a holy war against the sin and degradation, prostitution, drug usage and white slavery running rampant in the city's streets.

The Salvation Army is among the first on the scene when disaster strikes. (right and below) *Bottom left photo by Robert Clark.*

Booth abandoned the conventional concept of a church and a pulpit and took his message to the people. He preached to a small street congregation in the slums of London. His spirit was as militant as that of a professional soldier battling hopelessly against an almost overwhelming enemy.

When his fervor met with disagreement from church leaders in London, Booth withdrew and traveled throughout England conducting evangelistic meetings. It was in 1865 that he was invited to hold a series of meetings in the east end of London. He set up a tent in a Quaker graveyard and his services became an instant success.

His undaunted spirit attracted loyal followers whose numbers grew as the years went by. Thirteen years after its inception, The Salvation Army became a legal entity with a quasi-military structure.

The early days in England brought suffering, abuse and the threat of death to the dedicated members of The Salvation Army. But in spite of these initial difficulties, the work of the organization's social services departments flourished.

Based on Booth's philosophy of "soup, soap and salvation," The Salvation Army's soldiers fed and clothed the desperately poor, brought them Christian guidance and instruction and helped the converts to find a new mode of existence and a chance for a brighter life.

These converts became the soldiers of Christ and are known as Salvationists. They launched an offensive throughout the British Isles. In some instances, there were real battles as organized gangs mocked and attacked soldiers as they went about their work. In spite of the violence and persecution, some 250,000 persons were converted under the ministry of the Salvationists between 1881 and 1885.

In 1880, George Scott Railton, a follower of Booth, bought seven "Hallelujah Lassies" from England to New York City to officially begin the work of the Army in America. In 1887, The Salvation Army was established in Los Angeles with a tent meeting held on a vacant lot at the corner of Temple Street and Broadway.

The Salvation Army's work expanded in Los Angeles with the opening of corps and facilities for social welfare services. The Corps Community Centers, which are the heart of The Salvation Army, serve the spiritual, social and recreational needs of the whole neighborhood with their programs for pre-school children, youth, singles, family groups and senior citizens.

Although the paramount objective of The Salvation Army has always been to lead men and

women into a proper relationship with God, the organization recognizes that physical, emotional and social restoration must go hand-in-hand with spiritual rebirth.

To that end, The Salvation Army is dedicated to caring for the poor, feeding the hungry, clothing the naked, loving the unlovable and befriending those who have no friends. This dedication has produced an international network of helpful ministries which provide a variety of local programs including religious services, family counseling, day care centers, youth, teen and community centers, adult rehabilitation and senior centers, shelter for the homeless, emergency disaster relief and women's ministries.

"Because Caring Shouldn't Stop When Work Starts," The Salvation Army Day Care Center in downtown Los Angeles provides the elements necessary for child development, including proper nutrition, rest and recreation. The 76-year-old program also offers latch-key and full-time summer day care for school age children. With over 250 children enrolled, the center is the oldest and largest Salvation Army day care operation in Los Angeles County.

The Red Shield Youth and Community Center in Los Angeles, gives all who enter its doors the opportunity to reach their full potential. Youth of all ages learn the value of cooperation, discipline and respect as they engage in a variety of educational and recreational activities. Youth who need special help with their

The number of youth and adults using computers at the Red Shield Youth and Community Centers continues to increase.
Photo by Nina Pratt Photography

Veteran actor Ed Asner and local NBC weather anchor Fritz Coleman "ring a bell" to collect holiday funds for the Salvation Army.
Photo by Judy Lawne Photography

school work are tutored in an after-school program. In the Learning Center at the Red Shield, the number of youth and adults using computers continues to increase. Guided by an accredited teacher, adults learn new skills and students receive intense academic instruction with an emphasis on English, math and science.

As the Hollywood Way In program for homeless and runaway teens. evolved, the need for more comprehensive services resulted in the building of a 20-bed

youth shelter in 1994, providing emergency and transitional shelter. Reunification with the family is the program's objective, when appropriate. When reuniting is not the answer, a variety of life skills for independent living is taught. The young people served by The Way In range from 12-17 years of age. The program also has an important drop-in center component that offers a wide spectrum of support services.

"Each year, thousands of men and women lose their way in this troubled, stress-filled world. Helping the lost of our communities find their way back to useful, productive lives — allowing them to dream again of brighter, hopeful futures." This is the mission of The Salvation Army Adult Rehabilitation Centers (ARC).

This nationwide network represents one of the largest single associations of alcohol and substance abuse programs in America. Men and women with identifiable and treatable needs come to these centers for help when they are no longer able to cope with their problems. At a residential treatment program, they receive housing, nourishing meals, medical care and engage in work therapy. They have the benefits of group therapy, spiritual guidance and skilled counseling in clean and wholesome surroundings.

Changing times have called for major changes in The Salvation Army's traditional programs to help families. Efforts toward the rehabilitation of men are now paralleled by aid to women and their children with the expansion of housing programs and AIDS counseling services.

The need for maternity homes to shelter single mothers has actually decreased in recent years. But out-patient and after-care for the young mother, and counseling to help avoid repeated unwanted pregnancies are a major part of the newer programs.

Meeting the needs of young and old alike is the aim of The Salvation Army and the growing needs of older Americans are met with a variety of community programs designed to provide older adults with companionship, comfort, care and a renewed interest and zest for life.

Major natural disasters affect thousands of people as they occur across the country. Minor local disasters may not affect as many people, but are equally devastating to those who are involved. The Salvation Army is always available because of their everyday presence in communities across the country and is among the first on the scene when disaster strikes. Officers are trained to meet all kinds of emergencies by providing food, shelter, clothing and spiritual comfort to victims.

An international movement, The Salvation Army continues to be an evangelical part of the universal Christian Church. Its message is based on the Bible. Its ministry is motivated by the love of God. Its mission is to preach the gospel of Jesus Christ and to meet human needs in His name without discrimination.

Its doctrinal basis is of the Wesleyan-Armenian tradition. It is comprised of persons who are united by the love of God and man, and share the common purpose of bringing others to Jesus Christ. The word "salvation" indicates the overall purpose of the organization — to motivate all people to embrace the salvation provided to them in Christ.

The word "army" indicates that the organization is a fighting force, constantly at war with the powers of evil. Battles are effectively waged through an integrated ministry which gives heed to both body and spirit. It is a total ministry for the total person. Cooperation is maintained with churches of all denominations to meet the need in the religious life of the community.

Even though The Salvation Army has been active in the United States for over a century, its spirit is still young and in tune with contemporary needs. New knowledge and technologies are sought in carrying out an integrated ministry to the whole person. Improved operational procedures are required as changing times dictate the adoption of new programs and services and upgrading existing ones.

Serving the community is the basis for programs which are designed to meet the specific needs as they are identified. Each community is different, and The Salvation Army is located in neighborhoods all across America, supported by volunteers and contributors who help make these services possible.

Today, the Army's religious and social activities serve millions of men, women and children in almost 100 nations around the world.

The young people served by *The Way In* range from 12-17 years of age.
Photo by Nina Pratt Photography

Transitional housing programs are available for families.
Photo by Tara Patty Photography

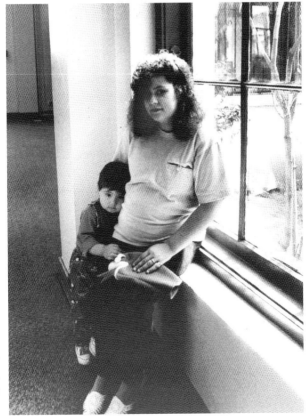

St. Vincent Medical Center

Courage, compassion and commitment led to the founding of the first hospital in Los Angeles. More than 140 years after six Catholic nuns received their first patients, St. Vincent Medical Center has evolved into one of the most progressive medical centers in Southern California. St. Vincent has a unique identity: It is both a notable pioneer in the forefront of modern medical advances and an advocate for the less fortunate. St. Vincent Medical Center traces its heritage directly back to that small band of courageous Catholic nuns whose work graced a great city with an enduring legacy of faith, duty and determination, beginning with their dramatic arrival in what was then a lawless cow town.

In the middle of the 19th century, when travel was treacherous and tedious, six nuns left the security of their convent in Maryland and began a three-month journey to California. They arrived at El Pueblo de la Senora la Reina de Los Angeles on January 6, 1856. The sisters were members of the Daughters of Charity, founded in 17th century France by St. Vincent de Paul, and their profound commitment to the sacredness of service inspired their incredible odyssey.

In the 1850s, Los Angeles was a primitive pueblo, a town of dusty roads menaced by mongrel dogs. Money was made sending beef to the hungry gold miners up north, and money was spent on drinking, gambling and other unsavory activities. Dwellings were made of adobe with tar roofs that leaked in the rain. The sisters, garbed in their long blue habits with broad white collars and swooping white headpieces, must have appeared as angels of mercy. Mercy was, indeed, their mission, wherever the need was greatest. They imagined it would be teaching. But the sick needed them more. Their Mother Superior, Sister Mary Scholastica Logsdon, D.C. answered the appeal from the community with divinely simple logic, "Our friends are anxious for us to take charge of the sick poor."

The sisters' first infirmary was established in 1858 at Alameda and Macy streets, and the county paid the nuns $1.00 per day for each indigent patient. During the next decade, more nuns arrived to assist their sisters, and a stately two-story building, opposite the train station at Main and San Fernando, expanded the hospital's capacity. In 1869 the facility was incorporated as the Los Angeles Infirmary, and the Daughters of Charity became the first women in Los Angeles to organize to protect both their business and charity interests. In 1877 and 1886, small pox ravaged the rapidly growing city, and the sisters showed extraordinary courage in remaining to nurse the afflicted, losing two of their nuns to the devastating disease.

As the years passed, Los Angeles prospered, and the population dramatically expanded. To respond to the increasing numbers of patients, the Daughters of Charity paid $10,000 for six and one-half acres of land at Sunset and Beaudry and built their third hospital. During the first two decades of the 20th century, the surrounding city was transformed into a booming metropolis whose population, by 1918, approached one million. In that year, the Daughters of Charity named their infirmary St. Vincent's Hospital in honor of their founding father.

A Daughter of Charity in the traditional habit with its signature cornette. "The Shadow and the Line" by Robert Vickrey, 1964. Part of the permanent collection of the Indianapolis Museum of Art.

In 1927, the hospital's upper floors were swept by fire, but catastrophe was averted since construction had already begun at the hospital's fourth and final location, the corner of Third and Alvarado streets. The new incarnation was a 304-bed hospital, described then as ultramodern and magnificent, with solid oak doors, terrazzo floors and an exquisite chapel. But it was the magnificence of the medical care that made St. Vincent's Hospital a landmark in the city, while the financial acumen of Sister Fidelis Klein, D.C. maintained the institution in sound fiscal health. Financial security and a prominent position in the civic life of Los Angeles enabled St. Vincent's to assume a leading role in the impressive progress of 20th century medicine.

In 1971, ground was broken for the last new facility in the hospital's history. Today, St. Vincent Medical Center (renamed in 1974) is a not-for-profit, 380-bed regional acute care medical facility with nationally recognized specialties in several areas of medicine. The sisters' core values guide the policies of the medical center which is a member of the large family of hospitals operated by Catholic Healthcare West. As a result of this alliance, a very special philosophy of excellence and compassion directs the operations of St. Vincent, guided by the core values of Dignity, Collaboration, Justice, Stewardship and Excellence.

The prominent position of St. Vincent Medical Center, while a reflection of its commitment to compassionate care, is equally a result of its commitment to the pioneering practice of medicine. The list of the hospital's innovations, including many medical firsts, is long and impressive. During World War II, the hospital's nursing school admitted cadet nurses as its contribution to the war effort, while in 1942, the Daughters of Charity successfully fought back a mayoral effort to treat hospitals like for-profit organizations, citing among other reasons, their treat-ment of war casualties at their own expense. The first eye research bank was established as the Estelle Doheny Eye Foundation in the late 1940s, and in 1947 the Department of Electroencephalography and a Tumor Clinic were established. They were joined by the Foundation of Otology, subsequently incorporated with the House Ear Institute, which later inaugurated new surgical techniques to restore hearing, including the cochlear implant and the auditory brain stem implant.

From the 1950s forward, several breakthroughs and innovations marked the growth of the medical center. The hospital expanded the School of Nursing, introduced a Department of Electromyography, a Department of Isotopic Medicine, and the Department of Nuclear Medicine, the first in Los Angeles. The West Coast's first successful open heart surgery took place at St. Vincent in 1957. During the 1960s, the medical center established its reputation as one of the nation's top cardiac care hospitals with its innovative coronary artery bypass surgery, while in 1988, St. Vincent surgeons completed the hospital's first heart transplant. In the 1970s St. Vincent Medical Center began kidney transplants, becoming the first state-certified institution in California. St. Vincent was one of the first medical centers in the country to utilize stereotactic implants into inoperable brain tumors, increasing survival and quality of life.

St. Vincent Medical Center in 1996, the year of its 140th Anniversary.

St. Vincent Meals on Wheels delivers its eight millionth meal in February, 1998. At left is Sister Alice Marie Quinn, D.C., R.D., Founder and Executive Director, who was joined by the Mayor of Los Angeles, Richard J. Riordan. *Photo by Rick Powell.*

The delivery of outstanding cardiac care for children and adults established St. Vincent as one of the most prominent and busy cardiac centers in the nation. Today, a comprehensive array of invasive and non-invasive diagnostic techniques and therapeutic modalities is available, including heart transplantation. The Los Angeles Heart Institute at St. Vincent Medical Center has supported education, clinical care and research since 1974, while its Miracles Across Miles program offered charitable heart care to infants and children from around the world.

St. Vincent is renowned for its expertise in the treatment of hearing disorders. Through the House Ear Institute and the House Ear Clinic, St. Vincent performs rare and delicate surgeries and has pioneered surgical techniques that improve hearing quality and save lives. Seventy-five percent of the world's cochlear implants have been performed at St. Vincent, while those patients who are not helped by the procedure have had partial hearing sensation restored through the use of a central electroauditory prosthesis. The House Ear Clinic offers many highly specialized treatments for ears, facial nerves, skull base, otologic allergy, balance and other related disorders.

More than 40 years ago, St. Vincent organized one of the first hospital cancer programs in the state, and today the medical center continues to offer comprehensive, state-of-the-art cancer services. The St. Vincent Cancer Treatment Center is a unique facility offering outpatient chemotherapy and radiation therapy along with coordinated, multidisciplinary patient support and rehabilitative services. Through the Los Angeles Oncologic Institute, leading-edge clinical research contributes to the battle against cancer by offering advanced investigational therapies to patients at St. Vincent and throughout the region.

St. Vincent is home to the National Institute of Transplantation. The hospital began its transplant program with kidneys, and today provides procedures for heart, liver, lung and pancreas. In 1977, St. Vincent established the Southern California Organ Procurement Center to assist in matching patients with donor organs. It serves hospitals throughout Southern California. St. Vincent Medical Center's innovative kidney transplant program includes such breakthroughs as donor-specific blood transfusion which builds up the kidney recipient's tolerance. This procedure widens the scope of potential donors, and in 1989, the hospital performed the first successful transplant between incompatible blood individuals, enabling more patients to benefit from this life-saving procedure. The medical center also specializes in simultaneous heart/kidney and kidney/pancreas transplants.

The St. Vincent Medical Center Comprehensive Liver Disease Center is a leading institute treating patients with all forms of liver disease. A wide program of treatment options is available, including liver transplantation. The Liver Center specializes in aggressive research while incorporating an individualized management approach to ensure that every patient receives a highly personalized care plan and improved access.

While life-saving techniques comprise much of the activity in the acute-care medical center, in service to its surrounding community, St. Vincent devotes impressive attention to disease-prevention and quality of life issues. More than one million people live within a five-mile radius of St. Vincent Medical Center, many of them in the densely-populated Pico-Union/Westlake area. Each year, St. Vincent offers more than $15 million in community benefit services and medical care for the poor.

In 1990, in response to increased gang activity, St. Vincent Medical Center met with the Los Angeles Police Department and the Los Angeles City Council to organize the community to take back the streets. Throughout the decade, programs such as graffiti removal, parenting classes, neighborhood watch, teen counseling, crime walks, a community garden, computer classes and team sports have made the area safer by reducing crime and enriching the lives of its citizens. The hospital considers this commitment to be so important, that in 1993 it established a full-time community liaison position and later donated a 5,000 square foot building, Casa Amigos de San Vicente, to be used as a community youth center.

Through the St. Vincent Community Mammography Program, Liver Cancer Screening Program, and the African American Men's Health Project, which offers low-cost health screening for prostate cancer, diabetes and high blood pressure, the hospital collaborates with a dozen medical clinics in the community to offer culturally sensitive cancer control services to a diverse, medically under-served population. Other programs include health fairs, education seminars, and a hospice volunteer program for people with AIDS.

The Japanese and Korean communities also receive special attention from St. Vincent. The 16-bed Nikkei Pavilion provides a culturally sensitive environment with Japanese-speaking physicians and a Japanese menu. Similarly, the Korean Pavilion is a 16-bed inpatient hospital nursing area for patients of Korean heritage. The Korean Pavilion includes a Korean patient-physician representative, Korean-speaking nurses and a specialized menu.

Through its Meals on Wheels program, St. Vincent serves more than 2,000 seniors in crisis who receive nourishing meals through a daily home delivery program. For many of these elderly, their entire food requirements are supplied by Meals on Wheels which depends on a network of volunteers and financial supporters to maintain and expand its program.

With compassion, charity and medical expertise, St. Vincent Medical Center contributes greatly to the good of the community. It is the role of the St. Vincent Medical Center Foundation to encourage the community to contribute back to St. Vincent. Private philanthropic support supplements the income of the medical center through an ambitious fundraising program, and donations are encouraged through several avenues.

Annual giving is the primary support for the center's community benefits programs and is funded through direct mail programs and major gifts from individuals. Patrons of The Circle of Angels contribute annually to Meals on Wheels, from $500 to $10,000. Members of

the Pioneer Estate and Trust Society name St. Vincent Medical Center in their wills or charitable remainder trusts, private foundations sponsor grants for specific programs at the center, and corporate donations include gifts-in-kind, matching gifts and community service programs. The bi-annual Cornette Gala is a successful fundraising event cosponsored by the St. Vincent Auxiliary.

The St. Vincent Medical Center Auxiliary is a dedicated group of volunteers whose work directly supports the financial health of the medical center. The Auxiliary has sponsored successful fundraising events and manages the "Hour Glass" gift shop in the hospital lobby. Other volunteers generously donate their time by working in the hospital, offering assistance to the nursing staff and comfort to the patients.

Given its eventful history, it was a logical outgrowth of the medical center's 140th anniversary to organize the St. Vincent Medical Center Historical Conservancy, a project of the St. Vincent Auxiliary, to document both the history of the hospital and the history of medical care in Los Angeles.

Throughout its extraordinary history, St. Vincent Medical Center has served the citizens of Los Angeles with its unswerving commitment to quality and compassion. Since those desperate days when six Daughters of Charity were the only refuge for the sick and needy, St. Vincent has devoted itself to medical excellence and community charity. The need is as great today as it was when the Daughters of Charity first opened an infirmary for the indigent, and St. Vincent serves its community with as much energy and compassion as did its founding nuns. The sponsoring sisters have never wavered in their core values, and their legacy is a great medical center, diligent in its care for both the body and the soul.

The main building of St. Vincent Medical Center and the Institute Plaza span Third Street, just west of Downtown Los Angeles.

WOODBURY UNIVERSITY

A specialized university committed to providing professional education in its bachelor's and master's programs, Woodbury University takes an innovative approach to its curriculum by offering both theory and extensive practical experience.

In 1884, F. C. Woodbury, an educator and entrepreneur from San Francisco, recognized the need for a school offering practical business training in Los Angeles. His vision was realized with the Woodbury Business College situated in the heart of the city's developing business district.

The demand for bright employees with practical business skills fueled the institution's success. By World War I, Woodbury had established a solid reputation for individual instruction — an approach that continues today.

In 1924, Woodbury broadened its educational scope and created a program in professional arts. In 1961, the Western Association of Schools and Colleges (WASC) granted accreditation and in the 1970s, Woodbury went from proprietary to non-profit status, established an independent Board of Trustees and changed its name to Woodbury University.

Today, Woodbury offers bachelor's degrees in architecture plus design, business plus management and arts plus sciences. The University's Weekend and Evening College programs allow working adults to earn business degrees. The institution continually updates majors in each of the degree programs to meet the needs of a changing workplace.

After relocating within the downtown area several times to accommodate a growing student body, Woodbury settled in as a quiet residential campus nestled below the Vergudo Foothills in Burbank in 1987. The current campus offers a pool, gymnasium and athletic field, on-campus housing, state-of-the-art computer labs, design studios for architecture, animation, fashion, graphic and interior design majors and traditional as well as on-line resources at the University's *Los Angeles Times* Library.

Since its inception, Woodbury's approach to personalized education has been a Los Angeles tradition and stands ready to serve an increasingly demanding and ethnically diverse student population.

School of Architecture and Design

Woodbury University offers students both a broad general education and strong professional preparation. Students develop their talents and abilities in a supportive climate which encourages individual creative and critical thinking, thoughtful analysis and purposeful innovation.

Advanced computer applications are integrated with courses providing the full range of skills and abilities required to excel in entrepreneurial and rapidly evolving professions. Students graduate prepared for leadership roles in their chosen fields and able to contribute to positive change.

1887 — Woodbury College's first graduation class

Founder Francis C. Woodbury served as president of the college from 1884 to 1903.

The School of Architecture and Design is built around the premise that a creative and balanced education is the most valuable education. This philosophy guides each of the majors that fall under the School's broad — and colorful — umbrella, including Animation Arts, Architecture, Fashion Design, Graphic Design and Multimedia, and Interior Design.

Animation is everywhere: feature films, TV commercials, computer games and on the Internet. While there is no shortage of computer animators, the industry is desperately seeking talented young artists who can actually draw.

For this reason, the Animation Arts major emphasizes a rigorous and formal approach to the study of drawing, painting, color and composition by stressing theory as well as traditional techniques. This four-year program is designed to prepare graduates to enter the animation profession with the required skills and abilities. Topics covered include storyboarding, background painting and story development. While computer animation and camera techniques are also covered, the emphasis is on talent, not tools.

Woodbury's Department of Architecture is a professional program, offering a five-year, nationally accredited Bachelor of Architecture degree designed to educate students in the practice and discourse of architecture.

Central to this is the belief that a creative environment encourages critical thinking, innovative research and experimental design and is essential in order to redefine the future. The precursor to this exploration is an understanding of history, theory and the fundamental principles and techniques pertaining to all architecture.

Los Angeles, which serves as the learning laboratory for the Department of Architecture, presents a vital context within which to examine architecture in the urban condition. The role of the architect and architecture are thus analyzed and debated in order to arrive at alternatives for tomorrow.

The Community Design and Urban Research Center of Woodbury University's Department of Architecture takes the study of urban design right into the heart of Hollywood. The 2,500-square-foot facility houses a design studio and space for community design projects and offers a series of lectures, panel discussions and exhibits.

Woodbury University's department of Fashion Design utilizes the knowledge and talents of instructors who are practicing professionals in the fashion and entertainment industries. The curriculum offers a strong balance between design and technical courses, allowing students to create and execute their ideas from concept to final product.

Students master the basic skills of pattern drafting, drawing, illustration, tailoring and draping and then move on to courses that develop creativity and professionalism. The program takes a progressive approach with an emphasis on conceptual and critical thinking, experimental design, thorough research and strong technical skills. Students are encouraged to investigate and practice the latest trends and movements in textiles, technology and design to prepare for two of the world's most challenging industries: fashion and entertainment.

1940 — All aboard for the ocean, only 18 miles away. What fun after a hard day's work...swimming and lying around on the beach! Next Saturday off to the mountains for a delightful weekend of skiing, skating, and tobogganing. Woodbury students had lots of good times mixed in with their serious work.

May 31, 1937 — This building became the new home of Woodbury College under the leadership of President "Pop" Whitten. It extended an entire half block on Wilshire Boulevard and was one of the most distinctive structures in Los Angeles. It represented the latest in construction, arrangement and equipment. Every provision was made for the convenience, comfort, health and happiness of students. With the new equipment and added facilities, Woodbury was able to give even better training than the training that had made them famous nationally for more than 50 years.

1894: This picture was taken during the Fiesta, an early day Los Angeles celebration. Woodbury's location at the time was 226 S. Spring Street. The building on the left is where the school moved temporarily after the fire in 1893.

For the graphics art major, the study of graphics, typography, advertising, packaging and computer imaging is complemented by course work in business and the liberal arts and prepares students for career opportunities including: Graphic Designer, Art or Creative Director, Illustrator, Marketing and Corporate Communications Executives.

As a $10 billion growth industry, entertainment graphics is a major economic force that employs thousands of skilled artists, designers and technicians. Woodbury University remains on the cutting edge of education by offering courses in the study of film and theater marketing, posters and promotional graphics to prepare students for entry into the entertainment industry.

The concentration in Multimedia prepares students to design and create original interactive projects using text, animation, photography, video, narration and music. This area of digital design teaches students how to create, conceive, write, design, edit and animate various interactive multimedia projects using Macintosh Power Mac workstations with Macromedia Director software.

The Interior Design major, accredited by the Foundation for Interior Design Education Research (FIDER), focuses on the three-dimensional study of all types and scales of spatial environments. A dynamic and diverse faculty of practicing architects and designers exposes students to multiple design methods and theories.

The goal of the interior design curriculum is to produce graduates who are skillful technicians, and future leaders in the profession. Opportunities are available in commercial and institutional interiors, the design of manufactured and custom elements, as well as exhibit, set and entertainment design.

School of Arts and Sciences

Woodbury's School of Arts and Sciences is all about access. Students here have access to majors that creatively balance intellectual adventure with marketable career skills.

Woodbury offers innovative learning from team teaching to Internet research projects and collaborative presentations. The institution focuses on a curriculum and faculty with the unusual flexibility to blend the traditions of liberal arts with the front edge of contemporary life.

The History & Government major offers students an understanding of how the past and present shape the future. Courses focus on the development of human societies and political organizations, emphasizing the ways cultural practices, economic structures, social organizations and political institutions rise and fall over time.

The Humanities & Management major is a course of study that is both an unusual and powerful collaboration — investigating accepted ideas in art, literature and philosophy and integrating them with cutting-edge business, multicultural and technological issues.

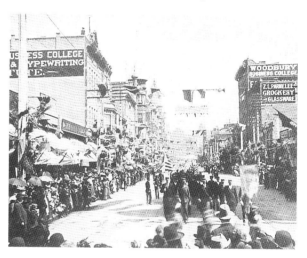

A practical degree in psychology brings a sharp focus to the broad phenomenon of human behavior. For this reason, the Psychology & Management major focuses on aspects of human behavior that students will need in tomorrow's workplace. The major concentrates on the behavior of human beings both as individuals and as members of communities. It investigates the nature of leadership and group dynamics, social influence and persuasion, the psychology of gender, human motivation, cognition and personality.

Through course work and internships, students learn to function in diverse settings, work effectively with persons from various backgrounds, form and lead cohesive, productive teams or turn dysfunctional work environments into productive ones. This degree in psychology can be put to use immediately upon graduation or prepare students for graduate school.

School of Business and Management

The business world that exists today is not the business world that will exist tomorrow. It is this reality that drives the faculty, the curriculum and the educational philosophy of the School of Business and Management.

The undergraduate and graduate business programs provide Woodbury's students with a professional education and practical entrepreneurial skills to compete effectively and ethically in a dynamic global environment characterized by rapid technological and social change.

The nationally accredited School of Business and Management offers the Bachelor of Science degree in four majors: Accounting, Business and Management, Computer Information Systems and Fashion Marketing.

Woodbury University's MBA is known as an eminently practical degree. In today's corporate milieu — where changes are virtually instantaneous — Woodbury offers an MBA grounded in the realities of the marketplace, the constantly erupting information explosion and the increasing global dimension of business.

Woodbury University offers the serenity of a campus in the hills above Burbank, the vividness of nearby downtown Los Angeles, the energy of the beaches, the calm of the desert and the excitement of nearby attractions like Disneyland and the Dodger Stadium.

The serious side of Woodbury's Southern California locale is just as impressive. The institution and its students are valued members of the community. As a result, internship connections are strong. Leaders from all walks of business come to the campus as speakers, adjunct professors and project reviewers. And, after graduation, Woodbury alumni find themselves perfectly positioned in a thriving area filled with opportunity from corporate to creative.

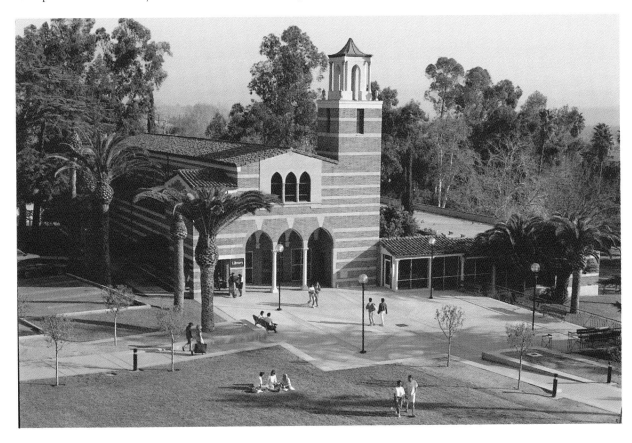

Woodbury University's *Los Angeles Times* Library and campus as it appears today.

AMERICAN MEDICAL RESPONSE

merican Medical Response (AMR) is the leading emergency medical service and ambulance transportation company in Los Angeles. The company was created from a series of mergers with more than a dozen L.A. county ambulance companies, including Med-

Trans, Crippen, AME and Goodhew Ambulance Services. This new combined company represents progressive leadership in the delivery of high-quality, cost-effective healthcare and medical transportation services. With community-based operations in 37 states and over 22,000 employees, AMR has the national resources, technology and financial strength to be an industry leader in integrated healthcare.

Prior to its merger with AMR, MedTrans Southern California had invested significant personnel and financial resources in the development of new, state-of-the-art communications technology, service request procedures and response priority protocols. AMR combines these tools with a proven track record as an innovator in pre-hospital and out-of-hospital managed care, physician proactive management, triage pathways creation and emergency medicine delivery.

AMR provides 911 emergency backup service for the city of Los Angeles and for Orange County, although several surrounding cities, including Glendale and Santa Monica, contract with AMR as a private 911 provider. AMR also provides 911 transportation throughout Los Angeles County, including the San Gabriel Valley, San Fernando Valley, and the L.A. Metro area; the company is also the primary

Turn-of-the-century
horse-drawn ambulance

Cadillac ambulances,
circa 1950s

paramedic provider for Ventura County.

AMR had 16 back-up ambulances at the scene of the infamous Bank of America robbery shootout in the San Fernando Valley in 1997, and the company responded to a mass drug overdose at a 1996 New Years Eve concert at the L.A. Sports Arena with a fleet of 20 ambulances. When the LA/Northridge earthquake occurred, MedTrans brought in units from surrounding counties to help with the emergency, for which it received a commendation from St. John's Hospital in Santa Monica for the company's prompt assistance.

Things were considerably calmer in Los Angeles in 1919 when James H. Goodhew founded Goodhew Ambulance Services, AMR's oldest acquisition. Goodhew was one of the first ambulance drivers for the Los Angeles County Hospital, and continued to work for them while establishing his own company. His first ambulance was a Pierce-Arrow, but after several years Goodhew purchased several rival ambulance companies and added to his fleet of ambulances. In the mid 1930s, Goodhew moved his headquarters to a house on Park Grove near the Harbor Freeway and Santa Monica Freeway interchange, and in 1947 relocated to the corner of Washington and Hoover, where Goodhew stayed for many years.

In 1941, Goodhew purchased Ace Ambulance Service, which brought with it preferred provider status for Good Samaritan Hospital. Additional ambulance company acquisitions over the next ten years offered similar status with other local hospitals. The acquisitions also continued to increase the number of ambulances operated by Goodhew. In the mid 1950s, most ambulances were made by Cadillac or Eureka. There was no air conditioning, just a fan in the patient compartment. Two red lights were mounted near the front of the ambulance, and a siren was mounted on the left front fender. A Beacon ray light was added to the roof several years later.

James Goodhew's son, William Goodhew, took over as president of Goodhew Ambulance Services in 1955. The company continued to grow through acquisitions of other ambulance companies, and branched out to service surrounding cities in the greater South Bay area. The company's first air-conditioned vehicle was purchased in 1963, and trip fare meters similar to those used in taxis were installed in most ambulances. By the 1970s, paramedic service was established, and van-type vehicles were incorporated into the Goodhew fleet.

By 1985, Goodhew had 65 ambulances running at peak hours in Los Angeles, and was a major ambulance service provider for the Los Angeles County Fire Department. The company continued its growth pattern, acquiring more ambulance companies and expanding its service. In 1995, Goodhew was purchased by MedTrans, which merged with AMR in 1997.

With a rich history of service to the Los Angeles community, AMR is looking to the future by increasing its services and continuing to add up to date technology and advanced dispatch centers. State-of-the-art equipment and modern techniques and concepts keep AMR at the forefront of the health care industry. Ambulances are tracked by global position satellite (GPS) tracking in the communications center in the Harbor Gateway area of Los Angeles, where dozens of call takers and dispatchers staff the center 24 hours a day. AMR personnel use a computer aided dispatch (CAD) system to ensure a rapid response time. A call is automatically displayed on a computer screen, and as the information is relayed from the caller into the computer, an ambulance is dispatched. That's a far cry from the old days, when call takers would write the information down and hand it to a dispatcher. The CAD saves time, and saves lives.

AMR is also a leader in the use of a state-of-the-art vehicle deployment technique called system status management (SSM). SSM determines where in Los Angeles calls for service are generated during a given time period in a given week, and keeps ambulances posted in that area to ensure a quick response time for every call.

AMR treats and transports an average of 1,000 patients each day from calls routed to the main communications center. Some calls may be as simple as hospital discharges or as complex as critical care transports, and some may be fast paced emergencies, but none are routine. All calls are managed by emergency dispatchers who are nationally certified, and handled by fully trained health care professionals, all of whom quickly determine the seriousness of each call and are ready to respond.

The Harbor Gateway is also home to the AMR billing department, where a staff of 150 medical billing professionals handle Medicare, Medi-Cal, and contract facilities for the ambulance transportation services.

Nationwide, AMR's 22,000 healthcare professionals and 4,700-vehicle fleet serves over 5 million patients every year; four hundred AMR physicians staff more than 30 hospital emergency departments, treating 500,000 patients each year, and the scope of AMR's reach continues to grow.

The new AMR, in partnership with other leading industry groups, is applying its national resources, community-based operations and management expertise to the continuous improvement of today's healthcare system. AMR is paving a progressive new road for healthcare and medical transportation.

AMR communications center

Modern AMR ambulances and paramedics

CHARLES R. DREW UNIVERSITY OF MEDICINE AND SCIENCE

Charles R. Drew University of Medicine and Science was founded as a postgraduate medical school in 1966 by a group of community physicians and residents who sought to build a comprehensively equipped facility devoted to the "highest quality of care, teaching and research" for the residents of South Central Los Angeles.

Located just across the street, the King/Drew Medical Center is a 500-bed acute care medical facility that has since its inception, served as the primary "teaching hospital" for Drew's students.

The community the hospital and medical school initially sought to serve has been characterized by poverty, higher morbidity and mortality rates in the major disease categories than the rest of the county, high unemployment, little or no health insurance or coverage and one of the lowest physician/patient ratios in the entire state.

As a result, the Drew University has made its mission to "conduct medical education and research in the context of service to a defined population so as to train persons to provide care with competence and compassion to this and other underserved populations."

Since the start, this academic entity has expanded its purpose from a postgraduate school offering specialist programs in traditional clinical disciplines and continuing graduate education to that of a fully accredited health services university with undergraduate as well as postgraduate training in medicine and a wide range of programs in allied health disciplines.

Drew University is accredited by the Western Association of Schools and Colleges. Additionally, in conjunction with UCLA, Drew University offers students a Doctor of Medicine degree. The institution also awards baccalaureate and associate degrees as well as certificates of completion to students in several allied health disciplines, including Diagnostic Medical Sonography, Health Information Management, Nuclear Medicine Technology, Substance Abuse Counseling and Physician Assistant primary care (the first program of its kind in California).

Drew University also provides training to interns, residents and fellows in 14 clinical programs as well as a program of continuing medical education for Drew faculty and community physicians. All of Drew's programs have accreditations in their professional discipline.

The University's Colleges of Medicine and Allied Health have been able to attract a multiethnic faculty who have devoted careers to inner city teaching, practice and research.

The University's research portfolio is extensive, focusing primarily on illnesses and diseases that affect medically underserved populations, such as hypertension, kidney disease, diabetes, cancer and HIV. Drew University has the only inner city telemedicine project in the U.S., enabling them to perform eye examinations via a sophisticated telecommunications network on patients 15 miles away. The data collected through the research provides valuable insight into causes and management of diseases.

Drew's College of Allied Health has consistently responded to the community's need for education and

Graduation Day '98 — A graduate of Drew University's College of Allied Health is shown with family members.

employment opportunities. Drew University has been noteworthy for its nontraditional approach to training people to meet the needs of the underserved, because it believes that a healthier community has to be more than training doctors and dispersing them to needy areas.

Former dean of the post graduate medical school and current US Surgeon General Dr. David Satcher is among the individuals who embrace the University's approach to teaching. Because good health hinges on proper nutrition, Drew University offers a comprehensive program in community nutrition as well as a degree for registered dieticians.

The institution's history reflects a recognition of social, environmental and cultural factors influencing health and disease. In its community-based training and service programs, Drew reaches out to the mentally and physically disabled, the incarcerated, alcohol and drug abusers, gang members and teen parents, among others.

These community-based programs have been developed by clinical departments, including Family Medicine, Internal Medicine, Pediatrics, OB/GYN and Psychiatry, in an attempt to build partnerships with families and community agencies.

Mobile transportation is also used to provide services such as HIV testing and services to senior citizens in the community. In a collaborative effort with the Watts Health Foundation, health education and preventive services are also provided.

The university's philosophy of "building a healthier community *with* rather than *for* local residents" has made it possible for Drew to work with agencies like the Los Angeles Unified School District in establishing a medical magnet high school near the University campus. The University views the high school as part of its "science pipeline" continuum.

One of these pipeline programs, the Saturday Science Academy, through hands-on experience, introduces youngsters (aged seven to 14) to medicine and science to "demystify the notion that science and math are too difficult to master." Weekly sessions include the metamorphoses of a butterfly, fetal pig dissection and the "Doctor for a Day" program, in which the children pretend to be physicians.

Drew University's W. Montague Cobb Medical Education Building and William M. Keck Foundation Allied Health Building. *Photo credit: John Davis*

Drew emphasizes early exposure of youngsters to role models and learning experiences in the sciences through extended programs including the Johnnie Tillmon Child Care Center. Drew also sponsors a plethora of child development programs which have served to provide a context for the pursuit of science and research in addition to education.

The Drew-sponsored Headstart program, which currently encompasses 1,700 students and their families, is designed to offer children basic exposure to science in the hope that these students will one day matriculate as students of the University.

These "pipeline" programs are open to the public and provide extracurricular educational support and a medically-oriented educational continuum for persons ages six months through adulthood.

Since its founding, Charles R. Drew University of Medicine and Science has sought to improve the health profile of a rapidly changing community. It successfully accomplishes its mission through medical education, training and research in the context of service to a defined population and its principle of working in concert with its community to solve issues.

CHURCH OF SCIENTOLOGY

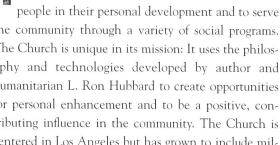

The Church of Scientology began in Los Angeles on February 18, 1954 with a commitment to serve people in their personal development and to serve the community through a variety of social programs. The Church is unique in its mission: It uses the philosophy and technologies developed by author and humanitarian L. Ron Hubbard to create opportunities for personal enhancement and to be a positive, contributing influence in the community. The Church is centered in Los Angeles but has grown to include millions of people throughout the world.

The Church of Scientology established an early headquarters in Downtown Los Angeles, but quickly outgrew its limits. In 1976, it found the space it needed and purchased the former Cedars of Lebanon hospital in East Hollywood. Since that time, the complex has been upgraded through the efforts of staff and parishioners. It is now the center of a community beautification program and a landmark presence in the neighborhood. As the Church grew, so did its presence in Los Angeles, both physically and culturally. The Church added other prestigious sites to house expanding social programs and worked hard to become an integral part of the Los Angeles community.

So impressive have the Church's accomplishments been, using Hubbard's technologies, that the Los Angeles City Council recognized these humanitarian efforts and impact on the city by authorizing a name change of the street adjacent to the main Church site.

L. Ron Hubbard, world-renowned author, humanitarian and founder of the Scientology religion spent his life researching and developing Dianetics and Scientology.

Grand opening of L. Ron Hubbard Way

Formerly Berendo Street, it was renamed, "L. Ron Hubbard Way." The Church responded with a significant renovation project, completing the upgrade and beautification of the street in April 1997. The grand opening was attended by thousands of neighbors and Church members as well as city officials and celebrities.

One of the most distinctive locations of the Church of Scientology in the area is its Celebrity Centre, housed in the historic and majestic Château Elyseé, an impressive landmark from the Golden Age of Hollywood. Celebrity Centre assists artists to achieve their goals through application of Dianetics and Scientology. It offers services to artists and professionals in fields such as the performing arts, sports and business. The Centre's *Garden Pavilion* is also a beautiful venue for many charitable events held throughout the year. Such events include the annual *Christmas Stories* Show for underprivileged children and the benefit for the Hollywood Police Support Association and Police Activities League. Other programs conducted at Celebrity Centre include efforts to promote literacy and drug education.

One of L. Ron Hubbard's writings states, "A culture is only as great as its dreams, and its dreams are dreamed by artists." Mr. Hubbard felt strongly that artists have enormous influence in society, both for good and for bad. It is the aim of the Church to encourage that influence for good by improving the lives of artists so that they may, in turn, have a stronger, more positive impact on society. The Church maintains that artists imbued with strong communication talents and high moral standards will impart that positive influence to many others. Believing that artists can have a beneficial effect on society, the Church of Scientology Celebrity Centre is dedicated to helping them help other people by focusing on such important agendas as improving the environment and helping people lead drug-free lives.

That commitment to helping people help others arises from the moral teachings of the Mr. Hubbard.

It offers many of the answers to human suffering, and those answers are available to everyone. The goals of Scientology are to replace intolerance with kindness, criminality with decency and degradation with dignity. It offers all its members, not just artists, tools for personal ethics and a nonreligious moral code.

While artists play a prominent role in the Church's efforts to enrich the lives of people, it is the Church's volunteers who are on the front lines of the many immensely successful programs. Some are Church-based. Some are secular. The programs range from drug education and after-school tutoring to neighborhood watch and anti-crime efforts, as well as recycling programs, public park cleanups, highway beautification programs, graffiti paint-outs, tree plantings, wildlife projects and disaster relief. Many of the programs have been in place for more than a quarter of a century.

These volunteers bring tremendous spirit to the tasks at hand, but they also contribute sophisticated practical skills which they use to remedy conflict and restore personal integrity. Many of them are Volunteer Ministers for their local Churches, offering help and compassion through simple, basic assistance. Helping people overcome difficulties they may be having in life is a large part of the volunteer effort. It is part of the Church's philosophy that communities are made of people and people are the richest resource for growth and change. From the success of individual efforts comes success of the communities.

In Los Angeles, one of the most successful efforts of the Church of Scientology is the Los Angeles Community Program which, over the years, has contributed more than 60,000 hours of work to the Los Angeles County Department of Children and Family Services. Those hours have gone to providing assistance to thousands of foster children. The children also benefit from the annual L. Ron Hubbard *Winter Wonderland* where the community's largest Christmas tree, nearly eight stories high, is Santa's home in Hollywood.

Caring for the environment is another vital concern of volunteer Church of Scientology members. Throughout the city, Scientologists have created murals to beautify the urban landscape so that the community is more attractive and enjoyable for everyone. The Church's campaign to reduce pollution is intended to improve lifestyle quality for everyone.

The Church of Scientology takes a hands-on approach to drug education. It provides young people with a complete understanding of the dangers of drugs so that they will make the decision to remain drug-free. The Drug-Free Marshals program deputizes children who have pledged to keep themselves, their friends and their families drug-free. The program began in 1993 when several officials from the U.S. Marshalls and FBI swore in 200 children between the ages of six and 13. Those first 200 were followed by thousands, and, from its headquarters in Hollywood, the program has spread around the world.

As impressive as these efforts are, there are others of equal importance, specifically social betterment organizations supported by the Church, whose programs are based on L. Ron Hubbard's humanitarian discoveries and breakthroughs. Narconon (no drugs), drug rehabilitation and education program, has highly effective results. The World Literacy Crusade helps resolve study problems. The Criminon Program (no crime) works with inmates in more than 750 prisons and detention centers around the world to reverse criminal behavior.

From the personal to the global, the Church of Scientology plays a prominent role in the lives of millions. From its modest beginnings in Los Angeles, the Church has expanded rapidly to become a significant moral force throughout the world. Los Angeles remains its headquarters, and the Church is a visible presence throughout the city. From its architectural landmarks to the activism of its members, the Church of Scientology contributes its philosophy and its talent to the neighborhood, the community, the city, the country and the world.

The beautifully renovated Church of Scientology Celebrity Centre International is located in Hollywood in what was formerly the Château Elyseé.

In 1983 L. Ron Hubbard donated the first 60-foot Christmas tree in a gesture that became the annual *Winter Wonderland* to benefit children everywhere.

COVENANT HOUSE CALIFORNIA

ovenant House California is an affiliate of the international organization Covenant House Inc., the largest program of its kind serving runaway, homeless and at-risk youth.

In 1988, a small group of Covenant House volunteers began work in Los Angeles on a program needs assessment. In addition to consulting with community leaders and other youth services providers, Covenant House staff began conducting street outreach throughout the greater Los Angeles area.

Through these efforts, it soon became apparent that there were a great number of older youth (18-20 years old) living on the streets of Hollywood. These youth were too old for existing shelters for minors, yet too young and inappropriate for traditional adult homeless shelters operating in downtown Los Angeles. In order to address this unmet service need, Covenant House California (CHC) was incorporated as a non-profit organization and, in October 1989, opened a temporary 24-bed shelter for older youth on Sunset Boulevard in Hollywood.

In 1990, planning began for the construction of expanded and permanent facilities to better meet the needs of homeless youth in Hollywood. After an extensive search of properties and buildings, Covenant House California signed an agreement with the Assistance League of Southern California in 1991 for the purchase of a 1.3 acre site on Western Avenue, in Hollywood. The architectural firm of Meyer & Allen was engaged to begin a detailed facility-planning process. After careful study and consultation with other ser-

vice providers, the plan for the new shelter and transitional living program was approved by the Board of Covenant House California.

Groundbreaking for the first phase of the building project occurred in May 1993. Twelve months later, the Phase I new shelter building opened, providing Covenant House California with its first permanent home in Hollywood. Construction on the Phase II building began in the spring of 1995. On May 30, 1996 the new residential center was officially opened, in a ceremony attended by the First Lady, Hillary Rodham Clinton, Senator Dianne Feinstein, Cardinal Roger Mahony and the President of Covenant House Inc., Sister Mary Rose McGeady, D.C. The center was named "Rose House," in honor of Sister Mary Rose, a fitting tribute to an individual who has dedicated over 40 years of service to homeless and disturbed children and their families.

In the spirit of open intake, Covenant House services are offered to all youth seeking help, with priority given those at greatest risk and for whom no other service is available. No one is ever turned away on the first visit and *each youth* is accepted on a "no questions asked" basis.

Covenant House California has carefully designed a Continuum of Care, with a progression of programs and services from one level to the next. The goal is to provide homeless and at-risk youth with greater opportunities to transition from street life to independent living situations.

The first contact many youth have with Covenant House California is with the members of the Van Outreach team who travel the streets of Los Angeles every night. The blue van is a familiar sight in places where youth congregate. The outreach program is designed to first gain trust by providing food, drink, crisis counseling and a sympathetic ear. Youth may then be transported to the Crisis Shelter, or referred to another program that can meet their special needs.

The 48-bed Crisis Shelter is always open when there's nowhere else to turn. The Crisis Shelter staff provide homeless youth with emergency needs first: food; clothing; and emergency medical care. Once their immediate physical needs are met, the work begins to keep them off the streets permanently. Each youth receives individual attention from specially trained case managers who provide hope and the opportunity to start a new life. Support services include health care, psychological services, substance abuse counseling, employment skills training and job placement, educational assistance and a variety of cultural and recreational activities.

A Rights of Passage Program (transitional living) can accommodate up to 24 young people who have progressed through the Crisis Shelter and will benefit from a long-term transitional living program to prepare them for adult independent living. This 12 to 18-month program helps them develop the skills they need to become fully responsible, contributing members of society. All participants in this program either work and/or attend school full time. In addition, they attend workshops in which they learn money management and decision-making skills. All participants are assigned a mentor from the community, who serves as a positive role model by providing guidance, advice and encouragement.

Two programs, the Health Services Center and the Employment Skills Program, are available to youth at any time while they are residents in the program. The Health Services Center provides comprehensive medical services and health education free of charge. (This program is also open to nonresident youth.) The Employment Skills Program assists youth so they may explore their career interests, identify educational and vocational opportunities, learn how to conduct an effective job search and ultimately find work. In March 1998, the employment program was relocated to leased space across the sreet

from the residential center to meet the demand for increased program services.

In early 1998, Covenant House California also opened a supportive Apartments Program, in Hollywood, where ten youth live in five, two-bedroom apartments — taking another step toward independent living. The program will again be expanded in the fall of 1998, when CHC will begin operating supportive apartments for emancipating foster youth.

Funded primarily by individual donors, and supplemented with support from other diversified funding sources including corporations and foundations, the services provided by Covenant House California are desperately needed but never enough. In Los Angeles alone, over 200 youth receive assistance each day — nearly 10,000 each year — and there is never an empty bed. The future will bring additional program development and new strategies that lend a helping hand to the homeless and at-risk youth of our communities.

Courtesy of Meyer & Allen Associates, Architects, Planners: Photos by Paul Bielenberg.

GOOD SAMARITAN HOSPITAL

Renowned for its hightech, high-touch approach, Los Angeles' Good Samaritan Hospital has been providing outstanding primary care and specialized medical services to the community since 1885.

ocated in downtown Los Angeles, Good Samaritan Hospital has been serving the Southern California community since 1885, when Sister Mary Wood of the Episcopal Church founded a nine-bed infirmary known as Los Angeles Hospital and Home for Invalids. In 1896, the hospital moved to larger quarters and was renamed Good Samaritan Hospital in honor of Mrs. Mark Severance, who donated the funds needed to purchase the new property. As Los Angeles grew, so did the hospital, which moved to its current location in 1911. New facilities were completed in 1927, with an addition in 1953 to enable care for more than 400 patients. A new hospital building opened in 1976, with a medical office addition in 1981 and a new surgery and intensive care wing in 1990.

Good Samaritan houses many regional centers of excellence, which yearly draw thousands of patients from throughout Southern California and the western United States. The facility includes a comprehensive heart care program; a neurosciences program with new treatments for brain cancer, Parkinson's disease and other brain disorders; an extensive women's health program; an orthopaedic surgical program; ophthalmologic care; an oncology program; a digestive diseases program; kidney stone treatment; and many other outstanding specialized medical services. Above all, Good Samaritan offers personalized care to ease patients' concerns. The hospital's staff knows that a reassuring touch and comforting words play a powerful part in the healing process. That's why compassion goes hand in hand with a commitment to the best in medical technologies.

Heart Institute

Boasting some of the nation's finest cardiologists and cardiac surgeons, Good Samaritan is home to one of California's busiest and most comprehensive heart programs. Specializing in high-risk cases, Good Samaritan's cardiac surgeons perform approximately

1,100 open heart operations annually, including bypass surgeries, valve repairs and aortic dissections. They are known for their expertise in high-risk cases and transfusion-free procedures. Using a fleet of specially equipped ambulances and aircraft, the Good Samaritan cardiac care team has rushed more than 9,500 heart patients to the hospital in time to receive lifesaving treatments.

Each year, more than 10,000 cardiology patients come to Good Samaritan to take stress tests, receive the latest drug therapies and undergo procedures to dissolve blood clots and resolve other heart conditions. The hospital's cardiologists excel in non-invasive as well as interventional techniques, and they are particularly well recognized in electrophysiologic procedures, such as radio frequency ablation, a highly effective treatment for abnormal heart rhythms. The physician/scientists at the Good Samaritan Heart Institute Research Laboratories conduct studies that allow patients to benefit from the latest breakthrough treatments.

Neurosciences Institute

Good Samaritan has emerged as one of the country's premier centers for the research and treatment of neurological disorders. The hospital's Neurosciences Institute offers the expertise, compassion and support that patients need to cope with brain tumors and brain malformations, movement disorders, Parkinson's disease, and other daunting neurologic conditions. The hospital was among the first in the nation to acquire the Gamma Knife, a revolutionary non-surgical device that has safely and successfully been applied in approximately 1,000 neurological therapy cases. Good Samaritan is also one of the few medical facilities in the country to offer neurotransplantation as a treatment for Parkinson's disease — and the only hospital in the nation to provide it as a therapy for Huntington's disease. At the Neurosciences Institute's research facilities, scientists continue to examine promising treatments for a number of illnesses, including cellular approaches to combat brain cancer.

Other Services

From routine gynecological exams to high-risk obstetrical services to gynecologic oncology, Good Sam offers women expert, personalized care. The hospital's multidisciplinary Breast Cancer Center provides a full range of diagnostic breast services, including mammography, ultrasound and stereotactic core biopsy. Good Samaritan's Board-certified radiologists and its highly trained technicians ensure that diagnoses are made swiftly and efficiently.

The reopening of Good Samaritan's Perinatal Center in 1989 marked its return to obstetrical care after a 17-year hiatus. The new obstetrical unit was one of the first in Los Angeles equipped with single labor-delivery-recovery rooms (LDRs), where patients may go through the entire birth experience in the same room. The hospital's state-of-the-art Neonatal Intensive Care Unit, staffed around the clock by specialists in the field, ranks as one of the best facilities in Los Angeles for babies born prematurely or with acute medical conditions.

Good Samaritan's orthopaedic surgeons provide many services, from treating sprains and broken bones to performing complicated pelvic reconstruction and knee and hip replacement operations. A comprehensive physical and occupational rehabilitation program helps patients recover from injuries. Recently, the hospital opened The Center for Wound Care to provide comprehensive care for chronic non-healing wounds in a single setting using a team of specialized physicians and nurses. The hospital's ophthalmologists use the latest technologies to treat a wide range of eye disorders, including near-and far-sightedness, cataracts, glaucoma and astigmatism. Several eye specialists excel in the surgical treatment of the retina and vitreous. Hospital oncologists, oncologic surgeons and radiation specialists offer compassionate and effective care to many cancer patients.

At Good Samaritan, the hospital's gastroenterologists are renowned for their expertise in endoscopic procedures. They effectively treat many conditions of the biliary tract, pancreas and common duct. The hospital's Kidney Stone Service is one of the busiest in California for treating kidney stones with lithotripsy, a non-surgical procedure that breaks up stones. Good Samaritan's pulmonology services include treatment for acute and chronic respiratory diseases, including asthma, emphysema and bronchitis. The hospital's medical staff also boasts highly trained urologists, dermatologists, reconstructive plastic surgeons, otolaryngologists and primary care specialists, including internists and family and general practitioners.

Reaching Out To The Future

Good Samaritan provides a number of outreach programs that benefit thousands of neighbors and former patients, homemaker and social services for the low-income elderly, a follow-up clinic for former patients of its Neonatal Intensive Care Unit, and a series of free lectures, exercise classes and blood pressure screenings for the senior community.

As a high-tech, high-touch institution, Good Samaritan continues to move forward in science, technology and medical advances while retaining the personalized care for which it is known. Serving an ever-growing community and constantly developing programs to meet patients' needs, the hospital is leading the way into a new era of health care for the 21st century.

Excelling in cutting-edge research and a wide array of cardiology and cardiac surgical services, Good Samaritan's Heart Institute recently celebrated a decade of exceptional care. Its cardiologists, cardiac surgeons, research scientists, nurses, technicians and other team members gathered for a commemorative photo.

LOS ANGELES ORTHOPAEDIC HOSPITAL

Orthopaedic Hospital has been confidently ahead of its time from the start. The hospital is internationally recognized as the site of research breakthroughs, physician education, complex specialized procedures and the realization of many children's dreams of walking and running.

In 1904, Dr. Charles LeRoy Lowman, visionary founder of Orthopaedic Hospital, arrived in Los Angeles. He brought with him a commitment to improving the future of disabled children and a mere $10 in his pocket. He opened an orthopaedic care office, the first of its kind in the Southwest, on North Broadway in Downtown Los Angeles. In a time when public health care programs and private insurance plans were unheard of, Dr. Lowman spent long hours helping hundreds of patients, regardless of their ability to pay.

His quiet personal passion for aiding crippled children would eventually evolve into a comprehensive facility where topnotch treatment would be coupled with a philosophy of treating "the whole child" by attending to each patient's psychological, social, educational and vocational needs.

Singleton Estate carriage house served as the first hospital building.

Orthopaedic medical care is often lengthy, complex and costly, necessitating a partnership between dedicated volunteers, community leaders and medical professionals. Dr. Lowman had the expertise and the vision, but needed considerable financial backing. With the monetary support of John Brockman, Lowman's landlord and mentor, the fund-raising efforts of Occidental College professor Mary Carruth Cunningham, and the astute legal advice of attorney George W. Dryer, a plan for Orthopaedic Hospital began to crystallize.

In January of 1918, the Los Angeles Orthopaedic Foundation was incorporated. John Brockman supplied the missing piece of the puzzle — the location: a parcel of land on the corner of Flower and Hope Streets, known as the Singleton Estate. The only condition was that the bulk of the project had to be completed within 36 months.

Fund raising and planning were pushed into full-swing to meet the deadline, and the Singleton Estate's 3.5 acres were quickly transformed after the initial groundbreaking in 1921. On April 1, 1922, the first hospital in the western United States devoted exclusively to orthopaedics opened its doors.

Orthopaedic Hospital and its unique philosophy of treating the whole child was an immediate success. By 1926, the demand for care began to strain available facilities and plans to raise funds and expand kicked into full gear. The Memorial Building opened in 1929, adding indoor treatment pools, occupational and physical therapy facilities, outpatient services and even a dental clinic.

After the rollicking pace of the 1920s, the early 1930s were relatively calm at Orthopaedic Hospital. But these quiet years eventually collapsed into turbulence with the start of WWII as volunteers made bandages and slings for wounded troops.

After 40 years, both the hospital and its locale had been transformed — Los Angeles was now a booming metropolis, and the hospital grew right along with it. The 1950s saw enormous advances in orthopaedic care, including the first successful polio vaccine. In 1954, The League for Crippled Children raised funds to build a new Rehabilitation Center. The most forward-looking facility of its time, the center continues helping patients today.

The next year saw a great change in the training of orthopaedic medical students when J. Vernon Luck Sr., MD, almost single-handedly reinvented professional

medical education by organizing training for medical residents and developing an orthopaedic residency examination in an effort to assure uniform high standards across the country.

In 1956, Dr. Luck built upon his revolutionary surgical activities by proposing the construction of a new hospital complex that would contain expanded clinical services and space dedicated to education and research facilities. Orthopaedic Hospital was able to raise the necessary funds and the building opened its doors in 1959.

The J. Vernon Luck Sr., MD, Orthopedic Research Center, named for the man who helped unify education, research and patient care at Orthopaedic Hospital, has established Orthopaedic Hospital as an international research leader.

Over the 80 years since its inception, Orthopaedic Hospital has compiled a stunning list of accomplishments. Its well-orchestrated combination of research, education, care and innovative facilities has made the hospital renowned in nearly every aspect of orthopaedic care.

The Joint Replacement Institute, established in 1991, is a state-of-the-art treatment center and, in conjunction with the Luck Center, uses the latest technology to conduct research on artificial joint wear via computer modeling, biological studies and biomechanical investigations. The Pacific Coast Tissue Bank, founded in 1987, supplies demineralized bone products used to accelerate bone regeneration, while the addition of NovaCare Orthotics & Prosthetics provides patients with braces, supports and advanced prosthetic devices. The Orthopaedic Hospital Occupational Medicine Center, opened in 1988, provides around-the-clock treatment of complex workplace injuries.

The hospital sponsors educational programs for physicians, pediatricians, nurses, physical therapists and technicians. Faculty, medical students and residents from premier local hospitals take part in Orthopaedic Hospital medical education. Fellowship programs attract promising international students, and a series of major programs, annual symposia and monthly conferences and lectures round out the hospi-

tal's orthopaedic education curriculum.

In 1997, the hospital began sponsoring the International Center for Orthopaedic Education in cooperation with the American Orthopaedic Association as an effort to coordinate postgraduate education and international interchange. The hospital also recently received designation as the World Health Organization Collaborating Center for the Control of Hemophilia throughout the Western Hemisphere as a result of its groundbreaking blood clotting research.

"Our past leads us directly into the future," Dr. Lowman once said. And as such, the Orthopaedic Hospital continues to narrow the gap in research between someday and today by educating physicians with the advanced techniques needed to further the quality of patient care.

In 1977, Dr. Lowman passed away at the age of 97 in the very hospital he had dreamed of building more than half a century before. The institution continues in the optimistic manner in which Dr. Lowman lived by rising to the challenge of changes in health care with leadership, excellence and service in charity care, research and education.

Today, as it always has, Orthopaedic Hospital relies upon the foresight of its leadership and generosity of caring individuals to support the hospital as it continues to transform hope into healing; leading the way from the past into the future.

LOYOLA MARYMOUNT UNIVERSITY

et on a magnificent bluff overlooking the Pacific Ocean, Loyola Marymount University is a comprehensive Catholic independent university emphasizing undergraduate liberal arts in the educational traditions of the Society of Jesus (Jesuits) and the Religious of the Sacred Heart of Mary (R.S.H.M.). Its mission to combine rigorous academic work with ethical values has led to Loyola Marymount University being recognized as a world-class learning institution.

The school follows the Jesuit and Marymount educational traditions, emphasizing scholarship, ethics, service to others and the rich heritage of the Catholic Church. It characterizes itself as a "thinking shop" and promulgates the notion that life consists of taking one's highest standards and putting them into practice in the community. The Loyola Marymount mission has been defined as the encouragement of learning, the education of the whole person, the service of faith and the promotion of justice.

The University was founded in 1911 when Bishop Thomas J. Conaty brought the Jesuits — famed for their orthodoxy and intellectual rigor — to Los Angeles to administer St. Vincent's High School and College. The school then consisted of three small buildings in Highland Park, and in its first six years graduated 149 students. In 1917, St. Vincent's changed its name to Loyola College, and in 1930 it became Loyola University.

Loyola Law School, originally known as St. Vincent's School of Law, opened its doors on September 8, 1920, as an evening program. It was founded to afford access to many for whom existing law schools were in effect closed, including Catholics and Jews. The first graduating class consisted of seven men and — a rarity at that time — one woman.

In 1928, real estate developer Harry Culver, for whom Culver City was named, offered to give any Los Angeles private school 100 acres of land overlooking the ocean. His proviso: the school must erect a permanent building within one year and maintain the land for 50 years. Loyola College accepted his offer, even after Culver changed the terms and required the construction of two buildings in two years.

The Jesuits proved more than equal to the challenge. On May 20, 1928, in front of a grandstand jammed with supporters and an on-site radio announcer broadcasting the historic event, Los Angeles Archbishop John Cantwell broke ground for the new campus. At that time, the surrounding land featured sewer ditches, bean fields, a dump and an endless stream of rats. Undaunted, the Jesuits secured money to build the first two buildings with fund raisers featuring Hollywood stars. By September, 1929, with both Xavier Hall (now the Jesuit residence) and St. Robert's Hall (consisting of classrooms and administrative offices) completed, the first group of students arrived to

Loyola Marymount University's Westchester campus

attend classes. That same year, Loyola Law School added a day division and moved to downtown Los Angeles in order to allow students to be closer to the courts.

One month after moving onto the Westchester campus, the Wall Street crash wreaked havoc with the College's plans. Financial pledges, many from the motion picture industry, were withdrawn. Students found themselves unable to pay for even the barest necessities. To keep them in school, the newly renamed Loyola University afforded students a "pay what you can" approach to tuition. In some cases a barter system resulted, with one family paying for their son's education by providing a steady supply of fresh eggs.

Loyola University grew during the 1930s, but World War II decimated the student body. In 1943, enrollment fell to 85, and 1945 produced only one graduate. This situation dramatically reversed itself after the war ended, when the influx of veterans swelled campus enrollment to almost 2,000 students. Quonset huts, pressed into service as classrooms and "temporary housing" in 1946, remained on campus for 14 years.

Charles S. Casassa, S.J., president from 1949 to 1969, rethought and essentially reinvented the University with an unprecedented 20 program of reorganization, building and expansion. He also laid the groundwork for the affiliation of the all-male Loyola University and the all-female Marymount College in

1968. By 1973, the two schools merged to become Loyola Marymount University, and for the first time a significant number of women arrived on the Westchester campus.

Today, undergraduate instruction is provided in four colleges — Liberal Arts, Business Administration, Communication and Fine Arts, and Science and Engineering — and the School of Education. The University offers 30 master's degree programs and seven education credential programs, and Loyola Law School grants the juris doctor degree. More than 4,000 undergraduates and 1,200 graduates attend the Westchester campus, and more than 1,400 others participate at the Law School's downtown campus, which was designed by renowned architect Frank O. Gehry. These students represent all 50 states and more than 70 foreign countries, and though Loyola Marymount is a Catholic university, there are students and faculty from all religious and ethnic backgrounds.

The tradition of giving back to others continues. Members of the Loyola Marymount community dedicate 100,000 hours each year to working with more gang members, helping the sick, easing the lot of battered women and the homeless, working at AIDS hospices and caring for abused children. The Law School was among the first in the nation to institute a pro bono requirement for graduation, which calls for each student to volunteer a minimum of 40 hours of his or her time for the good of people in the community.

The University is prepared to take its educational mission into the 21st century. Success begets success, and continuing efforts by administrators, faculty, alumni and students alike assure Loyola Marymount University of its ongoing place as the preeminent institution of Catholic higher education in the Western United States.

Los Angeles Archbishop John Cantwell breaks ground for Loyola college's new campus on May 20, 1928.

MOUNT ST. MARY'S COLLEGE

ount St. Mary's College, the only independent Catholic women's college west of the Mississippi River, offers a values-based liberal arts education for women as well as innovative programs for professional men and women on two historical Los Angeles campuses.

For more than 70 years, the college has maintained a tradition of excellence in education based on key values that will guide the institution toward its future as well: intellectual rigor, compassionate faith, individual leadership and dedicated service.

Founded in 1925 by the Sisters of St. Joseph of Carondelet, the original campus was housed at St. Mary's Academy, at Slauson and Crenshaw Boulevards in Los Angeles. Property was purchased in the Santa Monica Mountains in 1927 and that site in Brentwood became the Chalon Campus, which is home to the baccalaureate degree programs, a master's program in physical therapy and a Weekend College, which gives working men and women an opportunity to earn a bachelor's degree by attending school every third weekend.

The Doheny Campus near downtown Los Angeles was originally a neighborhood of Victorian homes built in the 1890s. The oil pioneering family of Carrie Estelle and Edward Doheny purchased nine of the homes over a period of years. Edward died in 1935 and when Carrie Estelle died in 1958, the 15-acre estate was left to the Los Angeles Archdiocese, which deeded it the Sisters

A student on a balcony overlooking the Chalon Campus of Mount St. Mary's College, Los Angeles. The view from the hillside campus stretches from Downtown Los Angeles to the Pacific Ocean. *Courtesy Brad Elliott*

An organic chemistry class during the 1940s at Mount St. Mary's College

of St. Joseph. Mount St. Mary's College opened the Doheny Campus at this site in 1962 and now offers graduate, educational credential and associate degree programs there. Many of the graduate and credential programs are offered in an evening and weekend format.

In order to facilitate travel between the two campuses, the college offers free shuttle service. Students can also take College shuttles into surrounding communities where they are minutes from cultural enrichment, recreation, internships and community service opportunities.

The nearly 2,000-member student body benefits from a student-centered faculty that provides a challenging and supportive learning environment in classes and labs averaging 16 students. Ninety-eight percent of the full time faculty have Ph.D.s or terminal degrees in their field. But what the faculty offers goes far beyond advanced degrees from prestigious universities. Teaching is their first priority. They feel the educational process occurs on an individual, human scale fed by lively debate and hands-on opportunities.

Courses are offered in health, liberal arts, education, business and other subjects. There are seven associate, 22 baccalaureate, two Weekend College and four graduate degrees offered. The nursing program, which graduated its inaugural class in 1952, was Southern California's first baccalaureate degree program in nursing. Since the start, the College has granted more than 12,800 degrees.

The College, which ranks among the top regional universities in the West in U.S. *News & World Report*, is

committed to providing educational opportunities for under-served women. The Doheny Campus accepts educationally disadvantaged students into the two-year "alternative access" program and more than half of those who enter this rigorous program complete the associate degree and/or transfer into a baccalaureate program.

The College offers extensive student services including tutoring, counseling, fitness facilities, health services, career planning and campus ministry. This personal attention contributed to the College being named one of two institutions in the nation that are models for graduating minority students at above-average rates by the American Council on Education.

Another key aspect of the Mount St. Mary's philosophy is its goal to prepare women for positions of leadership. The Women's Leadership Program has been nationally recognized for the dynamic skills and opportunities it creates for students. Leadership courses and seminars are directly related to community and national service activities, ensuring that Mount St Mary's students are among those participating in the most exciting projects in their fields.

Students with exceptional ability in every academic area are encouraged to enjoy special academic challenges through participation in the Honors Program. While undergraduate-level research is often unheard of at larger institutions where only graduate level students conduct research, many undergraduate students at Mount St. Mary's find themselves conducting research. They also present their results at conferences, giving them an obvious advantage when applying to graduate programs at other institutions. Students also participate in internships locally and nationally, including Washington, D.C., and attend Study Abroad programs throughout the world.

Community outreach is a significant part of the mission of the College. The Catholic tradition of Mount St. Mary's offers a value orientation for the student's personal life and career, laying the foundation for a commitment that views professional life as service. Students obviously take this lesson to heart because more than 87 percent of Mount St. Mary's seniors report they are actively involved in volunteering and the institution was named a Character Building College by the John Templeton Foundation. Just a few examples of community outreach opportunities include:

- The Social Action Program on the Doheny campus ensures that every student in the associate degree program provides at least 25 hours of service to the community.
- The Urban Engagement and Civic Responsibility Program makes the College a resource for the community by involving students directly in community organizations.
- The Center for Cultural Fluency is designed to provide K-12 teachers with cultural diversity resources and workshops.

While tradition remains an important and bonding element at Mount St. Mary's, the challenges of educating new generations of women for the next millennium are not being overlooked. The new Sister Magdalen Coughlin Learning Complex serves as one example of the efforts the College is taking to provide facilities to meet the growing needs of its students. Named for the prominent Los Angeles leader who served as Mount St. Mary's president from 1976-1989 and chancellor from 1989 until her death in 1994, the complex houses a library, Cultural Fluency Center, Academic Building and Learning Resource Center.

The College's $40 million comprehensive capital campaign is raising funds to maintain the high quality of facilities, continue providing excellent financial aid resources, enhance academic program offerings and add to the Annual Fund. It will conclude in 1999.

It is an exciting and enriching time for this institution that is a haven of peace, belonging and educational excellence in the center of an urban area with an ongoing need for those values to be reinforced. With lessons taught from both the past and the present, Mount St. Mary's College prepares for the future with innovative solutions for a changing world.

Doheny Campus students take a break between classes. *Courtesy Brad Elliott*

SERVICE EMPLOYEES INTERNATIONAL UNION LOCAL 660

Service Employees International Union Local 660 represents approximately 40,000 Los Angeles County employees, protecting their interests and serving as their political voice.

Local 660 members serve Los Angeles in a variety of capacities. They groom and maintain the county's beaches, care for the sick in public hospitals, protect the quality of the drinking water, keep records in the courts, administer benefits for the poor and homeless, maintain the library system, help run the jails and work with parolees, and perform many other tasks that keep Los Angeles running and its residents well-served. Local 660 also represents workers in the Sanitation Districts, the Los Angeles County Office of Education, the Santa Monica/Malibu Unified School District, the Los Angeles City Housing Authority, the city of South El Monte, and in private, nonprofit health clinics.

Local 660 was founded in 1911 as the Los Angeles County Employees Association. For decades, the Association protected the interests of its workers as the county expanded. In 1971, the Association affiliated with the Service Employees International Union, becoming part of one of the most active labor organizations in the United States. Today, SEIU claims over one million members, and Local 660 is the largest public sector union in Southern California.

Over the past several decades, Local 660 has led the way in many Southern California labor causes. In 1985, the union won the right for California public employees to strike. When the recession and the resulting fiscal crisis threatened to destroy the County's health care system in 1995, Local 660 was instrumental in obtaining Federal funds to help preserve services. In 1997, the union managed the successful campaign to approve Proposition L, which provided additional funds to keep County libraries open.

Local 660 fights to rebuild LAC/USC at a larger 750 bed size.

The union keeps LA running by organizing its yearly Emergency Relief Run and Walk fund-raiser.

Local 660 leads L.A. County workers in successful 1997 fight for long-overdue wage increases.

Through a combination of concerted mass action and political pressure, Local 660 has pursued and won many battles to protect its members' jobs and preserve County services. It has been instrumental in forming many county-wide alliances, including labor organizations, community groups, and political forces, who align to fight for a variety of causes, from opposing divisive Propositions 187 and 209, to preserving County services. In 1998, Local 660 led the coalition that defeated Proposition 226, an initiative intended to silence the political voice of working people.

In the days of shrinking government, tight budgets, and a changing economy, Local 660 faces many new challenges. In seeking to protect the jobs and working conditions of its members, the Local also speaks for a large portion of the Los Angeles community in demanding accessible quality health care for all, decent and humane treatment for the homeless and the indigent, and a preservation of traditional community services. It is also constantly redefining itself to better meet the needs of its members and the community. The tendency toward privatization of County services has led Local 660 to follow its members' work and launch aggressive organizing campaigns in the private sector. The future is likely to see

Local 660 representing many more workers in both the public and private sectors.

Throughout its history, SEIU Local 660 has struggled to bring better wages and working conditions to its members and to improve the community in which we all live. The Local continues to be committed to that fight. Its mission is to "improve the lives of working people and their families, and lead the way to a more just and humane society."

Local 660 fights to keep Rancho Los Amigos Hospital public and accessible.

THE UNIVERSITY OF CALIFORNIA, LOS ANGELES

y any measure, the University of California, Los Angeles (UCLA), ranks among the world's preeminent universities. From its celebrated faculty to its super-high-achieving students, from its distinguished alumni to its myriad contributions to the community, UCLA has attained a stature to which most institutions of higher education can only aspire.

It is a remarkable achievement for a university that measures its life span in decades rather than centuries. And it is even more extraordinary given the humble nature of its origins. In 1913, Edward A. Dickson, a 33-year-old reporter for the *Los Angeles Express*, was appointed to the Board of Regents of the University of California, his alma mater. Dickson was a Southern California booster. With its rapid population growth in the early years of the 20th century, Southern California was starting to tilt the state's balance of political power away from the north. A determined cadre of Los Angeles-area citizens had concluded that a public university was essential to the future of the region. Until Dickson's appointment, however, their efforts had been stymied by a Board of Regents who feared that a second campus would weaken the University and compete for resources.

Dickson and his constituents launched a crusade for a southern campus of the University of California, and in 1916, after extensive political maneuvering and under escalating public pressure, the Regents grudgingly opened a branch of University Extension in downtown Los Angeles. A summer session followed in 1917. In 1919, amid unrelenting demands, the Regents voted to take over the campus of the Los Angeles State Normal School, a teacher training institution, to establish the Southern Branch of the University of California. By the mid-1920s, the Southern Branch, like the region it served, had experienced phenomenal

growth that had outstripped its capacity. With the help of bond measures passed by the state and four local communities, and a special appropriation by the Los Angeles County Board of Supervisors, the University purchased a new site on the outskirts of Los Angeles, in Westwood. There, a new campus was built, and to signal the Southern Branch's coming of age, its name was changed to the University of California at Los Angeles — UCLA for short.

UCLA's fortunes, like those of Los Angeles, waxed and waned and waxed over the next few decades. During the 1940s and 1950s, the university grew by a number of professional schools, but it was not until Franklin Murphy became chancellor in 1960 that UCLA emerged as an academic and cultural leader. Murphy set out to transform what was then a modest regional institution into an outstanding research university of national stature. His initiatives, which included building a new library and other much-needed facilities and the advancement of interdisciplinary organized research units, attracted the first-rate faculty necessary to effect the metamorphosis.

Charles Young was Murphy's protégé. He succeeded Murphy as chancellor in 1969 and built on his mentor's

foundation over the next three decades. Faculty hiring was accelerated during the 1980s, specifically in areas not currently fashionable but that UCLA's academic leaders believed would prove essential in the near future. The strategy produced world-class programs in such emerging fields as political economy, women's studies and Chicano Studies.

During the same period, UCLA's stature as a center for innovation and discovery was established. The university was the birthplace of the Internet in 1969, and home of the nation's first departments of dance and ethnomusicology. UCLA researchers played pivotal roles in research that led to the discovery of the "top quark," the last in a set of subatomic building blocks; engineering faculty were among the first to identify smog particles; and UCLA scholars opened a window into the ancient world through the analysis of 2,000-year-old scrolls.

Other UCLA researchers were responsible for developing new methods of tissue typing to reduce the likelihood of rejection in organ transplantation; PET scanning to track functional changes within the body's biochemistry also originated at the University. It was at UCLA that AIDS was first described as a new disease, and at UCLA's Jonsson Comprehensive Cancer Center that a gene believed to play an active role in some human breast cancer was implicated in ovarian cancer. UCLA doctors performed the first combined small bowel/liver transplant in the Western United States.

By the time Chancellor Young passed the mantle of leadership to his successor, Albert Carnesale, in 1997, UCLA was ranked among the top ten U.S. research universities and was a preeminent cultural and intellectual center — an achievement it had attained in less than 80 years, making it a virtual prodigy among its peer institutions. UCLA had also become one of the largest employers in Southern California and one of the most successful public universities at attracting private support.

Today the university that owes its very existence to the will of the people continues to give back to the community, the nation and the world in innumerable ways. It educates more students than any other California university, offering degree programs in more than 100 fields.

Since 1990-91, the UCLA Medical Center has regularly been rated the best hospital in the West, and the UCLA library is consistently ranked among the top five university libraries in the nation. The UCLA Film and Television Archive is the largest university-based archive in the world, second only to the Library of Congress. UCLA's Center for the Performing Arts is one of the largest arts presenters in the nation, and UCLA Extension is the largest urban-based continuing education program in the United States.

Home to some of the finest minds in the world, UCLA numbers four Nobel laureates among its faculty, as well as numerous Guggenheim and several MacArthur fellows. Some 31 of UCLA's Ph.D. programs are ranked among the top 20 in their field — the third best showing in the nation. UCLA also ranks sixth in federal research support, and 29 faculty members belong to the National Academy of Sciences.

It is a proud heritage, but UCLA remains a work in progress. As long as there are mysteries to solve, communities to help and frontiers to explore, UCLA will build on its tradition of excellence, striving for ever greater distinction.

The Right Chemistry — UCLA biochemist Paul Boyer, recipient of a Nobel Prize in Chemistry, discusses his pioneering work in investigating how ATP (adenosine triphosphate) — the cellular energy that drives all biological reactions — is formed.

Student Life — Students have always found unique solutions to parking on campus.

Graduation Day — Two women, Amy Boyle and Lucille Kirkpatrick, take a moment away from 1930 graduation ceremonies. Theirs was the first class to graduate on the new Westwood campus.

UNITED FIREFIGHTERS OF LOS ANGELES CITY

One hundred-five firefighters were called to a stubborn blaze in the Los Feliz area as flames raced through a vacant four-story apartment building..."

"An explosion at a Texaco refinery rocked the harbor area Monday and ignited an intense, 90-minute fire in a processing unit..."

"Fire burned through grass, brush and trees in rugged Griffith Park, stubbornly resisting efforts to bring it under control. Helicopters made water-dropping runs as more than 200 firefighters were marshaled against the blaze in the nation's largest municipal park..."

"The LA City Fire Department had gone 14 years without a violent death in the line of duty when within a two week span in March, four firefighters died in two separate incidents..."

These true scenarios are typical of the hazardous conditions Los Angeles City firefighters face each time they respond to emergency calls. It's expected of these highly skilled men and women to risk life and limb battling blazes and saving lives and property.

But in an era of economic recession, downsizing and government cutbacks have significantly impacted the ranks of the nation's fire and police departments. For this reason, organizations like the United Firefighters of Los Angeles City (UFLAC) are all the more critical to ensure the rights of those whose job it is to "protect and serve."

UFLAC, IAFF Local 112, began as two separate entities: the Firefighter's Union, founded in 1906, received its charter from the International Association of Firefighters in 1918; and the Los Angeles Fire and Police Protective League.

The local union was responsible for legislation that would guarantee the firefighters the right to organize. Although the law forbade strikes, the organization served as the city model and case law for organizing all California public employees.

Since its inception, the goals of UFLAC have remained essentially the same: fair pay for a skillful, difficult and often dangerous profession; protection for a firefighter's family and a pension tailored to his/her limited working years; improved and lightweight protective clothing and equipment such as breathing apparatus and turn out gear and better legal protection for injuries which result in permanent disability. Additionally, UFLAC strives to ensure each firefighter's basic rights of a reasonable workweek, vacation, medical care and a fair promotional system.

Firefighters from Engine 82 help a woman out of a burning structure.
Photo by Mike Meadows

During the late 70s and early 80s, the union won the long sought-after establishment of minimum safety standards, under CAL-OSHA, for the state's firefighters. These standards incorporated safer helmets, mandatory gloves and safety shoes and a requirement that each firefighter wear a personal alarm device when fighting structure fires. The standard also required that the employer provide all personal protective clothing for each firefighter.

UFLAC was also responsible for launching an extensive public education campaign through a union-community coalition, "Citizens for Better Fire Protection Committee." This committee included members of some of the most influential homeowner groups, chambers of commerce, business and service clubs, retired fire chiefs and organized labor.

UFLAC was the first union to achieve city funding of health benefits for dependents, a dental insurance program, a uniform allowance and host of other rule changes designed to improve the firefighters' profession and economic security for their families.

It was through the union's efforts that state legislators recognized that some chemicals are carcinogenic and presumed responsible for certain kinds of cancer in firefighters, which led to the passage of Assembly Bill 3011. This new law acknowledged that if a firefighter contracted any of these cancers, it would be presumed that the disease resulted from job-related exposure to the chemicals in question.

UFLAC established one of the first employee assistance programs in the nation to assist firefighters with issues of substance abuse, smoking cessation and any other problems which might impact their health and job performance.

The union's newspaper, the *Los Angeles Firefighter*, has won countless awards for outstanding achievement in the field of labor journalism from The Greater Los Angeles Press Club, the Western Labor Communications Association, the International Labor Communications Association and the IAFF.

Through the hard work and dedication of its officers, past and present members and strict adherence to the union's objectives, UFLAC has become one of the largest and most respected organizations among the nation's fire departments and labor unions.

UNITED WAY OF GREATER L.A.

Since 1962, the United Way of Greater Los Angeles has been the best way to help the most people.

Although no single charity can solve all of a community's needs, the United Way funds a wide variety of health and human services for people from every walk of life in the greater Los Angeles metropolitan area.

Since its inception, the United Way's mission has been to serve as a "voluntary organization dedicated to helping people, by uniting individuals and institutions — government, private and voluntary — in a communitywide effort to plan, support, deliver and evaluate effective human service programs that are responsive to changing community needs."

The county's largest nongovernmental provider of funds for health and human services organizations, the United Way of Greater L.A.'s roots can be traced back to 1854 with the advent of the Hebrew Benevolent Society, which is believed to be the city's first social agency. Nearly 40 years later, the Associated Charities was formed, incorporating 13 separate agencies.

The first Community Chest campaign, launched in L.A. in 1924 as a combined appeal of 166 agencies, raised nearly $2.5 million by 168,000 citizens. Subsequent Community Chests campaigns followed until 1962, when 38 Community Chests consolidated to form the United Way Inc.

Priority issues include child care and development, youth education and development, families in crises and homelessness and community health.

The first Community Chest campaign, launched in L.A. in 1924 as a combined appeal of 166 agencies, raised nearly $2.5 million by 168,000 citizens. Subsequent Community Chests campaigns followed until 1962, when 38 Community Chests consolidated to form the United Way Inc.

By 1977, the then-$40 million campaign partnership included nine major health care organizations. Three years later, the United Way merged with AID/United Givers, an association of employee and corporate funding campaigns. During the same time period, the nonprofit adopted a five-year admissions plan to enlarge the United Service network with the addition of 75 agencies.

In 1995, the United Way headquarters moved to its current location in downtown Los Angeles on West Sixth Street. The same year, Joe Haggerty stepped in as executive director and began implementing innovative new programs to expand the organization's already-extensive vision and outreach.

Highlights of these endeavors include the Crenshaw Corridor Report, the launch of an Asian Pacific Profiles report, serving as the lead on the selection of the community torchbearers for the Olympic Torch Relay in 1996 and winning the United Way of America's National Diversity Award the next year for the organization's support of diversity in all areas, including staffing, staffing policies/benefits, volunteer involvement, funding and fund raising.

The United Way is the area leader in bringing together local business, government, social services and community leaders to help assess and address a wide variety of community needs. Priority issues include child care and development, youth education and development, families in crises and homelessness and community health.

More than four million Los Angeles County residents, spread across the 5,500 square miles that make up the Antelope Valley, Westside, Downtown, San Fernando/Santa Clarita Valleys, San Gabriel Valley and the Harbor area, are served through a network of over 250 charities focused on health and human services.

These charities include local chapters of well-known organizations such as the American Cancer Society, the American Heart Association, the Boys and Girls Club and the Y.M.C.A to community-based charities like the Long Beach Community Improvement League, AIDS Project L.A. and the Literacy Network of Greater L.A. Inc.

UNIVERSITY OF SOUTHERN CALIFORNIA

os Angeles was little more than a frontier town in the 1870s when members of the Methodist Episcopal Conference first sought to establish a university in the region. In 1879, three community leaders — O.W. Childs, a Protestant horticulturalist; former California Governor John G. Downey, an Irish-Catholic businessman; and I.W. Hellman, a German-Jewish banker and philanthropist — deeded to the Board of Trustees of the University of Southern California 308 lots in what was then known as West Los Angeles. A portion of the land, which was located within the original land grant establishing "El Pueblo de la Reina de Los Angeles," was to be reserved for the actual campus. More than an act of generosity, the gift of land was an expression of the confidence in the future of the growing City of Los Angeles.

As the only major comprehensive university in Southern California for nearly 50 years, USC was called upon to provide the knowledge and training for a burgeoning region. By 1930, most of the Southland's doctors, lawyers, judges, teachers, dentists, pharmacists, urban planners and government officials were USC-trained. The nation's first schools in international relations and cinema were established at USC. By the late 1940s, USC's School of Architecture played an instrumental role in solving the postwar housing crisis, and USC graduates virtually designed the Los Angeles skyline, including such well-known edifices as City Hall, the Department of Water and Power Building, St. Basil's Catholic Church, and Cedars-Sinai Medical Center.

Today, USC is the oldest and largest private research university in the American West and a member of the prestigious Association of American Universities, an organization of the top 62 universities in the United States and Canada. It ranks among the top ten private universities in sponsored research and development, has one of the fastest growing endowments in the nation and

Since its unveiling in 1930, the statue of the bronzed Trojan warrior has served as a popular meeting place for students on campus.

is Los Angeles' largest private employer. USC's student body has grown from a class size of 53 in 1880 to more than 28,000 undergraduate, graduate and doctoral students pursing degrees in hundreds of fields. USC has 240,000 living alumni, extending the Trojan family across the nation and around the world. Graduates of USC have walked on the moon (Neil Armstrong '70), influenced international affairs (Warren Christopher '45 and Norman Schwarzkopf '64), shaped the face of architecture (Frank Gehry '54) and entertained the world (David Wolper '49, George Lucas '66, and Herb Alpert '54).

The USC University Park Campus, located three miles south of Downtown Los Angeles, features numerous parks, eateries, libraries, museums and galleries which the general public is invited to visit. The USC School of Music offers 500 productions annually in addition to performances offered by USC's School of Theatre, exhibitions hosted by USC's School of Fine Arts, and lecture programs sponsored by a variety of schools. The USC Health Sciences Campus, located northeast of the main campus, is home to the USC Norris Comprehensive Cancer Center, the USC University Hospital [see following page] and the Doheny Eye Institute. USC's medical faculty staffs five of the city's premier hospitals including the region's largest — LA County+USC Medical Center.

In just this past decade, USC has already marked a number of major milestones including the establishment of the only national research center in multimedia, the establishment of the Annenberg Center for Communication (the result of the largest single cash gift in higher education from Ambassador Walter Annenberg), the endowment of the $100 million Alfred E. Mann Institute for Biomedical Engineering, and the bestowing of a Nobel Prize to USC faculty member George Olah. As the university prepares to enter a new century, it remains committed to the foundation of excellence forged by its founders.

USC UNIVERSITY HOSPITAL

ew people had heard of Moebius syndrome, a rare birth defect that robs its victims of the facial muscles necessary for smiling, until surgeons at USC University Hospital gave 11-year-old Mallory Wofford her first smile. This and other leading-edge surgeries are what take place every day at USC University Hospital.

The opening in 1991 of the Richard K. Eamer Medical Plaza and its cornerstone, USC University Hospital, marked an exciting new beginning in Southern California by uniting private enterprise with one of the nation's leading universities. This collaboration between entrepreneurship and education has advanced medicine while meeting the future needs of health care and medical education.

The University of Southern California (USC), a private institution founded in 1880, entered into the partnership with Tenet Healthcare Corporation (then National Medical Enterprises [NME]) to expand resources for patient care, medical research and physician training. For almost a century, the USC School of Medicine has been affiliated with Los Angeles County medical facilities, in particular, the LAC+USC Medical Center, one of the largest teaching hospitals in the nation. The School supported some 850 full-time faculty and 3,000 voluntary faculty, but there were few ways for patients outside the county system to take advantage of USC medical expertise — some of the best in the nation.

It was increasingly evident that in order to attract the best new clinicians and to provide a setting where students and residents could experience a diversity of patients and medical conditions, USC needed a private practice hospital.

By 1985, the USC Board of Trustees and the NME Board of Directors had approved the plan. The 275-bed hospital — complete with private practice offices in the form of a Healthcare Consultation Center, a heliport and more than $32 million in equipment — opened to patients in May of 1991.

Providing options — for patient care, for physician research, and for student training at the USC School of Medicine — was the vision behind the development of USC University Hospital. Beyond medical care, the hospital has also added more than 1,000 new jobs and contributed millions of tax dollars to the community.

The now 284-bed facility is operating at staffed capacity; and additional patients are treated daily at an adjacent outpatient surgery center, opened in 1995, and transitional care unit. The Healthcare Consultation Center, which houses medical offices for USC physicians, is filled to overflowing.

"USC University Hospital plays an essential role in expanding the reputation of the USC School of Medicine and USC in general," says Stephen J. Ryan, dean of the USC School of Medicine, "while at the same time significantly advancing the state of the art of medicine."

The opening of USC University Hospital also enhanced the university's ability to attract and retain many respected clinical specialists, which is vital to maintaining and expanding its standard and reputation of excellence.

Patients from all over the world are drawn to USC University Hospital because of the knowledge and skill of our doctors. That, coupled with the outstanding care from a committed and talented staff, has made the hospital a place that people seek out for their medical and surgical needs.

Among the hospital's specialty diagnostic and treatment services are: Gamma Knife, Positron Emission Tomography (PET), open-heart surgery, cardiac catheterization and interventional cardiology, arthritis & joint implant surgery, spine surgery, complex neurosurgeries and multi-organ transplantation (liver, heart, heart-lung, lung, kidney). The hospital also has specialty centers in the areas of liver disease, stroke, lung disease, athletic medicine and arthritis and joint implant surgery.

USC University Hospital, which opened in 1991, is the cornerstone of the Richard K. Eamer Medical Plaza near downtown Los Angeles.

WATTSHEALTH SYSTEMS, INC.

ounded in 1967, WATTSHealth Systems (WHS) is a community services enterprise that has celebrated over 30 years of community commitment. Literally rising from the ashes of the 1965 Watts rebellion, WHS now serves over 200,000 people each year of all races, creeds, colors, national origins and economic statuses.

In three decades, a small health clinic that many people gave no chance of surviving has grown into a major conglomerate. In 1997, the WATTSHealth Systems was organized as an umbrella organization for about 23 different health programs and organizations dedicated to building and maintaining individual, group and community health and well being.

Quality health care involved more than meeting the medical needs of the community. For this reason, WATTSHealth Systems takes a holistic approach that includes business development, financial opportunities and cultural activities that reflect the ethnic diversity of Southern California.

With nearly 800 employees, WATTSHealth Systems is one of the largest nonprofit employers in South Central Los Angels. Area residents have always been given consideration for employment and have received on-the-job training for positions.

The WATTSHealth Center is the first and flagship program within the Systems. Original funding for the health center came from an Office of Economic Opportunity (OEO) grant for more than $2 million and included the provision that a medical school sponsor the program. The University of Southern California (USC) agreed to accept responsibility for the program and let the fledgling community organization use space in a warehouse on university property.

The Center was named the South Central Multi-Purpose Health Services Center when it was dedicated in 1967. It was the first comprehensive medical facility built to serve the 30,000 residents of Watts who, until then, had been faced with a two-hour bus ride to traverse the almost 12 miles to the Los Angeles County General Hospital, the nearest treatment center.

Once there, they sometimes waited all day for treatment. At the time, the physician-patient ratio in Watts was one physician for every 4,200 residents, sadly inadequate for a community in the richest nation in the world.

The Center was renamed the Watts Health Center in 1979 when a new building was constructed. WATTSHealth Center is now one of the largest community health centers in the United States, providing comprehensive primary and urgent care services to over 170,000 patients annually.

The Center was founded on the premise that physicians must be concerned with each patient as an individual and simultaneously maintain an awareness of the medical, social strengths and weakness of the patient's entire family. Issues surrounding the delivery of health care took a high priority, such as transportation, reducing the waiting period, language barriers and other social needs that impact on health care access.

During the 1992 civil unrest, while other parts of the city burned, the WATTSHealth Center remained untouched. It is a glowing symbol of the great things that can be accomplished when everyone works together for the good of the community.

The changing demographics of Watts from predominately African American to predominately Latino, as well as the influx of Korean merchants has sometimes caused tension and friction among the three groups.

WATTSHealth Systems works hard to open the avenues of communication by exposing each ethnic group to the customs, traditions and beliefs of the others. Center facilities are used for art and other cultural displays, meetings, conferences, seminars and educational sessions open to community professionals and the general public.

A major milestone in the history of WATTSHealth Systems was the establishment of UHP Healthcare in 1973. In 1982, it received certification as an HMO. This nonprofit, federally qualified and state-licensed health maintenance organization provides services to its 90,000 members through a network of medical groups and private physicians. Patients range from Medicare and Medi-Cal recipients to individuals, families and employees of small businesses.

One of the goals of WATTSHealth Systems is to serve as a facilitator of social and economic development in underdeveloped areas of Southern California. This is part of a long-term program to enhance the health and general quality of life within the community.

Toward this end, in 1996 WATTSHealth Systems made two major moves. First, it acquired a controlling interest in Family Savings Bank to provide full banking services with an emphasis on home loans. Family Savings Bank had a long history of serving the financial needs of the Watts community from its founding in 1948.

Also in 1996, WHS purchased the Los Angeles Black Business Expo & Trade Show. This exposition is held annually at the Los Angeles Convention Center and provides the opportunity for small businesses with limited advertising budgets to present their products and services to thousands of potential customers.

Following this acquisition, WATTSHealth Systems started a year-round business development center providing assistance in event planning, seminar development, public relations and marketing to help entrepreneurs improve their operations and also their Expo presentations.

Some of the many other services offered by WATTSHealth Systems are: mobile units for radiology, pediatrics, dental and other services; comprehensive residential and outpatient substance abuse rehabilitation treatment; prenatal care, family planning and health education; and AIDS prevention, early intervention and treatment services.

Building on more than 30 years of providing quality health care for undeserved populations, WATTSHealth Systems stands poised to help residents of Los Angles, Orange, Riverside and San Bernardino counties live happier and healthier lives well into the new millennium.

WATTSHealth Center, Los Angeles

R&D LABORATORIES, INC.

Although renal dialysis patients constitute a small segment of the population (fewer than a quarter million), their medical needs are great. The kidneys function to remove toxic substances from the bloodstream. Dialysis, a process by which a machine is used to remove toxins, is required when the kidneys fail. The major causes of kidney failure are uncontrolled high blood pressure and diabetes.

While dialysis is a vital tool in prolonging the lives of kidney patients, it also creates specific nutritional needs. It is the goal of R&D Laboratories, Inc. to increase a dialysis patient's quality of life by providing pharmaceuticals and nutritionals formulated specifically for their needs.

Major pharmaceutical companies often fail to produce formulations specific to the needs of the dialysis patient. Recognizing the need for someone to fill this niche, Rhoda Makoff, Ph.D. founded R&D Laboratories, Inc. in 1983. Makoff earned her Ph.D. in biochemistry from UCLA and subsequently worked in the Department of Medicine at UCLA's Center for Health Sciences doing research in diabetes and kidney disease. She is an acknowledged expert whose experience and understanding of kidney disease led to the founding of R&D Laboratories, Inc.

R&D Laboratories, Inc. enlisted the aid of recognized renal nutrition authorities, incorporating the latest medical research in the development of its products. The company's initial product was a vitamin supplement, Nephro-Vite®.

The success of the initial product led to research and production of more renal-specific pharmaceuticals and nutritionals. Fifteen years after the introduction of Nephro-Vite®, R&D's product line had grown to include 20 prescription and over-the-counter renal-specific products, available through pharmacies and hospitals nationwide and internationally.

As a result of its innovation and niche marketing, R&D Laboratories, Inc. has experienced rapid growth. For three consecutive years, it has been included in the roster of the INC. list of the 500 fastest-growing privately held companies in the United States. Additionally, R&D has been honored as one of the most rapidly advancing technology companies in Southern California and across the nation.

Initially, R&D formulated all of its own products, but its current growth strategy incorporates licensing products from other companies as well. Since the company outsources its manufacturing, packaging, sample fulfillment and shipping to outside suppliers, its capacity to license in new products and realize sales is flexible.

The company has a commitment to excellence, innovation, efficiency and making the company a great place to work because of its creative environment. The expectation is that every employee will do more than their best, for the company and the customer.

At R&D Laboratories, Inc., years of research and innovation have resulted in a company that serves its clients with aggressive and creative products formulated to enhance the quality of their lives. It is the goal of R&D Laboratories, Inc. to provide cutting-edge leadership in the nutritional and pharmaceutical management of kidney disease. With such a successful strategy, the company faces the 21st century with a record of achievement, a commitment to excellence and an exceptional, motivated staff who create the zeal to be a major healthcare company in its field.

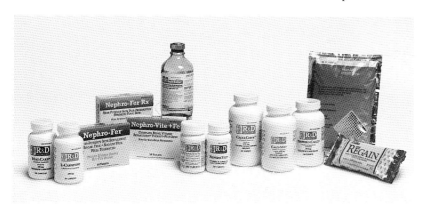

GOODWILL INDUSTRIES

oodwill Industries of Southern California has been providing job training, education and job placement services to people with disabilities and vocational disadvantages throughout Los Angeles County for over 79 years.

In 1916, Katherine B. Higgins started what is today Goodwill Industries of Southern California near the plaza of the old Pueblo in Los Angeles. In the plaza, known as Olvera Street, Goodwill started its mission by collecting, repairing and selling clothing garments to poverty-stricken residents.

Over the years, Goodwill has expanded and now serves more than 2,000 people per year through its various educational and job training services. Many of the individuals helped by Goodwill are physically, mentally or emotionally disabled adults or parents of children with severe disabilities. Others are reformed and reforming addicts, ex-convicts, former gang members, veterans, welfare recipients and the homeless. Goodwill believes that with the proper training and support, many of these individuals can find and retain jobs to build independent lives.

Goodwill offers people a means to achieve this end through its education, training and work experience programs. The first step is to evaluate the needs and strengths of the individual. Then, the trainee is taught to develop basic work habits in Goodwill's retail program or through the organization's industrial services contract program. Goodwill's 25 retail stores in the greater Los Angeles area not only provide a place of employment for over 1,000 people daily, but also provide low-cost quality merchandise to its customers and have aided Goodwill to become nearly 90 percent self-supporting.

Accountability, compassion, inclusion, integrity, service, spirituality and vision. These seven organizational values shape Goodwill's daily operations and long-term goals. Because Goodwill Industries realizes that community support makes their operation possible, the organization operates with integrity and

remains fully accountable to the community.

Goodwill strives to provide excellent service to its clients, donors, and customers through its recruitment of highly-skilled and professional staff and volunteers. The organization makes a conscious, systematic and active effort to encourage the inclusion of people with disabilities in community life. As a part of this effort, each individual who is helped by Goodwill is encouraged at every step of the way and is treated with dignity and respect at all times. A healthy spirituality is also encouraged as a part of the organization's overall mission.

Throughout this century, Goodwill has readjusted its programs to meet the changing needs of its surrounding communities. The ability to adapt to society's changes has enabled Goodwill to continue to enhance the quality of the lives of people who have disabilities and other vocational disadvantages by assisting them to become productive and self-sufficient through education, training and job opportunities.

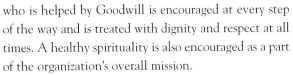

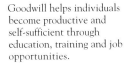

Goodwill helps individuals become productive and self-sufficient through education, training and job opportunities.

Goodwill believes that with the proper training and support, many individuals with disabilities and other vocational disadvantages can find and retain jobs to build independent lives.

NEW ECONOMICS FOR WOMEN

ew Economics for Women (NEW) began when a group of Latinas came together to discuss designing affordable housing for single parents and their families. Their dream was to design housing in a way that made an economic difference in these families' lives. They understood from their own individual experiences that public policy leaders and others had paid little attention to assisting poor Latinas meet the challenges of being the family's primary caretaker and sole financial supporter.

Based on that initial grassroots meeting, these Latina community leaders formed a central philosophy for NEW: they would address poverty from the economic perspective of women by designing safe, affordable housing with the support services that families need to attain economic self-sufficiency. Their programs would be based on two principles: the needs of women and children had to be an economic priority in order for any neighborhood to prosper; and community support and participation had to be the cornerstone of any affordable housing program. With this framework established, NEW incorporated in 1985. The volunteer leaders began to fundraise and search for a site for their first housing development.

NEW President Bea Olvera-Stotzer, founding Board member Maria Rodriguez and NEW's Executive Director Maggie Cervantes pictured in one of the play areas for the children of La Villa Mariposa.

Soon after, NEW received funding for their first housing development when the City of Los Angeles Community Redevelopment Agency awarded them $5.3 million. This sizable grant paved the way for future funding from local and national banks, lending institutions and private foundations.

Five years after incorporating, NEW broke ground for Casa Loma, a 110-unit housing development, located just west of downtown Los Angeles. Casa Loma provided its residents with an array of educational and support programs such as an on-site daycare center, English literacy classes, programs for seniors, case management services, a computer homework center and an after school youth program. It was the first of many developments designed by NEW to integrate affordable housing with educational and economic programs, and as a result, helping families move realistically from poverty to economic self-reliance.

With the immediate local and national success of Casa Loma, NEW began expanding its housing and economic development efforts. It opened other housing developments, including La Posada, a 60-unit development for teen mothers and their children. La Posada was the first and only program in the nation to offer teen mothers a unique combination of support services to help them emotionally and economically care for their children.

In addition, an economic development center was launched, offering micro-lending services, home ownership seminars and technical training to nearby residents and others. Each step of the way, NEW's leaders and staff set the standards for developing a comprehensive strategy for affordable housing and economic development.

NEW's innovative work has influenced how solutions to poverty are formed in Los Angeles and California, and throughout the nation. While their industry peers turn to them as the model to replicate, agencies such as the U.S. Departments of Housing and Urban Development and Commerce acknowledge NEW's work for its success in increasing a family's long-term earning potential. In less than two decades, NEW's founders had realized their dream to help single parents become self-reliant.

BARLOW RESPIRATORY HOSPITAL

he story of Barlow Respiratory Hospital starts with Walter Jarvis Barlow, an extraordinary man who dedicated his life to meeting the health needs of his community. Born in New York in 1868, he received his A.B. degree in 1889 and his M.D. in 1892. After interning at Mt. Sinai Hospital, he opened his own practice, and the future looked bright for the new doctor. However, in 1895 his life's path took a sharp turn when he contracted tuberculosis.

Demonstrating courage, practicality and optimism, Dr. Barlow headed west for a dry, sunny climate. His infection was mild and soon cured, but thousands of others afflicted with pulmonary disease were far less fortunate. Dr. Barlow's firsthand experience with the disease filled him with the desire to build a sanatorium so he could give proper care to the afflicted and conduct research. In 1902, Dr. Barlow discovered the ideal location — 25 acres of untouched meadowland in Los Angeles set amidst rolling hills adjacent to the city-owned Elysian Park. The conditions were perfect for the imagined facility.

The Barlow Sanatorium turned from dream to reality when it admitted its first patient in 1903. During that first year, 75 applications were received and 34 were accepted. Success bred achievements, and the intervening years saw the facility continue to grow and prosper with its reputation. The years since have brought many changes, but the needs of the surrounding community are still considered and met with the same enthusiasm that originally inspired Barlow to build his great sanatorium.

The facility changed its name to Barlow Respiratory Hospital in 1989 to better reflect its focus toward pulmonary disease. Today, the hospital is recognized as one of the nation's leading centers for ventilator weaning and pulmonary care. A University of Southern California (USC) Medical School affiliated teaching facility, Barlow pulmonologists train students in leading-edge research and technology, providing some of the finest pulmonary education in the country. Furthermore, the hospital has one of the country's best pulmonary research centers dedicated to clinical studies.

With this vast background of experience, the Barlow program has expanded to encompass treatment of other medical concerns such as diabetes, renal disease, heart complications, paralysis and special nutritional demands. Barlow's board-certified specialists develop medical and therapy programs which address a wide variety of issues, including physical, occupational and respiratory therapy, dietary planning and assistance with psychological and social challenges.

To better meet the needs of these patients, the hospital instituted a satellite program of Barlow Respiratory Hospital acute care units within other hospitals. The first such satellite opened in March of 1997 at Presbyterian Intercommunity Hospital in Whittier. This increased proximity has led to a marked improvement in the lives of many patients, allowing them to live more independently.

Soon, Barlow Respiratory Hospital will begin its second century of service. From 1902 to the present, the combination of committed staff, adaptability and unparalleled knowledge of patients' needs has led to the hospital's current status as a leader and visionary in the medical field and laid the groundwork for continued accomplishments into the next millennium.

(Top) Patients convalescing at the hospital in 1914.

Barlow Respiratory Hospital more than 80 years later.

PARTNERS IN LOS ANGELES
TECHNOLOGY

A large and diverse group of businesses have gathered to make Los Angeles one of the world's leading centers of technology innovation, development, manufacturing and employment.

DELTA TAU DATA SYSTEMS INC.

elta Tau Data Systems Inc. may not be a household name, but it's a given that homes and offices in nearly every corner of the world have been touched by the company's cutting-edge technology.

Delta Tau's motion controllers sew, shape and stitch a variety of consumer products, including quilts, box springs and even pajamas. The firm's handiwork can be found in clothing from slippers to suits, and furniture from lamps to tables. Bathroom items such as disposable razors and toilet paper were likely assembled and packaged by the company's PMAC (Programmable Multi-Axis Controller) technology.

PMAC grinds coffee; bakes, slices and packages bread; even filets fish with high-pressure jets; and carefully packages cereal according to weight.

Before sliding behind the wheel of an automobile, PMAC technology has formed the cam shafts, tested the engine, ignited the spark plugs and even painted the exterior.

At the office, PMAC Motion Controllers could be responsible for the manufacture or packaging of an array of items from copier paper and plastic and aluminum products to the disk drive, semiconductors, connectors and even the LCD display on a computer.

More than 50,000 PMACs are at work around the world, productive every day. Applications, in virtually every industry imaginable, are endless: examples include machine tools, welding, food processing, vehicular control, camera control, robotics, material handling, general automation, telescopes, woodworking, surgery, etc.

Over the years, Delta Tau Data Systems has emerged as one of the nation's leading providers of high-tech, innovative motion control hardware, software and solutions for general automation, machine tool, robotics and more.

Given its rich history, rapid growth and position in the global marketplace, it's hard to imagine that this successful operation literally began life as a garage-based business.

Even when working from the garage of his Northridge home in 1975, the firm's visionary founder, Dimitri S. Dimitri always believed in "providing good engineering solutions and services for industrial problems."

Within a few years, the growing company "spilled from the garage into the kitchen and living room" before Dimitri's "better-half," (wife Tammy), moved the no-longer fledgling firm out of the house and into the first of many office spaces, a 2,000-square-foot facility in Canoga Park.

By 1981, Dimitri had made an important decision which would affect the future of the company and redefine its long-term vision. He decided to focus on providing "motion control products" rather than just design services and proceeded to make the transition into this niche market. Delta Tau owes its growth to this simple decision.

Company founders Dimitri and Tammy Dimitri

The company's product line covers motion controllers, servo controllers, motor controllers, MACRO controllers, servo amplifiers, CNC controllers and CNC systems. Delta Tau Data Systems' products are adaptable to a wide variety of leading technologies, providing open architecture and easy-to-use solutions.

The high-tech company's PMAC product, when put to use by other like-minded organizations resulted in the creation of the Hubbel Telescope's corrective lenses. Delta Tau recently forayed into previously "unchartered waters" in the movie industry by providing an eight-axis motion controller as one component of an impressive hydraulic power system which allowed director James Cameron to literally "raise and sink" a two-million-pound scale model of the *Titanic* in the blockbuster film of the same name.

By 1989, Delta Tau had released its first PMAC card and by the early 90s, research led to the creation of a CNC specific package based around an IBM PC which incorporates the spirit of open architecture that currently dominates the PC market.

Delta Tau delivered its first PMAC NC system to NIST in 1992, as a proof of concept for open architecture, PC-based CNC control. The company began selling its machining package the following year and introduced its turning package in 1994. Having survived the Northridge earthquake, the company decided to remain in the L.A. area.

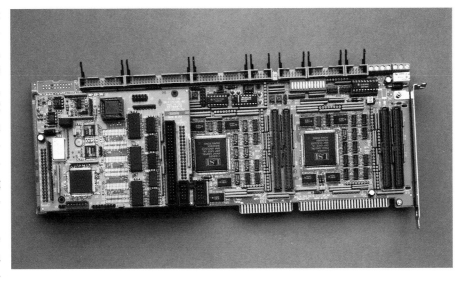

Programmable multi-axis controller cards are the stars of Delta Tau's product lineup.

PMAC NC Pack

Currently operating from a newly acquired state-of-the-art 120,000-square-foot facility, Delta Tau Data Systems is entirely self-financed, and is solely owned by its principals and a few of its 130 employees, some of whom have been with the firm since its inception.

To provide its customers with the latest technologies, Delta Tau works with the leaders in the fields of motion control, CNC, and factory automation and is continually improving the state-of-the-art in both PC-based systems and open architecture standards. The company's greatest assets are its pool of outstanding engineering and production talent which are self-motivated and collectively committed to excellence in service.

Chances are, no matter the location, Delta Tau's leadership products in the Motion Control industry is

A few years after its inception, the growing company "spilled from the garage into the kitchen and living room" of the Dimitris' home before moving into the first of many office spaces, a 2,000-square-foot facility in Canoga Park.

already there, improving productivity and product quality, while simultaneously lowering manufacturing costs.

The company's success to date can be directly traced to a combination of factors including reliability, speed, accuracy, versatility and overall capability of the product. A major strength of the company lies in its ability to efficiently design, produce, sell and maintain a complex product line while continuously developing state-of-the-art motion control products at very high technology levels with significant innovations.

Strategic alliances with major companies worldwide have proven instrumental in Delta Tau's growth. Recent international expansion efforts include branch offices in the Netherlands, France, Switzerland, Korea, U.K. and Japan.

PMAC / PMAC 2

Programmable Multi-Axis Controller cards are the stars of Delta Tau's product lineup. In a few short years, Delta Tau's motion controllers (particularly the PMAC) have reached into almost every aspect of daily life. From sunrise to sunset, the company's motion

controllers have made, inspected and packaged hundreds of common (and not so common) products, such as those previously mentioned.

Recently the company has expanded its arsenal to encompass new system level products which are complementary to the PMAC and offer a fresh variety of choices to the user.

Turbo PMAC is the latest in a series of PMAC controllers which further raises the "technology bar" and provides unprecedented capabilities in a board level motion control technology. Some of the features are Multi-Block, high speed look ahead, built-in inverse kinematics, 32-axis simultaneous motion control, etc. Delta Tau plans to follow this up with PCI-based controllers to serve the new generation of PC's.

MACRO-Ring

MACRO is an acronym for "Motion and Control Ring Optical," a nonproprietary digital interface developed by Delta Tau Data Systems for connection of multi-axis motion controllers, amplifiers, and I/O on a fiber optic or twisted pair copper ring. Advantages

Digital Quad Amplifier

Delta Tau Data Systems recently introduced a new family of universal four-axis three-phase servo drives, the Delta Tau Quad Amplifier. This "Quad Amp" utilizes the latest in smart power technology from the world's leading vendors, and mates with the cutting-edge control algorithms of the new PMAC2 controller family. This combination results in previously unobtainable levels of performance with both permanent-magnet and induction motors.

The Quad Amp is based upon direct digital PWM (Pulse Width Modulation) of power devices for controlling a variety of motors directly in digital domain rather than the already established analog methods. PWM improves performance, reduces system costs and allows much easier setup and maintenance. Reliability is also increased due to the drive's simplification.

The privately held firm remains very much a family operation. Tammy serves as the executive vice president and all four of their children, who began in the business as weekend janitors, currently contribute to various engineering, marketing and financial activities within the company.

As Delta Tau heads into the new millennium, the firm is getting ready to extend its leadership role in control technology and with this, hopes to make the world a better place in which to live.

include noise immunity, speed and simplicity.

Fiber-optic cable transmits light, not electricity. Unlike electricity, light is immune to electromagnetic noise, capacitive coupling, ground loops and other wiring problems.

One of MACRO's most impressive features is its high speed rate of data transmission, which is many times faster than any other available serial bus protocol.

MACRO lends itself well to large multi-axis applications where the amplifiers and I/O are spread out in several cabinets around the machine. Packaging, converting, processing and textiles machinery as well as robotics systems, and automated assembly lines all can benefit from MACRO's advantages.

Delta Tau's new, state-of-the-art 120,000-square-foot facility.

ADLINK

*Making the L.A. Connection –
Los Angeles cable pioneer, Adlink,
unites advertisers with the nation's
most diverse market*

os Angeles is the place where the future takes shape. From cars to culture, L.A. sets the standards, starts the trends, molds the way the society is going. And it is here in Southern California — with almost 15 million residents and five million television households — that a pioneering cable television advertising company called Adlink® is shaping the future of TV.

Adlink, which turned ten years old in 1998, was the nation's first cable "interconnect." The company innovation was to technologically link cable networks and systems so that advertisers only had to produce one tape and place one "buy" in order for their commercial to reach the entire market.

Adlink could only exist in L.A., the city of innovation and the nation's most diverse and multicultural market. But, like any new idea, it wasn't an easy sell at first.

The Connecting Point

Cable television first came on the scene 50 years ago, as a mechanism for getting TV signals to mountainous or remote areas of the country where regular reception was poor or impossible. In 1950, there were already 70 cable systems but only a handful of subscribers — 14,000 nationwide.

By the 80s, however, the nation was cabling up at a furious rate, as the demand for more programming exploded. Spurring the trend was the 1984 Cable Act, which effectively deregulated the industry. From 1984 to 1992, in fact, the cable industry spent more than $15 billion on connecting American households to the cable universe. It was the largest private construction project since World War II.

Still, while consumers were signing up at a furious rate, advertisers remained dubious. Advertisers who wanted to run ads on cable television in Los Angeles had to deal with literally dozens of different entities, each with their own billing systems, ad formats and policies. But in 1988, a group of cable system operators

in L.A. banded together and, using satellite technology, formed Adlink to "interconnect" their sales and technological efforts. (Today, Adlink's equity partners include some of the nation's leading cable and telecommunications companies: Century Communications, Charter Communications, Comcast Cablevision, Cox Cable Communications, Falcon Communications, MediaOne, Time Warner and TCI.)

Opening the Digital Door

Initially, Adlink inserted TV commercials on five cable networks. By 1990, the company had 14 networks on its roster with a handful of L.A. headends linked by a satellite delivery of analog video. But advertisers were still reluctant. Analog technology limited the number of networks and systems that could be interconnected, and resulted in video quality unacceptable in the sophisticated L.A. market. To grow out of its infancy, Adlink needed to innovate again.

In 1995, Adlink pioneered the industry's transition from analog to digital video technology by investing more than $10 million to create the world's first digital interconnect. This uniquely designed digital platform provides for the simultaneous, accurate and high quality insertion of commercial advertising across more than 70 cable systems, 24 hours a day, seven days a week. For the first time, advertisers could reach viewers in the entire Los Angeles market on more than 24 cable networks with customized messages from a single buy and a single tape. From that digital breakthrough, Adlink then created two groundbreaking products: Adtag™ and Adcopy™. In effect, Adlink's innovations defined the beginning of "targeted TV" — advertisers could now target specific audiences with selected messages aimed, virtually, to the neighborhood level — something broadcast television cannot offer.

With Adtag, retail marketers can customize their commercials across all the different L.A. "geographies" and demographic segments. The first 25 seconds of the spot is the same on every cable system, but then it is "tagged" with a specific dealer or store location. This customization means, for example, that viewers in Beverly Hills see an auto commercial with a local dealer's address, while at the same time cable watchers in Torrance see the same spot, but with a South Bay dealer's address.

Another innovation is Adcopy, which takes targeted advertising one step further. With Adcopy, advertisers can place a market-wide ad, yet tailor the content to different areas. Suppose an airline wants to run flight-specific spots for Los Angeles. That means running different flight information for LAX, Burbank, Ontario and John Wayne International. With Adcopy, Adlink carves the regions around the area's airports, and different messages can be delivered to different areas simultaneously. All with one buy.

Throughout its short but storied life, Adlink has helped redefine how cable advertising is used. Its partnerships with such blue-chip advertisers as General Motors have pioneered new ways to use cable networks to promote products. Its research has identified new opportunities, most recently through Adlink's precedent-setting use of Polk automotive registration data that, for example, reveals that folks who live in the 92677 zip code in Laguna Nigel are more likely to drive a Chevy Suburban and watch Fox Sports West, while residents who live in the 92821 zip code in Brea prefer driving Dodge's RAM and Caravan — and all those minivan moms are watching Lifetime television.

Additionally, Adlink continues to invent integrated marketing opportunities, including program sponsorships, network co-branding opportunities, promotional and multimedia packages that continue to set the industry's standard for creative, high-impact, cutting edge ways to use cable television to advertise effectively.

Adlink, in fact, is something of a living laboratory for the cable industry. Indeed, the term "Adlink" is sometimes used as a generic term for interconnects by ad agencies.

An Even Brighter Tomorrow

Not coincidentally, Adlink is poised for spectacular growth — the company's 1997 gross revenues totaled $61

million, up from $40 million the previous year, and the company is on pace to generate $80 million in 1998. Adlink now reaches more than three million cable households, with a 62 percent penetration of all television viewers in the L.A. market. And it inserts commercials on 24 cable networks, including ESPN, A&E, MTV and CNN. More than 300 top national and regional advertisers, including Kraft, Disney, General Motors/Chevrolet, Macy's and AirTouch Cellular use Adlink to reach their prospective customers.

But the real impact of this L.A.-born pioneer may be yet to come. The cable industry is undergoing tremendous consolidation, with half the nation's cable system owners disappearing in just the past decade. At the same time, the audience is splitting up into literally hundreds of different fragments with hundreds of viewing options. In the process, interconnects like Adlink, which have spent years listening to advertisers' needs in their respective markets and putting solutions into practice, have become more important than ever.

"Designed to make a confusing and expensive process simple, Adlink is much more than the technological tool it was when the company was first born," concludes Adlink President and Chief Executive Officer, Charlie Thurston. "It is an invaluable marketing entity providing precise and efficient tools for reaching a fragmented audience, and it is particularly effective in a diverse market like L.A. Adlink is, in fact, what the future of television will look like."

Adlink's West Los Angeles headquarters reflects its pioneering cable television heritage.

APTX

September 24, 1997 may never be a day which schoolchildren memorize as historic moments in world history, but the sewn products and home furnishing industries will soon come to revere the day as the start of a multi-faceted revolution. It was on that day that Apparel Technologies, now called APTX, acquired the Digital Group, thereby linking progressive state-of-the-art digital printing technology with apparel design and manufacturing.

"Digital printing creates the opportunity to change the formula from sales push to demand pull," says Grier.

As a pioneer in the development and application of digital printing, APTX is uniquely positioned to be at the forefront of commercialization of digital printing in the textile business. Industry experts already expect APTX to revolutionize apparel design and production. Utilizing advanced proprietary and patent-pending digital technology, APTX can print high resolution designs with no limitations to color or graphic placement. The process can print on several synthetic blends and surfaces which produce a permanent colorfast product. They are in the process of developing the technology for natural fibers.

The voice of the technology of APTX, President of the Digital Group, Bill Grier, explains, "APTX has made tremendous strides in several markets with our digital applications. Every day we are challenged, not only in apparel and home furnishings, but in accessories, automotive and footwear. The possibilities are endless."

With offices in Los Angeles, New York and Paris, APTX is poised to make a significant impression on apparel and printing industries. In an industry which has undergone very little change in the past century, APTX is the lone company pursuing digital printing on a large scale. While other companies have shied away from the challenge of bringing this technology to the marketplace, APTX has already put out a product so far superior to any other clothing that it has to be seen to be believed.

As an environmentally conscious company, APTX has gone to great lengths to make sure their process is "Green Technology." The environment for using digital printing is actually considered both "white" and "green." White; because of the efficient use of printing on only white fabrics, and green; because virtually every step in the process is done by computers, thereby eliminating much of the waste of traditional design methods.

On the high end of clothing manufacturing, digital printing can produce clothing never before imagined. Images can be continuous throughout the garment, from sleeves to collars to front and back. This can only be achieved because the actual printing of the image is done on each individual piece of the shirt, instead of the traditional method of printing limited patterns on rolls of material which is then cut and sewn, leaving a great deal of waste. APTX can, for example, take famous works of art, scan them, and reproduce them on a piece of clothing with continuous resolution and fine attention to detail, like an artist's rendering. The only other way to achieve this effect is to have an artist paint the art by hand on the finished product.

With offices in Los Angeles, New York and Paris, APTX is poised to make a significant impression on apparel and printing industries.

The process may seem complex, and technically it is, but APTX simplifies everything for the client. It can take a product from design to production to the marketplace with incredible speed and efficiency. Traditionally, the design concept needs to be drawn up, the materials need to be ordered and the whole production takes about six months before the product reaches the shelves. That means clothing designers have to use the archaic "crystal ball method" to predict what people will want to wear six months in advance. With APTX's digital printing, the demand for a particular style or art can be sold to consumers in anywhere from 48 hours to three days. The client only needs to inventory white materials which are cut, printed and then assembled.

"Digital printing creates the opportunity to change the formula from sales push to demand pull," says Grier.

"APTX has made tremendous strides in several markets with our digital applications. Every day we are challenged, not only in apparel and home furnishings, but in accessories, automotive and footwear. The possibilities are endless."

Some well known retailers purchased an order of women's blouses made by APTX's new technology in April of 1998, thereby becoming the first national retailer to test the marketability of the product. And while there is always a certain amount of risk involved in trying something new, using APTX cuts that risk significantly. Stores can order a small amount of any product and replenish as the demand arises. With the traditional method of clothing supply and demand, a company's warehouse can be filled with volumes of unsellable finished products.

"While other companies have shied away from the challenge of bringing this technology to the marketplace, APTX has already put out a product so far superior to any other clothing that it has to be seen to be believed."

Because of the efficiency of the digital printing, clients can order one swatch for sampling or proofing purposes, or large orders of tens of thousands of finished products. And because APTX is the sole company to use this technology on this scale, it provides education and customer service to help clients understand the workings and requirements of digital printing. It's a new world for APTX, a world where one can "just make what you sell."

CLEGG INDUSTRIES, INC.

Timothy P. Clegg, founder and president of Clegg Industries, Inc.

Talking magazine insert for Mars' TWIX candy bar using Clegg microelectronic technology. When readers open the insert, they hear the advertising slogan: "TWIX. Two for me, none for you."

n the competitive world of advertising, it's all about getting noticed. Clegg Industries, makers of microelectronic promotional products, creates advertising that demands to be seen and heard.

The Torrance-based company's products blink, make sound effects, and even talk.

Using patented microelectronic technology, Clegg Industries adds lights, music and voices to point-of-purchase retail displays, print advertising products, such as greeting cards, brochures and packaging, and promotional products such as talking calculators, talking mouse pads and talking pens.

A business card is just a business card until a client pops it into one of Clegg's holders. When the recipient flips it open, it emits the sound of a telephone ringing with the saying, "When you're looking for the best... Give me a ring!"

A baseball card comes to life when Clegg combines lenticular motion technology to achieve a moving, 3-D image of Cal Ripkin swinging a game-winning home run. When baseball card enthusiasts press a button, they hear the actual recorded voice of the sportscaster announcing the play.

This innovative, high-tech marketing strategy is the brainchild of Timothy P. Clegg, who was born in the Bronx and raised with his six siblings in Chagrin Falls, Ohio. He double-majored in economics/business management and Spanish at Albion College in Albion, Michigan. After graduating in 1985, he went to work selling microcomputer chips for his cousins' company in Houston, where Clegg got his first taste of entrepreneurship. By watch-

ing his two hardworking cousins, he learned the discipline needed to start a successful business from scratch.

It was there, while tinkering with company logos printed on paper and LED lights used in computers, that he realized microcomputer chip technology could be put to use to add a new, powerful dimension to advertising and promotional products.

Clegg's first idea was simple, yet something entirely different than had ever been done before: a blinking button that draws attention to itself better than a standard lapel pin. McDonald's bought the idea. Employees wore pins with four blinking lights that highlighted the phrase, "Try Double Fries."

In the beginning, Clegg ran his fledgling company out of his apartment, working late at night handling design, sales, manufacturing and distribution. It wasn't long before he had other customers. Promoters for a Frank Sinatra show bought blinking buttons that looked like minimarquees. Anheuser-Busch ordered blinking bottle-caps.

"At this point, I knew this was going to be big," he said.

In 1988, technology made another leap and it became possible to digitally encode microcomputer chips with not only lights, but music, sound effects and talking messages. Clegg combined these talking integrated circuits with several watch batteries and a tiny speaker. He called his invention a sound card and in 1992 put it to use in what would become among his best-selling products, audio business cards holders, the first of many patented products.

While consumers were already familiar with greeting cards that play a song when opened, the business card created the first use for sound cards in the lucrative corporate-advertising world. A whole new array of

possibilities presented themselves, and Clegg capitalized on the technological advance.

He began building a sound library that has since grown to 60 stock sounds, including a drum roll, car crash, fire engine siren, trumpet fanfare, a beverage pouring, a ship's horn, children giggling, ocean waves and applause. His company also manufacturers sound cards with custom messages of up to 60 seconds per chip.

Now, not only could companies identify themselves to customers with a logo, but with sound.

"Doesn't it make sense, if you're BMW, for example, that your print advertisements would sound like a revving engine?" he reasoned. "Sprint or MCI or AT&T should have print advertising that rings to reinforce the essence of their product."

He developed a uniquely 90s concept, coining the term "audio logo." Clegg reasoned that in today's fast-paced, multimedia, remote-controlled world, old-style corporate jingles that might last 20 or 30 seconds took too long to deliver a company message, namely, having the consumer audibly connect the sound immediately with the product, brand or company.

His new audio logos last only a second or two and achieve the same result but more effectively.

The technology's cost-effectiveness has enabled Clegg to convince clients that the expense of micro-electronics is worth the money. Direct-mail advertisers usually consider a one to two percent response rate to be successful for bulk mailings. With sound cards, direct-mail advertisers report up to a 50 percent response rate, according to Clegg.

Clegg was rewarded with a growing client list. In 1989, he moved to Los Angeles to be closer to film studios and video distributors who had started hiring his firm to add movie theme songs to promotional materials. The "Clegg Audio Logo Chip" is used in printed promotional materials for major computer, telecommunications, automobile, food and entertainment companies, including Intel, Microsoft, Hewlett-Packard, Nike,

General Motors, Ford, Coca-Cola, Seagrams, Disney, Warner Bros., Mattel, Kellogg's, Sony and Hallmark Cards.

In 11 years, Clegg Industries has grown from a one-man operation to a multimillion dollar corporation. At the 30,000-square-foot Torrance location, Clegg Industries employs nearly 100 people in sales, design and manufacturing. In 1997, Clegg added computer programmers and engineers to his staff who program the microcomputer chips in-house, thereby cutting the time it takes to deliver his finished products to clients from ten weeks to less than ten days.

He recently launched a consumer products division to design and manufacture gift products, toys and movie merchandise such as talking pens, mouse pads, postcards, calculators, calendars, key chains and greeting cards.

His family, which Clegg credits with instilling in him the drive and determination to succeed, has joined him in business. His younger brother, Kevin, is the company attorney, and his older brother John heads the point-of-purchase division. The fourth Clegg brother, Jim, recently gave up his job in the banking industry to head Clegg Industries' investment division, with the long-term goal of acquiring companies that use technology that will complement Clegg already successful products. His parents, who live in Chagrin Falls, Ohio work as sales representatives there.

Clegg's passion is to continue finding new ways to integrate microelectronic technology with consumer and advertising products.

"The future of our company is continuing to grow market share as the world wide leader of audio-visual-print communication," says Clegg.

The first talking baseball card designed and developed by Clegg for Topps. Baseball card collectors can hear the recorded voice of the sportscaster announcing the play pictured in lenticular motion on the front of the card.

(Top left) This talking, interactive brochure for Absolut Vodka lets clients hear a two minute message describing Absolut's history and unique distillation process.

(Opposite page, top right) Gillette's World Cup 98 pen set features one of Clegg's patented sounds, "Ole!"

Talking retail display featuring Coca-Cola's latest jingle.

LITTON INDUSTRIES, INC.

When Charles Bates "Tex" Thornton founded Litton Industries, Inc. in California in 1953, he did so with this strategy: to expand a company with a technological orientation to develop new products and to improve existing products for all markets. That strategy helped Litton become a multi-industry, multinational manu-facturing company with sales of $4.2 billion at the end of the 1997 fiscal year.

But Litton didn't become a manufacturing trend-setter overnight. The growth of the company has steadily risen and restructuring over the years has led to its current position. The company recognizes the following four distinct phases that occurred since its inception to make it what it is today.

Litton ranks among the leaders in navigation, guidance and control systems for military and commercial aircraft, spacecraft, helicopters, ships, land vehicles and missiles.

Throughout its 60-year history, Litton's Ingalls Shipbuilding Division's basic strategy has been to maintain sufficient flexibility to respond quickly and effectively to changes in its markets.

The Beginning

In the early 1950s, during the postwar experience, electronics was a rapidly emerging technolo-gy with potentially far reaching applications. Even though there were both large and small com-panies already involved in elec-tronics, most of the large companies were slow to turn the new tech-nology into useful products while the small companies lacked the capital to do so. Thornton took this opportunity to create a new type of company that was tech-nologically oriented and could develop and apply these advanced technologies, primarily electron-ics, to different types of products and industries.

In the company's first year, sales reached nearly $3 million, primarily from one product — a state-of-the-art magnetron for radar systems. This product came from the company's first acquisition, a small electron tube compa-ny. After this acquisition, the company was renamed Litton Industries. Litton was one of the first companies to get involved in electronics through acquisitions and its own research and development.

The company continued to acquire other compo-nent companies and began its in-house research and development program for new electronic and other high-tech products. One of its first new concepts was adapting inertial navigation technology for aircraft. This technology was developed into a $1 billion annual busi-ness and Litton continues to be a leader and innovator in that market.

Expansion Through Acquisitions and Internal Growth

At the beginning of the 1970s, Litton had grown to about 120 divisions with nearly 120,000 employees. In its first two decades, Litton had acquired well over 100 companies. It developed the first space suits in the Sputnik era and provided a number of sophisticated scientific instruments like a gas chromatograph mass spectrometer for the Mars Viking space mission. It also developed and built scientific submarines for deep sea diving and oceanographic research. One of these subs, Alvin, became world famous when it was used to detect and recover a U.S. hydrogen bomb lost off the coast of Spain. The company had acquired a reputation in aerospace and defense electronics, shipbuilding, office equipment and furniture, paper and publishing, seismic exploration, machine tools and many others.

Streamlining for High Profitability

The state of the economy of the 1970s — surging inflation, excessive governmental control, export restrictions and costly labor increases — led to the third phase which had a goal of making Litton a strong operating company with high profitability. During this phase, the company eliminated some product lines, consolidated operations, sold off some businesses, closed down a number of factories and implemented a strong cost-reduction program companywide.

Restructuring for the Future

A restructuring strategy to raise shareholder values during this fourth phase was accomplished by reducing Litton to three core businesses: aerospace and defense electronics and shipbuilding; high-tech resource exploration services; and industrial automation systems. In 1994, Litton strengthened and focused its commitment to defense by splitting the company through a spinoff of Western Atlas — which consists of Litton's former commercial operations.

In the marine business, Litton revolutionized shipbuilding by introducing modular concepts and replacing the traditional construction approach with modern manufacturing production line techniques in the building process.

Today, Litton is continuing to grow through selective acquisition and is rapidly strengthening its market leadership position in information technology, marine systems and electronics. Since 1994, it has acquired companies with a combined annual revenue of about $2 billion. The company's current acquisition strategy is intended to grow its non-defense business, particularly in information technology and commercial electronics.

By continuing with the company's original philosophy — applying electronics and advanced technology to all types of products — Litton has become a world leader in technological innovation. Today, the company is a multi-billion dollar aerospace, defense and commercial electronics company with technological and market leadership in its principal businesses located throughout the United States, Canada, Germany and Italy.

STADCO

As the nation's leading producer of large, complex, high-precision tooling and parts, Stadco prides itself on *setting*, rather than following, industry standards.

In operation since 1945, Nat Handel and Reginald King were at the helm of what was then known as Stadco Precision Fabricators, Inc. when in 1981, Neil Kadisha and Parviz Nazarian purchased the company. Kadisha and Nazarian were as committed to quality and service as the original founders, which contributed to the continued growth of the firm.

The University of Rochester target chamber for nuclear fusion reactor.

Operating in the same location since its inception, Stadco presently utilizes approximately 300,000 square feet of building and employs over 200 individuals — an impressive growth from what was originally a 2,000-square-foot facility with only eight employees.

From the beginning, Stadco's niche was in aviation and defense. Over the years, the company's fortunes have substantially followed those of the aerospace and defense industries. Stadco has been providing the high technology aviation, aerospace, energy, machine tool and communications industries with guidance and assistance in their most demanding projects.

Stadco's public successes speak for themselves: extremely close tolerance components weighing 30 tons; major sections of the space shuttle booster hardware for NASA/Thiokol Corporation; critical sections of the mobile transporter of the International Space Station for NASA/McDonnell Douglas Corporation; complex assembly and composites tooling for Northrop Corporation's military aviation programs; large and challenging structural components for the USAF/Lockheed Martin F-22 Air Superiority Fighter; and the high-tech vacuum chamber for inertial fusion testing for the University of Rochester.

A testament to Stadco's successes are the various contracts and awards presented to the company over the years. In 1989, Stadco was awarded its first "Supplier Excellence Award" for its participation in Thiokol Corporation's Space Operations Program. Stadco produced and delivered its first redesigned solid rocket motor case stiffener segment ahead of schedule with no nonconformance. More recently, Boeing contracted with Stadco to be its supplier

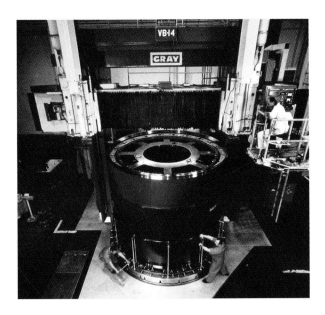

Space Shuttle Booster
Hardware

for various pieces of launch vehicle hardware for satellite deployment, the contract to carry over into the year 2002.

Stadco also enjoys a long association with the U.S. Navy and Hughes Missile Systems as a supplier of Phalanx gun mounts and Ram launchers. For more than 13 years, Stadco has had the distinction of being the sole source in the United States for machining and assembly of Sikorsky CH-53 "D" and "E" model helicopter transmission housings. Various other Supplier Appreciation Awards have since been received from McDonnell Douglas, Northrop Grumman and ROHR, to name a few.

Stadco has aggressive plans for the future, focusing not only in the aerospace field, but in serving the commercial sector as well by offering heavy fabrication and machining of intricate parts and exotic materials to other industries. In serving this sector of the market, Stadco will continue to keep its number one priority which is to produce quality products and services for its customers. Its Quality Control Department is equipped and trained to ensure quality and accuracy in its standard manufacturing processes. Total Quality Management is a company-wide program in place to achieve excellence in quality and increased productivity through the utilization of a continuous process improvement plan.

One key ingredient to Stadco's success is the adaptability of its skilled personnel. They continually evaluate and target new technologies and are trained to evolve its services, processes and procedures enabling this ISO 9002 certified company to offer unique capabilities that are rarely matched. The Stadco Engineering Group is nationally recognized as one of the finest of its kind and their designs are now being shipped internationally.

In keeping with its vision for the future, Stadco's management has plans under consideration to increase its 300,000-square-foot facility and $100 million of unique assets. Entering a new era with the impact of automation and information technology in manufacturing processes, the role of Stadco has grown to include digital-design activities for its customers. This is in addition to its capabilities in high-technology manufacturing, test and assembly, fabrication, engineering and program management. Stadco now takes responsibility for the entire life cycle of some very sophisticated products and systems.

With over half a century's presence in Los Angeles, Stadco's future in this city and in this industry is very promising. It vows to remain competitive in today's global market by performing due diligence, taking calculated risks as necessary through partnering, alliances or acquisitions, for the continued realization of its successes and progress.

The principals of Stadco

THOMAS BROS. MAPS

or over 82 years, Thomas Bros. Maps has produced maps and related products based on the high standards set by its founders. The company has grown from a pioneer in street map book publishing to a leader in state-of-the-art digital street mapping. This story spans the company history and offers a glimpse into its spirit, quality and leadership.

In 1915, company founder George Coupland Thomas and his two brothers began mapping parcel plots for the County of Alameda in northern California. Later, they produced pocket street maps and wall maps for retail customers. After a few years, George Thomas, a skilled cartographer, continued expanding the busi-

Founder George Coupland Thomas.

Owner and Chief Executive Officer Warren Wilson (standing) and Tom Tripodes.

ness while his brothers pursued careers in civil engineering.

In the late 1920s and early 30s, the map business grew as California's major cities grew. Mr. Thomas developed the innovative idea of a map book bound with individual map pages which include an index of the street location by page and grid. The map books covered the geographical area of an entire county. It soon became the cornerstone of the Thomas Bros. business. By the end of the 1940s, Thomas Bros. Maps published guides for northern and southern California counties. Major cities in Washington and Oregon were added during the 50s.

Mr. Thomas moved the company's headquarters to Los Angeles in the early 1940s, where he managed the business as a sole proprietor, with a manager in the Oakland office publishing the Bay Area counties. After his death in 1955, the company was incorporated under the leadership of Warren Wilson as CEO and Tom Tripodes as CFO, both long-time advisors to Thomas' widow and his family.

Under the leadership of Mr. Wilson and Mr. Tripodes, and with the assistance of Barry Elias, a young city planner, Thomas Bros. Maps continued to map new counties and provide the exploding population of the West Coast with accurate, easy-to-read maps. Mindful of the needs voiced by customers, the company continued to grow and prosper.

In 1980, having outgrown its Los Angeles facility, the company built and moved into its present headquarters in Irvine, which is recognized as an artistic showplace in contemporary, rustic design. Not only does the building offer exceptional working conditions for its 200+ employees, but also provides a tranquil setting in which to enjoy the work environment. At that time, Mr. Wilson developed the company philosophy

which focuses on human relationships and self-development of its employees, with the common goal of publishing the best in street maps.

In 1986, envisioning the future of street mapping, Thomas Bros. Maps began implementing the conversion of its Thomas Guides from manual cartography to digital computer mapping. In doing so, the company established a network of grid systems encompassing the contiguous United States. This conversion to highly accurate computer data enables the company to provide a wide variety of geographical maps tailored to the needs of individual businesses and organizations. This conversion offers users such as public utility companies, government agencies and others Thomas Guides with 10 foot spatial accuracy.

The firm's entry into the Baltimore/Virginia corridor provides an opportunity for Thomas Bros. Maps to offer users technological advances and products. The Thomas Bros. family of products brings users the most up-to-date street maps available, including the Thomas Guides, wall maps, Express Maps, Thomas Guide CD-ROMS, Geofinder and Digital licensing.

Thomas Bros. Maps also delivers its corporate tradition of mapping excellence and its Corporate Philosophy of caring.

Thomas Bros. Maps was once located on Main Street in Los Angeles before moving to its new corporate headquarters in Irvine, California.

USER TECHNOLOGY
ASSOCIATES, INC.

ser Technology Associates, Inc. (UTA) was founded by Yong K. Kim in 1985 to close the gap between the user and technology. UTA's operating divisions, Acquisition and Program Management, Advanced Technology, Systems Support/Information Technology, Information Resource Management, LAN, WAN & Telecommunications, and Engineering and Logistics provide solutions to customers who require the highest return on their use of technology — cheaper, faster and better.

Mr. Kim is president and CEO of UTA; a company that is dedicated to helping business people derive maximum benefit from the use of their technology. He has spent over 30 years inventing technology and managing technology companies. By 1985, he was convinced that the only way businesses could truly profit from their technology was to make sure that employees became proficient in the use of the technology — a conviction documented by a *Washington Times* article "UTA Advances in High-Tech Field by Caring About Low-Tech Users" and a *Washington Post* article "Successful Entrepreneur Offers Real World Advice."

Since its founding in 1985, UTA has created a complete suite of user/technology improvement tools, including a "Total User Support Model," a complete, "just-in-time" support system that meets five key operational objectives. It helps managers define their technological support requirements; select, acquire and install appropriate and effective technology and associated support; develop and implement operational applications; develop documentation and

user manuals; and train and assist personnel in program operations and maintenance.

UTA has been recognized as one of the most successful privately owned companies in the United States. Mr. Kim and his company have garnered a list of over 300 commendations and awards in the past ten years, including the *Ernst & Young/Inc.* Magazine Entrepreneur of the Year (1992), the SBA Small Business Person of the Year (1995) and the KPMG Peat Marwick High Tech Entrepreneur (1993), and have received extensive press coverage to include CBS and ABC-TV, and *Inc.* and *Fortune* magazines. *UTA* has received the ABBIE Award as a "Best Business" in Arlington County, Virginia.

Mr. Kim has participated in such international appointments as Department of Commerce Trade Missions to Northern Ireland and the Border Counties of Ireland, and a Trade Mission to Mexico City in support of the Clinton Administration's NAFTA efforts. He participated in the Business Development Trade Mission to the Persian Gulf in support of the Bush Administration reconstruction efforts immediately following the Persian Gulf War.

UTA has worked with economic development and trade entities in Canada, Mexico, Korea, the Philippines and Nigeria, and has offices in Korea and Great Britain, setting the pace for global technology trading. Mr. Kim is an involved national and community leader and has served on the Department of Commerce's US-Korea Committee on Business Cooperation and as a Special Advisor to the Congressional Advisory Board.

UTA was named by Washington Technology's Fast 50 as the fastest growing company in the Washington DC area in 1991 when the company experienced 13,500 percent growth, and was also named to the Fast 50 for 1992-1994. *Inc.* magazine named UTA one of America's fastest growing private companies from 1992-1994.

Yong Kim, president and CEO of UTA, puts his employees first. He says it's just smart business in a healthy economy, when computer-savvy employees are at a premium.

Mr. Kim earned a bachelor's degree in Electronic Engineering from KIT, Korea, and a master's degree in Technology of Management with a major in Management Information Systems and a minor in Computer Systems from American University. He attended the Harvard Business School, Owner/President Management Program from 1992 until graduation from that program in 1994. He pursued doctoral studies in Public Administration at Nova Southeastern University.

In 1994, UTA opened its Pasadena, California office to support NASA's Jet Propulsion Laboratory (JPL). The company's initial contract was valued at $18 million and has since grown to over $45 million. In 1997, UTA growth required the opening of a second office in Pasadena to accommodate its technical personnel. Today, UTA West has over 135 employees. The men and women behind UTA's phenomenal success in California support over 26 missions including Galileo, Cassini, Shuttle Radar Topography Mission (SRTM) and Mars Pathfinder. These professionals provide services such as software engineering, systems analysis, program analysis, system engineering, system administration, technical documentation and web development.

UTA is continually expanding to bring its vision of user technology to emerging IT markets. Realizing the impact of the Internet on businesses today, UTA started a new division, Internet Solutions, based in Pasadena with a Washington DC branch office, focused on providing Internet and Intranet technology to federal, commercial and global customers.

One of UTA's major focuses is the impending year 2000 computing crisis. Realizing the significant implications of year 2000 computing impact on the international economy, UTA formed a joint venture with Greenwich Mean Time Ltd. (GMT), the global authority on the year 2000 PC and client/server problem. Greenwich Mean Time-UTA L.C. markets, sells and distributes Check 2000 in North America. GMT-UTA's flagship product, Check 2000 Client Server, addresses year 2000 issues in PC hardware, software, operating systems, data files and exchange of data between users. Check 2000 PC is sold in over 4,000 stores in the US and Canada.

Another commercial company, UTA Business Systems, develops and markets retail point of sale software for the restaurant and other delivery industries. Its products, including flagship product Head Driver, is in use in 40 states by franchises of major fast food restaurants including Domino's and Little Caesars.

Realizing the need for employees to receive ongoing technical and managerial training, Kim developed UTA Institute of Technology, an accredited program to enhance the skills of UTA's current workforce while providing continuing education credits. UTA Professional Associates provides temporary professional support to UTA and its clients.

Since 1985, User Technology's revenues have grown substantially — from $50,000 per year to annual revenue over $60 million.

Mr. Kim ties UTA's success to programs that provide value to local communities. UTA's Pasadena office has made a commitment to enhance the educational experience of children by donating computer equipment to various schools within the community. UTA has adopted Glassell Park Elementary School and has provided financial support to send their fifth grade class to Space Camp. In Arlington, Virginia, UTA headquarters supports Washington-Lee High School through its Partnership Program, provides computers to Arlington County schools and supports the Arlington County Economic Development Commission, the Ballston Partnership, the League of Korean Americans and other organizations built for the betterment of community.

Mr. Kim serves on the Board of the Boy Scouts of America, sits on the Board of Visitors of Marymount University, and is a member of the MIS Advisory Council at American University. He is a dynamic proponent that "education and training is the insurance for the future of America."

Writing this manuscript over a twelve-month period, I came to accept that certain materials were not readily available, and that the editorial process nevertheless must continue. Please be advised, therefore, that my source list is far from comprehensive. Footnotes originally bound the references (and explanations) to the text. Though less exact, the present endnote format still parallels the order of the manuscript. Finally, I should explain that the articles and books below were most often used for factual information or to further my interpretations. On occasion, however, I derived considerably different conclusion from these sources; I will attempt to highlight such variations.

CHAPTER 1 MULTICULTURAL MELANGE

A discussion on the multicultural aspects of philanthropy may be found in Lynn Kronzek, "Fund-Raising Execs See Broader Donor Bases as Essential," California Education Funding Alert, Vol. I, Number 3, March 31, 1996, p. 10. The advice about new constituencies is attributable to Emmett Charson, Ph.D., president and CEO of the Minneapolis Foundation.

The motivating passion behind Christine Sterling's first preservation campaign is explained in Christine Sterling, "A Mexican Street of Yesterday in a City of Today," (Los Angeles: June Sterling Park, 1947), p. 24.

Please note that for most of the Native American material, the dates that I use pertain to Southern California, not just the City of Los Angeles. I also apply broad ranges, since specific time periods are debated.

A comprehensive source on the Gabrielino/Tongva people is William McCawley's The First Angelenos (Banning and Novato, CA: A Malki Museum Press/Ballena Press Cooperative Publication, 1996). McCawley, an anthropologist, seems to have reviewed most studies on the topic, and woven them into an excellent narrative/ reference work. (I wish I had had similar source material for every chapter). Of particular relevance here were pp. 10-11, 25, 101, 108, 123-124, 134, 171, 195, 196, and 205-206.

A fine reference on the Chumash is Chester King/Topanga Anthropological Consultants, "Prehistoric Native American Cultural Sites in the Santa Monica Mountains," prepared for the Santa Monica Mountains and Seashore Foundation, National Park Service Western Region, Santa Monica Mountains National Recreation Area, July 18, 1994. King's work is useful for other reasons. For example, he provides a 12-month calendar showing when a variety of edible local plants were available for gathering. (He also indicates a year round supply of "near-shore resident fish" and marsh/lake plants). Finally, King analyzes a number of local Native sites and assesses whether their inhabitants were Chumash, Tongva — or mixed. See pp. 7-8, 11, 15, 17-18, 23, 43, 46, and 89-92.

Readers wishing a more detailed, but nevertheless concise, discussion of the four micro-climates and their relationship to culture should consult Dee T. Hudson, "Proto-Tongva Patterns of Territorial Organization in South Coast California," Pacific Coast Archaeological Society Quarterly, Vol. 7, No. 2 (April, 1971), pp. 56-57, 61-62.

Antonio Rios-Bustamante provides very useful information about the push-pull factors that drove early Mexican immigration northward, and about the early settlers generally, in Mexican Los Angeles (Encino: Floricanto Press, 1992). I drew on this source heavily. See pp. 35-38, 45, and 49.

The relationships between the settlers from Mexico and the Native population is presented in Rios-Bustamante, as well as Richard Griswold del Castillo, The Los Angeles Barrio 1850-1890, A Social History (Berkeley, Los Angeles, and London: University of California Press, 1979), pp. 1-2, 11, 13, and 46. My interpretations vary at times. Although Griswold del Castillo talks about adoptions of Native orphans by the Mexican settlers, it should be emphasized that some of these young people were employed as slaves and manual laborers. On a related topic, both Griswold del Castillo and Rios-Bustamante explore issue of class. Griswold del Castillo's work is interesting, too, in its use of quantitative sources to paint a demographic picture of Mexican-Americans in early Los Angeles.

Deflating romantic images, I did not stoop over disintegrating census records — or microforms — to obtain comparative information about the Cherokee census and cultural blending in the Southeast. See the (United States) National Archives and Records Administration, Teaching With Documents: Using Primary Sources From the National Archives (Washington: National Archives Trust Fund Board, 1989), pp. 13-15. The book contains copies of historic documents, as well as suggestions about utility for bringing a more tangible, real past to students. Please note, however, that the designations mulato, mestizo, chino, etc. are authentic to the Spanish census.

An engaging presentation of creole culture, both L.A.-style and from a historic perspective, appears in Lynell George, No Crystal Stair: African Americans in the City of Angels (London and New York: Verso, 1992). Of particular interest is an essay titled, " 'Who's Your People?' La to L.A. — The Creolization of Los Angeles," pp. 220-243. More generally, each chapter of George's book examines a different facet of the African-American experience here.

A discussion of blacks during the Spanish colonial era may be found in Kenneth Goode, California's Black Pioneers: A Brief Historical Survey (Santa Barbara: McNally & Loftin, Publishers, 1973), pp. 4 and 7.

Cultural blending in the Central American was not universal phenomenon. Some indigenous populations — particularly in the remote regions Mexico — remained insular, while segments of the urban elite viewed the mestizos/Indians as less than equals, and did not readily marry them. See George Sanchez, *Becoming Mexican American: Ethnicity, Culture, and Identity in Chicano Los Angeles, 1900-1945* (New York and Oxford: Oxford University Press, 1993), pp. 29-30.

For oral history-based accounts and direct observations of Native American life at around the time of Statehood, readers might turn to: Hugo Reid, *The Indians of Los Angeles County*. The edition used here was edited and annotated by Robert F. Heizer, and subtitled "Hugo Reid's Letters of 1852" (Los Angeles: Southwest Museum, 1968).

The changing ethnic/racial identities of the pobladores is the subject of Mary Jane Hewitt's "The Long Black Line," California History, Vol. 60, No. 1 (Spring, 1981), p. 12.

Additional sources for the sidebar on Victoria Reid include: Susanna Bryant Dakin, *A Scotch Paisano: Hugo Reid's Life in California* (Berkeley: University of California Press, 1939); Dee Dixon, "The Indian Maid and Her Scott," *Los Angeles Examiner*, March 24, 1964, pp. 1 and 3; Laura Evertson King, "Reminiscences of Mission San Gabriel," Historical Society of Southern California Annual Publications, 1920, pp. 58-62; Anna H. Wallace, "Hugo Reid's wife, Victoria — a life of grief, fear," *Arcadia Tribune*, November 24, 1977, no page given.

For the section on pioneer Jewish Angelenos, please refer to: Max Vorspan and Lloyd Gartner, *History of the Jews of Los Angeles*. (San Marino: Huntington Library, 1970), pp. 5-6, 8, 20-21, 46, and 86; Stephen J. Sass, editor, *Jewish Los Angeles: A Guide*, Second Edition (Los Angeles: Council on Jewish Life, Jewish Federation Council of Greater Los Angeles, 1982), pp. 8-11; Norton B. Stern, "The Location of Los Angeles Jewry at the Beginning of 1851," in Norton B. Stern, ed., *The Jews of Los Angeles: Urban Pioneers* (Los Angeles: Southern California Jewish Historical Society, 1981), pp. 103-107; Norton B. Stern, "Jews in the 1870 Census," in Norton B. Stern, ed., *The Jews of Los Angeles: Urban Pioneers* (Los Angeles: Southern California Jewish Historical Society, 1981), pp. 129-144; and, Norton B. Stern, "Los Angeles Jewry and Stow's Anti-Semitism," *Bicentennial Digest: A Perspective of Pioneer Los Angeles Jewry* (Los Angeles: Jewish Federation-Council of Greater Los Angeles, 1976), p. 25. The internal diversification of the L.A. Jewish community is discussed in Lynn C. Kronzek, *Fairfax...A Home, A Community, A Way of Life* (Los Angeles: Jewish Historical Society of Southern California, 1990), pp. 46-52.

Unique cross-cultural perspectives may be cleaned from Gerald D. Turbow and Suellen Cheng, "Chinese Americans and Jewish Americans in Los Angeles: Timetable" (Los Angeles: Published for "Intertwining Trails," a joint program of the Chinese and Jewish Historical Societies of Southern California hosted by El Pueblo Historic Monument, August 29, 1993).

The "push" factors that operated in China and caused many to emigrate are thoroughly examined by Jack Chen, *The Chinese of America* (San Francisco: Harper and Row, 1980), pp. 9-25.

Much of the information on Chinese Angelenos from 1850-1940 comes from: Lynn C. Kronzek, "Historical Background," in *Cultural Resources Impact Mitigation Program for the Los Angeles Metro Red Line Segment One (Chinatown)*, October, 1993 (Los Angeles: Los Angeles County Metropolitan Transportation Authority, 1993), pp. 21-81; Lynn C. Kronzek, "Historical Background," in *Down by the Station: Los Angeles Chinatown 1883-1933*, edited by Roberta S. Greenwood (Los Angeles: UCLA Institute of Archaeology, 1996), pp. 5-40; and, Thomas Allen McDannold, "Development of the Los Angeles Chinatown, 1850-1970," (unpublished Master's thesis, California State University-Northridge, 1973).

Charles Choy Wong and Kenneth Klein explore the painful, personal facets of exclusion in "False Papers, Lost Lives," *Origins and Destinations: 41 Essays on Chinese America* (Los Angeles: Chinese Historical Society of Southern California and UCLA Asian American Studies Center: 1994), pp. 355 and 359.

The story of Biddy Mason appears has been told by Dolores Hayden, Gail Dubrow, and Carolyn Flynn in the "Power of Place: Los Angeles" (Los Angeles: Power of Place, undated brochure).

CHAPTER 2 ERSTWHILE MIDWESTERNERS

The thumbnail sketch of Oscar Hudson was taken from Kenneth G. Goode, *California's Black Pioneers, A Brief Historical Survey* (Santa Barbara: McNally & Loftin, Publishers, 1979), p. 112 and 116.

The Swedish-American community is described in Lars Ljungmark (translated by Kermit B. Westerberg), *Swedish Exodus* (Carbondale and Edwardsville, Ill.: Southern Illinois University Press, 1979), pp. 95-96.

In presenting my statistics on the Easterners and Midwesterners, I refer to the largest contingent, the nine states aggregated by census takers: New York, Missouri, Massachusetts, Ohio, Illinois, Pennsylvania, Maine, Iowa, and Indiana. (See 1880 Census of Population, Population by Race and Nativity, page 498.) A more detailed assessment would require a perusal of the handwritten rolls, a task unfortunately beyond the scope of this book.

Social changes arising from the influx of Midwesterners are discussed by Leonard Pitt in "The Modernization of a Cow Town," *California History*, Volume 60, Number 1 (Spring, 1981), pp. 28-49. I obtained useful information from this article (the founding dates of local colleges, some statistics, etc). etc.), but I obviously believe that the definition of Midwesterners has been simplified over time and that their influence has been overstated.

Insights into public attitudes toward immigrants were gleaned from the Commission of Immigration and Housing of California, "A Community Survey Made in Los Angeles City" (San Francisco: Commission of Immigration and Housing, 1919?), pp. 14-19. Please note that when I used italics to highlight a direct quotation, the emphasis was mine.

Personal communications with Marcelino Ugalde, Basque Studies Center, University of Nevada, Reno, October, 1997 were helpful in clarifying the immigration status of Basques. Their presence lingers locally, though it is scattered and elusive. A curator at the Leonis Adobe told me that a small community of shepherds tended their flocks in the western San Fernando Valley, and I later came upon a long-gone Basque sheep camp in the Arroyo Seco. Over L.A.'s eastern border, the unincorporated city of Vernon contains a landmark Basque restaurant.

Main references on Japanese-Americans were from William M. Mason and John A. McKinstry, *The Japanese of Los Angeles* (Los Angeles: Los Angeles County Museum of Natural History, 1969), and Ronald Takaki, *A Different Mirror, A History of Multicultural America* (Boston: Little, Brown and Company, 1993), pp. 246-247, 250, 273. Takaki's work discusses the push-pull factors leading to Japanese immigration. His quote on restrictive housing comes from Arthur A. Hansen and Betty F. Mitson (eds.), *Voices Long Silent: An Oral Inquiry into the Japanese American Evacuation* (Fullerton, 1974), pp. 84 and 90.

With regard to Korean-Americans, I used Eui-Young Yu, Earl H. Phillips, and Eun Sik Yang, eds., *Koreans in Los Angeles: Prospects and Promises* (Los Angeles: Koryo Research Institute, Center for Korean-American and Korean Studies, California State University Los Angeles, 1982), pp. 5-6 and 9, and Helen Lewis Givens, *The Korean Community in Los Angeles* (San Francisco: R and E Research Associates, 1974), pp. 22-24, 34. The latter monograph originally was the author's masters thesis, written in 1939 at the University of Southern California.

L.A.'s Filipino community is explored by two sources, the first being Valentin R. Aquino, *The Filipino Community in Los Angeles* (San Francisco: R and E Research Associates, 1974), p. 14, 41-42, 47, 59. This monograph originally was the author's masters thesis, written in 1952 at the University of Southern California. The second source is Severino F. Corpus, *An Analysis of the Racial Adjustment Activities and Problems of the Filipino-American Christian Fellowship in Los Angeles* (San Francisco: R and E Research Associates, 1975). Corpus' work likewise has been derived from his 1938 masters thesis at USC. With regard to the loneliness of Filipino male immigrants — and the environment downtown — he sites the testimony of one D.F. Gonzalo.

To place the Filipino intermarriage factor in context, I drew on George Sanchez, *Becoming Mexican American: Ethnicity, Culture, and Identity in Chicano Los Angeles, 1900-1945* (New York and Oxford: Oxford Univerity Press, 1993), p.139. Comparisons between Mexican and Filipino Angelenos are not perfect, however, because Sanchez provides no specific dates. Nevertheless, he cites other studies of the Mexican-American population, roughly from 1924 onward, that parallel his own.

Information about Mexican immigration and the development of an identifiable community during this era owes to Richard Griswold del Castillo, *The Los Angeles Barrio 1850-1890, A Social History* (Berkeley, Los Angeles, and London: University of California Press, 1979), pp. 117, 119, 124-138, 139-148, and to George Sanchez, op. cit., pp. 41 and 45. (Beside having different approaches, note that the authors deal with successive time periods). Sanchez also utilizes the research of Oscar J. Martinez, *Border Boom Town: Ciudad Juarez since 1848* (Austin: University of Texas Press, 1975), p. 161 when discussing the border town phenomenon.

A discussion of Jewish migration patterns within the city appears in Lynn C. Kronzek, *Fairfax: A Home, A Community, A Way of Life* (Los Angeles: Jewish Historical Society of Southern California), p. 12. Here, I quote Mitchell Brian Gelfand, "Chutzpah in El Dorado: Social Mobility of Jews in Los Angeles, 1900-1920" (Pittsburgh: PhD dissertation/Carnegie Mellon University, 1981), pp. 104 and 160. Allow me to add a footnote to the topic of Jewish cultural diversity: Preferences for English or Ladino aside, both Ashkenazim and Sephardim used Hebrew for much of their services. Some Eastern/Central European immigrant congregations chose the familiar Yiddish rather than English — at least initially.

Information on L.A.'s Armenian community comes from Sheila E. Henry, *Cultural Persistence and Socio Economic Mobility: A Comparative Study of Assimilation Among Armenians and Japanese in Los Angeles* (San Francisco: R & E Research Associates, 1978), pp. 34-37, and Leonard Pitt and Dale Pitt, *Los Angeles A to Z, An Encyclopedia of the City and County* (Berkeley, Los Angeles, and London: University of California Press, 1997), p. 26.

Sources on the African-American Community of this era are: Lonnie G. Bunch, "A Past Not Necessarily Prologue: The Afro-American in Los Angeles," in Norman M. Klein and Martin J. Schiesl, eds., *Twentieth Century Los Angeles, Power, Promotion and Social Conflict* (Claremont: Regina Books, 1990), p. 101; Lawrence Brooks de Graaf, *Negro Migration to Los Angeles, 1930 to 1950* (San Francisco: R and E Research Associates, 1974), pp. 3, 21, 74, 80-82., with the original manuscript published as a Ph.D. dissertation at UCLA, 1962; and, Kenneth Goode, *California's Black Pioneers: A Brief Historical Survey* (Santa Barbara: McNally & Loftin, Publishers: 1973), p. 109. The approaches are different, and useful together. Bunch clearly writes in a 1990s public history style. De Graaf successfully intersperses census data and other demographic information with contemporary accounts, while Goode uses trailblazers and historic events to illustrate his work.

Knowledge about the town of Allensworth owes to a personal visit and to Craig Cook, who responded to an H-NET California Studies inquiry, July 14,

1997. H-Net is an Internet humanities/ history resource containing upwards of 80 special interest "discussion lists." For further details, contact http://www.h-net.msu.edu. The California Studies list, H-California, focuses on the history and culture of this state.

The results of public opinion polls regarding Japanese-Americans during World War II are cited in Audrie Girdner and Anne Loftis, *The Great Betrayal: The Evacuation of Japanese-Americans during World War II* (London and Toronto: Macmillan, 1969), p. 355. Individually expressed anti-evacuation sentiment is captured by Judith Branfman's forthcoming manuscript on Boyle Heights; the author uses oral history and different sets of statistics.

The story about the Lopez Farm Ranch was told to me by Chris Lopez in an interview conducted on November 4, 1997.

CHAPTER 3 GOVERNANCE

Among other articles, the issue of neighborhood councils was raised in Ted Rorhlich, "Riordan Taps Into Mood for City Panels," *Los Angeles Times*, Metro Section, Thursday April 16, 1998, p. B10. It should be noted here that there are two Charter Reform Commissions, one elected and the other appointed.

Raphael J. Sonenshein, Ph.D., Executive Director of the Charter Reform Commission, spoke briefly about neighborhood secession movements in response to a question raised during a panel discussion sponsored by the American Jewish Committee, November 13, 1997.

Allow me to explain my mathematical calculations regarding the citizen advisory boards. In many instances, the website indicated that the number of members per committee varied. My method was to calculate a membership of five per board, the lowest number of any cited. Note, too, that with the limited figures in my possession, I chose not to tabulate involvement in park advisory boards, which exist "one per rec. center and major park" (however those terms are defined). Therefore, my estimate is very conservative.

Several different sources were useful in understanding local government history. I relied heavily on Burton L. Hunter, *The Evolution of Municipal Organization and Administrative Practice in the City of Los Angeles* (Los Angeles: Parker, Sone & Baird Company, Publishers, 1933). This book highlights internal organization, such as staffing and the structural changes that evoked incorporation, charter revisions, etc. In surveying early L.A. government, Hunter frequently utilizes the early 20th century historian, J.M. Guinn. Citations are incomplete, however. Anne V. Howell's "History and Description: Los Angeles City Government (1781-1998), (Los Angeles: Los Angeles Department of City Planning, Central Publications Unit, June, 1998) commences with the early colonial governments, and notes changing politics (colonial revolutions, etc.) and political philosophies (Progressivism). She defines current city offices, agencies, and commissions, too. An emphasis on the bureaus and transformations that the city government has undergone also may be found in Irene Jerison, editor, *Los Angeles: Structure of a City* (Los Angeles: League of Women Voters, 1976). Another work by Anne V. Howell — "City Planners and Planning in Los Angeles (1781-1998)," (Los Angeles: Los Angeles Department of City Planning, Central Publications Unit, June, 1998) — directs itself toward urban infrastructural development, as well as the evolution of centralized planning and zoning. In addition, Howell outlines the contributions of the each of the city's planning directors. For a general introduction to local government concepts, see Owen Newcomer's textbook, *Governing Los Angeles*, Second Edition (New York: McGraw Hill, 1993). This work devotes separate chapters to Los Angeles County and the cities of El Monte, South El Monte, Pico Rivera, Whittier, and Santa Fe Springs.

Information about the friction between the Mission soldiers and the local Native American population (and neophytes) is taken from: William McCawley, *The First Angelenos: The Gabrielino Indians of Los Angeles* (Banning and Novato, CA:

A Malki Museum Press/Ballena Press Cooperative Publication, 1996), pp. 189-190 and 197-198.

The "La Pronunciamiento Contra Los Norte Americanos" was excerpted from and translated by Antonio Rios-Bustamante, *Mexican Los Angeles: An Illustrated History* (Encino: Floricante Press, 1992), pp. 147-149.

Newcomer, op. cit., p. 98 talks about the extended service of early civic leaders here: their simultaneous election to both municipal governments, and participation in several committees. The multiple commitments of school board members, as discussed in *Place of Possibilities*, apparently was an exaggerated version of the standard practice. According to Anne V. Howell, city committees typically were chaired by a councilmember; a citizen and possibly a second councilmember served with him. See Howell, "History and Description: Los Angeles City Government (1781-1998)," op. cit., p. 9.

Information on the Sisters of Charity schools comes from a city directory: A.J. King and Alonzo Waite, *The First Los Angeles City and County Directory*, originally published in 1872 and reproduced by Ward Ritchie, Los Angeles, 1963. Historian Michael E. Engh, S.J. verified for me the enrollment of Jewish children in these Catholic-operated school (personal communications, April 2, 1998). The phone call was necessitated by the fact that as I was writing this chapter, I was unable to find my copy of Engh's book. I heartily recommend *Frontier Faiths: Church, Temple, and Synagogue in Los Angeles 1846-1888* (Albuquerque: University of New Mexico Press, 1992). One final note on the Sisters of Charity: their historic Boyle Heights buildings were later purchased by County Hospital.

Dolores Haydn, Gail Dubrow, and Carolyn Flynn write about George Bright and African-American firefighters in "The Power of Place" (Los Angeles: Power of Place, undated brochure). I take responsibility for the summary remarks.

Willard's quote was excerpted from Hunter, op. cit., p. 70.

Anne V. Howell, "City Planners and Planning in Los Angeles (1781-1998)," op. cit., p. 8, reports on the Gas Company's pricing methods. However, the conclusions reached about government, utilities and franchising are solely mine.

The quotes on conditions in the Macy Street District and Chinatown originally appeared in (California) Commission on Immigration and Housing, "Report on Unemployment," Supplement to the First Report (Sacramento: State Printing Office, 1914), pp. 263-264. This was an earlier report than the one mentioned in Chapter III, though obviously produced by the same state agency and with the same reformist intent. The Macy Street District overlaps, too. Therefore, the paragraph immediately before the quote uses descriptions from both reports.

Information about the Associated Charities, and the fundraising activities of the Hebrew Benevolent Society and the Ladies Hebrew Benevolent Society owe to John E. Baur, "Philanthropy in Nineteenth Century Southern California," in *Southern California Quarterly*, Special Edition (Los Angeles: Historical Society of Southern California, 1989), Vol. LXXI, Number 2-3, pp. 127, 135-136.

Please note that I use the term "women's club" both literally and more broadly. Progressive-era women's clubs were a type of association that educated their members to organizational effectiveness and public involvement. Each local group worked on its own issues, and many built "club houses" in which to hold their functions. (Some are still standing and a considerable number have attained historic landmark status). Other women's groups had more specific goals: rescuing women from prostitution, providing safe respite and recreational facilities, etc.

Information about Caroline Severance and about women's residences (YWCA, etc.) comes from Gloria Ricci Lothrop, "Strength Made Stronger: The Role of Women in Southern California Philanthropy," in *Southern California Quarterly*, Special Edition (Los Angeles: Historical Society of Southern California, 1989), Vol. LXXI, Number 2-3, p. 159.

I came across Estelle Lawton Lindsey for the first time in Anne V. Howell, "History and Description: Los Angeles City Government (1781-1998)," op. cit., p. 13.

Sanchez, op. cit., p. 132, talks about the system of godparenting, *compadrazgo*, among Mexican-Americans.

Landsmenschaften were clubs composed of Jews from the same European *shtetl* (village) or occasionally, region. While groups offered aide and social activities, a major thrust after World War II was charitable giving to Israel. In fact, some *landsmenschaften* chose specific Israeli towns, akin to the "sister city" concept.

For information on Chinese family associations beyond the short quotation I have excerpted, please see Kit Fong Tom, *Participation of the Chinese in the Community Life of Los Angeles* (San Francisco: R and E Research Associates, 1974), p. 34. This work is a reprint of Tom's master's thesis, written at the University of Southern California 30 years earlier.

The close affinity that "Southern Branch" students held for Berkeley was explained by Dr. Clyde Johnson, former Assistant Dean of Undergraduates at UCLA and historian of the Associated Students, in his doctoral dissertation, "Student Self-Government, A Preliminary Survey of the Background and Development of Extra-Class Activities at the University of California, Los Angeles." Dr. Johnson is quoted in an alumni publication, *UCLA Magazine*, Fall, 1994.

An authoritative article on John Randolph Haynes is Tom Sitton, "California's Practical Idealist John Randolph Haynes," in *California History*, March 1988. I cited information from pages 3-17 and 67-69. Please note that Haynes was the best known local Progressive— but hardly the only one. Caroline Severance is another fine example.

Mulholland's impressions of the natural beauty here were quoted from Department of Water and Power, "William Mulholland: The Man Who Built the Los Angeles-Owens River Aqueduct" (Los Angeles: DWP pamphlet, originally printed in 1939, revised 1987).

The history of the Owens River controversy is told in intricate detail by Marc Reisner in Cadillac Desert, *The American West and Its Disappearing Water* (New York: Penguin Books, 1993). Discussion about the early relationship and differing conservation philosophies of Eaton and Mulholland may be found on pp. 60-62. Also, see pp. 62-69.

An excellent report about the 1925 plague (and a manuscript that tells much about the evolution of health care services in Los Angeles County) is Helen Eastman Martin, *The History of the Los Angeles County Hospital (1878-1968) and the Los Angeles County-University of Southern California Medical Center (1968-1978)*, (Los Angeles: University of Southern California Press, 1979). I obtained information from pp. 67-69.

Differential health care for Mexican-Americans has been examined in Gloria E. Miranda, "The Mexican Immigrant Family: Economic and Cultural Survival in Los Angeles, 1900-1945," in Norman M. Klein and Martin J. Schiesl, eds., *Twentieth Century Los Angeles, Power, Promotion, and Social Conflict* (Claremont: Regina Books, 1990), p. 45. Here, Miranda quotes: "Health, Relief, and Delinquency Conditions among the Mexicans of California" in Manuel P. Servin, ed., *An Awakened Minority: The Mexican Americans*, second edition (Beverly Hills: Glencoe Press, 1974), p. 72.

Newcomer, op. cit. , p. 101 talks about municipal responsibility for health care, especially the state-mandated transfer of authority to the counties.

Those interested in housing issues might read Don Parsons, "Los Angeles' 'Headline-Happy Public Housing War,'" *Southern California Quarterly* (Los Angeles: Historical Society of Southern California, Fall 1983) Vol. LVI, No. 3, p. 252. Parsons quotes Leonard Leader's unfinished UCLA doctoral dissertation (1972), "Los Angeles and the Great Depression," p. 183, with reference to general community organizing activities.

A final footnote: African-American and Euroamerican youth sported the same styles as the Mexican-American zoot suiters. A much smaller number of the former were brutalized, too.

CHAPTER 4 INDUSTRY

The Primary Report and the Building, Structure, and Object Report on 2401 S. Santa Fe Avenue, dated August 18, 1994, are on file at the State Office of Historic Preservation, Sacramento. Richard Starzak, of Myra L. Frank & Associates, did the architectural/historic assessment of the building for an environmental impact report connected with the Alameda Corridor project. He also provided additional insights on the more recent history of the former furniture factory (now the Santa Fe Arts Colony), during an August 3, 1998 telephone conversation.

Aggregated data about L.A. artists — and their contribution to the local economy — comes from Laura Zucker, "The Artist in Los Angeles County," in *The Arts: A Competitive Advantage for California*, prepared by the Policy Economics Group of KPMG Peat Marwick for the California Arts Council (Sacramento: California Arts Council, 1992). I specifically refer to pp. 25, 27-30. Note that some statistical overlap exists, due to the interdisciplinary nature of art. Also, study is limited to actors/ performers/directors, dancers, musicians and composers, visual artists, and writers/authors. Photographers, art educators, producers, designers, and architects have NOT been included, but constitute an additional estimated workforce of 49,393. Please note, too, that of artists' total incomes, 53 percent was derived from arts-related activities.

Much of my information — and quotations — on the early livestock industry owes to Robert Glass Cleland, *The Cattle on a Thousand Hills: Southern California 1850-1880* (San Marino: The Huntington Library, 1975). The letter from the vaquero to his brother may be found in the Cave J. Couts manuscript collection at the Huntington Library.

The assessment about livestock being insufficient to meet local consumer needs is taken from: George P. Clements, M.D., "The Agricultural Future of Los Angeles County," *Los Angeles Realtor*, Vol. IV, March, 1925, p. 17.

Burton L. Hunter, *The Evolution of Municipal Organization and Administrative Practice in the City of Los Angeles* (Los Angeles: Parker, Sone & Baird Company, Publishers, 1933), p. 7 cites Guinn on what we would now call "sin taxes" and related issues.

The information concerning Matthew Keller and the early wine industry here comes from Lynn C. Kronzek, "Historical Background," in *Cultural Resources Impact Mitigation Program for the Los Angeles Metro Red Line Segment One (Chinatown)*, October, 1993 (Los Angeles: Los Angeles County Metropolitan Transportation Authority, 1993), pp. 17, 23, and 33. Among the sources I used were a personal interview with Keller's granddaughter, Marion Francis. I also quote from the newspaper obituary of the vintner, April 11, 1881.

Some details about early citrus growing and cooperative marketing (including the *Riverside Press and Horticulturalist* quotation) appear in Ed Ainsworth, *Journey with the Sun, The Story of Citrus in Its Western Pilgrimage* (Los Angeles: 1968).

The statistics on the breadth of the citrus industry are attributable to: C.C. Teague, "The Growth and Development of California Fruit Culture," *Los Angeles Realtor*, Vol. IV, March, 1925, pp. 18 and 19.

Information about the San Fernando Valley wheat empire may be found in Remi Nadeau, "Wheat Ruled the Valley," *Westways*, April, 1963.

Statistics pertaining to Chinese-American mobility through agricultural industries come from Kronzek, op. cit., pp. 53-54.

The history of Louie Gwan's market has been explored by Dolores Hayden, Gail Dubrow, and Carolyn Flynn, *The Power of Place, Los Angeles* (Los Angeles: Power of Place, undated brochure).

Gordon L'Allemand, "Chinatown Passes," *Los Angeles Times Sunday Magazine*, March 11, 1933, pp. 12-13, describes his visit to the Yee Sing Chong Market.

Ivan Light, *Ethnic Enterprise in America: Business and Welfare Among Chinese, Japanese and Blacks* (Berkeley, Los Angeles, and London: University of California Press, 1972), p. 76, discusses the economic benefits of marketing to both ethnic and general population. He also writes about Japanese-American cooperatives, agricultural networks, and relief funds (p. 77). Please note that Light's individual footnotes often draw on more than one source. Since I wanted to avoid being too academic here, I am not listing all of them. Instead, I refer you to the author's work directly.

The Bogardus quote on Mexican farm labor comes from Gloria E. Miranda, "The Mexican Immigrant Family: Economic and Cultural Survival in Los Angeles, 1900-1945," in Norman M. Klein and Martin J. Schiesl, eds., *Twentieth Century Los Angeles, Power, Promotion, and Social Conflict* (Claremont: Regina Books, 1990), pp. 45-46.

Details about the early twentieth century homebuilding industry owe to Hayden, Dubrow, and Flynn, op. cit.

George P. Clements, op. cit., p. 17, provides the assessment of truck farming's success in Los Angeles.

Cleland, op cit., pp. 111-112 lists some of the debts owed by L.A.'s largest landowners at the time.

For information on the early finance industry, see Robert Glass Cleland and Frank B. Putnam, *Isaias W. Hellman and the Farmers and Merchants Bank* (San Marino: The Huntington Library, 1965), p. 12. The authors are quoting from a recollection by Hellman associate Jackson A. Graves in Ira B. Cross, *Financing an Empire: History of Banking in California*, p. 536-537.

Cleland, op. cit. p. 233, aggregated the professional/trade affiliations listed in the 1875 *Los Angeles Directory*.

I found very useful Ira B. Cross' *A History of the Labor Movement in California* (Berkeley, Los Angeles, London: The University of California Press, 1935). See pages 207, 229, 269, 278, and 282 for direct citations.

Some information on the L.A. Chamber of Commerce, comes from Pitt and Pitt, *Los Angeles A to Z* (Berkeley, Los Angeles, London: University of California Press, 1997), p. 84.

George Sanchez, *Becoming Mexican American: Ethnicity, Culture, and Identity in Chicano Los Angeles, 1900-1945* (New York and Oxford: Oxford University Press, 1993) offers a good discussion of cross-border labor relations (pp. 230-231) and the Mexican railroad system (pp. 22 and 230). The "double entendre" interpretation is mine, however.

African-American involvement in railroad-related unions is described by Thomas C. Fleming, "Joining the Union"/Column 41, written for the San Francisco *Sun-Reporter* June or July, 1998. My copy was obtained through the H-Net California Studies List, July 2, 1998.

The section on mining, including the quotation, owes to Robert Glass Cleland, *Cattle on a Thousand Hills*, p. 145. Among other sources, Cleland uses contemporary newspapers advertisements. He obtained his estimate on the number of prospectors from the *Southern Vineyard* (p. 149).

The technical aspects — and progress — of early oil drilling and refinement are explained in Olaf P. Jenkins, "Geological Formations and Economic Development of the Oil and Gas Fields of California," Bulletin 118, (San Francisco: State of California, Department of Natural Resources, Division of Mines, 1943; reprinted 1948), pp. 4-6.

Hayden, Dubrow, and Flynn, op. cit., write about Emma Summers and provide statistics on the oil industry of that time. Because the authors utilize footnotes extensively, I refer you directly to their work.

Robert Glass Cleland and Osgood Hardy, *March of Industry* (San Francisco, Los Angeles, Chicago: Powell Publishing Company, 1929), provide data on the prominence and economic worth of what I call the early "technology-dependent" industries. See pp. 148, 150, and 266.

My narrative on the film industry benefitted from many sources. For a detailed analysis of the transition from local theatre and subsequent union issues, read Michael C. Nielsen, "Labor Power and Organization in the Early U.S. Motion Picture Industry," *Film History*, Volume 2 (1988), pp. 121-131. Cleland and Hardy, op. cit., p. 157 incorporate the *Times* reporter's chart of regional locations and their suitability as simulated environments. In addition, (on p. 163 of their work), Pitt and Pitt, op. cit., p. 337, offer some details on the film pioneers of the Teens. Marc Wanamaker, *History of the Jewish Presence in Hollywood — From Cowboy to Corporate Leader* (Los Angeles: Jewish Historical Society of Southern California, 1987), pp. 8-9 discusses Sid Grauman's influence — and a variety of subjects. (His book is part of JHSSC's Legacy journal series, Volume I, No. 1). Douglas Gomery examines the commercial connections between production, distribution, and exhibition. See, "U.S. Film Exhibition: The Formation of a Big Business" in Tino Balio, ed., *The American Film Industry* (Madison and London: The University of Wisconsin Press, 1985 revised edition), pp. 221-222. Gomery likens theatre dynasties to the grocery and drugstore chains which, with their innovative marketing techniques, were simultaneously sweeping the country. His work also details the strategies employed by the Balaban & Katz organization. The film industry's economic contributions, both locally and nationally, are quantified in Thurston H. Ross and Ellis G. Fulton, Project Directors, *An Economic Survey of Hollywood* (Los Angeles: University of Southern California Bureau of Business Research, 1938), pp. 102, 104, 106 and an unmarked page titled "Highlight Facts — Hollywood and Its Major Trade Area." William S. Paley's quote also comes from this source.

There are many facets to the port's history. Information on the Free Harbor fight is provided in: Lanier Bartlett, "The Battle for South Pacific Ports," Part II, *Westways*, August, 1935; and Charles F. Queenan, "San Pedro Emerged the Winner in the Great Free Harbor Fight," *Los Angeles Times*, May 17, 1992, Section B/South Bay News, p. B5. Donald Teruo Hata, Jr. and Nadine Ishitani Hata report on the Japanese fishing industry. See "Asian-Pacific Angelenos: Model Minorities and Indispensible Scapegoats" in Norman M. Klein and Martin J. Schiesl, eds., *Twentieth Century Los Angeles, Power, Promotion, and Social Conflict* (Claremont: Regina Books, 1990), p. 72. Gloria E. Miranda, op. cit., p. 48, briefly discusses the fish cannery workers. She quotes the definitive study, Vicki L. Ruiz's *Cannery Women, Cannery Lives: Mexican Women,*

Unionization, and the California Food Processing Industry, 1930-1950 (Albuquerque: University of New Mexico Press, 1987), p. 14. Helpful, too, were entries on Fort McArthur and shipbuilding from Pitt and Pitt, op. cit., pp. 155 and 465, respectively.

Regarding aviation and aeronautics, it is important to note that until the conclusion of World War II, most facilities technically were not within city limits. This regional industry is too important, however, to omit from the text. My sources were varied. The first-hand experience of flying in a World War I plane owes to George F. Kennan, *Sketches From A Life* (New York: Pantheon Books, 1989), pp. 28-29. Dana Slawson and Judith A. Rasson, "Howard Hughes Industrial Complex Historic American Building Survey," prepared for Maguire Thomas Partners by Greenwood and Associates, December, 1995, pp. 1-3 offered insights into technological progress, as well as how government procurement practices affected the industry. A good historic overview also appears in Patt Morrison, "Payloads, Paydays, Palm Trees," *Los Angeles Times*, December 5, 1993, p. A 28. Adding to the story of Los Angeles International Airport are: Pitt and Pitt, op. cit., p. 294; and, Robert P. Olislagers, *Fields of Flying: An Illustrated History of Airports in the Southwest*, with a foreword by Brigadier General Charles E. "Chuck" Yeager (Encinitas: Heritage Media Corporation, 1996), p. 55.

CHAPTER 5 COMMUNITIES

I cited two population studies, 45 years apart, that included the Fairfax district. The earlier one was Fred Massarik's "A Report on the Jewish Population of Los Angeles," (Los Angeles: Los Angeles Jewish Community Council, 1953), p. 11. According to "best estimates," Beverly-Fairfax then claimed 24,848 Jewish resident and Wilshire-Fairfax, 26,608. The density (percentage of Jewish households) per 100 was slightly higher in Beverly-Fairfax, however: 59 percent to 53.5 in the southern area. Today's demographics were explored by Pini Herman, Ph.D., Principal Investigator, "Los Angeles Jewish Population Survey 1997" (Los Angeles: Planning and Allocations Department, Jewish Federation of Greater Los Angeles, 1998), p. 16.

Glatt kosher represents a new type of supervision that holds no basis in traditional Jewish law and has been introduced in the United States only within the past 20 or so years.

Disparaging names for the community during the early 1970s are reported in Lynn C. Kronzek, *Fairfax...A Home, A Community, A Way of Life* (Los Angeles: Jewish Historical Society of Southern California, 1990), pp. 71 and 86.

From this point, most of the sources pertain to various communities. The endnotes will be organized to underscore this relationship.

Sonoratown: Gloria E. Miranda, "The Mexican Immigrant Family: Economic and Cultural Survival in Los Angeles, 1900-1945," in Norman M. Klein and Martin J. Schiesl, eds., *Twentieth Century Los Angeles, Power, Promotion, and Social Conflict* (Claremont: Regina Books, 1990), p. 43.

Chinatown: "Removing Chinatown," *Los Angeles Times*, August 10, 1887, p. 4 describes the likely arson that obliterated the first Chinatown. Details about the second Chinatown, its earliest inhabitants, and the population influx during the 1880s come from: Lynn C. Kronzek, "Historical Background," Cultural Resources Impact Mitigation Program, Los Angeles Metro Red Line Segment One (Chinatown), op. cit., p 37. Matthew Keller's land was to the immediate south of this new Chinatown. Marion Francis, Keller's granddaughter, states that as she heard it, most of the field hands there were Mexican-Americans. We also know that Native Americans had been likewise engaged by local enologists/vintners. Keller died and his land was subdivided before the new Chinatown emerged. Therefore, it is fair to deduce similar labor demographics on the Keller and Apablasa estates. Nora Sterry lends insight into the "Housing Conditions in Chinatown Los Angeles," *Journal of Applied Sociology*, November-December, 1922, p. 71. Much of the information about China City and New Chinatown developments originally appeared in my study, op. cit., pp. 78-79. Edwin R. Bingham in "The Saga of the Los Angeles Chinese" (Los Angeles: unpublished Master's thesis, Department of History and Government, Occidental College, 1942), pp. 148-152, gives a physical description of New Chinatown. Data about investments in that community owe to: Thomas Allen McDannold, "Development of the Los Angeles Chinatown, 1850-1970" (Northridge: Unpublished Master's thesis, Department of Geography, California State University-Northridge, 1973), p. 107.

Little Tokyo: A historic overview of developing land uses, as well as information about Molokan residents, is provided by Judith A. Rasson in "Metro Rail Red Line Eastern Extension: Historical and Archaeological Evaluation of Seven Stations," prepared for the Cordoba Corporation by Greenwood and Associates, March, 1994. See pp. 5-8. When describing the Molokans, Rasson refers to John K. Berokoff's *Molokans in America* (Stockton, Whittier: Doty Trade Press, 1969), pp. 33-36. William M. Mason and John A. McKinstry chronicle the Japanese experience and interactions with other immigrant groups situated in or near Little Tokyo. Refer to their work, *The Japanese of Los Angeles* (Los Angeles: Los Angeles County Museum of Natural History, 1969), pp. 7-13.

An essential reference on L.A.'s transportation history is Robert C. Post, *Street Railways and the Growth of Los Angeles* (San Marino: Golden West Books, 1989). I obtain information on the early system from pp. 17-19.

Angelino Heights: Murray Burns, "Angelino Heights Tour" (Los Angeles: Los Angeles Conservancy, 1997), p. 1.

Boyle Heights/East Los Angeles: Rasson, op. cit., pp. 13-14,17-18, and 38 examines in depth early surveys and, more generally, land settlement, development, and population patterns. To highlight William Workman's role, she quotes Thompson and West (publishers), *History of Los Angeles County* (Oakland: Howell-North, 1959 reprint of the original 1880 text). The development philosophies of Louis Lewin and Charles Jacoby are reported in Southern California Jewish Historical Society, "A Sourcebook for Tour Guides" (Los Angeles: Southern California Jewish Historical Society, 1988), p. 26. Jewish population statistics likewise come from this publication; those pertaining to Mexican-Americans may be found in Ricardo Romo's *History of a Barrio, East Los Angeles* (Austin: University of Texas Press, 1983), p. 5. The original source for Hy Solomon's City Terrace oral history is Lynn C. Kronzek, *Fairfax*, op. cit., p. 12. I spoke with Norma Alvarado during 1991 about her Boyle Heights childhood.

The Arroyo Seco: Betty Welcome, *The History of Eagle Rock* (Los Angeles: Printed courtesy of Councilman Richard Alatorre's office, undated, sometime during the late 1980s to late 1990s), pp. 3-4; and, Highland Park Branch of the Security Trust & Savings Branch, *The Story of Greater Highland Park* (Highland Park: 48-page pamphlet, produced in 1923), pp. 7,14-15. Note that among other sources, Welcome draws on on an October 24, 1909 article in the *Los Angeles Herald Sunday Magazine*.

South Central: Pitt and Pitt, *Los Angeles from A to Z* (Berkeley, Los Angeles, London: University of California Press, 1997), p. 537, write about early Watts. Lonnie G. Bunch, "A Past Not Necessarily Prologue: The Afro-American in Los Angeles" in Norman M. Klein and Martin G. Schiesl, eds., *Twentieth Century Los Angeles: Power, Promotion, and Social Conflict* (Claremont: Regina Books, 1990) describes this community, too. Additionally, he explores how and why neighborhoods consolidated into South Central, and changing attitudes toward African-Americans. See pp. 103-104 and 115. The cultural and architectural scene has been observed by Carson A. Anderson and Ronald Lewis, "Avenues, Arts, and Architecture of South Central Los Angeles," (Los Angeles: Walking tour brochures produced by the Los Angeles Conservancy, 1993).

San Pedro/Wilmington: Wilmington's reluctance to give up its independence — particularly its school board — was conveyed to Camille Baxter during a December 4, 1972 oral history interview with local residents Thomas J. Garcia and Mary Garcia Guerrero. Further information may be obtained from the Historical File, Los Angeles Harbor College Library.

The "Great Age of Hiking" and outdoor discovery were discussed in Richard A. Flom and Lynn C. Kronzek, "Presentation of Interpretive Themes for the West Fork Ranger Station, Angeles National Forest," prepared by Lynn C. Kronzek & Associates under contract to the U.S. Department of Agriculture Forest Service, January, 1993, pp. 21-22.

Among others, Robert M. Fogelson, *The Fragmented Metropolis: Los Angeles, 1850-1930* (Berkeley, Los Angeles, London: University of California Press, 1967), pp. 166-167, talks about early signs of the electric cars' demise.

"The Boulevards": See Gary Libman, "Sunset Boulevard: Epitome of Los Angeles," *Los Angeles Times* reprint, taken from the View Section/Part 6, December 18, 1988. Libman quotes Joe Kennelley and Roy Hankey in the 1981 book, *Sunset Boulevard: America's Dream Street*. Moving to Wilshire, a standby has been Ralph Hancock's, *Fabulous Boulevard* (New York, Funk & Wagnalls Company, 1949), pp. 159-160. Lynn C. Kronzek, *Fairfax*, op. cit., pp. 15, 27 and 30, has information about Ross, the Miracle Mile, and the Wilshire corridor generally.

Westwood: Johnson Heumann Research Associates, "Westwood: North and East Villages," Cultural Resources Documentation Report Prepared for the City of Los Angeles Department of Planning, 1987, pp. 6-8. The goal of making the community palatable to homeowner-investors is illustrated by a real estate advertisement (after page 11 of the report) taken from the *Los Angeles Times*, March 17, 1929, Part V, p. 9.

Pacific Palisades: Robert M. Fogelson, op . cit., pp. 89, 105, and 155 includes Robert C. Gillis in his discussion. Also, see Pitt and Pitt, op. cit., p. 375.

Venice and Playa del Rey: A densely-packed source is Patricia Adler, "A History of the Venice Area," prepared as part of the Venice Community Plan Study for the Los Angeles Department of City Planning, 1969. Pages 5, 8, and 14 were used here. Information on the early Machado holdings comes from W.W. Robinson's *Ranchos Become Cities* (Pasadena: San Pasqual Press, 1939), p. 118. Adler also uses E.J. Wright's "Official Map of the County of Los Angeles, California, 1898" to describe the rail connections that facilitated development. The pros and cons of Venice's consolidation with Los Angeles are evoked through the *Los Angeles Times* of October 1, 1925, and Richard Bigger and James D. Kitchen, *How the Cities Grew* (Los Angeles: The Haynes Foundation, 1952), p. 181.

San Fernando Valley: A good overview may be obtained by way of W.W. Robinson, *The Story of the San Fernando Valley* (Los Angeles: Title Insurance and Trust Company, 1961). My footnotes are taken from pp.19, 27, 55. Interesting nuggets also appeared in "Owensmouth to be Opened," *Van Nuys News*, p. 1, undated clipping from Los Angeles Conservancy files, and "Canoga Park History 1912-1929", typewritten article from the files of the Canoga Park Branch Library, undated. For information on Valley planning and zoning, mostly during the 1940s, see: (Anne V. Howell), "City Planners and Planning in Los Angeles (1781-1998), (Los Angeles: Central Publications Unit, Los Angeles Department of City Planning, 1998), pp. 16-19.

INDEX